Machine Learning With Noisy Labels

Machine Learning With Noisy Labels

Definitions, Theory, Techniques, and Solutions

Gustavo Carneiro
Centre for Vision, Speech and Signal Processing (CVSSP)
Surrey Institute for People-centred Artificial Intelligence
Department of Electrical and Electronic Engineering
The University of Surrey
Guildford, United Kingdom

ACADEMIC PRESS
An imprint of Elsevier

Academic Press is an imprint of Elsevier
125 London Wall, London EC2Y 5AS, United Kingdom
525 B Street, Suite 1650, San Diego, CA 92101, United States
50 Hampshire Street, 5th Floor, Cambridge, MA 02139, United States

Notices

Knowledge and best practice in this field are constantly changing. As new research and experience broaden our understanding, changes in research methods, professional practices, or medical treatment may become necessary.

Practitioners and researchers must always rely on their own experience and knowledge in evaluating and using any information, methods, compounds, or experiments described herein. In using such information or methods they should be mindful of their own safety and the safety of others, including parties for whom they have a professional responsibility.

To the fullest extent of the law, neither the Publisher nor the authors, contributors, or editors, assume any liability for any injury and/or damage to persons or property as a matter of products liability, negligence or otherwise, or from any use or operation of any methods, products, instructions, or ideas contained in the material herein.

ISBN: 978-0-443-15441-6

For information on all Academic Press publications
visit our website at https://www.elsevier.com/books-and-journals

Publisher: Mara Conner
Acquisitions Editor: Tim Pitts
Editorial Project Manager: Emily Thomson
Production Project Manager: Gomathi Sugumar
Cover Designer: Christian Bilbow

Typeset by VTeX

Working together
to grow libraries in
developing countries

www.elsevier.com • www.bookaid.org

I dedicate this book to my beautiful wife Mari

Contents

Biography

Gustavo Carneiro

Gustavo Carneiro has been a Professor of AI and Machine Learning at the University of Surrey, UK, since December 2022. He is also a member of the Centre for Vision, Speech and Signal Processing (CVSSP) and the Surrey Institute for People-centred Artificial Intelligence. Before that, from 2019 to 2022, he was a Professor at the School of Computer Science at the University of Adelaide, an ARC Future Fellow, and the Director of Medical Machine Learning at the Australian Institute for Machine Learning. He joined the University of Adelaide as a Senior Lecturer in 2011, became an Associate Professor in 2015 and a Professor in 2019. In 2014 and 2019, he joined the Technical University of Munich as a visiting professor and a Humboldt fellow. From 2008 to 2011 Prof Carneiro was a Marie Curie International Incoming Fellow and a visiting Assistant Professor at the Instituto Superior Tecnico (Lisbon, Portugal) within the Carnegie Mellon University-Portugal program (CMU-Portugal). From 2006 to 2008, Prof Carneiro was a research scientist at Siemens Corporate Research in Princeton, USA. In 2005, he was a post-doctoral fellow at the University of British Columbia and at the University of California San Diego. Prof Carneiro received his Ph.D. in computer science from the University of Toronto in 2004. His main research interest is in the fields of computer vision, medical image analysis, and machine learning, and, according to Google Scholar in November 2023, he has more than 14400 citations, with an h-index of 55.

Preface

Historically, machine learning models have been trained with well-curated training sets that contain negligible amount of label noise. Even though these clean-label training sets represent one of the main pillars behind the success of machine learning, such careful curation is a process that does not scale to the large datasets that are becoming increasingly available in the field. In fact, as the dataset size increases, the probability of including noisy-label samples also increases due to the considerable costs associated with the careful curation. Moreover, in certain machine learning scenarios, such as the interpretation of medical images for disease diagnosis, it is common for expert labelers to exhibit natural disagreements regarding specific labels. The inherent uncertainty caused by expert disagreements in these problems makes them susceptible to a significant amount of label noise that cannot be entirely eliminated, even with an exceedingly careful labeling process. Therefore, the development of new machine learning models that can explore extremely large-scale datasets that, perhaps, have not been carefully labeled, or datasets that possess intrinsically uncertain labels, relies on the development of algorithms and models that exhibit robustness to noisy labels.

Such development of noisy-label learning algorithms and models has attracted a fair amount of attention by the research community, leading to the publication of a large number of excellent papers. Consequently, students, researchers, and practitioners who want to be able to read and understand the noisy-label problem would have to navigate through this large amount of papers published in the last 5 to 10 years, which is not an easy task even for experienced professionals. This book has been proposed to facilitate this task, providing students, researchers, and practitioners with a useful source of information in the topic.

The book starts by defining the noisy-label learning problem, then it introduces different types of label noise and the theory behind the problem. It also presents the main techniques and methods that enable the effective use of noisy-label training sets. With this book, the reader will have the tools to be able to understand, reproduce, and design regression, classification, segmentation, and detection models that can be trained with large-scale noisy-label training sets. Advanced machine learning courses that cover topics in learning with noisy-label and real-world datasets will greatly benefit from the insights provided in this book.

To summarize, with this book the reader will be able to:

1. Successfully design and reproduce regression, classification, detection, and segmentation models using large-scale noisy-label training sets;
2. Understand the theory and motivation of noisy-label learning;
3. Analyze noisy-label learning methods with respect to a set of core techniques;
4. Describe the current state-of-the-art methods and benchmarks available in the field;
5. Know how to access the codes and datasets on the internet;

6. Know how to discover the best methods for current and future noisy-label problems; and

7. Propose innovative noisy-label learning methods.

Survey papers and books on the same topic

We are not aware of other authored books published in the topic of machine learning with noisy labels. Recently, Caiafa et al. (2021) edited a book that contains a collection of papers in machine learning with imperfect training sets, i.e., not only noisy-label learning, but also learning with incomplete and small datasets. That book presents several machine learning methods applied to specific medical and industrial problems, and a couple of more fundamental approaches. Nevertheless, differently from that edited book, our book aims to provide a more didactic presentation of the topic with basic principles, theoretical explanations, and the main strategies proposed for the problem of noisy-label with machine learning.

There have been excellent surveys published in the last decade on this topic. One of the most influential surveys (Frénay and Verleysen, 2014) assumed the feature space to be pre-defined and focused on the study of classic statistical learning methods, such as naive Bayes, boosting, and support vector machines. That survey is quite relevant because it defined the sources of label noise, a taxonomy of label noise (both the label noise sources and taxonomy were presented in Section 1.2), and introduced the impact of noisy label on those classic machine learning classifiers. The pre-defined feature space assumption made by Frénay and Verleysen (2014) makes it difficult to translate some of their results to deep learning models (Han et al., 2020b), which learn both the features and the classifier during the training process.

The surveys by Algan and Ulusoy (2021), Karimi et al. (2020), Nigam et al. (2020), and Cordeiro and Carneiro (2020) present classic label noise definitions and a summary of methods with a especial focus on applications. As mentioned in Section 1.2, one of the sources of label noise is crowdsourcing by non-experts, and the survey by Zhang et al. (2016) studies this problem, where they focus on basic concepts of label quality and learning models and algorithms. An extensive survey on label noise representation learning (LNRL) is provided by Han et al. (2020b), which defines the LNRL problem, explains how noisy labels affect the generalization of deep learning models, and provides a taxonomy of LNRL approaches in terms of input data, objective functions, and optimization policies. The survey published by Song et al. (2022) presents a comprehensive comparison of noisy-label learning methods based on their proposed taxonomy of methods.

Throughout this book, we refer to many of the surveys mentioned above when explaining the concepts pertinent to the topic of learning with noisy labels. Nevertheless, we cover some of the topics in significantly more detail than the surveys, presenting the theory behind the problem, introducing critical technical developments, and presenting the main results and applications. We hope that after reading this book the reader will be able to successfully design and reproduce regression, classification, detection, and segmentation models using large-scale noisy-label training sets.

Book organization

This book starts with **Chapter 1**, where we provide an informal definition of label noise, a discussion of sources of label noise, and a simplified description of the taxonomy of label noise currently accepted by machine learning researchers and practitioners. Then, we discuss the main challenges faced by researchers in label noise learning.

Chapter 2 provides a formal definition of the noisy-label learning problem focusing on four tasks: classification, regression, segmentation, and detection. Then we define symmetric, asymmetric, and instance-dependent closed and open-set label noise problems. Moreover, we define methods to assess label noise learning methods. The chapter also presents the main computer vision, medical image analysis, and non-image datasets and benchmarks used to assess noisy-label learning methods.

In **Chapter 3**, we introduce theoretical aspects of the label noise learning problem. In particular, we describe in detail the label noise generation process when defining the noisy-label learning problem with a label transition matrix. We then explain how the same label noise generation process is performed when assuming the label noise distribution definition. The chapter is concluded with a brief introduction of probably approximately correct (PAC) learning bounds in the context of learning with label noise.

Chapter 4 presents the main technical developments in the study of learning with label noise. In particular, we focus our explanations on the main techniques in terms of loss function design, training algorithms, data processing, and model architecture. Even though the methods in this chapter can be applied to machine learning methods in general, we focus our attention on deep learning methods since they show the best results in virtually all applications.

Next in **Chapter 5**, we introduce modern approaches that present state-of-the-art results in the main noisy-label learning benchmarks. We explain each approach, and present their code repository (if available). We also present their results on the main benchmarks in the field. This chapter concludes with a ranking of the top methods for each benchmark and a summary of the most successful techniques used to handle noisy-label learning problems.

The book concludes in **Chapter 6**, where we discuss the main findings and limitations of the methods presented in the field, followed by a presentation of possible future directions.

Acknowledgments

Numerous sections of this book have evolved through discussions and collaborative efforts with esteemed researchers. I would like to express my gratitude for the invaluable contributions and feedback provided by the following individuals: Cuong Cao Nguyen, Filipe Cordeiro, Ian Reid, Vasileios Belagiannis, Fengbei Liu, Yuyuan Liu, Yuanhong Chen, Chong Wang, Yuan Zhang, Arpit Garg, Thanh-Toan Do, Rafael Felix Alves, Dung Anh Hoang, Brandon Smart, David Butler, Miguel Angel Gonzalez Ballester, Yu Tian, Adrian Galdran, Hu Wang, Renato Hermoza Aragones, Jacinto Nascimento, Fabio Faria, Lauren Oakden-Rayner, Ragav Sachdeva, Hoang Son Le, Tim Chen, Dileepa Pitawela, Helen Frazer, Louise Hull, and Rajvinder Singh.

Gustavo Carneiro

Mathematical notation

We have used a relatively standard mathematical notation. It is expected that the reader has an undergraduate level of understanding of basic concepts of calculus, linear algebra, optimization, and probability theory. Nevertheless, we try to explain the concepts while introducing the formulations.

We represent vectors with lower case bold Roman letters such as $\mathbf{x}$. While $\mathbf{x}$ is a column vector, its transpose $\mathbf{x}^\top$ is a row vector. A row vector with M elements can be explicitly represented with their elements, as in $\mathbf{x}^\top = (\mathbf{x}_1, ..., \mathbf{x}_M)$, where a column vector is represented with $\mathbf{x} = (\mathbf{x}_1, ..., \mathbf{x}_M)^\top$.

Matrices are represented with uppercase bold Roman letters, like $\mathbf{M}$. Matrices can also be represented with column vectors, as in $\mathbf{M} = [\mathbf{x}_1, ..., \mathbf{x}_M]$, where the $(m, n)^{th}$ element of the matrix $\mathbf{M}$ is denoted by the element $\mathbf{x}_{m,n}$.

A closed interval from a to b is denoted by $[a, b]$, while an open interval is represented with (a, b). Intervals can also be open in one end and closed in the other end, such as $(a, b]$.

Sets are represented with calligraphic Roman letters, such as $\mathcal{X}$. A function from a set $\mathcal{X}$ to a set $\mathcal{Y}$ is represented by $f : \mathcal{X} \to \mathcal{Y}$. Variables are represented by lowercase Roman letters, like x. The expectation of a function $f(x)$ is denoted by $\mathbb{E}_x[f(x)]$.

Random variables are represented with uppercase Roman letters, such as X, Y. The probability distribution of random variable is denoted with $p(X)$, where sampling from this distribution is achieved with $\mathbf{x} \sim p(X)$, and the computation of the probability of a particular value $\mathbf{x}$ is done with $p(X = \mathbf{x})$. Also, we denote the simplex probability space of the class label set $\mathcal{Y}$ that contains $|\mathcal{Y}|$ one-hot representations, with $\Delta^{|\mathcal{Y}|-1}$. Each point $\mathbf{p} \in \Delta^{|\mathcal{Y}|-1}$ in this simplex probability space denotes a categorical probability distribution among the $|\mathcal{Y}|$ labels.

Problem definition

Motivation, introduction, and challenges

1.1 Motivation

The last couple of decades have witnessed an unprecedented development of machine learning (ML) (Bishop, 2006) and deep learning (DL) (LeCun et al., 2015) methods that are now integral part of many image classification (Druzhkov and Kustikova, 2016), speech recognition (Nassif et al., 2019), text classification (Minaee et al., 2021), and medical image analysis (Litjens et al., 2017) techniques. In turn, these techniques are being used for the development of several systems, such as self-driving cars (Daily et al., 2017), e-commerce (Laudon and Traver, 2013), chatbots (Adamopoulou and Moussiades, 2020), recommendation systems (Karimi et al., 2018), and spam filters (Bhowmick and Hazarika, 2018), which are shaping many aspects of our society.

Arguably, the successful development of ML and DL methods critically depends on the existence of well-curated large-scale labeled datasets. Such datasets are typically formed by carefully collecting and labeling each data sample that is guaranteed to belong to a pre-defined set of classes, with a label that reliably represents the sample contents. However, we are starting to witness the availability of an increasing number of minimally-curated large-scale datasets. In such datasets, each sample may have been annotated with a noisy label that does not reliably represent the sample contents. Hence, the development of ML and DL methods that are robust to label noise is attracting much research activity.

Dataset curation can be defined as the processes of data collection and labeling. The first step in the data collection process is to define the data source and the criteria to select the samples to be included in the dataset. For example, if the goal is to build a natural image dataset, then we can collect data based on the results returned by image search engines. Another example is if we want to build a dataset of chest X-ray (CXR) images, then it is necessary to collect the CXR images available from hospitals' picture archiving and communication systems (PACS). After collecting data, the next step is the data labeling, which consists of identifying relevant classes in each data sample. For example, Fig. 1.1 shows examples of images and different types of labeling, namely: 1) multi-class (top row), where each image contains a single visual class, e.g., the image with a piggy bank is labeled with the class 'piggy bank', the image of a teapot is labeled with the class 'teapot', etc.; 2) multi-label (second row, top to bottom), with each image annotated with a set of labels, e.g., an image of a park with trees, grassy field, and a river is labeled with the classes 'tree', 'river', and 'grass';

Machine Learning With Noisy Labels. https://doi.org/10.1016/B978-0-44-315441-6.00010-1

FIGURE 1.1 Labeling examples.

Top row shows how multi-class images are labeled, with each image belonging to a single class. The second row displays examples of multi-label images, where each image can be annotated with a set of labels. While the segmentation label (third row) consists of a single label per image pixel, the detection label (fourth row) has not only the label of the object inside the region of interest (ROI), represented by a rectangle, but also the ROI coordinates.

3) segmentation (third row, top to bottom), where each pixel is labeled with a single visual class, so an image of a kangaroo sitting on the ground has each pixel labeled as 'kangaroo' or 'background', depending if the pixel is part of the former or latter visual class; and 4) detection (last row), with the label consisting of the bounding box coordinates and a single visual class, so an image of a bat flying in the sky is labeled with a bounding box that covers the whole bat and is annotated with the class 'bat'. When the curation process is carefully done, with well-designed and well-executed data collection and labeling processes, it is rare, but not impossible, to find label noise in the dataset. Fig. 1.2 shows a carefully collected dataset of handwritten digits that contains images which represent well the distribution of handwritten digits, and the dataset does not contain outliers (i.e., images that do not contain handwritten digits). Fig. 1.2 also displays a few ways that the labeling process can be implemented (e.g., crowdsourcing, expert annotation, or semi-automated annotation), where the amount of label noise can be negligible if the labeling is done by experts. However, when the

Unlabeled data set   Labeling strategy   Labeled data set

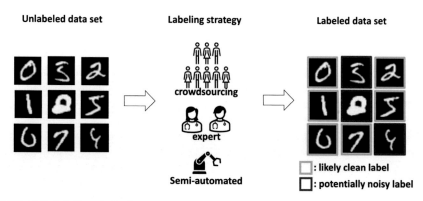

FIGURE 1.2 Labeling strategies.

The main strategies to label a dataset are: crowdsourcing (i.e., employing crowdworkers to label data samples), hiring experts who can label especial types of data samples (e.g., medical data), and semi-automated labeling based on systems that can provide labels with minimal human intervention. While the expert-labeling strategy enables a more careful labeling process, where labels can be assumed to be clean, they tend to be expensive and slow. On the other hand, crowdsourcing and semi-automated strategies tend to produce datasets with non-negligible amount of label noise, but they also enable the quick labeling of substantially larger datasets than the expert-labeling strategy.

labeling is executed by crowdsourcing or semi-automated tools, such amount of label noise can reach relatively high rates.

An example of a carefully curated dataset is ImageNet (Deng et al., 2009), which is a popular computer vision dataset that has 15 million images annotated, with more than 20,000 labels by 49,000 labelers from 167 countries, in a labeling process that took 2.5 years to complete. Another example is PadChest (Bustos et al., 2020), which is a large-scale Chest X-ray dataset containing 160,000 images from 67,000 patients, collected from 2009 to 2017. This dataset has 27% of its images manually labeled by trained physicians (i.e., experts), with the remaining images being semi-automatically labeled and manually verified. Although datasets like ImageNet (Deng et al., 2009) and PadChest (Bustos et al., 2020) have been extremely important for the development of DL and ML methods, the time and cost involved in preparing similar datasets represent a major roadblock in the development of new ML and DL applications. As a result, the field is now working on alternative ways to build large-scale datasets.

There are currently numerous examples of large-scale datasets that have been prepared with considerably less manual curation than ImageNet (Deng et al., 2009) and PadChest (Bustos et al., 2020). For instance, Google[1] has built the private dataset JFT-300M (Sun et al., 2017), which has 300M images that have been labeled by semi-automated tools using 18,000 labels. JFT-300M has recently been extended

---

[1] https://www.google.com/.

to form the JFT-3B (Zhai et al., 2022) that contains 3 billion images, annotated with 30k labels. Both JFT-300M and JFT-3B have noisy labels as a consequence of the mistakes made by the semi-automated tools. Another example is the dataset YFCC100M (Thomee et al., 2016), which is a large-scale natural image dataset with 100 million media objects collected from Flickr,[2] with annotations extracted from inherently noisy meta data, such as title, tags, and automatically generated labels. Similarly prepared large-scale datasets have been collected for speaker recognition (VoxCeleb2 with 1M utterances from over 6k speakers) (Chung et al., 2018), video classification (Sports-1M with more than 1M videos from 487 sports-related) (Karpathy et al., 2014), activity recognition (HowTo100M with 136M video clips from 1.2M YouTube[3] videos from 23k activities) (Miech et al., 2019), and medical image analysis (Chest X-Ray14 (Wang et al., 2017b) with more than 100k Chest X-Ray images from 32k patients, and CheXpert (Irvin et al., 2019) with more than 200k Chest X-Ray images from 65k patients).

The datasets above have been minimally curated, allowing them to be larger and available at a faster rate than previous well-curated datasets (Bustos et al., 2020; Deng et al., 2009). These two advantages have the potential to enable a quicker development of ML and DL models that can be trained more robustly because of the larger size of the training sets. However, these advantages are counter-balanced with many issues that can affect these datasets such as: label noise (Frénay and Verleysen, 2014; Han et al., 2020b; Song et al., 2022), data noise (Frénay and Verleysen, 2014), imbalanced distribution of samples per class (Johnson and Khoshgoftaar, 2019), missing labels (Yu et al., 2014), multiple labels per sample (Liu et al., 2021), out-of-distribution (OoD) data (Bengio et al., 2011), domain shift (Wang and Deng, 2018), etc. Hence, one of the main challenges that the machine learning community currently faces is the following: **how can we use these large-scale minimally-curated datasets to robustly train ML and DL models?**

Although all the issues raised above are important and need to be addressed, in this book we focus only on the label noise issue. The relevance of focusing on the label noise issue resides in the evidence shown by Zhang et al. (2021a), who demonstrate that DL models can easily overfit label noise. Overfitting happens when the model perfectly fits the training samples, but performs poorly on testing samples. Fig. 1.3 shows the modeling of a binary classifier using a noisy-label training set, where the model overfits the training data, producing a boundary (purple solid curve) that does not represent well the true boundary of the problem (black dashed curve). This poor representation of the true boundary forces the overfit model to produce inaccurate classification for testing data, particularly for samples lying in regions where the true classification boundary and the overfit classification boundary do not match. In fact, Zhang et al. (2021a) show an extreme case where the modeling of a DL classifier can overfit the entire training data, even when all training samples have their

---

2 https://www.flickr.com/.
3 https://www.youtube.com/.

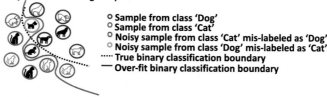

Feature space with training samples

○ Sample from class 'Dog'
○ Sample from class 'Cat'
○ Noisy sample from class 'Cat' mis-labeled as 'Dog'
○ Noisy sample from class 'Dog' mis-labeled as 'Cat'
···· True binary classification boundary
— Over-fit binary classification boundary

FIGURE 1.3 Overfitting the label noise.

Modeling of a binary classifier from training images of dogs and cats that contain a few noisy-label samples (i.e., samples that have been mislabeled, as indicated in the legend), where the model overfits the training data producing a boundary (purple solid curve) that represents poorly the true (latent) boundary of the problem (black dashed curve). Such overfit model will provide low accuracy classification for unseen test samples that lie close to the true boundary.

original labels randomly flipped to other labels. However, these models will have low prediction accuracy on previously unseen correctly labeled testing data. Therefore, the successful handling of label noise will facilitate the exploration of many of the existing minimally curated datasets that are currently available in the field.

1.2 Introduction

Let us informally introduce the label noise learning problem using multi-class image classification as an example. In this task, images are annotated with one label that is selected from a set of training labels. A common example of a multi-class image classification dataset is MNIST (LeCun, 1998), which contains black and white images of handwritten digits that are labeled using the set of labels $\{0, 1, ..., 8, 9\}$. Fig. 1.4, top frame, shows examples of MNIST images. For most MNIST images, the image is clear enough and can be easily labeled – such images are defined to have clean labels (see top frame of Fig. 1.4). According to Frénay and Verleysen (2014), there are four sources of label noise (Fig. 1.5, frame on the left): 1) the information in the image is not sufficiently reliable for a precise labeling; 2) the labeler is not reliable; 3) there is intrinsic variability among labelers; and 4) data encoding or communication error. The middle frame of Fig. 1.4 (titled closed-set noise) contains noisy label samples, where the first two images show examples of the first source of label noise (i.e., insufficiently reliable information), the third and fourth images display unreliable labeling, the next two examples (fifth and sixth) show intrinsically ambiguous images that can lead to large variability among labelers, and the last two images show encoding or communication errors. The main difference between the label noise from unreliable labeling versus encoding or communication errors is that in the former case, even though the labeler clearly made a mistake, the wrong label can be justified by a relatively ambiguous image. However, label noise from encoding or communi-

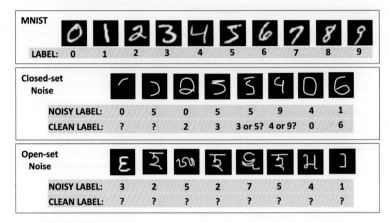

FIGURE 1.4 Types of label noise.

Top frame shows samples from the MNIST handwritten digit dataset (LeCun, 1998). The middle frame displays different types of closed-set label noise, where images belong to one of the classes in the training set. In this frame the first two images show images with insufficient information to enable a reliable annotation, the next two images show challenging images that were mislabeled, then the next two images display intrinsically ambiguous cases, and the final two images show cases of data encoding or communication error. The bottom frame shows open-set label noise, where the images do not belong to any of the MNIST classes.

cation errors happen randomly, where in general, the label noise cannot be explained from image ambiguities.

While we explain the sources of label noise above, below we discuss the characterization of label noise, which was originally proposed by Frénay and Verleysen (2014), but has suffered changes in naming and scope over the last few years. In (Frénay and Verleysen, 2014), label noise was characterized as (Fig. 1.5, frame on the right): 1) noise completely at random (NCAR), 2) noise at random (NAR), and 3) noise not at random (NNAR). In NCAR, the noise consists of flipping the class label from its original label to any of the other labels completely at random, where the new noisy label can switch to any of the wrong labels with equal probability. This NCAR model is related to the fourth source of label noise in Fig. 1.5, which happens from encoding or communication errors. NCAR is currently referred to as symmetric or uniform label noise (Han et al., 2020b; Song et al., 2022). NAR models the relationship of the class labels without taking into account any information available from the data, so using MNIST as an example, NAR estimates the probability that any image of digit '1' can be mislabeled as '7' (and vice-versa). In other words, NAR models a transition matrix (applicable to any training sample) with the probability of switching between correct and noisy labels. NAR is currently referred to as asymmetric, pair-flipping, label-dependent noise, or instance-independent noise (Han et al., 2020b; Song et al., 2022). NNAR extends NAR to also depend on the data, resulting in a

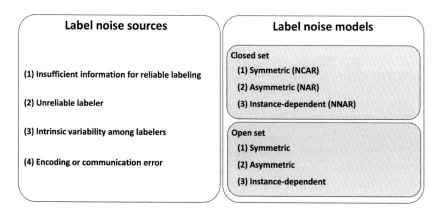

FIGURE 1.5 Label noise sources and models.

The left hand side frame shows the sources of label noise (Frénay and Verleysen, 2014), while the right hand side frame displays the noise label models being studied in the field (Frénay and Verleysen, 2014; Han et al., 2020b; Song et al., 2022).

unique transition matrix per sample. This takes into account that some samples can be harder to label than others, as shown in Fig. 1.4. Currently, NNAR is referred to as instance-dependent noise or semantic label noise (Han et al., 2020b; Song et al., 2022). Both NAR and NNAR happen when either the labeler is not reliable, or when there is intrinsic variability among labelers, accounting for error sources (2) and (3) above. These three label noise models are collectively referred to as closed-set label noise models because the dataset only contains in-distribution (ID) images that belong to classes that are in the set of training labels.

When the dataset contains OoD samples, which do not belong to any of the classes that are in the set of training labels, then we have the open-set label noise model (Wang et al., 2018). For example, considering the MNIST dataset in Fig. 1.4, this problem happens when images from a different dataset, such as OMNIGLOT (Lake et al., 2015) (containing 1623 different handwritten characters from 50 different alphabets) are placed in the dataset – see Fig. 1.4 (bottom frame titled open-set noise). Similarly to the closed-set label noise, open-set label noise can be symmetric, asymmetric or instance-dependent. In symmetric open-set label noise, the OoD samples are randomly labeled with any of the training labels – this type of noise would assign any of the 10 MNIST classes to each image of the bottom frame of Fig. 1.4 with probability 10%. The asymmetric open-set label noise models the relationship from the OoD labels to the ID labels (i.e., the training labels) without considering the input data information. An example of such noise model would label the 2nd, 4th, and 6th characters of the bottom frame of Fig. 1.4 with MNIST labels '2' or '5', each with probability 50%. Furthermore, the instance-dependence open-set label noise works similarly as the asymmetric case above, but taking into account the input data information, so taking the bottom frame of Fig. 1.4, the 2nd character is arguably more likely to be labeled as '2' (and less likely as '5'), while the 6th character is more likely to be labeled as '5' (and less likely as '2'). Note that open-set models are related to the error source (1) above because there is insufficient information to reliably label the image.

The sources and models of label noise presented above can be easily found not only in uncurated datasets, but also in well-curated datasets. In fact, it is estimated that publicly available (curated and uncurated) datasets have around between 5.0% and 38.5% of label noise rate (Frénay and Verleysen, 2014; Song et al., 2022). For instance, curated datasets, such as ImageNet (Deng et al., 2009), CalTech-256,[4] MNIST (LeCun, 1998) and IMDB (Maas et al., 2011), which are usually assumed to have only clean labels, actually contain label noise, as demonstrated by Northcutt et al. (2021)[5] – see Fig. 1.6 for a few examples. The annotation of large-scale computer vision datasets, like ImageNet (Deng et al., 2009), usually relies on crowdsourcing labeling from Amazon Mechanical Turk.[6] Crowdsourcing labeling is generally provided by unreliable labelers, which as described in Fig. 1.5, are considered a potential source of label noise. In medical image analysis, it is harder to obtain crowdsourcing labeling given the expertise needed to perform the annotation task. Instead, medical image labeling needs to be done by radiologists who tend to be expensive and to suffer from significant time constraints. Considering this scenario, Wang et al. (2017b) proposed an automated way to label a hospital-scale Chest X-ray (CXR) dataset, containing more than 100,000 images, based on the use of natural language processing (NLP) techniques to automatically extract the multiple disease labels from the radiological report associated with each image. As noted by Oakden-Rayner (2020), this dataset has a non-negligible proportion of label noise not only because of the NLP mistakes, but also because of the difficulty of diagnosing some diseases from CXR images. Speech recognition is another domain with datasets containing label noise. For example, the dataset collected by Reddy et al. (2019) contains Voice-over-Internet-Protocol (VoIP) calls with different types speech impairments and labels related to the cause of bad audio quality. However, these labels are noisy since they do not precisely identify the impairment in the speech.

We argue that label noise is an intrinsic problem in any machine learning task, which explains why even well-curated datasets are affected by it. This argument is supported by the bias-variance decomposition of the predictive training loss used to train a model, as follows:

$$\text{Mean}(\text{TrainingLoss}) = \text{IrreducibleError} + \text{Bias} + \text{Variance}, \qquad (1.1)$$

where Bias and Variance represent terms that depend on the training algorithm, but IrreducibleError denotes as unavoidable component of the loss that is independent of the learning algorithm (Domingos, 2000). Such IrreducibleError is in part function of the label noise present in the problem, with its rate depending on the source

---

[4] https://paperswithcode.com/dataset/caltech-256.

[5] https://labelerrors.com/.

[6] https://www.mturk.com/.

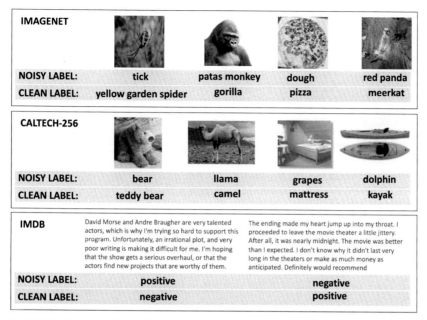

FIGURE 1.6 Label noise in public datasets.

Public datasets contain label noise even after careful annotation. All label noise examples are extracted from https://labelerrors.com/, where the top frame shows mislabeled images from ImageNet (Deng et al., 2009), the second frame displays images from CalTech-256 (https://paperswithcode.com/dataset/caltech-256), and the third frame shows samples from the movie review IMDB dataset (Maas et al., 2011).

and model of label noise. Hence, well-curated datasets have small intrinsic noise, enabling more effective training. Nevertheless, the realization that the IrreducibleError is unavoidable leads to interesting challenges in ML and DL, that we introduce in the next section.

1.3 Challenges

In this section, we define a list of challenges in the study of learning with label noise. Since they represent open research problems in the field, we hope that this book will provide potential directions to address these challenges.

The first challenge (see Fig. 1.7) lies in the definition of the process to generate a label noise. There are two competing strategies, one based on a label transition process (Lawrence and Schölkopf, 2001; Pérez et al., 2007), and the other based on label distribution (Domingos, 2000; Thiel, 2008). In the label transition definition, it is assumed that each sample has a latent clean-label probability distribution

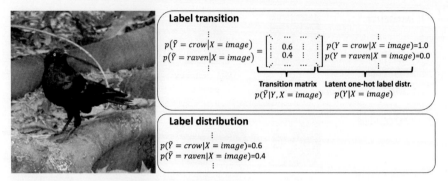

FIGURE 1.7 First Challenge: definition of label noise.

Label noise can be defined using two different processes. In the label transition process, we assume that the sample has a latent clean-label probability distribution, denoted by $p(Y|X = \mathbf{x})$, and that we also have a label transition matrix, represented by $p(\tilde{Y}|Y = \mathbf{y}, X = \mathbf{x})$ to form a label distribution $p(\tilde{Y}|X = \mathbf{x}) = \sum_{\mathbf{y}} p(\tilde{Y}|Y = \mathbf{y}, X = \mathbf{x})p(Y = \mathbf{y}|X = \mathbf{x})$. In the label distribution process, we assume that each image has a latent noisy-label distribution $p(\tilde{Y}|X = \mathbf{x})$. In both cases, the one-hot noisy label is obtained by sampling from $p(\tilde{Y}|X = \mathbf{x})$.

$p(Y = \mathbf{y}|X = \mathbf{x}) \in [0, 1]$, with $\mathbf{y} \in \mathcal{Y} \subset \{0, 1\}^{|\mathcal{Y}|}$ denoting the one-hot clean label (i.e., $\sum_{c=1}^{|\mathcal{Y}|} \mathbf{y}(c) = 1$ and $\mathbf{y}(c) \in \{0, 1\}$ for $c \in \{1, ..., |\mathcal{Y}|\}$), $\mathbf{x} \in \mathcal{X}$ representing the data, Y and X being the random variables for the clean label and data, and $\sum_{\mathbf{y} \in \mathcal{Y}} p(Y = \mathbf{y}|X = \mathbf{x}) = 1$. This latent clean-label distribution is multiplied by a hidden label transition model $p(\tilde{Y} = \tilde{\mathbf{y}}|Y = \mathbf{y}, X = \mathbf{x})$, where $\tilde{Y}$ denotes the random variable for the noisy label and $\tilde{\mathbf{y}} \in \mathcal{Y}$. Using this label transition model, the noisy label distribution is defined by

$$p(\tilde{Y} = \tilde{\mathbf{y}}|X = \mathbf{x}) = \sum_{\mathbf{y} \in \mathcal{Y}} p(\tilde{Y} = \tilde{\mathbf{y}}|Y = \mathbf{y}, X = \mathbf{x})p(Y = \mathbf{y}|X = \mathbf{x}), \qquad (1.2)$$

with $p(\tilde{Y} = \tilde{\mathbf{y}}|X = \mathbf{x}) \in [0, 1]$ and $p(\tilde{Y} = \tilde{\mathbf{y}}|Y = \mathbf{y}, X = \mathbf{x}) \in [0, 1]$. Alternatively, the label distribution definition directly assumes the existence of a latent distribution $p(\tilde{Y} = \tilde{\mathbf{y}}|X = \mathbf{x}) \in [0, 1]$ for $\tilde{\mathbf{y}} \in \mathcal{Y}$. In both definitions, we assume that the one-hot noisy label available from each training point is sampled from the categorical label distribution defined by $p(\tilde{Y}|X = \mathbf{x})$. Notice that the main difference between these two definitions lies in the assumptions made about the latent distributions, which results in different strategies to address the noisy label problem. In Chapters 2 and 3, we clarify how to use each type of label noise when defining particular types of label noise problems.

The second challenge consists of the definition of an experimental setup that is useful to benchmark models for handling different types of label noise. The literature has a large number of datasets to assess label noise robustness (Albert et al., 2022;

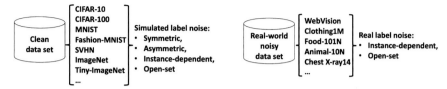

FIGURE 1.8 Second Challenge: datasets and benchmarks.

The development of datasets and benchmarks that cover all types of label noise described in Section 1.2 can lead to a combinatorial explosion in the number of benchmarks, which can challenge the progress of the field due to the intractability of assessing all models in all benchmarks.

Bossard et al., 2014; Deng et al., 2009; Gu et al., 2021; Jiang et al., 2020; Karpathy et al., 2016; Krizhevsky et al., 2014; LeCun, 1998; Lee et al., 2019; Li et al., 2017; Netzer et al., 2011; Song et al., 2019; Wang et al., 2018; Xia et al., 2020; Xiao et al., 2017, 2015; Zhang et al., 2021c) – see examples of synthetic and real-world datasets in Fig. 1.8. Such experimental setup comprises a training set containing samples with labels affected by one or more of the noise types described in Section 1.2, while the testing set contains samples with clean labels only. The definition of the noise types and rates, dataset, size of training set, distribution of training samples per classes, and task (multi-label or multi-class classification, regression, etc.) can lead to a combinatorial explosion in the number of benchmarks, which may not facilitate progress since it will be virtually impossible to evaluate all proposed models on all benchmarks. Furthermore, another issue related to the definition of the experimental setup is the requirement that all elements of the testing set need to have clean labels. For real-world datasets such requirement may be expensive and time-consuming to obtain, but in many cases, such as in medical image analysis datasets, it may be impossible to obtain given that these datasets will have an unavoidable amount of label noise because of the intrinsic variability among labelers.

Chapter 2 introduces the most explored experimental setups being used in computer vision, medical image analysis, and machine learning. However, the issues around the combinatorial explosion of benchmarks and the use of noisy testing sets are still open research problems.

The third challenge is related to the complete understanding of the impact of label noise on the training and testing of machine learning models. One of the first papers to study this problem was published by Angluin and Laird (1988), who presented a theoretical investigation on how training is affected by symmetric label noise. The main conclusion was that the learning algorithm for a binary classification problem is robust to symmetric noise, as long as the label noise rate is less than 50%. Lachenbruch (1966) studied the effect of symmetric label noise on binary classification problems, where effects become noticeable when noise rates in each class are different. The effects of label noise on normal discriminant and logistic regression are studied by Michalek and Tripathi (1980) and Bi and Jeske (2010). Uniform label noise also damages the generalization of a single-unit perceptron, as shown in (Heskes, 2000). Furthermore, the robustness of K Nearest Neighbors (KNN) classifiers is shown to depend on the value of K and the noise rate, where larger noise rates depend on higher values for K (Sánchez et al., 1997; Wilson and Martinez, 2000).

Before the advent of deep learning, Nettleton et al. (2010); Pechenizkiy et al. (2006) studied the effect of label noise on naive Bayes, decision trees induced by C4.5, KNN, and support vector machine (SVM) classifiers, and results show that SVM tends to be less robust due to its reliance on support vectors and the feature interdependence assumption. The adaptive boosting algorithm (AdaBoost) also tends to be sensitive to label noise, as demonstrated by Dietterich (2000). Ensemble learning classifiers are also shown to be sensitive to high noise rate because models can severely disagree in some cases (Ali and Pazzani, 1996). Spam filters can also overfit to the training samples with label noise because of their online update rules that quickly adapt to new spam (Sculley and Cormack, 2008).

Ever since deep learning models have become dominant in machine learning applications, with the groundbreaking paper by Krizhevsky et al. (2012), several researchers noticed that such models were particularly prone to overfit any complex function, even when the training set had corrupted labels (Krause et al., 2016). In particular, Arpit et al. (2017) show that higher label noise leads to slower convergence and poorer generalization to a test set that contains 100% clean label samples. Similarly, Zhang et al. (2021a) demonstrate that deep learning models can easily fit an entire training dataset with any rate of corrupted labels, which eventually resulted in poor generalizability on a clean test dataset.

Although we understand the theory in some specific label noise problems (Angluin and Laird, 1988), and the practical effect of different types and rates of label noise on many machine learning models (Han et al., 2020b; Song et al., 2022), we still do not have comprehensive studies that can predict, for example, the performance gap caused by different types and combinations of label noise. Chapter 3 presents more details about theoretical aspects of the impact of label noise on the training and testing of machine learning models.

The fourth challenge involves the development and evaluation of techniques capable of making machine learning models robust to label noise (see Fig. 1.9). The main strategies being developed in the field, which will be detailed in Chapter 4 are based on (Cordeiro and Carneiro, 2020; Frénay and Verleysen, 2014; Han et al., 2020b; Song et al., 2022): 1) loss function design, 2) training algorithm development, 3) training data processing, and 4) model architecture planning. These techniques have been shown to provide robustness to several types of label noise, where even though the papers claim to be "robust to label noise", they tend to focus only on the few benchmarks that the proposed method shows state-of-the-art results. Nevertheless, given the many different types of label noise, and the potentially large number of benchmarks presented in the first challenge, it is likely that some techniques are more adequate to particular types of label noise, but most papers fail to discuss such trade offs. Hence, it is difficult to confidently make a connection between label noise types and effective machine learning techniques.

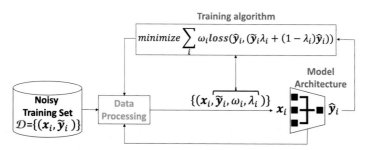

FIGURE 1.9 Fourth Challenge: techniques.

The main strategies developed in the field to handle label noise focus their contributions on: 1) loss function design, 2) training algorithm development, 3) training data processing, and 4) model architecture planning. In the diagram, the training set with samples and noisy labels is denoted by $\mathcal{D} = \{(\mathbf{x}_i, \tilde{\mathbf{y}}_i)\}$. As examples of data processing outputs, we display $\omega_i > 0$, which weights the training sample importance, and $\lambda_i \in [0, 1]$ that mixes the training label $\tilde{\mathbf{y}}_i \in \mathcal{Y}$ and model output $\hat{\mathbf{y}}_i \in \Delta^{|\mathcal{Y}|-1}$, with $\Delta^{|\mathcal{Y}|-1} = \{\mathbf{p}|\mathbf{p} \in [0, 1]^{|\mathcal{Y}|}$, and $\sum_{c=1}^{|\mathcal{Y}|} \mathbf{p}(c) = 1\}$ representing the probability simplex (Boyd et al., 2004).

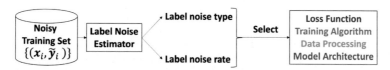

FIGURE 1.10 Fifth Challenge: label noise type and rate estimation.

The estimation of label noise type and rate can be used to select or estimate the parameters of label noise methods, namely: 1) loss function, 2) training algorithm, 3) training data, and 4) model architecture.

   The fifth challenge consists of estimating the noise rate and type(s) of label noise present in real-world datasets (see Fig. 1.10). Such estimate involves the characterization of the whole noisy-label training set, which is a process that is not usually performed in machine learning. This challenge is linked to the third challenge presented above because its utility depends on our ability to clearly establish which label noise learning methods are more adequate to specific rates and types of label noise. Even though this challenge is briefly covered by Frénay and Verleysen (2014), it has been under-explored in the field. A remarkable exception is the method presented by Xiao et al. (2015) that tries to estimate the label noise type (but not the label noise rate) affecting each training sample. Methods based on the estimation label transition models (Liu and Tao, 2015) aim to find the label noise rate, but not the type since they assume a specific type of label noise (e.g., asymmetric label noise).

1.4 **Conclusion**

With this first chapter, we hope to have convinced the reader about the importance of studying the label noise problem. The study of this problem will facilitate the development of machine learning and deep learning methods that can robustly use noisy-label datasets. We also described the process of labeling data and how label noise is introduced into large-scale training sets. The challenges associated with the label noise problem were then briefly explained, but we will discuss these challenges in more detail in Chapter 2.

Noisy-label problems and datasets

2

Tasks, taxonomy, datasets, and evaluation

2.1 Introduction

As explained in Fig. 1.5, there are four sources of label noise. To facilitate the formal definition of label noise in this chapter, we will cluster these four sources into two sources, namely: 1) the intrinsic noise associated with the difficulty of labeling the data (i.e., the insufficient information for reliable labeling, and the intrinsic variability among labelers from Fig. 1.5); and 2) the noise introduced by the labeler or by the encoding process (i.e., unreliable labeler and encoding/communication error from Fig. 1.5). It is important to consider these two noise clusters because the type and rate of label noise usually depends on both sources, as we will explain in this chapter. Fig. 2.1 shows a fictitious example[1] of an image that has an intrinsic label noise given the inherently uncertain label distribution (i.e., the distribution does not show a 100% conditional probability for any of the labels) based on the information available in the picture, where this distribution is commonly hidden in real-world problems. More specifically, the intrinsic label distribution shows that even though the probability of labeling the image with the class "yellow-crested cockatoo" is 80% (which is the correct class in this case), there is still a 10% probability of labeling it with "salmon-crested cockatoo" or "umbrella cockatoo". If we take this image and request 100 expert labelers (i.e., labelers who do not introduce noise beyond the intrinsic label distribution of the image) to provide one-hot labels (i.e., multi-class labels that contain a single class annotated with '1' and all other classes annotated with '0'), the histogram of labels will reflect the original intrinsic label distribution. However, if that image is labeled by 100 layman labelers (i.e., people who may introduce label noise beyond the intrinsic label distribution of the image), the 100 one-hot labels will have additional mistakes introduced by the labelers, as depicted by the histogram of labels that shows a different distribution from the original intrinsic label distribution.

In this chapter, we first define the regression, classification, segmentation, and detection problems assuming that data samples have an underlying intrinsic label dis-

---

[1] By fictitious, we mean that we did not consult with experts to estimate the probabilities mentioned in the text. Instead, we list the probabilities to facilitate the understanding of label noise sources explained in this chapter.

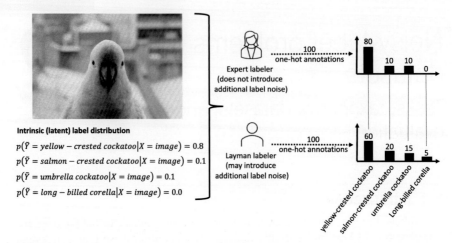

FIGURE 2.1 Label noise: intrinsic error and labeler/encoding error.

The four sources of label noise defined in Fig. 1.5 can be clustered into the following two sources: the intrinsic noise from the latent label distribution, and the noise introduced by labeling mistakes. Let us assume that the image on the left has the displayed intrinsic (latent) label distribution, then if we take 100 one-hot labels provided by expert labelers who do not introduce additional label noise, we will have a label histogram that mirrors the intrinsic label distribution. On the other hand, if we request 100 one-hot labels by layman labelers who may introduce additional label noise, we will have a label histogram that deviates from the intrinsic label distribution.

tribution. Then, we explain the main types of label noise processes studied in the field, i.e., closed-set, open-set, symmetric, asymmetric, and instance-dependent, which are introduced by the labeling process. We then present the main datasets and benchmarks used to assess methods that are designed to address label noise problems, and we conclude the chapter with approaches to assess noisy-label classification, segmentation, and detection problems.

2.2 Regression, classification, segmentation, and detection problems

In this section, we provide a more formal description of the label noise learning problem, where we focus on regression, classification, segmentation, and detection problems.

2.2.1 Regression

For the regression problem, we have $\mathbf{x} \in \mathcal{X}$ denoting the input data sample (e.g., image, text, sound) and $\tilde{\mathbf{y}} \in \mathcal{Y}$ representing the noisy label in a continuous space, which for regression problems is generally represented by $\mathcal{Y} \subset \mathbb{R}$. Each training sample is drawn from a joint probability distribution defined by $p(X, \tilde{Y})$ that is generally latent, unless we are dealing with toy problems where we can define such distribution. This probability distribution $p(X, \tilde{Y})$ can be defined in the joint $\mathcal{X} \times \mathcal{Y}$ space, where data $\mathbf{x}$ and noisy label $\tilde{\mathbf{y}}$ are drawn simultaneously, but such joint distribution complicates the definition of label noise since the noise affecting the data is entangled with the noise affecting the label. Hence, we decompose $p(X, \tilde{Y})$ into $p(\tilde{Y}|X)p(X)$ using the fundamental rule for probability calculus, which suggests a 2-stage sampling process, where we first draw $\mathbf{x}$ from $p(X)$, and then a noisy label $\tilde{\mathbf{y}}$ from $p(\tilde{Y}|X = \mathbf{x})$.

Without loss of generality, let us assume that both terms can be represented by normal distributions, so the joint probability distribution can be denoted as follows:

$$p(X = \mathbf{x}, \tilde{Y} = \tilde{\mathbf{y}}) = p(\tilde{Y} = \tilde{\mathbf{y}}|X = \mathbf{x}) \times p(X = \mathbf{x})$$
$$= \mathcal{N}(\tilde{\mathbf{y}}; \mu_X(\mathbf{x}), \Sigma_X(\mathbf{x})) \times \mathcal{N}(\mathbf{x}; \mu, \Sigma),$$

(2.1)

where

$$\mathcal{N}(\mathbf{x}; \mu, \Sigma) = \frac{\exp\{-\frac{1}{2}(\mathbf{x} - \mu)^\top \Sigma^{-1}(\mathbf{x} - \mu)\}}{\sqrt{(2\pi)^{|X|}|\Sigma|}}$$

(2.2)

represents a multivariate normal distribution, with $\mathcal{N}(\tilde{\mathbf{y}}; \mu_X(\mathbf{x}), \Sigma_X(\mathbf{x}))$ being similarly defined, $\mu_X : \mathcal{X} \to \mathcal{Y}$ denotes the function that returns the mean label in $\mathcal{Y}$ given $\mathbf{x}$, $\Sigma_X : \mathcal{X} \to \mathcal{Y} \times \mathcal{Y}$ is the function that returns the label covariance in $\mathcal{Y}$ given $\mathbf{x}$, and μ and Σ are the mean and covariance for the multivariate normal distribution in $\mathcal{X}$. The sampling process then happens in two stages:

1. $X = \mu + \Sigma \times \epsilon_X$
2. $\tilde{Y} = \mu_X(\mathbf{x}) + \Sigma_X(\mathbf{x}) \times \epsilon_y,$

(2.3)

where $\epsilon_X \sim n(\mathbf{0}_X, \mathbf{I}_X)$ is a normally distributed pseudo-random vector in $\mathcal{X}$ (with zero mean $\mathbf{0}_X \in \mathcal{X}$ and identity covariance $\mathbf{I}_X \in \mathcal{X} \times \mathcal{X}$), and similarly for $\epsilon_y \sim n(\mathbf{0}_y, \mathbf{I}_y)$ in $\mathcal{Y}$.

To introduce the concept of a latent clean label in regression problems, we consider another representation for the joint probability with $p(X, \tilde{Y}) = \int p(Y, \tilde{Y}|X) \times p(X)dY = \int p(\tilde{Y}|Y, X)p(Y|X)p(X)dY$, where Y denotes the latent clean label variable. An example of this representation is:

$$p(X = \mathbf{x}, \tilde{Y} = \tilde{\mathbf{y}}) = \int p(\tilde{Y} = \tilde{\mathbf{y}}|Y, X = \mathbf{x}) \times p(Y|X = \mathbf{x}) \times p(X = \mathbf{x})dY$$

$$= \int \mathcal{N}(\tilde{\mathbf{y}}; \mu_{yX}(Y, \mathbf{x}), \Sigma_{yX}(Y, \mathbf{x})) \times \mathcal{N}(Y; \mu_X(\mathbf{x}), \Sigma_X(\mathbf{x})) \times \mathcal{N}(\mathbf{x}; \mu, \Sigma)dY,$$

(2.4)

where $\mu_{YX} : \mathcal{Y} \times \mathcal{X} \to \mathcal{Y}$, $\Sigma_{YX} : \mathcal{Y} \times \mathcal{X} \to \mathcal{Y} \times \mathcal{Y}$, and other definitions are as explained in (2.1). The sampling follows a 3-stage process:

$$
\begin{aligned}
&1.\ X = \mu + \Sigma \times \epsilon_X \\
&2.\ Y = \mu_X(\mathbf{x}) + \Sigma_X(\mathbf{x}) \times \epsilon_Y \\
&3.\ \tilde{Y} = \mu_{YX}(\mathbf{y}, \mathbf{x}) + \Sigma_{YX}(\mathbf{y}, \mathbf{x}) \times \epsilon_Y,
\end{aligned}
\tag{2.5}
$$

where $\epsilon_X \sim n(\mathbf{0}_X, \mathbf{I}_X)$ and $\epsilon_Y \sim n(\mathbf{0}_Y, \mathbf{I}_Y)$, following the same definitions as in (2.3).

In a regression problem, we define a model $f_\theta : \mathcal{X} \to \mathcal{Y}$, parameterized by $\theta \in \Theta$, that is trained to produce the output in $\mathcal{Y}$ given an input in $\mathcal{X}$. This training is based on an optimization that minimizes a loss function denoted by $\ell : \mathcal{Y} \times \mathcal{Y} \to \mathbb{R}$, which is designed to penalize mistakes made by the model. Two examples of losses that are usually considered in regression problems are:

$$
\begin{aligned}
\ell_{L1}(\tilde{\mathbf{y}}, f_\theta(\mathbf{x})) &= \|\tilde{\mathbf{y}} - f_\theta(\mathbf{x})\|_1, \text{ and} \\
\ell_{L2}(\tilde{\mathbf{y}}, f_\theta(\mathbf{x})) &= \left\|\tilde{\mathbf{y}} - f_\theta(\mathbf{x})\right\|_2,
\end{aligned}
\tag{2.6}
$$

which denote the $L1$ and $L2$ losses, respectively. The training of the regression model using the joint probability of sample X and noisy label $\tilde{Y}$ is then based on optimizing the model parameters that minimize the expectation of the loss function:

$$
\theta^* = \arg\min_{\theta \in \Theta} \mathbb{E}_{(\mathbf{x}, \tilde{\mathbf{y}}) \sim p(X, \tilde{Y})}[\ell(\tilde{\mathbf{y}}, f_\theta(\mathbf{x}))].
\tag{2.7}
$$

However, the optimization in (2.7) cannot be performed because in general the distribution $p(X, \tilde{Y})$ is unknown. This issue is solved by optimizing a Monte-Carlo approximation of the expectation of the loss function (2.7), by averaging the loss on the training set containing noisy labels $\mathcal{D} = \{(\mathbf{x}, \tilde{\mathbf{y}})_i\}_{i=1}^{|\mathcal{D}|}$, where $(\mathbf{x}, \tilde{\mathbf{y}}) \sim p(X, \tilde{Y})$. This optimization is referred to as empirical risk minimization (ERM), which is defined as:

$$
\theta^* = \arg\min_{\theta \in \Theta} \frac{1}{|\mathcal{D}|} \sum_{(\mathbf{x}, \tilde{\mathbf{y}}) \in \mathcal{D}} \ell(\tilde{\mathbf{y}}, f_\theta(\mathbf{x})).
\tag{2.8}
$$

We show the results of two regression experiments, with one relying on the 2-step sampling process described in (2.3) (see Fig. 2.2), and the other based on the 3-step sampling process from (2.5) (see Fig. 2.3). Both approaches relied on a model $f_\theta(.)$ that consists of a multi-layer perceptron (2 hidden layers, each with 10 nodes and Exponential Linear Unit (ELU) activation functions, and an output layer with a single linear output), which is trained with the ERM in (2.8) that minimizes the L2 loss in (2.6).

2.2.2 Classification

For the **multi-class classification problem** (see Fig. 2.4(a)), we assume to have input data $\mathbf{x} \in \mathcal{X}$ labeled with $\tilde{\mathbf{y}} \in \mathcal{Y} = \{\mathbf{p} | \mathbf{p} \in \{0, 1\}^{|\mathcal{Y}|}, \text{ and } \sum_{c=1}^{|\mathcal{Y}|} \mathbf{p}(c) = 1\}$, which is a

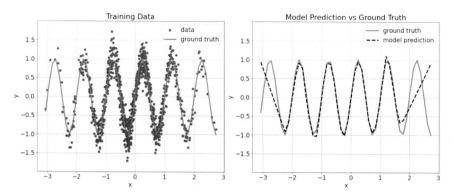

FIGURE 2.2 Regression problem using a 2-stage sampling process from (2.3).

The graph on the left shows the training samples (blue dots) drawn from $X = \mu + \Sigma \times \epsilon_X$, where $\mu = 0$ and $\Sigma = 1$, and noisy labels sampled from $\tilde{Y} = \mu_X(\mathbf{x}) + \Sigma_X \times \epsilon_y$, where $\mu_X(\mathbf{x}) = \sin(2\pi\mathbf{x})$ (solid red curve) and $\Sigma_X = 0.25$. On the right, we plot $\mu_X(\mathbf{x})$ (red, solid) and the prediction of the model (black, dashed) trained with the data (blue dots) from the left graph.

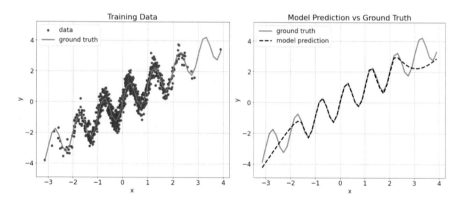

FIGURE 2.3 Regression problem using a 3-stage sampling process from (2.5).

The graph on the left shows the training samples (blue dots) drawn from $X = \mu + \Sigma \times \epsilon_X$, where $\mu = 0$ and $\Sigma = 1$, clean labels sampled from $Y = \mu_X(\mathbf{x}) + \Sigma_X \times \epsilon_y$, where $\mu_X(\mathbf{x}) = \sin(2\pi\mathbf{x})$ and $\Sigma_X = 0.25$, and noisy labels are drawn from $\tilde{Y} = \mu_{y_X}(\mathbf{y}, \mathbf{x}) + \Sigma_{y_X}(\mathbf{y}, \mathbf{x}) \times \epsilon_y$, where $\mu_{y_X}(\mathbf{y}, \mathbf{x}) = \mathbf{x} + \mathbf{y}$ (red solid line) and $\Sigma_{y_X} = 0.25$. On the right, we plot $\mu_{y_X}(\mathbf{y}, \mathbf{x})$ (red, solid) and the prediction of the model (black, dashed) trained with the data (blue dots) from the left graph.

one-hot classification label, where the dimension $|\mathcal{Y}|$ denotes the number of classes. Compared to the regression problem, the main difference in the classification problem is that $\mathcal{Y}$ is a discrete (instead of continuous) space representing the presence or absence of the classes in the input data.

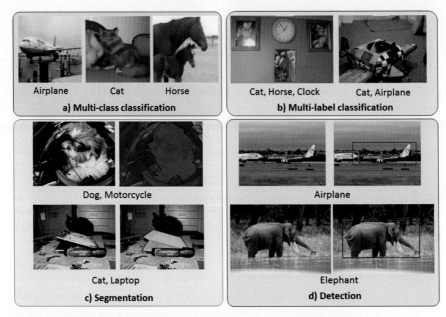

Airplane   Cat   Horse
a) Multi-class classification

Cat, Horse, Clock   Cat, Airplane
b) Multi-label classification

Dog, Motorcycle

Cat, Laptop
c) Segmentation

Airplane

Elephant
d) Detection

FIGURE 2.4 Examples of classification, segmentation, and detection problems.

a) Multi-class classification examples from the Pascal VOC2012 dataset (Everingham et al., 2010), b) Multi-label classification, c) Segmentation, and d) Detection from the COCO dataset (Lin et al., 2014).

Similarly to the regression problem, for the multi-class classification problem, a more direct representation of the label noise is achieved from the decomposition $p(X, \tilde{Y}) = p(\tilde{Y}|X)p(X)$. For example, we can have

$$
\begin{aligned}
p(X = \mathbf{x}, \tilde{Y} = \tilde{\mathbf{y}}) &= p(\tilde{Y} = \tilde{\mathbf{y}}|X = \mathbf{x}) \times p(X = \mathbf{x}) \\
&= p(\tilde{\mathbf{y}}; t_\mathcal{X}(\mathbf{x})) \times \mathcal{N}(\mathbf{x}; \mu, \Sigma),
\end{aligned}
\tag{2.9}
$$

where $t_\mathcal{X} : \mathcal{X} \to \Delta^{|\mathcal{Y}|-1}$ represents a function that outputs the categorical distribution at each $\mathbf{x} \in \mathcal{X}$, with $\Delta^{|\mathcal{Y}|-1} = \{\mathbf{p}|\mathbf{p} \in [0, 1]^{|\mathcal{Y}|}, \text{ and } \sum_{c=1}^{|\mathcal{Y}|} \mathbf{p}(c) = 1\}$ being the probability simplex (Boyd et al., 2004), $p(\tilde{\mathbf{y}}; t_\mathcal{X}(\mathbf{x})) = \prod_{c=1}^{|\mathcal{Y}|} \mathbf{t}(c)^{\tilde{\mathbf{y}}(c)}$ (with $\mathbf{t} = t_\mathcal{X}(\mathbf{x})$) (Bishop, 2006), and μ and Σ are the mean and covariance for the multivariate normal distribution in $\mathcal{X}$. The sampling process is based on two stages:

$$
\begin{aligned}
&1.\ X = \mu + \Sigma \times \epsilon_\mathcal{X} \\
&2.\ \tilde{Y} = T_\mathcal{X}^{-1}(u; \mathbf{x}),
\end{aligned}
\tag{2.10}
$$

where $\epsilon_\mathcal{X} \sim n(\mathbf{0}_\mathcal{X}, \mathbf{I}_\mathcal{X})$, following the definitions in (2.3), $u \sim \mathcal{U}(0, 1)$ denotes a number in $[0, 1]$ sampled from a uniform distribution, and $T_\mathcal{X}^{-1} : [0, 1] \times \mathcal{X} \to \mathcal{Y}$

represents the inverse cumulative distribution function computed from $t_X(\mathbf{x})$ (Olver and Townsend, 2013).

The clean label variable Y can be explicitly introduced into the formulation with $p(X, \tilde{Y}) = p(\tilde{Y}|X)p(X) = \sum_Y p(Y, \tilde{Y}|X)p(X) = \sum_Y p(\tilde{Y}|Y, X)p(Y|X)p(X)$. In this representation, we also introduce the transition probability function that estimates the noisy categorical distribution of $\tilde{Y}$ given Y and X. An example of this representation is

$$p(X = \mathbf{x}, \tilde{Y} = \tilde{\mathbf{y}}) = \sum_{y \in \mathcal{Y}} p(\tilde{Y} = \tilde{\mathbf{y}}|Y = \mathbf{y}, X = \mathbf{x}) \times p(Y = \mathbf{y}|X = \mathbf{x}) \times p(X = \mathbf{x})$$

$$= \sum_{y \in \mathcal{Y}} p(\tilde{\mathbf{y}}; t_{y_X}(\mathbf{y}, \mathbf{x})) \times p(\mathbf{y}; t_X(\mathbf{x})) \times \mathcal{N}(\mathbf{x}; \mu, \Sigma),$$

$$(2.11)$$

where $p(\mathbf{y}; t_X(\mathbf{x}))$ and $\mathcal{N}(\mathbf{x}; \mu, \Sigma)$ are as defined in (2.9), and $t_{y_X} : \mathcal{Y} \times \mathcal{X} \to \Delta^{|\mathcal{Y}|-1}$ represents the transition probability function that outputs a categorical distribution for the label $\tilde{\mathbf{y}}$ given $\mathbf{y}$ and $\mathbf{x}$. The sampling process is based on three stages:

$$1.\ X = \mu + \Sigma \times \epsilon_X$$
$$2.\ Y = T_X^{-1}(u; \mathbf{x}) \qquad\qquad (2.12)$$
$$3.\ \tilde{Y} = T_{y_X}^{-1}(u; \mathbf{y}, \mathbf{x}),$$

where, as in (2.10), $\epsilon_X \sim n(\mathbf{0}_X, \mathbf{I}_X)$ and $u \sim \mathcal{U}(0, 1)$, and $T_X^{-1}(.)$ and $T_{y_X}^{-1}(.)$ represent the inverse cumulative distribution functions computed from $t_X(\mathbf{x})$ and $t_{y_X}(\mathbf{y}, \mathbf{x})$.

The classifier is defined as $f_\theta : \mathcal{X} \to \Delta^{|\mathcal{Y}|-1}$, which is trained to output the probability for each class in $\mathcal{Y}$ given an input in $\mathcal{X}$. This training process minimizes a loss function $\ell : \mathcal{Y} \times \Delta^{|\mathcal{Y}|-1} \to \mathbb{R}$ that penalizes misclassifications. Examples of losses that are usually considered in classification problems are:

$$\ell_{01}(\mathbf{y}, f_\theta(\mathbf{x})) = \delta(\mathbf{y} \neq \mathsf{OneHot}(f_\theta(\mathbf{x}))),$$
$$\ell_{CE}(\mathbf{y}, f_\theta(\mathbf{x})) = -\mathbf{y}^\top \log(f_\theta(\mathbf{x})),$$
$$\ell_{BCE}(\mathbf{y}, f_\theta(\mathbf{x})) = -\mathbf{y}^\top \log(f_\theta(\mathbf{x})) - (1 - \mathbf{y})^\top \log(1 - f_\theta(\mathbf{x})), \qquad (2.13)$$
$$\ell_{HNG}(\mathbf{y}, f_\theta(\mathbf{x})) = \max(0, 1 - \mathbf{y}^\top f_\theta(\mathbf{x})),$$
$$\ell_{NLL}(\mathbf{y}, f_\theta(\mathbf{x})) = -\log(f_\theta^{(\mathbf{y})}(\mathbf{x})),$$

which are the 0-1 loss, the cross-entropy (CE) loss, the binary cross-entropy (BCE) loss, the hinge loss, and the negative log-likelihood (NLL) loss, where $\mathsf{OneHot} : \Delta^{|\mathcal{Y}|-1} \to \mathcal{Y}$ returns a binary vector with a '1' in the class of maximum probability from $f_\theta(\mathbf{x})$, and '0' for all other classes, $\delta(.)$ denotes the indicator function, and $f_\theta^{(\mathbf{y})}(\mathbf{x})$ returns the output from the model $f_\theta(\mathbf{x})$ for the class indexed by the one-hot vector $(\mathbf{y})$. The training of the classifier to estimate the optimal parameter $\theta \in \Theta$

using the joint probability of sample X and noisy label $\tilde{Y}$ is achieved by minimizing the loss function:

$$\theta^* = \arg\min_{\theta \in \Theta} \mathbb{E}_{(\mathbf{x},\tilde{\mathbf{y}}) \sim p(X,\tilde{Y})}[\ell(\tilde{\mathbf{y}}, f_\theta(\mathbf{x}))], \tag{2.14}$$

which is unfeasible since $p(X, \tilde{Y})$ is unknown. This is mitigated by using the training set containing noisy labels $\mathcal{D} = \{(\mathbf{x}, \tilde{\mathbf{y}})_i\}_{i=1}^{|\mathcal{D}|}$, where $(\mathbf{x}, \tilde{\mathbf{y}}) \sim p(X, \tilde{Y})$, to minimize the empirical risk with

$$\theta^* = \arg\min_{\theta \in \Theta} \frac{1}{|\mathcal{D}|} \sum_{(\mathbf{x},\tilde{\mathbf{y}}) \in \mathcal{D}} \ell(\tilde{\mathbf{y}}, f_\theta(\mathbf{x})). \tag{2.15}$$

We show the results of two multi-class classification experiments, with one relying on the 2-step sampling process described in (2.10), and the other based on the 3-step sampling process from (2.12) (see Fig. 2.5). In both experiments, the 2-D data is generated by a Gaussian mixture model (GMM) using four components, with each component representing a separate class, where the class means are $(-2, -2)$, $(-2, 2)$, $(2, -2)$, $(2, 2)$, covariances are denoted by an identity matrix of size 2×2, and mixture weights are equal to 0.25. The two experiments use a model $f_\theta(.)$ that consists of a multi-layer perceptron (1 hidden layer with 5 nodes and Exponential Linear Unit (ELU) activation functions, and an output layer with a softmax output), which is trained with ERM in (2.15) that minimizes the BCE loss in (2.13).

For **multi-label classification problems** (see Fig. 2.4(b)), the training samples $\mathbf{x}$ are annotated with $\tilde{\mathbf{y}} \in \mathcal{Y} \subset \{0, 1\}^{|\mathcal{Y}|}$, with $0 \leq \sum_{c=1}^{|\mathcal{Y}|} \tilde{\mathbf{y}}(c) \leq |\mathcal{Y}|$, so each sample can be labeled with no classes or multiple classes. This modification from the multi-class classification scenario requires some changes in the definitions presented above.

First, the model needs to be redefined as $f_\theta : \mathcal{X} \to [0, 1]^{|\mathcal{Y}|}$, which means that each label can have a separate probability of being present in the data. The noisy-label distribution also needs a redefinition with $p(\tilde{Y} = \tilde{\mathbf{y}}|X = \mathbf{x}) = p(\tilde{\mathbf{y}}|t_X^{\mathcal{P}}(\mathbf{x}))$, where $t_X^{\mathcal{P}}$: $\mathcal{X} \to \Delta^{2^{|\mathcal{Y}|}-1}$ outputs a categorical distribution at each $\mathbf{x} \in \mathcal{X}$, with $\Delta^{2^{|\mathcal{Y}|}-1}$ denoting the probability simplex for the label power set $\mathcal{P}$. In this power set, each of the $2^{|\mathcal{Y}|}$ labels in $\mathcal{P}$ denotes a different label combination from the classes in $\mathcal{Y}$ (Spolaôr et al., 2013). Following the idea above, we extend $p(\tilde{\mathbf{y}}; t_X^{\mathcal{P}}(\mathbf{x})) = \prod_{c \in \mathcal{P}} t^{\mathcal{P}}(c)^{\delta(\mathcal{P}(c)=\tilde{\mathbf{y}})}$, with $t^{\mathcal{P}} = t_X^{\mathcal{P}}(\mathbf{x})$, $\delta(.)$ being the indicator function, and $\mathcal{P}(c)$ representing the cth element of the power set $\mathcal{P}$.

For training the classification model, we could consider the same loss functions from (2.13) if we regard the problem as a multi-class problem, where the classes are the label combinations in the power set $\mathcal{P}$. However, the size of this power set quickly becomes intractable, so in practice, multi-label problems use the BCE loss from (2.13) and the class-wise 0-1 loss defined by $\ell_{01-ML}(\mathbf{y}, f_\theta(\mathbf{x})) = \prod_{c=1}^{|\mathcal{Y}|} \delta\left(\mathbf{y}(c) \neq \text{Squash}\left(f_\theta^{(\mathbf{y}_c)}(\mathbf{x}), \tau\right)\right)$, where $\mathbf{y}(c) \in \{0, 1\}$ represents the cth element of the label vector $\mathbf{y}$, $\text{Squash} : [0, 1] \times [0, 1] \to \{0, 1\}^{|\mathcal{Y}|}$ is a function that thresholds the cth output of the model to be either 0 or 1 per label (using a threshold

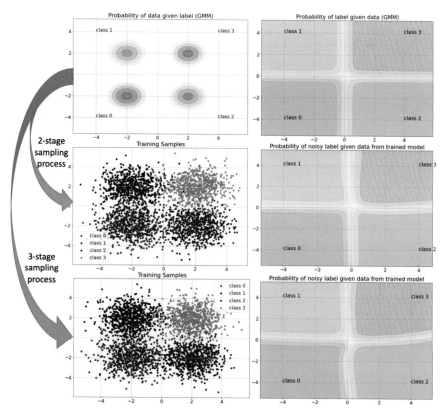

FIGURE 2.5 Classification using a 2-stage and a 3-stage sampling processes from (2.10) **and** (2.12)**, respectively.**

The top-left figure shows the underlying GMM distribution of the four classes (each Gaussian model represents by a different class) with means $(-2, -2), (-2, 2), (2, -2), (2, 2)$, identity covariances, and mixture weights of 0.25. The top-right figure shows the label distribution given data, where higher color saturation denotes larger probability. Using the 2-stage sampling process from (2.10), we draw (from the GMM) the data samples $X = \mu + \Sigma \times \epsilon_X$, which are then labeled with noisy labels sampled from $\tilde{Y} = T_X^{-1}(u; \mathbf{x})$ using label distribution given data from the top-right figure. After training the model $f_\theta(\mathbf{x})$ to minimize the ERM in (2.15) with the BCE loss in (2.13) using the samples in the middle-left figure, the classification predictions are shown in the middle-right figure. Relying on the 3-stage process from (2.12), we again draw data samples labeled with noisy labels, first sampled from $Y = T_X^{-1}(u; \mathbf{x})$ and then sampled from $\tilde{Y} = T_{Y|X}^{-1}(u; \mathbf{y}, \mathbf{x})$, both using label distribution given data from the top-right figure. The bottom-right figure shows the outputs of the model trained with the data from the bottom-left figure.

$\tau \in [0, 1]$), with this c^{th} model output denoted by $f_\theta^{(\mathbf{y}_c)}(\mathbf{x})$. Training is similarly done by minimizing the empirical risk in (2.15).

2.2.3 Semantic segmentation

The semantic segmentation problem mainly applies to images, as shown in Fig. 2.4(c), where the input image is denoted by $\mathbf{x} \in \mathcal{X} \subset \mathbb{R}^{H \times W \times R}$ (with $H = $ height, $W = $ width, $R = $ number of color channels), which is labeled by $\tilde{\mathbf{y}} \in \mathcal{Y} \subset \{0, 1\}^{H \times W \times C}$ (with $C = $ being number of segmentation classes, and $\sum_{c=1}^{C} \tilde{\mathbf{y}}(\omega, c) = 1$ for $\omega \in \Omega$ indexing the image lattice of size $H \times W$). The segmentation model, parameterized by $\theta \in \Theta$, is defined by $f_\theta : \mathcal{X} \to \{\Delta_\omega^{|\mathcal{Y}|-1}\}_{\omega \in \Omega}$, which outputs a pixel-wise categorical distribution for the image $\mathbf{x} \in \mathcal{X}$. The segmentation problem is an extension of the whole image classification problem from Section 2.2.2 to a pixel-wise classification. Hence all definitions in Section 2.2.2 can be extended to the segmentation problem, but with the modifications explained below.

The joint probability from (2.9) needs to redefine the categorical distribution function from $t_\mathcal{X} : \mathcal{X} \to \Delta^{|\mathcal{Y}|-1}$ to $t_{\Omega\mathcal{X}} : \mathcal{X} \to \{\Delta_\omega^{|\mathcal{Y}|-1}\}_{\omega \in \Omega}$, which represents a function that outputs a pixel-wise categorical distribution. Furthermore, we also redefine $p(\tilde{\mathbf{y}}; t_{\Omega\mathcal{X}}) = \prod_{\omega \in \Omega} \prod_{c=1}^{|\mathcal{Y}|} \mathbf{t}(\omega, c)^{\tilde{\mathbf{y}}(\omega, c)}$, where $\mathbf{t}(\omega, c)$ denotes the probability of the cth class at the pixel ω computed from $\mathbf{t} = t_{\Omega\mathcal{X}}(\mathbf{x})$, $\tilde{\mathbf{y}}(\omega, c)$ represents the label of the cth class at ω, and it is assumed that the pixel-wise categorical distribution is independent within the image lattice Ω. The sampling process for the segmentation problem is similar to the one for classification in (2.10) with the same step 1, and step 2 performed in a pixel-wise manner with $\tilde{Y}(\omega) = T_{\Omega\mathcal{X}}^{-1}(u; \mathbf{x})$ for $\omega \in \Omega$ and $u \sim \mathcal{U}(0, 1)$, which is the inverse cumulative distribution function computed from $t_{\Omega\mathcal{X}}(\mathbf{x})$. When introducing the latent clean label variable Y, the joint distribution $p(X, \tilde{Y})$ from (2.11) needs to use $t_{\Omega\mathcal{X}\mathcal{Y}} : \mathcal{Y} \times \mathcal{X} \to \{\Delta_\omega^{|\mathcal{Y}|-1}\}_{\omega \in \Omega}$, where sampling in (2.12) is done with $\tilde{Y}(\omega) = T_{\Omega\mathcal{X}\mathcal{Y}}^{-1}(u; \mathbf{y}, \mathbf{x})$, which is the inverse cumulative distribution function computed from $t_{\Omega\mathcal{X}\mathcal{Y}}(\mathbf{y}, \mathbf{x})$.

Another difference is in the definition of the loss functions, where the losses in (2.13) are now defined in a pixel-wise manner, but a global loss can also be considered, such as the Dice loss (Milletari et al., 2016):

$$\ell_{Dice}(\mathbf{y}, \hat{\mathbf{y}}) = \frac{2 \sum_{\omega \in \Omega} \mathbf{y}(\omega)^\top \hat{\mathbf{y}}(\omega)}{\sum_{\omega \in \Omega} \mathbf{y}(\omega)^\top \mathbf{y}(\omega) + \sum_{\omega \in \Omega} \hat{\mathbf{y}}(\omega)^\top \hat{\mathbf{y}}(\omega)}, \qquad (2.16)$$

where $\hat{\mathbf{y}} = f_\theta(\mathbf{x})$. Segmentation problems are constrained to a single label per pixel, so we do not consider the multi-label classification for segmentation problems. Training with a noisy label dataset $\mathcal{D} = \{(\mathbf{x}, \tilde{\mathbf{y}})_i\}_{i=1}^{|\mathcal{D}|}$ is usually done by minimizing a combination of a pixel-wise loss and a global loss, as with the ERM in:

$$\theta^* = \arg\min_{\theta \in \Theta} \frac{1}{|\mathcal{D}|} \sum_{(\mathbf{x}, \tilde{\mathbf{y}}) \in \mathcal{D}} \left(\frac{1}{|\Omega|} \sum_{\omega \in \Omega} \ell(\tilde{\mathbf{y}}(\omega), \hat{\mathbf{y}}(\omega)) \right) + \lambda \times \ell_{Dice}(\tilde{\mathbf{y}}, \hat{\mathbf{y}}), \qquad (2.17)$$

where $\hat{\mathbf{y}} = f_\theta(\mathbf{x})$, and λ weights the contribution of the Dice loss.

2.2.4 Detection

To deal with the detection of visual objects from images (see Fig. 2.4(d)), we define the input image as $\mathbf{x} \in X \subset \mathbb{R}^{H \times W \times R}$ (with H = height, W = width, R = number of color channels), which is associated with B bounding boxes, each represented by the top-left and bottom-right two-dimensional coordinates denoted by $\mathbf{b} \in \mathcal{B} \subset \mathbb{R}^4$ and labeled with the object class $\tilde{\mathbf{y}} \in \mathcal{Y} \subset \{0, 1\}^{|\mathcal{Y}|}$. The detection model, parameterized by $\theta \in \Theta$, is defined by $f_\theta : X \to \left\{ \Delta_a^{|\mathcal{Y}|-1} \times \mathcal{B}_a \right\}_{a=1}^{A}$, where A is the fixed number of detections produced by the model. The detection problem can be seen as an extension of the image classification and regression problems, where we aim to regress a set of A bounding boxes of visual objects, together with their classification.

The joint distribution includes image, noisy bounding boxes, and labels, as follows:

$$p(X = \mathbf{x}, \tilde{Y}_1 = \tilde{\mathbf{y}}_1, \tilde{B}_1 = \tilde{\mathbf{b}}_1, ..., \tilde{Y}_A = \tilde{\mathbf{y}}_A, \tilde{B}_A = \tilde{\mathbf{b}}_A)$$

$$= p(\tilde{Y}_1 = \tilde{\mathbf{y}}_1, \tilde{B}_1 = \tilde{\mathbf{b}}_1, ..., \tilde{Y}_A = \tilde{\mathbf{y}}_A, \tilde{B}_A = \tilde{\mathbf{b}}_A | \mathbf{x}) \times p(X = \mathbf{x})$$

$$= \prod_{a=1}^{A} p(\tilde{Y}_a = \tilde{\mathbf{y}}_a, \tilde{B}_a = \tilde{\mathbf{b}}_a | X = \mathbf{x}) \times p(X = \mathbf{x})$$

$$= \prod_{a=1}^{A} p(\tilde{Y}_a = \tilde{\mathbf{y}}_a | \tilde{B}_a = \tilde{\mathbf{b}}_a, X = \mathbf{x}) \times p(\tilde{B}_a = \tilde{\mathbf{b}}_a | X = \mathbf{x}) \times p(X = \mathbf{x})$$

$$= \prod_{a=1}^{A} p(\tilde{\mathbf{y}}_a; t_X(\mathbf{x}(\tilde{\mathbf{b}}_a))) \times \mathcal{N}(\tilde{\mathbf{b}}_a; \mu_{\mathcal{B}}(\mathbf{x}), \Sigma_{\mathcal{B}}(\mathbf{x})) \times \mathcal{N}(\mathbf{x}; \mu, \Sigma),$$

$$(2.18)$$

where the A bounding boxes are assumed to be independent from each other, $t_X(\mathbf{x}(\tilde{\mathbf{b}}_a))$ is the categorical distribution, defined in (2.9), at the image region inside the bounding box $\tilde{\mathbf{b}}_a$ (denoted by $\mathbf{x}(\tilde{\mathbf{b}}_a)$), $p(\tilde{\mathbf{y}}_a; t_X(\mathbf{x}(\tilde{\mathbf{b}}_a)))$ is defined in (2.9), $\mu_{\mathcal{B}} : X \to \mathcal{B}$ returns the bounding box mean in image $\mathbf{x}$ and $\Sigma_{\mathcal{B}} : X \to \mathcal{B} \times \mathcal{B}$ returns the bounding box covariance for the multivariate normal distribution $\mathcal{N}(.)$, and $\mathcal{N}(\mathbf{x}; \mu, \Sigma)$ is defined in (2.1).

The sampling process for each bounding box happens in three stages:

$$1. \ X = \mu + \Sigma \times \epsilon_X$$

$$2. \ \tilde{B} = \mu_{\mathcal{B}}(\mathbf{x}) + \Sigma_{\mathcal{B}}(\mathbf{x}) \times \epsilon_{\mathcal{B}} \qquad (2.19)$$

$$3. \ \tilde{Y} = T_X^{-1}(u; \mathbf{x}(\tilde{\mathbf{b}})),$$

where $\epsilon_X \sim n(\mathbf{0}_X, \mathbf{I}_X)$ is defined as in (2.3), $\epsilon_{\mathcal{B}} \sim n(\mathbf{0}_{\mathcal{B}}, \mathbf{I}_{\mathcal{B}})$ follow the definitions from (2.3), $u \sim \mathcal{U}(0, 1)$ denotes a uniform random number in $[0, 1]$, and $T_X^{-1}(.)$ is the inverse cumulative distribution from t_X, as defined in (2.10).

Similarly to the regression problem in Section 2.2.1 and the classification problem in Section 2.2.2, we can introduce the clean label variable Y and clean bounding box variable B. We then define the transition probability function that estimates the noisy bounding box given X with $p(\tilde{B}|X) = \int p(B, \tilde{B}|X)dB = \int p(\tilde{B}|B, X)p(B|X)dB$. We also need to define the transition probability function that estimates the noisy categorical distribution of $\tilde{Y}$ given Y, $\tilde{B}$, and X with $p(\tilde{Y}|\tilde{B}, X) = \sum_Y p(\tilde{Y}|Y, \tilde{B}, X)p(Y|\tilde{B}, X)$. Hence, we have

$$
\begin{aligned}
p(\tilde{Y} &= \tilde{\mathbf{y}}, \tilde{B} = \tilde{\mathbf{b}}|X = \mathbf{x}) \\
&= \sum_{\mathbf{y}\in\mathcal{Y}} p(\tilde{Y} = \tilde{\mathbf{y}}|Y = \mathbf{y}, \tilde{B} = \tilde{\mathbf{b}}, X = \mathbf{x}) \times p(Y = \mathbf{y}|\tilde{B} = \tilde{\mathbf{b}}, X = \mathbf{x}) \times \\
&\quad \int p(\tilde{B} = \tilde{\mathbf{b}}|B, X = \mathbf{x}) \times p(B|X = \mathbf{x})dB \\
&= \sum_{\mathbf{y}\in\mathcal{Y}} p(\tilde{\mathbf{y}}; t_{\mathcal{Y}X}(\mathbf{y}, \mathbf{x}(\tilde{\mathbf{b}}))) \times p(\mathbf{y}; t_X(\mathbf{x}(\tilde{\mathbf{b}}))) \times \\
&\quad \int \mathcal{N}(\tilde{\mathbf{b}}; \mu_{\mathcal{B}X}(B, \mathbf{x}), \Sigma_{\mathcal{B}X}(B, \mathbf{x})) \times \mathcal{N}(B; \mu_{\mathcal{B}}(\mathbf{x}), \Sigma_{\mathcal{B}}(\mathbf{x}))dB,
\end{aligned}
\tag{2.20}
$$

where we follow the same definitions as in (2.4) and (2.11).

The sampling process for each bounding box is based on five stages:

$$
\begin{aligned}
&1.\ X = \mu + \Sigma \times \epsilon_X \\
&2.\ B = \mu_{\mathcal{B}}(\mathbf{x}) + \Sigma_{\mathcal{B}}(\mathbf{x}) \times \epsilon_{\mathcal{B}} \\
&3.\ \tilde{B} = \mu_{\mathcal{B}X}(\mathbf{b}, \mathbf{x}) + \Sigma_{\mathcal{B}X}(\mathbf{b}, \mathbf{x}) \times \epsilon_{\mathcal{B}X} \\
&4.\ Y = T_X^{-1}(u; \mathbf{x}(\tilde{\mathbf{b}})) \\
&5.\ \tilde{Y} = T_{\mathcal{Y}X}^{-1}(u; \mathbf{y}, \mathbf{x}(\tilde{\mathbf{b}})),
\end{aligned}
\tag{2.21}
$$

where we follow the definitions from (2.5), (2.12), and (2.19).

The detector is trained to minimize a combination of regression and classification loss functions using a noisy label dataset $\mathcal{D} = \left\{(\mathbf{x}_i, \{\tilde{\mathbf{b}}_{i,j}, \tilde{\mathbf{y}}_{i,j}\}_{j=1}^{B_i})\right\}_{i=1}^{|\mathcal{D}|}$, with the ERM defined as follows:

$$
\begin{aligned}
\theta^* = \arg\min_{\theta\in\Theta} \frac{1}{A|\mathcal{D}|} \sum_{\left(\mathbf{x}_i, \{\tilde{\mathbf{b}}_{i,j}, \tilde{\mathbf{y}}_{i,j}\}_{j=1}^{B_i}\right)\in\mathcal{D}} \sum_{a=1}^{A} \\
\left(\ell_C(\mathbf{y}_{i,a}^*, \hat{\mathbf{y}}_{i,a}) + \delta(\mathbf{y}_{i,a}^* \neq \mathbf{0}_{\mathcal{Y}}) \times \ell_R(\mathbf{b}_{i,a}^*, \hat{\mathbf{b}}_{i,a})\right),
\end{aligned}
\tag{2.22}
$$

where $\{\hat{\mathbf{y}}_{i,a}, \hat{\mathbf{b}}_{i,a}\}_{a=1}^{A} = f_\theta(\mathbf{x}_i)$, $\mathbf{b}_{i,a}^* = \arg\max_{\mathbf{b}\in\{\tilde{\mathbf{b}}_{i,j}\}_{j=1}^{B_i}} \mathsf{IoU}(\mathbf{b}, \hat{\mathbf{b}}_{i,a})$, with $\mathsf{IoU}(A, B) = \frac{|A\cap B|}{|A\cup B|}$ denoting the intersection over union operator and $\{\tilde{\mathbf{b}}_{i,j}\}_{j=1}^{B_i}$ representing the

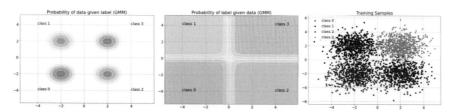

FIGURE 2.6 Intrinsic classification label noise.

Example of the training data (rightmost graph) sampled from the GMM (leftmost graph shows the probability of data given label, and middle figure shows the probability of label given data) from Fig. 2.5, where the label is affected only by the intrinsic label noise.

noisy bounding box annotation. Also in (2.22), we have

$$\mathbf{y}_{i,a}^* = \begin{cases} \tilde{\mathbf{y}}_{i,j}, & \text{if } \mathsf{IoU}(\mathbf{b}_{i,a}^*, \hat{\mathbf{b}}_{i,a}) > \tau \\ \mathbf{0}_{\mathcal{Y}}, & \text{otherwise} \end{cases}, \tag{2.23}$$

where each bounding box in $\{\tilde{\mathbf{b}}_{i,j}, \tilde{\mathbf{y}}_{i,j}\}_{j=1}^{B_i}$ can be associated with only one detection in $\{\hat{\mathbf{b}}_{i,a}, \hat{\mathbf{y}}_{i,a}\}_{j=1}^{A}$, and $\mathbf{0}_{\mathcal{Y}}$ is a vector with zeros of size $|\mathcal{Y}|$. In (2.22), the loss $\ell_C(.)$ is represented by one of the classification losses in (2.13), and the loss $\ell_R(.)$ is one of the regression losses in (2.6).

2.3 Label noise problems

Recall that the label noise discussed in Section 2.2 is represented by the joint probability distribution $p(X, \tilde{Y})$, which can be decomposed in two ways, one depending on the intrinsic label distribution $p(\tilde{Y}|X)$, and the other relying on the latent transition distribution $p(\tilde{Y}|Y, X)$ and clean distribution $p(Y|X)$. The intrinsic label noise for classification and regression problems is shown in Figs. 2.6 and 2.7. Also recall that label noise can be decomposed into two types, namely: an irreducible term that is associated with the difficulty of the annotation and therefore impossible to eliminate, and a labeling error introduced by human or semi-automated labelers. The algorithms presented in this book target to mitigate the second type of noise since the first type is in principle impossible to eliminate.

To define the label noise process made by labelers, we introduce the **noise rate** $\eta \in [0, 1]$, and the **noise type** ν, which can be **symmetric, asymmetric, and instance-dependent**. To account for this noise, we need to re-define the joint probabilities from Section 2.2. First, let us re-define the decomposed joint probability by conditioning it on η and ν, as follows:

$$\begin{aligned} p(X, \tilde{Y}|\eta, \nu) &= p(\tilde{Y}|X, \eta, \nu) \times p(X) \\ &= \big((1-\eta) \times p(\tilde{Y}|X) + \eta \times p(\tilde{Y}|X, \nu)\big) \times p(X), \end{aligned} \tag{2.24}$$

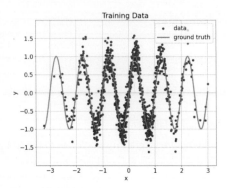

FIGURE 2.7 **Intrinsic regression label noise.**

Example of the training data sampled from the ground truth regression model from
Fig. 2.2, containing only intrinsic label noise.

where $p(\tilde{Y}|X)$ denotes latent conditional label distribution defined in (2.1) for regression problems and (2.9) for classification problems, and $p(\tilde{Y}|X, v)$ represents the latent conditional noisy label distribution of type v. By taking the transition distribution into account, the joint probability is re-defined as

$$p(X, \tilde{Y}|\eta, v) = \sum_{Y \in \mathcal{Y}} p(\tilde{Y}|Y, X, v, \eta) \times p(Y|X) \times p(X)$$

$$= \sum_{Y \in \mathcal{Y}} \left((1 - \eta) \times p(\tilde{Y}|Y, X) + \eta \times p(\tilde{Y}|Y, X, v)\right) \times p(Y|X) \times p(X),$$

$$(2.25)$$

where the latent transition probability $p(\tilde{Y}|Y, X)$ is as defined in (2.4) for regression and in (2.11) for classification, while $p(\tilde{Y}|Y, X, v)$ represents the latent noisy transition distribution of type v, and the sum is replaced by an integral for the regression problem of (2.4). This joint distribution can then be used to build the noisy training set with samples $(\mathbf{x}, \tilde{\mathbf{y}}) \sim p(X, \tilde{Y}|\eta, v)$.

The definitions in (2.24) and (2.25) are related to the definition of the label noise process explained in the first challenge presented in Section 1.3, which is related to definition of the label noise generation process that can be based on a label distribution (Thiel, 2008; Domingos, 2000) as in (2.24), or a label transition process (Pérez et al., 2007; Lawrence and Schölkopf, 2001) as in (2.25).

2.4 Closed set label noise problems

The defining property of closed-set label noise problems is that the hidden clean label of the data is always in the set (for classification) or range (for regression) of training

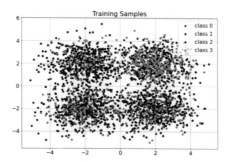

FIGURE 2.8 Closed-set symmetric classification label noise.

Example of the training data sampled from the GMM from Fig. 2.6, where the label is affected by symmetric label noise with $\eta = 50\%$. Note that the label noise is uniformly distributed among the training samples.

labels $\mathcal{Y}$. Below we present closed-set label noise problems for classification and regression problems since both subsume the other applications (i.e., segmentation and detection).

2.4.1 Symmetric

In closed-set symmetric *classification* label noise, the noise is uniform and independent of the input data X and label Y, so this type of noise can be explained by encoding or communication errors, as mentioned in Section 1.2. Essentially, given a data sample X, with label distribution $p(\tilde{Y}|X)$, a symmetric label noise will mix a uniform distribution with the label distribution, so that the labeling process produces a noisy label that can produce an arbitrary random label. Fig. 2.8 shows an example of a training set with symmetric label noise in a classification problem, where it is clear that labels are corrupted in an uniform manner. Also, in Fig. 2.9, we see how a uniform label noise affects a regression problem, with an η rate of samples showing a uniform distribution of labels. This type of noise is defined by the latent conditional noisy label distribution of type $v = sym$ from (2.24), with

$$p(\tilde{Y}|X, v = sym) = \mathcal{U}(\mathcal{Y}), \tag{2.26}$$

where $\mathcal{U}(\mathcal{Y})$ represents a uniform distribution, where the probability for each label is $\frac{1}{|\mathcal{Y}|}$. Similarly, if we are working with the latent transition distribution $p(Y|\tilde{Y}, X)$ as in (2.25), we define the latent noisy transition as

$$p(\tilde{Y}|Y, X, v = sym) = \mathcal{U}(\mathcal{Y}). \tag{2.27}$$

The closed-set symmetric *regression* label noise is similarly defined, but we need to establish a closed-set domain for the labels, which is in principle unbounded for regression problems. Therefore, we use a common definition of inlier from statistics (Wilcox, 2011) which defines that the closed set for the labels is $1.5\times$ the

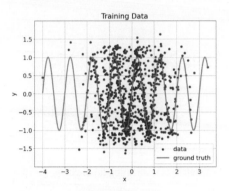

FIGURE 2.9 Closed-set symmetric regression label noise.

Example of the training data sampled from the ground truth regression model from Fig. 2.2, containing symmetric label noise with $\eta = 50\%$. Notice how the y-values are uniformly distributed within the IQR as defined in (2.28) and (2.29).

interquartile range (IQR), where

$$IQR(p(\tilde{Y})) = Q3(p(\tilde{Y})) - Q1(p(\tilde{Y})), \tag{2.28}$$

with $Q3(p(\tilde{Y}))$ being the upper quartile defined as the median of the second half of $p(\tilde{Y})$, and $Q1(p(\tilde{Y}))$ denoting the lower quartile defined as the median of the first half of $p(\tilde{Y})$, and $p(\tilde{Y}) = \int p(X, \tilde{Y})dX$. For the purpose of defining regression label noise, we consider a low outlier value $\tilde{Y}$ for $p(\tilde{Y})$ to be less than $Q1(p(\tilde{Y})) - 1.5 \times IQR(p(\tilde{Y}))$, and a high outlier to be more than $Q3(p(\tilde{Y})) + 1.5 \times IQR(p(\tilde{Y}))$. Hence, for closed-set symmetric *regression* label noise, the latent conditional noisy label distribution of (2.24) is defined by

$$p(\tilde{Y}|X, v = sym) = \mathcal{U}\big(Q1(p(\tilde{Y})) - 1.5 \times IQR(p(\tilde{Y})),$$
$$Q3(p(\tilde{Y})) + 1.5 \times IQR(p(\tilde{Y}))\big), \tag{2.29}$$

where $\mathcal{U}(a, b) = \frac{1}{b-a}$ if $\tilde{Y} \in [a, b]$ and 0 otherwise. Similarly, if we are working with the latent transition distribution $p(\tilde{Y}|Y, X)$ as in (2.25), we define the latent noisy transition as

$$p(\tilde{Y}|Y, X, v = sym) = \mathcal{U}\big(Q1(p(\tilde{Y})) - 1.5 \times IQR(p(\tilde{Y})),$$
$$Q3(p(\tilde{Y})) + 1.5 \times IQR(p(\tilde{Y}))\big). \tag{2.30}$$

2.4.2 Asymmetric

In closed-set asymmetric *classification* label noise, the label noise depends only on the true label denoted by Y, but not on the data X. In image classification, typical examples are the inherent ambiguity in classifying visual classes that are nat-

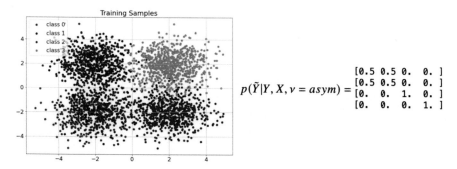

$$p(\tilde{Y}|Y, X, v = asym) = \begin{matrix} [0.5 & 0.5 & 0. & 0. \ ] \\ [0.5 & 0.5 & 0. & 0. \ ] \\ [0. & 0. & 1. & 0. \ ] \\ [0. & 0. & 0. & 1. \ ] \end{matrix}$$

FIGURE 2.10 Closed-set asymmetric classification label noise.

Example of the training data sampled from the GMM from Fig. 2.6, where the label is affected by asymmetric label noise using the label transition matrix depicted on the right hand side of the image. Note from the transition matrix that the labels of classes 0 (red) and 1 (blue) can be flipped with 50% probability, while the labels from classes 2 (purple) and 3 (gray) do not flip.

urally similar, such as 'wolf' and 'coyote', or 'crow' and 'raven', as explained in Section 2.1. This noise type can happen due to unreliable labeling or the intrinsic variability among labelers. In this type of error, given the data X with label distribution $p(\tilde{Y}|X)$ and noisy label transition distribution $p(\tilde{Y}|Y, X)$, an asymmetric label noise will increase the probability of pre-defined pairwise label flippings. This type of noise can only be defined with the transition distribution and the latent conditional noisy label distribution of type $v = asym$ from (2.25), as follows

$$p(\tilde{Y}|Y, X, v = asym) = \mathbf{T}, \tag{2.31}$$

where $\mathbf{T} \in [0, 1]^{|\mathcal{Y}| \times |\mathcal{Y}|}$ is a stochastic matrix with the label flipping probabilities

$$\mathbf{T}_{i,j} = p(\tilde{Y} = \mathbf{y}_i | Y = \mathbf{y}_j), \tag{2.32}$$

for $\mathbf{y}_i, \mathbf{y}_j \in \mathcal{Y}$ denoting the one-hot label with the ith and j^{th} labels active, respectively. Fig. 2.10 shows an example of asymmetric label noise using the transition distribution depicted on the right-hand side of the image.

The closed-set asymmetric *regression* label noise can be similarly defined with the latent transition distribution in (2.25) as in:

$$p(\tilde{Y}|Y, X, v = asym) = p(\tilde{Y}|Y), \tag{2.33}$$

where $p(\tilde{Y}|Y)$ is similarly defined as in (2.4), i.e.,

$$p(\tilde{Y}|Y) = \mathcal{N}(\tilde{Y}; \mu_y(Y), \Sigma_y(Y)), \tag{2.34}$$

where $\mu_y : \mathcal{Y} \to \mathcal{Y}$ and $\Sigma_y : \mathcal{Y} \to \mathcal{Y} \times \mathcal{Y}$. Fig. 2.11 displays an asymmetric label noise regression problem with a simple $p(\tilde{Y}|Y)$ defined as a Gaussian with mean $2 \times Y$.

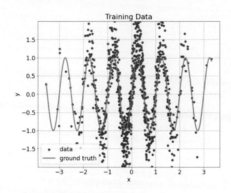

FIGURE 2.11 Closed-set asymmetric regression label noise.

Example of the training data sampled from the ground truth regression model from
Fig. 2.2, containing asymmetric label noise, where $\mu_y(\mathbf{y}) = 2 \times \mathbf{y}$ and $\Sigma_y(\mathbf{y}) = 1$ in (2.34).

2.4.3 Instance-dependent

Instance dependent *classification* label noise consists of a noisy labeling process
that depends on the data X and possibly on Y. Compared with the symmetric and
asymmetric noise types above, instance-dependent noise is more realistic since the
label noise distribution depends on the input data, taking into account that some instances are harder to label than other instances. This noise type can happen due to
insufficient information in the data for a reliable labeling, unreliable labeling or the
intrinsic variability among labelers. From (2.24), given an instance X, with label
distribution $p(\tilde{Y}|X)$, instance-dependent noise (IDN) adds a noisy label distribution
$p(\tilde{Y}|X, v = idn)$, defined as:

$$p(\tilde{Y}|X, v = idn) = p(\tilde{Y}; t_X^{idn}(X)), \tag{2.35}$$

where $t_X^{idn} : X \rightarrow \Delta^{|\mathcal{Y}|-1}$ is a function that returns a categorical noisy-label distri-
bution for instance X. For the latent transition distribution $p(\tilde{Y}|Y, X)$ in (2.25), we
define the latent noisy transition as

$$p(\tilde{Y}|Y, X, v = idn) = p(\tilde{Y}; t_{y_X}(Y, X)) = \mathbf{T}(X), \tag{2.36}$$

where $t_{y_X} : \mathcal{Y} \times X \rightarrow \Delta^{|\mathcal{Y}|-1}$ is a function that returns a categorical noisy-label
transition for instance X, and $\mathbf{T} \in [0, 1]^{|\mathcal{Y}| \times |\mathcal{Y}|}$ is a stochastic matrix with instance-
dependent label flipping probabilities defined as

$$\mathbf{T}_{i,j}(X) = p(\tilde{Y} = \mathbf{y}_i | Y = \mathbf{y}_j, X), \tag{2.37}$$

for $\mathbf{y}_i, \mathbf{y}_j \in \mathcal{Y}$ denoting the one-hot vector with the ith and j^{th} labels active, respectively. Fig. 2.12 shows an example of instance dependent label noise, where the IDN
increases the chances of a sample to be corrupted by a symmetric label noise if it is
closer to the origin.

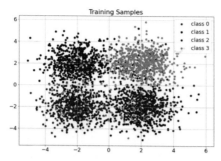

FIGURE 2.12 Closed-set instance-dependent classification label noise.

Example of the training data sampled from the GMM from Fig. 2.6, where the label is affected by instance-dependent label noise with samples closer to the origin being more likely to be affected by a symmetric label noise.

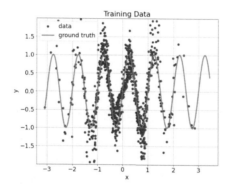

FIGURE 2.13 Closed-set instance-dependent regression label noise.

Example of the training data sampled from the ground truth regression model from Fig. 2.2, containing instance-dependent label noise, where $\mu_{yx}(\mathbf{y}, \mathbf{x}) = 2 \times \mathbf{y} \times |\mathbf{x}|$ and $\Sigma_{yx}(\mathbf{y}, \mathbf{x}) = 1$ in (2.39).

The closed-set instance-dependent *regression* label noise is similarly defined using the label distribution $p(\tilde{Y}|X)$ from (2.24), given an instance X, as follows:

$$p(\tilde{Y}|X, \nu = idn) = \mathcal{N}(\tilde{Y}; \mu_X(X), \Sigma_X(X)), \tag{2.38}$$

where $\mu_X : \mathcal{X} \to \mathcal{Y}$ and $\Sigma_X : \mathcal{X} \to \mathcal{Y} \times \mathcal{Y}$. For the latent transition distribution $p(\tilde{Y}|Y, X)$ in (2.25), we define the latent noisy transition as

$$p(\tilde{Y}|Y, X, \nu = idn) = p(\tilde{Y}; \mu_{yx}(Y, X), \Sigma_{yx}(Y, X)), \tag{2.39}$$

where $\mu_{yx} : \mathcal{Y} \times \mathcal{X} \to \mathcal{Y}$ and $\Sigma_{yx} : \mathcal{Y} \times \mathcal{X} \to \mathcal{Y} \times \mathcal{Y}$. Fig. 2.13 shows an instance-dependent label noise regression problem with $\mu_{yx}(\mathbf{y}, \mathbf{x}) = 2 \times \mathbf{y} \times \mathbf{x}$ and $\Sigma_{yx}(\mathbf{y}, \mathbf{x}) = 1$ in (2.39).

2.5 Open-set label noise problems

Open-set label noise problems are defined by having data instances whose clean labels are not in the set (for classification) or range (for regression) of training labels $\mathcal{Y}$. For classification problems containing open-set label noise, the training set contains samples from both the closed and open sets, where closed-set samples are defined by

$$X_\eta^c = \left\{ \mathbf{x} \in X \middle| \sum_{\mathbf{y} \in \mathcal{Y}} p(Y = \mathbf{y}|X = \mathbf{x}) = 1 \text{ and } \sum_{\mathbf{y} \notin \mathcal{Y}} p(Y = \mathbf{y}|X = \mathbf{x}) = 0 \right\}, \quad (2.40)$$

where $P(Y|X)$ is the latent distribution of clean labels, and open-set samples are defined by

$$X_\eta^o = \left\{ \mathbf{x} \in X \middle| \sum_{\mathbf{y} \in \mathcal{Y}} p(Y = \mathbf{y}|X = \mathbf{x}) = 0 \text{ and } \sum_{\mathbf{y} \notin \mathcal{Y}} p(Y = \mathbf{y}|X = \mathbf{x}) = 1 \right\}, \quad (2.41)$$

with $X = X_\eta^c \bigcup X_\eta^o$ and $\eta = \frac{|X_\eta^o|}{|X|}$.

For regression problems, the training set also contains samples from both the closed and open sets, where closed-set samples are defined by

$$X_\eta^c = \left\{ \mathbf{x} \in X \middle| \int_{Y \in \mathcal{Y}} p(Y|X = \mathbf{x})dY = 1 \text{ and } \int_{Y \notin \mathcal{Y}} p(Y|X = \mathbf{x})dY = 0 \right\}, \quad (2.42)$$

where $\mathcal{Y} = \mathcal{U}(Q1(p(Y)) - 1.5 \times IQR(p(Y)), Q3(p(Y)) + 1.5 \times IQR(p(Y)))$, with $p(Y) = \int p(X, Y)dX$ and $Q1(p(Y))$, $IQR(p(Y))$ and $Q3(p(Y))$ being defined in (2.29), and open-set samples are defined by

$$X_\eta^o = \left\{ \mathbf{x} \in X \middle| \int_{Y \in \mathcal{Y}} p(Y|X = \mathbf{x})dY = 0 \text{ and } \int_{Y \notin \mathcal{Y}} p(Y|X = \mathbf{x})dY = 1 \right\}, \quad (2.43)$$

with $X = X_\eta^c \bigcup X_\eta^o$ and $\eta = \frac{|X_\eta^o|}{|X|}$.

In open-set classification and regression noise, the noise rate η defines the proportion of samples belonging to the open set X_η^o, so the latent conditional noisy label distribution from (2.24) is re-defined as

$$p(X, \tilde{Y}|\eta, v) = \left(\delta(X \in X_\eta^c) \times p(\tilde{Y}|X) + \delta(X \in X_\eta^o) \times p(\tilde{Y}|X, v) \right) \times p(X), \tag{2.44}$$

where η is as defined in (2.41), and $\delta(.)$ denotes an indicator function. Similarly, if we are working with the latent transition distribution $p(\tilde{Y}|Y, X)$ as in (2.25), we define

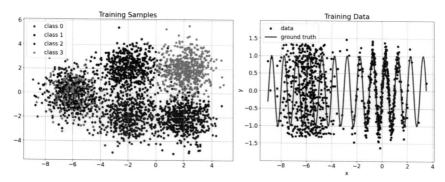

FIGURE 2.14 Open-set symmetric label noise.

For the classification problem on the left, we take the training data sampled from the GMM of Fig. 2.6 and introduce data sampled from an open-set distribution with a unimodal multi-dimensional Gaussian with mean $(-6, 0)$ and identity covariance, where each sample is randomly labeled with one of the 4 training labels. For the regression problem on the right, we take the training data sampled from the regression model of Fig. 2.2 and add data sampled from an open-set distribution with a Gaussian of mean -6 and unit variance, with each sample randomly labeled with any value in the range of inliers, as described in (2.48) and (2.49).

the latent noisy transition as

$$p(X, \tilde{Y}|\eta, v) = p(X) \times \Big(\delta(X \in \mathcal{X}_\eta^c) \times \sum_{Y \in \mathcal{Y}} p(\tilde{Y}|Y, X) \times p(Y|X) +$$
$$\delta(X \in \mathcal{X}_\eta^o) \times \sum_{Y \notin \mathcal{Y}} p(\tilde{Y}|Y, X, v) \times p(Y|X) \Big),$$

(2.45)

where η is defined in (2.41), and $\delta(.)$ denotes the indicator function. For regression problem, the sums in (2.44) and (2.45) are replaced by integrals.

2.5.1 Open-set symmetric

The open-set symmetric *classification* label noise is uniform and independent of the input data X and clean label Y, where an open-set data sample in $\mathcal{X}_\eta^o$ is labeled with any of the closed-set labels by sampling a uniform distribution (see Fig. 2.14, on the left). Considering the latent conditional noisy label distribution for the open set samples of type $v = sym^o$ from (2.44), we have

$$p(\tilde{Y}|X, v = sym^o) = \mathcal{U}(\mathcal{Y}),$$

(2.46)

where $\mathcal{U}(\mathcal{Y})$ is a uniform distribution with label probability equal to $\frac{1}{|\mathcal{U}|}$. When working with the latent transition distribution from (2.45), we have

$$p(\tilde{Y}|Y, X, v = sym^o) = \mathcal{U}(\mathcal{Y}).$$

(2.47)

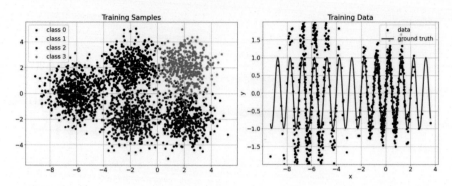

FIGURE 2.15 Open-set asymmetric label noise.

For the classification problem on the left, we take the training data sampled from the GMM of Fig. 2.6 and introduce data sampled from an open-set distribution with a unimodal multi-dimensional Gaussian with mean $(-6, 0)$ and identity covariance, where each sample is randomly labeled with training labels of classes 0 or 1, each with 50% probability. For the regression problem on the right, we take the training data sampled from the regression model of Fig. 2.2 and add data sampled from an open-set distribution with a Gaussian of mean -6 and unit variance, with each sample affected by an asymmetric label noise with $\mu_y(\mathbf{y}) = 2 \times \mathbf{y}$ and $\Sigma_y(\mathbf{y}) = 1$.

For the open-set symmetric *regression* (see Fig. 2.14, on the right), the latent conditional noisy label distribution of (2.44) is defined by

$$
\begin{aligned}
p(\tilde{Y}|X, v = sym^o) = \mathcal{U}\big(Q1(p(\tilde{Y})) - 1.5 \times IQR(p(\tilde{Y})), \\
Q3(p(\tilde{Y})) + 1.5 \times IQR(p(\tilde{Y}))\big),
\end{aligned}
\tag{2.48}
$$

where $p(\tilde{Y}) = \int_{X \in \mathcal{X}_\eta^c} p(X, \tilde{Y}|\eta, v)dX$, $IQR(p(\tilde{Y})) = Q3(p(\tilde{Y})) - Q1(p(\tilde{Y}))$, and $\mathcal{U}(a, b) = \frac{1}{b-a}$ if $\tilde{Y} \in [a, b]$ and 0 otherwise. With the latent transition distribution $p(\tilde{Y}|Y, X)$ from (2.45), we define the latent noisy label transition as

$$
\begin{aligned}
p(\tilde{Y}|Y, X, v = sym^o) = \mathcal{U}\big(Q1(p(\tilde{Y})) - 1.5 \times IQR(p(\tilde{Y})), \\
Q3(p(\tilde{Y})) + 1.5 \times IQR(p(\tilde{Y}))\big),
\end{aligned}
\tag{2.49}
$$

where $X \in \mathcal{X}^o$.

2.5.2 Open-set asymmetric

Similarly to the closed-set asymmetric classification noise, the open-set asymmetric label noise depends only on the true label denoted by Y, as shown in Fig. 2.15, on the left. Asymmetric label noise will affect the latent conditional noisy label distribution of type $v = asym^o$ from (2.44)

$$p(\tilde{Y}|Y, X, v = asym^o) = \mathbf{T}, \tag{2.50}$$

where $\mathbf{T} \in [0, 1]^{|\mathcal{Y}| \times |\mathcal{Y}^o|}$ is a stochastic matrix with the label flipping probabilities between the labels inside and outside the set $\mathcal{Y}$, with the outside labels denoted by $\mathcal{Y}^o$ and

$$\mathbf{T}_{i,j} = p(\tilde{Y} = \mathbf{y}_i | Y = \mathbf{y}_j), \tag{2.51}$$

for $\mathbf{y}_i \in \mathcal{Y}$ and $\mathbf{y}_j \in \mathcal{Y}^o$ denoting the one-hot vectors with the ith and j^{th} labels active, respectively.

The open-set asymmetric *regression* label noise can also be defined with the latent transition distribution in (2.24), as displayed on the right graph of Fig. 2.15, as in:

$$p(\tilde{Y}|Y, X, v = asym^o) = p(\tilde{Y}|Y), \tag{2.52}$$

where $p(\tilde{Y}|Y)$ can be defined as in (2.4), i.e.,

$$p(\tilde{Y}|Y) = \mathcal{N}(\tilde{Y}; \mu_{\mathcal{Y}}(Y), \Sigma_{\mathcal{Y}}(Y)), \tag{2.53}$$

where $\mu_{\mathcal{Y}} : \mathcal{Y}^o \to \mathcal{Y}$ and $\Sigma_{\mathcal{Y}} : \mathcal{Y}^o \to \mathcal{Y} \times \mathcal{Y}$.

2.5.3 Open-set instance-dependent

Open-set instance dependent *classification* label noise consists of a noisy labeling process that depends on the data X and possibly on Y, as displayed on the left of Fig. 2.16. From (2.44), given an instance X, with label distribution $p(Y|X)$, instance-dependent noise (IDN) adds a noisy label distribution $p(\tilde{Y}|X, v = idn^o)$, defined as:

$$p(\tilde{Y}|X, v = idn^o) = p(\tilde{Y}; t_X^{idn^o}(X)), \tag{2.54}$$

where $t_X^{idn^o} : \mathcal{X}_\eta^o \to \Delta^{|\mathcal{Y}|-1}$ is a function that returns a categorical open-set noisy-label distribution for instance X. For the latent transition distribution $p(\tilde{Y}|Y, X)$ in (2.45), we define the latent noisy transition as

$$p(\tilde{Y}|Y, X, v = idn^o) = p(\tilde{Y}; t_{\mathcal{Y}X}^{idn^o}(Y, X)) = \mathbf{T}(X), \tag{2.55}$$

where $t_{\mathcal{Y}X}^{idn^o} : \mathcal{Y}^o \times \mathcal{X}_\eta^o \to \Delta^{|\mathcal{Y}|-1}$ is a function that returns a categorical noisy-label distribution for instance X, and $\mathbf{T}(X) \in [0, 1]^{|\mathcal{Y}| \times |\mathcal{Y}^o|}$ is a stochastic matrix with instance-dependent label flipping probabilities defined as

$$\mathbf{T}_{i,j}(X) = p(\tilde{Y} = \mathbf{y}_i | Y = \mathbf{y}_j, X), \tag{2.56}$$

for $\mathbf{y}_i \in \mathcal{Y}$ and $\mathbf{y}_j \in \mathcal{Y}^o$ denoting the one-hot vectors with the ith and j^{th} labels active, respectively, and $X \in \mathcal{X}^o$.

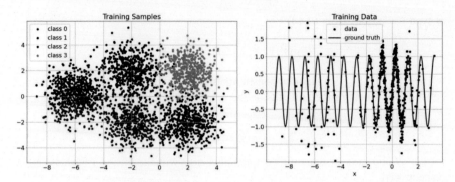

FIGURE 2.16 Open-set IDN label noise.

For the classification problem on the left, we take the training data sampled from the GMM of Fig. 2.6 and introduce data sampled from an open-set distribution with a unimodal multi-dimensional Gaussian with mean $(-6, 0)$ and identity covariance, where each sample is labeled by sampling the probability of label given the data from the original 4-class of Fig. 2.6. For the regression problem on the right, we take the training data sampled from the regression model of Fig. 2.2 and add data sampled from an open-set distribution with a Gaussian of mean -6 and unit variance, with each sample affected by an asymmetric label noise with $\mu_{y\chi}(\mathbf{y}, \mathbf{x}) = 2 \times \mathbf{y} \times |\mathbf{x}|$ and $\Sigma_{y\chi}(\mathbf{y}, \mathbf{x}) = 1$.

The open-set instance-dependent *regression* label noise (see right of Fig. 2.16) is similarly defined using the label distribution $p(Y|X)$ from (2.44), given an instance X, as follows:

$$p(\tilde{Y}|X, v = idn^o) = \mathcal{N}(\tilde{Y}; \mu_X(X), \Sigma_X(X)), \tag{2.57}$$

where $\mu_X : \mathcal{X}_\eta^o \to \mathcal{Y}$ and $\Sigma_X : \mathcal{X}_\eta^o \to \mathcal{Y} \times \mathcal{Y}$. For the latent transition distribution $p(\tilde{Y}|Y, X)$ in (2.45), we define the latent noisy transition as

$$p(\tilde{Y}|Y, X, v = idn^o) = p(\tilde{Y}; \mu_{y\chi}(Y, X), \Sigma_{y\chi}(Y, X)), \tag{2.58}$$

where $\mu_{y\chi} : \mathcal{Y}^o \times \mathcal{X}_\eta^o \to \mathcal{Y}$ and $\Sigma_{y\chi} : \mathcal{Y}^o \times \mathcal{X}_\eta^o \to \mathcal{Y} \times \mathcal{Y}$.

2.6 Label noise problem setup

The label noise problems discussed in Sections 2.4 and 2.5 generally have a setup involving three datasets:

- a **training set** $\mathcal{D} = \{(\mathbf{x}, \tilde{\mathbf{y}})_i\}_{i=1}^{|\mathcal{D}|}$, where $(\mathbf{x}, \tilde{\mathbf{y}})_i \sim p(X, \tilde{Y}|\eta, v)$, with unknown $\eta > 0$ and $v \in \{sym, asym, idn, sym^o, asym^o, idn^o\}$;
- a **testing set** that is formed with a noise rate $\eta = 0$ and represented by $\mathcal{T} = \{(\mathbf{x}_i, \tilde{\mathbf{y}}_i)\}_{i=1}^{|\mathcal{T}|}$, where $(\mathbf{x}_i, \tilde{\mathbf{y}}_i) \sim p(X, \tilde{Y})$; and

- a **validation set**, with a noise rate $\eta = 0$, denoted by $\mathcal{V} = \{(\mathbf{x}_i, \tilde{\mathbf{y}}_i)\}_{i=1}^{|\mathcal{V}|}$, where $(\mathbf{x}_i, \tilde{\mathbf{y}}_i) \sim p(X, \tilde{Y})$.

Hence, the main challenge is on how to train a model using a noisy-label training set $\mathcal{D}$ with unknown noise rate η and type v, and to test the trained model with the testing set $\mathcal{T}$ with $\eta = 0$. Some problems also rely on the validation set $\mathcal{V}$, where $|\mathcal{V}| << |\mathcal{D}|$, that is formed with a noise rate $\eta = 0$ to facilitate the adaptation of the trained model to the testing set.

Another important point is that some problems may have a combination of E different noise types at different noise rates, so effectively, the joint distribution for these problems is denoted by $p(X, \tilde{Y} | \{\eta_e, v_e\}_{e=1}^E)$. When all noise types in $\{\eta_e, v_e\}_{e=1}^E$ are closed-set label problems, the decomposed joint probability from (2.24) is re-defined as

$$p(X, \tilde{Y} | \{\eta_e, v_e\}_{e=1}^E) = p(\tilde{Y} | X, \{\eta_e, v_e\}_{e=1}^E) \times p(X)$$

$$= \left(\left(1 - \sum_{e=1}^E \eta_e\right) \times p(\tilde{Y} | X) + \sum_{e=1}^E \eta_e \times p(\tilde{Y} | X, v_e) \right) \times p(X),$$

$$(2.59)$$

and by taking the transition distribution into account, the joint probability is re-defined as

$$p(X, \tilde{Y} | \{\eta_e, v_e\}_{e=1}^E) = \sum_{Y \in \mathcal{Y}} p(\tilde{Y} | Y, X, \{\eta_e, v_e\}_{e=1}^E) \times p(Y | X) \times p(X)$$

$$= \sum_{Y \in \mathcal{Y}} \left(\left(1 - \sum_{e=1}^E \eta_e\right) \times p(\tilde{Y} | Y, X) + \sum_{e=1}^E \eta_e \times p(\tilde{Y} | Y, X, v_e) \right) \times p(Y | X) \times p(X).$$

$$(2.60)$$

When all noise types in $\{\eta_e, v_e\}_{e=1}^E$ are open-set label noise problems, the latent conditional noisy label distribution from (2.44) is re-defined as

$$p(X, \tilde{Y} | \{\eta_e, v_e\}_{e=1}^E) =$$

$$\left(\delta(X \in \mathcal{X}_{\sum \eta_e}^c) \times p(\tilde{Y} | X) + \sum_{e=1}^E \delta(X \in \mathcal{X}_{\eta_e}^o) \times p(\tilde{Y} | X, v_e) \right) \times p(X),$$

$$(2.61)$$

where $\sum \eta_e = \frac{\sum_{e=1}^E |\mathcal{X}_{\eta_e}^o|}{|\mathcal{X}|}$ represents the sum of all E noise rates, so this means that the proportion of closed-set samples $\mathcal{X}_{\sum \eta_e}^c \in \mathcal{X}$ is $\left(1 - \sum_{e=1}^E \eta_e\right)$. When working with the latent transition distribution $p(\tilde{Y} | Y, X)$ as in (2.45), we define the latent noisy transition as

$$p(X, \tilde{Y}|\{\eta_e, \nu_e\}_{e=1}^E) = p(X) \times \left(\delta(X \in \mathcal{X}_{\sum \eta_e}^c) \times \sum_{Y \in \mathcal{Y}} p(\tilde{Y}|Y, X) \times p(Y|X) + \right.$$

$$\left. \sum_{e=1}^E \delta(X \in \mathcal{X}_{\eta_e}^o) \times \sum_{Y \notin \mathcal{Y}} p(\tilde{Y}|Y, X, \nu_e) \times p(Y|X) \right).$$

$$(2.62)$$

We can also have a combination of closed-set and open-set label noise. Let us represent the closed-set noise set with $\{\eta_e, \nu_e\}_{e=1}^E$ and the open-set noise with $\{\eta_e^o, \nu_e^o\}_{e=1}^{E^o}$, then the latent conditional noisy label distribution is defined as

$$p(X, \tilde{Y}|\{\eta_e, \nu_e\}_{e=1}^E, \{\eta_e^o, \nu_e^o\}_{e=1}^{E^o}) =$$

$$\left(\delta(X \in \mathcal{X}_{\sum \eta_e^o}^c) \times \left(\left(1 - \sum_{e=1}^E \eta_e \right) \times p(\tilde{Y}|X) + \sum_{e=1}^E \eta_e \times p(\tilde{Y}|X, \nu_e) \right) + \right.$$

$$\left. \sum_{e=1}^{E^o} \delta(X \in \mathcal{X}_{\eta_e^o}^o) \times p(\tilde{Y}|X, \nu_e^o) \right) \times p(X),$$

$$(2.63)$$

and the latent noisy transition as

$$p(X, \tilde{Y}|\{\eta_e, \nu_e\}_{e=1}^E, \{\eta_e^o, \nu_e^o\}_{e=1}^{E^o}) = p(X) \times$$

$$\left(\delta(X \in \mathcal{X}_{\sum \eta_e^o}^c) \times \sum_{Y \in \mathcal{Y}} \left(\left(1 - \sum_{e=1}^E \eta_e \right) \times p(\tilde{Y}|Y, X) + \sum_{e=1}^E \eta_e \times p(\tilde{Y}|Y, X, \nu_e) \right) \times \right.$$

$$\left. p(Y|X) + \sum_{e=1}^{E^o} \delta(X \in \mathcal{X}_{\eta_e^o}^o) \times \sum_{Y \notin \mathcal{Y}} p(\tilde{Y}|Y, X, \nu_e^o) \times p(Y|X) \right).$$

$$(2.64)$$

The second and fifth challenges from Section 1.3 are related to the setup of the problem. In particular, the second challenge is about the experimental setup of the problem, where the datasets, noise rate, and noise type can lead to a combinatorial explosion in the number of benchmarks, which can hinder progress given the impossibility of assessing all proposed models on all benchmarks. Another point highlighted in the second challenge is the possible presence of label noise in the testing and validation sets. This issue can happen in real-world datasets since it may not be possible to acquire clean-label testing and validation sets. For instance, the diagnosis of certain conditions from medical images can be challenging, leading to high-level of label noise due the uncertainty of the diagnosis, making it impossible to have a clean label, unless we use a different source of information for the labels, such as pathology or surgery. The fifth challenge is about the estimation of the label noise rate and type present in a dataset, which is hard to obtain, but can be useful during the training process (Xiao et al., 2015; Liu and Tao, 2015). Frénay and Verleysen (2014) introduced a generic way to use such noise estimation information with a graphical model to explain closed-set symmetric, asymmetric, and instance-dependent noise, where a binary random variable represents the presence of error in the labeling process.

2.7 Datasets and benchmarks

In this section, we introduce the main datasets and benchmarks used to assess noisy label learning methods. We present the amount of training, validation, and testing images present in each dataset and benchmark, the estimated proportion and type of noise present, and the task (e.g., classification, segmentation, detection, etc.) used in the assessment. We divided the datasets into Computer Vision Datasets, Medical Image Analysis Datasets, and Non-image Datasets.

2.7.1 Computer vision datasets and benchmarks

Let us first introduce the datasets that contain approximately 0% of intrinsic label noise in the training, validation, and testing sets. **MNIST** (LeCun, 1998)[2] is a handwritten digit dataset to evaluate multi-class classifiers. MNIST contains 10 classes, 60K training and 10K testing images of small size (28×28 pixels). **Fashion-MNIST** (Xiao et al., 2017)[3] is used to evaluate multi-class classifiers and has essentially the same data structure as MNIST, with 60K training and 10K testing images of size 28×28 pixels, 10 classes (types of garments), and approximately no label noise. **CIFAR-10** (Krizhevsky et al., 2014) and **CIFAR-100** (Krizhevsky et al., 2014)[4] are also used to assess multi-class classifiers. Both contain 50K training and 10K testing images of size 32×32 pixels. The main difference between them is the number of classes (10 for CIFAR-10 and 100 for CIFAR-100). **SVHN** (Netzer et al., 2011)[5] is a dataset for multi-class classification, containing 32×32 pixel RGB images of printed digits cropped from pictures of house number plates. SVHN has 10 classes, 73K training and 26K testing images.

   Tiny-ImageNet (Karpathy et al., 2016)[6] is a dataset for multi-class classification that has 200 classes, 100K training, 10K validation, and 10K testing RGB images of size 64×64 pixels. The **Mini-ImageNet** (Vinyals et al., 2016)[7] is a coarse-grained multi-class classification dataset, containing 100 classes, 50K training images, and

---

[2] https://data.deepai.org/mnist.zip.

[3] https://github.com/zalandoresearch/fashion-mnist.

[4] https://www.cs.toronto.edu/~kriz/cifar.html.

[5] http://ufldl.stanford.edu/housenumbers/.

[6] https://www.kaggle.com/c/tiny-imagenet.

[7] https://www.kaggle.com/datasets/whitemoon/miniimagenet.

Table 2.1 Datasets used for assessing noisy-label learning computer vision algorithms and models. The table shows the number of training, validation, and testing images, the number of classes, the task (MC = multi-class classification, ML = multi-label classification, SG = segmentation, DT = detection), if it is class-balanced (Y = yes, N = No, ? = unknown), the estimated noise rate η and noise type ν (CSSYM = closed-set symmetric, CSASM = closed-set asymmetric, CSIDN = closed set instance dependent noise, OSSYM = open-set symmetric, OSASM = open-set asymmetric, OSIDN = open-set instance dependent noise, INT = intrinsic) in the training set.

Dataset	# Training	# Validation	# Testing	# Classes	Task	Balanced	Noise Rate η (%)	Noise Type ν
MNIST	60K	–	10K	10	MC	Y	≈0.0	INT
Fashion-MNIST	60K	–	10K	10	MC	Y	≈0.0	INT
CIFAR-10	50K	–	10K	10	MC	Y	≈0.0	INT
CIFAR-100	50K	–	10K	10	MC	Y	≈0.0	INT
SVHN	73K	–	26K	10	MC	Y	≈0.0	INT
Tiny-ImageNet	100K	10K	10K	200	MC	Y	≈0.0	INT
Mini-ImageNet	50K	–	10K	100	MC	Y	≈0.0	INT
Stanford Cars	8K	–	8K	196	MC	Y	≈0.0	INT
Cats vs Dogs	9K	1K	–	2	MC	Y	≈0.0	INT
ImageNet	1.3M	50K	50K	1000	MC	Y	≈0.0	INT
ANIMAL-10N	50K	–	5K	10	MC	Y	≈8.0	INT+CSIDN
CIFAR-10N	50K	–	10K	10	MC	Y	≈9.0,18.0,40.2	INT+CSIDN
CIFAR-100N	50K	–	10K	10	MC	Y	≈25.6,40.2	INT+CSIDN
Food-101N	310K	5K	25K	101	MC	?	≈18.4	INT+CSIDN
Clothing1M	1M	14K	10K	14	MC	N	≈38.5	INT+CSIDN
WebVision	2.4M	50K	50K	1000	MC	N	≈20.0	INT+CSIDN+OSIDN
Cityscapes	25K	–	–	30	SG,DT	N	> 0, but not reported	INT+CSIDN
COCO	118K	5K	81K	171	SG,DT	N	≈0	INT
PASCAL VOC	2501	2510	15943	21	SG,DT	N	≈0	INT
Potsdam+Vaihingen	30	10	31	6	SG	N	≈0	INT

10K testing RGB images of size 84 × 84 pixels. The **Stanford Cars** (Krause et al., 2013)[8] is a fine-grained image multi-class classification dataset with 196 classes of cars, 8144 training and 8041 testing RGB images of size 360 × 240 pixels. The **Cats vs Dogs** (Elson et al., 2007)[9] is a binary classification dataset containing 9302 training and 1184 validation images, which are sub-sampled from the original dataset that has balanced distributed 25K images. The **ImageNet** (Deng et al., 2009)[10] dataset has 1000 classes, 1.3M training, 50K validation, and 50K testing RGB images of mean size 482 × 418 pixels.

While the datasets above have negligible amount of noise, the next datasets were collected in such a way that they naturally contain label noise introduced by the labeling process in the training set, but the validation and testing sets still contains approximately 0% of intrinsic label noise. **Animal-10N** (Song et al., 2019)[11] is a multi-class classification image dataset containing 10 classes, with 5 pairs of confusing animals, namely: (cat, lynx), (jaguar, cheetah), (wolf, coyote), (chimpanzee, orangutan), and (hamster, guinea pig). Animal-10N has 50K training and 5K testing images, collected from online search engines (e.g., Bing and Google) using the labels above, and annotated by 15 people, where each annotator labeled 600 images per class (i.e., a total of 6K images per annotator). This is followed by removing irrelevant images, forming a training set of 50K and a testing set of 5K RGB images of size 64 × 64 pixels.

The **CIFAR-10N, CIFAR-100N** (Wei et al., 2021a)[12] introduce noisy labels to the training images of CIFAR-10 and CIFAR-100 (Krizhevsky et al., 2014). These noisy labels are produced by human annotations from Amazon Mechanical Turk, where CIFAR-10 relied on three independent workers for each training image, and CIFAR-100 used one worker for each training image. Using the annotations above, CIFAR-10N has different types of noisy label sets for training, defined as: 1) aggregate from majority voting from the three labels per image (if there are 3 different labels, the aggregate label will consist of a random selection among the three labels); 2) random selection of the label produced by one of the three annotators; and 3) worst label from the annotator with the highest noise rate. For CIFAR-100N, each annotator provides a coarse label, belonging to one of the 20 super-classes, and a fine label, belonging to one of the 100 classes, forming the two noisy label sets for training.

Food-101N (Lee et al., 2018)[13] is a multi-class classification dataset containing 310009 images of 101 classes of food recipes. Food-101N and Food-101 (Bossard et al., 2014) datasets share the same 101 classes. Food-101 has 1000 RGB images (with maximum side length of 512 pixels) per class (collected from the site foodspotting.com, which is no longer available), with 750 for training and 250 for testing.

---

[8] https://paperswithcode.com/dataset/stanford-cars.

[9] https://www.microsoft.com/en-us/download/details.aspx?id=54765.

[10] https://www.image-net.org/.

[11] https://dm.kaist.ac.kr/datasets/animal-10n/.

[12] http://www.noisylabels.com/.

[13] https://kuanghuei.github.io/Food-101N/.

While Food-101N's testing images are the same as the ones in Food-101, the training images are collected from Google, Bing, Yelp, and TripAdvisor websites using the Food-101 classes, where verification labels were manually assigned to 52868 images (approximately 523 images per class) for training and 4741 images (approximately 47 images per class) for validation, where this verification label indicates if the class label is correct for an image.

The dataset **Clothing1M** (Xiao et al., 2015)[14] contains 1M images from 14 fashion classes. These images are collected from online shopping websites, where the image annotation is automatically done using a noisy label from the keywords in the image's surrounding text. Clothing1M also contains 50K training, 14K validation, and 10K testing images with clean labels. Note that there is image overlap between the three clean sets and the original set with label noise, and images are of variable sizes.

WebVision (Li et al., 2017)[15] contains 2.4M training images of web crawled images (1M from Google Image search and 1.4M from Flickr) using queries formed from the 1000 labels of ImageNet (Deng et al., 2009). WebVision also contains meta data for each image (e.g., title, description, tags, etc.). This dataset has 50K validation and 50K testing images, containing clean labels produced by annotators from the Amazon Mechanical Turk platform. Note that the images in all sets are of variable sizes, and experiments follow the setting proposed by Chen et al. (2019) that uses only the first 50 classes of the Google image subset when testing the methods on the human-annotated WebVision validation set and the ImageNet validation set.

For the assessment of noisy-label methods for segmentation and detection problems, the main datasets used are Cityscapes (Cordts et al., 2016), COCO (Lin et al., 2014), PASCAL VOC (Everingham et al., 2010), and Potsdam+Vaihingen (Potsdam, 2018; Vaihingen, 2018). The **Cityscapes** (Cordts et al., 2016)[16] dataset contains images from urban street scenes from 50 cities at different day times and in different seasons (spring, summer, fall) and weather conditions. It contains semantic, instance-wise, and dense pixel annotations for 30 classes grouped into 8 categories (flat surfaces, humans, vehicles, constructions, objects, nature, sky, and void), with 5K images with fine semantic annotations, and 20K images with coarse annotations. The **COCO** dataset (Lin et al., 2014)[17] contains 328K images and is used for noisy-label segmentation and detection problems, and contains 80 classes of "things" (e.g., cat, pen, fridge, etc.) and 91 classes of "stuff" (e.g., road, sky, water, etc.). There are many versions available, with the first one, released in 2014, containing 83K images for training, 41K for validation, and 41K for testing. In 2015, the testing set was augmented to contain a total of 81K images. Then in 2017, the training/validation split changed to 118K/5K, and a new set of 123K un-annotated images were added. The

---

[14] https://github.com/Cysu/noisy_label.

[15] https://data.vision.ee.ethz.ch/cvl/webvision/download.html.

[16] https://www.cityscapes-dataset.com/.

[17] https://cocodataset.org/#home.

PASCAL VOC dataset (Everingham et al., 2010)[18] is used for noisy-label segmentation and detection problems, and contains 2501 images for training, 2510 images for validation, and 4952/10991 testing images for PASCAL VOC 2010/PASCAL VOC 2012. The dataset contains 21 visual object classes (e.g., vehicles, household objects, animals, person, background), where each image is annotated with pixel-level segmentation annotations, bounding box annotations, and object class annotations. The **Potsdam+Vaihingen** datasets (Potsdam, 2018; Vaihingen, 2018)[19],[20] have very high resolution airborne multi-spectral (RGB + NIR) images and Digital Surface Model (DSM) generated from Light Detection and Ranging (LiDAR) point clouds from top view and dense urban scenes. The images from both datasets have been manually labeled into the following six classes: impervious surfaces, building, low vegetation, tree, car, and clutter/background. For the Potsdam dataset, there are 38 annotated images of 6000 × 6000 pixels, split as 18/6/14 for training/validation/testing. The Vaihingen dataset has 33 images of different sizes, split as 12/4/17 for training/validation/testing.

2.7.1.1 Classification benchmarks

The real-world classification benchmarks are represented by the datasets Animal-10N (Song et al., 2019), CIFAR-10N, CIFAR-100N (Wei et al., 2021a), Food-101N (Lee et al., 2018), Clothing1M (Xiao et al., 2015), and WebVision (Li et al., 2017). These datasets contain specific types and rates of label noise, and methods are compared by verifying their classification accuracy on their clean testing sets. Even though useful, the real-world noisy label datasets above have fixed label noise rates and types, which do not allow for a systematic evaluation of the methods. To address this issue, many benchmarks have been proposed, where different types and rates of label noise are artificially introduced to the clean label datasets from Table 2.1 (i.e., all datasets that have noise rate $\eta \approx 0$). Such artificially built benchmarks enable a systematic assessment of the methods with respect to label noise.

The most common artificial benchmark explored in the field is the one proposed by Tanaka et al. (2018); Patrini et al. (2017), comprising **symmetric and asymmetric label noise applied to CIFAR-10 and CIFAR-100** (first four rows in Table 2.2), which are applied as explained in Sections 2.4.1 and 2.4.2, respectively. For the asymmetric label noise in CIFAR-10, Tanaka et al. (2018); Patrini et al. (2017) proposed the following four pairs of label transitions to be used in the transition matrix described in Section 2.4.2: TRUCK → AUTOMOBILE, BIRD → AIRPLANE, DEER → HORSE, CAT ↔ DOG. These transitions are parameterized by $\eta \in [0, 1]$, where the probability of the ground truth (in the diagonal of the transition matrix) and noisy-label transition are $\eta - 1$ and η, respectively. The asymmetric label noise for CIFAR-100 (Karim et al., 2022) relies on a transition matrix that contains label flip-

---

[18] http://host.robots.ox.ac.uk/pascal/VOC/.
[19] https://www.isprs.org/education/benchmarks/UrbanSemLab/2d-sem-label-potsdam.aspx.
[20] https://www.isprs.org/education/benchmarks/UrbanSemLab/2d-sem-label-vaihingen.aspx.

Table 2.2 Benchmarks used for assessing noisy-label learning computer vision classification algorithms and models. The table shows the dataset(s) used, the estimated noise rate η and noise type ν (CSSYM = closed-set symmetric, CSASM = closed-set asymmetric, CSIDN = closed set instance dependent noise, OSSYM = open-set symmetric, OSASM = open-set asymmetric, OSIDN = open-set instance dependent noise, INT = intrinsic) in the training set.

Benchmark	Dataset	Noise Rate η (%)	Noise Type ν
Symmetric CIFAR-10	CIFAR-10	$\approx$ 20.0 to 90.0	INT+CSSYM
Asymmetric CIFAR-10	CIFAR-10	$\approx$ 10.0 to 49.0	INT+CSASM
Symmetric CIFAR-100	CIFAR-100	$\approx$ 20.0 to 90.0	INT+CSSYM
Asymmetric CIFAR-100	CIFAR-100	$\approx$ 10.0 to 40.0	INT+CSASM
IDN	F-MNIST,SVHN,CIFAR-10	$\approx$ 10.0 to 50.0	INT+CSIDN
PMD	CIFAR-10/-100	$\approx$ 35.0, 70.0	INT+CSIDN
Red Mini-ImageNet	Mini-ImageNet	$\approx$ 0.0 to 80.0	INT+CSIDN+OSIDN
Red Stanford Cars	Stanford Cars	$\approx$ 0.0 to 80.0	INT+CSIDN+OSIDN
Blue Mini-ImageNet	Mini-ImageNet	$\approx$ 0.0 to 80.0	INT+CSSYM
Blue Stanford Cars	Stanford Cars	$\approx$ 0.0 to 80.0	INT+CSSYM
Deepmind Benchmark	CIFAR-10/-100, PatchCamelyon,CatsVsDogs	$\approx$ 13%, 21.7%, 52.4%	INT+CSIDN
RoG	CIFAR-10/-100	$\approx$ 32% to 38%	INT+CSIDN
Open-set	CIFAR-10/-100,ImageNet32,SVHN	$\approx$ 20% to 40%	INT+OSSYM+CSSYM
EDM	CIFAR-10/-100,ImageNet32	$\approx$ 30%, 60%	INT+CSSYM+OSSYM
DSOS	CIFAR-10/-100,ImageNet32	$\approx$ 40% to 80%	INT+CSSYM+OSSYM
FSR/RoLT/INOLML	Imbalanced CIFAR-10/-100	$\approx$ 10% to 50%	INT+CSSYM

pings for each class to the next one within the super-classes (note that the 100 classes in the CIFAR-100 are grouped into 20 super-classes).

The **instance-dependent noise (IDN)** generator from (Xia et al., 2020)[21] aims to produce noisy labels with a mean noise rate η, where each instance has a different noise rate sampled from a Gaussian (with mean η) truncated to be in $[0, 1]$. Then, the probability of assigning an incorrect label to the training image is increased by the sampled noise rate above, while the probability of assigning the correct label to the training image is decreased by the same sampled noise rate. IDN is applied to Fashion-MNIST (Xiao et al., 2017), SVHN (Netzer et al., 2011), and CIFAR-10 (Krizhevsky et al., 2014) using $\eta \in \{10\%, 20\%, 30\%, 40\%, 50\%\}$. Another instance-dependent noise benchmark is the **Polynomial Margin Diminishing (PMD)** label noise (Zhang et al., 2021c),[22] where only the instances close to the classification decision boundary can have their labels switched to the wrong label available from that boundary. Zhang et al. (2021c) assume that the decision boundary is recovered from a classifier trained with clean labels, and that each instance can only switch between its most confident and second most confident classifications, where the closer a sample is to the boundary, the closer the probabilities of its most and second most confident classifications. PMD has three polynomial functions that define the bound for the label noise near the decision boundary, and it also defines two noise rates $\eta \in \{35\%, 70\%\}$ applied to CIFAR-10 and CIFAR-100. Furthermore, Zhang et al. (2021c) proposed a combination of PMD with symmetric (30% and 60%) and asymmetric (30%) label noises.

The controlled web label noise proposed by Jiang et al. (2020)[23] introduced four instance-dependent noise benchmarks using the Mini-ImageNet (Vinyals et al., 2016) and Stanford Cars (Krause et al., 2013) datasets. The **Red Mini-ImageNet and Red Stanford Cars** benchmarks are based on noisy web label acquisition using a 3-step process: (1) image collection, (2) de-duplication, and (3) manual annotation. The first step collects images from Google text-to-image and image-to-image search engines, then near-duplicates to images in the validation set are removed, with the remaining images being annotated using the Google Cloud labeling platform. In this annotation process, labelers are asked if the original label is correct for the collected image, with each image being annotated by 3 to 5 labelers, and final label being produced by majority voting. From this 3-step process, 212588 images are collected, where 54400 images are found to have incorrect labels on Mini-ImageNet and 12629 images on Stanford Cars. The benchmark dataset with noise rate $\eta \in \{0\%, 5\%, 10\%, 15\%, 20\%, 30\%, 40\%, 50\%, 60\%, 80\%\}$ is formed by replacing $\eta\%$ of the original training images with the collected images with incorrect labels. Note that these two benchmarks can have not only closed-set, but also open-set instance dependent noise because the image collection in the first step can include images that do not belong to any of the training classes. The **Blue Mini-ImageNet and**

---

[21] https://github.com/xiaoboxia/Part-dependent-label-noise.
[22] https://github.com/pxiangwu/PLC.
[23] http://www.lujiang.info/cnlw.html.

Blue Stanford Cars benchmarks are formed by producing symmetric label noise, as explained in Section 2.4.1, with rates $\eta \in \{0\%, 5\%, 10\%, 15\%, 20\%, 30\%, 40\%, 50\%, 60\%, 80\%\}$.

The **Deepmind** benchmark[24] uses the datasets CIFAR-10 (Krizhevsky et al., 2014), CIFAR-100 (Krizhevsky et al., 2014), PatchCamelyon (Bejnordi et al., 2017; Veeling et al., 2018) (shown below in Table 2.4), and Cats vs Dogs (Elson et al., 2007). This benchmark uses a simulation framework that takes a subset of the clean-labeled training set (around 50% of the original training set) to train a set of models (referred to as rater models), which generate multiple instance-dependent noisy labels for the rest of the training set. The rater models have different characteristics (number of training epochs, number of training samples, validation performance, and number of parameters) and consequently can produce multiple labels with different noise rates. Three pseudo-labeled training sets are created for each dataset, containing a low ($\eta = 13\%$), medium ($\eta = 21.7\%$), and high ($\eta = 52.4\%$) amount of noise, which are formed by the rater models above. The instance-dependent label noise benchmark **RoG** (Lee et al., 2019)[25] is based on training a DenseNet-100 (Huang et al., 2017), a ResNet-34 (He et al., 2016a), and a VGG-13 (Simonyan and Zisserman, 2015) classifier with 5% and 20% of CIFAR-10 and CIFAR-100 training samples (using their clean labels), respectively. These three trained models will then pseudo-label the remaining training samples, with different rates of label noise, as follows: 1) for CIFAR-10, DenseNet-100 has $\eta = 32\%$, ResNet-34 has $\eta = 38\%$, and VGG-13 has $\eta = 34\%$; 2) for CIFAR-100, DenseNet-100 has $\eta = 34\%$, ResNet-34 has $\eta = 37\%$, and VGG-13 has $\eta = 37\%$.

The **Open-set benchmark** (Wang et al., 2018)[26] introduces an open-set noisy-label dataset by randomly replacing some training images in CIFAR-10 by outlier images, but keeping the original labels and number of images per class unchanged. The outlier images can either be of type I, i.e., from CIFAR-100, ImageNet32 (comprising 32×32 ImageNet images), and SVHN, where they only consider images whose labels exclude CIFAR-10 classes; or type II with images being damaged by Gaussian random noise (mean 0.2 and variance 1.0), corruption (75% of an image is set to black or white), and resolution distortion (an image resized to 4×4 and dilated back to 32×32). This benchmark combines 40% open-set symmetric noise with 20% to 40% symmetric closed-set noise. The **EDM** benchmark (Sachdeva et al., 2021)[27] combines open-set and closed-set symmetric label noise, with the rate of noisy samples defined by $\eta \in \{30\%, 60\%\}$ and the rate of open-set noise in $\{0\%, 25\%, 50\%, 75\%, 100\%\}$. The closed-set symmetric noise dataset is CIFAR-10, and the open-set symmetric noise datasets are CIFAR-100 and ImageNet32. The **DSOS** benchmark (Albert et al., 2022)[28] is similar to the EDM benchmark, but it

---

[24] https://github.com/deepmind/deepmind-research/tree/master/noisy_label.

[25] https://github.com/pokaxpoka/RoGNoisyLabel.

[26] https://github.com/YisenWang/ONL.

[27] https://github.com/ragavsachdeva/EvidentialMix.

[28] https://github.com/PaulAlbert31/DSOS.

uses CIFAR-100 as closed set symmetric noise (noise rate from 20% to 40%) and ImageNct32 as open set (noise rate from 20% to 60%) symmetric noise, so the total noise rate η is a sum of the open- and closed-set rates.

All benchmarks above assume an unrealistic balanced distribution of samples per class, which facilitates the learning process of various techniques explored for noisy-label learning. The **FSR/RoLT/INOLML** benchmark (Zhang and Pfister, 2021; Hoang et al., 2022; Wei et al., 2021b) proposes to combine symmetric noise on CIFAR-10 and CIFAR-100, with rates in $\{10\%, 20\%, 30\%, 40\%, 50\%\}$ with an imbalanced learning problem, with imbalance ratio $\rho \in \{10, 50, 100, 200\}$. The imbalance ratio is the ratio between the sample sizes of the largest majority class and the smallest minority class.

2.7.1.2 Segmentation and detection benchmarks

The **Symmetric Cityscapes** segmentation benchmark proposed by Luo et al. (2022)[29] to assess noisy-label learning segmentation algorithms takes the Cityscapes dataset (Cordts et al., 2016), shown in Table 2.3, and synthetically modify the original labels of the training set with symmetric label noise with rate $\eta \in \{50\%, 70\%, 90\%\}$ and remove the label of the pixels with rate $\eta \in \{50\%, 70\%, 90\%\}$.

The detection benchmarks **Flickr-VOC** and **Flickr-COCO** (Shen et al., 2020)[30] are built to simulate label noise for training visual object detectors for the PASCAL VOC (Everingham et al., 2010) and COCO (Lin et al., 2014) datasets listed in Table 2.1. Flickr-VOC and Flickr-COCO use the classes from PASCAL VOC and COCO, respectively, to retrieve images from the Flickr photo-sharing website. For each class, the first 4K images per class are collected, forming 83905 and 335327 images, without any postprocessing, for Flickr-VOC and Flickr-COCO, respectively. **Flickr-Clean** (Wei et al., 2016) is also constructed by taking the classes from PASCAL VOC and crawling Flickr to produce 41625 images in total, but differently from Flickr-VOC, the images in Flickr-Clean are post-processed by a salient object detector (Jiang et al., 2013) and saliency-cut segmentation (Cheng et al., 2014) to filter out noisy images. In general, Flickr-VOC is more challenging than Flickr-Clean, given its more realistic label noise. When using Flickr-VOC and Flickr-Clean as training sets, the detector is tested on the PASCAL VOC 2007 and 2012 (Everingham et al., 2010) testing sets, containing 4092 and 10991 test images over 20 categories, respectively, where none of the PASCAL VOC images is in the training sets. Also, when training on Flickr-COCO, the detector is assessed on COCO (Lin et al., 2014) validation dataset that has 80 object categories and 5000 images.

The **noisy-label instance segmentation** benchmark proposed by Yang et al. (2020)[31] artificially corrupts visual object class labels using **symmetric** (with $\eta \in \{20\%, 40\%, 60\%, 80\%\}$) and **asymmetric** (with $\eta \in \{20\%, 40\%\}$) noise on **PASCAL VOC** (Everingham et al., 2010), **COCO** (Lin et al., 2014), and **Cityscapes** (Cordts

---

[29] https://github.com/YaoruLuo/Meta-Structures-for-DNN.
[30] https://github.com/shenyunhang/NA-fWebSOD.
[31] https://github.com/longrongyang/LNCIS.

Table 2.3 Benchmarks used for assessing noisy-label learning computer vision segmentation and detection algorithms and models. The table shows the dataset(s) used, the estimated noise rate η, and noise type ν (CSSYM = closed-set symmetric, CSASM = closed-set asymmetric, CSIDN = closed set instance dependent noise, OSSYM = open-set symmetric, OSASM = open-set asymmetric, OSIDN = open-set instance dependent noise, INT = intrinsic) in the training set.

Benchmark	Dataset	Noise Rate η (%)	Noise Type ν
Symmetric Cityscapes	Cityscapes	$\approx$ 50.0, 70.0, 90.0	INT+CSSYM
Flickr-VOC	PASCAL VOC	> 0, but not reported	INT+CSIDN
Flickr-COCO	COCO	> 0, but not reported	INT+CSIDN
Flickr-Clean	PASCAL VOC	> 0, but not reported	INT+CSIDN
Symmetric Instance Segmentation	PASCAL VOC,COCO,Cityscapes	$\approx$ 20.0, 40.0, 60.0, 80.0	INT+CSSYM
Asymmetric Instance Segmentation	PASCAL VOC,COCO,Cityscapes	$\approx$ 20.0, 40.0	INT+CSASM
Symmetric Pixel Potsdam+Vaihingen	Potsdam+Vaihingen	$\approx$ 5.0, 10.0	INT+CSSYM
Symmetric Region Potsdam+Vaihingen	Potsdam+Vaihingen	$\approx$ 5.0, 10.0	INT+CSSYM
Spatial Shift Potsdam+Vaihingen	Potsdam+Vaihingen	> 0 (5,10-pixel label shift)	INT+CSIDN

et al., 2016) datasets. For the asymmetric noise, labels are flipped between the following classes from each dataset: PASCAL VOC (Bird → Aeroplane, Diningtable → Chair, Bus → Car, Sheep → Horse, Bicycle ↔ Motorbike, Cat ↔ Dog), COCO (the 80 classes are grouped into 12 super-classes and flipping can occur between two random classes within each super-class), and Cityscapes (Person ↔ Rider, Bus ↔ Truck, Motorcycle ↔ Bicycle).

Using the **Potsdam+Vaihingen** dataset (Potsdam, 2018; Vaihingen, 2018) listed in Table 2.1, Maiti et al. (2022) proposed three noisy-label segmentation benchmarks. The first is the **symmetric pixel-wise** label noise, where randomly selected pixels have their labels switched to another random labels, with $\eta \in \{5\%, 10\%\}$. The second is the **symmetric region-wise** label noise, where randomly selected contiguous regions have their labels switched to another random labels, with $\eta \in \{5\%, 10\%\}$. The third is the **relative shift of object boundaries**, where labels are spatially shifted in random direction by 5 or 10 pixels.

2.7.2 Medical image analysis datasets and benchmarks

The datasets used in medical image analysis for the study of learning with label noise are summarized in Table 2.4. The **Chest X-ray14** (Wang et al., 2017b)[32] dataset contains 112120 frontal view chest X-ray images from 30805 patients, labeled with the presence or absence of 14 diseases. Given that each patient can have multiple diseases and that these diseases are distributed in an imbalanced manner among patients, this dataset represents a multi-label imbalanced classification problem. The dataset is divided into 70% training, 10% validation, and 20% testing, and the annotation process is based on the automatic detection of disease concepts from specific sections of the radiology report. The annotation accuracy of this process was found to produce an F1 score[33] of 0.90 (Wang et al., 2017b) using radiology reports and clean labels from OpenI (Demner-Fushman et al., 2016), so label noise is present in the whole dataset, including training, validation, and testing sets. Similarly, the CheXpert (Irvin et al., 2019)[34] dataset has 220K multi-view chest X-ray images (out of which, 191010 are frontal view chest X-rays) from 65240 patients, where each image can be labeled with multiple diseases from a set of 14 diseases. The labeling process for the training set followed an approach that can automatically extract positive, negative, and uncertain labels for each disease. The uncertain label reflects the intrinsic noise present in the image-based disease diagnosis or the noise in extracting the positive or negative label from the report. The Micro-F1 result of this labeling process is around 0.95 for positive and negative labels, and 0.85 for the uncertain labels.[35] The validation set

---

[32] https://www.kaggle.com/datasets/nih-chest-xrays/data.

[33] The F1 score is computed by the harmonic mean of precision and recall, where precision is calculated by dividing the correctly annotated labels by all annotated labels, and recall is computed by dividing the correctly annotated labels by the amount of samples that should have been annotated.

[34] https://stanfordmlgroup.github.io/competitions/chexpert/.

[35] Micro-F1 is type of average F1 score covering over all labels.

Table 2.4 Datasets used for assessing noisy-label learning medical image analysis algorithms and models. The table shows the number of training, validation, and testing images, the number of classes, the task (MC = multi-class classification, ML = multi-label classification, SG = segmentation, DT = detection), if it is class-balanced (Y = yes, N = No), the estimated noise rate η, and noise type ν (CSSYM = closed-set symmetric, CSASM = closed-set asymmetric, CSIDN = closed set instance dependent noise, OSSYM = open-set symmetric, OSASM = open-set asymmetric, OSIDN = open-set instance dependent noise, INT = intrinsic) in the training set.

Dataset	# Training	# Validation	# Testing	# Classes	Task	Balanced	Noise Rate η (%)	Noise Type ν
ChestX-ray14	78,484	11,211	22,425	14	ML	N	$\approx$ 10.0 (all sets)	INT+CSIDN
CheXpert	224,316	200	500	14	ML	N	$\approx$ 5	INT+CSIDN
OpenI	–	–	7,470	19	ML	N	$\approx$ 0	INT
PadChest	121,829	–	39,039	28	ML	N	$\approx$ 7	INT+CSIDN
ISIC 2017	$\approx$ 2,000	$\approx$ 150	$\approx$ 600	3	MC	N	$\approx$ 0	INT
ISIC 2019	25,331	–	–	8	MC	N	$\approx$ 0	INT
PatchCamelyon	262,144	32,768	32,768	2	MC	Y	$\approx$ 0	INT
Gleason 2019	247	–	86	4	MC	N	> 0, not reported	INT+CSIDN
DigestPath2019	48435	–	9318	2	MC	Y	> 0, not reported	INT+CSIDN
Camelyon16	22314	–	9548	2	MC	Y	$\approx$ 0	INT
Chaoyang	4021	–	2139	4	MC	N	$\leq$ 40%	INT+CSIDN
ER	157	28	38	2	SG	N	$\approx$ 0	INT
MITO	165	8	10	2	SG	N	$\approx$ 0	INT
NUC	841	–	–	2	SG	N	$\approx$ 0	INT
SegTHOR	40	–	20	4	SG	N	$\approx$ 0	INT
ISBI15 MS	21	–	59	2	SG	N	> 0, not reported	INT+CSIDN
BraTS2019	335	125	166	4	SG	N	> 0, not reported	INT+CSIDN
LIDC-IDRI	1018	–	–	3	SG	N	> 0, not reported	INT+CSIDN
JSRT	247	–	–	5	SG	N	$\approx$ 0	INT

has 200 chest X-ray images that were labeled by three board-certified radiologists, and the test set has 500 chest X-ray images annotated by a consensus (majority vote) of five board-certified radiologists. For the datasets above, the chest X-ray images may also show signs of diseases that are not in the set of 14 labels, so we consider that they can also contain open-set label noise. However, considering that the open-set labels may be correlated with the closed-set labels, their effect is not as dramatic as for multi-class classification problems.

Clean-labeled chest X-ray image datasets have also been used to test the ability of models trained with the noisy-label datasets above to translate to an environment containing not only clean labels, but also images captured from different machines (i.e., a domain translation problem). For instance **OpenI** (Demner-Fushman et al., 2016)[36] contains 7470 multi-view chest X-rays (3643 frontal view and 3827 lateral view images) and radiology reports, labeled with 19 key findings by human annotators. Furthermore, **PadChest** (Bustos et al., 2020)[37] is a large-scale multi-view chest X-ray dataset containing 160868 images (out of which, 108722 are frontal view chest X-rays) from 67625 patients, with 27% (i.e., 39039 images) of images being manually labeled by trained physicians and the remaining 73% (i.e., 121829 images) automatically labeled by a recurrent neural network with attention mechanisms that achieves 0.93 Micro-F1 score on an independent test set. The reports are labeled with 174 different radiographic findings, 19 differential diagnoses, and 104 anatomic locations, but the benchmark focuses on 28 labels available for training and testing.

The international skin imaging collaboration (ISIC) has organized many workshops and challenges for the analysis of skin images. The **ISIC 2017** (Codella et al., 2018)[38] has been used to build noisy label learning benchmarks. This dataset contains around 2750 dermoscopy color images, split into 2000 for training, 150 for validation, and 600 for testing. These images are annotated with three classes (melanoma, nevus, seborrheic kerathosis), and the dataset has an imbalanced distribution of samples per classes. The **ISIC 2019** (Tschandl et al., 2018) dataset[39] has also been considered to build benchmarks with synthetic label noise. ISIC 2019 contains 25331 dermoscopic color images, which have been used in a challenge to predict eight skin disease classes, with a highly imbalanced class distribution.

Pathological images have also been used in benchmarks to assess noisy-label learning methods. For instance, the **PatchCamelyon** dataset (Bejnordi et al., 2017; Veeling et al., 2018)[40] is a binary image classification dataset that contains of 327680 color images, split as 262144 for training, 32768 for validation, and 32768 for testing. The images have size 96×96 pixels, and are extracted from histopathologic scans of lymph node sections, with each image being labeled with the presence or absence of metastatic tissue. The images are extracted from 400 Hematoxylin and

---

[36] https://www.kaggle.com/datasets/raddar/chest-xrays-indiana-university.
[37] https://bimcv.cipf.es/bimcv-projects/padchest/.
[38] https://challenge.isic-archive.com/landing/2017/.
[39] https://challenge.isic-archive.com/landing/2019/.
[40] https://github.com/basveeling/pcam.

Eosin stained whole slide imaging of sentinel lymph node sections, with each slide being acquired and digitized at 2 different centers using a 40x objective (producing a pixel resolution of 0.243 microns), and a positive label indicates that the center of the image has at least one pixel of tumor tissue. **Gleason 2019** (Nir et al., 2018)[41] has a training set with 333 tissue microarray (TMA) images (247 for training and 86 for testing) of prostate cancer, sampled from 231 radical prostatectomy patients. These images are annotated at the pixel-level by six pathologists (with different experience levels) for different Gleason grades, from benign (0) to cancerous (3 to 5). Approximately 16K image patches are extracted from the TMA images for training, where each patch has six separate labels, one provided by each pathologist using the four classes mentioned above. Hence, this is a real-world amount of label noise because of inter-observer variability, where Xue et al. (2022) reported that the inter-observer Cohen's kappa coefficient is between 0.4 and 0.6, with 0.0 indicating chance agreement and 1.0 representing perfect agreement.

DigestPath2019 (Da et al., 2022)[42] is another pathology image dataset containing 250 malignant images with pixel level annotation and 410 benign images. Images are cropped into patches of 256×256 pixels using a stride of 64 pixels. Malignant patches are defined as having a malignant lesion area of more than 95% inside the patch, which adds an unknown amount of instance-dependent label noise. Benign patches are cropped from benign images according to the method explained in (Zhu et al., 2021a), which divides the patches into easy and hard. The number of training samples is 29334 malignant samples and 28419 benign samples, where the setup consists of randomly partition them into 24611 malignant, 23824 benign, and 4723 malignant, 4595 benign samples for training and testing, respectively. The dataset **Camelyon16** (Bejnordi et al., 2017)[43] contains 400 whole-slide images (WSIs) of sentinel lymph node from two independent datasets collected from the Radboud University Medical Center and the University Medical Center Utrecht. The dataset is constructed according to the protocol by Zhu et al. (2021a), which builds a dataset with 110 WSIs of normal cases and 110 WSIs of tumor cases. By cropping patches as done above for DigestPath2019 (Zhu et al., 2021a), it is possible to extract 16050 malignant samples and 14812 negative samples, which are split into 11262 malignant and 11052 benign training patches, and 4788 malignant and 4760 benign testing samples, where training and testing patches are from different WSIs. Furthermore, the dataset **Chaoyang** (Zhu et al., 2021a)[44] is built with colon slides from Chaoyang hospital, where the patch size is 512×512 pixels. These patches were labeled by three pathologists, where the testing set is formed with patches that have consistent label from the three pathologists, and the training set has patches with consistent (about 60% of the patches) and inconsistent (around 40% of patches) results, where

41 https://bmiai.ubc.ca/research/miccai-automatic-prostate-gleason-grading-challenge-2019/gleason2019-data.
42 https://digestpath2019.grand-challenge.org/Home/.
43 https://camelyon16.grand-challenge.org/.
44 https://bupt-ai-cz.github.io/HSA-NRL/.

the noisy labels for the training patches are obtained by randomly selecting one of the three doctors' diagnoses. For training, Chaoyang has 1111 normal, 842 serrated, 1404 adenocarcinoma, and 664 adenoma patches; and for testing, it has 705 normal, 321 serrated, 840 adenocarcinoma, 273 adenoma patches.

The **ER** and **MITO** datasets (Luo et al., 2020)[45] are used to assess binary segmentation of fluorescence microscopy images. These images show intracellular organelle networks, such as the endoplasmic reticulum (ER) network and the mitochondrial (MITO) network. The label of each image has an accurate binary segmentation of these complex network structures. Images are cropped into 256×256 pixel patches with overlap for training and without overlap for validation and testing. The ER dataset is split into 157/28/38 images for training, validation, and testing; and the MITO dataset is split into 165/8/10 images for training, validation, and testing.

The **NUC** dataset (Caicedo et al., 2019)[46] consists of a variety of 2D light microscopy images showing manually annotated nuclei from a range of different organisms, e.g., humans, mice, and flies. In particular, the dataset contains 37333 manually annotated nuclei in 841 images obtained from more than 30 experiments across different samples, operators, microscopy instruments, imaging conditions, varying quality of illumination, cell lines, magnifications, staining protocols, and research facilities.

The **SegTHOR** (Lambert et al., 2020)[47] dataset contains the segmentations of organs surrounding a tumor that must be preserved from irradiations during radiotherapy. These organs are known as organs at risk (OARs) in the thorax, which comprise: heart, trachea, aorta, and the esophagus. The dataset has 60 3D computed tomography (CT) scans, split as 40/20 for training and testing. The CT volumes are from 60 patients (with or without IV contrast) with non small cell lung cancer referred for radiotherapy with curative intent at the Centre Henri Becquerel, Rouen, France (CHB, regional anti-cancer center). The CT scans have 512×512 pixels with in-plane resolution varying between 0.90 mm and 1.37 mm per pixel, and number of slices varying from 150 to 284 with a z-resolution between 2 mm and 3.7 mm.

The **ISBI15 multiple sclerosis (MS)** lesion segmentation dataset (Jesson and Arbel, 2015)[48] contains 3D brain magnetic resonance images (MRI) with labeled MS lesions. The training data has longitudinal images from 5 patients, and the testing data contains longitudinal images from 14 patients, but only the training data has the MS annotations. Each longitudinal dataset has T1-weighted, T2-weighted, PD-weighted, and T2-weighted fluid attenuated inversion recovery (FLAIR) MRI with 3-5 time points acquired on a 3T MR scanner, where the T1-weighted has a 1 mm^3 voxel resolution, while the other scans have 1 mm in-plane resolution with 3 mm

---

[45] https://ieee-dataport.org/documents/fluorescence-microscopy-image-datasets-deep-learning-segmentation-intracellular-orgenelle#files.

[46] https://bbbc.broadinstitute.org/BBBC038/.

[47] https://competitions.codalab.org/competitions/21145.

[48] https://smart-stats-tools.org/lesion-challenge-2015.

sections. All images are rigidly co-registered to the baseline T1-weighted image with automatic skull stripping masks. The MS lesions were segmented by two annotators.

The **brain tumor segmentation (BraTS)** (Menze et al., 2014)[49] dataset is designed to test segmentation methods from multimodal magnetic resonance imaging (MRI) scans, where one of the goals is to evaluate tumor segmentation uncertainty. The training dataset contains 259 subjects with high-grade gliomas (HGG) and 76 subjects with low-grade gliomas (LGG), where each subject has four $240 \times 240 \times 155$ MRIs (acquired with different clinical protocols and various scanners from 19 institutions) of the following types: native (T1), post-contrast T1-weighted (T1Gd), T2-weighted (T2), and T2 Fluid Attenuated Inversion Recovery (FLAIR). The segmentations, done by one to four annotators, consist of $240 \times 240 \times 155$ maps with four classes, i.e., necrotic (NCR) and the non-enhancing tumor core (NET), edema (ED), enhancing tumor (ET), and everything else. Furthermore, the validation set has 125 unlabeled subjects and the testing set contains 166 unlabeled subjects. The data are co-registered to the same anatomical template, interpolated to the resolution 1 mm^3, and skull-stripped.

The lung image database consortium image collection (**LIDC-IDRI**) dataset (Armato et al., 2011)[50] contains 1018 low-dose diagnostic and lung cancer screening thoracic computed tomography (CT) scans, from 1010 lung patients, with lesions annotated by four experienced thoracic radiologists. Lesions are labeled into one of the three classes: nodule ≥ 3 mm, nodule < 3 mm, and non-nodule ≥ 3 mm.

The **JSRT** (Shiraishi et al., 2000)[51] dataset, created by the Japanese Society of Radiological Technology Database in cooperation with the Japanese Radiological Society (JRS), has 247 chest X-rays, with 154 chest X-rays containing lung nodules (split into 100 malignant and 54 benign nodules, classified into five groups according to their subtlety degrees) and 93 without nodules. The chest X-rays have been digitized to form an image of 2048×2048 pixels and a 12-bit gray scale. The dataset also has non-image data, e.g., patient age, gender, diagnosis (malignant or benign), X and Y coordinates of nodule, and a simple diagram of nodule location.

2.7.2.1 Classification benchmarks

The benchmarks to assess noisy-label learning medical image analysis classifiers are shown in Table 2.5. The real-world **IDN Chest X-ray14** and **IDN CheXpert** benchmarks (Liu et al., 2022a)[52] in medical image classification are represented by training using datasets that naturally contain instance-dependent noise (e.g., Chest X-ray14 (Wang et al., 2017b) or CheXpert (Irvin et al., 2019)) and testing using clean-label test sets (e.g., CheXpert (Irvin et al., 2019), OpenI (Demner-Fushman et al., 2016), or PadChest (Bustos et al., 2020)). A similar real-world benchmark, referred to as **Computer-generated Noisy Label**, was proposed by Xue et al. (2022)

---

[49] https://www.med.upenn.edu/cbica/brats-2019/.
[50] https://wiki.cancerimagingarchive.net/display/Public/LIDC-IDRI.
[51] http://db.jsrt.or.jp/eng.php.
[52] https://github.com/FBLADL/NVUM.

Table 2.5 Benchmarks used for assessing noisy-label learning medical image analysis classification algorithms and models. The table shows the dataset(s) used, the estimated noise rate η, and noise type ν (CSSYM = closed-set symmetric, CSASM = closed-set asymmetric, CSIDN = closed set instance dependent noise, OSSYM = open-set symmetric, OSASM = open-set asymmetric, OSIDN = open-set instance dependent noise, INT = intrinsic) in the training set.

Benchmark	Dataset	Noise Rate η (%)	Noise Type ν
IDN Chest X-ray14	ChestX-ray14,OpenI,PadChest	≈ 10	INT+CSIDN
IDN CheXpert	CheXpert,OpenI,PadChest	≈ 5	INT+CSIDN
Computer-generated Noisy Label	Chest X-ray14	≈ 10	INT+CSIDN
Inter-observer Variability	Gleason 2019	≈ 10	INT+CSIDN
IDN Chaoyang	Chaoyang	≤ 40	INT+CSIDN
Symmetric ISIC	ISIC 2019	$\approx 10, 20, 40$	INT+CSSYM
Asymmetric ISIC	ISIC 2019	≈ 10	INT+CSASM
Random Noise ISIC	ISIC 2017	$\approx 5, 10, 20, 40$	INT+CSSYM
Random Noise PCam	PatchCamelyon	$\approx 5, 10, 20, 40$	INT+CSSYM
Symmetric DigestPath2019	DigestPath2019	$\approx 10, 20, 30, 40$	INT+CSSYM
Symmetric Camelyon16	Camelyon16	$\approx 10, 20, 30, 40$	INT+CSSYM

using the Chest X-ray14's training set (Wang et al., 2017b) and a subset of the testing set containing 1962 images (Majkowska et al., 2020) that have been manually re-labeled by radiologists using four labels (pneumothorax, opacity, nodule or mass, and fracture). Xue et al. (2022) also presented another real-world benchmark using the Gleason 2019 dataset (Nir et al., 2018), namely the **Inter-observer Variability** benchmark. Gleason 2019 is annotated by six pathologists with high inter-observer variation, where the ground-truth clean label is estimated by applying the Simultaneous Truth and Performance Level Estimation (STAPLE) algorithm (Warfield et al., 2004), and the label of one of the six pathologists is assumed to be the noisy label. The benchmark uses 80% of the dataset for training and the rest for testing. Another real-world benchmark is available from the dataset **IDN Chaoyang** (Zhu et al., 2021a),[53] explained in Table 2.4, which contains closed-set instance-dependent label noise.

Medical image classification benchmarks containing synthetically added label noise have also been proposed by Zhang et al. (2021d), where they took the ISIC 2019 dataset (Tschandl et al., 2018) and balanced it by randomly sampling 628 images for each of the 8 classes (all images were selected from the classes that have less than 628 images). This allows the construction of a training set with 4260 images that are split into 80% training and 20% testing. Then closed-set symmetric noise with rates $\eta \in \{10\%, 20\%, 40\%\}$ and closed-set asymmetric noise with rates $\eta = 10\%$ are applied to the training set above, with labels flipping from each class to the next one, forming the benchmarks **Symmetric ISIC** and **Asymmetric ISIC**. Synthetic benchmarks based on symmetric noise on ISIC 2017 and PatchCamelyon have been introduced by Xue et al. (2022). For instance, the benchmark **Random Noise ISIC** uses extra 1582 training images from the ISIC archive, and the **Random Noise PCam** relies on the original training set. On these two datasets, the symmetric noise has rate $\eta \in \{5\%, 10\%, 20\%, 40\%\}$. The **Symmetric DigestPath2019** and **Symmetric Camelyon16** (Zhu et al., 2021a)[54] benchmarks use the training and testing sets described for DigestPath2019 and Camelyon16 in Table 2.4, but add symmetric label noise with $\eta \in \{10\%, 20\%, 30\%, 40\%\}$ for the training samples.

2.7.3 Medical image analysis segmentation benchmarks

The medical image analysis noisy-label segmentation benchmarks are listed in Table 2.6. The benchmark by Luo et al. (2022)[55] is developed for binary segmentation problems using the images from ER and MITO (Luo et al., 2020), and NUC (Caicedo et al., 2019) datasets, described in Table 2.4. There are three types of label noise considered: 1) randomized clean label (RCL), 2) perturbed clean label (PCL), and 3) random label (RL). **RCL** consists of two types of perturbations: i) in **random sampling**, a noise rate $\eta \in \{10\%, 30\%, 50\%, 70\%, 100\%\}$ represents the percentage of

---

[53] https://bupt-ai-cz.github.io/HSA-NRL/.

[54] https://bupt-ai-cz.github.io/HSA-NRL/.

[55] https://github.com/YaoruLuo/Meta-Structures-for-DNN.

Table 2.6 Benchmarks used for assessing noisy-label learning medical image analysis segmentation algorithms and models. The table shows the dataset(s) used, the estimated noise rate η, and noise type ν (CSSYM = closed-set symmetric, CSASM = closed-set asymmetric, CSIDN = closed set instance dependent noise, OSSYM = open-set symmetric, OSASM = open-set asymmetric, OSIDN = open-set instance dependent noise, INT = intrinsic) in the training set.

Benchmark	Dataset	Noise Rate η (%)	Noise Type ν
RCL-random sampling	ER,MITO,NUC	$\approx 10, 30, 50, 70, 100$	INT+CSSYM
RCL-random flipping	ER,MITO,NUC	$\approx 0, 20, 40, 45, 49$	INT+CSSYM
PCL	ER,MITO,NUC	> 0, not reported	INT+CSIDN
RL	ER,MITO,NUC	$\approx 10, 30, 50$	INT+CSSYM
IDN SegTHOR	SegTHOR	> 0, reported mIoU noisy vs. clean	INT+CSIDN
IDN ISBI2015 MS	ISBI2015 MS	> 0, reported mIoU noisy vs. clean	INT+CSIDN
IDN BraTS	BraTS2019	> 0, reported mIoU noisy vs. clean	INT+CSIDN
IDN LIDC-IDRI	LIDC-IDRI	> 0, reported mIoU noisy vs. clean	INT+CSIDN
IDN JSRT	JSRT	$\approx 30, 50, 70$	INT+CSIDN

pixels that are randomly selected to be discarded from training; and ii) in **random flipping**, a noise rate $\eta \in \{0\%, 20\%, 40\%, 45\%, 49\%\}$ represents the percentage of pixels that are randomly selected to have their labels flipped. **PCL** relies on morphological operators to introduce more structured noise, where 3×3 template image dilation or erosion or one-pixel-wide skeletonization are applied to the image annotation. **RL** relies on a noise rate $\eta \in \{10\%, 30\%, 50\%\}$ of pixels that are randomly selected to have their labels randomly switched, without considering the original pixel label. The benchmark proposed in (Luo et al., 2022) was designed to show that deep learning models are able to learn meta-structures from noisy labels instead of to systematically test the robustness of segmentation models.

The segmentation benchmark **IDN SegTHOR** (Liu et al., 2022b)[56] uses the SegTHOR dataset (Lambert et al., 2020), listed in Table 2.4, which has 3D CT scans with voxels labeled into the classes esophagus, heart, trachea, aorta, or background. The benchmark uses 2D slices (resized to 256×256 pixels) of the 3D scans by randomly splitting them into a training set of 3638 slices, a validation set of 570 slices, and a test set of 580 slices, with each patient appearing once in one of these subsets. The training set is affected by a label noise generated by applying random degrees of dilation and erosion to the original labels, where the noisy annotation has a mean intersection over union mIoU $\in \{0.28, 0.39, 0.52, 0.61, 0.73, 0.91, 1.0\}$[57] with respect to the original labels. The validation and testing sets maintain their original clean labels.

---

[56] https://github.com/Kangningthu/ADELE.
[57] mIoU is defined below in (2.73).

The noisy-label benchmarks proposed in (Zhang et al., 2020a)[58] form the **IDN ISBI2015 MS** lesion segmentation (Jesson and Arbel, 2015) and **IDN BraTS** (Menze et al., 2014). These benchmarks are formed by applying morphological operations (e.g., thinning, thickening, fractures, etc.) to generate synthetic noisy labels to the original annotation maps for binary (IDN ISBI2015 MS) and multi-class segmentation problems (IDN BraTS). With the operations above, a group of five annotators are simulated as follows: 1) *good-segmentation* with approximate ground truth segmentation, 2) *over-segment*, 3) *under-segment*, 4) small fractures and over-segmentation ("wrong-segmentation"), and 5) "blank-segmentation" that annotates everything as the background. The training data is created from the simulated annotators above, and for the IDN ISBI2015 MS benchmark, the training label has a varying degree of noise, where the original training set with 5 patients and 21 volumes is split into 10 volumes for training (sub-divided into 8 for training and 2 for validation) and 11 for testing. The IDN BraTS benchmark uses the 259 high grade glioma (HGG) cases in the training data of BraTS2019, where volumes are divided into 2D images with 1600/300/500 images split in a case-wise manner into training/validation/testing sets. Images are pre-processed by case-wise normalization and center-cropping to size 192×192 pixels, where all available modalities are concatenated. The synthetic label noise in this multi-class segmentation problem is performed by first choosing a target class, and then applying the morphological operators to produce one of the five simulated annotators mentioned above. The **IDN LIDC-IDRI** benchmark uses the LIDC-IDRI dataset (Armato et al., 2011) that contains 1018 lung CT scans from 1010 lung patients with manual lesion segmentations by four thoracic radiologists. The dataset is split as 722/144/144 patients for training/validation/testing, where the volumes are broke down into 2D images and re-sampled to 1 mm $\times$ 1 mm in-plane resolution, and images are center-cropped into 180×180 pixels around the lesion position labeled by at least one of the radiologists. This forms 5000/1000/1000 images for training/validation/testing. A gold standard segmentation is created by aggregating the labels via STAPLE (Warfield et al., 2004).

The benchmark in (Zhang et al., 2020b) uses the **JSRT** dataset (Shiraishi et al., 2000) that contains 247 chest X-rays of size 2048×2048 pixels, which are annotated with three anatomical structures, namely: clavicle, heart, and lung. Images are resized to 256×256 pixels, and the original set is split into 197 training and 50 validation images. Similarly to the methods above, the label noises are simulated with various morphological operators (e.g., dilating, eroding, and edge-distorting) applied to the original manual annotations. By varying the proportion and extent of the synthesized label noise, the benchmark aims to systematically assess methods using the variables η and β. The variable η defines the proportion of corruption, where each mask is dilated, eroded, or edge-distorted by $\beta \pm 3$. The training sets have $\eta \in \{30\%, 50\%, 70\%\}$. The benchmark also proposes two sets of values for β, with the first set defined by $\beta_{clavicle} = 5$, $\beta_{heart} = 10$, $\beta_{lung} = 15$; and the second set defined by $\beta_{clavicle} = 10$, $\beta_{heart} = 15$, $\beta_{lung} = 20$.

---

[58] https://github.com/moucheng2017/Learn_Noisy_Labels_Medical_Images.

2.7.4 **Non-image datasets and benchmarks**

Even though we focus on image datasets for noisy-label learning, we can also find non-image datasets available for the same task, as displayed in Table 2.7. For instance, the dataset **NEWS** (Lang, 1995)[59] contains 13997 training texts and 6000 test texts manually annotated with 20 classes. The **AG News** dataset (Zhang et al., 2015) has 120K training and 7600 testing texts, cleanly annotated with four classes. **Amazon reviews** (Xie et al., 2020) has 3M training and 650K testing texts, cleanly annotated with five classes. **Yelp reviews** (Yang et al., 2016) has 650K training and 50K testing texts, cleanly annotated with five classes. **Yahoo answers** (Conneau et al., 2016) has 1.4M training and 60K testing texts, cleanly annotated with 10 classes. **TREC question-type dataset** (Li and Roth, 2002) contains 4949 training, 503 validation, and 50 test texts, cleanly annotated with 6 classes. The **Docred** dataset (Yao et al., 2019) contains 101873 distantly labeled documents (Mintz et al., 2009) and 5053 human-annotated documents, split as 3053/1000/1000 for training/validation/testing, with 96 classes and an estimated label noise rate of $\eta > 41.4\%$. For noisy multi-label learning problems using non-image data, we have many datasets available,[60] such as: sound classification (**music emotion** (Trohidis et al., 2008) and **birds** (Briggs et al., 2013)); protein classification (**genbase** (Diplaris et al., 2005) and **Yeast** (Elisseeff and Weston, 2001)); and text classification (**medical** (Pestian et al., 2007) and **bibtex** (Katakis et al., 2008)).

Next we present in Table 2.8 some of the recent benchmarks proposed to assess non-image label noise learning problems. The benchmark **IDN NEWS** (Xia et al., 2020)[61] uses the dataset NEWS (Lang, 1995) with the instance-dependent noise (IDN) label noise explained in Section 2.7.1.1. The benchmarks for symmetric (**UNIF**) and asymmetric (**FLIP**) noisy-label text classification (Zheng et al., 2021) use the datasets AG News (Zhang et al., 2015), Amazon reviews (Xie et al., 2020), Yelp reviews (Yang et al., 2016), and Yahoo answers (Conneau et al., 2016). For all these datasets, a subset of the training image is guaranteed to be clean (400 for AG News, 500 for Amazon reviews, 500 for Yelp reviews, and 1000 for Yahoo answers), while the rest of the dataset is affected by symmetric and asymmetric label noise with $\eta \in \{0\%, 10\%, 20\%, ..., 80\%, 90\%, 100\%\}$. The **random noise** benchmark in (Garg et al., 2021) applies symmetric label noise with $\eta \in \{10\%, 20\%, 30\%, 40\%, 50\%\}$ in the training and validation sets, while keeping the original clean test set, of the datasets TREC (Li and Roth, 2002) and AG News (Zhang et al., 2015). Garg et al. (2021) also proposed the introduction of input-conditional noise (ICN) on TREC and AG News datasets, where for TREC the noise is inserted as follows: 1) by selectively corrupting the labels of inputs that contain the words 'How' or 'What'; and 2) in the longest inputs in the dataset. For AG-news, the random label noise is added for inputs containing the token 'AP' or 'Reuters'. In all cases, this IDN label

---

[59] https://drive.google.com/drive/folders/1Y0ewJGCGNal1xLjK6QS2Wak7UQo0VxwJ.
[60] http://mulan.sourceforge.net/datasets-mlc.html.
[61] https://github.com/xiaoboxia/Part-dependent-label-noise.

Table 2.7 Datasets used for assessing noisy-label learning algorithms and models applied to non-image data. The table shows the number of training, validation, and testing images, the number of classes, the task (TMC = text multi-class classification, SMC = sound multi-class classification, TML = text multi-label classification, SML = sound multi-label classification, PML = protein multi-label classification), if it is balanced (Y = yes, N = No, ? = unknown), the estimated noise rate η, and noise type ν (CSSYM = closed-set symmetric, CSASM = closed-set asymmetric, CSIDN = closed set instance dependent noise, OSSYM = open-set symmetric, OSASM = open-set asymmetric, OSIDN = open-set instance dependent noise, INT = intrinsic) in the training set.

Dataset	# Training	# Validation	# Testing	# Classes	Task	Balanced	Noise Rate η (%)	Noise Type ν
NEWS	13,997	–	6,000	20	TMC	?	≈ 0	INT
AG News	120,000	–	7,600	4	TMC	?	≈ 0	INT
Amazon reviews	3M	–	650K	5	TMC	?	≈ 0	INT
Yelp reviews	650K	–	50K	5	TMC	?	≈ 0	INT
Yahoo answers	1.4M	–	60K	10	TMC	?	≈ 0	INT
TREC question-type dataset	4949	503	50	6	TMC	?	≈ 0	INT
Docred	104926	1000	1000	96	TMC	Y	> 41.4	INT+CSIDN
music emotion	593	–	–	6	SML	N	> 0, not reported	INT+CSIDN
birds	645	–	–	19	SML	N	≈ 0	INT
genbase	662	–	–	27	PML	N	≈ 0	INT
Yeast	2417	–	–	14	PML	N	> 0, not reported	INT+CSIDN
medical	978	–	–	45	TML	N	≈ 0	INT
bibtex	7395	–	–	159	TML	N	≈ 0	INT

Table 2.8 Benchmarks used for assessing noisy-label learning algorithms and models applied to non-image data. The table shows the datasets, the estimated noise rate η, and noise type ν (CSSYM = closed-set symmetric, CSASM = closed-set asymmetric, CSIDN = closed set instance dependent noise, OSSYM = open-set symmetric, OSASM = open-set asymmetric, OSIDN = open-set instance dependent noise, INT = intrinsic) in the training set.

Benchmark	Dataset	Noise Rate η (%)	Noise Type ν
IDN NEWS	NEWS	$\approx$ 10, 20, 30, 40, 50	INT+CSIDN
UNIF	AG News, Amazon reviews, Yelp reviews, and Yahoo answers	$\approx$ 0, 10, 20, ..., 80, 90, 100	INT+CSSYM
FLIP	AG News, Amazon reviews, Yelp reviews, and Yahoo answers	$\approx$ 0, 10, 20, ..., 80, 90, 100	INT+CSASM
random noise	TREC, AG News	$\approx$ 10, 20, 30, 40, 50	INT+CSSYM
IDN	TREC, AG News	from 7.8% to 50%	INT+CSIDN
SYM artificially noised dataset	Docred	$\approx$ {20, 40, 60, 80}	INT+CSSYM
ASM artificially noised dataset	Docred	$\approx$ {20, 40, 60}	INT+CSASM
Noisy multi-label	music emotion, birds, genbase, Yeast, medical, bibtex	> 0	INT+CSIDN

noise is based on rate η that varies from 7.8% to 50% in the training and validation sets, and testing set remains clean. The **artificially noised dataset** benchmark proposed by Deng et al. (2021) uses the Docred dataset (Yao et al., 2019) that contains 105K noisy-label training samples and 1000 validation samples annotated by humans with clean labels. The artificially noised dataset is obtained by changing the human-annotated set, with symmetric and asymmetric noise. For symmetric noise, the rate is $\eta \in \{20\%, 40\%, 60\%, 80\%\}$, and for the asymmetric noise, the entity pairs in the human-annotated dataset are labeled through wikidata knowledge base, then labels are flipped using noise rate $\eta \in \{20\%, 40\%, 60\%\}$.

Non-image **Noisy multi-label** benchmarks have been proposed in (Xie and Huang, 2021),[62] with a support vector machine (SVM) classifier trained on original supervised multi-label datasets that simulates the human annotator. More specifically, the SVM classifier is trained on the multi-label data, and an $\alpha \in \{50\%, 100\%, 150\%\}$ percentage of noisy labels is introduced to the training samples based on their SVM classification confidence.

2.8 Evaluation

Noisy-label learning methods are assessed using many of the measures already used in the field to test regular classification, segmentation, and detection methods, but using the noise rate η as an independent variable, when it is available. When η is not available or fixed at a specific value, e.g., for real-world datasets, then comparisons are done with pre-defined training and testing sets. For the evaluations described below, the training is performed with a training set containing noisy labels $\mathcal{D} = \{(\mathbf{x}, \tilde{\mathbf{y}})_i\}_{i=1}^{|\mathcal{D}|}$, with noise rate $\eta > 0$, while the evaluation measure is computed using the clean testing set denoted by $\mathcal{T} = \{(\mathbf{x}, \tilde{\mathbf{y}})_i\}_{i=1}^{|\mathcal{T}|}$, which as explained in Section 2.6, is formed with a noise rate $\eta = 0$. Below, we list the most common measures to assess multi-class and multi-label classification, segmentation, and detection approaches.

2.8.1 Classification evaluation

For multi-class classification problems (see Fig. 2.17), the most common measure is the accuracy in the testing set, computed from:

$$\text{Accuracy} = \frac{1}{|\mathcal{T}|} \sum_{(\mathbf{x}, \tilde{\mathbf{y}}) \in \mathcal{T}} \tilde{\mathbf{y}}^\top \hat{\mathbf{y}}, \tag{2.65}$$

where the test image label produced by the model is represented by $\hat{\mathbf{y}} = \text{OneHot}(f_\theta(\mathbf{x}))$, with $f_\theta : \mathcal{X} \to \Delta^{|\mathcal{Y}|-1}$ being the trained model and OneHot :

---

[62] http://milkxie.github.io/code/PMLNIcode.zip.

$\Delta^{|\mathcal{Y}|-1} \to \mathcal{Y}$ denoting a function to produce a one-hot prediction from the model (2.13). Accuracy represents a sample-wise measure that works well when the number of samples per class in the testing set $\mathcal{T}$ is balanced. However, when the number of samples per class is imbalanced, accuracy can provide a result that is biased toward the classes that contain the majority of samples. For instance, assume that we have a binary classification problem with 90 samples for class 1 and 10 samples for class 2, and the model predicts the correct class for all 90 samples of class 1, but predicts the correct class for only 5 samples of class 2, so even though the accuracy from (2.65) is 95%, the accuracy for class 2 is only 50%. Hence, in problems where we have highly imbalanced distributions of samples per class, the label-wise measures that we explain below are preferred.

A common label-wise measure is the area under the receiver-operating characteristic curve (AUROC), which is displayed in Fig. 2.17. To compute this curve, we need to compute the following the true positive rate (TPR, also known as recall or sensitivity) and the false positive rate (FPR or 1-specificity) per class $c \in \{1, ..., |\mathcal{Y}|\}$ at several classification thresholds $\tau \in [0, 1]$,

$$
\begin{aligned}
\text{TPR}(c, \tau) &= \frac{\text{TP}(c, \tau)}{\text{TP}(c, \tau) + \text{FN}(c, \tau)} \\
\text{FPR}(c, \tau) &= \frac{\text{FP}(c, \tau)}{\text{TN}(c, \tau) + \text{FP}(c, \tau)},
\end{aligned}
\tag{2.66}
$$

with

$$
\begin{aligned}
\text{TP}(c, \tau) &= \sum_{(\mathbf{x}, \tilde{\mathbf{y}}) \in \mathcal{T}} \tilde{\mathbf{y}}(c) \times \delta(f_\theta^{(\mathbf{y}_c)}(\mathbf{x}) \geq \tau), \\
\text{FN}(c, \tau) &= \sum_{(\mathbf{x}, \tilde{\mathbf{y}}) \in \mathcal{T}} \tilde{\mathbf{y}}(c) \times \delta(f_\theta^{(\mathbf{y}_c)}(\mathbf{x}) < \tau), \\
\text{FP}(c, \tau) &= \sum_{(\mathbf{x}, \tilde{\mathbf{y}}) \in \mathcal{T}} (1 - \tilde{\mathbf{y}}(c)) \times \delta(f_\theta^{(\mathbf{y}_c)}(\mathbf{x}) \geq \tau), \\
\text{TN}(c, \tau) &= \sum_{(\mathbf{x}, \tilde{\mathbf{y}}) \in \mathcal{T}} (1 - \tilde{\mathbf{y}}(c)) \times \delta(f_\theta^{(\mathbf{y}_c)}(\mathbf{x}) < \tau),
\end{aligned}
\tag{2.67}
$$

where $\delta(.)$ is an indicator function, and $f_\theta^{(\mathbf{y}_c)}(\mathbf{x})$ represents the probability of classification for the cth class. The ROC curve per class c is computed by interpolating the values of $\text{TPR}(c, \tau)$ as a function of $\text{FPR}(c, \tau)$ by varying the threshold τ from 1 to 0. The AUROC for c is then computed as the area under the ROC curve for the class c, and the result for all classes is computed from the mean of the AUROC for all classes.

Another common label-wise measure used in classification problems is the area under the precision and recall curve (AUPRC), shown in Fig. 2.17, and the mean average precision (mAP). Both measures need the plotting of the precision-recall

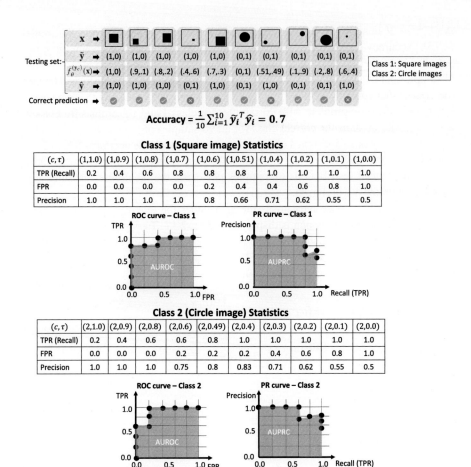

FIGURE 2.17 Classification evaluation.

Using a simple binary classification problem (images of square versus images of circle), we show example of the following classification evaluations: accuracy from (2.65), AUROC and AUPRC computed from TPR (or Recall) and FPR in (2.66), and Precision from (2.68).

curve, where $\text{Recall}(c, \tau) = \text{TPR}(c, \tau)$ in (2.66), and

$$\text{Precision}(c, \tau) = \frac{\text{TP}(c, \tau)}{\text{TP}(c, \tau) + \text{FP}(c, \tau)}, \tag{2.68}$$

where $\text{TP}(.)$, $\text{FP}(.)$ are defined in (2.67). The PR curve is then computed by interpolating the values of $\text{Precision}(c, \tau)$ as a function of $\text{Recall}(c, \tau)$ by varying the threshold τ from 1 to 0. Even though PR and ROC curves are equivalent, PR curves are preferred for datasets that show highly imbalanced label distributions (Davis and Goadrich, 2006). From the PR curves, there are two label-wise measures that are usually computed to summarize the performance of methods. The AUPRC is the area under the PR curve, while the mAP is calculated from the average precision (AP), estimated as the weighted sum of precision values, where recall increases, as follows:

$$AP(c) = \sum_{t=1}^{|\mathcal{R}|-1} \big(\text{Recall}(c, \tau(t)) - \text{Recall}(c, \tau(t+1))\big) \times \text{Precision}(c, \tau(t)), \quad (2.69)$$

where $\mathcal{R}$ denotes the set of threshold values where recall increases, $\tau(t)$ is the threshold at position t in $\mathcal{R}$, $\text{Recall}(c, \tau(|\mathcal{R}|)) = 0$, and $\text{Precision}(c, \tau(|\mathcal{R}|)) = 1$. The mAP is then computed as the mean of the $AP(c)$ over the classes $c \in \{1, ..., |\mathcal{Y}|\}$.

Multi-label classification problems are generally evaluated with AUROC, mAP, and AUPRC since these measures can be computed in a class-wise manner and then summarized over the classes. Nevertheless, other measures have also been used by noisy-label multi-label learning approaches (Xie and Huang, 2021), such as the following (Zhang and Zhou, 2013):

$$\text{HammingLoss}(\tau) = \frac{1}{|\mathcal{T}| \times |\mathcal{Y}|} \sum_{(\mathbf{x}, \tilde{\mathbf{y}}) \in \mathcal{T}} \sum_{c \in \{1, ..., |\mathcal{Y}|\}} \delta\big(\tilde{\mathbf{y}}(c) \neq \hat{\mathbf{y}}^\tau(c)\big),$$

$$\text{OneError} = \frac{1}{|\mathcal{T}|} \sum_{(\mathbf{x}, \tilde{\mathbf{y}}) \in \mathcal{T}} \tilde{\mathbf{y}}(\arg \max_{c \in \{1, ..., |\mathcal{Y}|\}} f_\theta^{(y_c)}(\mathbf{x})) = 0,$$

$$\text{Coverage} = \frac{1}{|\mathcal{T}|} \sum_{(\mathbf{x}, \tilde{\mathbf{y}}) \in \mathcal{T}} \max_{c: \tilde{\mathbf{y}}_i(c)=1} \text{rank}(f_\theta^{(y_c)}(\mathbf{x})) - 1,$$

$$\text{RankLoss} = \frac{1}{|\mathcal{T}|} \sum_{(\mathbf{x}, \tilde{\mathbf{y}}) \in \mathcal{T}} \frac{1}{\#(\tilde{\mathbf{y}}=1) \times \#(\tilde{\mathbf{y}}=0)} |\mathcal{K}(f_\theta(\mathbf{x}), \tilde{\mathbf{y}})|,$$

(2.70)

where $\hat{\mathbf{y}}_i^\tau = \text{Squash}(f_\theta(\mathbf{x}), \tau)$ with the $\text{Squash}(.)$ defined in Section 2.2.2 as a function that thresholds the output using $\delta(f_\theta(\mathbf{x}) > \tau)$, $\text{rank}(f_\theta^{(y_c)}(\mathbf{x}))$ returns the rank of the label c according to the classification confidence $f_\theta^{(y_c)}(\mathbf{x})$, $\#(\tilde{\mathbf{y}}=1)$ is a function that returns the number of labels in $\tilde{\mathbf{y}}$ annotated with "1", $\#(\tilde{\mathbf{y}}=0)$ returns the number of labels annotated with "0", and $\mathcal{K}(f_\theta^{(y_c)}(\mathbf{x}), \tilde{\mathbf{y}}) = \{(c', c'') | f_\theta^{(y_{c'})}(\mathbf{x}) < f_\theta^{(y_{c''})}(\mathbf{x}), \tilde{\mathbf{y}}(c') = 1, \tilde{\mathbf{y}}(c'') = 0\}$ is the set of mis-ranked labels.

2.8.2 Segmentation evaluation

The evaluation of noisy-label segmentation methods can in principle be done with pixel-wise accuracy, using the formula in (2.65). However, segmentation problems tend to present extremely imbalanced distributions of classes, so accuracy is not well suited. A particularly interesting measure that is robust to such imbalanced distributions is the intersection over union (IoU), or also known as the Jaccard index. Recall that the pixel-wise segmentation label is denoted by $\tilde{\mathbf{y}}(\omega, c) \in \{0, 1\}$ where $\omega \in \Omega$ and $c \in \{1, ..., |\mathcal{Y}|\}$, and the segmentation model produces a pixel-wise classification

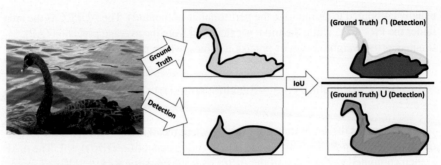

FIGURE 2.18 Segmentation evaluation.

Computation of the segmentation evaluation measure IoU to assess the performance of the segmentation of the visual object 'Swan'. Given the ground truth annotation (top-middle) and detection (bottom-middle), the IoU is computed by dividing the intersection (top-right) and the union (bottom-right) of the ground truth annotation and detection segmentation maps.

$\hat{\mathbf{y}} = \text{OneHot}(f_\theta(\mathbf{x}))$, where $\hat{\mathbf{y}}(\omega, c) \in \{0, 1\}$. The IoU is computed for each image and class c as follows (see Fig. 2.18):

$$\text{IoU}(\tilde{\mathbf{y}}^c, \hat{\mathbf{y}}^c) = \frac{\hat{\mathbf{y}}^c \bigcap \tilde{\mathbf{y}}^c}{\hat{\mathbf{y}}^c \bigcup \tilde{\mathbf{y}}^c}$$

$$= \frac{\text{TP}(\hat{\mathbf{y}}^c, \tilde{\mathbf{y}}^c)}{\text{TP}(\hat{\mathbf{y}}^c, \tilde{\mathbf{y}}^c) + \text{FP}(\hat{\mathbf{y}}^c, \tilde{\mathbf{y}}^c) + \text{FN}(\hat{\mathbf{y}}^c, \tilde{\mathbf{y}}^c)}, \tag{2.71}$$

where $\hat{\mathbf{y}}^c$ denotes the cth channel of the segmentation map $\hat{\mathbf{y}}$ (similarly for $\tilde{\mathbf{y}}^c$), and

$$\text{TP}(\hat{\mathbf{y}}^c, \tilde{\mathbf{y}}^c) = \sum_{\omega \in \Omega} \hat{\mathbf{y}}(\omega, c) \times \tilde{\mathbf{y}}(\omega, c),$$

$$\text{FP}(\hat{\mathbf{y}}^c, \tilde{\mathbf{y}}^c) = \sum_{\omega \in \Omega} \hat{\mathbf{y}}(\omega, c) \times (1 - \tilde{\mathbf{y}}(\omega, c)), \tag{2.72}$$

$$\text{FN}(\hat{\mathbf{y}}^c, \tilde{\mathbf{y}}^c) = \sum_{\omega \in \Omega} (1 - \hat{\mathbf{y}}(\omega, c)) \times \tilde{\mathbf{y}}(\omega, c).$$

In (2.71), elements that have division by zero are generally ignored. Then, the mean IoU (mIoU) is computed with

$$\text{mIoU} = \frac{1}{|\mathcal{T}| \times |\mathcal{Y}|} \sum_{c \in \{1, \dots, |\mathcal{Y}|\}} \sum_{(\mathbf{x}, \tilde{\mathbf{y}}) \in \mathcal{T}} \text{IoU}(\tilde{\mathbf{y}}^c, \hat{\mathbf{y}}^c). \tag{2.73}$$

Another measure commonly used to assess semantic segmentation methods is the Dice measure, computed for each image and class c as

$$\text{Dice}(\tilde{\mathbf{y}}, \hat{\mathbf{y}}, c) = \frac{2 \times \text{IoU}(\tilde{\mathbf{y}}^c, \hat{\mathbf{y}}^c)}{1 + \text{IoU}(\tilde{\mathbf{y}}^c, \hat{\mathbf{y}}^c)}, \tag{2.74}$$

and the mean Dice over testing images and classes provides the final measure for the method. Dice and IoU allow similar interpretation of methods, but notice that Dice is larger than IoU, particularly when IoU is small, when Dice is two times larger.

In segmentation problems, it is possible that we have a set of labels per image (Zhang et al., 2020a) and that the method also produces a set of predictions per image, allowing us to estimate a distribution of labels instead of a single binary mask per class. The measure used for such cases is the class-wise generalized energy distance (GED) (Székely and Rizzo, 2013; Salimans et al., 2018; Bellemare et al., 2017; Zhang et al., 2020a), computed as

$$D^2_{GED}\big(p(\tilde{Y}|X=\mathbf{x}), p(\hat{Y}|X=\mathbf{x}), c\big) =$$
$$2 \times \mathbb{E}\big[d(\tilde{\mathbf{y}}, \hat{\mathbf{y}}, c)\big] - \mathbb{E}\big[d(\hat{\mathbf{y}}, \hat{\mathbf{y}}', c)\big] - \mathbb{E}\big[d(\tilde{\mathbf{y}}, \tilde{\mathbf{y}}', c)\big], \tag{2.75}$$

where $\tilde{\mathbf{y}}, \tilde{\mathbf{y}}' \sim p(\tilde{Y}|X=\mathbf{x})$ denote samples from the ground truth annotation distribution, $\hat{\mathbf{y}}, \hat{\mathbf{y}}' \sim p(\hat{Y}|X=\mathbf{x}) = f_\theta(\mathbf{x}_i)$ represent samples from the distribution learned by the trained model, and $d(\tilde{\mathbf{y}}, \hat{\mathbf{y}}, c) = 1 - \text{IoU}(\tilde{\mathbf{y}}, \hat{\mathbf{y}}, c)$ is a distance measure. Then, by averaging $D^2_{GED}\big(p(\tilde{Y}|X=\mathbf{x}_i), p(\hat{Y}|X=\mathbf{x}_i), c\big)$ over the classes, we obtain the GED measure for the method.

2.8.3 Detection evaluation

The evaluation of detectors depends not only on the correct localization of the visual object, but also on the classification of the detected region. Recall from Section 2.2.4 that the detection testing set is denoted by $\mathcal{T} = \big\{\mathbf{x}_i, \{\tilde{\mathbf{b}}_{i,j}, \tilde{\mathbf{y}}_{i,j}\}_{j=1}^{B_i}\big\}_{i=1}^{|\mathcal{T}|}$, and the model outputs $\{\hat{\mathbf{b}}_{i,a}, \hat{\mathbf{y}}_{i,a}\}_{a=1}^{A} = f_\theta(\mathbf{x}_i)$, where $\tilde{\mathbf{b}}_{i,j}, \hat{\mathbf{b}}_{i,a} \in \mathbb{R}^4$, $\tilde{\mathbf{y}}_{i,j} \in \{0, 1\}^{|\mathcal{Y}|}$, and $\hat{\mathbf{y}}_{i,a} \in \Delta^{|\mathcal{Y}|-1}$. Detection methods are usually evaluated with mAP, but with the following re-definitions of precision and recall:

$$\text{Precision}(c, \tau, \tau_{IoU}) = \frac{\text{TP}(c, \tau, \tau_{IoU})}{\text{TP}(c, \tau, \tau_{IoU}) + \text{FP}(c, \tau, \tau_{IoU})},$$
$$\text{Recall}(c, \tau, \tau_{IoU}) = \frac{\text{TP}(c, \tau, \tau_{IoU})}{\text{TP}(c, \tau, \tau_{IoU}) + \text{FN}(c, \tau, \tau_{IoU})}, \tag{2.76}$$

where

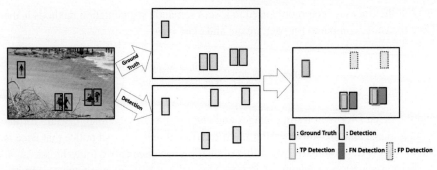

FIGURE 2.19 Detection evaluation.

Examples of TP_Detection, FP_Detection, and FN_Detection for the detection of people from images, using the ground truth in top-middle and detection in bottom-middle.

$$TP(c, \tau, \tau_{IoU}) = \sum_{i=1}^{|\mathcal{T}|} \sum_{j=1}^{B_i} TP\_Detection(\tilde{\mathbf{b}}_{i,j}^c, \tilde{\mathbf{y}}_{i,j}^c, \{\hat{\mathbf{b}}_{i,a}^c, \hat{\mathbf{y}}_{i,a}^c\}_{a=1}^A, \tau, \tau_{IoU}),$$

$$FP(c, \tau, \tau_{IoU}) = \sum_{i=1}^{|\mathcal{T}|} \sum_{a=1}^{A} FP\_Detection(\hat{\mathbf{b}}_{i,a}^c, \hat{\mathbf{y}}_{i,a}^c, \{\tilde{\mathbf{b}}_{i,j}^c, \tilde{\mathbf{y}}_{i,j}^c\}_{j=1}^{B_i}, \tau, \tau_{IoU}), \quad (2.77)$$

$$FN(c, \tau, \tau_{IoU}) = \sum_{i=1}^{|\mathcal{T}|} \sum_{j=1}^{B_i} FN\_Detection(\tilde{\mathbf{b}}_{i,j}^c, \tilde{\mathbf{y}}_{i,j}^c, \{\hat{\mathbf{b}}_{i,a}^c, \hat{\mathbf{y}}_{i,a}^c\}_{a=1}^A, \tau, \tau_{IoU}).$$

In (2.77), we have

- TP_Detection$(\tilde{\mathbf{b}}_{i,j}^c, \tilde{\mathbf{y}}_{i,j}^c, \{\hat{\mathbf{b}}_{i,a}^c, \hat{\mathbf{y}}_{i,a}^c\}_{a=1}^A, \tau, \tau_{IoU})$ first checks if $\tilde{\mathbf{y}}_{i,j}^c = 1$, then if at least one of the detections in $\{\hat{\mathbf{b}}_{i,a}^c, \hat{\mathbf{y}}_{i,a}^c\}_{a=1}^A$ has $IoU(\tilde{\mathbf{b}}_{i,j}^c, \hat{\mathbf{b}}_{i,a}^c) > \tau_{IoU}$ and $\hat{\mathbf{y}}_{i,a}^c \geq \tau$, then returns "1"; otherwise returns "0";
- FP_Detection$(\hat{\mathbf{b}}_{i,a}^c, \hat{\mathbf{y}}_{i,a}^c, \{\tilde{\mathbf{b}}_{i,j}^c, \tilde{\mathbf{y}}_{i,j}^c\}_{j=1}^{B_i}, \tau, \tau_{IoU})$ first checks if $\hat{\mathbf{y}}_{i,a}^c \geq \tau$, then if all annotations in $\{\tilde{\mathbf{b}}_{i,j}^c, \tilde{\mathbf{y}}_{i,j}^c\}_{j=1}^{B_i}$ have $\tilde{\mathbf{y}}_{i,j}^c = 0$ or $\tilde{\mathbf{y}}_{i,j}^c = 1$ and $IoU(\tilde{\mathbf{b}}_{i,j}^c, \hat{\mathbf{b}}_{i,a}^c) < \tau_{IoU}$, then returns "1"; otherwise returns "0";
- FN_Detection$(\tilde{\mathbf{b}}_{i,j}^c, \tilde{\mathbf{y}}_{i,j}^c, \{\hat{\mathbf{b}}_{i,a}^c, \hat{\mathbf{y}}_{i,a}^c\}_{a=1}^A, \tau, \tau_{IoU})$ first check if $\tilde{\mathbf{y}}_{i,j}^c = 1$, then if all detections in $\{\hat{\mathbf{b}}_{i,a}^c, \hat{\mathbf{y}}_{i,a}^c\}_{a=1}^A$ have $\hat{\mathbf{y}}_{i,a}^c < \tau$ or $\hat{\mathbf{y}}_{i,a}^c \geq \tau$ and $IoU(\tilde{\mathbf{b}}_{i,j}^c, \hat{\mathbf{b}}_{i,a}^c) < \tau_{IoU}$, then returns "1"; otherwise returns "0".

Given the precision and recall computed from (2.76), we can compute $AP(c)$ per class as from (2.69), and then the mAP as the mean of $AP(c)$ over all classes at a particular IoU threshold τ_{IoU}. Fig. 2.19 shows examples of TP_Detection, FP_Detection, and FN_Detection for the detection of people from images.

2.9 **Conclusion**

In this chapter, we presented the formal definition of the different types of label noise for classification, regression, segmentation, and detection problems. We then presented the datasets and benchmarks relevant for the study of label noise, followed by an explanation of the main methods used to assess the performance of methods designed to address label noise problems. Next, we focus on theoretical aspects of noisy-label learning, then on noisy-label learning techniques and proposed methods.

Theoretical aspects of noisy-label learning

3

Bias-variance decomposition, label transition distribution, and PAC learning

3.1 Introduction

This chapter introduces useful tools to improve the theoretical understanding of the learning with noisy-label problem. We start with an analysis of the problem from the bias-variance decomposition viewpoint, which divides the error estimated by machine learning methods into components that can explain the different types of error affecting the learning of a model. Even though the bias-variance decomposition formulation has been valuable to explain machine learning methods, it has been under-utilized for clarifying noisy-label learning problems. In this chapter, we first define the bias-variance decomposition for regression and classification problems (Domingos, 2000; Zhu et al., 2022), and then use this decomposition to explain how label noise affects the minimization of the expected loss and the learning difficulty of data.

Another tool that has been used to theoretically explain label noise learning is the study of the identifiability of the label transition matrix needed for dealing with the asymmetric and instance-dependent noisy-label learning problems (Natarajan et al., 2013; Patrini et al., 2017; Han et al., 2020a; Scott et al., 2013). Such study investigates the necessary and sufficient conditions to enable the identification of the exact parameters of the transition matrix from the training data (Scott et al., 2013; Liu, 2022; Blanchard et al., 2010). These conditions are based on the number of labels that are needed to be sampled from the label distribution of each training data, which results on the development of a different style of learning algorithms that can use training sets containing label noise.

We conclude the chapter with an overview of the use of probably approximately correct (PAC) model of learning (Valiant, 1984) to explain noisy-label learning. PAC learning studies the learnability of certain types of classifiers on different categories of noisy-label binary classification learning problems. Even though the results from this PAC-learning analysis are limited to binary classification problems, they contain important bounds that can improve our understanding of the noisy-label learning problem.

Machine Learning With Noisy Labels. https://doi.org/10.1016/B978-0-44-315441-6.00012-5

3.2 Bias variance decomposition

The training of classifiers and regressors relies on the minimization of loss functions, as explained in Chapter 2. Recall that the training set is represented by $\mathcal{D} = \{(\mathbf{x}, \tilde{\mathbf{y}})_i\}_{i=1}^{|\mathcal{D}|}$ and that the goal of the training process is to estimate the parameter $\theta \in \Theta$ for the model $f_\theta(.)$ that minimizes the loss:

$$\theta^* = \arg\min_{\theta \in \Theta} \frac{1}{|\mathcal{D}|} \sum_{(\mathbf{x}, \tilde{\mathbf{y}}) \in \mathcal{D}} \ell(\tilde{\mathbf{y}}, f_\theta(\mathbf{x})), \tag{3.1}$$

where the loss is a function that is minimized when the output from $f_\theta(\mathbf{x})$ approximates the label $\tilde{\mathbf{y}}$ (some examples for regression and classification losses are represented in (2.6) and (2.13)). Therefore, the goal of the training process is to estimate the model parameter that minimizes the mean loss of the training samples. As described in Chapter 2, the label $\tilde{\mathbf{y}}$ is in fact the result of a non-deterministic process that depends on the data $\mathbf{x}$ by sampling the function $p(\tilde{Y}|X = \mathbf{x})$. The optimal prediction for the data sample $\mathbf{x}$, denoted by $\mathbf{y}$, is the following (Domingos, 2000):

$$\mathbf{y} = \arg\min_{\hat{\mathbf{y}}} \mathbb{E}_{p(\tilde{Y}|X=\mathbf{x})}[\ell(\tilde{\mathbf{y}}, \hat{\mathbf{y}})], \tag{3.2}$$

where the domain for $\hat{\mathbf{y}}$ can be a continuous space $\mathcal{Y} \subset \mathbb{R}$ for regression problems or the probability simplex $\mathcal{Y} \subset \Delta^{|\mathcal{Y}|-1}$ for classification problems. Following this definition, the optimal model is the one that outputs the optimal prediction $\mathbf{y}$ with $f_\theta(\mathbf{x})$. Note that different training sets will enable the learning of different models, but this dependency of the model on the training set can be removed by averaging the training process over all possible training sets of a particular size $|\mathcal{D}|$. Let us represent this set of all training sets of size $|\mathcal{D}|$ by $\mathcal{S}$, so we can now compute the expected loss for a data sample $\mathbf{x}$ as the expectation with respect to $p(\tilde{Y}|X = \mathbf{x})$ and training sets $\mathcal{D} \in \mathcal{S}$, denoted by

$$\mathbb{E}_{p(\tilde{Y}|X=\mathbf{x}), \mathcal{S}}[\ell(\tilde{\mathbf{y}}, f_{\theta^{\mathcal{D}}}(\mathbf{x}))], \tag{3.3}$$

where $\theta^{\mathcal{D}}$ is the model parameter estimated for training set $\mathcal{D} \in \mathcal{S}$.

The general bias-variance decomposition breaks the expected loss in (3.3) into three components: bias, variance, and irreducible noise. Both bias and variance require the definition of the main prediction, as follows (Domingos, 2000):

$$\bar{\mathbf{y}} = \arg\min_{\hat{\mathbf{y}}} \mathbb{E}_{\mathcal{S}}[\ell(\hat{\mathbf{y}}, f_{\theta^{\mathcal{D}}}(\mathbf{x}))], \tag{3.4}$$

which represents the prediction that has a minimum mean loss relative to all predictions obtained from models trained with each training set $\mathcal{D} \in \mathcal{S}$ using the regression and classification domains described in (3.2). The bias of the training process for a data sample $\mathbf{x}$ is defined as the loss between the main prediction $\bar{\mathbf{y}}$ and the optimal prediction $\mathbf{y}$, defined as (Domingos, 2000):

$$\text{Bias}(\mathbf{x}) = \ell(\mathbf{y}, \bar{\mathbf{y}}), \tag{3.5}$$

where $\mathbf{y}$ is the optimal prediction from (3.2) and $\bar{\mathbf{y}}$ is the main prediction from (3.4). The variance of the training process for a data sample $\mathbf{x}$ is represented by fluctuations around a mean response for different training sets, computed from the mean loss produced by predictions from $f_\theta(\mathbf{x})$ with respect to the main prediction $\bar{\mathbf{y}}$, as in (Domingos, 2000):

$$\mathsf{Var}(\mathbf{x}) = \mathbb{E}_S[\ell(\bar{\mathbf{y}}, f_{\theta\mathcal{D}}(\mathbf{x}))]. \tag{3.6}$$

The irreducible noise independent of the training process is defined as

$$\mathsf{N}(\mathbf{x}) = \mathbb{E}_{p(\tilde{Y}|X=\mathbf{x})}[\ell(\tilde{\mathbf{y}}, \mathbf{y})], \tag{3.7}$$

where $\mathbf{y}$ is the optimal prediction from (3.2). Note that $\mathsf{Bias}(\mathbf{x})$ does not depend on any specific training set and reduces to zero when the main prediction is equal to the optimal prediction, $\mathsf{Var}(\mathbf{x})$ does not depend on the optimal prediction and reduces to zero when the model outputs the same prediction independently of training set in S, and $\mathsf{N}(\mathbf{x})$ is independent of the training algorithm and model (Domingos, 2000).

Given an example $\mathbf{x}$ with label distribution $p(\tilde{Y}|X=\mathbf{x})$ and a training process that produces a model $f_{\theta\mathcal{D}}(\mathbf{x})$ using one of the training sets in $\mathcal{D} \in S$, then for some loss functions, the expected loss for $\mathbf{x}$ from (3.3) is decomposed as follows (Domingos, 2000):

$$\mathbb{E}_{S, p(\tilde{Y}|X=\mathbf{x})}[\ell(\tilde{\mathbf{y}}, f_{\theta\mathcal{D}}(\mathbf{x}))] = c1 \times \mathsf{N}(\mathbf{x}) + \mathsf{Bias}(\mathbf{x}) + c2 \times \mathsf{Var}(\mathbf{x}), \tag{3.8}$$

where $c1$ and $c2$ vary for different loss functions. The extension of the sample-wise bias-variance decomposition in (3.8) to the whole data space $\mathcal{X}$ is obtained with

$$\mathbb{E}_{p(X), S, p(\tilde{Y}|X=\mathbf{x})}[\ell(\tilde{\mathbf{y}}, f_{\theta\mathcal{D}}(\mathbf{x}))] = \mathbb{E}_{p(X)}[c1 \times \mathsf{N}(\mathbf{x}) + \mathsf{Bias}(\mathbf{x}) + c2 \times \mathsf{Var}(\mathbf{x})]. \tag{3.9}$$

In this section, we first describe the bias-variance decomposition for regression and classification problems, and then we explain how label noise affects this decomposition. Zhu et al. (2022) show that this decomposition can be used to identify sample learning complexity, which in turn can suggest the presence of label noise.

3.2.1 Regression

Let us first consider a regression problem to minimize the mean squared error (MSE) loss, with $\ell(\tilde{\mathbf{y}}, f_{\theta\mathcal{D}}(\mathbf{x})) = (\tilde{\mathbf{y}} - f_{\theta\mathcal{D}}(\mathbf{x}))^2$. Using Theorem 1 from (Domingos, 2000), we have

$$\begin{aligned}
\mathbb{E}_{S, p(\tilde{Y}|X=\mathbf{x})}[(\tilde{\mathbf{y}} - f_{\theta\mathcal{D}}(\mathbf{x}))^2] = &\mathbb{E}_{p(\tilde{Y}|X=\mathbf{x})}[(\tilde{\mathbf{y}} - \mathbb{E}_{p(\tilde{Y}|X=\mathbf{x})}[\tilde{\mathbf{y}}])^2] + \\
&(\mathbb{E}_{p(\tilde{Y}|X=\mathbf{x})}[\tilde{\mathbf{y}}] - \mathbb{E}_S[f_{\theta\mathcal{D}}(\mathbf{x})])^2 + \\
&\mathbb{E}_S[(\mathbb{E}_S[f_{\theta\mathcal{D}}(\mathbf{x})] - f_{\theta\mathcal{D}}(\mathbf{x}))^2],
\end{aligned} \tag{3.10}$$

where the first, second, and third terms represent the irreducible noise $\mathsf{N}(\mathbf{x})$ from (3.7), $\mathsf{Bias}(\mathbf{x})$ from (3.5), and $\mathsf{Var}(\mathbf{x})$ from (3.6), respectively, the optimal prediction in (3.2) is $\mathbf{y} = \mathbb{E}_{p(\tilde{Y}|X=\mathbf{x})}[\tilde{\mathbf{y}}]$, and the main prediction in (3.4) is $\bar{\mathbf{y}} = \mathbb{E}_S[f_{\theta\mathcal{D}}(\mathbf{x})]$ (Domingos, 2000). Hence, the formulation in (3.10) is equal to the one in (3.8) by setting $c1 = c2 = 1$.

The decomposition of the expected MSE loss above implies that variance and irreducible noise are always additive, which means that biased (i.e., $\bar{\mathbf{y}} \neq \mathbf{y}$) and unbiased (i.e., $\bar{\mathbf{y}} = \mathbf{y}$) training samples will increase the expected loss with an increase of their variance or irreducible noise.

3.2.2 Classification

For a binary classification problem trained with a loss function $\ell : \Delta^1 \times \Delta^1 \to \mathbb{R}$ where $\forall \mathbf{y} \in \mathcal{Y}$, $\ell(\mathbf{y}, \mathbf{y}) = 0$ and $\forall \hat{\mathbf{y}} \in \mathcal{Y}$ such that $\hat{\mathbf{y}} \neq \mathbf{y}$, $\ell(\mathbf{y}, \hat{\mathbf{y}}) \neq 0$, the bias-variance decomposition is defined from (3.8) using Theorem 1 in (Domingos, 2000) as:

$$c1 = P_S(f_{\theta\mathcal{D}}(\mathbf{x}) = \mathbf{y}) - \frac{\ell(\mathbf{y}, f_{\theta\mathcal{D}}(\mathbf{x}))}{\ell(f_{\theta\mathcal{D}}(\mathbf{x}), \mathbf{y})} \times P_S(f_{\theta\mathcal{D}}(\mathbf{x}) \neq \mathbf{y}),$$

$$c2 = \begin{cases} +1, & \text{if } \bar{\mathbf{y}} = \mathbf{y}, \\ -\frac{\ell(\mathbf{y}, f_{\theta\mathcal{D}}(\mathbf{x}))}{\ell(f_{\theta\mathcal{D}}(\mathbf{x}), \mathbf{y})}, & \text{otherwise,} \end{cases} \tag{3.11}$$

where $P_S(f_{\theta\mathcal{D}}(\mathbf{x}) = \mathbf{y})$ represents the probability over training sets in S that the model outputs the optimal prediction $\mathbf{y}$ from (3.2), and $\bar{\mathbf{y}}$ denotes the main prediction from (3.4). Note in (3.11) that when the loss is symmetric, i.e., $\ell(\mathbf{y}, f_{\theta\mathcal{D}}(\mathbf{x})) = \ell(f_{\theta\mathcal{D}}(\mathbf{x}), \mathbf{y})$, then $c1 = 2 \times P_S(f_{\theta\mathcal{D}}(\mathbf{x}) = \mathbf{y}) - 1$ and $c2 = 1$ when $\bar{\mathbf{y}} = \mathbf{y}$, and $c2 = -1$, otherwise. Hence, in such symmetric loss scenario, the decomposition described in (3.8) with multiplicative factors from (3.11) shows that variance is additive (i.e., it increases the expected loss) in unbiased examples (i.e., $\bar{\mathbf{y}} = \mathbf{y}$) and subtractive (i.e., it decreases the expected loss) in biased examples (i.e., $\bar{\mathbf{y}} \neq \mathbf{y}$). This is an interesting result because if the model is biased for $\mathbf{x}$, then increasing the variance reduces the expected loss. Furthermore, the irreducible noise term $N(\mathbf{x})$ in (3.8) becomes subtractive for training samples $\mathbf{x}$ where $P_S(f_{\theta\mathcal{D}}(\mathbf{x}) = \mathbf{y}) < 0.5$ since this implies $c1 < 0$ in (3.11), so a high irreducible noise $N(\mathbf{x})$ in (3.7) for these samples will reduce the expected loss, which means that a high noise level can be beneficial to performance under these circumstances (Domingos, 2000).

The definition in (3.11) can be extended to the multi-class classification problem that relies on the 0-1 loss from (2.13), as follows (Theorem 3 in Domingos, 2000):

$$c1 = P_S(f_{\theta\mathcal{D}}(\mathbf{x}) = \mathbf{y}) - P_S(f_{\theta\mathcal{D}}(\mathbf{x}) \neq \mathbf{y}) \times P_{\tilde{Y}}(f_{\theta\mathcal{D}}(\mathbf{x}) = \tilde{\mathbf{y}}|\mathbf{y} \neq \tilde{\mathbf{y}}),$$

$$c2 = \begin{cases} +1, & \text{if } \bar{\mathbf{y}} = \mathbf{y}, \\ -P_S(f_{\theta\mathcal{D}}(\mathbf{x}) = \mathbf{y}|f_{\theta\mathcal{D}}(\mathbf{x}) \neq \bar{\mathbf{y}}), & \text{otherwise,} \end{cases} \tag{3.12}$$

where $P_{\tilde{Y}}(f_{\theta\mathcal{D}}(\mathbf{x}) = \tilde{\mathbf{y}}|\mathbf{y} \neq \tilde{\mathbf{y}}) = 1 - \mathbb{E}_{p(\tilde{Y}|X=\mathbf{x})}[\ell_{01}(f_{\theta\mathcal{D}}(\mathbf{x}, \tilde{\mathbf{y}}))|\mathbf{y} \neq \tilde{\mathbf{y}}]$ and $P_S(f_{\theta\mathcal{D}}(\mathbf{x}) = \mathbf{y}|f_{\theta\mathcal{D}}(\mathbf{x}) \neq \bar{\mathbf{y}}) = 1 - \mathbb{E}_S[\ell_{01}(f_{\theta\mathcal{D}}(\mathbf{x}, \mathbf{y}))|f_{\theta\mathcal{D}}(\mathbf{x}, \mathbf{y}) \neq \bar{\mathbf{y}}]$.

For the multi-class classification problems that optimize the 0-1 loss, the samples whose variance contribute to reduce the loss are the ones that have $f_{\theta\mathcal{D}}(\mathbf{x}) = \mathbf{y}$

for all training sets in $\mathcal{S}$, where $f_{\theta^{\mathcal{D}}}(\mathbf{x}) \neq \bar{\mathbf{y}}$. This means that for 0-1 loss, the tolerance for variance decreases with an increasing number of classes (Domingos, 2000). The results above for 0-1 loss are useful, but unfortunately, the empirical risk minimization of this loss for training modern deep learning models is known to be intractable (Feldman et al., 2012). Recently, researchers have worked on approximations to the zero-one loss (Hasan and Pal, 2019) that can alleviate this issue, but the bias-variance decomposition for this approximation is still to be developed.

An alternative solution for this issue is to consider the bias-variance decomposition for multi-class classification problems that minimize a tractable loss function, such as the negative log-likelihood (NLL) loss defined in (2.13). The decomposition is as follows (Heskes, 1998):

$$\mathbb{E}_{\mathcal{S}, p(\tilde{Y}|X=\mathbf{x})}[\ell_{NLL}(\tilde{\mathbf{y}}, f_{\theta^{\mathcal{D}}}(\mathbf{x}))] = \mathbb{E}_{p(\tilde{Y}|X=\mathbf{x})}[-\log(p(\tilde{Y}|X=\mathbf{x}))] + KL[\tilde{\mathbf{y}}\|\bar{\mathbf{y}}] + \mathbb{E}_{\mathcal{S}}[KL[\bar{\mathbf{y}}\| f_{\theta^{\mathcal{D}}}(\mathbf{x})]],$$

$$(3.13)$$

where $KL[\tilde{\mathbf{y}}\|\bar{\mathbf{y}}]$ is the Kullback-Leibler divergence between $\tilde{\mathbf{y}}$ and $\bar{\mathbf{y}}$, $\tilde{\mathbf{y}}, \bar{\mathbf{y}} \in \Delta^{|\mathcal{Y}|-1}$, $f_{\theta^{\mathcal{D}}} : \mathcal{X} \to \Delta^{|\mathcal{Y}|-1}$, and the main prediction is defined as

$$\bar{\mathbf{y}} = \arg \min_{\hat{\mathbf{y}} \in \Delta^{|\mathcal{Y}|-1}} \mathbb{E}_{\mathcal{S}}[KL[\hat{\mathbf{y}}\| f_{\theta^{\mathcal{D}}}(\mathbf{x})]] = \frac{1}{Z} \exp(\mathbb{E}_{\mathcal{S}} \log(f_{\theta}(\mathbf{x}))), \quad (3.14)$$

with Z being a normalization factor independent of $f_{\theta}(\mathbf{x})$.

The bias-variance decomposition above shows that an increase in irreducible noise and variance can decrease the expected loss under the conditions denoted in (3.11) and (3.12). Such decomposition has also been explored by Zhu et al. (2022) to detect hard training samples, which are relevant because such samples have a higher likelihood of containing noisy labels, even though they may just be located close to classification boundaries, but annotated with clean labels.

3.2.3 Explaining label noise with bias variance decomposition

Fig. 3.1 shows the following examples of the sample-wise bias-variance decomposition: 1) Fig. 3.1a presents a regression problem unaffected by labeling noise (i.e., containing only the intrinsic noise from Fig. 2.7); 2) Fig. 3.1b displays a regression affected by the symmetric noise explained in Fig. 2.9; 3) Fig. 3.1c shows another regression problem affected by the asymmetric noise from Fig. 2.11; and 4) Fig. 3.1d displays a regression problem affected by the instance-dependent noise shown in Fig. 2.13. Note that the irreducible noise $N(\mathbf{x})$ (denoted by the blue points in the Noise Decomposition graphs in Fig. 3.1) can reasonably measure the amount of labeling noise in each label, but that measure requires access to multiple labels sampled from $p(\tilde{Y}|X=\mathbf{x})$, which is problematic given that it is rarely the case that we have access to $p(\tilde{Y}|X=\mathbf{x})$, and noisy training samples tend to have a single label drawn from that distribution, limiting our ability to compute the expected value in (3.10) to obtain $N(\mathbf{x})$. The bias $B(\mathbf{x})$ term can also identify samples with labeling noise, but it

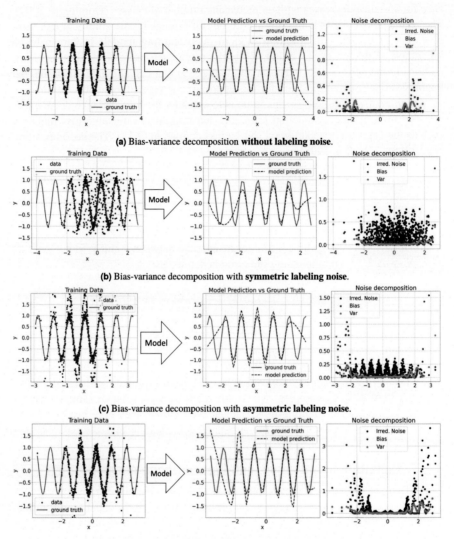

(a) Bias-variance decomposition **without labeling noise**.

(b) Bias-variance decomposition with **symmetric labeling noise**.

(c) Bias-variance decomposition with **asymmetric labeling noise**.

(d) Bias-variance decomposition with **instance-dependent labeling noise**.

FIGURE 3.1 Bias-variance decomposition in regression problems.

Examples of decomposition for regression problems affected by different types of labeling noise. The graphs on the left show the training samples in blue, with the ground truth in dashed red curve, the graphs in the middle display the model prediction (dashed black curve), and the graphs on the right show the sample-wise bias-variance decomposition (blue = irreducible noise, red = bias, green = variance).

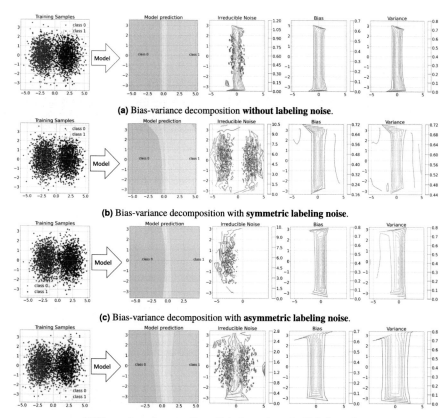

(a) Bias-variance decomposition **without labeling noise**.

(b) Bias-variance decomposition with **symmetric labeling noise**.

(c) Bias-variance decomposition with **asymmetric labeling noise**.

(d) Bias-variance decomposition with **instance-dependent labeling noise**.

FIGURE 3.2 Bias-variance decomposition in classification problems.

Examples of decomposition for classification problems affected by different types of label-ing noise. From left to right, the graphs on the first column show the training samples in red (class 0) and blue (class 1), the second column graphs display the prediction from the model trained with the samples from the first column, and the graphs in the third, fourth, and fifth columns show contour plots representing the components (irreducible noise, bias, and variance, respectively) of the sample-wise bias-variance decomposition.

is less effective since it cannot estimate symmetric noise as reliably as the irreducible noise, as clearly displayed in Fig. 3.1b. The variance term $V(\mathbf{x})$ is effective to identify poor model predictability for samples at the edge of training set support, but it is not reliable to estimate label noise. Hence, to estimate the noise present in the labeling process, one needs to approximate the computation of $N(\mathbf{x})$ with multiple labels per training sample drawn from $p(\tilde{Y}|X = \mathbf{x})$ that are affected by the intrinsic noise, but not the labeling nose.

Fig. 3.2 shows several examples of the sample-wise bias-variance decomposition for a binary classification problem using a model trained with the cross-entropy loss, which satisfies the criterion for Theorem 1 in (Domingos, 2000). The examples considered are the following: 1) Fig. 3.2a presents a classification problem unaffected by labeling noise (i.e., containing only the intrinsic noise, like the one in Fig. 2.6); 2) Fig. 3.2b displays a classification affected by the symmetric noise explained from Fig. 2.8; 3) Fig. 3.1c shows another classification problem affected by the asymmetric noise similar to the one from Fig. 2.11, but using the following transition matrix

$$p(\tilde{Y}|Y, X, v = asym) = \begin{bmatrix} 0.5 & 0.5 \\ 0.0 & 1.0 \end{bmatrix};$$ and 4) Fig. 3.1d displays a classification problem affected by an instance-dependent noise similar to the one in Fig. 2.12, where samples closer to the classification boundary are more likely to be affected by a symmetric label noise. Similarly to the regression problems, the irreducible noise $N(\mathbf{x})$ (graphs in the third column of Fig. 3.2) produces a reliable map of the training samples affected by the labeling noise. However, this irreducible noise needs to access multiple labels sampled from $p(\tilde{Y}|X = \mathbf{x})$ that are affected by the intrinsic but not the labeling noise, so it is unlikely to be available. Also, noisy-label training samples tend to have a single label drawn from that distribution, which does not allow a robust computation of the expected value in (3.10) to obtain $N(\mathbf{x})$. The bias and variance terms, $B(\mathbf{x})$ and $V(\mathbf{x})$ respectively, tend to have overwhelmingly higher values at the classification boundary than at labeling noise regions, making these measures relatively ineffective at identifying samples containing label noise. Similarly to the conclusion for the regression problem above, the estimation of the noise present in the labeling process requires the approximation of the computation of $N(\mathbf{x})$ using multiple labels per training sample drawn from $p(\tilde{Y}|X = \mathbf{x})$.

A recent pre-print paper by Zhu et al. (2022) explored the bias-variance decomposition to identify samples containing label noise based on a theoretical definition of sample learning difficulty. Zhu et al. (2022) assume that bias decreases and variance increases with model complexity, where this complexity can be computed with the mean square values of the network weights. Hence, the expected error in (3.9) first decreases and then increases as a function of model complexity, as shown in Fig. 3.3. Such decomposition can be plot for the whole training set and for individual training samples, and the optimal model complexity is estimated by minimizing the expected error in (3.9). Therefore, we can define easy and hard learning samples by looking at the ratio between the optimal complexity of the training sample and the whole training set, where a value larger than one represents a hard sample to learn, and smaller than one, an easy sample to learn. Hard samples to learn are more likely to contain noisy labels, but as observed from our examples in Fig. 3.2, there is no guarantee that these samples contain label noise.

3.3 The identifiability of the label transition distribution

As explained in Section 2.2.1 and Section 2.2.2, the joint probability $p(X, \tilde{Y})$ can be computed from the label transition distribution $T(X) = p(\tilde{Y}|Y, X)$ that represents the transition probability from Y to $\tilde{Y}$ given X and the clean label distribution $p(Y|X)$.

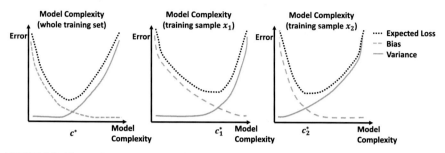

FIGURE 3.3 Bias-variance decomposition to define sample learning difficulty.

From left to right, we show a representation of the bias-variance decomposition as a function of model complexity, where the first graph shows this decomposition for the whole training set, with the optimal complexity denoted by c^*. The second and third graphs show the decomposition for training samples $(\mathbf{x}_1, \tilde{\mathbf{y}}_1)$ and $(\mathbf{x}_2, \tilde{\mathbf{y}}_2)$, with respective optimal complexity $c_1^* > c^*$, indicating a hard sample to learn, and $c_2^* < c^*$, defining an easy sample to learn. According to Zhu et al. (2022), samples with noisy labels are hard to learn and can be detected using the condition $c_1^* > c^*$.

The challenging estimation of this transition distribution has been widely studied to address noisy-label learning problems (Natarajan et al., 2013; Patrini et al., 2017; Han et al., 2020a; Scott et al., 2013), but its inaccurate estimation can lead to poor performance (Natarajan et al., 2013; Liu and Wang, 2021; Xia et al., 2019; Zhu et al., 2021c). Hence, it is important to understand if $T(X)$ can be accurately estimated (such accurate estimation is generally known as the identifiability problem), which leads to a learnable noisy-label problem.

We start by studying the problem of the class-conditional (i.e., instance independent) label transition distribution identifiability (Scott et al., 2013), where $T(X) = p(\tilde{Y}|Y)$, $\forall \mathbf{x} \in X$. Scott et al. (2013) prove that the identifiability of $T(X)$ for a binary classification problem depends on: 1) the majority of the observed labels being correct, and 2) the true class-conditional distributions being "mutually irreducible" (such condition is defined to limit the similarity between two distributions). Following the formulation in (Scott et al., 2013) and assuming a binary classification problem, we define P_0 and P_1 as the class-conditional distributions for classes 0 and 1, and η_0, η_1 as the noise rates affecting samples in classes 0 and 1, respectively, as follows:

$$\begin{aligned}\tilde{P}_0 &= (1 - \eta_0) P_0 + \eta_0 P_1, \\ \tilde{P}_1 &= (1 - \eta_1) P_1 + \eta_1 P_0.\end{aligned} \tag{3.15}$$

The necessary and sufficient conditions to uniquely define P_0, P_1, η_0, η_1 given samples drawn from $\tilde{P}_0$, $\tilde{P}_1$ are:

- *Total noise level*: $\eta_0 + \eta_1 < 1$,
- *Mutual irreducibility*: It is not possible to write P_0 as a nontrivial mixture of P_1 and some other distribution, and vice versa.

The first condition roughly means that the majority of the labels are correct on average, leading to the following proposition 1 from (Scott et al., 2013):

$$\frac{p_1(X)}{p_0(X)} > \gamma \iff \frac{\tilde{p}_1(X)}{\tilde{p}_0(X)} > \lambda, \text{ where}$$
$$\lambda = \frac{\eta_1 + \gamma(1 - \eta_1)}{1 - \eta_0 + \gamma\eta_0},$$

(3.16)

where $p_0(X)$ and $p_1(X)$ represent the densities of P_0 and P_1, $\tilde{p}_0(X) = (1 - \eta_0)p_0(X) + \eta_0 p_1(X)$, and $\tilde{p}_1(X) = (1 - \eta_1)p_1(X) + \eta_1 p_0(X)$. According to this proposition, the likelihood ratio test (LRT) described in (3.16) of the true densities is identical to the LRT of the noisy densities using a different threshold, but note that the LRT using the noisy densities forms a classifier for the noisy samples that is not necessarily optimal for the clean samples. Hence, it is necessary to estimate the clean classifier performance using estimates of the label noise proportions, as shown below.

To enable the estimation of such performance, we first introduce the alternate contamination model using Lemma 2 from (Scott et al., 2013), which assumes that $P_0 \neq P_1$ and that the *Total noise level* condition holds (i.e., $\eta_0 + \eta_1 < 1$), then $\tilde{P}_1 \neq \tilde{P}_0$ and there is a unique $\tilde{\eta}_0, \tilde{\eta}_1 \in [0, 1)$, such that:

$$\tilde{P}_0 = (1 - \tilde{\eta}_0)P_0 + \tilde{\eta}_0\tilde{P}_1,$$
$$\tilde{P}_1 = (1 - \tilde{\eta}_1)P_1 + \tilde{\eta}_1\tilde{P}_0,$$

(3.17)

where $\tilde{\eta}_0 = \frac{\eta_0}{1 - \eta_1} < 1$, and $\tilde{\eta}_1 = \frac{\eta_1}{1 - \eta_0} < 1$. Furthermore, Lemma 3 from (Scott et al., 2013) assumes that (3.17) holds and $\tilde{P}_1 \neq \tilde{P}_0$, which allows us to conclude that $P_1 \neq P_0$, $\eta_0 = \frac{\tilde{\eta}_0(1 - \tilde{\eta}_1)}{1 - \tilde{\eta}_0\tilde{\eta}_1}$, and $\eta_1 = \frac{\tilde{\eta}_1(1 - \tilde{\eta}_0)}{1 - \tilde{\eta}_0\tilde{\eta}_1}$, and the *Total noise level* condition holds. The Lemmas 2 and 3 defined above imply that for $P_0 \neq P_1$, we have a one-to-one correspondence between (η_0, η_1) and $(\tilde{\eta}_0, \tilde{\eta}_1)$, assuming the *Total noise level* condition holds and $\tilde{\eta}_0, \tilde{\eta}_1 \in [0, 1)$. The alternate representations for $\tilde{P}_0$ and $\tilde{P}_1$ in (3.17) motivate the mutual irreducibility between P_0 and P_1 that with the *Total noise level* condition ensures that $\tilde{\eta}_0$ and $\tilde{\eta}_1$ are identifiable. In particular, $\tilde{\eta}_0$ and $\tilde{\eta}_1$ are separately estimated by reducing it to the problem of mixture proportion estimation (MPE).

The MPE problem is defined by taking independent and identically distributed (i.i.d.) samples from probability distributions F and H defined over a Hilbert space $\mathcal{Z}$ to estimate κ for (Scott et al., 2013):

$$F = (1 - \kappa)J + \kappa H,$$

(3.18)

where J is an unknown probability distribution in $\mathcal{Z}$, and $\kappa \in [0, 1]$. The identifiability problem in this MPE context consists of finding the mixture proportion κ in (3.18), using the Proposition 1 from (Liu, 2022; Blanchard et al., 2010), which states that κ is identifiable if J is irreducible with respect to H (i.e., J cannot be written as $J = \gamma H + (1 - \gamma)F'$, where $\gamma \in [0, 1]$ and F' is another distribution). By noting that the two problems in (3.17) are MPE problems, and assuming that P_0 is irreducible with respect to $\tilde{P}_1 = (1 - \eta_1)P_1 + \eta_1 P_0$ and P_1 is irreducible with respect to $\tilde{P}_0 = (1 - \eta_0)P_0 + \eta_0 P_1$, then we can estimate $\tilde{\eta}_0$ and $\tilde{\eta}_1$ from the proposition above. Then, the one-to-one correspondence defined above enables the identification of η_0 and η_1. Next, P_0 and P_1 are recovered from (3.17). A stronger result can follow, which is that for any arbitrary $\tilde{P}_0 \neq \tilde{P}_1$, there is a unique solution P_0, P_1, η_0, η_1 (referred to as the mutually irreducible solution) that satisfies the (Total noise level) and (Mutual irreducibility) conditions.

The results above provided theoretical guarantees for the identification of label transition distributions for noisy-label classification problems, and many methods have been developed based on such theory (Yao et al., 2020b; Zhu et al., 2021c; Li et al., 2021). Nevertheless, these theoretical results are limited to binary classification problems, and class-dependent transition distributions.

Recently, a pre-print paper by Liu (2022) proposed a new theoretical result to address these two issues by elaborating a more general solution that can be applied to noisy-label multi-class classification problems on instance-dependent transition distribution. The result in (Liu, 2022) explores Kruskal's identifiability (Kruskal, 1976, 1977) to establish that multiple noisy labels per training sample are needed to show the identifiability of the instance-dependent transition distribution. Kruskal's identifiability defines a hidden variable, which we consider to be the clean label variable Y that takes values from a discrete domain $\mathcal{Y}$ with prior $P(Y = \mathbf{y}) > 0$, for all $\mathbf{y} \in \mathcal{Y}$. Instead of observing Y, we observe L variables represented by $\{\tilde{Y}_i\}_{i=1}^{L}$ that takes values from $\mathcal{Y}$. We can represent the matrix $\mathbf{M}_i$ of size $|\mathcal{Y}|^2$ containing rows denoted by vectors $[P(\tilde{Y}_i = \mathbf{y}_1 | Y = \mathbf{y}_j), ..., P(\tilde{Y}_i = \mathbf{y}_{|\mathcal{Y}|} | Y = \mathbf{y}_j)]$, where $\mathbf{y}_i \in \mathcal{Y}$ denotes a one-hot label vector, with the ith class active. Hence, $[\mathbf{M}_1, ..., \mathbf{M}_L]$ and prior $P(Y = \mathbf{y}_i)$ represent the hidden parameters required to generate the observations. The Kruskal's identifiability results depend on the Kruskal rank of a matrix, denoted by $\mathsf{Kr}(\mathbf{M})$, defined as the largest number I such that every set of I rows from $\mathbf{M}$ are linearly independent, and a theorem (Kruskal, 1976, 1977; Liu, 2022) that states that $[\mathbf{M}_1, ..., \mathbf{M}_L]$ are identifiable, up to label permutation, if

$$\sum_{i=1}^{L} \mathsf{Kr}(\mathbf{M}_i) \geq 2|\mathcal{Y}| + L - 1. \tag{3.19}$$

Below, we describe the main steps of the demonstration to reach a result based on using $L = 3$ labels drawn from $p(\tilde{Y}|X = \mathbf{x})$ per training sample $\mathbf{x} \in X$ to enable the identification of the transition distribution $T(X) = p(\tilde{Y}|Y, X)$ and clean distribution $p(Y|X)$.

This demonstration assumes that the noisy label is informative, which is achieved with $\mathsf{rank}(T(X)) = |\mathcal{Y}|$ (i.e., $T(X)$ is full rank) (Liu, 2022). Based on this assumption, Liu (2022) proposes a theorem that states that $L = 3$ informative i.i.d. noisy labels are both sufficient and necessary to identify $T(X)$. Recalling that $\tilde{Y}_i$ corresponds to $\mathbf{M}_i$, where $\mathbf{M}_i[j, k] = p(\tilde{Y}_i = \mathbf{y}_k | Y = \mathbf{y}_j, X)$, we have that $\mathbf{M}_i = T(X)$ for all $i \in \{1, 2, 3\}$. If $T(X)$ is full rank, then all rows in $\{\mathbf{M}_i\}_{i=1}^{3}$ are independent, so the

Kruskal ranks satisfy $\mathrm{Kr}(\mathbf{M}_1) = \mathrm{Kr}(\mathbf{M}_2) = \mathrm{Kr}(\mathbf{M}_3) = |\mathcal{Y}|$, leading to

$$\sum_{i=1}^{3} \mathrm{Kr}(\mathbf{M}_i) = 3|\mathcal{Y}| \geq 2|\mathcal{Y}| + 2, \qquad (3.20)$$

which proves sufficiency (Liu, 2022). The necessity is proven only for binary classification by showing that less than 3 informative labels do not guarantee identifiability (Liu, 2022). Such necessity part of the proof still appears to be incomplete since it shows only the binary classification problem. In addition, the assumption that $L = 3$ informative i.i.d. noisy samples may be hard to meet in practice.

A similar identifiability result has been achieved from extensions of the Dawid-Skene model (Dawid and Skene, 1979) that was designed to learn from crowd-sourced data. This problem assumes to have M annotators labeling the training samples, where the goal of the model is to estimate the latent true label of the training samples. Under the Dawid-Skene model, we have:

$$p(\tilde{\mathbf{y}}_{i,1}, ..., \tilde{\mathbf{y}}_{i,M} | \mathbf{x}_i) = \sum_{y} \prod_{m} p(\tilde{\mathbf{y}}_{i,m} | \mathbf{y}_i, \mathbf{x}_i) p(\mathbf{y}_i | \mathbf{x}_i), \qquad (3.21)$$

which assumes that the crowd-sourced labels $\{\tilde{\mathbf{y}}_{i,m}\}_{m=1}^{M}$ are independent given the true sample label $\mathbf{y}_i$. The estimation of the transition matrices $\{p(\tilde{\mathbf{y}}_{i,m} | \mathbf{y}_i, \mathbf{x}_i)\}_{m=1}^{M}$ and prior $p(\mathbf{y}_i | \mathbf{x}_i)$ has been proposed with the Expectation-Maximization algorithm (Dempster et al., 1977). More reliable methods that do not make the conditional independence assumption from (3.21) have been proposed (Traganitis et al., 2018; Ibrahim et al., 2019), but they are based on higher-order statistics that are harder to estimate given the usual limited amount of training labels per sample. Using tensor algebra, Traganitis et al. (2018) show that the identifiability of the transition matrices requires that at least three transition matrices in $\{p(\tilde{\mathbf{y}}_{i,m} | \mathbf{y}_i, \mathbf{x}_i)\}_{m=1}^{M}$ have full column ranks, or in other words, that at least three annotators have different responses to different classes, resulting in at least three matrices that do not have two co-linear columns. Note that this identifiability result agrees with the one proposed by Liu (2022), even though they were proposed to solve slightly different, but related problems, namely: noisy-label learning (Liu, 2022) and crowd-sourced true label (Traganitis et al., 2018).

Another recently published pre-print paper (Nguyen et al., 2023) has a similar motivation to solve the identifiability problem by stating that a single noisy label per training sample does not allow the learning of a unique solution unless that clean label samples are available or strong assumptions are made. Nguyen et al. (2023) define identifiability as the ability to recover the exact distribution parameters given a set of observed variables, where $\forall \theta, \theta' \in \Theta$; if $\theta \neq \theta'$ then $p(X|\theta) \neq p(X|\theta')$, where $p(X|\theta)$ represents a distribution of X using a function parameterized by $\theta \in \Theta$. The noisy label learning problem can then be formulated as a multinomial mixture model (Nguyen et al., 2023), as follows:

$$p(\tilde{Y}|X = \mathbf{x}) = \sum_{\mathbf{y}\in\mathcal{Y}} p(Y = \mathbf{y}|X = \mathbf{x})\, p(\tilde{Y}|Y = \mathbf{y}, X = \mathbf{x})$$
$$= \sum_{\mathbf{y}\in\mathcal{Y}} p(Y = \mathbf{y}|X = \mathbf{x})\mathsf{Mult}(\tilde{Y}; N, \rho_{\mathbf{y}}),$$

(3.22)

where $p(Y = \mathbf{y}|X = \mathbf{x})$ is the mixture coefficient, and $\mathsf{Mult}(\tilde{Y}; N, \rho_{\mathbf{y}})$ is a mixture component formed by a multinomial distribution with number of trials denoted by $N \in \mathbb{N}$ and success probability vector represented by $|\mathcal{Y}|$ classes $\rho_{\mathbf{y}} \in \Delta^{|\mathcal{Y}|}$. Such mixture model formulation of the noisy-label learning problem in (3.22) allows us to borrow the identifiability constraints from the study of mixture models. More specifically, using Lemma 2.2 from (Kim, 1984) and Theorem 4.2 from (Elmore and Wang, 2003), we can conclude that the mixture model (3.22) is identifiable (up to label permutation) if $N \geq 2|\mathcal{Y}| - 1$. In other words, the noisy label learning formulated as a mixture of multinomial models is identifiable, if we have at least $2|\mathcal{Y}| - 1$ noisy labels per training sample.

Note that the result by Nguyen et al. (2023) is more conservative than the results by Liu (2022) and Traganitis et al. (2018) since (Nguyen et al., 2023) requires a number of labels that is linear in the number of classes, instead of the fixed number of labels per class from Liu (2022); Traganitis et al. (2018). However, note that the identifiability result in (Liu, 2022; Traganitis et al., 2018) requires a minimum number annotators to have different responses to different classes, which can be hard to achieve in practice, while (Nguyen et al., 2023) does not make such strong assumption. Nevertheless, all results (Liu, 2022; Traganitis et al., 2018; Nguyen et al., 2023) show that in order to accurately estimate the model parameters, we need to obtain multiple noisy labels for each training sample. Interestingly, the need for multiple noisy labels per training sample is a result that was also informally concluded from the bias-variance decomposition from Section 3.2.3 to enable the estimation of the intrinsic noise function $N(\mathbf{x})$. The results in this section suggest that noisy-label training algorithms should need multiple labels per training sample, which is generally known as a multi-rater problem.

3.4 PAC learning and noisy-label learning

This section is based on the literature review provided by Jabbari (2010) on the use of Valiant's probably approximately correct (PAC) model of learning (Valiant, 1984) to explain noisy-label learning. PAC learning aims to find a learning algorithm that estimates an accurate binary target concept using a finite number of training examples. The learning algorithm estimates the target concept by selecting from a set of binary valued concept functions, where this set is called the concept class. Even though the learning algorithm aims to find highly accurate target concept estimates, the stochasticity of the sampling of training examples means that the learning algorithm can fail with some probability. During this process, the learning algorithm can use a number of examples that is polynomial in the inverse of its estimation error and the inverse of its probability of failure. The original PAC-learning model (Valiant, 1984) assumes that the labels of training examples are clean, so the theory needs adaptation when dealing with label noise.

In this section, a concept is defined by $c : X \rightarrow \{0, 1\}$, where the concept class C is a set of concepts over X, or a probabilistic concept defined by $c : X \rightarrow [0, 1]$. The set of all probability distributions in X is denoted by $\mathcal{D}_X$. Assuming that we have a specific $\mathcal{D} \in \mathcal{D}_X$ and c is a probabilistic concept, then the oracle $\mathsf{EX}(c, \mathcal{D})$ is a procedure that produces examples $(\mathbf{x}, \mathbf{y}) \in X \times \{0, 1\}$, where the instance $\mathbf{x} \sim \mathcal{D}$, the label $\mathbf{y} \sim \mathsf{Bernoulli}(c(\mathbf{x}))$, and repeated calls to $\mathsf{EX}(c, \mathcal{D})$ produce independent samplings. The support of $\mathcal{D}$, denoted by $\mathsf{supp}(\mathcal{D})$, is the smallest closed set $\hat{X} \subseteq X$ with $\Pr[\mathbf{x} \in X \setminus \hat{X}] = 0$, so all instances of examples produced by $\mathsf{EX}(c, \mathcal{D})$ are in $\mathsf{supp}(\mathcal{D})$. Multi-sets S of elements in $X \times \{0, 1\}$ are called samples over X, where the multiplicity that examples occur in a sample contains important information. Furthermore, in a binary classification task where the target concept $c : X \rightarrow \{0, 1\}$, the training set is represented by a sample of examples produced by $\mathsf{EX}(c, \mathcal{D})$, and a procedure (i.e., the learning algorithm) predicts the labels of potentially unseen instances from $\mathcal{D}$ (forming the test set).

PAC-learning can be defined as follows (Valiant, 1984; Jabbari, 2010): A concept class C is PAC-learnable if there is a learning algorithm $\mathcal{L}$ and $m : (0, 0.5) \times (0, 0.5) \rightarrow \mathbb{N}$ such that for any $c^* \in C$, for all $\epsilon, \delta \in (0, 0.5)$ and for any $\mathcal{D} \in \mathcal{D}_X$, if $\mathcal{L}$ can access $\mathsf{EX}(c^*, \mathcal{D})$ and inputs ϵ and δ, then with probability at least $1 - \delta$, after seeing a sample S of $m(\epsilon, \delta)$ examples, where $m(\epsilon, \delta)$ is polynomial in $\frac{1}{\epsilon}$ and $\frac{1}{\delta}$, $\mathcal{L}$ outputs a concept $c \in C$ that satisfies $\Pr_{\mathbf{x} \sim \mathcal{D}}[c(\mathbf{x}) \neq c^*(\mathbf{x})] \leq \epsilon$. Note that the error ϵ happens because $\mathcal{L}$ only sees a finite number of examples. Also, the learning algorithm does not need to succeed all the time. In fact, it can fail with probability at most δ, which happens when the examples poorly represent the distribution $\mathcal{D}$. Increasing the sample size results in a reduction of ϵ and δ. Learning complexity depends on the Vapnik-Chervonenkis dimension (VC-dimension) of the concept class, defined below.

The VC-dimension d of a concept class C over the input space X is defined as follows (Vapnik and Chervonenkis, 2015; Jabbari, 2010): if arbitrarily large finite sets $\hat{X} \subseteq X$ can be shattered by C, then the VC-dimension is ∞; otherwise, the VC-dimension is the cardinality of the largest $\hat{X} \subseteq X$ that can be shattered by C, where shattering is defined as (Kearns and Vazirani, 1994; Jabbari, 2010): let $\hat{X} = \{\mathbf{x}_1, ..., \mathbf{x}_m\} \subseteq X$ and $\Pi_C(X) = \{(c(\mathbf{x}_1), ...c(\mathbf{x}_M))|c \in C\}$. If $\Pi_C(X) = \{0, 1\}^M$, then $\hat{X}$ is shattered by C. Finally, a concept class C is PAC-learnable if and only if it has VC-dimension $d < \infty$ (Blumer et al., 1986; Jabbari, 2010).

We now extend PAC-learning to problems involving label noise. The label noise model over X is a mapping $\Phi : 2^X \times \mathcal{D}_X \times X \rightarrow 2^{[0,1]}$, which is deterministic if $|\Phi(c, \mathcal{D}, \mathbf{x})| = 1$ for all $c \in 2^X$, $\mathcal{D} \in \mathcal{D}_X$, $\mathbf{x} \in X$, else it is non-deterministic. When we fix the distribution $\mathcal{D}$ and concept c, we can define the Φ-noisy concept with the function $\Phi_{c,\mathcal{D}} : X \rightarrow [0, 1]$, which allows the definition of the oracle with

$EX_{\Phi}(c, \mathcal{D}) = EX(\Phi_{c,\mathcal{D}}, \mathcal{D})$ (Jabbari, 2010). This noisy concept defines a probabilistic concept from c by applying a label noise process according to $\Phi_{c,\mathcal{D}}$ and $\mathcal{D}$ via $EX(\Phi_{c,\mathcal{D}}, \mathcal{D})$. For example, assume that $c(\mathbf{x}) = 1$, then if $\Phi(c, \mathcal{D}, \mathbf{x}) = 0.4$, then $EX_{\Phi}(c, \mathcal{D})$ labels $\mathbf{x}$ with 1 with probability 40%, which results in a probability of 60% of mislabeling $\mathbf{x}$. The probability of mislabeling can be defined as the noise rate $nr_{c,\mathcal{D}}(\mathbf{x}) = |c(\mathbf{x}) - \Phi_{c,\mathcal{D}}(\mathbf{x})|$ (Jabbari, 2010).

The noisy concept $\Phi_{c,\mathcal{D}} : \mathcal{X} \to [0, 1]$ can be deterministic or non-deterministic. For the deterministic case, the oracle $EX(\Phi_{c,\mathcal{D}}, \mathcal{D})$ runs the following steps (Jabbari, 2010):

1. Draw example $(\mathbf{x}, c(\mathbf{x}))$ from oracle $EX(c, \mathcal{D})$
2. With probability $nr_{c,\mathcal{D}}(\mathbf{x})$, let $\mathbf{y} = 1 - c(\mathbf{x})$, else $\mathbf{y} = c(\mathbf{x})$
3. Return $(\mathbf{x}, \mathbf{y})$

For the non-deterministic case, the oracle $EX(\Phi_{c,\mathcal{D}}, \mathcal{D})$ runs the following steps (Jabbari, 2010):

1. Draw example $(\mathbf{x}, c(\mathbf{x}))$ from oracle $EX(c, \mathcal{D})$
2. Non-deterministically, pick a value $p' \in \Phi(c, \mathcal{D}, \mathbf{x})$
3. With probability $p' = |c(\mathbf{x}) - p'|$, let $\mathbf{y} = 1 - c(\mathbf{x})$, else $\mathbf{y} = c(\mathbf{x})$
4. Return $(\mathbf{x}, \mathbf{y})$

Using the label noise model defined above, we define a variant of Valiant's PAC learning model.

A concept class C is $PAC_{\epsilon,\delta}$-learnable with respect to label noise model Φ, $\epsilon, \delta \in [0, 0.5)$, and a class of distributions $\hat{\mathcal{D}} \subseteq \mathcal{D}_{\mathcal{X}}$ if there exists a learning algorithm $\mathcal{L}$ and function $m : (0, 0.5) \times (0, 0.5) \to \mathbb{N}$ such that for all $\epsilon \in (\underline{\epsilon}, 0.5)$ (assuming $\underline{\epsilon} \in [0, 0.5)$), for all $\delta \in (\underline{\delta}, 0.5)$ (assuming $\underline{\delta} \in [0, 0.5)$), for all $\mathcal{D} \in \hat{\mathcal{D}}$, and for all target concepts $c^* \in C$, the following property is fulfilled (Jabbari, 2010): $\mathcal{L}$, given ϵ and δ, requests a sample S of $m(\epsilon, \delta)$ independent draws from $EX(\Phi_{c,\mathcal{D}}, \mathcal{D})$, where $m(\epsilon, \delta)$ is polynomial in $\frac{1}{\epsilon}$ and $\frac{1}{\delta}$; then $\mathcal{L}$, with probability $\geq (1 - \delta)$, returns a concept $c \in C$, such that $\Pr_{\mathbf{x} \sim \mathcal{D}}[c(\mathbf{x}) - c^*(\mathbf{x})] \leq \epsilon$ (Jabbari, 2010).

Based on the formulation above, we present some basic label noise models such as the random classification noise (RCN) model $\Phi_{rcn(\eta)}$ by Angluin and Laird (1988), which is a deterministic label noise model defined as

$$\Phi_{rcn(\eta)}(c, \mathcal{D}, \mathbf{x}) = \begin{cases} (1 - \eta), & \text{if } c(\mathbf{x}) = 1, \\ \eta, & \text{if } c(\mathbf{x}) = 0, \end{cases} \tag{3.23}$$

where $c \in 2^{\mathcal{X}}$, $\mathcal{D} \in \mathcal{D}_{\mathcal{X}}$, $\mathbf{x} \in \mathcal{X}$. With this model, a learning algorithm $\mathcal{L}$ draws an example $(\mathbf{x}, \mathbf{y})$ from $EX_{\Phi_{rcn(\eta)}}(c, \mathcal{D})$ and $\mathbf{y} = c(\mathbf{x})$ with probability $1 - \eta$, and $\mathbf{y} = 1 - c(\mathbf{x})$ with probability η. Note that this model defines the symmetric noise model for a binary classification problem, where the noisy concept for $\mathbf{x} \in \mathcal{X}$ only depends on $c(\mathbf{x})$. With this model, and assuming C to be a finite concept class, $\eta \in [0, 0.5)$, Angluin and Laird (1988) proved that C is $PAC_{0,0}$-learnable with respect to the η-random classification noise and $\mathcal{D}_{\mathcal{X}}$. Laird (2012) extends the $PAC_{0,0}$-

learnable with respect to this η-random classification noise for concept classes of finite VC-dimension.

Such random classification noise model has been generalized to allow different noise rates in different partitions of the space $X \times \{0, 1\}$ (Decatur, 1997). More specifically, assuming $k \in \mathbb{N}$, $\eta = (\eta_1, ..., \eta_k) \in [0, 1]^k$, $\pi = (\pi_1, ..., \pi_k) \subseteq X \times \{0, 1\}$ denotes a k-tuple of pairwise disjoint sets such that $\pi_1 \bigcup ... \bigcup \pi_k = X \times \{0, 1\}$, then the (η, π)-constant-partition classification noise (CPCN) model is defined by

$$\Phi_{cpcn(\eta)}(c, \mathcal{D}, \mathbf{x}) = \begin{cases} (1 - \eta_i), & \text{if } c(\mathbf{x}) = 1, \\ \eta_i, & \text{if } c(\mathbf{x}) = 0, \end{cases} \tag{3.24}$$

where $c \in 2^X$, $\mathcal{D} \in \mathcal{D}_X$, $\mathbf{x} \in X$, and $i \in \{1, ..., k\}$ with $(\mathbf{x}, c(\mathbf{x})) \in \pi_i$. The PAC-learnability of CPNC was proven by Ralaivola et al. (2006) by showing the equivalence between CPNC from (3.24) and RCN from (3.23) (Jabbari, 2010).

Another important basic model is the non-deterministic malicious classification noise (MCN) model (Sloan, 1995), defined by

$$\Phi_{mcn(\eta)}(c, \mathcal{D}, \mathbf{x}) = \begin{cases} [1 - \eta, 1], & \text{if } c(\mathbf{x}) = 1, \\ [0, \eta], & \text{if } c(\mathbf{x}) = 0, \end{cases} \tag{3.25}$$

where $c \in 2^X$, $\mathcal{D} \in \mathcal{D}_X$, and $\mathbf{x} \in X$. With this model, a learning algorithm $\mathcal{L}$ draws an example $(\mathbf{x}, \mathbf{y})$ from $\text{EX}_{\Phi_{mcn(\eta)}}(c, \mathcal{D})$ and $\mathbf{y} = c(\mathbf{x})$ with probability at least $1 - \eta$, and $\mathbf{y} = 1 - c(\mathbf{x})$ with probability η. Assuming that C is a finite concept class, and $\eta \in [0, 0.5)$, Sloan (1995) proved that C is $\text{PAC}_{0,0}$-learnable with respect to $\Phi_{mcn(\eta)}$ and $\mathcal{D}_X$ (Jabbari, 2010).

The label noise models above mostly assume that the noise is independent of the instances, distribution, and target concept, but as we have already seen particularly with instance-dependent label noise, this does not apply to real-world problems (Jabbari, 2010). For example, instances are more likely to be mislabeled if the target concept labels part of the instances in their local neighborhood with label 0 and the other part with label 1. An instance-dependent label noise model shown by Jabbari (2010) is the ρ-distance random classification noise model, defined by

$$\Phi_{drball(\rho)}(c, \mathcal{D}, \mathbf{x}) = \{\text{Pr}_{\mathbf{x}' \sim \mathcal{D}}[c(\mathbf{x}') = 1 | \mathbf{x}' \in \text{DB}_\rho(\mathbf{x})]\}, \tag{3.26}$$

where $c \in 2^X$, $\mathcal{D} \in \mathcal{D}_X$, $\mathbf{x} \in \text{supp}(\mathcal{D})$, and $\text{DB}_\rho(\mathbf{x}) = \{\mathbf{x}' \in X | \text{dist}(\mathbf{x}, \mathbf{x}') \leq \rho\}$, with dist(.) being a metric on X. Note that $\Phi_{drball(\rho)}(c, \mathcal{D}, \mathbf{x}) = \{0\}$ for $\mathbf{x} \notin \text{supp}(D)$. With this model, a learning algorithm $\mathcal{L}$ draws an example $(\mathbf{x}, \mathbf{y})$ from $\text{EX}_{\Phi_{drball(\rho)}}(c, \mathcal{D})$ and $\mathbf{y} = c(\mathbf{x})$ if all points in the ρ-distance ball around $\mathbf{x}$ have the same label under c, otherwise, if points of the two classes lie in the ρ-distance ball around $\mathbf{x}$, the $\mathbf{y}$ will be drawn from $\{0, 1\}$ following the distribution of labels within the ρ-distance ball around $\mathbf{x}$ (Jabbari, 2010). This model is proven to be $\text{PAC}_{0,0}$-learnable with respect to $\Phi_{drball(\rho)}$ and $\mathcal{D}_X$, assuming $\rho \geq 0$ (Jabbari, 2010).

If we do not make any geometric assumptions about the noise, like in (3.26) which assumes that noise is potentially large if the nearest neighbors have mixed labels, then we can refer to the Massart (Diakonikolas et al., 2019) and Tsybakov Noise (Diakonikolas et al., 2021) models. The Massart Noise (Diakonikolas et al., 2019; Massart and Nédélec, 2006) is defined by

$$\Phi_{mas(\alpha)}(c, \mathcal{D}, \mathbf{x}) = \begin{cases} (1 - \eta(\mathbf{x}, \alpha)), & \text{if } c(\mathbf{x}) = 1, \\ \eta(\mathbf{x}, \alpha), & \text{if } c(\mathbf{x}) = 0, \end{cases} \tag{3.27}$$

where $c \in 2^X$, $\mathcal{D} \in \mathcal{D}_X$, $\mathbf{x} \in X$, $\alpha \in [0, 0.5)$, and $\eta(\mathbf{x}, \alpha) \in [0, \alpha]$. Hence, the Massart noise in (3.27) is a noise model that has an instance-dependent upper-bounded noise rate $\eta(\mathbf{x}, \alpha) \leq \alpha$ that extends the RCN noise in (3.23) which has a fixed $\eta(\mathbf{x}) = \eta$ for all $\mathbf{x} \in X$. The Tsybakov noise (Diakonikolas et al., 2021; Mammen and Tsybakov, 1999) generalizes the Massart noise by replacing the fixed upper bound α by a probability that is arbitrarily close to 0.5 for a fraction of the examples, as follows:

$$\Phi_{tsy(\alpha, A)}(c, \mathcal{D}, \mathbf{x}) = \begin{cases} (1 - \eta(\mathbf{x}; \alpha, A)), & \text{if } c(\mathbf{x}) = 1, \\ \eta(\mathbf{x}; \alpha, A), & \text{if } c(\mathbf{x}) = 0, \end{cases} \tag{3.28}$$

where $c \in 2^X$, $\mathcal{D} \in \mathcal{D}_X$, $\mathbf{x} \in X$, and for any $t \in (0, 0.5]$ we have $\Pr_{\mathbf{x} \sim \mathcal{D}_X}[\eta(\mathbf{x}; \alpha, A) \geq 0.5 - t] \leq At^{\frac{\alpha}{1-\alpha}}$.

Many papers studied the PAC learnability of the halfspace concept class for the Massart and Tsybakov noise models defined above in (3.27) and (3.28). The halfspace concept class C is defined by $c(\mathbf{x}) = \text{sign}(\mathbf{w}^\top \mathbf{x} - \theta)$, where $\mathbf{w} \in \mathbb{R}^d$ is a weight vector, $\theta \in \mathbb{R}$ is a threshold, and $\text{sign}(u) = +1$ if $u \geq 0$ and $\text{sign}(u) = -1$ otherwise. The learnability with the halfspace concept class is a fundamental machine learning problem (Rosenblatt, 1958), which has been proved to be PAC-learnable (Valiant, 1984) if no label noise is present. However, with agnostic noise (Kearns et al., 1992; Haussler, 2018), where an arbitrary $\eta < 0.5$ fraction of the labels are corrupted, the learning of the halfspace concept class becomes computationally intractable (Diakonikolas et al., 2019; Guruswami and Raghavendra, 2009; Feldman et al., 2006; Daniely, 2016). With the simpler RCN noise model presented in (3.23), where labels are perturbed in an instance-independent manner with a fixed probability $\eta \in [0, 0.5)$, the learning of the halfspace concept class becomes feasible (Diakonikolas et al., 2019; Blum et al., 1998).

The Massart noise model in (3.27) (Massart and Nédélec, 2006) is more challenging than RCN, but it is not as complicated as the agnostic learning, and for this reason it has become an important instance-dependent noise model to be studied. Diakonikolas et al. (2019) successfully proved the PAC-learnability of the halfspace concept class by presenting a learning algorithm $\mathcal{L}$ for all $\alpha \in (0, 0.5)$, on a set of i.i.d. examples from $\text{EX}_{\Phi_{mas(\alpha)}}(c^*, \mathcal{D})$, where c^* is an unknown halfspace on $\mathbb{R}^d$. $\mathcal{L}$ is polynomial in d, b, $\frac{1}{\epsilon}$, where b is an upper bound on the bit complexity of the examples, and outputs a concept c that satisfies $\Pr_{\mathbf{x} \sim \mathcal{D}}[c(\mathbf{x}) \neq c^*(\mathbf{x})] \leq \eta + \epsilon$. It is important to mention that many other papers provided similar results for the Massart noise model (Awasthi et al., 2015, 2016; Zhang et al., 2017c; Yan and Zhang,

2017; Zhang, 2018), with the results above being one of the latest to be published and making less restrictive assumptions on the distribution.

The Tsybakov noise in (3.28) is more challenging than the Massart noise, particularly when α decreases, where previous papers recognized that a necessary and sufficient condition to learn halfspaces with this noise model is a number of examples that is exponential in $1/\alpha$ (Diakonikolas et al., 2021). The proposal of a tractable learning algorithm for the homogeneous halfspaces concept class[1] in the presence of Tsybakov noise under *well-behaved* distributional assumptions has been studied by Diakonikolas et al. (2021). A well-behaved distribution is defined as (Diakonikolas et al., 2021): for $L, R, U > 0$ and $k \in \mathbb{Z}_+$, a distribution $\mathcal{D}$ on $\mathbb{R}^d$ is called (k, L, R, U)-well-behaved if for any projection $(\mathcal{D})_V$ of $\mathcal{D}$ on a k-dimensional subspace V of $\mathbb{R}^d$, the probability distribution function $\gamma_V(\mathbf{x})$ satisfies: 1) $\gamma_V(\mathbf{x}) \geq L$ for all $\mathbf{x} \in V$ where $\|\mathbf{x}\|_2 < R$, and 2) $\gamma_V(\mathbf{x}) \leq U$ for all $\mathbf{x} \in V$. In addition, if there exists $\beta \geq 1$, such that for any $t > 0$ and unit vector $\mathbf{w} \in \mathbb{R}^d$, we have $\Pr_{\mathbf{x} \sim \mathcal{D}}[|\mathbf{w}^\top \mathbf{x}| \geq 1] \leq e^{\frac{1-t}{\beta}}$, then $\mathcal{D}$ is referred to as (k, L, R, U)-well-behaved. Assuming that $\mathcal{D}$ is an isotropic[2] well-behaved distribution on $\mathbb{R}^d$, satisfying the (α, A)-Tsybakov noise condition w.r.t. a homogeneous halfspace $c^*(\mathbf{x}) = \text{sign}(\mathbf{w}_*^\top \mathbf{x})$, there is a learning algorithm $\mathcal{L}$ that draws $N = O_{A,\alpha}(d/\epsilon)^{\frac{1}{\alpha}}$ examples from $\mathcal{D}$ and runs in polynomial time in N and d to estimate a homogeneous halfspace $c(\mathbf{x})$ such that $\Pr_{\mathbf{x} \sim \mathcal{D}}[c(\mathbf{x}) - c^*(\mathbf{x})] \leq \epsilon$ (Diakonikolas et al., 2020, 2021).

The use of Valiant's PAC learning model (Valiant, 1984) is a powerful tool to unequivocally establish the learnability of certain concept classes for some data distributions under particular noise models. While the noise models presented in this section can adequately represent the noise models explained in previous sections, the concept classes tend to be too simple to represent the complex classifiers based on deep learning models. In general, finite concept classes or finite VC dimension concept classes are assumed in the problems above, but it is unclear if deep learning models can in general be considered to be a member of such concept classes. Hence, it is important that theoretical and applied noisy-label learning researchers collaborate more to enable new discoveries that can improve our general understand of noisy-label learning.

3.5 Conclusion

The theoretical tools presented in this chapter represent the initial attempts to better understand the noisy-label learning problem. Many results achieved from the bias-variance decomposition and the identifiability of the label transition distribution matrix suggest that there may be a need for multiple labels per training sample. A similar problem has been studied by many computer vision and machine learning

---

[1] A halfspace is homogeneous if the hyperplane defined by $\mathbf{w}$ contains the origin.

[2] In isotropic distributions, variance is uniformly distributed across all dimensions.

researchers for addressing an issue that is related to the noisy-label learning problem, which is the multi-rater learning (Guan et al., 2018; Jensen et al., 2019; Jungo et al., 2018; Baumgartner et al., 2019; Sudre et al., 2019; Yu et al., 2020a). In multi-rater learning, each training instance has many labels provided by multiple annotators (who may disagree on the annotation), and the goal is to train a model that uses such uncertainty information to better understand the reasoning behind the disagreement among annotators. There are clear similarities between the two problems, so it is expected that these two problems will merge in the near future. The use of PAC learning to study the types of classifiers that can be learned under certain types of label noise is interesting, but the classifiers and classification problems being investigated are still not as complex as what applied researchers are studying. Therefore, it is necessary that applied and theoretical researchers actively collaborate to improve our understanding of noisy-label learning problem.

Noisy-label learning techniques

4

Loss function design, training algorithm, training data processing, and model architecture

---

4.1 Introduction

In this chapter, we explain the main techniques developed to address the learning with noisy-label problem. Our explanation follows the hierarchy presented in Fig. 4.1, which provides an organization of the main approaches proposed by many researchers to solve the problem of learning with label noise. Such hierarchy in Fig. 4.1 and the explanations present in this chapter also follow some of the material introduced by recently published surveys (Han et al., 2020b; Song et al., 2022; Karimi et al., 2020; Cordeiro and Carneiro, 2020), but we propose new materials and insights.

As explained in Chapter 1, the motivation to design new techniques to handle noisy-label learning problems stems from the overfitting issue generally experienced by regression and classification models based on conventional model architectures (e.g., a multi-layer perceptron) and optimizers (e.g., Adam optimizer (Kingma and Ba, 2014)) trained on datasets containing label noise, as shown in Fig. 4.2 for regression and Fig. 4.3 for classification. Note that to facilitate the visualization of the overfitting issue, we reduced the original number of training samples for the instance-dependent noise for a regression problem presented in Fig. 2.13 from 1000 to 200 and increased the number of hidden nodes from 10 to 100. For the classification problem, we also reduced the number of training samples for the instance-dependent noise presented in Fig. 2.13 from 3000 to 300 and increased the number of hidden nodes from 4 to 50.

The training with noisy labels for regression and classification in Figs. 4.2 and 4.3 show the overfitting issue, where the loss in the noisy-label training set decreases and stabilizes at a low value, while the loss in the clean-label testing set reduces at the beginning of the training, and then starts to increase after a certain point in the training. Such problem has been investigated by Zhang et al. (2017a) and Zhang et al. (2021a), who concluded that deep artificial neural networks can easily fit a random labeling of the training data, which can be considered to be the symmetric label noise presented in Section 2.4.1. An interesting phenomenon that can be observed in Figs. 4.2 and 4.3 is the early-learning phenomenon (Liu et al., 2020), which divides the noisy-label training process into two stages: the early learning stage, where the model learns

Machine Learning With Noisy Labels. https://doi.org/10.1016/B978-0-44-315441-6.00013-7

93

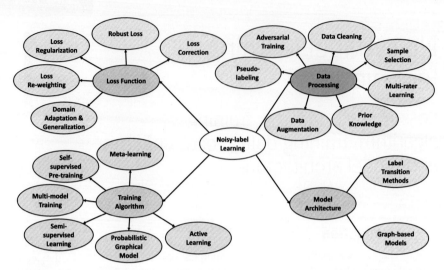

FIGURE 4.1 Hierarchical structure of the techniques developed to solve noisy-label learning problems.

to predict the clean labels even when trained with noisy labels (note the testing loss going down at the beginning of the training), followed by the memorization stage, where the model memorizes the noisy labels and makes incorrect predictions for the testing samples containing clean labels (this is when the testing loss starts to rise in the later training stages).

To mitigate the overfitting to the noisy-label training samples, many papers in the field have proposed many techniques, summarized in Fig. 4.1, that modify one or more of the following core components of regressors and classifiers:

- Loss Function,
- Training Algorithm,
- Data Processing, and
- Model Architecture.

The loss function strategy aims to change regression and classification losses in order to automatically correct mislabelings (Patrini et al., 2017), weight training samples (Liu and Tao, 2015), make the loss robust to noisy labels (Long and Serve-dio, 2008), or regularize the loss according to the early-learning phenomenon (Liu et al., 2020). The training algorithm strategy focuses on changing several stages of the training process, such as by adding a self-supervised pre-training (Zheltonozh-skii et al., 2022), introducing meta-parameters to handle noisy-label samples in a bi-level meta-learning optimization (Ren et al., 2018), detecting noisy-label samples, and estimating clean labels with co-teaching (Han et al., 2018c) and co-training (Yu et al., 2007), or by transforming noisy-label learning into a semi-supervised learning problem, where confidently-labeled training samples form the labeled set and the re-

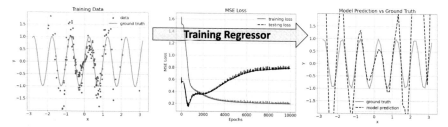

FIGURE 4.2 Overfitting of a regressor.

The training of a regressor overfits a training set containing instance-dependent label noise from Fig. 2.13, where we increased the number of nodes from 10 to 100 and decreased the number of training samples from 1000 to 200. The left-most graph shows the training samples (blue points) and the ground truth (red curve), while the right-most graph shows the model output (dashed black line) and the ground truth (red curve), and the middle graph shows the training and testing MSE losses as a function of the number of training epochs.

maining training samples are assumed to be un-labeled. The data-processing strategy aims to modify the training data, with for example adversarial training (Goodfellow et al., 2014), or data augmentation (Nishi et al., 2021). The model architecture strategy introduces new layers trained to learn the label transition model (Goldberger and Ben-Reuven, 2017), or graph-based models (Iscen et al., 2020).

In this chapter, we explain each one of the strategies in Fig. 4.1, highlighting the most representative papers for each strategy.

4.2 Loss function

Recalling from Section 2.2, the optimization for the regression and classification problems consists of optimizing the model parameters to minimize the following empirical risk:

$$\theta^* = \arg\min_{\theta \in \Theta} \mathbb{E}_{(\mathbf{x}, \tilde{\mathbf{y}}) \sim p(X, \tilde{Y})}[\ell(\tilde{\mathbf{y}}, f_\theta(\mathbf{x}))],$$

defined in (2.7), where the loss function can be, for example, the L1 and L2 losses, respectively defined in (2.6) as

$$\ell_{L1}(\tilde{\mathbf{y}}, f_\theta(\mathbf{x})) = \|\tilde{\mathbf{y}} - f_\theta(\mathbf{x})\|_1,$$
$$\ell_{L2}(\tilde{\mathbf{y}}, f_\theta(\mathbf{x})) = \|\tilde{\mathbf{y}} - f_\theta(\mathbf{x})\|_2,$$

or the 0-1 loss, the cross-entropy (CE) loss, the binary cross-entropy (BCE) loss, the hinge loss, and the negative log-likelihood (NLL) loss for the classification problem,

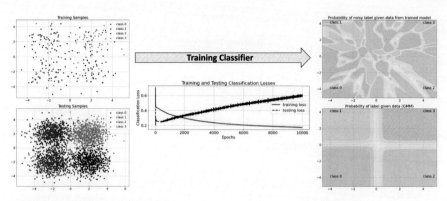

FIGURE 4.3 Overfitting of a classifier.

The training of classifier overfits a training set containing the instance-dependent label noise from Fig. 2.12, where we increased the number of nodes from 4 to 50 and decreased the number of training samples from 3000 to 300. The left-most top plot shows the training samples (each represented by a different color) and the bottom plot shows the testing samples with clean labels, while the right-most top map shows the model output (region colors represent different classes) and the bottom map displays the ground truth, and the middle graph shows the training and testing binary cross-entropy (BCE) losses as a function of the number of training epochs.

respectively defined in (2.13) as

$$
\begin{aligned}
\ell_{01}(\tilde{\mathbf{y}}, f_\theta(\mathbf{x})) &= \delta(\mathbf{y} \neq \mathsf{OneHot}(f_\theta(\mathbf{x}))), \\
\ell_{CE}(\tilde{\mathbf{y}}, f_\theta(\mathbf{x})) &= -\mathbf{y}^\top \log(f_\theta(\mathbf{x})), \\
\ell_{BCE}(\tilde{\mathbf{y}}, f_\theta(\mathbf{x})) &= -\mathbf{y}^\top \log(f_\theta(\mathbf{x})) - (1-\mathbf{y})^\top \log(1 - f_\theta(\mathbf{x})), \\
\ell_{HNG}(\tilde{\mathbf{y}}, f_\theta(\mathbf{x})) &= -\max(0, 1 - \mathbf{y}^\top f_\theta(\mathbf{x})), \\
\ell_{NLL}(\tilde{\mathbf{y}}, f_\theta(\mathbf{x})) &= -\log(f_\theta^{(\mathbf{y})}(\mathbf{x})).
\end{aligned}
\tag{4.1}
$$

In general the methods described in this section are based on modifying the loss functions above to make them more robust to the noise present in the labels of the training samples. We start by describing label noise robust losses that are designed in such a way that they do not penalize too much samples that cannot be fitted by the model, which tends to mitigate overfitting. Then, we explain different strategies to regularize loss functions to make them less prone to overfitting noisy-label samples. The re-weighting of training samples is then discussed, where the goal is to automatically up-weight clean-label samples and down-weight noisy-label samples, where the challenge is on how to design weighting functions that can reliably identify clean and noisy-label samples. Next, we discuss techniques that change the model prediction so it can fit the noisy-label learning, but at the same time produce a clean-label model. Alternatively, training labels can be automatically modified to represent their most

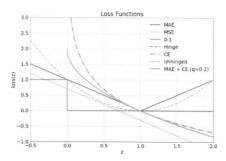

FIGURE 4.4 Loss functions.

Typical loss functions used for classification problems, and some examples of robust losses, such as MSE, MAE, Unhinged, and MAE + CE.

likely latent clean-label. We conclude the chapter with the presentation of loss functions designed to adapt from a noisy-label training domain to a clean-label domain.

4.2.1 Label noise robust loss

The design of loss functions that are intrinsically robust to noisy labels aims to avoid the need to estimate noise rate, particularly regarding the transition between ambiguous labels (e.g., estimating the probability of mislabeling an image of a cat with the label dog). We start the discussion on robust loss with a theoretically motivated loss function by Van Rooyen et al. (2015), who studied the paper (Long and Servedio, 2008), which claims that convex losses are not robust to the random classification noise (RCN) (Angluin and Laird, 1988) defined in (3.23) over the concept class of linear classifiers. This means that training under these conditions can produce a classification performance equivalent to random guessing. However, Van Rooyen et al. (2015) show that a convex loss that is negatively unbounded, formed by modifying the hinge loss to not be clamped at zero avoids the robustness issue described in (Long and Servedio, 2008). Such a loss is the unhinged loss defined by

$$\ell_{UNH}(\tilde{\mathbf{y}}, f_\theta(\mathbf{x})) = 1 - \tilde{\mathbf{y}}^\top f_\theta(\mathbf{x}). \tag{4.2}$$

Fig. 4.4 shows the graphs of a few examples of classification losses, including the unhinged loss from (4.2). Also, Fig. 4.5 shows an example of the training of a classifier with the robust loss function in (4.2). Although the result above was limited to binary classification problems and linear classifiers, it inspired many researchers to study other types of robust loss functions that could avoid overfitting noisy-label training samples.

Manwani and Sastry (2013) define the noise tolerance as a property of learning methods that can produce a binary classifier with the same classification accuracy, independently if they are trained with or without label noise. They concluded that risk minimization under 0-1 loss function has outstanding noise tolerance and MSE loss is robust only to symmetric noise. Then Ghosh et al. (2017) extended the work above by defining the noise tolerance property for learning methods that can produce a multi-class deep-learning classifier. This work concluded that the MAE loss is tolerant to symmetric and asymmetric label noise, cross-entropy (CE) loss is not tolerant to any label noise, and MSE loss is in between MAE and CE losses. Kumar et al. (2020) extended the noise tolerance property for learning methods that can produce a multi-label classifier and concluded that Hamming loss is robust to symmetric multi-label noise.

Even though MAE is known to be a robust training loss, it suffers from slow convergence, with poor fitting of hard classification problems (Song et al., 2022). Hence, to combine the convergence of CE loss and robustness of MAE loss, Zhang and Sabuncu (2018) proposed the noise-robust loss that combines CE and MAE losses, as follows (see MAE+CE in Fig. 4.4):

$$\ell_{MAE+CE}(\tilde{\mathbf{y}}, f_\theta(\mathbf{x})) = \frac{1 - (\tilde{\mathbf{y}}^\top f_\theta(\mathbf{x}))^q}{q}, \qquad (4.3)$$

where $q \in (0, 1]$. In (Zhang and Sabuncu, 2018), it is shown that when $\lim_{q \to 0} \ell_{MAE+CE}(\tilde{\mathbf{y}}, f_\theta(\mathbf{x})) = \ell_{CE}(\tilde{\mathbf{y}}, f_\theta(\mathbf{x}))$ and when $q = 1$, (4.3) approximates the unhinged loss, so a small value for q facilitates training convergence, but risks overfitting, and large q leads to slower convergence, but better robustness to label noise. The loss in (4.3) has been empirically shown to work well for closed-set and open-set label noise. It is possible to find loss functions that have been proposed to have good convergence and solid robustness to label loss, such as the two-temperature loss based on the Tsallis divergence (Amid et al., 2019b), bi-tempered loss based on the Bregman divergence (Amid et al., 2019a), and the symmetric cross entropy (SCE) loss (Wang et al., 2019c) that is defined by

$$\ell_{SCE}(\tilde{\mathbf{y}}, f_\theta(\mathbf{x})) = -\alpha(\tilde{\mathbf{y}}^\top \log(f_\theta(\mathbf{x}))) - \beta(f_\theta(\mathbf{x})^\top \log(\tilde{\mathbf{y}})), \qquad (4.4)$$

where $\log(0) = A$, with $A < 0$ being a constant. In the loss in (4.4), the first term is the CE loss, while the second term is the reverse CE loss, which is proved in (Wang et al., 2019c) to be robust to label noise.

As already discussed above by Manwani and Sastry (2013), the 0-1 loss has outstanding label noise tolerance. Such tolerance is achieved by noting that the 0-1 loss minimizes the (worst-case) adversarial risk (Lyu and Tsang, 2019; Hu et al., 2018), assuming that the model is trained from the noisy-label training distribution, and the model should perform well on the worst case estimate of the clean-label testing distribution that is unknown during training. Unfortunately, the 0-1 loss is non-differentiable and has zero gradients almost everywhere, which makes is hard to minimize. Therefore, Lyu and Tsang (2019) proposed a surrogate for the 0-1 loss based in curriculum learning. Ma et al. (2020) introduced the active passive loss that combines an active (a.k.a. positive) loss that maximizes the confidence of belonging to the labeled class and a passive (a.k.a. negative) loss that minimizes the confidence of belonging to the non-labeled classes. A similar loss function that explores negative and positive learning was explored by Kim et al. (2019).

Gradient clipping is a widely known technique to provide generic robustness to training, but Menon et al. (2020) showed that this technique is not helpful for training with noisy-label samples. Instead, a more helpful method is based on loss clipping, which provides a better robustness to label noise than CE loss (Menon et al., 2020).

Symmetric losses (i.e., losses where $\ell(z) + \ell(-z) = $ constant) have been studied by Charoenphakdee et al. (2019), who theoretically demonstrated that such losses are robust to label noise. Their paper corroborates the label noise robustness of the unhinged loss (Van Rooyen et al., 2015), which is a symmetric loss. However, in practice, the use of unhinged loss to train complex deep learning models is observed to perform poorly, most likely because of the negative unboundedness of the unhinged loss. They then proposed a new convex barrier hinge loss that is robust to label noise, but not negatively unbounded, even though it is not symmetric everywhere.

Abstention learning has been explored to prevent the model from training from confusing samples, while training from the non-abstained examples (Thulasidasan et al., 2019; Sachdeva et al., 2021). This type of learning relies on the deep abstaining classifier (DAC) that adds an abstention class $|\mathcal{Y}| + 1$, with a loss

$$
\ell_{DAC}(\tilde{\mathbf{y}}, f_\theta(\mathbf{x})) = \left(1 - f_\theta^{(|\mathcal{Y}|+1)}(\mathbf{x})\right)\left(-\tilde{\mathbf{y}}^\top \log \frac{f_\theta^{(1..|\mathcal{Y}|)}(\mathbf{x})}{1 - f_\theta^{(|\mathcal{Y}|+1)}(\mathbf{x})}\right)
$$
$$
+ \alpha \log \frac{1}{1 - f_\theta^{(|\mathcal{Y}|+1)}(\mathbf{x})}, \tag{4.5}
$$

where $f_\theta^{(|\mathcal{Y}|+1)}(\mathbf{x})$ denotes the abstention class prediction, and $f_\theta^{(1..|\mathcal{Y}|)}(\mathbf{x})$ the training classes' predictions. In (4.5), a large α leads the model to not abstain, and on the contrary, when α is small, then the model abstains from training all training samples. In general, Thulasidasan et al. (2019) showed that DAC works well for many types of noisy-label learning, and Sachdeva et al. (2021) demonstrated that abstention learning enables the detection of open-set label noise.

A new family of label noise robust loss functions, referred to as peer loss functions, has been introduced by Liu and Guo (2020). These peer loss functions are based on peer prediction mechanisms, where we assume to have multiple classification tasks. The peer loss function is defined by

$$
\ell_{peer}(\tilde{\mathbf{y}}, f_\theta(\mathbf{x})) = \ell(\tilde{\mathbf{y}}, f_\theta(\mathbf{x})) - \ell(\tilde{\mathbf{y}}_i, f_\theta(\mathbf{x}_j)), \tag{4.6}
$$

where $(\mathbf{x}_i, \tilde{\mathbf{y}}_i)$ and $(\mathbf{x}_j, \tilde{\mathbf{y}}_j)$ are two training samples randomly sampled from $\mathcal{D}$ with replacement. In general, the first term of the peer loss (4.6) aims to maximize the stochastic correlation between the noisy labels $\tilde{\mathbf{y}}$ and model predictions $f_\theta(\mathbf{x})$, while minimizing the risk of overfitting by penalizing incorrect correlations between samples and labels from different tasks in the second term of the peer loss. This peer loss is shown to lead to optimal or a near-optimal classifier as if training with the clean-label training set.

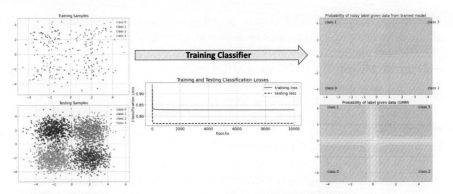

FIGURE 4.5 Classifier trained with a loss function robust to label noise.

The training of classifier with the unhinged loss from (4.2) using the same problem described in Fig. 4.3. Note that this noisy-label robust loss no longer overfits to the noisy-label training set and produces a model output (region colors represent different classes) that is reasonably similar to the ground truth at the bottom map on the right.

Xu et al. (2019) proposed the $\mathcal{L}_{\text{DMI}}$, which is a determinant-based mutual-information loss function that is robust to asymmetric label noise. This paper shows that by training with the loss:

$$\mathcal{L}_{\text{DMI}}(\mathcal{D}, \theta) = -\log(\text{DMI}(\tilde{Y}, f_\theta(X))) = -\log(|\det(\mathbf{Q})|), \qquad (4.7)$$

where $\mathbf{Q}$ is a $|\mathcal{Y}| \times |\mathcal{Y}|$ matrix representing the joint distribution between $\tilde{Y}$ and $f_\theta(X)$ computed with

$$\mathbf{Q}_{\tilde{c},c} = \frac{1}{|\mathcal{D}|} \sum_{(\mathbf{x},\tilde{\mathbf{y}}) \in \mathcal{D}} f_\theta^{(\mathbf{y}_c)}(\mathbf{x}) \times \delta(\tilde{\mathbf{y}}(\tilde{c}) = 1), \qquad (4.8)$$

with $f_\theta^{(\mathbf{y}_c)}(\mathbf{x})$ denoting the cth output from the model and $\delta(\tilde{\mathbf{y}}(\tilde{c}) = 1)$ representing the indicator function that is equal to one when $\tilde{\mathbf{y}}(\tilde{c}) = 1$, and zero otherwise. Xu et al. (2019) show that by training with $\mathcal{L}_{\text{DMI}}(\mathcal{D}, \theta)$ from (4.7), it is possible to prove that

$$\mathcal{L}_{\text{DMI}}(\text{noisy data}, \theta) = \mathcal{L}_{\text{DMI}}(\text{clean data}, \theta) + \text{noise rate.} \qquad (4.9)$$

Robust losses have been intensively studied, with many papers showing solid theoretical foundations with certain performance guarantees. The main idea explored by the proposed methods is focused on reducing the influence of the loss from misclassified samples and, at the same time, allow well-classified samples to influence the training even after they have already been successfully fit. The main advantage of these robust loss functions, with respect to other techniques that will be presented in the next sections, is that they do not require the estimation of noise rate. However, a

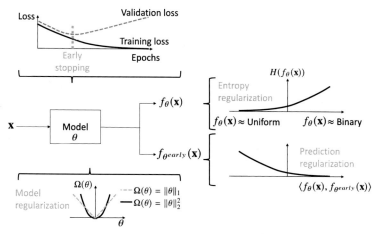

FIGURE 4.6 Loss regularization.

Different types of loss regularization to make training robust to noisy labels. Model regularization constrains model parameters to specific values, as in (4.10). Entropy regularization constrains model predictions to have high entropy, as in (4.11). Early stopping halts training before model convergence using the training loss. Prediction regularization constrains model predictions to be similar to outputs from the model trained at the early training epochs, as in (4.14).

major challenge of this strategy is the difficulty to determine if a misclassified sample is mislabeled or is just a hard sample to fit. Consequently, these approaches are limited to problems that are not naturally hard, where the noise rate is not too high and the number of classes is relatively small (Song et al., 2022). Nevertheless, robust loss function can be explored as part of complex noisy-label learning methods that include other techniques to handle label noise.

4.2.2 Loss regularization

Loss regularization represents a straightforward way to make the empirical risk minimization (ERM) of (2.8) more robust by avoiding overfitting in general. The optimization using loss regularization is defined as follows

$$\theta^* = \arg\min_{\theta \in \Theta} \frac{1}{|\mathcal{D}|} \sum_{(\mathbf{x}, \tilde{\mathbf{y}}) \in \mathcal{D}} \ell(\tilde{\mathbf{y}}, f_\theta(\mathbf{x})) + \Omega(\theta), \tag{4.10}$$

where $\Omega(\theta) = \|\theta\|_2^2$ for the Tikhonov regularization (ℓ_2-norm) or $\Omega(\theta) = \|\theta\|_1$ for the ℓ_1-norm regularization for the model parameters (Tibshirani, 1996). Fig. 4.6 shows a few examples of loss regularization functions. One of the first papers to propose a deep learning method robust to noisy labels was (Azadi et al., 2015) that introduced a new auxiliary image regularizer (AIR), which is a group sparse norm.

This regularizer automatically selects relevant training samples for training and gives them higher learning weights, while irrelevant or noisy samples are forced to have near zero learning weight. This means that only the selected samples will contribute to model learning. The penalization of low entropy predictions is also a common way to regularize the loss function (Pereyra et al., 2017), with

$$\theta^* = \arg\min_{\theta \in \Theta} \frac{1}{|\mathcal{D}|} \sum_{(\mathbf{x},\tilde{\mathbf{y}}) \in \mathcal{D}} \ell(\tilde{\mathbf{y}}, f_\theta(\mathbf{x})) + \beta H(f_\theta(\mathbf{x})), \qquad (4.11)$$

where $H(f_\theta(\mathbf{x}))$ measures the negative entropy of the prediction from $f_\theta(\mathbf{x}_i)$. Such entropy regularization prevents the model to become over-confident in the prediction of the training samples, mitigating the overfitting of the training set.

A simple, but powerful regularization technique for noisy-label learning is early-stopping (Rolnick et al., 2017; Li et al., 2020b), which we already discussed informally in Figs. 4.2 and 4.3. Li et al. (2020b) show that by running empirical risk minimization with CE or MSE loss functions using a small number of epochs (i.e., early stopping) allows the learning of a model that fits well the clean labels and ignores the noisy label. Naturally, because of the small number of epochs, the learned model will be close to its initialization, and the farther it moves from this initialization, the more likely it fits the noisy label. Estimating the number of epochs is not straightforward, but Li et al. (2020b) showed that this number is a linear function of the number of data clusters $K > |\mathcal{Y}|$ in the training set. Hu et al. (2019b) extended this idea with the regularization function:

$$\theta^* = \arg\min_{\theta \in \Theta} \frac{1}{|\mathcal{D}|} \sum_{(\mathbf{x},\tilde{\mathbf{y}}) \in \mathcal{D}} \ell(\tilde{\mathbf{y}}, f_\theta(\mathbf{x})) + \lambda \|\theta - \theta(0)\|_2^2, \qquad (4.12)$$

where $\theta(0)$ denotes the model initialization, which explicitly forces the learning to keep the estimated θ^* close to its initialization $\theta(0)$. Alternatively, Hu et al. (2019b) proposed the introduction of a sample-wise training variable $\mathbf{b}_i$ to be used when fitting the ith training label, as follows:

$$\theta^* = \arg\min_{\theta \in \Theta, \{\mathbf{b}_i\}_{i=1}^{|\mathcal{D}|}} \frac{1}{|\mathcal{D}|} \sum_{(\mathbf{x}_i,\tilde{\mathbf{y}}_i) \in \mathcal{D}} \ell(\tilde{\mathbf{y}}_i, f_\theta(\mathbf{x}_i) + \lambda \mathbf{b}_i), \qquad (4.13)$$

where $\mathbf{b}_i$ is initialized as a $|\mathcal{Y}|$-vector of zeros. The regularization in (4.13) worked better than the one in (4.12) and the early stopping of (Li et al., 2020b). Early-stopping was also explored in the early-learning regularization (ELR) by Liu et al. (2020), who introduced a regularization to boost the gradient of training samples with clean labels and to dampen the gradient of training samples with noisy labels, once the training passes the early-learning phase. This is reached with

$$\theta^* = \arg\min_{\theta \in \Theta} \frac{1}{|\mathcal{D}|} \sum_{(\mathbf{x}_i,\tilde{\mathbf{y}}_i) \in \mathcal{D}} \ell(\tilde{\mathbf{y}}_i, f_\theta(\mathbf{x}_i)) + \lambda \log \left(1 - f_\theta(\mathbf{x}_i)^\top \mathbf{t}_i\right), \qquad (4.14)$$

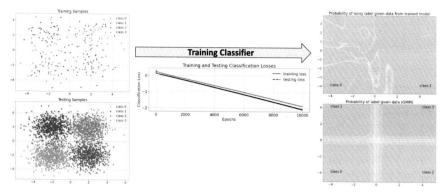

FIGURE 4.7 Classifier trained with a regularized loss function.

The training of classifier with the ELR loss from (4.14) using the same problem described in Fig. 4.3. Note that the ELR loss is robust to the noisy-label samples and produces a model output (region colors represent different classes) that is relatively similar to the ground truth at the bottom map on the right. Also note how the loss reduces boundlessly.

where $\langle ., . \rangle$ represents the inner product operator, and $\mathbf{t}_i \in \Delta^{|\mathcal{Y}|-1}$ denotes a target probability for sample i, which is estimated with a moving average at iteration k with $\mathbf{t}_i^{(k)} = \beta \mathbf{t}_i^{(k-1)} + (1 - \beta) f_\theta^{(k)}(\mathbf{x}_i)$, with $\beta \in [0, 1)$. When fitting a clean label, the loss term of (4.14) goes to zero, but the regularizer becomes negative because $f_\theta(\mathbf{x}_i) \approx \mathbf{t}_i$, boosting the gradient of clean-label samples, forcing the continuing learning from the clean-label samples. On the other hand, for a noisy label, the loss term of (4.14) increases, which is compensated by the regularizer that becomes negative since the target $\mathbf{t}_i$ tends to keep the early learning fitted label, which is likely to be the clean label that coincides with the model output $f_\theta(\mathbf{x}_i)$ (see Fig. 4.7).

An alternative form of regularization can be achieved via the general-purpose dropout (Jindal et al., 2016) or nested dropout (Chen et al., 2021b) regularizers. Dropout (Jindal et al., 2016) randomly selects nodes to be switched off during a training iteration, which means that these nodes do not contribute to the forward pass and their weights are not updated during the backward pass. On the other hand, nested dropout (Chen et al., 2021b) drops feature activations instead of nodes. Both types of regularization have been proposed in the context of regularizing the training of a model to avoid overfitting the training data. As a result, their application to noisy-label learning is quite natural and has produced interesting results, especially when combined with sophisticated noisy-label learning techniques (Chen et al., 2021b).

4.2.3 Loss re-weighting

In the loss re-weighting approach, each training sample is weighted differently during training, where samples with noisy labels are assigned smaller weights, while samples with clean labels are assigned larger weights (Wang et al., 2017a; Liu and

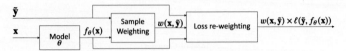

FIGURE 4.8 **Loss re-weighting.**

The basic architecture of loss re-weighting techniques consists of leveraging information from the model prediction $f_\theta(\mathbf{x})$ and training noisy label $\tilde{\mathbf{y}}$ to produce a weight for the training sample. In general, samples that are likely to contain noisy labels are weighted down to prevent overfitting to those samples, while clean-label samples are weighted up.

Tao, 2015). As shown in Figs. 4.8 and 4.9, the optimization problem is defined as

$$\theta^* = \arg\min_{\theta \in \Theta} \frac{1}{|\mathcal{D}|} \sum_{(\mathbf{x},\tilde{\mathbf{y}}) \in \mathcal{D}} w(\mathbf{x}, \tilde{\mathbf{y}}) \times \ell(\tilde{\mathbf{y}}, f_\theta(\mathbf{x})), \tag{4.15}$$

where $w(\mathbf{x}, \tilde{\mathbf{y}})$ is the function that returns the weight assigned to the training sample $(\mathbf{x}, \tilde{\mathbf{y}}) \in \mathcal{D}$. Therefore, the noisy-label training samples with smaller values of $w(\mathbf{x}, \tilde{\mathbf{y}})$ in (4.15) will have smaller influence to the training of the model $f_\theta(\mathbf{x})$.

Assuming a binary classification problem, Liu and Tao (2015) formulate noisy-label learning as a domain adaptation problem, where the source domain is represented by the noisy-label training set, and the target domain, by the clean-label testing set. Then, (Liu and Tao, 2015) propose the use of importance re-weighting (Gretton et al., 2009), which re-weights the loss expectation with respect to the joint probability distribution of the sample and true label, as follows:

$$\mathbb{E}_{(\mathbf{x},y) \sim p(X,Y)}[\ell(y, f_\theta(\mathbf{x}))] = \mathbb{E}_{(\mathbf{x},\tilde{y}) \sim p(X,\tilde{Y})}\left[\frac{p(X=\mathbf{x}, Y=\tilde{\mathbf{y}})}{p(X=\mathbf{x}, \tilde{Y}=\tilde{\mathbf{y}})} \ell(\tilde{\mathbf{y}}, f_\theta(\mathbf{x})) \right] \tag{4.16}$$
$$= \mathbb{E}_{(\mathbf{x},\tilde{y}) \sim p(X,\tilde{Y})}\left[w(\mathbf{x}, \tilde{\mathbf{y}}) \ell(\tilde{\mathbf{y}}, f_\theta(\mathbf{x})) \right],$$

where

$$
\begin{aligned}
w(\mathbf{x}, \tilde{\mathbf{y}}) &= \frac{p(X=\mathbf{x}, Y=\tilde{\mathbf{y}})}{p(X=\mathbf{x}, \tilde{Y}=\tilde{\mathbf{y}})} \\
&= \frac{p(Y=\tilde{\mathbf{y}}|X=\mathbf{x})\,p(X=\mathbf{x})}{p(\tilde{Y}=\tilde{\mathbf{y}}|X=\mathbf{x})\,p(X=\mathbf{x})} \\
&= \frac{p(Y=\tilde{\mathbf{y}}|X=\mathbf{x})}{p(\tilde{Y}=\tilde{\mathbf{y}}|X=\mathbf{x})}.
\end{aligned}
\tag{4.17}
$$

Then, (Liu and Tao, 2015) proves that

$$p(Y=\tilde{\mathbf{y}}|X=\mathbf{x}) = \frac{p(\tilde{Y}=\tilde{\mathbf{y}}|X=\mathbf{x}) - \rho_{-\tilde{y}}}{(1 - \rho_{+1} - \rho_{-1})}, \tag{4.18}$$

where

$$\rho_{-1} = p(\tilde{Y} = +1 | Y = -1),$$
$$\rho_{+1} = p(\tilde{Y} = -1 | Y = +1),$$ (4.19)
$$\rho_{-\tilde{\mathbf{y}}} = \min_{\mathbf{x} \in \mathcal{X}} p(\tilde{Y} = \tilde{\mathbf{y}} | X = \mathbf{x})$$

with $\rho_{-\tilde{\mathbf{y}}}$ representing a consistent estimator of noise rate. The paper (Liu and Tao, 2015) shows how to estimate $p(\tilde{Y} = \tilde{\mathbf{y}} | X = \mathbf{x})$ and the label transition probabilities in (4.19) to allow the computation of the weight $w(\mathbf{x}, \tilde{\mathbf{y}})$ in (4.17).

Selecting easy samples (Bengio et al., 2009; Kumar et al., 2010) or hard samples (Shrivastava et al., 2016) for the early learning part of the training of a general classifier has been shown to improve the learning of neural networks in different scenarios. In noisy-label learning, these strategies have pros and cons. For instance, learning from easy samples first provides more guarantees that the training will be done with clean-label samples, but these easy samples will have small losses and gradients, which can compromise convergence. On the other hand, learning from hard samples first may force the model to learn from not only the hard samples, but also from the noisy-label samples, which can result in overfitting.

Active bias (Chang et al., 2017) aims to place high weights to samples containing high variance in their prediction probability over the last H training iterations, which implies that these samples are neither easy, nor hard because we should observe small variance for easy and hard training samples. Such strategy is similar to how active learning selects informative samples to be labeled (Settles, 2012). One of the strategies presented in (Chang et al., 2017) defines the weight in (4.15) as

$$w(\mathbf{x}, \tilde{\mathbf{y}}) = \frac{1}{Z}(s(\mathbf{x}, \tilde{\mathbf{y}}) + \epsilon),$$ (4.20)

with Z denoting a normalization factor, ϵ representing a smoothness constant, and

$$s(\mathbf{x}, \tilde{\mathbf{y}}) = \sqrt{\text{var}\left(\left\{f_{\theta^t}^{(\tilde{\mathbf{y}})}(\mathbf{x})\right\}_{t=T-H+1,\ldots,T}\right) + \frac{\text{var}\left(\left\{f_{\theta^t}^{(\tilde{\mathbf{y}})}(\mathbf{x})\right\}_{t=T-H+1,\ldots,T}\right)^2}{H-1}},$$ (4.21)

where $\text{var}\left(\left\{f_{\theta^t}^{(\tilde{\mathbf{y}})}(\mathbf{x})\right\}_{t=T-H+1,\ldots,T}\right)$ denotes the prediction variance for class $\tilde{\mathbf{y}}$ for the last H training iterations.

The open-set noisy label problem was introduced by Wang et al. (2018), who proposed a loss re-weighting mechanism to enable the learning from clean-label samples and avoid the learning from noisy-label samples. Their method has a noisy-label detection method called probabilistic and cumulative Local Outlier Factor algorithm (pcLOF) based on the features of the network, which we will describe in more detail in (4.69) of Section 4.3.3. This algorithm estimates the probability that a training sample is an outlier, denoted by $\mathsf{pcLOF}(\mathbf{x})$ that outputs a score in $[0, 1]$. This is followed by the estimation that a training sample belongs to the set of clean-label samples, defined by $\mathcal{D}_c$ that contains samples with $\mathrm{pcLOF}(\mathbf{x}) \approx 0$, or the set of noisy-label samples, defined by $\mathcal{D}_n$ that contains samples with $\mathrm{pcLOF}(\mathbf{x}) \approx 1$. The model parameters are learned with a loss function that weighs the samples in $\mathcal{D}_n$ with $w(\mathbf{x}, \tilde{\mathbf{y}}) = 1 - \mathrm{pcLOF}(\mathbf{x})$ as follows (Wang et al., 2018):

$$\theta^* = \arg\min_{\theta \in \Theta} \frac{1}{|\mathcal{D}_c| + |\mathcal{D}_n|} \Big(\sum_{(\mathbf{x}, \tilde{\mathbf{y}}) \in \mathcal{D}_c} \ell(\tilde{\mathbf{y}}, f_\theta(\mathbf{x})) + \sum_{(\mathbf{x}, \tilde{\mathbf{y}}) \in \mathcal{D}_n} w(\mathbf{x}, \tilde{\mathbf{y}}) \times \ell(\tilde{\mathbf{y}}, f_\theta(\mathbf{x})) \Big). \tag{4.22}$$

Li et al. (2019) propose a loss re-weighting mechanism specifically designed for the WebVision dataset (Li et al., 2017). The weighting function is defined based on five challenges present in large-scale noisy datasets, namely: 1) high class imbalances, 2) ambiguity between certain pairs of classes, 3) label noise, 4) training samples that poorly represent classes, and 5) training samples that can belong to multiple classes. The challenges above motivate the design of particular weighting functions that are multiplied together to form the final $w(\mathbf{x}, \tilde{\mathbf{y}})$ in (4.15). Unfortunately, this loss was only tested in the WebVision dataset, and still needs to be verified in other datasets.

The use of Bayesian learning for up-weighting clean-label samples and down-weighting noisy-label samples is explored by Wang et al. (2017c). The Reweighted Probabilistic Model (RPM) optimizes the following model Wang et al. (2017c):

$$\theta^* = \arg\min_{\theta \in \Theta, \mathbf{w} \in \mathcal{W}} -\log p_\theta(\theta) - \log p_w(\mathbf{w}) + \frac{1}{|\mathcal{D}|} \Big(\sum_{i=1}^{|\mathcal{D}|} \mathbf{w}_i \ell(\tilde{\mathbf{y}}_i, f_\theta(\mathbf{x}_i)) \Big), \tag{4.23}$$

where $p_\theta(\theta)$ is a prior on model parameters, $p_w(\mathbf{w})$ is a prior on the weights for the $|\mathcal{D}|$ samples denoted by $\mathbf{w} \in \mathcal{W} \subset \mathbb{R}_+^{|\mathcal{D}|}$. The paper (Wang et al., 2017c) proposes three types of priors on the weights, namely a bank of Beta distributions, a scaled Dirichlet distribution, and a bank of Gamma distributions, where this prior encourages weights to be close to one, unless the sample appears to be noisy which pushes the weight to be close to zero.

Arazo et al. (2019) proposed an influential method to weight samples using a 2-component Beta mixture model (BMM) to automatically cluster clean-label and noisy-label samples. With this method, it is possible to weight each training sample based on its probability of belonging to the clean-label set. More specifically, given the loss values for sample i and its respective loss function value $\ell_i = \ell(\tilde{\mathbf{y}}_i, f_\theta(\mathbf{x}_i))$, the BMM is computed as

$$p(\ell_i) = \sum_{k \in \{\text{noisy}, \text{clean}\}} \lambda_k \times p(\ell_i | k), \tag{4.24}$$

where λ_k denoted the mixing weights for the $k \in \{noisy, clean\}$, and $p(\ell_i|k)$ is modeled by the Beta distribution:

$$p(\ell_i|k) = \frac{\Gamma(\alpha_k + \beta_k)}{\Gamma(\alpha_k) + \Gamma(\beta_k)} \ell_i^{\alpha_k-1} (1-\ell_i)^{\beta_k-1}, \qquad (4.25)$$

with $\alpha_k, \beta_k > 0$ and $\Gamma(.)$ representing the Gamma function. The sample weight is computed from the posterior probability that the sample i was generated by mixture component $k = $ clean, as follows:

$$\mathbf{w}_i = \frac{\lambda_{k=\text{clean}} \times p(\ell_i|k = \text{clean})}{\sum_{j \in \{\text{noisy,clean}\}} \lambda_j \times p(\ell_i|j)}. \qquad (4.26)$$

In (Arazo et al., 2019), this sample weight is not used as in (4.15), but as way to smooth the training label (Reed et al., 2014), as in:

$$\theta^* = \arg\min_{\theta \in \Theta} \frac{1}{|\mathcal{D}|} \sum_{(\mathbf{x}_i, \tilde{\mathbf{y}}_i) \in \mathcal{D}} \ell(\mathbf{w}_i \times \tilde{\mathbf{y}}_i + (1 - \mathbf{w}_i) \times \text{OneHot}(f_\theta(\mathbf{x}_i))), f_\theta(\mathbf{x}_i)), \qquad (4.27)$$

where $\mathbf{w}_i$ is the sample weight from (4.26).

A modified gradient-based optimization algorithm is proposed in (Han et al., 2020a, 2018a), which relies on stochastic gradient descent for reliable data and learning-rate-reduced gradient ascent on unreliable data. This paper explores the idea that training is divided into two stages. An initial stage where the model learns reliable data patterns (Arpit et al., 2017), followed by a second stage where the model learns unreliable data such as outliers and noisy-label data. To learn from reliable data, while avoiding the learning from unreliable data, Han et al. (2020a, 2018a) propose the stochastic integrated gradient under-weighted ascent (SIGUA) and the Pumpout losses that can be summarized as follows:

$$\mathcal{L}_{\text{SIGUA}} = \frac{1}{|\mathcal{D}|} \sum_{(\mathbf{x}, \tilde{\mathbf{y}}) \in \mathcal{D}} \mathcal{R}(\mathbf{x}, \tilde{\mathbf{y}}) \times \ell(\tilde{\mathbf{y}}, f_\theta(\mathbf{x})) - \gamma \times \mathcal{U}(\mathbf{x}, \tilde{\mathbf{y}}) \times \ell(\tilde{\mathbf{y}}, f_\theta(\mathbf{x})), \qquad (4.28)$$

where $\mathcal{R}(\mathbf{x}, \tilde{\mathbf{y}})$ returns 1 if the training data $(\mathbf{x}, \tilde{\mathbf{y}})$ belongs to the set of reliable samples (otherwise it returns 0), $\mathcal{U}(\mathbf{x}, \tilde{\mathbf{y}})$ returns 1 if the training data $(\mathbf{x}, \tilde{\mathbf{y}})$ belongs to the set of unreliable samples (otherwise it returns 0), and γ weights negatively the loss for the unreliable samples. The sets of reliable and unreliable samples are formed using sample selection techniques that will be introduced in Section 4.3.3.

Another method to weight training samples is the improved MAE (IMAE) (Wang et al., 2019b), which down-weights samples that are either too easy or too hard to learn, and simultaneously up-weights challenging training samples with

$$w(\mathbf{x}, \tilde{\mathbf{y}}) = \exp\left(T \times \left(\tilde{\mathbf{y}}^\top f_\theta(\mathbf{x})\right) \times \left(1 - \tilde{\mathbf{y}}^\top f_\theta(\mathbf{x})\right)\right), \qquad (4.29)$$

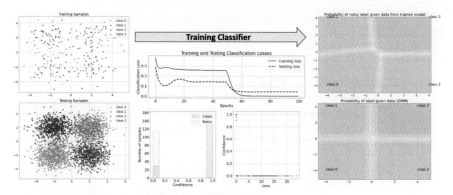

FIGURE 4.9 Classifier trained with loss re-weighting.

The training of classifier with the loss re-weighting in (4.15) using the same problem described in Fig. 4.3. We train for 100 iterations, where the first 50 iterations are with unweighted samples, and the remaining are with weighted samples, using a Gaussian mixture model to classify samples into clean or noise based on their loss values. At the bottom, in the middle, we also show a histogram of confidence for the clean and noisy-label samples and a scatter plot of the weight versus loss (note that samples with large loss value have zero weight).

where $T > 0$ is a constant that controls the exponential base. Essentially, when $\tilde{\mathbf{y}}^\top f_\theta(\mathbf{x}) \approx 1$ or $\tilde{\mathbf{y}}^\top f_\theta(\mathbf{x}) \approx 0$, $w(\mathbf{x}, \tilde{\mathbf{y}}) \approx 1$, and when $\tilde{\mathbf{y}}^\top f_\theta(\mathbf{x}) \approx 0.5$, then $w(\mathbf{x}, \tilde{\mathbf{y}}) > 1$.

The definitions of the sample weighting functions provided in this section tend to be intuitive, but arbitrary, and to depend on hyper-parameters that are hard to define. The papers by Wang et al. (2017c) and Arazo et al. (2019) started the discussion about the small-loss hypothesis, which links small loss values with clean labels and high-loss values with noisy labels. Many papers followed the idea of using the small-loss hypothesis to weight or select clean samples (Jiang et al., 2017; Li et al., 2020a), but in most cases, the Beta mixture model was replaced by the Gaussian mixture model.

In Fig. 4.8, we show an example of the training process using the loss re-weighting from (4.15). In this example, the posterior probability that the sample i was generated by mixture component $k =$ clean of a Gaussian mixture model estimated from the training loss values with $p(\ell_i | k) = \mathcal{N}(\ell_i; \mu_k, \sigma_k)$, where μ_k and σ_k denote the mean and standard deviation of the component k of the mixture model (the component with smaller mean denotes the clean label component), where the first 50 training iterations rely on the unweighted training samples to stabilize the model. The results shown by loss re-weighting tend to be reasonably good, but it is usually explored in combination with other methods to provide competitive noisy-label learning results.

Another form of loss re-weighting is proposed in meta-learning methods, which are described in more detail below in Section 4.4.1. In meta-learning, the weights are defined as a meta-parameter that can be automatically learned using a bi-level optimization and a validation set, which mitigates the two issues mentioned above

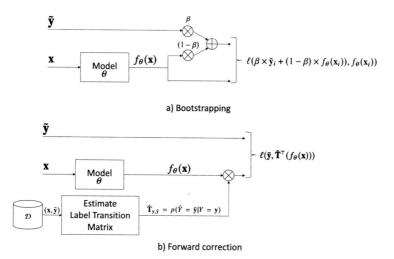

FIGURE 4.10 Loss correction.

In loss correction approaches, the loss is modified either with a modification of the training label (a – bootstrapping (Reed et al., 2014)), or a modification of the model prediction (b – forward prediction (Patrini et al., 2017)).

about the arbitrariness of the weight function and the hyper-parameters. However, the downside of meta-learning approaches is that they tend to take much longer to train than other methods.

4.2.4 Loss correction

Loss correction methods enable the learner to re-label a sample when the trained model disagrees with the label from the training set. One of the earliest works in the field that explored this idea was the method called bootstrapping (Reed et al., 2014), shown in Fig. 4.10(a), where the learner bootstraps itself by re-labeling training samples with a convex combination of the model's prediction and the training label. The intuition of bootstrapping is that as training progresses, the model's predictions become more consistent and if these predictions agree with the training label, then the loss becomes a trivial cross-entropy loss with a "one-hot" training label. When predictions disagree with the training label, then the loss becomes a cross entropy with multiple targets, namely the training label and the model prediction. Two types of bootstrapping were proposed: 1) the soft bootstrapping that uses the predicted class probabilities from $f_\theta(\mathbf{x})$ for the loss, as in:

$$\theta^* = \arg\min_{\theta \in \Theta} \frac{1}{|\mathcal{D}|} \sum_{(\mathbf{x},\tilde{\mathbf{y}}) \in \mathcal{D}} \ell(\beta \times \tilde{\mathbf{y}} + (1 - \beta) \times f_\theta(\mathbf{x}), f_\theta(\mathbf{x})), \qquad (4.30)$$

where $\beta \in [0, 1]$ weights the training label and model prediction; and 2) the hard bootstrapping which is trained with

$$\theta^* = \arg\min_{\theta \in \Theta} \frac{1}{|\mathcal{D}|} \sum_{(\mathbf{x}, \tilde{\mathbf{y}}) \in \mathcal{D}} \ell(\beta \times \tilde{\mathbf{y}} + (1 - \beta) \times \text{OneHot}(f_\theta(\mathbf{x}))), f_\theta(\mathbf{x})), \quad (4.31)$$

where $\text{OneHot} : \Delta^{|\mathcal{Y}|-1} \to \mathcal{Y}$ was defined in (2.13) to return a one-hot vector with a '1' in the class of maximum probability from $f_\theta(\mathbf{x})$, and '0' for all other classes.

Patrini et al. (2017) proposed the forward and backward loss correction methods to address the problem of asymmetric label noise (Fig. 4.10(b) shows the forward loss correction method). Recall from Section 2.4.2 that asymmetric label noise is defined by a label transition matrix $\mathbf{T}_{\mathbf{y}, \tilde{\mathbf{y}}} = p(\tilde{Y} = \tilde{\mathbf{y}} | Y = \mathbf{y})$ for $\mathbf{y}, \tilde{\mathbf{y}} \in \mathcal{Y}$ indexing the rows and columns of $\mathbf{T}$, respectively. The backward approach corrects the loss with the inverse $\mathbf{T}^{-1}$ by first approximating this transition matrix with a prediction using a model trained without correction, leading to the estimate $\hat{\mathbf{T}}$. Then, the model is re-trained by correcting the label of training sample $(\mathbf{x}, \tilde{\mathbf{y}}) \in \mathcal{D}$ with a linear combination of the losses for class labels and the estimated inverse transition matrix $\hat{\mathbf{T}}^{-1}$, as in

$$\theta^* = \arg\min_{\theta \in \Theta} \frac{1}{|\mathcal{D}|} \sum_{(\mathbf{x}, \tilde{\mathbf{y}}) \in \mathcal{D}} \overleftarrow{\ell}(\tilde{\mathbf{y}}, f_\theta(\mathbf{x})), \quad (4.32)$$

where

$$\overleftarrow{\ell}(\tilde{\mathbf{y}}, f_\theta(\mathbf{x})) = \tilde{\mathbf{y}}^\top \left(\hat{\mathbf{T}}^{-1} \left[\ell(\mathbf{y}_1, f_\theta(\mathbf{x})), ..., \ell(\mathbf{y}_{|\mathcal{Y}|}, f_\theta(\mathbf{x})) \right]^\top \right) \quad (4.33)$$

with $\mathbf{y}_k \in \mathcal{Y}$ denoting the one-hot vector of $|\mathcal{Y}|$ dimensions with the kth dimension equal to one, and $\ell(.)$ representing any of the losses in Chapter 2. The forward correction works similarly, but instead of relying on the inverse of the transition matrix, it works directly with the estimated $\hat{\mathbf{T}}$. The re-training in this forward approach relies on a linear combination of the model predictions as follows:

$$\theta^* = \arg\min_{\theta \in \Theta} \frac{1}{|\mathcal{D}|} \sum_{(\mathbf{x}, \tilde{\mathbf{y}}) \in \mathcal{D}} \overrightarrow{\ell}(\tilde{\mathbf{y}}, f_\theta(\mathbf{x})), \quad (4.34)$$

where

$$\overrightarrow{\ell}(\tilde{\mathbf{y}}, f_\theta(\mathbf{x})) = \ell(\tilde{\mathbf{y}}, \hat{\mathbf{T}}^\top(f_\theta(\mathbf{x}))). \quad (4.35)$$

The forward/backward correction methods in (4.32) and (4.34) critically depend on an accurate estimation of $\mathbf{T}$, which is challenging particularly for problems with large noise rates or a large number of classes. This motivated the gold loss correction (GLC) approach that proposes the use of a clean-label validation set $\bar{\mathcal{D}}$, which is also referred to as anchor points, to estimate $\mathbf{T}$, with (Hendrycks et al., 2018):

$$\hat{\mathbf{T}}_{\mathbf{y}, \tilde{\mathbf{y}}} = \frac{1}{|\bar{\mathcal{D}}_{\mathbf{y}}|} \sum_{\mathbf{x} \in \bar{\mathcal{D}}_{\mathbf{y}}} p_\theta(\tilde{Y} = \tilde{\mathbf{y}} | X = \mathbf{x}), \quad (4.36)$$

where $\bar{\mathcal{D}}_{\mathbf{y}}$ is the set of clean-label data of label $\mathbf{y} \in \mathcal{Y}$, and $p_\theta(\tilde{Y} = \tilde{\mathbf{y}} | X = \mathbf{x})$ is trained using the original noisy-label training set. Empirically, a more accurate estimate of $\mathbf{T}$ enables a more robust result by the GLC model trained with the forward correction method from (4.34).

A simpler alternative to the estimation of the transition matrix is based on smoothing the training label with a uniform label vector (Szegedy et al., 2016). Lukasik et al. (2020) extended this idea to the noisy-label learning problem with a label smearing framework that is related to the backward approach in (4.32), with

$$\theta^* = \arg\min_{\theta \in \Theta} \frac{1}{|\mathcal{D}|} \sum_{(\mathbf{x},\tilde{\mathbf{y}}) \in \mathcal{D}} \ell_{\text{SM}}(\tilde{\mathbf{y}}, f_\theta(\mathbf{x})), \qquad (4.37)$$

where

$$\ell_{\text{SM}}(\tilde{\mathbf{y}}, f_\theta(\mathbf{x}_i)) = \tilde{\mathbf{y}}^\top \left(\mathbf{M} \left[\ell(\mathbf{y}_1, f_\theta(\mathbf{x})), ..., \ell(\mathbf{y}_{|\mathcal{Y}|}, f_\theta(\mathbf{x})) \right]^\top \right). \qquad (4.38)$$

In (4.38), $\mathbf{M}$ denotes a smearing matrix that is defined in three ways:

- As the identity matrix $\mathbf{I}$, i.e., $\mathbf{M} = \mathbf{I}$, forming the standard training;
- As the label smoothing matrix $\mathbf{M} = (1 - \alpha)\mathbf{I} + \frac{\alpha \mathbf{J}}{|\mathcal{Y}|}$, where $\mathbf{J}$ is the all-ones matrix and $\alpha \in [0, 1]$ is a tuning parameter;
- As the inverse of a symmetric noise transition matrix, defined by $\mathbf{M} = \frac{1}{1-\alpha} \times \left(\mathbf{I} - \frac{\alpha \mathbf{J}}{|\mathcal{Y}|} \right)$.

Fig. 4.11 displays an example of a classifier trained with the loss correction in (4.37) for the problem described in Fig. 4.3 using the label smoothing smearing matrix $\mathbf{M} = (1 - \alpha)\mathbf{I} + \frac{\alpha \mathbf{J}}{|\mathcal{Y}|}$, with $\alpha = 0.5$.

Loss correction techniques are heavily used as an auxiliary method to address the learning with noisy-label problem given their simple implementation and relative efficacy. However, it is not a technique that alone can provide competitive results for noisy-label learning. Among the challenges faced by loss correction methods, we have: 1) difficult estimation of β in (4.30) and (4.31); 2) challenging estimation of the label transition matrix $\hat{\mathbf{T}}$ in (4.33) and (4.35); and 3) over-smoothing of the decision boundaries with (4.38), as shown in Fig. 4.11.

4.2.5 Domain adaptation/generalization

The noisy-label learning problem can be seen as an instance of the domain adaptation/generalization problem (Wang and Deng, 2018; Zhou et al., 2022), where the source domain $\mathcal{S}$ is the one that produces the noisy-label training set, while the target domain $\mathcal{T}$ is the one that generates the clean-label target set (Konstantinov and Lampert, 2019). In fact, as shown in Fig. 4.12, it is possible to have multiple source domains $\{\mathcal{S}_i\}_{i=1}^N$, each generating a separate training set denoted by $\mathcal{D}(\mathcal{S}_i)$, where

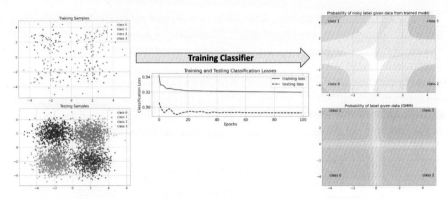

FIGURE 4.11 Classifier trained with loss correction.

The training of classifier with the loss correction in (4.37) using the same problem described in Fig. 4.3. We train for 100 iterations using the label smoothing smearing matrix $\mathbf{M} = (1-\alpha)\mathbf{I} + \frac{\alpha \mathbf{J}}{|\mathcal{Y}|}$, with $\alpha = 0.5$.

the α-weighted empirical risk of the model $f_\theta(.)$ is:

$$\mathcal{L}_\alpha\left(\theta, \{S_i\}_{i=1}^N\right) = \sum_{i=1}^N \alpha_i \mathcal{L}(\theta, S_i)$$

$$= \sum_{i=1}^N \frac{\alpha_i}{|\mathcal{D}(S_i)|} \sum_{(\mathbf{x},\tilde{\mathbf{y}}) \in \mathcal{D}(S_i)} \ell(\tilde{\mathbf{y}}, f_\theta(\mathbf{x})), \tag{4.39}$$

where $\sum_{i=1}^N \alpha_i = 1$ and $\alpha_i \geq 0$ for all $i \in \{1, ..., N\}$. The discrepancy between one of the source distributions $\mathcal{D}(S_i)$ and the target distribution $\mathcal{D}(\mathcal{T})$ is computed as follows:

$$d_\theta(S_i, \mathcal{T}) = \sup_{\theta \in \Theta}(|\mathcal{L}(\theta, S_i) - \mathcal{L}(\theta, \mathcal{T})|), \tag{4.40}$$

where $\mathcal{L}(\theta, S_i)$ denotes the empirical loss of the training set from the source domain S_i and $\mathcal{L}(\theta, \mathcal{T})$ is the empirical loss of the testing set from the target domain $\mathcal{T}$. The discrepancy in (4.40) between S_i and $\mathcal{T}$ is large if there is at least one model that performs well on one and badly on the other, but it is small if all models perform similarly on S_i and $\mathcal{T}$. The model is learned from the multiple sources by first estimating the domain weights with

$$\alpha^* = \arg\min_{\{\alpha_i\}_{i=1}^N} \sum_{i=1}^N \alpha_i d_\theta(S_i, \mathcal{T}) + \lambda \sqrt{\sum_{i=1}^N \frac{\alpha_i^2}{|\mathcal{D}(S_i)|}}$$

$$s.t. \sum_{i=1}^N \alpha_i = 1, \text{ and } \alpha_i \geq 0 \text{ for all } i, \tag{4.41}$$

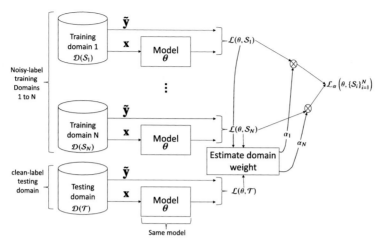

FIGURE 4.12 Domain adaptation/generalization.

Domain adaptation/generalization methods assume the availability of N noisy-label training domains $\{S_i\}_{i=1}^{N}$, each generating a separate training set denoted by $\mathcal{D}(S_i)$, and a
clean-label testing domain $\mathcal{T}$ that produces a testing set $\mathcal{D}(\mathcal{T})$ (Konstantinov and Lampert,
2019). The goal is to learn a model that can generalize well to the testing domain using a
combination of training domains weighted by $\{\alpha_i\}_{i=1}^{N}$.

where $\lambda > 0$ is a hyper-parameter. Then, the model is learned with $\theta^* = \arg\min_\theta$
$\mathcal{L}_{\alpha^*}\left(\theta, \{S_i\}_{i=1}^{N}\right)$ from (4.39). Note that the optimization in (4.41) implies that we
need to access a clean testing set (sampled from the target clean-label distribution $\mathcal{T}$)
and multiple noisy-label training sets (sampled from source noisy-label distributions
$\{S_i\}_{i=1}^{N}$). We show the results of a training using this domain adaptation in Fig. 4.13.
Similarly, Han et al. (2020c) and Yu et al. (2020b) propose relatively similar domain adaptation approaches, but with the difference of formulating a re-weighted
loss in (4.39), like the approaches presented in Section 4.2.3 to mitigate the negative
influence of label noise.

　　Domain adaptation and generalization techniques (Wang and Deng, 2018; Zhou
et al., 2022) are promising for addressing noisy-label learning problems since it is
quite clear that noisy-label training samples and clean-label testing samples represent data from different domains. Despite that, the field has not widely explored
domain adaptation and generalization methods for noisy-label learning. There may
be some reasons behind that, such as the operational difficulties to set up domain
adaptation/generalization problems. For instance, the need for testing set samples is
not widely adopted in noisy-label learning benchmarks, making the comparison with
domain adaptation/generalization approaches hard. Nevertheless, we believe that domain adaptation and generalization techniques should still be explored in noisy-label
learning problems in the future.

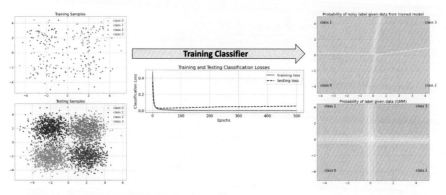

FIGURE 4.13 Classifier trained with domain adaptation.

Using the problem described in Fig. 4.3, we train a domain adaptation model for 500 epochs using the classification loss in (4.39) and domain adaptation loss (4.41) that targets the minimization of loss discrepancy between the single source noisy-label domain and the target clean-label domain. Note that we keep only the training samples from the source domain that have small losses with the condition $\ell(\tilde{\mathbf{y}}, f_\theta(\mathbf{x})) < 10 \times \frac{t}{T}$, where t is the current epoch, while T is the total number of epochs.

4.3 Data processing

In this section, we will discuss strategies that involve the processing of data to facilitate the training with noisy-label samples. We start by discussing adversarial training (Miyato et al., 2018; Goodfellow et al., 2014; Fawzi et al., 2016), which is a method designed to improve the robustness of models to data noise by applying small perturbations to the input training samples (Alayrac et al., 2019; Fatras et al., 2019; Zhu et al., 2021b). Alternatively, the selection of clean-label and informative samples from the training set by an external method is explored by data cleaning methods (Jiang et al., 2017; Shen and Sanghavi, 2019; Chen et al., 2019; Han et al., 2018c). These selected samples form a new training set to be used in the training of a regular classifier. Sample selection methods (Ding et al., 2018; Huang et al., 2020; Li et al., 2020a; Arazo et al., 2019; Kim et al., 2021) also aim to select clean-label samples, but the training of the classifier relies on both the selected clean-label samples and the samples classified as noisy, with algorithms that follow different strategies for the two sets. Another possible way of modifying the training data is by including multiple labels per training sample, in a problem known as multi-rater learning (Tanno et al., 2019). The exploration of prior knowledge about the data, for example by building super-classes that will have significantly less label noise (Seo et al., 2019) or by constraining label transition matrix structures (Han et al., 2018b), is another way of processing the input data to handle label noise. A widely explored data processing approach consists of relying on data augmentation techniques for training and testing. Such data augmentation methods can also work together with semi-supervised learning techniques. We conclude the section with the presentation

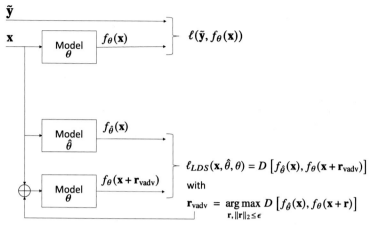

FIGURE 4.14 Adversarial training.

In adversarial training, the goal is to regularize the usual model training with an adversarial loss that estimates a noise vector $\mathbf{r}_{vadv}$ (of limited length $\|\mathbf{r}_{vadv}\|_2 < \epsilon$) to maximize the discrepancy $D[.\|.]$ between the prediction of the input data $\mathbf{x}$ from a model trained in a previous epoch (i.e., $f_{\hat{\theta}}(\mathbf{x})$) and the prediction of the noisy input data $\mathbf{x} + \mathbf{r}_{vadv}$ from the current model $f_\theta(.)$.

of pseudo-labeling techniques (Zhang et al., 2021c; Smart and Carneiro, 2023; Albert et al., 2022; Yao et al., 2021b; Wei et al., 2021b).

4.3.1 Adversarial training

While noisy-label learning addresses the problem of learning a robust model given that an unknown a subset of the training set is contaminated with label noise, adversarial training (Miyato et al., 2018; Goodfellow et al., 2014; Fawzi et al., 2016) generates small adversarial perturbations to the input training data to deceive the model to make mistakes (Song et al., 2022). Adversarial learning is a strategy usually adopted for safety-critical applications that need to be robust to challenging input data noise.

Let us introduce the virtual adversarial training (VAT) (Miyato et al., 2018) to exemplify adversarial training approaches. VAT proposes a loss to enforce a smooth model output distribution around each training sample without knowing the label information, resulting in robustness to small changes to input data. VAT assumes that the dataset is divided into labeled and unlabeled sets, represented by $\mathcal{D}_l, \mathcal{D}_u \subset \mathcal{D}$, and the model optimization is defined by:

$$\theta^* = \arg\min_\theta \frac{1}{|\mathcal{D}_l|} \sum_{(\mathbf{x}, \tilde{\mathbf{y}}) \in \mathcal{D}_l} \ell(\tilde{\mathbf{y}}, f_\theta(\mathbf{x})) + \frac{\lambda}{|\mathcal{D}_l| + |\mathcal{D}_u|} \times \sum_{\mathbf{x} \in \mathcal{D}_l \bigcup \mathcal{D}_u} \ell_{LDS}(\mathbf{x}, \hat{\theta}, \theta),$$

$$(4.42)$$

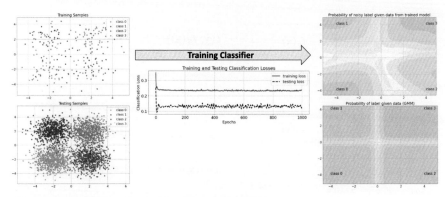

FIGURE 4.15 Classifier trained with adversarial training.

The training of classifier with adversarial training from (4.44) using the same problem described in Fig. 4.3. We train for 1000 iterations assuming that $\lambda = 0$ for the first 14 iterations, and $\lambda = 5$ between iterations 15 and 1000.

where $\hat{\theta}$ denotes a model parameter at a specific step in the training process, and the local distributional smoothness (LDS) is represented by

$$\ell_{LDS}(\mathbf{x}, \hat{\theta}, \theta) = D\left[f_{\hat{\theta}}(\mathbf{x}) \| f_{\theta}(\mathbf{x} + \mathbf{r}_{\text{vadv}})\right] \tag{4.43}$$

with $\mathbf{r}_{\text{vadv}} = \arg\max_{\mathbf{r}, \|\mathbf{r}\|_2 \leq \epsilon} D\left[f_{\hat{\theta}}(\mathbf{x}) \| f_{\theta}(\mathbf{x} + \mathbf{r})\right]$, and $D[.\|.]$ representing a nonnegative distribution divergence function (e.g., Kullback-Leibler (KL) divergence).

Surprisingly, the common goal of noisy-label learning and adversarial training, consisting of learning robust representations and models from noisy observations, has not attracted too much interest from the scientific community. Remarkable exceptions are the papers by Alayrac et al. (2019); Fatras et al. (2019); Zhu et al. (2021b). In (Alayrac et al., 2019), the authors show that adversarial training, such as the one in (4.42), makes the trained model $f_{\theta^*}(.)$ robust to label noise. We depict this approach in Fig. 4.14, where the optimization from (4.42) is updated for noisy-label learning as follows:

$$\theta^* = \arg\min_{\theta} \frac{1}{|\mathcal{D}|} \sum_{(\mathbf{x}, \tilde{\mathbf{y}}) \in \mathcal{D}} \ell(\tilde{\mathbf{y}}, f_{\theta}(\mathbf{x})) + \lambda \times \ell_{LDS}(\mathbf{x}, \hat{\theta}, \theta), \tag{4.44}$$

where $\hat{\theta}$ is the model parameter at a specific training epoch, and the $\ell_{LDS}(.)$ is defined in (4.43). The result from the optimization from (4.44) is shown in Fig. 4.15. The approach introduced in (Alayrac et al., 2019) motivated the Wasserstein adversarial regularization (WAR) on label noise (Fatras et al., 2019) that re-defines $D[.]$ in (4.43) as the Wasserstein distance computed in the label space $\mathcal{Y}$. Zhu et al. (2021b) analyzed the adversarial training in noisy-label learning problems and suggested that the number of projected gradient descent (PGD) steps to find an adversarial sample in the proximity of a training point is an effective way to decide the cleanliness of

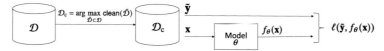

FIGURE 4.16 Data cleaning.

Data cleaning methods rely on an optimization that trains the model with a training set $\mathcal{D}_c \subset \mathcal{D}$ found by selecting training samples that are likely to have clean labels using the function clean(.)

its label. This paper follows the adversarial training from (Madry et al., 2017), which optimizes the model using just labeled data, as in

$$\theta^* = \arg\min_\theta \frac{1}{|\mathcal{D}|} \sum_{(\mathbf{x},\tilde{\mathbf{y}})\in\mathcal{D}} \ell(\tilde{\mathbf{y}},\, f_\theta(\tilde{\mathbf{x}})), \tag{4.45}$$

where $\tilde{\mathbf{x}}$ is an adversarial variant of input data inside the ϵ-ball centered at $\mathbf{x}$. The generation of adversarial variants, starting from initial sample $\mathbf{x}^{(0)} = \mathbf{x}$ follows the PGD steps, defined by

$$\mathbf{x}^{(t+1)} = \Pi_{\mathcal{B}(\mathbf{x}^{(0)},\epsilon)}\left(\mathbf{x}^{(t)} + \alpha \mathrm{sign}(\nabla_{\mathbf{x}^{(t)}}\ell(\tilde{\mathbf{y}},\, f_\theta(\mathbf{x}^{(t)})))\right) \tag{4.46}$$

where $\mathbf{x}^{(t)}$ is the adversarial sample at PGD step t, and $\Pi_{\mathcal{B}(\mathbf{x}^{(0)},\epsilon)}(.)$ denotes the function to project the adversarial sample into the ϵ-ball centered at $\mathbf{x}^{(0)}$. This paper (Zhu et al., 2021b) also concluded that the regularization from the adversarial training in (4.45) helps to make the training robust to noisy labels.

Adversarial training is a strategy that links label noise and data noise, which can be seen as two complementary aspects of a unified concept. This topic deserves more attention from the scientific community not only because it will allow a better understanding of how data and label noise affect the learning problem, but also because it may lead to more effective noisy-label learning mechanisms. Recently, Sanyal et al. (2020) studied how deep learning models become vulnerable to adversarial attacks. One of the reasons for that vulnerability was found to be the presence of label noise in the training set, while the other reason was the tendency of training procedures to learn simple classification boundaries.

4.3.2 Data cleaning

Data cleaning methods are designed to build a new training set by minimizing the likelihood that it contains data with noisy labels, as shown in Fig. 4.16. Thus the

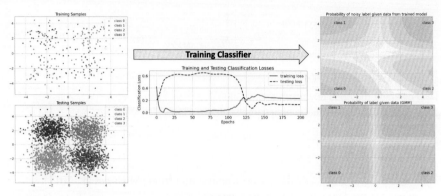

FIGURE 4.17 Classifier trained with data cleaning.

Using the classification problem described in Fig. 4.3, we train a classifier for 200 iterations with data cleaning from (4.47) and

$$\mathcal{D}_c = \begin{cases} \{(\mathbf{x}, \tilde{\mathbf{y}}) | (\mathbf{x}, \tilde{\mathbf{y}}) \in \mathcal{D}, \ell(\tilde{\mathbf{y}}, f_\theta(\mathbf{x})) < \frac{\tau \times \text{iteration}}{200}\}, & \text{if iteration} > 10 \\ \mathcal{D}, & \text{otherwise} \end{cases}, \text{ where } \tau = 10, \text{ and}$$

iteration $\in \{1, ..., 200\}$ denotes the training epoch.

model optimization is achieved with:

$$\theta^* = \arg\min_\theta \frac{1}{|\mathcal{D}_c|} \sum_{(\mathbf{x}, \tilde{\mathbf{y}}) \in \mathcal{D}_c} \ell(\tilde{\mathbf{y}}, f_\theta(\mathbf{x}))$$

$$\text{s.t. } \mathcal{D}_c = \arg\max_{\tilde{\mathcal{D}} \subset \mathcal{D}} \text{clean}(\tilde{\mathcal{D}}),$$

(4.47)

where $\text{clean}(\tilde{\mathcal{D}})$ represents a function that returns a measure of label cleanliness of $\tilde{\mathcal{D}} \subset \mathcal{D}$ that is maximized by including as many clean-label samples as possible and as little noisy-label samples as possible. Given that the selection of samples to be included into $\mathcal{D}_c$ consists of a combinatorial problem, it usually resorts to greedy optimization strategies, where the label cleanliness of each sample in $\mathcal{D}$ is studied to determine if that sample will be included or rejected from $\mathcal{D}_c$.

Before the advent of deep learning approaches, there have been many methods that aimed at producing such clean-label training sets by studying their weights in bagging or boosting approaches (Wheway, 2001; Sluban et al., 2014), their k-nearest neighbor classification (Delany et al., 2012), their compression measure (e.g., minimum description length) (Gamberger et al., 2000), or their outlier measure (Thongkam et al., 2008). Such ideas have been extended to deep learning approaches, as we explain below.

Data cleaning has been explored in deep learning, particularly with Mentor-Net (Jiang et al., 2017), Iterative Trimmed Loss Minimization (ITLM) (Shen and Sanghavi, 2019), Iterative Noisy Cross-Validation (INCV) (Chen et al., 2019), and Co-teaching (Han et al., 2018c). Even though these methods introduce different definitions for the function clean(.) in (4.47), all definitions are based on the assumption that large-loss samples are likely to have noisy labels. This assumption is based on the work by Arpit et al. (2017), who showed that deep learning models tend to learn simple patterns first (with clean-label samples showing small losses and noisy-label samples displaying large losses), and then gradually overfit to all training samples (with all samples presenting small losses). Such demonstration enables the formulation of the small-loss trick, which treats small-loss samples as clean-label samples. MentorNet uses a pre-trained a teacher model to select small-loss samples to be inserted into $\mathcal{D}_c$, which is used to train the student model. ITLM alternates between selecting small-loss samples and re-training the model with these samples. INCV breaks the training set into two halves, using one half to train the model and the other half to select clean samples (by checking if the prediction by the trained model matches the training label). Co-teaching uses two models, where each model selects a proportion of its small-loss training samples from $\mathcal{D}$ to train the other model. By avoiding noisy-labeled data, these models mitigate the risk of overfitting these mislabeled samples, but they also reduce the amount of informative training samples that are useful for training robustness even though they have a relatively large loss value (Shrivastava et al., 2016; Chang et al., 2017; Lin et al., 2017b).

The SELectively reFurbIsh unclEan samples (SELFIE) method (Song et al., 2019) addresses this issue by selecting not only clean, but also informative training samples (referred as refurbishable training samples), as follows:

$$
\begin{aligned}
\theta^* = \arg\min_{\theta} \frac{1}{|\mathcal{D}_c|} \sum_{(\mathbf{x},\tilde{\mathbf{y}})\in\mathcal{D}_c} \ell(\tilde{\mathbf{y}}, f_\theta(\mathbf{x})) + \frac{1}{|\mathcal{D}_r|} \sum_{(\mathbf{x},\tilde{\mathbf{y}}_r)\in\mathcal{D}_r} \ell(\tilde{\mathbf{y}}_r, f_\theta(\mathbf{x})) \\
s.t.\, \mathcal{D}_c = \left\{ (\mathbf{x},\tilde{\mathbf{y}}) | (\mathbf{x},\tilde{\mathbf{y}}) \in \mathcal{D}, \ell(\tilde{\mathbf{y}}, f_\theta(\mathbf{x})) < \tau \right\} \\
\mathcal{D}_r = \left\{ (\mathbf{x},\tilde{\mathbf{y}}_r) | (\mathbf{x},\tilde{\mathbf{y}}) \in \mathcal{D}, \frac{\mathbb{H}[f_{\theta^{(t-q)},\ldots,(t-1)}(\mathbf{x})]}{\delta} < \epsilon, \right. \\
\left. \tilde{\mathbf{y}}_r = \text{mode}\left(\text{OneHot}\left(f_{\theta^{(t-q)},\ldots,(t-1)}(\mathbf{x}) \right) \right) \right\}
\end{aligned}
\tag{4.48}
$$

where $\mathcal{D}_c \cap \mathcal{D}_r = \emptyset$, $\tilde{\mathbf{y}}_r$ is the most common label predicted in the last q iterations, $\mathbb{H}[f_{\theta^{(t-q)},\ldots,(t-1)}(\mathbf{x})]$ computes the entropy of the aggregated probability classification of the model from the previous q training iterations, τ and ϵ are thresholds used for sample selection, and δ is a normalization factor. Even with the improvement above, SELFIE still suffers from the inability to distinguish between samples with noisy labels and informative samples with clean labels because of limited information available from model predictions or loss values.

This issue has recently been addressed by considering prediction uncertainty with the use of interval loss estimation (Xia et al., 2021), where the goal is to distinguish between noisy-label samples and informative clean-label samples. Xia et al. (2021) propose the soft truncation and hard truncation robust mean estimators, where the soft truncation provides a robust mean loss estimation of a training sample's observed training losses $\mathcal{L}_t = \{\ell_i\}_{i=1}^t$ by changing the behavior of losses, as follows

$$\tilde{\mu}_s = \frac{1}{t} \sum_{\ell_i \in \mathcal{L}_t} \psi(\ell_i), \tag{4.49}$$

where $\psi(\ell_i) = \log(1 + \ell_i + \ell_i^2/2)$, with $\ell_i \geq 0$, is a non-decreasing influence function. The criterion to select samples for training is designed based on concentration inequalities (Xia et al., 2021) and the number of times a sample has been selected, with

$$\mathcal{D}_c = \left\{ (\mathbf{x}, \tilde{\mathbf{y}}) | (\mathbf{x}, \tilde{\mathbf{y}}) \in \mathcal{D}, s(\mathcal{L}_t) < \tau \right\}, \tag{4.50}$$

where

$$s(\mathcal{L}_t) = \tilde{\mu}_s - \frac{\sigma^2 \left(t + \frac{\sigma^2 \log(2t)}{t^2} \right)}{n_t - \sigma^2}, \tag{4.51}$$

with $\tilde{\mu}_s$ defined in (4.49), σ denoting the standard deviation of $\mathcal{L}_t$, and n_t representing the number of times a sample has been selected. The hard truncation first removes t_o outliers from the losses in $\mathcal{L}_t$, forming the set $\mathcal{L}_{t-t_o} \subset \mathcal{L}_t$, and then estimates the robust mean loss

$$\tilde{\mu}_h = \frac{1}{t - t_o} \sum_{\ell_i \in \mathcal{L}_{t-t_o}} \psi(\ell_i). \tag{4.52}$$

The hard truncation selection relies on the same criteria from (4.50) by replacing $s(\mathcal{L}_t)$ by

$$h(\mathcal{L}_t) = \tilde{\mu}_h - \frac{2\sqrt{2\tau_{min}} L(t + \sqrt{2}t_o)}{(t - t_o)\sqrt{t}} \sqrt{\frac{\log(4t)}{n_t}}, \tag{4.53}$$

where $\tilde{\mu}_h$ is defined in (4.52), L is an upper-bound for the loss, and τ_{min} represents the minimal mixing time. For the selection criteria in (4.51) and (4.53), the first term prioritizes samples with small robust mean loss, while the second term prioritizes samples with large σ^2 or τ_{min} (i.e. uncertain samples) and small n_t (i.e., less selected samples).

The problem mentioned above about the difficulty to differentiate between noisy-label samples from clean-label informative samples has been addressed in (Zhou et al., 2021) with the Robust Curriculum Learning (RoCL). More specifically, RoCL applies data cleaning at the beginning of the training, and gradually start training from noisy data that are pseudo-labeled using a time-ensemble of the model and data augmentation. Similarly to (Xia et al., 2021; Song et al., 2019), the data selection in (Zhou et al., 2021) relies on the history of the training process. In particular, Zhou et al. (2021) hypothesize that the training sample's label is more likely to be correct given a consistently low dynamic loss computed with

$$
\ell_i^{(t+1)} = \begin{cases} \gamma \ell(\tilde{\mathbf{y}}_i, f_{\theta^{(t)}}(\mathbf{x}_i)) + (1-\gamma)\ell_i^{(t)}, & \text{if } (\mathbf{x}_i, \tilde{\mathbf{y}}_i) \in \mathcal{D}_c \\ \ell_i^{(t)}, & \text{otherwise} \end{cases}, \qquad (4.54)
$$

where $\gamma \in [0, 1]$ represents a discounting factor, and t denotes the training epoch. RoCL also explores an empirical observation that the model output tends to be an accurate representation of the clean label if the output is consistent over the training history and across data augmentations of the training sample, as in

$$
c_i^{(t+1)} = \begin{cases} \gamma \zeta_i^{(t)} + (1-\gamma)c_i^{(t)}, & \text{if } (\mathbf{x}_i, \tilde{\mathbf{y}}_i) \in \mathcal{D}_c \\ c_i^{(t)}, & \text{otherwise} \end{cases}, \qquad (4.55)
$$

where $\gamma \in [0, 1]$ is a discounting factor, $\zeta_i^{(t)} = \frac{1}{m}\sum_{j=1}^{m} \ell(f_{\theta^{(t)}}(\mathbf{x}_i), \bar{f}_{\bar{\theta}^{(t)}}(\mathbf{x}_i^{(j)}))$ is the instantaneous consistency loss with $\bar{f}_{\bar{\theta}}(\mathbf{x}_i) = \frac{1}{m}\sum_{j=1}^{m} f_{\bar{\theta}^{(t)}}(\mathbf{x}_i^{(j)})$, and $\bar{\theta}^{(t)} = \gamma\theta^{(t-1)} + (1-\gamma)\bar{\theta}^{(t)}$. The selection of samples to be included into $\mathcal{D}_c$ is performed by drawing samples from $\mathcal{D}$ with the following probability distribution that combines the clean label detection and the consistency loss:

$$
\mathcal{P}_i^{(t)} = \gamma p_i^{(t)} + (1-\gamma)q_i^{(t)}, \qquad (4.56)
$$

where

$$
p_i^{(t)} = \frac{\exp(\tau_1 \ell_i^{(t)})}{\sum_{j=1}^{|\mathcal{D}|} \exp(\tau_1 \ell_j^{(t)})}, \quad q_i^{(t)} = \frac{\exp(\tau_2 c_i^{(t)})}{\sum_{j=1}^{|\mathcal{D}|} \exp(\tau_2 c_j^{(t)})}, \qquad (4.57)
$$

with τ_1, τ_2 being the curriculum parameters to prioritize the clean label detection and the consistency loss. When $\tau_1 < 0$, samples with clean labels tend to have high $p_i^{(t)}$; conversely, when $\tau_1 > 0$, samples with noisy labels tend to have high $p_i^{(t)}$. Also, when $\tau_2 < 0$, samples with smaller consistency loss tend to have high $q_i^{(t)}$, and with $\tau_2 > 0$, samples with higher consistency loss tend to have high $q_i^{(t)}$. Thus, when $\tau_1 < 0$, the training is focused on clean data already learned by the model, and when $\tau_2 < 0$, the training is focused on data that shows consistent losses. To motivate exploration of the data, τ_1 and τ_2 need to move toward zero. Alternatively, $\tau_1 < 0$ and $\tau_2 > 0$ focus on clean data that show inconsistent model outputs, while $\tau_1 > 0$ and $\tau_2 < 0$ strengthen noisy samples with consistent outputs. Zhou et al. (2021) suggest a curriculum learning starting from $\tau_1 < 0$ and $\tau_2 > 0$ that gradually move to $\tau_1 > 0$ and $\tau_2 < 0$, which suggests a training starting from the learning from clean data and finishing with the learning from consistent samples.

Other recently published methods propose data cleaning approaches based on early stopping (Bai et al., 2021), combined with test time augmentation (Wang et al., 2019a) and dropout (Srivastava et al., 2014) to select a balanced set of pseudo clean-label samples (Smart and Carneiro, 2023). Furthermore, Pleiss et al. (2020)

studied the training with noisy labels dynamics and introduced the area under the margin (AUM) statistic. In essence, they discovered that the average difference between the logits of a training sample's assigned class and its highest non-assigned class can characterize this sample, which is measured as follows:

$$\text{AUM}(\mathbf{x}, \tilde{\mathbf{y}}) = \sum_{t=1}^{T} f_{\theta^{(t)}}^{(\tilde{\mathbf{y}})}(\mathbf{x}) - \max_{\hat{\mathbf{y}} \neq \tilde{\mathbf{y}}} f_{\theta^{(t)}}^{(\hat{\mathbf{y}})}(\mathbf{x}), \tag{4.58}$$

where $f_{\theta^{(t)}}^{(\tilde{\mathbf{y}})}(\mathbf{x})$ denotes the $\tilde{\mathbf{y}}^{th}$ output from the model obtained at the tth training iteration. Clean-label samples tend to have larger AUM than noisy-label samples, so the method proposed in (Pleiss et al., 2020) removes the samples with AUM less than a threshold that is automatically set based on a clean set or on the use of a non-existing training class.

The detection of clean samples can also be done directly with the training samples' feature representations instead of loss values or model predictions, under mild assumptions (data density has a compact support, true conditional distributions of labels are continuous, and class-wise decision region of the Bayes optimal classifier is connected). For example, Wu et al. (2020) explore a high-order topological information of data that assumes that clean data are clustered together while noisy-label data are spread out and isolated. The proposed algorithm starts with an early-stopping trained model $f_\theta(.)$ using the whole $\mathcal{D}$. The next step builds a K-nearest neighbor graph for the training samples' representations using one of the intermediate layers of $f_\theta(.)$ and finds the class-wise largest components, which are likely to contain most of the clean labels for the class. Next, the outermost layer of each largest component is removed to mitigate the noisy-label samples present at the boundary of these clusters. Wu et al. (2020) prove the purity (selected data are likely to be clean) and abundancy (majority of clean data is collected by the method) properties of the algorithm.

The geometric structure of feature representations and model predictions have also been explored to reject noisy-label samples (Wu et al., 2021b) with the Noisy Graph Cleaning (NGC) approach. NGC builds a k-nearest neighbor graph that rejects open-set and closed-set noisy-label samples based on their low-confidence model predictions. Then, each class will be formed by a sub-graph that corresponds to the largest connected component for that class. During testing, this method can detect open-set data by calculating the distance between their representations and the representations of learned class prototypes. Data cleaning from the K-nearest neighbors of logit representations (Bahri et al., 2020) or data representations from an intermediate model layer (Feng et al., 2021) have also been explored by removing the samples that disagree with their neighbors.

More recently, the cleanlab studio[1] has been developed with the goal of improving the quality of training sets in a data-centric manner, by identifying samples with noise

---

[1] https://cleanlab.ai.

labels (Northcutt et al., 2021). Cleanlab is based on the confident learning (CL) concept that assumes asymmetric label noise, which implies that $p(\tilde{Y}|Y, X) = p(\tilde{Y}|Y)$, or that label transition is conditionally independent of the input data. CL studies the estimation of the joint distribution between noisy and clean labels, defined by $p(\tilde{Y}, Y)$, to characterize and identify label errors in datasets, estimate noise, and rank training samples. The estimation of $p(\tilde{Y}, Y)$ depends on the noisy labels $\tilde{y}$ present in the training set $\mathcal{D}$ and on a trained model $f_\theta : \mathcal{X} \rightarrow \Delta^{|\mathcal{Y}|-1}$, which means that cleanlab is model agnostic, but it needs a pre-trained model to clean the training set. The self-confidence of the model for a particular class $c \in \mathcal{Y}$ depends of a classification threshold, computed with

$$t_c = \frac{1}{|\mathcal{D}_c|} \sum_{x \in \mathcal{D}_c} f_\theta^{(c)}(x), \qquad (4.59)$$

where $\mathcal{D}_c = \{x|(x, \tilde{y}) \in \mathcal{D}_{out}, \tilde{y} = c\}$ (with $\mathcal{D}_{out}$ denoting an out-of-sample set), and $f_\theta^{(c)}(x)$ is the model (probabilistic) output for label $c \in \mathcal{Y}$. Then the set of samples for clean class k from noisy class c is defined by

$$\mathcal{D}_{c,k} = \left\{ x | x \in \mathcal{D}_c, f_\theta^{(k)}(x) \geq t_k, k = \arg \max_{y \in \mathcal{Y}, f_\theta^{(y)}(x) > t_y} f_\theta^{(y)}(x) \right\}, \qquad (4.60)$$

where $k \in \mathcal{Y}$. This allows us to estimate the joint distribution between noisy and clean labels, with

$$\hat{Q}_{=c,k} = \frac{|\mathcal{D}_{c,k}|}{\sum_{i,j \in \mathcal{Y}} |\mathcal{D}_{i,j}|}. \qquad (4.61)$$

The last step of CL is then to clean the data by ranking and pruning it, where Northcutt et al. (2021) suggest that samples belonging to the set $\{x|x \in \mathcal{D}_{c,k}, c \neq k\}$ are classified as noisy-label samples. The samples belonging to this noisy-label set are sorted by the normalized margin, defined with $f_\theta^{(\tilde{y})}(x) - f_\theta^{(y^*)}(x)$, where $y^* = \arg\max_{y \neq \tilde{y} \in \mathcal{Y}} f_\theta^{(y)}(x)$ (Wei et al., 2018).

Kuan and Mueller (2022) analyzed many different data-centric noisy-label scores that, similarly to cleanlab's CL, are independent of the model. The self-confidence score is the model's probability of the training label $\tilde{y}$, defined as $\text{Score}(x, \tilde{y}, \theta) = f_\theta^{(\tilde{y})}(x)$. The normalized margin score is computed from the difference between the training label $\tilde{y}$ and the most likely class that is not the training label, defined as $\text{Score}(x, \tilde{y}, \theta) = f_\theta^{(\tilde{y})}(x) - f_\theta^{(y^*)}(x)$, where $y^* = \arg\max_{y \neq \tilde{y} \in \mathcal{Y}} f_\theta^{(y)}(x)$. The confidence-weighted entropy is defined by the ratio of the self-confidence and the log normalized entropy of the model probabilities, defined by $\text{Score}(x, \tilde{y}, \theta) = \frac{f_\theta^{(\tilde{y})}(x)}{(1/\log(|\mathcal{Y}|))\mathbb{H}(f_\theta(x))}$. The negative entropy and least-confidence scores do not require the training label and are respectively defined as $\text{Score}(x, \tilde{y}, \theta) = -\mathbb{H}(f_\theta(x))$ and $\text{Score}(x, \tilde{y}, \theta) = f_\theta^{(y^*)}(x)$ where $y^* = \arg\max_{y \in \mathcal{Y}} f_\theta^{(y)}(x)$. These scores can be adjusted to account for model biases, with $\text{AdjustedScore}(x, \tilde{y}, \theta) = \text{Score}(x, \tilde{y}, \bar{\theta})$, where $f_{\tilde{\theta}}^{(c)}(\mathbf{x}) = f_\theta(\mathbf{x}) - \mathbf{t_c}$, with $\mathbf{t_c}$ defined in (4.59). We can also have an ensemble of K models that are aggregated with $\sum_{i=1}^{K} w_i \times f_{\theta_i}(\mathbf{x})$, with $\sum_{i=1}^{K} w_i = 1$. In this case, the ensemble label quality score is produced by $\mathsf{Score}(\mathbf{x}, \tilde{\mathbf{y}}, \{\theta_i\}_{i=1}^{K}) = \sum_{i=1}^{K} w_i \times \mathsf{Score}(\mathbf{x}, \tilde{\mathbf{y}}, \theta_i)$. Experiments in this paper show that confidence weighted entropy and self-confidence scores are the top-performing scores, while the least-confidence and negative entropy scores perform poorly overall.

In open set noise (Wang et al., 2018), recent methods formulate a data selection process to classify samples belonging to the closed and open sets (Sachdeva et al., 2021) with the following optimization

$$\theta^* = \arg\min_{\theta} \frac{1}{|\mathcal{D}_{\text{closed}}|} \sum_{(\mathbf{x}, \tilde{\mathbf{y}}) \in \mathcal{D}_{\text{closed}}} \ell(\tilde{\mathbf{y}}, f_\theta(\mathbf{x}))$$

$$s.t. \ \mathcal{D}_{\text{closed}} = \arg\max_{\tilde{\mathcal{D}} \subset \mathcal{D}} \mathsf{closed}(\tilde{\mathcal{D}}, \theta_{open}^*),$$

$$\theta_{open}^* = \arg\min_{\theta_{open}} \frac{1}{|\mathcal{D}|} \sum_{(\mathbf{x}, \tilde{\mathbf{y}}) \in \mathcal{D}} \ell_{open}(\tilde{\mathbf{y}}, f_{\theta_{open}}(\mathbf{x})),$$

(4.62)

where $\mathsf{closed}(.)$ represents a function that detects (clean- or noisy-label) samples belonging to one of the training classes, and $f_{\theta_{open}}(.)$ is a model trained to detect open-set samples. EvidentialMix (Sachdeva et al., 2021) uses the subjective logic (SL) loss function in $\ell_{open}(.)$ (Sensoy et al., 2018), defined in (4.5), to train $\mathsf{closed}(.)$. The SL loss is designed to quantify classification uncertainty, which tends to be small for clean-label samples, large for noisy-label samples, and of an intermediate value for open-set samples. This observation leads to a natural formulation of a 3-component Gaussian mixture model to represent the distribution of loss values of the training set, where the function $\mathsf{closed}(.)$ detects the samples belonging to the component with the smallest mean (i.e., the clean-label closed-set samples) or the largest mean (i.e., the noisy-label closed-set samples), and rejects all remaining samples classified as open-set.

Data cleaning is one of the most studied and utilized techniques in noisy-label learning, as can be seen from the number of methods explained in this section that depend on it. Nevertheless, defining a function that can reliably select clean-label samples from a training set with a minimum number of false positives and false negatives remains challenging. For this reason, data cleaning is rarely used isolated as a method for handling noisy-label samples. Furthermore, training only with the clean-label samples while disregarding the noisy-label samples may not be the best strategy since there is plenty of evidence, which we will show next in Section 4.3.3, that these noisy-label samples can improve the generalization of the model. Nevertheless, given the importance of this technique, we anticipate that many innovative methods will still depend on data cleaning methods.

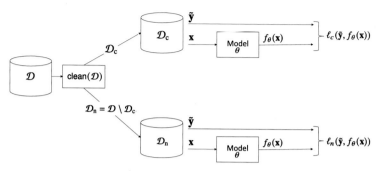

FIGURE 4.18 Sample selection.

Sample selection methods rely on the function clean($\mathcal{D}$) that forms the dataset $\mathcal{D}_c \subset \mathcal{D}$ with the training samples from $\mathcal{D}$ that are likely to contain clean labels, with the remaining samples forming the set $\mathcal{D}_n = \mathcal{D} \setminus \mathcal{D}_c$. The optimization uses a loss $\ell_c(.)$ for the samples in $\mathcal{D}_c$ and the loss $\ell_n(.)$ for the samples in $\mathcal{D}_n$.

4.3.3 Sample selection

Sample selection techniques classify samples into clean or noisy, but differently from the data cleaning methods in Section 4.3.2, they do not discard any subset of the training samples. In general, the optimization for sample selection approaches, depicted in Fig. 4.18 can be defined as:

$$\theta^* = \arg\min_\theta \frac{1}{|\mathcal{D}_c|} \sum_{(\mathbf{x},\tilde{\mathbf{y}}) \in \mathcal{D}_c} \ell_c(\tilde{\mathbf{y}}, f_\theta(\mathbf{x})) + \frac{1}{|\mathcal{D}_n|} \sum_{(\mathbf{x},\tilde{\mathbf{y}}) \in \mathcal{D}_n} \ell_n(\tilde{\mathbf{y}}, f_\theta(\mathbf{x}))$$
(4.63)
$$s.t. \mathcal{D}_c = \mathsf{clean}(\mathcal{D}), \mathcal{D}_n = \mathcal{D} \setminus \mathcal{D}_c,$$

where $\mathcal{D}_c, \mathcal{D}_n \in \mathcal{D}$ denote the clean and noisy-label training sets. Fig. 4.19 shows the training results of the optimization from (4.63), where $\ell_c(.)$ is defined as the cross-entropy loss and $\ell_n(.)$ as the mean absolute error loss. Some sample selection techniques work together with the data re-weighting methods from Section 4.2.3 by classifying clean-label and noisy-label samples and weighting them differently during training.

The most common sample selection approach applied in the definition of the function clean(.) in (4.63) is based on the small-loss trick (Arpit et al., 2017), which defines the function clean($\mathcal{D}$) to return the following set

$$\mathcal{D}_c = \left\{ (\mathbf{x}, \tilde{\mathbf{y}}) | (\mathbf{x}, \tilde{\mathbf{y}}) \in \mathcal{D}, \ell_c(\tilde{\mathbf{y}}, f_\theta(\mathbf{x})) < \tau \right\}.$$
(4.64)

Given the difficulty in defining a value for the threshold τ, many papers have proposed different ways to use this small-loss trick to select clean-label samples. As already described in Section 4.2.3 Arazo et al. (2019) proposed the use of a Beta mixture model to represent the distribution of the losses from the training samples in (4.24), where the component associated with the small loss values denotes

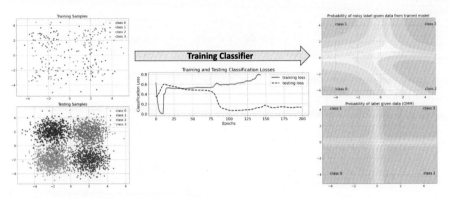

FIGURE 4.19 Classifier trained with sample selection.

Similarly to Fig. 4.17, we use the classification problem described in Fig. 4.3 to train a classifier for 200 iterations with sample selection from (4.63) and

$$\mathcal{D}_c = \begin{cases} \{(\mathbf{x}, \tilde{\mathbf{y}}) | (\mathbf{x}, \tilde{\mathbf{y}}) \in \mathcal{D}, \ell(\tilde{\mathbf{y}}, f_\theta(\mathbf{x})) < \frac{\tau \times \text{iteration}}{200}\}, & \text{if iteration} > 10 \\ \mathcal{D}, & \text{otherwise} \end{cases}, \text{ and } \mathcal{D}_n = \mathcal{D} \setminus \mathcal{D}_c,$$

where $\tau = 10$, and iteration $\in \{1, ..., 200\}$ denotes the training epoch. Also from (4.63), $\ell_c(.)$ is defined as the cross-entropy loss and $\ell_n(.)$ as the mean absolute error loss.

the clean-label component. Small-loss sample selection has also been applied in SIGUA (Han et al., 2020a) that relies on the loss function defined in (4.28). In this loss function, the training samples are ranked based on their loss values, then the p% smaller loss samples are inserted into the reliable set $\mathcal{R}$ for gradient descent, the mid-loss samples, composed by the next q% of ranked samples are inserted into the unreliable set $\mathcal{U}$ for weighted gradient ascent. SIGUA rejects the remaining higher loss samples, which means that it combines sample selection, loss re-weighting, and data cleaning technique. Similarly, PumpOut (Han et al., 2018a) also ranks the training samples in terms of their losses and uses the smallest p% samples for regular stochastic gradient descent, while the remaining $100\% - p\%$ of the training samples are used for weighted gradient ascent. The ProMix approach (Wang et al., 2022) introduced an extended small loss criterion by selecting not only samples that have small cross-entropy losses, but samples with high-confidence prediction for the training label. SELF (Huang et al., 2020) introduces a sample selection approach to select noisy-label samples using a temporal ensembling of predictions with $\hat{\mathbf{y}}^{(t+1)} = \alpha \times \hat{\mathbf{y}}^{(t)} + (1 - \alpha) \times f_\theta(\mathbf{x})$, where $\hat{\mathbf{y}}^{(0)} = \mathbf{0}$ and $\hat{\mathbf{y}}^{(t)}$ represents the prediction ensemble at training iteration t. Then, training samples where $\tilde{\mathbf{y}} \neq \text{OneHot}(\hat{\mathbf{y}}^{(t+1)})$ have their labels erased (i.e., they become un-labeled).

Sample selection has been effectively combined with semi-supervised learning (SSL), which will be described in more detail in Section 4.4.4, where $\ell_c(.)$ in (4.63) is formulated as a supervised loss and $\ell_u(.)$ denotes an unsupervised loss. Ding et al. (2018) introduced an SSL approach, where the clean(.) function in (4.63) selects the training samples that: 1) have the model predictions matching the training label, i.e.,

$\tilde{\mathbf{y}} = \arg\max_{\mathbf{y}} f_\theta^{(\mathbf{y})}(\mathbf{x})$; and 2) $f_\theta^{(\tilde{\mathbf{y}})}(\mathbf{x}) > 0.9$. If less than 10% of the training images of any of the classes are selected based on these conditions, then images that do not meet the second condition are added until we have 10% of the training images of that class. Kong et al. (2019) proposed an SSL method that, in every epoch t, selects a proportion $R(t)$ of the training samples with smallest losses for each class. DivideMix (Li et al., 2020a) introduced a sample selection approach that is based on an unsupervised classification using a 2-component Gaussian mixture model to represent the loss distribution. DivideMix's sample selection works in the same way as the 2-component Beta mixture model (BMM) (Arazo et al., 2019) in (4.24).

Most methods above need a warm-up stage, where the model is trained for a few epochs on the noisy-label training, so it can fit the clean-label samples without memorizing the noisy-label samples. An important question remains to be answered about this early-learning stage, which is why can a model trained on noisy-label data identify noisy-label samples based on prediction confidence? Zheng et al. (2020) provide a theoretical result that proves that such models indeed have low confidence on noisy-label data. They also propose an algorithm that finds noisy-label samples by thresholding the ratio $\mathsf{LR}(\theta, \mathbf{x}, \tilde{\mathbf{y}})$ between the model's prediction of the training label $f_\theta^{(\tilde{\mathbf{y}})}(\mathbf{x})$ and the model's maximum prediction $f_\theta^{(\mathbf{m})}(\mathbf{x})$, where $\mathbf{m} = \mathsf{OneHot}(f_\theta(\mathbf{x}))$. If $\mathsf{LR}(\theta, \mathbf{x}, \tilde{\mathbf{y}}) < \delta$, the sample label is flipped from $\tilde{\mathbf{y}}$ to $\mathbf{m}$.

The feature space present in intermediate model layers has also been used in sample selection. For instance, Ortego et al. (2021) added a projection model $g_\phi : \mathcal{V} \to \mathcal{Z}$ on top of the model backbone $f_{\hat{\theta}} : \mathcal{X} \to \mathcal{V}$, which is trained using the following sample-wise contrastive learning loss:

$$\ell(\mathbf{x}_i, \tilde{\mathbf{y}}_i) = \frac{1}{|\mathcal{D}_{\tilde{\mathbf{y}}_i}|} \sum_{(\mathbf{x}_j, \tilde{\mathbf{y}}_j) \in \mathcal{D}} \delta(i \neq j) \delta(\tilde{\mathbf{y}}_i = \tilde{\mathbf{y}}_j) \mathbf{P}_{i,j}, \qquad (4.65)$$

where

$$\mathbf{P}_{i,j} = -\log \frac{\exp(\mathbf{z}_i^\top \mathbf{z}_j / \tau)}{\sum_{(\mathbf{x}_k, \tilde{\mathbf{y}}_k) \in \mathcal{D}} \delta(k \neq i) \exp(\mathbf{z}_i^\top \mathbf{z}_k / \tau)}. \qquad (4.66)$$

$\mathcal{D}_{\tilde{\mathbf{y}}_i} \subset \mathcal{D}$ represents the training subset of the samples from class $\tilde{\mathbf{y}}_i$, $\mathbf{z}_i = g_\phi(f_{\hat{\theta}}(\mathbf{x}_i))$, $\mathbf{P}_{i,j}$ denotes the j-th component of the τ scaled normalized softmax distribution of the dot product of the representations from the samples i and j represented by $\mathbf{z}_i^\top \mathbf{z}_j$, and $\delta()$ is the indicator function. The proposed Multi-Objective Interpolation Training (MOIT) (Ortego et al., 2021) relies on three stages, namely: 1) regularization to prevent overfitting, 2) semi-supervised learning based on sample selection, and 3) model refinement. The sample selection process consists of the small-loss criterion using a K nearest neighbor classifier from the pseudo-labeled samples. The set of pseudo-clean samples is formed by:

$$\mathcal{D}_c = \{(\mathbf{x}, \tilde{\mathbf{y}}) | (\mathbf{x}, \tilde{\mathbf{y}}) \in \mathcal{D}, d(\mathbf{x}, \tilde{\mathbf{y}}) < \gamma\}, \qquad (4.67)$$

where

$$d(\mathbf{x}, \tilde{\mathbf{y}}) = -\tilde{\mathbf{y}}^\top \log \hat{\mathbf{p}}, \tag{4.68}$$

with $\hat{\mathbf{p}} \in \Delta^{|\mathcal{Y}|-1}$ representing the probability of finding samples of each of the $|\mathcal{Y}|$ classes withing the K nearest neighbors of $\mathbf{x}$ in the space $\mathcal{Z}$ produced by the projector $g_\phi(f_{\hat{\theta}}(\mathbf{x}))$. The Sample Selection and Relabeling (SSR) approach (Feng et al., 2021) follows a similar sample selection idea, where samples are classified as clean only if their K nearest neighbor classifier prediction matches with the training label.

A similar feature-based selection process, referred to as probabilistic and cumulative Local Outlier Factor algorithm (pcLOF), was proposed to filter out open-set samples in the loss re-weighting method in (Wang et al., 2018). The pcLOF score represents the probability that a sample is an outlier, which is defined as

$$\text{pcLOF}(\mathbf{x}) = g \left(\sum_{t=1}^{T} \text{LOF}^{(t)}(\mathbf{x}) \right), \tag{4.69}$$

where t denotes the training iteration, $g(.)$ represents a local Gaussian statistics transformation to scale the cumulative LOF score into $[0, 1]$,

$$\text{LOF}(\mathbf{x}) = \frac{\sum_{\mathbf{x}_j \in \mathcal{N}_k(\mathbf{x})} \frac{d(\mathbf{x}_j)}{d(\mathbf{x})}}{|\mathcal{N}_k(\mathbf{x})|}, \tag{4.70}$$

with $\mathcal{N}_k(\mathbf{x})$ being the set of k nearest neighbors of $\mathbf{x}$, and

$$d(\mathbf{x}) = \left(\frac{\sum_{\mathbf{x}_j \in \mathcal{N}_k(\mathbf{x})} \text{reach}_k(\mathbf{x}, \mathbf{x}_j)}{|\mathcal{N}_k(\mathbf{x})|} \right)^{-1} \tag{4.71}$$

representing the local reachability density of $\mathbf{x}$. In (4.71), $\text{reach}_k(\mathbf{x}, \mathbf{x}_j)$ returns the distance between $\mathbf{x}$ and $\mathbf{x}_j$, if they are far away from each other, but if they are close to each other, $\text{reach}(.)$ returns the distance of $\mathbf{x}_j$ to its k-th nearest neighbor.

The selection of samples belonging to closed-set and open-set samples, with a further differentiation of closed set samples into clean or noisy-label samples was proposed in (Albert et al., 2022), following a similar idea presented in the data cleaning method of (Sachdeva et al., 2021). Albert et al. (2022) proposed the Softening of Out-of-distribution Samples (DSOS) that is based on the collision entropy score, defined by:

$$s_{DSOS}(\mathbf{x}, \tilde{\mathbf{y}}) = \sum_{c=1}^{|\mathcal{Y}|} -\log\left(\mathbf{y}_{int}(c)\right)^2, \tag{4.72}$$

where $\mathbf{y}_{int}(c) = \frac{\tilde{\mathbf{y}}(c) + f_\theta^{(c)}(\mathbf{x})}{2}$ is the intermediate label, $\tilde{\mathbf{y}}(c)$ denotes the cth component of the label vector, and $f_\theta^{(c)}(\mathbf{x})$ represents the cth model output. The collision entropy score in (4.72) has the property that when the model is certain about an output that is different from the training label, then $\mathbf{y}_{int}$ will be 0 in all dimensions, except for the training label and model prediction dimensions, which will be 0.5, leading to $s_{DSOS}(\mathbf{x}, \tilde{\mathbf{y}}) = -\log(0.5)$. Such a score suggests that $s_{DSOS}(\mathbf{x}, \tilde{\mathbf{y}}) < -\log(0.5)$ represents closed-set clean-label sample. On the other hand, samples with $s_{DSOS}(\mathbf{x}, \tilde{\mathbf{y}}) > -\log(0.5)$ show a bimodal distribution that can be fit by a Beta mixture model, with the smaller score component containing closed-set noisy-label samples, and the larger score component containing open-set samples. The DSOS optimization roughly follows (4.63), with $\mathcal{D}_c$ containing the closed-set samples and $\mathcal{D}_n$ having the open-set samples.

A promising sample selection technique, referred to as filtering noisy instances via their eigenvectors (FINE) (Kim et al., 2021), relies on the eigen-decomposition of the gram matrix of each class $\mathbf{c} \in \mathcal{Y}$, with

$$\mathbf{U_c} \Lambda_\mathbf{c} \mathbf{U_c}^{-1} = \Sigma_\mathbf{c}, \tag{4.73}$$

where $\Sigma_\mathbf{c} = \sum_{(\mathbf{x}, \tilde{\mathbf{y}}) \in \mathcal{D}} \delta(\tilde{\mathbf{y}} = \mathbf{c}) f_{\hat{\theta}}(\mathbf{x}) f_{\hat{\theta}}(\mathbf{x})^\top$ denotes the gram matrix (with $f_{\hat{\theta}} : \mathcal{X} \to \mathcal{Z}$ producing an image representation $\mathbf{z} \in \mathcal{Z}$, and $\delta(.)$ representing the indicator function), and $\mathbf{U_c}$, $\Lambda_\mathbf{c}$ denote the matrices with eigenvectors and eigenvalues. The FINE score for each sample is computed with

$$\text{FINE}(\mathbf{x}, \tilde{\mathbf{y}}) = \langle \mathbf{u}_{\tilde{\mathbf{y}}}^{(1)}, f_{\hat{\theta}}(\mathbf{x}) \rangle^2, \tag{4.74}$$

where $\mathbf{u}_{\tilde{\mathbf{y}}}^{(1)}$ represents the eigenvector associated with the largest eigenvalue from the class $\tilde{\mathbf{y}}$. The class-wise scores are computed using a 2-component Gaussian mixture model, where the component with smallest mean denotes the clean-label component. Then, samples whose probability of belonging to the clean-label component is larger than a threshold τ are classified as clean. The selected samples can then be used in semi-supervised learning approaches or robust loss functions.

Sample selection based on the predictions from teacher and student models has been proposed in (Kaiser et al., 2022). This approach adopts a teacher-student architecture (Gou et al., 2021), where the teacher model is trained by minimizing a classification loss using the labels from the training set, while the student model is trained to reproduce the logits produced by the teacher for each training sample. Assuming the teacher model is denoted by $f_{\theta(t)} : \mathcal{X} \to \Delta^{|\mathcal{Y}|-1}$ and the student model is represented by $f_{\theta(s)} : \mathcal{X} \to \Delta^{|\mathcal{Y}|-1}$, their aggregate classification is denoted by

$$p(Y = \mathbf{y}|X = \mathbf{x}) = \frac{f_{\theta(t)}^{(\mathbf{y})}(\mathbf{x}) \times f_{\theta(s)}^{(\mathbf{y})}(\mathbf{x})}{\sum_{\hat{\mathbf{y}} \in \mathcal{Y}} f_{\theta(t)}^{(\hat{\mathbf{y}})}(\mathbf{x}) \times f_{\theta(s)}^{(\hat{\mathbf{y}})}(\mathbf{x})}, \tag{4.75}$$

where $f_{\theta(t)}^{(\mathbf{y})}(\mathbf{x})$ represents the probability prediction for class $\mathbf{y}$ from the teacher model (similarly for the student model $f_{\theta(s)}^{(\mathbf{y})}(\mathbf{x})$). Then the set of pseudo-clean images are the ones in the set $\{(\mathbf{x}, \tilde{\mathbf{y}})|(\mathbf{x}, \tilde{\mathbf{y}}) \in \mathcal{D}, p(Y = \tilde{\mathbf{y}}|X = \mathbf{x}) > \tau\}$, while the pseudo-noisy images are the ones in $\{(\mathbf{x}, \tilde{\mathbf{y}})|(\mathbf{x}, \tilde{\mathbf{y}}) \in \mathcal{D}, p(Y = \tilde{\mathbf{y}}|X = \mathbf{x}) \leq \tau\}$, where the threshold τ is estimated with the Otsu's algorithm (Otsu, 1979).

Another way of selecting noisy-label samples is based on the use of uncertainty measures (Köhler et al., 2019), such as variation-ratio or standard deviation of the predictions. These measures, computed from deep ensembles (Lakshminarayanan et al., 2017) or Monte-Carlo dropout (Gal et al., 2016), have shown to be relatively effective, where the more uncertain samples are assumed to have incorrect labels, and new pseudo-labels are applied to them. The use of peer loss has also been considered in (Cheng et al., 2020a) for the problem of sample selection, where samples that have the peer loss score in (4.6) below a certain threshold are selected for training.

A critical point present in all methods above is how to determine the threshold τ for the clean-label criterion in (4.64). A relatively common way is to set τ based on the pre-defined proportion $R(t)$ of training samples to be selected as noisy at each training epoch t. For instance, Han et al. (2018c) pre-define a curriculum, where at the first training iterations, $R(t) \approx 1$, which means that most of the training samples are classified as clean-label. This is sensible since the model has not started the overfitting process at this early training stage. As training progresses, $R(t)$ is reduced using a pre-defined function, to prevent the model to overfit the noisy-label training samples. More specifically, Co-teaching (Han et al., 2018c) introduced the following schedule:

$$R(t) = 1 - \tau \times \min(1, (t/t_k)^\alpha), \qquad (4.76)$$

where τ, α, t_k are hyper-parameters. A more principled way of designing $R(t)$ has been proposed in (Yao et al., 2020a), as the following bi-level algorithm:

$$
\begin{aligned}
R^* &= \arg\min_{R \in \mathcal{F}} \mathcal{L}_{val}(\theta^*, R, \mathcal{D}_{val}) \\
\text{s.t. } \theta^* &= \arg\min_{\theta} \mathcal{L}(\theta, R, \mathcal{D}),
\end{aligned}
\qquad (4.77)
$$

where $\mathcal{D}_{val}$ represents a clean-label validation set, $\mathcal{D}$ is the usual noisy-label training set, $\mathcal{L}_{val}$ and $\mathcal{L}$ denote validation and training loss functions, and $\mathcal{F}$ is a search space for R. This search space represents the prior for $R(t)$, explained above, where $R(t)$ should be large at the beginning of the training and it should reduce as training progresses. Yao et al. (2020a) suggested the use of K basis functions to build $\mathcal{F}$, each one following the prior about $R(t)$. Hence, the optimization for $R(t)$ comprises an estimation of the basis functions weights and parameters. Results show that the $R(t)$ learned is more effective than the one manually defined (Han et al., 2018c). In (Cheng et al., 2020a) the threshold is automatically defined at each training epoch with

$$\tau = \frac{1}{|\mathcal{Y}|} \sum_{\hat{\mathbf{y}} \in \mathcal{Y}} \ell_{peer}(\hat{\mathbf{y}}, f_\theta(\mathbf{x})), \qquad (4.78)$$

where $\ell_{peer}(.)$ is as defined in (4.6).

Sample selection has been a fertile research topic in noisy-label learning. The two main points of study in sample selection are the clean-label sample selection criteria and the threshold. Many techniques have been proposed for the selection criteria, ranging from small-loss trick approaches, to graph-based methods. The research into

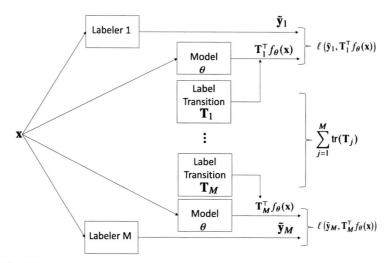

FIGURE 4.20 Multi-rater learning.

The multi-rater learning technique takes the annotation from M labelers for every data point, denoted by $(\mathbf{x}, \{\tilde{y}_j\}_{j=1}^{M}) \in \mathcal{D}$, to learn labeler-specific transition models, represented by $\{\mathbf{T}_j\}_{j=1}^{M}$, and the clean-label model predictor $f_\theta(\mathbf{x})$. The learning of the label transition models is usually regularized by some smoothing function, such as the minimization of the trace of the transition matrices.

the threshold has received comparatively less attention, where the focus is whether it should be manually defined (Han et al., 2018c), or automatically optimized (Yao et al., 2020a). Even though we do not have a standard sample selection method, this technique is ubiquitously present in noisy-label learning approaches, which suggests that this technique is an important stage in noisy-label learning methods.

4.3.4 Multi-rater learning

As presented in Section 3.3, there have been papers (Liu, 2022; Nguyen et al., 2023) that show that the identifiability of the learning from noisy-label problem requires a minimum number of labels per training sample. The experimental setup that relies on a certain number of labels per training sample is generally referred to as multi-rater learning (Sudre et al., 2019; Ji et al., 2021; Schaekermann et al., 2019; Becker et al., 2019; Tanno et al., 2019), and it has been usually studied from the perspective of uncertainty learning instead of noisy-label learning. Multi-rater learning tries to estimate the degree of uncertainty in the predictions of the model and the annotators and use this information to guide the learning process. Given the direct connection between multi-rater learning and noisy-label learning, we present some papers that provide links between the two problems.

In multi-rater learning, such as the one depicted in Fig. 4.20, the training set is defined as $\mathcal{D} = \{(\mathbf{x}_i, \{\tilde{\mathbf{y}}_{i,j}\}_{j=1}^{M})\}_{i=1}^{|\mathcal{D}|}$, with each image $\mathbf{x}_i$ having multiple labels

$\{\tilde{\mathbf{y}}_{i,j}\}_{j=1}^{M}$. The first methods designed to handle multi-rater learning explored two strategies, namely (Tanno et al., 2019): 1) two-stage, and 2) simultaneous. The first step in two-stage approaches (Smyth et al., 1994; Warfield et al., 2004; Whitehill et al., 2009; Welinder et al., 2010; Rodrigues et al., 2013) use the observed noisy labels to estimate the latent variables representing the true label and annotator skills. The second step consists of training a model using the estimated true labels. These methods are criticized for a few reasons, such as: 1) the input data is not explored when estimating the true label, 2) the trained models tend to underestimate uncertainty (Jungo et al., 2018; Jensen et al., 2019), and 3) the two-stage training is unlikely to provide an optimal optimization. On the other hand, simultaneous approaches (Raykar et al., 2009, 2010; Branson et al., 2017; Van Horn et al., 2018; Khetan et al., 2017) merge the two stages using expectation-maximization (EM) like algorithms and, except for (Khetan et al., 2017), they require a large number of labels per example, which constrains their application. Kaster et al. (2011) show an experimental evaluation of previously proposed multi-rater models using approximate variational techniques for inference.

The general learning of current multi-rater models can be summarized by the formulation by Tanno et al. (2019), where the multi-rater annotation probability is computed with

$$p\left(\{\tilde{\mathbf{y}}_j\}_{j=1}^{M}|\mathbf{x}\right) = \prod_{j=1}^{M}\sum_{\mathbf{y}\in\mathcal{Y}}p(\tilde{\mathbf{y}}_j|\mathbf{y},\mathbf{x})p(\mathbf{y}|\mathbf{x}), \qquad (4.79)$$

where $p(\mathbf{y}|\mathbf{x})$ is the true label distribution and $p(\tilde{\mathbf{y}}_j|\mathbf{y},\mathbf{x})$ is the transition probability from the true label to the jth noisy annotation. In (Tanno et al., 2019), the proposed optimization estimates the transition matrices and the model parameters, as in

$$\theta^*, \{\mathbf{T}_j^*\}_{j=1}^{M} = \arg\min_{\theta,\{\mathbf{T}_j\}_{j=1}^{M}} \frac{1}{|\mathcal{D}|} \sum_{\left(\mathbf{x},\{\tilde{\mathbf{y}}_j\}_{j=1}^{M}\right)\in\mathcal{D}} \ell\left(\tilde{\mathbf{y}}_j, \mathbf{T}_j^{\top}f_\theta(\mathbf{x})\right) + \lambda\sum_{j=1}^{M}\mathrm{tr}(\mathbf{T}_j),$$

$$(4.80)$$

where $\mathbf{T}_j$ denotes the label transition matrix for annotator $j \in \{1, ..., M\}$, and $\mathrm{tr}(\mathbf{T}_j)$ denotes the trace of matrix $\mathbf{T}_j$. This minimization of the trace of the label transition matrix in (4.80) encourages the annotators to be maximally unreliable to induce a maximal amount of confusion which explains the noisy labels (Tanno et al., 2019). We show an example of multi-rater noisy-label learning in Fig. 4.21.

The multi-rater optimization in (4.80) does not attempt to characterize the difficulty of labeling the image. For example, images where multi-rater labels show general consensus should be considered easy cases, while images where labels disagree should be considered hard cases (Paletz et al., 2016; Schaekermann et al., 2019). This fact is explored by Yu et al. (2020a) with multiple classification branches, each one representing predictions under three different sensitivity settings (high sen-

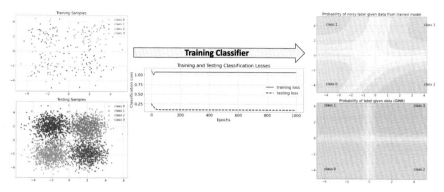

FIGURE 4.21 Classifier trained with multi-rater learning.

We use the classification problem described in Fig. 4.3 to train the classifier for multi-rater learning from (4.80) for 1000 epochs. The problem is modified to have three labelers, one with noise rate 0.25, another with rate 0.15, and the other rate 0.4.

sitivity, high specificity, and in-between the two settings). These three branches share a common feature extractor, referred to as $f_\theta : \mathcal{X} \to \mathcal{Z}$, but each branch has a separate output, with the high sensitivity branch denoted by $f_{\theta_{sn}} : \mathcal{Z} \to \Delta^{|\mathcal{Y}|-1}$, the high specificity branch represented by $f_{\theta_{sp}} : \mathcal{Z} \to \Delta^{|\mathcal{Y}|-1}$, and the in-between branch $f_{\theta_{fs}} : \mathcal{Z} \to \Delta^{|\mathcal{Y}|-1}$. The model is optimized with

$$\theta^*, \theta^*_{sn}, \theta^*_{sp}, \theta^*_{fs} = \arg \min_{\theta, \theta_{sn}, \theta_{sp}, \theta_{fs}}$$

$$\sum_{\left(\mathbf{x}, \{\tilde{\mathbf{y}}_j\}_{j=1}^M\right) \in \mathcal{D}_{sp}} \ell\left(\tilde{\mathbf{y}}_j, f_{\theta_{sp}}\left(f_\theta(\mathbf{x})\right)\right) + \ell_{con}\left(f_{\theta_{sp}}\left(f_\theta(\mathbf{x})\right), f_{\theta_{sn}}\left(f_\theta(\mathbf{x})\right), a\right) +$$

$$\sum_{\left(\mathbf{x}, \{\tilde{\mathbf{y}}_j\}_{j=1}^M\right) \in \mathcal{D}_{sn}} \ell\left(\tilde{\mathbf{y}}_j, f_{\theta_{sn}}\left(f_\theta(\mathbf{x})\right)\right) + \ell_{con}\left(f_{\theta_{sp}}\left(f_\theta(\mathbf{x})\right), f_{\theta_{sn}}\left(f_\theta(\mathbf{x})\right), a\right) +$$

$$\sum_{\left(\mathbf{x}, \{\tilde{\mathbf{y}}_j\}_{j=1}^M\right) \in \mathcal{D}} \ell_{fs}\left(\mathbb{E}_{\mathbf{w}}\left[\{\tilde{\mathbf{y}}_j\}_{j=1}^M\right], f_{\theta_{fs}}\left(f_\theta(\mathbf{x})\right), f_{\theta_{sp}}\left(f_\theta(\mathbf{x})\right), f_{\theta_{sn}}\left(f_\theta(\mathbf{x})\right)\right),$$

$$(4.81)$$

where $\mathcal{D}_{sp}, \mathcal{D}_{sn}$ denote the high specificity dataset (with twice more positive than negative labels) and high sensitivity dataset (with twice more negative than positive labels), respectively, $\ell(.)$ represents the cross-entropy loss,

$$\ell_{con}(\tilde{\mathbf{y}}_{sp}, \tilde{\mathbf{y}}_{se}, a) = \frac{a}{2}\|\tilde{\mathbf{y}}_{sp} - \tilde{\mathbf{y}}_{se}\|_2^2 + \frac{1-a}{2}\left(\max\left(0, 1 - \|\tilde{\mathbf{y}}_{sp} - \tilde{\mathbf{y}}_{se}\|\right)\right)^2 \quad (4.82)$$

is the consensus loss between the sensitivity and specificity branches denoted by $\tilde{\mathbf{y}}_{sp} = f_{\theta_{sp}}(f_\theta(\mathbf{x}))$ and $\tilde{\mathbf{y}}_{sn} = f_{\theta_{sn}}(f_\theta(\mathbf{x}))$, respectively,

$$\ell_{fs}(\hat{\mathbf{y}}, \tilde{\mathbf{y}}_{fs}, \tilde{\mathbf{y}}_{sp}, \tilde{\mathbf{y}}_{sn}) = u \times \mathsf{KL}(\hat{\mathbf{y}} \| \tilde{\mathbf{y}}_{fs}) \tag{4.83}$$

denotes the fusion loss weighted by the uncertainty $u = 0.5 \left(1 - \frac{\tilde{\mathbf{y}}_{sp}^\top \tilde{\mathbf{y}}_{sn}}{\|\tilde{\mathbf{y}}_{sp}\| \|\tilde{\mathbf{y}}_{sn}\|}\right)$, with $\hat{\mathbf{y}} = \mathbb{E}_{\mathbf{w}}\left[\{\tilde{\mathbf{y}}_j\}_{j=1}^M\right]$ calculating the average label weighted by $\mathbf{w} = \{\mathbf{w}_j\}_{j=1}^M$ that is the weight of the jth rater, determined by the rating accuracy against the ground-truth label.

When discussing uncertainty, it is important to differentiate between aleatoric and epistemic uncertainties (Der Kiureghian and Ditlevsen, 2009). The noise found in the data, such as the label noise, defines the aleatoric uncertainty, while the epistemic uncertainty is related to the noise in the estimation of the model parameters. Hu et al. (2019a) noticed that epistemic uncertainty is hard to estimate because we cannot access the groundtruth model to measure it. However, aleatoric uncertainty can be estimated from a multi-rater label with the variance $\mathbb{V}_{p(\mathcal{D})}[\tilde{\mathbf{y}}] = \frac{1}{M} \sum_{j=1}^M (\tilde{\mathbf{y}}_j - \bar{\mathbf{y}})^2$, where $\bar{\mathbf{y}} = \frac{1}{M} \sum_{j=1}^M \tilde{\mathbf{y}}_j$. The method in (Hu et al., 2019a) extends the Probabilistic U-Net (Kohl et al., 2018) by exploring multi-rater variability to account for aleatoric uncertainty and to estimate epistemic uncertainty. To explain the approach in (Hu et al., 2019a) in more detail, we first need to explain the posterior predictive distribution given by $p(Y|X, \mathcal{D}) = \int_\theta p(Y|X, \theta) p(\theta|\mathcal{D}) d\theta$, where $p(Y|X, \theta)$ denotes a prediction model parameterized by θ and $p(\theta|\mathcal{D})$ represents an intractable posterior distribution that is approximated by a tractable $q_\lambda(\theta)$, which is estimated with

$$\min_\lambda \mathsf{KL}\left(q_\lambda(\theta) \| p(\theta|\mathcal{D})\right) = \max_\lambda \mathbb{E}_{q_\lambda(\theta)}\left[\log \prod_{(\mathbf{x},\tilde{\mathbf{y}}) \in \mathcal{D}} p(\tilde{\mathbf{y}}|\mathbf{x}, \theta)\right] \\ - \mathsf{KL}\left(q_\lambda(\theta) \| p(\theta)\right), \tag{4.84}$$

where $p(\theta)$ is a prior on θ. The predictive uncertainty is the variance of the posterior predictive distribution, defined by the following decomposition

$$\underbrace{\mathbb{V}_{p(Y|X)}[\tilde{\mathbf{y}}]}_{\text{predictive uncertainty}} = \underbrace{\mathbb{E}_{q_\lambda(\theta)}\left[\mathbb{V}_{p(Y|X,\theta)}[\tilde{\mathbf{y}}]\right]}_{\text{aleatoric uncertainty}} + \underbrace{\mathbb{V}_{q_\lambda(\theta)}\left[\mathbb{E}_{p(Y|X,\theta)}[\tilde{\mathbf{y}}]\right]}_{\text{epistemic uncertainty}}. \tag{4.85}$$

In (4.85), the aleatoric uncertainty measures the average of the output variance, while the epistemic uncertainty measures fluctuations in the mean prediction. Putting all together, the model trained in (Hu et al., 2019a) extends the probabilistic U-net (Kohl et al., 2018) by adding a mechanism to measure epistemic uncertainty with the following loss function

$$\ell_{vd}(\lambda, \mathcal{D}) = -\frac{1}{|\mathcal{D}|} \sum_{(\mathbf{x}_i, \tilde{\mathbf{y}}_i) \in \mathcal{D}} \mathbb{E}_{q_\lambda(\theta) q_\lambda(Z|X=\mathbf{x}_i, Y=\tilde{\mathbf{y}}_i)} \left[\log p_\lambda(\tilde{\mathbf{y}}_i | \mathbf{x}_i, \mathbf{z}, \theta) \right]$$
$$+ \frac{\beta}{|\mathcal{D}|} \sum_{(\mathbf{x}_i, \tilde{\mathbf{y}}_i) \in \mathcal{D}} \mathrm{KL}\left(q_\lambda(\mathbf{z}|\mathbf{x}_i, \tilde{\mathbf{y}}_i) \| p_\lambda(\mathbf{z}\|\mathbf{x}_i) \right) + \frac{1}{|\mathcal{D}|} \mathrm{KL}\left(q_\lambda(\theta) \| p(\theta)) \right),$$

$$(4.86)$$

where $\mathbf{z} \in \mathcal{Z}$. In (4.86), the model uncertainty is minimized when $q_\lambda(\theta)$ approximates a delta peak on the maximum likelihood model parameters. The aleatoric uncertainty $\mathbf{p}_m = \mathbb{E}_{q_\lambda(\theta)} \left[\mathbb{V}_{p(Y|X,\theta)} [\tilde{\mathbf{y}}] \right]$ is then trained to approximate the multi-grader variability $\mathbf{p}_g = \mathbb{V}_{p(\mathcal{D})}[\tilde{\mathbf{y}}]$ with

$$\ell_{al} = -\frac{\gamma}{|\mathcal{D}|} \sum_{(\mathbf{x}_i, \tilde{\mathbf{y}}_i) \in \mathcal{D}} \left[\mathbf{p}_g \log \mathbf{p}_m + (1 - \mathbf{p}_g) \log(1 - \mathbf{p}_m) \right]. \quad (4.87)$$

A relatively different approach from the ones above is the Classifier Refinement Of croWD-sourced LABels (CROWDLAB) (Goh et al., 2022) that takes a trained classifier and estimates a consensus label (with a confidence score) per training sample, and a rating for each annotator to assess the correctness of their labels. CROWDLAB relies on a weighted ensemble of classifier predictions, where weights are estimated based on the trustworthiness of each annotator relative to the given classifier. After training a model $f_\theta : \mathcal{X} \to \Delta^{|\mathcal{Y}|-1}$ using consensus labels derived from majority voting using $\mathcal{D} = \{(\mathbf{x}_i, \{\tilde{\mathbf{y}}_{i,j}\}_{j=1}^M)\}_{i=1}^{|\mathcal{D}|}$, they first score the consensus label quality with:

$$f_{\theta_{CR}}^{(\hat{\mathbf{y}})}(\mathbf{x}) = \frac{w \times f_\theta^{(\hat{\mathbf{y}})}(\mathbf{x}) + \sum_{j=1}^M w_j \times f_{\theta_j}^{(\hat{\mathbf{y}})}(\mathbf{x})}{w + \sum_{j=1}^M w_j}, \quad (4.88)$$

where $\hat{\mathbf{y}}$ denotes the consensus label, $f_\theta^{(\hat{\mathbf{y}})}(\mathbf{x})$ represents the trained model prediction for class $\hat{\mathbf{y}}$,

$$f_{\theta_j}^{(\hat{\mathbf{y}})}(\mathbf{x}) = \begin{cases} P, & \text{if } \tilde{\mathbf{y}}_j = \hat{\mathbf{y}} \\ \frac{1-P}{|\mathcal{Y}|-1}, & \text{otherwise} \end{cases} \quad (4.89)$$

is the annotator-specific model prediction, with $P = \frac{1}{|\mathcal{D}|} \sum_{i=1}^{|\mathcal{D}|} \frac{1}{M} \sum_{j=1}^M \delta(\tilde{\mathbf{y}}_{i,j} = \hat{\mathbf{y}}_i)$ ($\delta(.)$ is the indicator function), and the trustworthiness weights w and $\{w_j\}_{j=1}^M$ represent the ensemble weights of the model and annotators, respectively, that are in general computed as 1 minus the estimated relative error of the trained model and annotator-specific models (Goh et al., 2022). Furthermore, CROWDLAB also ranks the annotators using the score $\{a_j\}_{j=1}^M$, with $a_j \in [0, 1]$ computed with the weighted average of the label quality score and the annotator agreement with consensus la-

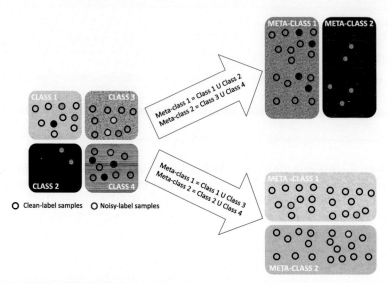

FIGURE 4.22 Prior knowledge with meta classes.

In the exploration of prior knowledge with meta classes, classes are merged to form new meta classes (e.g., the initial four classes are merged into two sets of two meta classes), which are guaranteed to have fewer mistakes than the original problem, as seen in this example (the original 4-class problem has 12 mislabeled samples, while the top 2-meta-class problem has nine mistakes, and the bottom 2-meta-class problem has three mistakes).

bels (Goh et al., 2022). Armed with the consensus labels, their confidence score, and the annotator ratings, it is then possible to eliminate the labels produced by low-ranked annotators and request the re-labeling of low-confidence labels.

Multi-rater learning is a fertile and relatively unexplored research topic, with applications in noisy-label learning and uncertainty estimation. The main issue with these approaches is the cost associated with the collection of multiple labels per image. Techniques that can generate new labels per image from its estimated label distribution (Nguyen et al., 2023) can mitigate this labeling cost problem if they can reliably substitute human labeling. The next years should witness an increasing investigation of multi-rater learning for noisy-label learning.

4.3.5 Prior knowledge

Prior information can be helpful when handling noisy-label learning, particularly when the information can constrain the optimization process. An interesting prior information about noisy-label learning is studied in (Seo et al., 2019) that explores the idea that by transforming the original problem containing $|\mathcal{Y}|$ classes into another problem where subsets of these classes are merged to form $|C| < |\mathcal{Y}|$ meta-classes, we reduce the noise rate in the training set (see Fig. 4.22). Consider that the original noise rate is provided by

$$\eta(\mathcal{D}) = \frac{1}{|\mathcal{D}|} \sum_{(\mathbf{x},\tilde{\mathbf{y}})\in\mathcal{D}} \delta(\mathbf{y} \neq \tilde{\mathbf{y}}), \tag{4.90}$$

where $\mathbf{y}$ is the hidden true label of $\mathbf{x}$, and $\delta(.)$ is the indicator function. Also assume that the new set of meta classes C^m merged a few of the classes from $\mathcal{D}$ to form a new training set $\mathcal{D}^m$, so the new noise rate is

$$\eta(\mathcal{D}^m) = \frac{1}{|\mathcal{D}^m|} \sum_{(\mathbf{x},\tilde{\mathbf{c}})\in\mathcal{D}^m} \delta(\mathbf{c}^m \neq \tilde{\mathbf{c}}^m), \tag{4.91}$$

where $\mathbf{c}_i^m$ and $\tilde{\mathbf{c}}_i^m$ are the hidden true and visible noisy meta class for $\mathbf{x}_i$ in $\mathcal{D}^m$. It is trivial to show that $\eta(\mathcal{D}^m) < \eta(\mathcal{D})$ (Seo et al., 2019). For instance, let us say that two samples $\mathbf{x}_i$ and $\mathbf{x}_j$ belong to the same class (i.e., $\mathbf{y}_i = \mathbf{y}_j$), but the label for $\mathbf{x}_j$ has been corrupted, which means that $\tilde{\mathbf{y}}_i \neq \tilde{\mathbf{y}}_j$. By merging $\tilde{\mathbf{y}}_i$ and $\tilde{\mathbf{y}}_j$ into the same meta class, we have $\tilde{\mathbf{c}}_i^m = \tilde{\mathbf{c}}_j^m$, i.e., the two samples share the same clean label again. Seo et al. (2019) propose the implementation of $\{\mathcal{D}^m\}_{m=1}^M$ meta-class sets and the training of M separate classifiers $\{f_{\theta^m} : \mathcal{X} \to C^m\}_{m=1}^M$ for those training sets. Inference is performed with

$$p(\mathbf{y}|\mathbf{x}) = \frac{\prod_{m=1}^M f_{\theta^m}^{\mathrm{meta}(\mathbf{y},m)}(\mathbf{x})}{\sum_{\hat{\mathbf{y}}\in\mathcal{Y}} \prod_{m=1}^M f_{\theta^m}^{\mathrm{meta}(\hat{\mathbf{y}},m)}(\mathbf{x})}, \tag{4.92}$$

where $\mathrm{meta}(\mathbf{y}, m)$ outputs the meta class from the mth set of meta classes that contains the label $\mathbf{y}$. The meta classes should be formed by merging the original classes that have common properties, which can be achieved by applying the k-means clustering algorithm. The prior information above is always true, but to properly explore this idea, one may need to have a large number of meta-class sets, with the inconvenience of needing to train one classifier per meta-class set.

A widely adopted noisy-label learning technique is the one that aims to estimate the noise transition matrix from clean-label to noisy-label learning, which will be explained in more detail in Section 4.5.1. The reliability of this estimation process requires clean-label samples or a large training set. An alternative based on a prior knowledge provided by humans is proposed in (Han et al., 2018b), where the idea is to constrain the optimization with a transition matrix mask that eliminates the possibility of estimating invalid class transition probabilities (e.g., images of beach cannot be confused with images of mountain), as shown in Fig. 4.23. In general, the optimization involving a transition matrix is formulated by

$$\theta^*, \mathbf{T} = \arg\min_{\theta,\mathbf{T}} \frac{1}{|\mathcal{D}|} \sum_{(\mathbf{x},\tilde{\mathbf{y}})\in\mathcal{D}} \ell(\tilde{\mathbf{y}}, \mathbf{T}^\top f_\theta(\mathbf{x}))$$

$$\text{s.t. } \mathbf{T} \in [0, 1]^{|\mathcal{Y}|\times|\mathcal{Y}|} \tag{4.93}$$

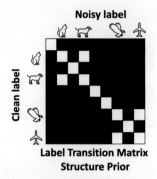

Noisy label

Clean label

**Label Transition Matrix
Structure Prior**

FIGURE 4.23 Prior knowledge with label transition matrix structure prior.

A prior on the possible label transitions can be provided by a prior with a binary label transition matrix, where 1 (white square) means a possible transition (e.g., label transition between dog and cat or between bird and plane), and 0 (black square) represents a prohibited transition (e.g., no label transition between dog and airplane).

where $\mathbf{T}$ represents the noisy-label transition matrix. In principle, this can be solved by adding an explicit structure constraint $s(\mathbf{T}) = \mathbf{S}_0$, with $s(.)$ extracting $\mathbf{T}$'s matrix structure $\mathbf{S}_0 \in \{0, 1\}^{|\mathcal{Y}| \times |\mathcal{Y}|}$. However, as pointed out in (Han et al., 2018b), such training strategy has a few issues, such as: 1) it is unclear which distance measure to use to compute the distance between the learned transition matrix $\mathbf{T}$ and the prior $\mathbf{S}_0$; and 2) the complexity of training (4.93) for large-scale problems using Lagrange multipliers. Han et al. (2018b) proposed the use of variational learning to maximize the following evidence lower bound (ELBO) that approximates the log-likelihood of the noisy data, as follows

$$\log p(\tilde{\mathbf{y}}|\mathbf{x}) \geq \mathbb{E}_{q(\mathbf{T})}\left[\log \sum_{\mathbf{y} \in \mathcal{Y}} p(\tilde{\mathbf{y}}|\mathbf{y}, \mathbf{T})p(\mathbf{y}|\mathbf{x}) - \log\left(q(\mathbf{S}_0)/p(\mathbf{S}_0)\right)\Big|_{\mathbf{S}_0 = s(\mathbf{T})}\right],$$
(4.94)

where $q(\mathbf{T})$ represents the variational distribution to approximate the posterior of the noise transition matrix $\mathbf{T}$, $q(\mathbf{S}_0) = q(\mathbf{T})\frac{d\mathbf{T}}{d\mathbf{S}_0}\Big|_{\mathbf{S}_0 = s(\mathbf{T})}$, and $p(\mathbf{S}_0)$ is the structure prior.

Another possible prior knowledge to explore in noisy-label learning is the fact that models with simpler hypothesis and smoother decision boundaries are less prone to overfit to the noisy-label samples, and consequently generalize better (Luo et al., 2019). The low dimensionality of the deep representation subspace of training samples is a way to represent such simpler hypothesis and smoother decision boundaries (Ma et al., 2018). The dimensionality can be measured with the Local Intrinsic Dimensionality (LID) of the underlying data subspace/submanifold (Houle, 2017). In practice, the LID of the deep representation $\mathbf{z}$ from a data point $\mathbf{x}$ can be estimated

Feature space with training samples

FIGURE 4.24 Prior knowledge with Local Intrinsic Dimensionality (LID).

The LID computed with $\widehat{\text{LID}}(\mathbf{z})$ from (4.95) is used to weight the re-labeling of training samples, as shown in (4.96), where high LID values suggest that the sample has been mislabeled, while low LID values indicate a clean label.

as follows (Levina and Bickel, 2004; Amsaleg et al., 2015):

$$\widehat{\text{LID}}(\mathbf{z}) = - \left(\frac{1}{K} \sum_{i=1}^{K} \log \frac{r_i(\mathbf{z})}{r_{\max}(\mathbf{z})} \right)^{-1} \tag{4.95}$$

where $r_i(\mathbf{z})$ represents the distance between $\mathbf{z}$ and its ith nearest neighbor, and $r_{\max}(\mathbf{z})$ is the maximum distance to all the K nearest neighbors from $\mathbf{z}$. In general, noisy-label learning has a LID compression in the early training stages, followed by a LID expansion in later training stages (Fig. 4.24 shows LID values for clean and noisy-label samples). On the contrary, when labels are clean, LID reduces continuously until the last training stages. Ma et al. (2018) proposed a training optimization with:

$$\theta_t^* = \arg\min_{\theta} \frac{1}{|\mathcal{D}|} \sum_{(\mathbf{x}, \tilde{\mathbf{y}}) \in \mathcal{D}} \ell \left(\alpha_t \times \tilde{\mathbf{y}} + (1 - \alpha_t) \times f_\theta(\mathbf{x}), f_\theta(\mathbf{x}) \right) \tag{4.96}$$

where t indexes the training epoch, and

$$\alpha_t = \exp\left(-(t/T) \frac{\widehat{\text{LID}}_t}{\min_{j=0}^{t-1} \widehat{\text{LID}}_j} \right), \tag{4.97}$$

with $\widehat{\text{LID}}_t = \frac{1}{|\mathcal{D}|} \sum_{i=1}^{|\mathcal{D}|} \widehat{\text{LID}}(\mathbf{z}_i)$ denotes the mean LID score at training epoch $t \in \{1, ..., T\}$. Hence, this optimization is a simulated annealing algorithm that finds a balance between LID and prediction performance. In particular, at the LID compression stage (early training epochs), $\alpha_t \to 1$ and training relies on the training labels. At the LID expansion stage (i.e., overfitting phase at later training epochs), $\alpha_t \to 0$, favoring model prediction. Fig. 4.25 shows a comparison between a training using the LID prior from (4.96) and a regular training with CE loss without any regularization. Notice that the probability map from the LID training looks closer to the clean-label

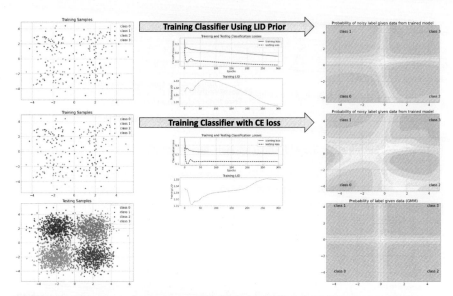

FIGURE 4.25 Classifier trained with Local Intrinsic Dimensionality (LID) prior knowledge.

Using the classification problem described in Fig. 4.3 to train a classifier for 300 iterations using the LID prior knowledge from (4.96), where $K = 50$ in (4.95). We show not only the final training losses and probability maps, but also the average LID values for the training samples using the optimization in (4.96), in comparison with a training that solely relies on CE loss without any regularization.

map, and the LID values tend to go down during training, differently from the LID values from the CE loss training.

Exploring prior data knowledge is a strategy that can lead to strong results. However, discovering sensible priors to explore is a challenging task that requires good knowledge of the problem and creativity. Furthermore, some priors may be specific to particular applications and do not generalize well to all possible applications. The optimization using priors can also introduce operational challenges, such as with the optimization presented in (Han et al., 2018b).

4.3.6 Data augmentation

Data augmentation (Shorten and Khoshgoftaar, 2019; Cubuk et al., 2019, 2020; De-Vries and Taylor, 2017; Hendrycks et al., 2019) is a method to generate new training samples from the original ones in the training set with the goal of increasing the diversity and size of the training set to regularize training and improve generalization. For images, this generation is based on applying relatively small transformations to the original training samples using several techniques, such as cropping, rotation, flipping, scaling, or image noise addition. The selection of data augmentation functions

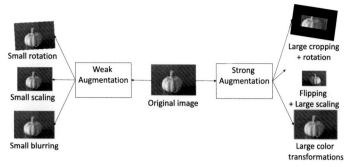

FIGURE 4.26 Data augmentation functions.

Examples of strong and weak data augmentation techniques.

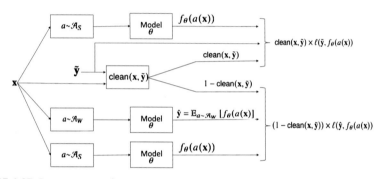

FIGURE 4.27 Data augmentation.

The training using data augmentation is based on learning a single model with both the weak augmentations in $\mathcal{A}_W$ and strong augmentations in $\mathcal{A}_S$ and a consistency loss between predictions affected by both augmentations, as explained in (4.98).

is a challenging task that can be automated (Cubuk et al., 2019, 2020) for specific datasets and learning tasks.

In noisy-label learning, data augmentation has been used mostly as a regularization technique (Song et al., 2022). For image-based problems, data augmentation usually relies on the traditional techniques of cropping, rotation, flipping, etc. However, Nishi et al. (2021) introduced the Augmented Descent (AugDesc) technique into noisy-label learning. AugDesc relies on two sets of data augmentation strategies: a weak augmentation based on traditional techniques of cropping, rotation, flipping, etc.; and a strong augmentation based on automated data augmentation selection methods (Cubuk et al., 2019, 2020) (see Fig. 4.26). Then, AugDesc uses the weak augmentation for sample selection and re-labeling, and the strong augmentation for the back-propagation step. The optimization of AugDesc is as follows (see Fig. 4.27):

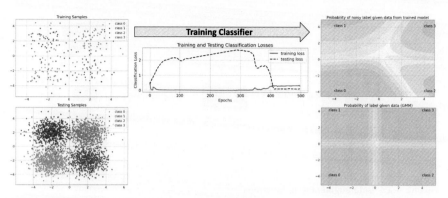

FIGURE 4.28 Classifier trained with data augmentation.

The data augmentation optimization AugDesc from (4.98), where $a(\mathbf{x}) = \mathbf{x} + \epsilon$, with $\epsilon \sim \mathcal{N}(\mu = \mathbf{0}, \Sigma = \mathbf{I} \times \sigma)$, where $\sigma = 0.001$ for weak augmentations in $\mathcal{A}_W$, and $\sigma = 0.01$ for strong augmentations in $\mathcal{A}_S$, and $\text{clean}(\mathbf{x}, \tilde{\mathbf{y}}) = \delta(\ell(\tilde{\mathbf{y}}, f_\theta(\mathbf{x})) < \frac{\tau \times \text{iteration}}{500})$.

$$\theta^* = \arg\min_\theta \frac{1}{|\mathcal{D}|} \sum_{(\mathbf{x}, \tilde{\mathbf{y}}) \in \mathcal{D}} \mathbb{E}_{a \sim \mathcal{A}_S} \Big[\text{clean}(\mathbf{x}, \tilde{\mathbf{y}}) \times \ell(\tilde{\mathbf{y}}, f_\theta(a(\mathbf{x}))+$$

$$(1 - \text{clean}(\mathbf{x}, \tilde{\mathbf{y}})) \times \ell(\hat{\mathbf{y}}, f_\theta(a(\mathbf{x})) \Big] \tag{4.98}$$

where

$$\hat{\mathbf{y}} = \mathbb{E}_{a \sim \mathcal{A}_W} [f_\theta(a(\mathbf{x}))], \tag{4.99}$$

with $\mathcal{A}_S$ and $\mathcal{A}_W$ representing the sets of strong and weak augmentation functions $a : \mathcal{X} \to \mathcal{X}$, and $\text{clean} : \mathcal{X} \times \mathcal{Y} \to \{0, 1\}$ being a function that classifies a training sample into clean (returns 1) or noisy (returns 0). We show an example of the optimization from (4.98) in Fig. 4.28. A similar idea has been explored in (Smart and Carneiro, 2023), where the proposed method uses weak augmentation to train with samples selected as clean and maximizes the consistency between the model predictions of the weakly and strongly augmented training samples classified as noisy, with

$$\theta^* = \arg\min_\theta \frac{1}{|\mathcal{D}|} \sum_{(\mathbf{x}, \tilde{\mathbf{y}}) \in \mathcal{D}} \text{clean}(\mathbf{x}, \tilde{\mathbf{y}}) \times \mathbb{E}_{a \sim \mathcal{A}_W} \Big[\ell(\tilde{\mathbf{y}}, f_\theta(a(\mathbf{x}))) \Big] +$$

$$(1 - \text{clean}(\mathbf{x}, \tilde{\mathbf{y}})) \times \ell \left(\mathbb{E}_{a \sim \mathcal{A}_S} [f_\theta(a(\mathbf{x}))], \mathbb{E}_{a \sim \mathcal{A}_W} [f_\theta(a(\mathbf{x}))] \right). \tag{4.100}$$

Another type of data augmentation explored for noisy-label learning is MixUp (Zhang et al., 2018) that trains on convex combinations of training samples and respective labels, such as

$$(\mathbf{x}, \tilde{\mathbf{y}}) = \text{MixUp}(\mathbf{x}_i, \tilde{\mathbf{y}}_i, \mathbf{x}_j, \tilde{\mathbf{y}}_j), \text{ where}$$

$$\mathbf{x} = \lambda \mathbf{x}_i + (1 - \lambda) \mathbf{x}_j, \tag{4.101}$$

$$\tilde{\mathbf{y}} = \lambda \tilde{\mathbf{y}}_i + (1 - \lambda) \tilde{\mathbf{y}}_j,$$

and $\lambda \sim \beta(a, b)$ representing a sample from a beta distribution parameterized by a and b. Arazo et al. (2019) proposed the use of MixUp in noisy-label learning with the following robust per-sample loss correction approach:

$$
\begin{aligned}
\ell(i, j) = -\lambda \times & \left[((1 - w_i) \times \tilde{\mathbf{y}}_i + w_i \times f_\theta(\mathbf{x}_i))^\top \log(h) \right] - \\
& (1 - \lambda) \times \left[((1 - w_j) \times \tilde{\mathbf{y}}_j + w_i \times f_\theta(\mathbf{x}_j))^\top \log(h) \right],
\end{aligned}
\tag{4.102}
$$

where $h = f_\theta(\lambda \times \mathbf{x}_i + (1 - \lambda) \times \mathbf{x}_j)$, and $w_i, w_j \in [0, 1]$ denote the confidence in the ground-truth labels and network predictions estimated from an unsupervised noise model.

Data augmentation has become a standard training technique in noisy-label learning. Virtually all modern approaches rely on some sort of data augmentation, ranging from simple approaches, such as with the use of regular augmentations during training, to sophisticated methods, like the ones described in this section. Consequently, we expect that data augmentation will continue to be explored in future methods as an essential technique to address noisy-label learning.

Test time augmentation (TTA) is a common post-hoc (i.e., applied after the training process is finished) machine learning technique used to improve generalization and robustness of models during testing. The basic idea is run the trained model on several augmented test samples, modified by applying several data transformations, and then the final prediction is based on aggregating the results from each augmented data (Shanmugam et al., 2021; Smart and Carneiro, 2023). The data augmentations, particularly when applied to image samples, consist of: random rotations, translations, scaling, flips, and color distortions. The application of these data transformations to the test samples followed by the calculation of the predictions for each augmented version effectively produces an ensemble of predictions. In particular, given a test image $\mathbf{x}$ and a set of image transformations denoted by $\mathcal{A}$, the TTA prediction is:

$$
\tilde{\mathbf{y}}^* = \mathbb{E}_{a \sim \mathcal{A}} \left[f_{\theta^*}(a(\mathbf{x})) \right].
\tag{4.103}
$$

Although quite simple, TTA shows substantial improvements in noisy-label classification (Smart and Carneiro, 2023). One can argue that this will significantly increase testing time, but since the data augmentations are mutually independent, they can in principle be applied in parallel, which means that this will not increase testing time. This is a topic that deserves further research.

4.3.7 Pseudo-labeling

Pseudo-labeling is a data-processing technique that is usually integrated with other methods, such as semi-supervised learning in Section 4.4.4. It is derived from the bootstrapping method (Reed et al., 2014) that modifies the training label with

$$
\hat{\mathbf{y}} = \beta \times \tilde{\mathbf{y}} + (1 - \beta) \times f_\theta(\mathbf{x}),
\tag{4.104}
$$

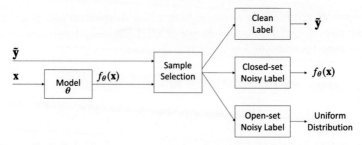

FIGURE 4.29 Pseudo-labeling.

Pseudo-labeling is usually used together with other techniques, such as sample selection (as shown in this diagram) and semi-supervised learning. The main idea is to first classify the training sample $(\mathbf{x}, \tilde{\mathbf{y}}) \in \mathcal{D}$ into clean label, closed-set noisy label, or open-set noisy label, and then modify the training label accordingly. For example, clean-label samples should keep their original training labels $\tilde{\mathbf{y}}$, closed-set noisy label samples should switch their labels to the model prediction, and open-set noisy label samples should replace their original labels to a uniform class distribution since they do not belong to any of the training classes.

where $\beta \in [0, 1]$. However, instead of indiscriminately changing the labels of all training samples, pseudo-labeling is more selective and modifies only the samples that are more likely to contain noisy labels. For instance, in (Zhang et al., 2021c; Smart and Carneiro, 2023), pseudo-labeling consists of updating the training sample $(\mathbf{x}, \tilde{\mathbf{y}}) \in \mathcal{D}$ with $(\mathbf{x}, \hat{\mathbf{y}})$, where $\hat{\mathbf{y}} = \text{OneHot}(f_\theta(\mathbf{x}))$ if $\tilde{\mathbf{y}} \neq \hat{\mathbf{y}}$ and $\max_{\mathbf{y} \in \mathcal{Y}} \left(f_\theta^{\mathbf{y}}(\mathbf{x}) \right) > \tau(t)$, where $\tau(t)$ is the prediction confidence threshold at training epoch t.

Modern pseudo-labeling methods tend to sub-divide the training set even more (e.g., clean-label, closed-set label noise, and open-set label noise) and apply different strategies to each sub-set, such as shown in Fig. 4.29. In DSOS (Albert et al., 2022), which addresses open and closed-set label noise problems, the pseudo-labeling is achieved by the function

$$h(\mathbf{x}_i, \tilde{\mathbf{y}}_i, u_i, v_i, \theta) = \frac{\exp\left(\frac{v_i \times \hat{\mathbf{y}}_i}{\alpha}\right)}{\sum_{c=1}^{|\mathcal{Y}|} \exp\left(\frac{v_i \times \hat{\mathbf{y}}_i(c)}{\alpha}\right)} \tag{4.105}$$

with $\alpha \in [0, 1]$, $v_i \in [0, 1]$, $u_i \in \{0, 1\}$, and

$$\hat{\mathbf{y}}_i = (1 - u_i) \times \tilde{\mathbf{y}}_i + u_i \times f_\theta(\mathbf{x}_i). \tag{4.106}$$

The optimization of DSOS (Albert et al., 2022) dynamically estimates $\{u_i\}_{i=1}^{|\mathcal{D}|}$ and $\{v_i\}_{i=1}^{|\mathcal{D}|}$, such that for open-set samples ($v_i \approx 0$), the pseudo-label is a uniform distribution over the class labels, for closed-set label noise, the pseudo-label is the model prediction, and for clean-label samples, the pseudo-label is the original training label. JoSRC (Yao et al., 2021b) proposes a similar pseudo-labeling technique as DSOS (Albert et al., 2022).

4.4 Training algorithms

This is one of the most fertile areas of research to address noisy-label learning. We begin by discussing meta-learning methods (Ren et al., 2018; Zhang et al., 2020c; Zhang and Pfister, 2021; Xu et al., 2021; Shu et al., 2019; Hoang et al., 2022; Dehghani et al., 2017) that automatically learn to weight and re-label training samples. Next, we present self-supervised pre-training techniques (Zheltonozhskii et al., 2022), which are present in virtually all methods that produce state-of-the-art results in the main benchmarks. Then, we describe multi-model approaches that use more than one model to mitigate the confirmation bias risk (Jiang et al., 2017; Malach and Shalev-Shwartz, 2017; Han et al., 2018c; Yu et al., 2019a; Wei et al., 2020), which is the risk of models learning from mistaken re-labellings and selected samples. Semi-supervised learning (SSL) is then presented (Ding et al., 2018; Nguyen et al., 2019; Li et al., 2020a; Zhou et al., 2021), where the goal is to separate the training samples into a labeled set and an unlabeled set, and then to treat the problem as an SSL task. Next, we present probabilistic graphical model techniques that aim to provide insightful understanding about the process of generating noisy labels for training samples (Lawrence and Schölkopf, 2001; Xiao et al., 2015; Vahdat, 2017; Yao et al., 2021a; Garg et al., 2023; Bae et al., 2022). We conclude the section with another type of training algorithm that has not received much attention for noisy-label learning, which is active learning (Bouguelia et al., 2018; Bernhardt et al., 2022; Goh and Mueller, 2023). Training algorithm techniques have been studied intensively in the field, and the most competitive noisy-label learning methods usually employ one of the algorithms presented in this section.

4.4.1 Meta-learning

In noisy-label learning problems, meta-learning algorithms (Ren et al., 2018; Zhang et al., 2020c; Zhang and Pfister, 2021; Xu et al., 2021; Shu et al., 2019; Hoang et al., 2022; Dehghani et al., 2017) are typically defined by two important features: 1) a bi-level optimization, and 2) the presence of a meta-parameter that weights the training samples. The bi-level optimization contains two nested optimization problems. The outer (or upper) optimization maximizes the performance of the meta-learner on the training task using a validation set, while the inner (or lower) optimization maximizes the performance of the model on the training task using the training set. The usual goal of the meta-learner is to automatically weight the training samples to facilitate the optimization of the training task, which usually results in down-weighting noisy-label samples and up-weighting clean-label samples.

An early example of a meta-learning method Dehghani et al. (2017) is shown in Fig. 4.30. In (Dehghani et al., 2017), the model architecture has a representation

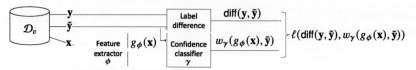

a) Train for feature extractor and confidence classifier

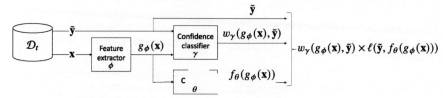

b) Train for feature extractor and classifier, keeping confidence classifier frozen

FIGURE 4.30 Meta-learning.

Meta-learning for dealing with noisy-label learning, as proposed in (Dehghani et al., 2017). (a) shows the optimization in (4.107) for training the feature extractor $g_\phi(.)$ and the sample confidence classifier $w_\gamma(.)$. (b) displays the optimization in (4.108) for training the feature extractor $g_\phi(.)$ and the classifier $f_\theta(.)$, while keeping the confidence classifier frozen.

learning network $g_\phi : \mathcal{X} \to \mathcal{Z}$ that extracts features $\mathbf{z} \in \mathcal{Z}$ from data $\mathbf{x} \in \mathcal{X}$. It also has the target network, denoted by $f_\theta : \mathcal{Z} \to \Delta^{|\mathcal{Y}|-1}$, and the confidence classifier $w_\gamma : \mathcal{Z} \times \mathcal{Y} \to \mathbb{R}$ that returns the confidence of matching the data $\mathbf{x} \in \mathcal{X}$ and label $\mathbf{y} \in \mathcal{Y}$. We also have a training set with noisy labels $\mathcal{D}_t = \{(\mathbf{x}, \tilde{\mathbf{y}})_i\}_{i=1}^{|\mathcal{D}_t|}$ and a small validation set containing both noisy and clean labels, defined by $\mathcal{D}_v = \{(\mathbf{x}, \tilde{\mathbf{y}}, \mathbf{y})_i\}_{i=1}^{|\mathcal{D}_v|}$, where $|\mathcal{D}_v| << |\mathcal{D}_t|$. Training is achieved in two stages, where the first stage optimizes the confidence model as follows:

$$\phi^*, \gamma^* = \arg\min_{\phi, \gamma} \frac{1}{|\mathcal{D}_v|} \sum_{(\mathbf{x}, \tilde{\mathbf{y}}, \mathbf{y}) \in \mathcal{D}_v} \ell(\text{diff}(\mathbf{y}, \tilde{\mathbf{y}}), w_\gamma(g_\phi(\mathbf{x}), \tilde{\mathbf{y}})), \qquad (4.107)$$

where $\text{diff}(\mathbf{y}, \tilde{\mathbf{y}})$ computes the difference between true label $\mathbf{y}$ and noisy label $\tilde{\mathbf{y}}$. The second training stage then optimizes the target network as follows:

$$\phi^*, \theta^* = \arg\min_{\phi, \gamma} \frac{1}{|\mathcal{D}_t|} \sum_{(\mathbf{x}, \tilde{\mathbf{y}}) \in \mathcal{D}_t} w_{\gamma^*}(g_\phi(\mathbf{x}), \tilde{\mathbf{y}}) \times \ell(\tilde{\mathbf{y}}, f_\theta(g_\phi(\mathbf{x}))). \qquad (4.108)$$

The trained target network is then using to label test data. This work was followed by more sophisticated meta-learning approaches described below.

Arguably the most representative meta-learning method for noisy-label learning is the learning to re-weight (L2R) by Ren et al. (2018). L2R divides the original training set containing noisy labels, denoted by $\mathcal{D}$, into mutually exclusive training and a validation sets $\mathcal{D}_t$ and $\mathcal{D}_v$, respectively, where $\mathcal{D}_t \bigcup \mathcal{D}_v = \mathcal{D}$ and the labels of $\mathcal{D}_v$ are guaranteed to be clean. L2R uses $\mathcal{D}_v$ to learn a meta-parameter $\mathbf{w} \in \Delta^{|\mathcal{D}_t|-1}$

which weights the loss $\ell(.)$ for each training sample in $\mathcal{D}_t$, similarly to the loss re-weighting technique in Section 4.2.3. This training sample weighting follows many utility criteria, such as informativeness, class-balanced distribution, and label cleanliness (Ren et al., 2018; Hoang et al., 2022). The meta-learning optimization is defined as:

$$\mathbf{w}^* = \arg \min_{\mathbf{w} \in \Delta^{|\mathcal{D}_t|-1}} \frac{1}{|\mathcal{D}_v|} \sum_{j=1}^{|\mathcal{D}_v|} \ell(\mathbf{y}_j, f_{\theta^*(\mathbf{w})}(\mathbf{x}_j))$$

$$\text{s.t.:} \ \theta^*(\mathbf{w}) = \arg \min_{\theta} \frac{1}{|\mathcal{D}_t|} \sum_{i=1}^{|\mathcal{D}_t|} \mathbf{w}_i \times \ell\left(\tilde{\mathbf{y}}_i, f_\theta(\mathbf{x}_i)\right), \quad (4.109)$$

where the label $\mathbf{y}_j$ from $\mathcal{D}_v$ is assumed to be clean. In (4.109), the inner (lower) optimization trains the model $f_\theta(.)$ using a weighted loss on the training set $\mathcal{D}_t$, while the outer (upper) optimization trains the meta-parameter $\mathbf{w} \in \Delta^{|\mathcal{D}_t|-1}$ that weights the training set losses in the inner level.

The optimization in (4.109) is performed iteratively with the inner and outer stages. The inner stage is based on a one-step-ahead model parameter estimation to produce $\theta^*(\mathbf{w})$ using the stochastic gradient descent (SGD) on the training subset $\mathcal{D}_t$, defined by:

$$\theta^*(\mathbf{w}) \approx \theta - \eta_\theta \nabla_\theta \frac{1}{|\mathcal{D}_t|} \sum_{i=1}^{|\mathcal{D}_t|} \mathbf{w}_i \times \ell\left(\tilde{\mathbf{y}}_i, f_\theta(\mathbf{x}_i)\right), \quad (4.110)$$

where η_θ is the learning rate. The outer stage consists of updating the meta-parameter $\mathbf{w}$ with a one SGD step on the loss computed from the validation set $\mathcal{D}_v$ using the model's parameter $\theta^*(\omega)$ from (4.110), as in

$$\mathbf{w}^* \approx \mathbf{w} - \eta_\mathbf{w} \nabla_\mathbf{w} \frac{1}{|\mathcal{D}_v|} \sum_{j=1}^{|\mathcal{D}_v|} \ell\left(\mathbf{y}_j, f_{\theta^*(\omega)}(\mathbf{x}_j)\right), \quad (4.111)$$

where $\eta_\mathbf{w}$ represents the step size to update $\mathbf{w}$. The learned meta-parameter $\mathbf{w}^*$ is then projected to the probability simplex $\Delta^{|\mathcal{D}_t|-1}$ before it is used to train the model in (4.109).

Ren et al. (2018) analyze the optimization in (4.109) and formulate the following expression on the weighting of each training sample loss:

$$\frac{1}{|\mathcal{D}_v|} \sum_{j=1}^{|\mathcal{D}_v|} \left[\frac{\partial}{\partial \mathbf{w}_i} \ell\left(\mathbf{y}_j, f_{\theta^*(\omega,\lambda)}(\mathbf{x}_j)\right) \right]\Bigg|_{\mathbf{w}_i=0}$$

$$\propto -\frac{1}{|\mathcal{D}_v|} \sum_{j=1}^{|\mathcal{D}_v|} \left[\sum_{l=1}^{L} (\mathbf{z}_{j,l-1}^{(v)})^\top \mathbf{z}_{i,l-1}^{(t)})(\mathbf{g}_{j,l}^{(v)})^\top \mathbf{g}_{i,l}^{(t)}) \right], \quad (4.112)$$

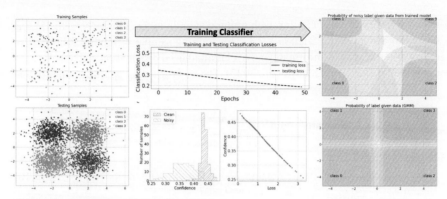

FIGURE 4.31 Classifier trained with meta-learning.

The training of classifier with the Meta-weight-net (MWN) (Shu et al., 2019) using the same problem described in Fig. 4.3. We train for 50 iterations using the optimization in (4.113). At the bottom, in the middle, we also show a histogram of confidence for the clean and noisy-label samples and a scatter plot of the weight versus loss (note that samples with large loss value have zero weight).

where $\mathbf{z}_{j,l-1}^{(v)}$ denotes the feature produced by model layer l for validation sample $\mathbf{x}_j$, $\mathbf{z}_{i,l-1}^{(t)}$ represents the lth-layer feature from the model for training sample $\mathbf{x}_i$, $\mathbf{g}_{j,l}^{(v)}$ is the lth-layer gradient for validation data $\mathbf{x}_j$, and $\mathbf{g}_{i,l}^{(t)}$ denotes the feature produced by model layer l for training data $\mathbf{x}_i$. Therefore, the loss reweighting factor $\mathbf{w}_i$ for training sample $\mathbf{x}_i$ is high if its feature and gradient are similar to at least one of the validation samples' feature and gradient; otherwise, $\mathbf{w}_i$ is low.

A similar approach to L2R above is the Meta-weight-net (MWN) (Shu et al., 2019) that introduces a sample weighting model parameterized by $\phi \in \Phi$ and represented with $w_\phi(.)$ that receives a loss value and returns a sample weight. The optimization is formulated as (see Fig. 4.31):

$$\phi^* = \arg\min_\phi \frac{1}{|\mathcal{D}_v|} \sum_{(\mathbf{x},\mathbf{y})\in\mathcal{D}_v} \ell(\mathbf{y}, f_{\theta_\phi^*}(\mathbf{x}))$$

$$\text{s.t.: } \theta_\phi^* = \arg\min_\theta \frac{1}{|\mathcal{D}_t|} \sum_{(\mathbf{x},\tilde{\mathbf{y}})\in\mathcal{D}_t} w_\phi(\ell\left(\tilde{\mathbf{y}}, f_\theta(\mathbf{x})\right)) \times \ell\left(\tilde{\mathbf{y}}, f_\theta(\mathbf{x})\right). \qquad (4.113)$$

This algorithm runs in three iterative steps. Assuming the current training epoch represented by t, MWN first updates $\hat{\theta}_\phi(t)$ with

$$\hat{\theta}_\phi(t) \approx \theta(t) - \eta_\theta \frac{1}{|\mathcal{D}_t|} \sum_{(\mathbf{x},\tilde{\mathbf{y}})\in\mathcal{D}_t} w_\phi\left(\ell\left(\tilde{\mathbf{y}}, f_{\theta(t)}(\mathbf{x})\right)\right) \nabla_\theta \ell\left(\tilde{\mathbf{y}}, f_\theta(\mathbf{x})\right)\Big|_{\theta(t)}, \qquad (4.114)$$

where η_θ represents the learning rate, and $\theta(t)$ denotes the model parameters at training iteration t. Then the parameter ϕ of the sample weighting model $w_\phi(.)$ is updated with:

$$\phi(t+1) \approx \phi(t) - \eta_\phi \frac{1}{|\mathcal{D}_v|} \sum_{(\mathbf{x},\mathbf{y})\in\mathcal{D}_v} \nabla_\phi \ell(\mathbf{y}, f_{\hat{\theta}_{\phi(t)}}(\mathbf{x})) \Big|_{\phi(t)}, \tag{4.115}$$

where η_ϕ represents the learning rate, and $\phi(t)$ is the sample weighting model's parameter at training iteration t. The last step consists of updating the model parameters with

$$\theta(t+1) \approx \theta(t) - \eta_\theta \frac{1}{|\mathcal{D}_t|} \sum_{(\mathbf{x},\tilde{\mathbf{y}})\in\mathcal{D}_t} w_{\phi(t+1)} \left(\ell\left(\tilde{\mathbf{y}}, f_{\theta(t)}(\mathbf{x})\right)\right) \nabla_\theta \ell\left(\tilde{\mathbf{y}}, f_\theta(\mathbf{x})\right) \Big|_{\theta(t)}. \tag{4.116}$$

The L2R approach is extended by Zhang et al. (2020c) with the introduction of a second meta-parameter $\beta_i \in [0,1]$, $i \in \{1,\ldots,|\mathcal{D}_t|\}$ that provides a re-labeling similar to the technique presented in Section 4.2.4. The re-labeling of training sample i is provided by

$$\hat{\mathbf{y}}_i(\beta_i) = \beta_i \times \tilde{\mathbf{y}}_i + (1-\beta_i) \times f_\theta(\mathbf{x}_i), \tag{4.117}$$

which is a convex combination between the original training label and label produced by the model. The optimization in (4.109) is then reformulated as follows:

$$\mathbf{w}^*, \beta^* = \arg\min_{\mathbf{w},\beta} \frac{1}{|\mathcal{D}_v|} \sum_{j=1}^{|\mathcal{D}_v|} \ell\left(\mathbf{y}_j, f_{\theta^*(\mathbf{w},\beta)}(\mathbf{x}_j)\right)$$

$$\text{s.t.: } \theta^*(\mathbf{w},\beta) = \arg\min_\theta \frac{1}{|\mathcal{D}_t|} \sum_{i=1}^{|\mathcal{D}_t|} \mathbf{w}_i \times \ell\left(\hat{\mathbf{y}}(\beta_i), f_\theta(\mathbf{x}_i)\right). \tag{4.118}$$

The meta-parameter $\mathbf{w}$ is optimized as explained in (4.111), but β is updated as follows:

$$\beta_i^* = \left[\text{sign}\left(-\frac{1}{|\mathcal{D}_v|} \sum_{j=1}^{|\mathcal{D}_v|} \left[\frac{\partial}{\partial\beta_i} \ell\left(\mathbf{y}_j, f_{\theta^*(\mathbf{w},\beta)}(\mathbf{x}_j)\right) \right] \right) \right]_+, \tag{4.119}$$

with $[.]_+$ representing the rectification operator. The loss function proposed by Zhang et al. (2020c) is defined as:

$$\ell(\tilde{\mathbf{y}}, \mathbf{x}) = \mathbf{w}^* \times \ell\left(\hat{\mathbf{y}}(\beta_0), f_\theta(\mathbf{x})\right) + \frac{\ell\left(\mathbf{y}^*(\beta^*), f_\theta(\mathbf{x})\right)}{B}$$

$$+ \rho \times \ell\left(\mathbf{y}^\gamma, f_\theta(\mathbf{x}^\gamma)\right) + \kappa \times \text{KL}\left[f_\theta(\mathbf{x}) \,\|\, f_\theta(\hat{\mathbf{x}})\right], \tag{4.120}$$

where $\hat{\mathbf{y}}(.)$ is the re-labeling defined in (4.117), $\beta_0 = 0.9$, B is the batch size,

$$\mathbf{y}^*(\beta^*) = \begin{cases} \tilde{\mathbf{y}} & \text{if } \beta^* > 0, \\ f_\theta(\mathbf{x}) & \text{otherwise,} \end{cases}$$

$\mathbf{y}^\gamma$ and $\mathbf{x}^\gamma$ are calculated from the mixup operator (Zhang et al., 2018) using the training and validation sets, KL[.||.] represents the Kullback-Leibler (KL) divergence, $\hat{\mathbf{x}}$ is an augmented sample of $\mathbf{x}$, and ρ and κ denote hyper-parameters.

All meta-learning methods above require a clean-label validation set $\mathcal{D}_v$, which is problematic to acquire, particularly in problems with many classes. Zhang and Pfister (2021) address this problem by replacing the clean-label dataset by a pseudo-clean validation set automatically built with a pusher function $u_\theta : \mathcal{X} \times \mathcal{Y} \to \mathbb{R}$, as in:

$$\mathcal{D}_v^* = \arg \max_{\mathcal{D}_v \in \mathcal{D}} \sum_{(\mathbf{x}, \tilde{\mathbf{y}}) \in \mathcal{D}_v} u_\theta(\mathbf{x}, \tilde{\mathbf{y}}), \qquad (4.121)$$

where $u_\theta(\mathbf{x}, \tilde{\mathbf{y}}) = \ell(\tilde{\mathbf{y}}, f_{\theta(t)}(\mathbf{x})) - \ell(\tilde{\mathbf{y}}, f_{\theta(t+1)}(\mathbf{x}))$. The maximization in (4.121) selects validation samples with the largest drops in losses between the models trained in steps t and $t + 1$, representing unstable samples that the model has started to fit, and leaves behind samples with continuous high or low losses because they are too hard or too easy to fit. Xu et al. (2021) propose a way to automatically detect a clean-label validation set by exploring the small-loss hypothesis with a Gaussian mixture model (GMM), similar to the approach in (4.24). Hoang et al. (2022) introduce a method to automatically select a clean-label validation set that has high-utility samples according to samples that maximize the gradient in (4.112).

Meta-learning methods provide a sound theoretical framework for the development of noisy-label learning methods since it automatically learns how to weight or re-label training samples to better optimize the target model. Nevertheless, such nice property comes with a relatively high computational cost since training takes 2 to 3 times longer compared with non meta-learning approaches, as can be seen from the 3-stage training in (4.114), (4.115), and (4.116), with each stage involving one-step SGD and the training of $\phi(t + 1)$ containing a second-order backpropagation. Additionally, the need for a clean (and balanced) validation set is a shortcoming that has recently been addressed (Zhang and Pfister, 2021; Xu et al., 2021; Hoang et al., 2022) with the caveat that the samples in this clean-label validation set may not actually be clean and may not be highly informative for the training process since these clean-label samples are likely to be the easy (or non-informative) samples to fit.

4.4.2 Self-supervised pre-training

Pre-training is a well-known technique to provide a strong initialization for a model by training it on a large amount of data using a general objective function to build effective representations of the training data (Erhan et al., 2010). These models can be trained using an external dataset (Krizhevsky et al., 2012), such as ImageNet (Deng et al., 2009), or they can rely on self-supervision (Noroozi and Favaro, 2016; Chen et al., 2020a; He et al., 2020). Self-supervised pre-training trains a model on a large amount of unlabeled data using a pretext task that does not require any labels. As shown in Fig. 4.32, examples of pretext tasks are the prediction of an image transfor-

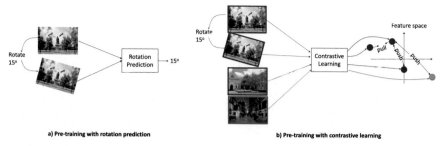

a) Pre-training with rotation prediction   b) Pre-training with contrastive learning

FIGURE 4.32 Self-supervised pre-training.

There are many ways to perform pre-training with self-supervision. For example, one way is based on predicting the transformations applied to input images, such as rotation (Gidaris et al., 2018) (a). Another example is contrastive learning (Chen et al., 2020a; He et al., 2020) (b), where feature representations are learned to pull together image embeddings from different views of the same image (e.g., one image is a rotated version of the other), while pushing apart embeddings coming from different images.

mation (Gidaris et al., 2018; Novotny et al., 2018), or the contrastive learning based on the maximization of the similarity of the representations obtained from two views of the same training image and the minimization of the similarity between the representations from different training images (Chen et al., 2020a; He et al., 2020).

The use of ImageNet pre-trained models in noisy-label learning methods is quite common (Li et al., 2020a), but more recently, sophisticated self-supervised pre-training techniques were explored with outstanding results (Zheltonozhskii et al., 2022). In contrast to divide (C2D), Zheltonozhskii et al. (2022) define the "warm-up obstacle" as the inability of early-stopping discriminative learning processes to produce effective model initialization that can prevent the overfitting of noisy-label training samples. Zheltonozhskii et al. (2022) also observed that ImageNet pre-training is not only impractical, given the difficulty in finding relevant large-scale training sets that can be helpful for certain applications, but it can also be detrimental in some cases. C2D consists of simply pre-training the noisy-label learning model with the contrastive learning pre-training method SimCLR (Chen et al., 2020a), and then train the model with a state-of-the-art noisy-label learning method (Li et al., 2020a; Liu et al., 2020).

Self-supervised pre-training has become a model initialization technique present in virtually all state-of-the-art approaches that we will study in Chapter 5. In fact, methods that do not rely on self-supervised pre-training are unlikely to produce competitive results in the main benchmarks in the field. Nevertheless, it is unlikely that new self-supervised pre-training methods will be proposed in noisy-label learning literature. Instead, what is usually seen in noisy-label learning is the utilization of self-supervised pre-training techniques developed for general downstream tasks.

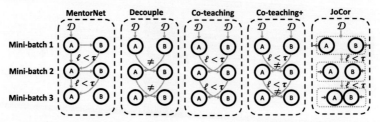

FIGURE 4.33 Multi-model training.

Multi-model training relies on the training of multiple models to address the issue of confirmation bias, where mistakes made by the model are reinforced during the training of the same model. MentorNet (Jiang et al., 2017) relies on the training of a teacher model Ⓑ that weights samples based on their losses for the training of a student model Ⓐ, as explained in (4.123). Decouple (Malach and Shalev-Shwartz, 2017) trains two models Ⓐ and Ⓑ, described in (4.122), where both models are trained with samples for which both models disagree. Co-teaching (Han et al., 2018c) and Co-teaching+ (Yu et al., 2019a) use a similar strategy, where models Ⓐ and Ⓑ are trained by swapping small-loss samples (Han et al., 2018c) as explained in (4.125), or swapping small-loss samples for which both models disagree (Yu et al., 2019a), as described in (4.126). JoCor (Wei et al., 2020) trains two models Ⓐ and Ⓑ with small-loss samples, and at the same time reduce the prediction divergence between the two models, as explained in (4.127).

4.4.3 Multi-model training

The use of multiple models in noisy-label learning is a dominant technique usually designed to work together with sample selection to mitigate an issue widely known as confirmation bias. In this issue, a noisy-label sample may be classified as clean, which encourages the model to overfit such noisy-label sample, so it is again classified as clean in the next training iteration. This issue is mitigated by the training of multiple models because of the difficulty that multiple models will overfit the same noisy-label samples at the same training epoch, as shown in Fig. 4.33.

Decouple (Malach and Shalev-Shwartz, 2017) is a pioneer multi-model training approach for noisy-label learning, where two networks $f_{\theta_1} : \mathcal{X} \to \Delta^{|\mathcal{Y}|-1}$ and $f_{\theta_2} : \mathcal{X} \to \Delta^{|\mathcal{Y}|-1}$ are trained only on the training samples that they disagree, with

$$\theta_1^* = \arg\min_{\theta_1} \frac{1}{|\mathcal{S}|} \sum_{(\mathbf{x},\tilde{\mathbf{y}})\in\mathcal{S}} \ell(\tilde{\mathbf{y}}, f_{\theta_1}(\mathbf{x}))$$

$$\theta_2^* = \arg\min_{\theta_2} \frac{1}{|\mathcal{S}|} \sum_{(\mathbf{x},\tilde{\mathbf{y}})\in\mathcal{S}} \ell(\tilde{\mathbf{y}}, f_{\theta_2}(\mathbf{x})) \tag{4.122}$$

$$\text{s.t. } \mathcal{S} = \left\{ (\mathbf{x}, \tilde{\mathbf{y}})|(\mathbf{x}, \tilde{\mathbf{y}}) \in \mathcal{D}, f_{\theta_1}(\mathbf{x}) \neq f_{\theta_2}(\mathbf{x}) \right\}.$$

The issue with decouple (Malach and Shalev-Shwartz, 2017) was that the disagreement set $\mathcal{S}$ in (4.122) could contain many noisy-label samples that can lead to overfitting and confirmation bias.

The multi-model in (Jiang et al., 2017) relies on a collaborative learning of two models, the MentorNet and the StudentNet, with the StudentNet optimizing a loss re-weighted function, where the sample weights are dynamically estimated by the MentorNet with a data-driven curriculum using the features from the StudentNet. The MentorNet, denoted by the model $g_\phi(.)$ parameterized by $\phi \in \Phi$, provides a data-driven curriculum learning to train the StudentNet. The MentorNet model is trained as follows:

$$\phi^*, \theta^* = \arg\min_{\phi,\theta} \frac{1}{|\mathcal{D}|} \sum_{i=1}^{|\mathcal{D}|} g_\phi(\mathbf{z}_i) \times \ell(\tilde{\mathbf{y}}_i, f_\theta(\mathbf{x}_i)) + G(g_\phi(\mathbf{z}_i); \lambda_1, \lambda_2) + \gamma \times |\theta\|_2^2,$$

(4.123)

where λ_1, λ_2 are regularization parameters for the penalization function $G(w_i; \lambda_1, \lambda_2) = 0.5\lambda_2^2 w_i - (\lambda_1 + \lambda_2)w_i$, and $\mathbf{z}_i = h(\mathbf{x}_i, \mathbf{y}_i, \theta)$ is a feature comprising the loss, loss difference to the moving average, label and epoch percentage. In (4.123), the first term denotes the curriculum-weighted loss, while the second term specifies the curriculum, defined by a sequence of samples and respective weights for training the StudentNet. The optimization of (4.123) leads to the following closed-form solution:

$$g_\phi(\mathbf{z}_i) = \begin{cases} \delta(\ell_i \leq \lambda_1), & \text{if } \lambda_2 = 0 \\ \min\left(\max\left(0, 1 - \frac{\ell_i - \lambda_1}{\lambda_2}\right), 1\right), & \text{if } \lambda_2 \neq 0 \end{cases},$$

(4.124)

where $\ell_i = \ell(\tilde{\mathbf{y}}_i, f_\theta(\mathbf{x}_i))$, and $\delta(.)$ represents an indicator function. Hence, when $\lambda_2 = 0$, we have a self-paced curriculum learning (Kumar et al., 2010), where the StudentNet is trained only with small-loss samples (i.e., samples with $\ell_i \leq \lambda_1$ will have $g_{\phi^*}(\mathbf{z}_i) = 1$). On the other hand, when $\lambda_2 \neq 0$, the StudentNet is not trained with large-loss samples where $\ell_i \geq \lambda_2 + \lambda_1$, but it will be trained with samples weighted linearly by $1 - \frac{\ell_i - \lambda_1}{\lambda_2}$. Hence, similarly to (Kumar et al., 2010), λ_1 and λ_2 control the learning pace. Also, similarly to the decouple method presented before in (4.122), if the MentorNet mistakenly weights up a noisy-label sample, confirmation bias will follow.

These issues motivated the development of co-teaching (Han et al., 2018c) that explores the small-loss hypothesis (Arpit et al., 2017) in a multi-model scenario. Motivated by co-training (Blum and Mitchell, 1998), co-teaching has two models that will continuously select small-loss samples to train the peer model, as follows:

$$\theta_1^* = \arg\min_{\theta_1} \frac{1}{|\mathcal{S}_2|} \sum_{(\mathbf{x},\tilde{\mathbf{y}})\in\mathcal{S}_2} \ell(\tilde{\mathbf{y}}, f_{\theta_1}(\mathbf{x}))$$

$$\theta_2^* = \arg\min_{\theta_2} \frac{1}{|\mathcal{S}_1|} \sum_{(\mathbf{x},\tilde{\mathbf{y}})\in\mathcal{S}_1} \ell(\tilde{\mathbf{y}}, f_{\theta_2}(\mathbf{x}))$$

(4.125)

$$\text{s.t. } \mathcal{S}_1 = \left\{(\mathbf{x}, \tilde{\mathbf{y}})|(\mathbf{x}, \tilde{\mathbf{y}}) \in \mathcal{D}, \ell(\tilde{\mathbf{y}}, f_{\theta_1}(\mathbf{x})) < \tau\right\},$$
$$\mathcal{S}_2 = \left\{(\mathbf{x}, \tilde{\mathbf{y}})|(\mathbf{x}, \tilde{\mathbf{y}}) \in \mathcal{D}, \ell(\tilde{\mathbf{y}}, f_{\theta_2}(\mathbf{x})) < \tau\right\},$$

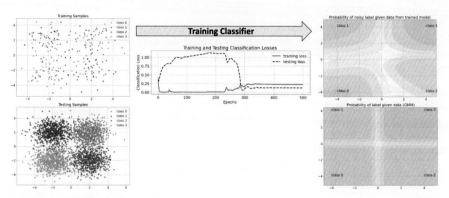

FIGURE 4.34 Multi-model training with co-teaching.

The training of classifier with Co-teaching (Han et al., 2018c) using the same problem described in Fig. 4.3. We train for 500 iterations using the optimization in (4.125).

where τ varies during the training. The two models in (4.125) filter different types of label noise, which makes it difficult that both models will overfit the same noisy-label samples. Furthermore, even though one model can give noisy-label samples to the peer model, the robustness of both models to noisy-label samples from the early learning stages (Arpit et al., 2017) will mitigate the overfit to these noisy-label samples. We show an example of co-teaching in Fig. 4.34. Nevertheless, the two models in co-teaching soon reach a consensus during training, which means that both models become too similar, leading to a self-training strategy that becomes vulnerable to confirmation bias. Such issue can be mitigated with the decouple strategy (Malach and Shalev-Shwartz, 2017), described in (4.122), which can slow down the convergence rate of the co-teaching models. This led to the development of co-teaching+ (Yu et al., 2019a), which updates the models using small-loss samples with prediction disagreement between the classifiers, with:

$$\theta_1^* = \arg\min_{\theta_1} \frac{1}{|\mathcal{S}_2|} \sum_{(\mathbf{x}, \tilde{\mathbf{y}}) \in \mathcal{S}_2} \ell(\tilde{\mathbf{y}}, f_{\theta_1}(\mathbf{x}))$$

$$\theta_2^* = \arg\min_{\theta_2} \frac{1}{|\mathcal{S}_1|} \sum_{(\mathbf{x}, \tilde{\mathbf{y}}) \in \mathcal{S}_1} \ell(\tilde{\mathbf{y}}, f_{\theta_2}(\mathbf{x}))$$

$$\text{s.t. } \mathcal{S} = \left\{(\mathbf{x}, \tilde{\mathbf{y}}) | (\mathbf{x}, \tilde{\mathbf{y}}) \in \mathcal{D}, f_{\theta_1}(\mathbf{x}) \neq f_{\theta_2}(\mathbf{x})\right\},$$

$$\mathcal{S}_1 = \left\{(\mathbf{x}, \tilde{\mathbf{y}}) | (\mathbf{x}, \tilde{\mathbf{y}}) \in \mathcal{S}, \ell(\tilde{\mathbf{y}}, f_{\theta_1}(\mathbf{x})) < \tau)\right\},$$

$$\mathcal{S}_2 = \left\{(\mathbf{x}, \tilde{\mathbf{y}}) | (\mathbf{x}, \tilde{\mathbf{y}}) \in \mathcal{S}, \ell(\tilde{\mathbf{y}}, f_{\theta_2}(\mathbf{x})) < \tau)\right\}. \tag{4.126}$$

Unfortunately, the combined constraints of small-loss and prediction disagreement in co-teaching+ (Yu et al., 2019a) can severely reduce the size of $\mathcal{S}_1$ and $\mathcal{S}_2$ in (4.126), particularly when the noise rate in $\mathcal{D}$ is too high. Such inefficient use of the training set can damage the training process, which motivated Wei et al. (2020) to develop Joint Training with Co-Regularization (JoCoR). JoCor moves away from the maximization of the prediction disagreement to the maximization of the prediction agreement between the two classifiers $f_{\theta_1}(.)$ and $f_{\theta_2}(.)$ using a joint training loss for the two models and a regularization that replaces the sampling proposed in (Han et al., 2018c). This joint loss is also used to select the small-loss samples, which complicates the selection of noisy-label samples since they will need to have a small loss in both models to be selected. JoCor (Wei et al., 2020) optimizes the following loss function:

$$\theta_1^*, \theta_2^* = \arg\min_{\theta_1, \theta_2} \frac{1}{|\mathcal{S}|} \sum_{(\mathbf{x}, \tilde{\mathbf{y}}) \in \mathcal{S}} \mathcal{L}(\mathbf{x}, \tilde{\mathbf{y}}, \theta_1, \theta_2)$$

$$\text{s.t. } \mathcal{S} = \left\{ (\mathbf{x}, \tilde{\mathbf{y}}) | (\mathbf{x}, \tilde{\mathbf{y}}) \in \mathcal{D}, \mathcal{L}(\mathbf{x}, \tilde{\mathbf{y}}, \theta_1, \theta_2) < \tau \right\},$$
(4.127)

where

$$\mathcal{L}(\mathbf{x}, \tilde{\mathbf{y}}, \theta_1, \theta_2) = (1 - \lambda) \times \left(\ell(\tilde{\mathbf{y}}, f_{\theta_1}(\mathbf{x})) + \ell(\tilde{\mathbf{y}}, f_{\theta_2}(\mathbf{x})) \right) +$$
$$\lambda \times \left(\mathsf{KL}[f_{\theta_1}(\mathbf{x}) \| f_{\theta_2}(\mathbf{x})] + \mathsf{KL}[f_{\theta_2}(\mathbf{x}) \| f_{\theta_1}(\mathbf{x})] \right),$$
(4.128)

with $\lambda \in [0, 1]$ and $\mathsf{KL}[.]$ representing the Kullback-Leibler (KL) divergence.

The use of the mean teacher model (Tarvainen and Valpola, 2017) that relies on a temporal ensembling of models, combined with the soft re-labeling of training samples based on a temporal ensembling of label and predictions are the two techniques explored by the self-ensemble label filtering (SELF) method (Nguyen et al., 2019). SELF filters out noisy-label samples by maintaining a temporal ensembling of predictions with $\hat{\mathbf{y}}^{(t+1)} = \alpha \times \hat{\mathbf{y}}^{(t)} + (1 - \alpha) \times f_\theta(\mathbf{y})$, where $\hat{\mathbf{y}}^{(0)} = \mathbf{0}$ and $\hat{\mathbf{y}}^{(t)}$ represents the prediction ensemble at training iteration t. Then, training samples where $\tilde{\mathbf{y}} \neq \mathsf{OneHot}(\hat{\mathbf{y}}^{(t+1)})$ have their labels erased (i.e., they become un-labeled). Given these un-labeled and the remaining labeled training samples, SELF trains the mean-teacher model (Tarvainen and Valpola, 2017), which is a semi-supervised teacher-student learning model that outputs $f_\theta(.)$. This model consists of the best teacher model, represented by the training epoch that provided the best accuracy in the validation set.

Multi-model training is one of the best tools developed to mitigate the confirmation bias problem, typically found in noisy-label learning methods. However, the need for training two separate models is generally seen as problematic given the larger run-time and memory complexity compared with other approaches based on a single model.

4.4.4 Semi-supervised learning

The experimental setup of semi-supervised learning (SSL) and noisy-label learning have one important commonality, which is that part of the dataset cannot be used for fully-supervised training. While in SSL, a subset of the training samples does not have labels, in noisy-label learning, a subset of the training set has wrong labels.

The major difference between SSL and noisy-label learning is that the un-labeled samples in SSL are clearly marked, but we do not have clear demarcation of the training samples that carry a noisy label. Therefore, if sample selection techniques work effectively, then we can simply keep the labels of the samples classified as clean, and remove the labels from the training samples classified as noisy, and apply one of the SSL techniques. There are two challenges in noisy-label SSL methods, namely: it is inevitable that the training samples classified as clean will contain a small subset of noisy-label samples, and the samples classified as noisy may just be the clean-label informative samples that are quite important for the training process. Hence, much of the work in the application of SSL in noisy-label learning focus on addressing these two challenges.

There are three assumptions explored by the SSL approaches (Van Engelen and Hoos, 2020) that are useful in noisy-label learning: 1) images with neighboring representations in the feature space have similar labels; 2) decision boundary passes through low-density areas of the feature space; and 3) representations sharing a low-dimensional manifold in the feature space also share the same label. The main techniques explored by SSL approaches are the pseudo-labeling (Berthelot et al., 2019; Sohn et al., 2020; Arazo et al., 2020) (such as the ones presented in Section 4.3.7) and consistency learning (Laine and Aila, 2016; Tarvainen and Valpola, 2017; Polyak and Juditsky, 1992). Pseudo-labeling methods work by progressively annotating part of the un-labeled dataset, while consistency-based approaches minimize prediction discrepancies produced by the model using different input views obtained, for example, from data perturbations produced by augmentation functions. It has been noted that consistency-learning approaches tend to outperform pseudo-labeling methods, most likely because pseudo-labeling methods disregard part of the training set during optimization (Liu et al., 2022d). In fact, SSL approaches applied to noisy-label learning are mostly based on consistency-learning techniques, as we present below.

The first method to use SSL for noisy-label learning was the one proposed by (Ding et al., 2018), which explored consistency learning with the loss (see Fig. 4.35):

$$\theta^* = \arg\min_{\theta} \frac{1}{|\mathcal{D}_c|} \sum_{(\mathbf{x}, \tilde{\mathbf{y}}) \in \mathcal{D}_c} \ell(\tilde{\mathbf{y}}, f_\theta(\mathbf{x})) + \frac{1}{|\mathcal{D}|} \sum_{(\mathbf{x}, \tilde{\mathbf{y}}) \in \mathcal{D}} \| f_\theta(\mathbf{x}) - f_{\hat{\theta}}(\mathbf{x}) \|_2^2, \quad (4.129)$$

where $\mathcal{D}_c = \{(\mathbf{x}, \tilde{\mathbf{y}}) | (\mathbf{x}, \tilde{\mathbf{y}}) \in \mathcal{D}, \delta(\tilde{\mathbf{y}} = \mathsf{OneHot}(f_\theta(\mathbf{x}))) = 1, f_\theta^{(\tilde{\mathbf{y}})}(\mathbf{x}) > \tau\}$ denotes the set of pseudo-clean label samples, $f_{\hat{\theta}}(\mathbf{x})$ represents the model prediction after being perturbed with dropout (Srivastava et al., 2014), and the second loss maximizes the consistency between the prediction outputs after dropout perturbation applied to the model. We show the result produced by this model in Fig. 4.36. The approach proposed by Kong et al. (2019) explored the SSL assumption about the decision boundary passing through low-density areas of the feature space, with the follow-

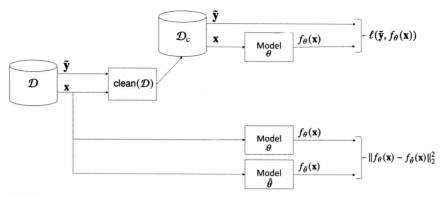

FIGURE 4.35 Semi-supervised learning.

Semi-supervised learning methods work by automatically selecting clean-label samples to form the set $\mathcal{D}_c$ that is used with a training loss $\ell(\tilde{\mathbf{y}}, f_\theta(\mathbf{x}))$, while the whole training set $\mathcal{D}$ (or sometimes just the set difference $\mathcal{D}_n = \mathcal{D} \setminus \mathcal{D}_c$) is trained with another loss that does not take the training label into account, such as the loss in this figure represented by $\| f_\theta(\mathbf{x}) - f_{\hat{\theta}}(\mathbf{x}) \|_2^2$, with $f_{\hat{\theta}}(.)$ being a model perturbed with dropout (Srivastava et al., 2014).

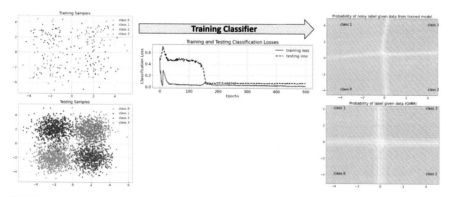

FIGURE 4.36 Semi-supervised learning.

Working with the problem described in Fig. 4.3, we show the functionality of the semi-supervised learning proposed by Ding et al. (2018) with a training of 500 iterations using the optimization in (4.129), where the clean-label dataset $\mathcal{D}_c$ is formed by only checking if $f_\theta^{(\tilde{\mathbf{y}})} > \tau$, with $\tau = 0.1$.

ing loss:

$$\theta^* = \arg\min_\theta \frac{1}{|\mathcal{D}_c|} \sum_{(\mathbf{x},\tilde{\mathbf{y}})\in\mathcal{D}_c} \ell(\tilde{\mathbf{y}}, f_\theta(\mathbf{x})) + \frac{1}{|\mathcal{D}_n|} \sum_{(\mathbf{x},\tilde{\mathbf{y}})\in\mathcal{D}_n} \mathbb{H}_r(f_\theta(\mathbf{x}), \alpha), \qquad (4.130)$$

where $\mathcal{D}_c$ is the set of pseudo-clean samples as defined in (4.64), $\mathcal{D}_n = \mathcal{D} \setminus \mathcal{D}_c$, and $\mathbb{H}_r(f_\theta(\mathbf{x}), \alpha)$ denotes the Renyi entropy, defined by

$$\mathbb{H}_r(f_\theta(\mathbf{x}), \alpha) = \frac{1}{1-\alpha} \log \left(\sum_{y \in \mathcal{Y}} \left(f_\theta^{(y)}(\mathbf{x}) \right)^\alpha \right), \tag{4.131}$$

with $\alpha > 0, \alpha \neq 1$.

As already explained in Section 4.4.3, the use of the mean teacher model (Tarvainen and Valpola, 2017) that relies on a temporal ensembling of models, combined with the soft re-labeling of training samples based on a temporal ensembling of predictions are the two techniques explored by the self-ensemble label filtering (SELF) method (Nguyen et al., 2019). SELF has the student and teacher models respectively denoted by $f_\theta : \mathcal{X} \times \mathbb{R} \to \Delta^{|\mathcal{Y}|-1}$ and $f_{\hat{\theta}} : \mathcal{X} \times \mathbb{R} \to \Delta^{|\mathcal{Y}|-1}$, where the student is optimized with

$$\theta^{(t)} = \arg\min_\theta \frac{1}{|\mathcal{D}_c|} \sum_{(\mathbf{x}, \tilde{\mathbf{y}}) \in \mathcal{D}_c} \ell(\tilde{\mathbf{y}}, f_\theta(\mathbf{x}, \eta)) + \frac{1}{|\mathcal{D}|} \sum_{(\mathbf{x}, \tilde{\mathbf{y}}) \in \mathcal{D}} \| f_\theta(\mathbf{x}, \eta) - f_{\hat{\theta}^{(t-1)}}(\mathbf{x}, \hat{\eta}) \|_2^2, \tag{4.132}$$

where $\eta, \hat{\eta} \in \mathbb{R}$ denote noise variables (e.g., noise to the inputs or noise applied to the model), and t denotes the training epoch. The teacher is trained by ensembling its previous model with the student model from epoch t, as follows:

$$\hat{\theta}^{(t)} = \alpha \times \hat{\theta}^{(t-1)} + (1 - \alpha) \times \theta^{(t)}. \tag{4.133}$$

SELF selects the samples to be inserted into $\mathcal{D}_c$ in (4.132) by maintaining a temporal ensembling of predictions with $\hat{\mathbf{y}}^{(t)} = \alpha \times \hat{\mathbf{y}}^{(t-1)} + (1 - \alpha) \times f_{\hat{\theta}}(\mathbf{x}, 0)$, where $\hat{\mathbf{y}}_i^{(0)} = \mathbf{0}$ and $\hat{\mathbf{y}}_i^{(t)}$ represents the prediction ensemble at training epoch t. Then, training samples where $\tilde{\mathbf{y}} = \text{OneHot}(\hat{\mathbf{y}}^{(t+1)})$ are inserted into $\mathcal{D}_c$. SELF also uses a noisy-label validation set to select the highest accuracy teacher model during the training process.

The application of the data augmentation technique MixUp (Zhang et al., 2018), defined in (4.101), into semi-supervised learning produced the MixMatch approach (Berthelot et al., 2019). MixMatch combines consistency learning and pseudo-labeling techniques and it was applied in noisy-label learning by the influential DivideMix method (Li et al., 2020a). MixMatch takes as input, a labeled and an un-labeled set. The labeled set is represented by training samples classified as clean-label and denoted by $\mathcal{D}_c = \{(\mathbf{x}, \tilde{\mathbf{y}}) | (\mathbf{x}, \tilde{\mathbf{y}}) \in \mathcal{D}, \text{clean}(\mathbf{x}, \tilde{\mathbf{y}}) = 1\}$, and the un-labeled set, represented by training samples classified as noisy-label and denoted by $\mathcal{D}_n = \{(\mathbf{x}) | (\mathbf{x}, \tilde{\mathbf{y}}) \in \mathcal{D}, \text{clean}(\mathbf{x}, \tilde{\mathbf{y}}) = 0\}$. Then, two sets of data augmented samples are built with

$$\begin{aligned} \hat{\mathcal{D}}_c &= \left\{ (\hat{\mathbf{x}}, \tilde{\mathbf{y}}) | \hat{\mathbf{x}} = a(\mathbf{x}), a \sim \mathcal{A}, (\mathbf{x}, \tilde{\mathbf{y}}) \in \mathcal{D}_c \right\}, \\ \hat{\mathcal{D}}_n &= \left\{ (\hat{\mathbf{x}}, \mathbf{q}) | \mathbf{q} = \text{sharpen}\left(\mathbb{E}_{a \sim \mathcal{A}} \left[f_\theta(\hat{\mathbf{x}}) \right] \right), \hat{\mathbf{x}} = a(\mathbf{x}), a \sim \mathcal{A}, \mathbf{x} \in \mathcal{D}_n \right\}, \end{aligned} \tag{4.134}$$

where $\mathcal{A}$ is a set of random horizontal flips and crops augmentation functions, denoted by $a : \mathcal{X} \rightarrow \mathcal{X}$, and sharpen : $\Delta^{|\mathcal{Y}|-1} \rightarrow \Delta^{|\mathcal{Y}|-1}$ denotes a function to sharpen the categorical distribution by adjusting the distribution's temperature. The next stage of MixMatch relies on augmenting the data from $\hat{\mathcal{D}}_c$ and $\hat{\mathcal{D}}_n$ with MixUp (Zhang et al., 2018) defined in (4.101), as

$$\mathcal{D}'_c = \left\{ (\mathbf{x}, \tilde{\mathbf{y}}) | (\mathbf{x}, \tilde{\mathbf{y}}) = \mathsf{MixUp}(\mathbf{x}_i, \tilde{\mathbf{y}}_i, \mathbf{x}_j, \tilde{\mathbf{y}}_j), (\mathbf{x}_i, \tilde{\mathbf{y}}_i) \in \hat{\mathcal{D}}_c, (\mathbf{x}_j, \tilde{\mathbf{y}}_j) \in \mathcal{W} \right\},$$

$$\mathcal{D}'_n = \left\{ (\mathbf{x}, \tilde{\mathbf{y}}) | (\mathbf{x}, \tilde{\mathbf{y}}) = \mathsf{MixUp}(\mathbf{x}_i, \tilde{\mathbf{y}}_i, \mathbf{x}_j, \tilde{\mathbf{y}}_j), (\mathbf{x}_i, \tilde{\mathbf{y}}_i) \in \hat{\mathcal{D}}_n, (\mathbf{x}_j, \tilde{\mathbf{y}}_j) \in \mathcal{W} \right\},$$

$$(4.135)$$

where $\mathcal{W} = \mathsf{shuffle}(\hat{\mathcal{D}}_c \bigcup \hat{\mathcal{D}}_n)$ is a set containing the shuffled contents of the union between the labeled and unlabeled sets from (4.134). The last step in MixMatch consists of the following optimization using the sets built in (4.135):

$$\theta^* = \arg\min_\theta \frac{1}{|\mathcal{D}'_c|} \sum_{(\mathbf{x}, \tilde{\mathbf{y}}) \in \mathcal{D}'_c} \ell(\tilde{\mathbf{y}}, f_\theta(\mathbf{x})) + \frac{\lambda_n}{|\mathcal{Y}| \times |\mathcal{D}'_n|} \sum_{(\mathbf{x}, \tilde{\mathbf{y}}) \in \mathcal{D}'_n} \|\tilde{\mathbf{y}} - f_\theta(\mathbf{x})\|^2_2,$$

$$(4.136)$$

where λ_U weights the loss from the un-labeled set.

Another type of SSL based on consistency loss for noisy-label learning is the RoCL (Zhou et al., 2021), introduced in Section 4.3.2. Essentially, the first stage of RoCL consists of a supervised learning from pseudo-clean samples, which is followed by a second stage represented by SSL on pseudo-labeled noisy samples produced by a time-ensemble of the model and data augmentations. The optimization of RoCL is defined by

$$\theta^{(t+1)} = \arg\min_\theta \left(\frac{\lambda}{\tau_1}\right) \times \log\left(\frac{1}{|\mathcal{D}_c|} \sum_{i=1}^{|\mathcal{D}_c|} \exp\left(\tau_1 \ell(\tilde{\mathbf{y}}_i, f_\theta(\mathbf{x}_i))\right)\right) +$$

$$\left(\frac{1-\lambda}{\tau_2}\right) \times \log\left(\frac{1}{|\mathcal{D}_c|} \sum_{i=1}^{|\mathcal{D}_c|} \exp\left(\tau_2 \times \zeta_i^{(t)}\right)\right),$$

$$(4.137)$$

where $\mathcal{D}_c$ is the dataset containing pseudo-clean samples defined in (4.56), and $\zeta_i^{(t)}$ is the instantaneous consistency loss defined in (4.55).

Some SSL methods developed for noisy-label learning are based on pseudo-labeling, as is the case with the modified co-teaching with self-supervision and re-labeling (mCT-S2R) (Mandal et al., 2020). The mCT-S2R approach extends co-teaching (Han et al., 2018c), presented in (4.125), by adding pseudo-labeling and re-training stages. The pseudo-labeling approach is done by selecting one of the models, say the one parameterized by θ_1, and dividing the training set into samples with small loss $\mathcal{D}_c$ with the remaining samples with large loss, forming the set $\mathcal{D}_n = \mathcal{D} \setminus \mathcal{D}_c$. Then, taking the features, denoted by $\mathbf{z} \in \mathcal{Z}$, from an intermediate layer of $f_{\theta_1}(\mathbf{x})$, we form the set of small-loss features $\mathcal{Z}_c = \{(\mathbf{z}, \tilde{\mathbf{y}}) | \mathbf{z} \text{ extracted from } f_{\theta_1}(\mathbf{x}), (\mathbf{x}, \tilde{\mathbf{y}}) \in \mathcal{D}_c\}$, and the set of large-loss features $\mathcal{Z}_n = \{(\mathbf{z}, \tilde{\mathbf{y}}) | \mathbf{z} \text{ extracted from } f_{\theta_1}(\mathbf{x}), (\mathbf{x}, \tilde{\mathbf{y}}) \in \mathcal{D}_n\}$. Next, we compute the class-wise prototype vectors, computed with the mean vector $\{\mu_{\mathbf{y}}\}_{\mathbf{y} \in \mathcal{y}}$ with $\mu_{\mathbf{y}} = \frac{1}{N} \sum_{(\mathbf{z}, \tilde{\mathbf{y}}) \in \mathcal{Z}_c} \delta(\tilde{\mathbf{y}} = \mathbf{y}) \times \mathbf{z}$, where $N = \sum_{(\mathbf{z}, \tilde{\mathbf{y}}) \in \mathcal{Z}_c} \delta(\tilde{\mathbf{y}} = \mathbf{y})$, and $\delta(.)$ is the indicator function. The new labels for the large-loss features are computed with:

$$\tilde{\mathbf{y}} = \mathsf{OneHot}\left(\mathsf{softmax}\left([-d_1, ..., -d_{|\mathcal{y}|}]\right)\right) \tag{4.138}$$

if $\max\left(\mathsf{softmax}\left([-d_1, ..., -d_{|\mathcal{y}|}]\right)\right) > \kappa$, where $d_{\mathbf{y}} = \|\mathbf{z} - \mu_{\mathbf{y}}\|_2^2$ represents the distance to the prototype of class $\mathbf{y}$, $\mathsf{softmax}(.)$ returns a categorical distribution using the softmax activation, and $\mathsf{OneHot}(.)$ returns the one-hot vector from this categorical distribution. The last step consists of taking $\mathcal{D}_c$ and the pseudo-labeled samples from $\mathcal{D}_n$ to fine-tune the model $f_{\theta_1}(.)$. The pseudo-labeling approach above has two weaknesses: 1) it only uses a single prototype per class, which may not allow a reliable representation of the feature distribution for each class when it has multiple modes; and 2) its non-iterative nature may under-utilize the training set if part of it never gets pseudo-labeled. Both issues have been addressed by Han et al. (2019), who proposed the estimation of multiple prototypes to represent each class, where the re-labeling and training follows an iterative process. Another interesting point explored in (Han et al., 2019) is that the loss function is represented by a convex combination of the loss with the original label and a loss with the pseudo-label, as in:

$$\theta^* = \arg\min_{\theta} \frac{1}{|\mathcal{D}_{pl}|} \sum_{(\mathbf{x}, \tilde{\mathbf{y}}, \hat{\mathbf{y}}) \in \mathcal{D}_{pl}} \alpha \times \ell(\tilde{\mathbf{y}}, f_{\theta}(\mathbf{x})) + (1 - \alpha) \times \ell(\hat{\mathbf{y}}, f_{\theta}(\mathbf{x})), \tag{4.139}$$

where $\alpha \in [0, 1]$ is close to 1 at the first training iterations and it decreases toward 0 as training progress, and $\hat{\mathbf{y}}$ is the pseudo-label for the training sample stored in $\mathcal{D}_{pl}$ that has both the original training label and the pseudo label.

Lately, the combination of pseudo-labeling and consistency learning has been explored in SSL methods for noisy label learning. The Sample Selection and Relabeling (SSR) approach (Feng et al., 2021), which has a sample selection technique discussed in Section 4.3.3 and a data cleaning method explained in Section 4.3.2, explores a consistency loss with

$$\theta^* = \arg\min_{\theta} \frac{1}{|\mathcal{D}_{pl}|} \sum_{(\mathbf{x}, \hat{\mathbf{y}}) \in \mathcal{D}_{pl}} \ell(\hat{\mathbf{y}}, f_{\theta}(\mathbf{x})) + \ell_{fc}(f_{\theta}(a_1(\mathbf{x})), f_{\theta}(a_2(\mathbf{x}))), \tag{4.140}$$

where $a_1, a_2 \sim \mathcal{A}$ denote data augmentation functions sampled from a set of functions $\mathcal{A}$, $\ell_{fc}(.)$ is a consistency loss represented by the cosine distance between two augmented views of the training data $\mathbf{x}$, and $\hat{\mathbf{y}}$ is the pseudo-label for training sample $\mathbf{x}$ obtained from the model if the confidence of the classifier in the pseudo-labeled class (i.e., $f_{\theta}^{(\hat{\mathbf{y}})}(\mathbf{x})$) is above a certain threshold, otherwise, $\hat{\mathbf{y}} = \tilde{\mathbf{y}}$.

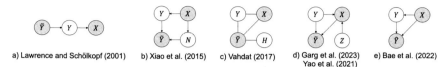

a) Lawrence and Schölkopf (2001)   b) Xiao et al. (2015)   c) Vahdat (2017)   d) Garg et al. (2023)   e) Bae et al. (2022)
                                                                              Yao et al. (2021)

FIGURE 4.37 Probabilistic graphical model.

Probabilistic graphical models (PGM) proposed in the field to address the noisy-label learning problem, where a shaded circle represents an observed variable, while the unshaded circle denotes a latent variable. In (a), the data X is generated by the clean label Y, which in turn is generated by the noisy label $\tilde{Y}$. (b) shows that the model uses the generated data X to produce the clean label Y and noise type N (i.e., no noise, symmetric, asymmetric), which are then explored to generate the noisy label $\tilde{Y}$. In (c), the undirected graphical model relies on the latent variable H that models the correlations between labels. (d) introduces a latent data representation Z that, together with the label Y, generates X that is in turn used with Y to generate $\tilde{Y}$. In (e) the clean label Y is generated only by data X, while the noisy label is generated by Y and X.

Semi-supervised learning is a technique that has been shown to produce outstanding results in noisy-label learning, particularly the methods based on consistency learning. The main issue with SSL-based approaches is the need to classify training samples into clean and noisy, which produces a non-negligible set of samples that are mistakenly classified as clean, but contain noisy labels, biasing the training process. It also mistakenly classifies hard clean-label samples as noisy-label ones, reducing the robustness of the classifier to those hard samples. Hence, much of the research in this area has focused on how to design the best possible classifier of clean and noisy-label samples.

4.4.5 Probabilistic graphical model

Probabilistic graphical models (PGM) have been used in the development of noisy-label learning methods even before deep learning started dominating the field (Krizhevsky et al., 2012). For example, the PGM introduced by Lawrence and Schölkopf (2001) for noisy-label learning using a kernel Fisher discriminant (KFD), was proposed with a random variable X representing the data, another random variable $\tilde{Y}$ denoting the noisy label, and a latent random variable Y representing the clean label, as shown in Fig. 4.37(a). The learning using such PGM is based on

$$\theta^* = \arg\max_{\theta} \sum_{(\mathbf{x},\tilde{\mathbf{y}})\in\mathcal{D}} \log p_\theta(\mathbf{x}|\tilde{\mathbf{y}}), \tag{4.141}$$

where θ parameterizes the class conditional density, and

$$\log p_\theta(\mathbf{x}|\tilde{\mathbf{y}}) = \sum_{\mathbf{y}\in\mathcal{Y}} q(\mathbf{y}|\mathbf{x},\tilde{\mathbf{y}}) \log p_\theta(\mathbf{x}|\tilde{\mathbf{y}}) \frac{q(\mathbf{y}|\mathbf{x},\tilde{\mathbf{y}})}{q(\mathbf{y}|\mathbf{x},\tilde{\mathbf{y}})}$$

$$= \sum_{\mathbf{y}\in\mathcal{Y}} q(\mathbf{y}|\mathbf{x},\tilde{\mathbf{y}}) \log \frac{p_\theta(\mathbf{x},\mathbf{y}|\tilde{\mathbf{y}})}{p_\theta(\mathbf{y}|\mathbf{x},\tilde{\mathbf{y}})} \frac{q(\mathbf{y}|\mathbf{x},\tilde{\mathbf{y}})}{q(\mathbf{y}|\mathbf{x},\tilde{\mathbf{y}})}$$

$$= \sum_{\mathbf{y}\in\mathcal{Y}} q(\mathbf{y}|\mathbf{x},\tilde{\mathbf{y}}) \log \frac{p_\theta(\mathbf{x},\mathbf{y}|\tilde{\mathbf{y}})}{q(\mathbf{y}|\mathbf{x},\tilde{\mathbf{y}})} + \sum_{\mathbf{y}\in\mathcal{Y}} q(\mathbf{y}|\mathbf{x},\tilde{\mathbf{y}}) \log \frac{q(\mathbf{y}|\mathbf{x},\tilde{\mathbf{y}})}{p_\theta(\mathbf{y}|\mathbf{x},\tilde{\mathbf{y}})} \quad (4.142)$$

$$= \underbrace{\mathbb{E}_{q(\mathbf{y}|\mathbf{x},\tilde{\mathbf{y}})}\left[\log \frac{p_\theta(\mathbf{x},\mathbf{y}|\tilde{\mathbf{y}})}{q(\mathbf{y}|\mathbf{x},\tilde{\mathbf{y}})}\right]}_{\text{ELBO}} + \underbrace{\text{KL}\left[q(\mathbf{y}|\mathbf{x},\tilde{\mathbf{y}}) \| p_\theta(\mathbf{y}|\mathbf{x},\tilde{\mathbf{y}})\right]}_{\geq 0}.$$

In (4.142), we have the evidence lower bound (ELBO) and the (non-negative term) Kullback-Leibler (KL) divergence between the variational posterior $q(\mathbf{y}|\mathbf{x},\tilde{\mathbf{y}})$ and the true posterior $p(\mathbf{y}|\mathbf{x},\tilde{\mathbf{y}})$. Note that variational posterior is designed to approximate the complex true posterior. The maximization in (4.141) relies on the expectation-maximization (EM) algorithm (Dempster et al., 1977), where in the tth iteration, the E-step consists of computing the posterior distribution of Y with

$$p_{\theta^{(t)}}(\mathbf{y}|\mathbf{x},\tilde{\mathbf{y}}) = \frac{p_{\theta^{(t)}}(\mathbf{x},\mathbf{y}|\tilde{\mathbf{y}})}{p_{\theta^{(t)}}(\mathbf{x}|\tilde{\mathbf{y}})}, \quad (4.143)$$

followed by setting $q(\mathbf{y}|\mathbf{x},\tilde{\mathbf{y}}) = p_{\theta^{(t)}}(\mathbf{y}|\mathbf{x},\tilde{\mathbf{y}})$ to make the KL divergence in (4.142) equal to zero. The M-step then maximizes the ELBO in (4.142) with respect to $\theta = \{\theta_1, \theta_2\}$, by representing

$$p_\theta(\mathbf{x},\mathbf{y}|\tilde{\mathbf{y}}) = p_{\theta_1}(\mathbf{x}|\mathbf{y}) p_{\theta_2}(\mathbf{y}|\tilde{\mathbf{y}}), \quad (4.144)$$

where $p_{\theta_1}(\mathbf{x}|\mathbf{y})$ is modeled with a normal distribution, and $p_{\theta_2}(\mathbf{y}|\tilde{\mathbf{y}})$ is a label transition modeled with a transition table. We show the functionality of this approach in Fig. 4.38.

The PGM in (Xiao et al., 2015) uses two latent variables, namely the clean label Y and the label noise type N, with the graph structure displayed in Fig. 4.37(b). The label noise type is a ternary random variable associated with the following semantic classes: 1) $\mathbf{n} = [1, 0, 0]$: label is noise free, which implies that $Y = \tilde{Y}$; 2) $\mathbf{n} = [0, 1, 0]$: symmetric noise, where the label has random noise, so $\tilde{Y}$ can take any possible label, except Y; and 3) $\mathbf{n} = [0, 0, 1]$: asymmetric noise, so $\tilde{Y}$ can take labels that are confusing with Y. Using the graph structure above, we can formulate the following decomposition:

$$p(\tilde{\mathbf{y}}, \mathbf{y}, \mathbf{n}|\mathbf{x}) = p(\tilde{\mathbf{y}}|\mathbf{y}, \mathbf{n}) p(\mathbf{y}|\mathbf{x}) p(\mathbf{n}|\mathbf{x}), \quad (4.145)$$

where

$$p(\tilde{\mathbf{y}}|\mathbf{y}, \mathbf{n}) = \begin{cases} \tilde{\mathbf{y}} \mathbf{I} \mathbf{y}, & \text{if } \mathbf{n} = [1, 0, 0] \\ \frac{1}{|\mathcal{Y}|-1}\tilde{\mathbf{y}}(\mathbf{U} - \mathbf{I})\mathbf{y}, & \text{if } \mathbf{n} = [0, 1, 0] , \\ \tilde{\mathbf{y}} \mathbf{C} \mathbf{y}, & \text{if } \mathbf{n} = [0, 0, 1] \end{cases} \quad (4.146)$$

FIGURE 4.38 Probabilistic graphical model.

The PGM approach from (Lawrence and Schölkopf, 2001) is tested on the problem described in Fig. 4.3 with a training of 1000 iterations using the optimization in (4.141) (Lawrence and Schölkopf, 2001), where the covariance of the normal distribution $p_{\theta_1}(\mathbf{x}|\mathbf{y})$ in (4.144) is constrained to be the same across all classes. Differently from other graphs in this chapter, we show the training and testing classification accuracies (as a function of number of epochs), with respect to their noisy and clean labels, respectively.

where $\mathbf{I}$ represents the $|\mathcal{Y}| \times |\mathcal{Y}|$ identity matrix, $\mathbf{U}$ denotes the $|\mathcal{Y}| \times |\mathcal{Y}|$ matrix with all elements equal to one, $\mathbf{C}$ is a $|\mathcal{Y}| \times |\mathcal{Y}|$ sparse stochastic matrix with $\mathrm{tr}(\mathbf{C}) = 0$, and $\mathbf{C}_{ij}$ represents the transition probability between classes i and j. The optimization maximizes the following log-likelihood

$$\theta^* = \arg\max_{\theta} \frac{1}{|\mathcal{D}|} \sum_{(\mathbf{x}, \tilde{\mathbf{y}}) \in \mathcal{D}} \log p_\theta(\tilde{\mathbf{y}}|\mathbf{x}), \qquad (4.147)$$

where we introduce the variational posterior $q(\mathbf{y}, \mathbf{n}|\mathbf{x}, \tilde{\mathbf{y}})$, with

$$\log p_\theta(\tilde{\mathbf{y}}|\mathbf{x}) = \underbrace{\mathbb{E}_{q(\mathbf{y},\mathbf{n}|\mathbf{x},\tilde{\mathbf{y}})}\left[\log \frac{p_\theta(\tilde{\mathbf{y}}, \mathbf{y}, \mathbf{z}|\mathbf{x})}{q(\mathbf{y}, \mathbf{n}|\mathbf{x}, \tilde{\mathbf{y}})}\right]}_{\text{ELBO}} + \underbrace{\mathrm{KL}\left[q(\mathbf{y}, \mathbf{n}|\mathbf{x}, \tilde{\mathbf{y}})||p_\theta(\mathbf{y}, \mathbf{z}|\mathbf{x}, \tilde{\mathbf{y}})\right]}_{\geq 0},$$

$$(4.148)$$

using the same derivation steps as in (4.142). This optimization is also based on the EM algorithm (Dempster et al., 1977), where in the E-step at the tth iteration, we set the KL divergence to zero, by setting $q(\mathbf{y}, \mathbf{n}|\mathbf{x}, \tilde{\mathbf{y}}) = p_{\theta^{(t)}}(\mathbf{y}, \mathbf{n}|\mathbf{x}, \tilde{\mathbf{y}})$, where

$$p_{\theta^{(t)}}(\mathbf{y}, \mathbf{n}|\mathbf{x}, \tilde{\mathbf{y}}) = \frac{p_{\theta^{(t)}}(\tilde{\mathbf{y}}, \mathbf{y}, \mathbf{n}|\mathbf{x})}{p_{\theta^{(t)}}(\tilde{\mathbf{y}}|\mathbf{x})}$$

$$= \frac{p_{\theta^{(t)}}(\tilde{\mathbf{y}}|\mathbf{y}, \mathbf{n})\, p_{\theta^{(t)}}(\mathbf{y}|\mathbf{x})\, p_{\theta^{(t)}}(\mathbf{n}|\mathbf{x})}{\sum_{\mathbf{y}',\mathbf{n}'} p_{\theta^{(t)}}(\tilde{\mathbf{y}}|\mathbf{y}', \mathbf{n}')\, p_{\theta^{(t)}}(\mathbf{y}'|\mathbf{x})\, p_{\theta^{(t)}}(\mathbf{n}'|\mathbf{x})}. \qquad (4.149)$$

The M-step maximizes the ELBO in (4.148) with respect to $\theta = \{\theta_1, \theta_2, \theta_3\}$ that is a set of parameters for the models $p_{\theta_1}(\tilde{\mathbf{y}}|\mathbf{y}, \mathbf{n})$, $p_{\theta_2}(\mathbf{y}|\mathbf{x})$, and $p_{\theta_3}(\mathbf{n}|\mathbf{x})$. While $p_{\theta_2}(\mathbf{y}|\mathbf{x})$ and $p_{\theta_3}(\mathbf{n}|\mathbf{x})$ are modeled with deep learning models, $p_{\theta_1}(\tilde{\mathbf{y}}|\mathbf{y}, \mathbf{n})$ is a label transition model trained with a separate set of data containing clean and noisy labels with $\mathcal{D}_c = \{(\mathbf{x}, \mathbf{y}, \tilde{\mathbf{y}})_i\}_{i=1}^{|\mathcal{D}_c|}$.

A similar PGM has been proposed by Vahdat (2017) that relies on an undirected graphical model depicted in with the graph structure of Fig. 4.37(c), where Y represents the latent clean label random variable and H denotes the random binary variable in the space $\mathcal{H}$ that models the correlations between labels. The model is estimated with the following optimization

$$\theta^* = \arg\max_\theta \frac{1}{|\mathcal{D}|} \sum_{(\mathbf{x},\tilde{\mathbf{y}})\in\mathcal{D}} \log p_\theta(\tilde{\mathbf{y}}|\mathbf{x}) + \frac{1}{|\mathcal{D}_c|} \sum_{(\mathbf{x},\mathbf{y},\tilde{\mathbf{y}})\in\mathcal{D}_c} \log p_\theta(\tilde{\mathbf{y}}, \mathbf{y}|\mathbf{x}), \quad (4.150)$$

where $\mathcal{D}$ is the original training set with noisy labels and $\mathcal{D}_c$ is a separate training set containing noisy and clean labels. The first term in (4.150) is decomposed as

$$\log p_\theta(\tilde{\mathbf{y}}|\mathbf{x}) = \underbrace{\mathbb{E}_{q(\mathbf{y},\mathbf{h}|\mathbf{x},\tilde{\mathbf{y}})}\left[\log \frac{p_\theta(\tilde{\mathbf{y}}, \mathbf{y}, \mathbf{h}|\mathbf{x})}{q(\mathbf{y}, \mathbf{h}|\mathbf{x}, \tilde{\mathbf{y}})}\right]}_{\text{ELBO}} + \underbrace{\mathsf{KL}\left[q(\mathbf{y}, \mathbf{h}|\mathbf{x}, \tilde{\mathbf{y}})||p_\theta(\mathbf{y}, \mathbf{h}|\mathbf{x}, \tilde{\mathbf{y}})\right]}_{\geq 0},$$

$$(4.151)$$

while the second term is decomposed as

$$\log p_\theta(\tilde{\mathbf{y}}, \mathbf{y}|\mathbf{x}) = \underbrace{\mathbb{E}_{q(\mathbf{h}|\tilde{\mathbf{y}})}\left[\log \frac{p_\theta(\tilde{\mathbf{y}}, \mathbf{y}, \mathbf{h}|\mathbf{x})}{q(\mathbf{h}|\tilde{\mathbf{y}})}\right]}_{\text{ELBO}} + \underbrace{\mathsf{KL}\left[q(\mathbf{h}|\tilde{\mathbf{y}})||p_\theta(\mathbf{h}|\tilde{\mathbf{y}})\right]}_{\geq 0}, \quad (4.152)$$

where $q(\mathbf{y}, \mathbf{h}|\mathbf{x}, \tilde{\mathbf{y}})$ is a variational posterior that approximates the true posterior $p_\theta(\mathbf{y}, \mathbf{h}|\mathbf{x}, \tilde{\mathbf{y}})$, and $q(\mathbf{h}|\tilde{\mathbf{y}})$ is another variational posterior to approximate the posterior $p_\theta(\mathbf{h}|\tilde{\mathbf{y}})$. Vahdat (2017) mentions that these variational distributions can overfit the data, particularly at the beginning of the training, so a regularization based on auxiliary (e.g., non-image) sources of information to extract the relationship between noisy and clean labels is proposed. This auxiliary distribution is denoted by the joint probability of noisy and clean labels and hidden binary states $p_{aux}(\tilde{\mathbf{y}}, \mathbf{y}, \mathbf{h})$, which is modeled by restricted Boltzmann machine (RBM). The regularization for (4.151) is $\alpha \times \mathsf{KL}\left[q(\mathbf{y}, \mathbf{h}|\mathbf{x}, \tilde{\mathbf{y}})||p_{aux}(\mathbf{y}, \mathbf{h}|\tilde{\mathbf{y}})\right]$, where $\alpha \geq 0$; and for (4.152) is $\alpha \times \mathsf{KL}\left[q(\mathbf{h}|\tilde{\mathbf{y}})||p_{aux}(\mathbf{h}|\tilde{\mathbf{y}})\right]$, where $\alpha \geq 0$. Finally, the training is based on the EM algorithm (Dempster et al., 1977), where the E-step during the tth iteration sets

$$q(\mathbf{y}, \mathbf{h}|\mathbf{x}, \tilde{\mathbf{y}}) \propto \left[p_{\theta^{(t)}}(\mathbf{y}, \mathbf{h}|\mathbf{x}, \tilde{\mathbf{y}}) \times p_{aux}^\alpha(\mathbf{y}, \mathbf{h}|\tilde{\mathbf{y}})\right]^{\frac{1}{\alpha+1}}, \quad (4.153)$$

and

$$q(\mathbf{h}|\tilde{\mathbf{y}}) \propto \left[p_{\theta^{(t)}}(\mathbf{h}|\tilde{\mathbf{y}}) \times p_{aux}^\alpha(\mathbf{h}|\tilde{\mathbf{y}})\right]^{\frac{1}{\alpha+1}}. \quad (4.154)$$

The M-step maximizes the ELBO terms in (4.151) and (4.152) with respect to θ by fixing $q(.)$ and following the direction of the gradients:

$$\frac{\partial}{\partial \theta} \mathbb{E}_{q(\mathbf{y},\mathbf{h}|\mathbf{x},\tilde{\mathbf{y}})}\left[\log p_\theta(\tilde{\mathbf{y}},\mathbf{y},\mathbf{h}|\mathbf{x})\right] \text{ ,and } \frac{\partial}{\partial \theta} \mathbb{E}_{q(\mathbf{h}|\tilde{\mathbf{y}})}\left[\log p_\theta(\tilde{\mathbf{y}},\mathbf{y},\mathbf{h}|\mathbf{x})\right], \quad (4.155)$$

where

$$p_\theta(\tilde{\mathbf{y}},\mathbf{y},\mathbf{h}|\mathbf{x}) = \frac{1}{Z_\theta(\mathbf{x})}\exp\left(-\mathsf{E}_\theta(\tilde{\mathbf{y}},\mathbf{y},\mathbf{h},\mathbf{x})\right), \quad (4.156)$$

with θ representing the bias terms $a_\phi(\mathbf{x})$, $b_\phi(\mathbf{x})$, $\mathbf{c}$ and the matrix $\mathbf{W}$ denoting the pairwise interactions, as follows

$$\mathsf{E}_\theta(\tilde{\mathbf{y}},\mathbf{y},\mathbf{h},\mathbf{x}) = -a_\phi(\mathbf{x})^\top\mathbf{y} - b_\phi(\mathbf{x})^\top\tilde{\mathbf{y}} - \mathbf{c}^\top\mathbf{h} - \mathbf{y}^\top\mathbf{W}\tilde{\mathbf{y}} - \mathbf{h}^\top\mathbf{W}\tilde{\mathbf{y}}. \quad (4.157)$$

Also in (4.156), the normalization is defined by

$$Z_\theta(\mathbf{x}) = \sum_{\tilde{\mathbf{y}}\in\mathcal{Y},\mathbf{y}\in\mathcal{Y},\mathbf{h}\in\mathcal{H}} \exp\left(-\mathsf{E}_\theta(\tilde{\mathbf{y}},\mathbf{y},\mathbf{h},\mathbf{x})\right). \quad (4.158)$$

The PGMs introduced in (Garg et al., 2023; Yao et al., 2021a) follow the model shown in Fig. 4.37(d), where Y is a latent clean random variable and Z is a latent image feature random variable. The optimization is performed by

$$\theta^* = \arg\max_\theta \frac{1}{|\mathcal{D}|}\sum_{(\mathbf{x},\tilde{\mathbf{y}})\in\mathcal{D}} \log p_\theta(\mathbf{x},\tilde{\mathbf{y}}), \quad (4.159)$$

where

$$\log p_\theta(\mathbf{x},\tilde{\mathbf{y}}) = \underbrace{\mathbb{E}_{q_\phi(\mathbf{z},\mathbf{y}|\mathbf{x},\tilde{\mathbf{y}})}\left[\log \frac{p_\theta(\mathbf{z},\mathbf{y},\mathbf{x},\tilde{\mathbf{y}})}{q_\phi(\mathbf{z},\mathbf{y}|\mathbf{x},\tilde{\mathbf{y}})}\right]}_{\text{ELBO}} + \underbrace{\mathsf{KL}\left[q_\phi(\mathbf{z},\mathbf{y}|\mathbf{x},\tilde{\mathbf{y}})\|p_\theta(\mathbf{z},\mathbf{y}|\mathbf{x},\tilde{\mathbf{y}})\right]}_{\geq 0}.$$

$$(4.160)$$

In (4.160), we have

$$p_\theta(\mathbf{z},\mathbf{y},\mathbf{x},\tilde{\mathbf{y}}) = p(\mathbf{y})p(\mathbf{z})p_{\theta_1}(\mathbf{x}|\mathbf{y},\mathbf{z})p_{\theta_2}(\tilde{\mathbf{y}}|\mathbf{y},\mathbf{x}), \quad (4.161)$$

where $p(\mathbf{z})$ is modeled by a multivariate normal distribution (zero mean, identity covariance), $p(\mathbf{y})$ by a uniform distribution, and $p_{\theta_1}(.)$ and $p_{\theta_2}(.)$ are the decoders modeled by deep learning networks. Also in (4.160), we have

$$q_\phi(\mathbf{z},\mathbf{y}|\mathbf{x},\tilde{\mathbf{y}}) = q_{\phi_1}(\mathbf{y}|\mathbf{x})q_{\phi_2}(\mathbf{z}|\mathbf{y},\mathbf{x}), \quad (4.162)$$

representing the encoders modeled by deep learning networks. The optimization in (4.159) consists of maximizing the ELBO, as follows:

$$
\begin{aligned}
\theta_1^*, \theta_2^*, \phi_1^*, \phi_2^* = \arg \max_{\theta_1, \theta_2, \phi_1, \phi_2} & \mathbb{E}_{q_{\phi_1}(\mathbf{y}|\mathbf{x})q_{\phi_2}(\mathbf{z}|\mathbf{y},\mathbf{x})} \left[\log p_{\theta_1}(\mathbf{x}|\mathbf{y},\mathbf{z})\right] \\
& + \mathbb{E}_{q_{\phi_1}(\mathbf{y}|\mathbf{x})}\left[\log p_{\theta_2}(\tilde{\mathbf{y}}|\mathbf{y},\mathbf{x})\right] - \mathrm{KL}\left[q_{\phi_1}(\mathbf{y}|\mathbf{x})\|p(\mathbf{y})\right] \quad (4.163) \\
& - \mathbb{E}_{q_{\phi_1}(\mathbf{y}|\mathbf{x})}\left[\mathrm{KL}\left[q_{\phi_2}(\mathbf{z}|\mathbf{y},\mathbf{x})\|p(\mathbf{z})\right]\right].
\end{aligned}
$$

In practice, this optimization leverages two sets of encoders and decoders, where $q_{\phi_1}(\mathbf{y}|\mathbf{x})$ is learned with co-teaching techniques, $q_{\phi_2}(\mathbf{z}|\mathbf{y},\mathbf{x})$ is trained as an encoder of a variational auto-encoder (VAE) (Kingma and Welling, 2013), conditioned on the input data and label sampled as $\mathbf{y} \sim q_{\phi_1}(\mathbf{y}|\mathbf{x})$, $p_{\theta_1}(\mathbf{x}|\mathbf{y},\mathbf{z})$ is learned using a reconstruction loss with the original image, similarly to how a VAE decoder is trained, and $p_{\theta_2}(\tilde{\mathbf{y}}|\mathbf{y},\mathbf{x})$ is trained as a classifier conditioned on the data and clean label to predict the noisy label.

Even though the Robust Generative classifier (RoG) (Lee et al., 2019) does not propose a new PGM, it transforms a discriminative model, represented by $f_\theta : \mathcal{X} \to \Delta^{|\mathcal{Y}|-1}$ and pre-trained on the noisy-label dataset, into a generative model that tends to be more robust to noisy data. Assuming that $f_\theta(\mathbf{x}) = h_{\theta_2}(g_{\theta_1}(\mathbf{x}))$, with $\theta = \{\theta_1, \theta_2\}$, $g_{\theta_1} : \mathcal{X} \to \mathcal{Z}$ and $h_{\theta_2} : \mathcal{Z} \to \Delta^{|\mathcal{Y}|-1}$, the central idea is to take the features from one of the hidden layers of the pre-trained model, say denoted by $\mathbf{z} = g_{\theta_1}(\mathbf{x})$, and learn $|\mathcal{Y}|$ Gaussian distributions with a tied covariance Σ (Fisher, 1936). More specifically, each class conditional distribution is denoted by

$$
p(Z = g_{\theta_1}(\mathbf{x})|Y = \mathbf{y}) = \mathcal{N}(g_\phi(\mathbf{x})|\mu_\mathbf{y}, \Sigma), \quad (4.164)
$$

with class prior $p(Y = \mathbf{y}) = \beta_\mathbf{y}$, where $\mathcal{N}(.)$ is a multivariate Gaussian distribution with mean $\mu_\mathbf{y}$ and covariance Σ. Then, the classifier is defined using the Bayes rule, as follows:

$$
p(Y = \mathbf{y}|X = \mathbf{x}) = \frac{p(Z = g_{\theta_1}(\mathbf{x})|Y = \mathbf{y})p(Y = \mathbf{y})}{\sum_{\mathbf{y}' \, in \mathcal{Y}} p(Z = g_{\theta_1}(\mathbf{x})|Y = \mathbf{y}')p(Y = \mathbf{y}')}. \quad (4.165)
$$

The class-conditional model parameters are learned with:

$$
\begin{aligned}
\mu_\mathbf{y} &= \frac{1}{\widehat{\mathcal{D}_\mathbf{y}}} \sum_{(\mathbf{x},\tilde{\mathbf{y}}) \in \widehat{\mathcal{D}_\mathbf{y}}} g_{\theta_1}(\mathbf{x}) \\
\beta_\mathbf{y} &= \frac{|\widehat{\mathcal{D}_\mathbf{y}}|}{|\widehat{\mathcal{D}}|} \quad (4.166) \\
\Sigma &= \frac{1}{|\widehat{\mathcal{D}}|} \sum_{\mathbf{y} \in \mathcal{Y}} \sum_{(\mathbf{x},\tilde{\mathbf{y}}) \in \widehat{\mathcal{D}_\mathbf{y}}} (g_{\theta_1}(\mathbf{x}) - \mu_\mathbf{y})(g_{\theta_1}(\mathbf{x}) - \mu_\mathbf{y})^\top,
\end{aligned}
$$

where

$$\widehat{\mathcal{D}_\mathbf{y}} = \arg\min_{\mathcal{D}'_\mathbf{y} \subset \mathcal{D}_\mathbf{y}} \det(\Sigma_\mathbf{y}) \text{ s.t. } |\mathcal{D}'_\mathbf{y}| = K_\mathbf{y} \tag{4.167}$$

for all $\mathbf{y} \in \mathcal{Y}$, where $\mathcal{D}_\mathbf{y} = \{(\mathbf{x}, \tilde{\mathbf{y}})|(\mathbf{x}, \tilde{\mathbf{y}}) \in \mathcal{D}, \tilde{\mathbf{y}} = \mathbf{y}\}$, $\det(.)$ denotes the matrix determinant operator, $\Sigma_\mathbf{y}$ is the sample covariance of $\mathcal{D}'_\mathbf{y}$, $K_\mathbf{y} \in (0, |\mathcal{D}_\mathbf{y}|)$.

The Noisy Prediction Calibration (NPC) approach (Bae et al., 2022) is a post-processing approach that assumes the presence of a classifier trained on a noisy-label training set to train a transition model from the trained classifier prediction to a clean label, as shown in Fig. 4.37(e). More specifically, assume that we have a classifier training with one of the algorithms presented in this chapter (e.g., Co-teaching (Han et al., 2018c), JoCoR (Wei et al., 2020), etc.), which is denoted by $\hat{\mathbf{y}} = f_{\hat{\theta}}(\mathbf{x})$, then the goal is to represent the clean label distribution with

$$p(\mathbf{y}|\mathbf{x}) = \sum_{\hat{\mathbf{y}} \in \mathcal{Y}} p(\mathbf{y}|\hat{\mathbf{y}}, \mathbf{x}) p_{\hat{\theta}}(\hat{\mathbf{y}}|\mathbf{x}), \tag{4.168}$$

where $p_{\hat{\theta}}(\hat{\mathbf{y}}|\mathbf{x}) = f_{\hat{\theta}}^{(\hat{\mathbf{y}})}(\mathbf{x})$ denotes the prediction probability for class $\hat{\mathbf{y}}$. Then, the goal is to learn the transition model $p(\mathbf{y}|\hat{\mathbf{y}}, \mathbf{x})$, which is referred to as NPC. Given the intractability of this model, Bae et al. (2022) introduce the variational model $q_\phi(Y|\hat{\mathbf{y}}, \mathbf{x})$ and a noisy-label reconstruction model $p_\theta(\hat{\mathbf{y}}|Y, \mathbf{x})$ that is learned with the minimization of the following KL divergence:

$$\begin{aligned}
KL&[q_\phi(\mathbf{y}|\hat{\mathbf{y}}, \mathbf{x}) \| p(\mathbf{y}|\hat{\mathbf{y}}, \mathbf{x})] \\
&= \int_Y q_\phi(Y|\hat{\mathbf{y}}, \mathbf{x}) \log \frac{q_\phi(Y|\hat{\mathbf{y}}, \mathbf{x})}{p(Y|\hat{\mathbf{y}}, \mathbf{x})} dY \\
&= \int_Y q_\phi(Y|\hat{\mathbf{y}}, \mathbf{x}) \log \frac{q_\phi(Y|\hat{\mathbf{y}}, \mathbf{x}) p(\hat{\mathbf{y}}|\mathbf{x})}{p_\theta(\hat{\mathbf{y}}|Y, \mathbf{x}) p(Y|\mathbf{x})} dY \\
&= \log p(\hat{\mathbf{y}}|\mathbf{x}) - \underbrace{\left(\mathbb{E}_{q_\phi(Y|\hat{\mathbf{y}}, \mathbf{x})} \left[\log p_\theta(\hat{\mathbf{y}}|Y, \mathbf{x}) \right] - KL \left[q_\phi(Y|\hat{\mathbf{y}}, \mathbf{x}) \| p(Y|\mathbf{x}) \right] \right)}_{\text{ELBO}}.
\end{aligned}$$

$$\tag{4.169}$$

Given that Y follows a Dirichlet distribution, Bae et al. (2022) propose the use of a reparameterization trick from (Joo et al., 2020) for maximizing the ELBO in (4.169).

As shown above, PGMs have been widely explored in noisy-label learning, with the latest results from (Garg et al., 2023) achieving state-of-the-art results in many benchmarks. However, there are many challenges involved with PGM-based approaches, such as the need for sampling variational posteriors, which tends to make the training much slower, and the learning of generative models that are generally harder to train than discriminative models.

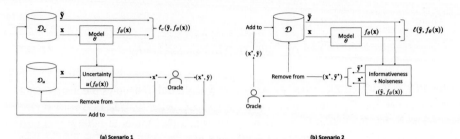

(a) Scenario 1　　　　　　　　　　　　　(b) Scenario 2

FIGURE 4.39 Active learning.

There are two possible scenarios for active learning in noisy-label learning problems, where in both scenarios it is assumed that the oracle can still make mistakes and provide noisy labels. In the first scenario, we have a small clean label dataset $\mathcal{D}_c$ and a large unlabeled dataset $\mathcal{D}_u$, where the model is iteratively trained with an updated $\mathcal{D}_c$ that includes a new training sample (selected by an uncertainty function that tends to select highly informative samples) transferred from $\mathcal{D}_u$ to $\mathcal{D}_c$ and labeled by the oracle. For the second scenario, samples from the training set $\mathcal{D}$ are selected, based on their informativeness and label noisiness, to be re-labeled by an oracle.

4.4.6 Active learning

In active learning, we assume the availability of a small labeled training set and a large unlabeled training set. The classifier is then trained with the labeled training set, and then it is used to select the most informative samples from the unlabeled set. An informative sample is typically defined by classification uncertainty (Settles, 2012) (e.g., a sample that produces a high-entropy classification prediction). Informative samples can also be identified based on how much they reduce overall classification uncertainty, change the probabilistic output of the model, or change the model after training on that sample (Settles, 2012). The selected samples are annotated by an oracle (e.g., a human expert), and used for re-training the classifier. The steps above are iterated until the training converges, where the expectation is that the classifier achieves a performance comparable with another classifier trained with a much larger labeled training set, where samples were randomly selected to be annotated by an oracle (Settles, 2012).

There are two possible scenarios for active learning in noisy-label learning. In scenario one (see Fig. 4.39(a)), we have a small set of clean-label training sets $\mathcal{D}_c = \{(\mathbf{x}, \mathbf{y})_i\}_{i=1}^{|\mathcal{D}_c|}$ and a large set of unlabeled samples $\mathcal{D}_u = \{\mathbf{x}_i\}_{i=1}^{|\mathcal{D}_u|}$. The model is trained with

$$\theta^* = \arg\min_\theta \frac{1}{|\mathcal{D}_c|} \sum_{(\mathbf{x},\mathbf{y})\in\mathcal{D}_c} \ell(\mathbf{y}, f_\theta(\mathbf{x})). \tag{4.170}$$

Then, informative samples from the unlabeled set are selected with

$$\mathbf{x}^* = \arg\max_{\mathbf{x}\in\mathcal{D}_u} u(f_{\theta^*}(\mathbf{x})), \tag{4.171}$$

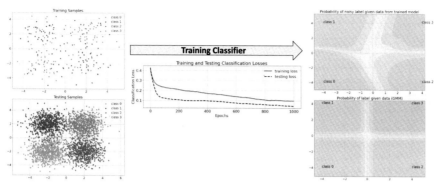

FIGURE 4.40 Active learning.

Using the problem in Fig. 4.3, we test active learning where a noisy oracle (same IDN noise rate as the original training set) is called to relabel the sample with largest loss every 10 epochs for a total of 1000 iterations, as described by the second scenario from (4.172) and (4.173).

where $u : \Delta^{|\mathcal{Y}|-1} \to \mathbb{R}$ represents the uncertainty function (e.g., $u(f_{\theta^*}(\mathbf{x}))$ can be represented by the entropy $\mathcal{H}(f_{\theta^*}(\mathbf{x})) = -f_{\theta^*}(\mathbf{x})^\top \log(f_{\theta^*}(\mathbf{x}))$. Next, the oracle provides a potentially noisy label $\tilde{\mathbf{y}}$ to $\mathbf{x}^*$, where datasets are then updated with $\mathcal{D}_c = \mathcal{D}_c \bigcup (\mathbf{x}^*, \tilde{\mathbf{y}})$ and $\mathcal{D}_u = \mathcal{D}_u \setminus (\mathbf{x}^*)$. The whole process starts over after this step, with a re-training of the classifier.

In scenario two (see Fig. 4.39(b) and Fig. 4.40), the classifier $f_\theta(\mathbf{x})$ is trained with the usual noisy-label dataset $\mathcal{D}$ to minimize classification loss. The next step is to select an informative noisy-label training sample, with

$$(\mathbf{x}^*, \tilde{\mathbf{y}}^*) = \arg \max_{(\mathbf{x}, \tilde{\mathbf{y}}) \in \mathcal{D}} \iota(\tilde{\mathbf{y}}, f_{\theta^*}(\mathbf{x})), \tag{4.172}$$

where $\iota : \mathcal{Y} \times \Delta^{|\mathcal{Y}|-1} \to \mathbb{R}$ measures the informativeness of the training sample and the noisiness of the training label $\tilde{\mathbf{y}}$. Next, the sample is re-labeled with a potentially noisy label $\tilde{\mathbf{y}}$ by an oracle and re-inserted into the training set with:

$$\mathcal{D} = \left(\mathcal{D} \setminus (\mathbf{x}^*, \tilde{\mathbf{y}}^*)\right) \bigcup (\mathbf{x}^*, \tilde{\mathbf{y}}), \tag{4.173}$$

which is then used to re-train the classifier. In scenarios one and two, it is assumed that we have a limited budget to access the oracle's labels.

The method proposed by Bouguelia et al. (2018) assumes scenario one above with a clean training set $\mathcal{D}_c$ and an un-labeled training set $\mathcal{D}_u$. The first stage in the approach consists of selecting informative samples, where a sample is informative if the re-training of the model using that sample disagrees significantly with the original model on the labeling of other samples. Hence, in (4.171), the uncertainty of $\mathbf{x} \in \mathcal{D}_u$

is measured with

$$u(f_{\theta^*}(\mathbf{x})) = \sum_{\mathbf{x}' \in \mathcal{D}_u} \delta\left(f_{\theta^*}(\mathbf{x}') \neq f_{\theta^*_{\mathbf{x}}}(\mathbf{x}')\right) \times w_{\mathbf{x}'}, \tag{4.174}$$

where $\delta(.)$ represents the indicator function, $f_{\theta^*_{\mathbf{x}}}(\mathbf{x})$ denotes the model from (4.174) that is re-trained using the training set $\mathcal{D}_c \bigcup (\mathbf{x}, f_{\theta^*}(\mathbf{x}))$, and

$$w_{\mathbf{x}'} = \left| \max_{\mathbf{y} \in \mathcal{Y}} \left(f_{\theta^*_{\mathbf{x}}}^{(\mathbf{y})}(\mathbf{x}')\right) - \max_{\mathbf{y} \in \mathcal{Y}} \left(f_{\theta^*}^{(\mathbf{y})}(\mathbf{x}')\right) \right|, \tag{4.175}$$

with $f_{\theta^*}^{(\mathbf{y})}(\mathbf{x}')$ representing the model prediction for the sample $\mathbf{x}'$ with respect to class $\mathbf{y}$. Hence, in (4.174), the uncertainty of selecting $\mathbf{x} \in \mathcal{D}_u$ is measured by not only how many instances are affected (i.e., their predicted label change), but also by how much those instances are affected. Then, the algorithm that selects the most informative un-labeled sample with

$$\mathbf{x}^* = \arg\max_{\mathbf{u} \in \mathcal{D}_u} u(f_{\theta^*}(\mathbf{x})) \tag{4.176}$$

where $u(.)$ is defined in (4.174), and the new clean training set is $\mathcal{D}_c \bigcup (\mathbf{x}^*, \tilde{\mathbf{y}})$, with $\tilde{\mathbf{y}}$ being the noisy label provided by the oracle. The model is then re-trained to produce the new parameter θ^* with the new clean training set, and after a few rounds of re-labeling, it detects which samples have been mislabeled by the oracle, using the measure

$$m(\mathbf{y}, f_{\theta^*}(\mathbf{x})) = \max_{\mathbf{y}' \in \mathcal{Y}} \sum_{\mathbf{x}' \in \mathcal{D}_u} \delta\left(\mathbf{y} \neq f_{\theta^*_{\mathbf{x}' \backslash \mathbf{x}}}(\mathbf{x})\right) \times f_{\theta^*_{\mathbf{x}' \backslash \mathbf{x}}}^{(\mathbf{y}')}(\mathbf{x}), \tag{4.177}$$

where $f_{\theta^*_{\mathbf{x}' \backslash \mathbf{x}}}(\mathbf{x})$ denotes the model re-trained using the training set $\left(\mathcal{D}_c \bigcup (\mathbf{x}', f_{\theta^*}(\mathbf{x}'))\right)$ $\backslash (\mathbf{x}, \mathbf{y})$. The mislabeled sample is detected with

$$(\mathbf{x}^*, \mathbf{y}^*) = \arg\max_{(\mathbf{x}, \mathbf{y}) \in \mathcal{D}_c} m(\mathbf{y}, f_{\theta^*}(\mathbf{x})), \tag{4.178}$$

which is then removed from $\mathcal{D}_c$ or re-labeled by the oracle.

The scenario two explained above is assumed in (Bernhardt et al., 2022), which selects noisy-label samples from $\mathcal{D}$ for re-annotation. However, the proposed method selects and allows multiple labels for samples based on estimated label correctness and labeling difficulty. Assuming a budget $B \in \mathbb{N}_+$, the goal of the method is the following

$$\max \frac{1}{|\mathcal{D}|} \sum_{i=1}^{|\mathcal{D}|} \delta(\text{OneHot}(\tilde{\mathbf{y}}_i) = \mathbf{y}_i)$$

$$\text{s.t.} \sum_{i=1}^{|\mathcal{D}|} \|\tilde{\mathbf{y}}\|_1 \leq B, \tag{4.179}$$

where $\mathbf{y}_i$ denotes the clean label for the ith sample, $\tilde{\mathbf{y}}_i \in \mathbb{N}^{|\mathcal{Y}|}$ is defined differently from previous approaches that usually assume $\tilde{\mathbf{y}}_i$ to be a one-hot vector, and consequently $\|\tilde{\mathbf{y}}_i\|_1$ represents the number of labels for the ith sample in $\mathcal{D}$. The training employed in (Bernhardt et al., 2022) first ranks the training samples according to predicted label correctness and annotation difficulty, with respect to the following measure:

$$m(\mathbf{x}, \tilde{\mathbf{y}}) = -\mathbb{E}_{\tilde{\mathbf{y}}/\|\tilde{\mathbf{y}}\|_1}\left[\log f_\theta(\mathbf{x})\right] - \left(-\mathbb{E}_{f_\theta(\mathbf{x})}\left[\log f_\theta(\mathbf{x})\right]\right), \qquad (4.180)$$

where the first term is the cross-entropy loss (larger values are associated with samples with noisy labels), and the second term is the negative classification entropy (larger values are associated with unambiguous samples). The training sample to be re-labeled is selected with

$$(\mathbf{x}^*, \tilde{\mathbf{y}}^*) = \arg \max_{(\mathbf{x},\tilde{\mathbf{y}})\in\mathcal{D}} m(\mathbf{x}, \tilde{\mathbf{y}}). \qquad (4.181)$$

This selected sample is re-labeled by requesting new labels from the oracle with

$$\tilde{\mathbf{y}}^* \leftarrow \tilde{\mathbf{y}}^* + \mathsf{Oracle}(\mathbf{x}^*), \qquad (4.182)$$

where $\mathsf{Oracle} : \mathcal{X} \rightarrow \mathcal{Y}$ draws a sample from the true categorical distribution of the data $\mathbf{x}$, until a majority is formed in $\tilde{\mathbf{y}}^*$ (i.e., one of the classes is selected more often than all others). The training set with the newly re-labeled sample is then used to re-train the model.

The method described in ActiveLab (Goh and Mueller, 2023) merges the two scenarios above, leveraging a dataset $\mathcal{D}$ containing noisy-label samples, together with a dataset $\mathcal{D}_u$ that has un-labeled samples. Note that each sample in $\mathcal{D}$ can contain multiple labels. The active learning algorithm proposed by ActiveLab assesses when the re-labeling of a sample in $\mathcal{D}$ will be more effective than the labeling of a sample $\mathcal{D}_u$. Such decision depends on the following acquisition score:

$$\text{If } \mathbf{x} \text{ in } \mathcal{D}: s(\mathbf{x}) = \frac{w_M \times f_\theta^{(\tilde{\mathbf{y}})}(\mathbf{x}) + \frac{w_A}{|\mathcal{Y}|} + \sum_{j=1}^{\mathcal{A}_\mathbf{x}} w_j p_j(\tilde{\mathbf{y}}|\mathbf{x})}{w_M + w_A + \sum_{j=1}^{\mathcal{A}_\mathbf{x}} w_j}$$

$$\text{If } \mathbf{x} \text{ in } \mathcal{D}_u: s(\mathbf{x}) = \frac{w_M \times \left(\max_{\mathbf{y}\in\mathcal{Y}} f_\theta^{(\mathbf{y})}(\mathbf{x})\right) + \frac{w_A}{|\mathcal{Y}|}}{w_M + w_A} \qquad (4.183)$$

where $\bar{\mathbf{y}}$ is the consensus label from CrowdLab (Goh et al., 2022) for the sample obtained using its multiple annotations, the classifier $f_\theta(\mathbf{x})$ is trained using the consensus label $\bar{\mathbf{y}}$, w_M is the model weight (Goh et al., 2022), $w_A = \frac{1}{A}\sum_{j=1}^{A} w_j$ represents the average annotator weight computed from the individual annotator weights $\{w_j\}_{j=1}^{A}$ (Goh et al., 2022), $\mathcal{A}_\mathbf{x}$ denotes the set of annotations for image $\mathbf{x}$, and $p_j(\bar{\mathbf{y}}|\mathbf{x})$ is the probability of the consensus label $\bar{\mathbf{y}}$ from the annotator j. From (4.183), the samples in $\mathcal{D}$ that have the lowest scores are the ones that have fewer annotations, where annotators disagree with the consensus label, or where the classifier predicts the consensus label to be unlikely. Also from (4.183), the samples in $\mathcal{D}_u$ that have the lowest scores are the ones that the classifier is least confident. In general, ActiveLab prefers to re-label a sample from $\mathcal{D}$ than to label a sample from $\mathcal{D}_u$, except when annotations disagree, classifier has low confidence in its prediction, or the classifier is confident in a prediction that disagrees with the annotations. The B samples that have the lowest scores $s(\mathbf{x})$ are selected, with each one receiving one additional label, and the sets $\mathcal{D}$ and $\mathcal{D}_u$ being updated with the new labels.

Active learning is a relatively unexplored area in noisy-label learning. One possible reason is the difficulty in setting up an experiment with real-world datasets involving an oracle to re-label samples. Another reason is the lack of a well-defined experimental setup that is widely available for other researchers. Nevertheless, active learning studies many important aspects of noisy-label learning, such as the need to explicitly identify samples that are hard to fit (i.e. ambiguous) and samples that have noisy labels. Another interesting aspect of active learning is the discussion of the utility of re-labeling a new sample versus the utility of labeling a new un-labeled sample.

4.5 Model architecture

In this section, we present methods that effectively change the model architecture by adding new modules to the network. We focus on two approaches, namely: label transition methods and graph-based models. Label transition models add a module (e.g., a network or a matrix) to learn the transition from clean to noisy labels. On the other hand, graph-based models rely on graph neural networks (GNN) that generalize convolutional networks to a non-Euclidean space to allow a more reliable selection of noisy-label training samples using a graph built from the training set. Label transition is likely to be the most studied topic in noisy-label learning, for reasons that are explained below, so we believe that the understanding of this technique is critical for the progress of the field.

4.5.1 Label transition methods

In Section 4.2.4, we have presented loss correction approaches, where the method by Patrini et al. (2017) leverages a label transition matrix $\mathbf{T}$ and its estimate $\hat{\mathbf{T}}$, defined in (4.36), to formulate a loss function that takes into account the transition from the latent clean label to the observed noisy label. In other words, it builds a risk-consistent estimator via loss correction (Han et al., 2020b). A risk-consistent method has a statistically consistent estimator of the clean risk, which means that by increasing the size of the noisy-label training set, the empirical risk computed from the noisy-label samples and the modified loss function converges to the expected risk computed from the clean-label samples and original loss function (Xia et al., 2019).

FIGURE 4.41 Label transition methods.

In label transition models, we usually learn two models, i.e., the clean label classifier denoted by $p(\mathbf{y}|\mathbf{x}, \theta_2)$ and the label transition model $p(\tilde{\mathbf{y}}|\mathbf{y}, \mathbf{x}, \theta_1)$.

In this section, we provide an alternative strategy to the loss correction approach by (Patrini et al., 2017) for the use of label transition methods to build a classifier-consistent estimation via hypothesis correction (Han et al., 2020b; Xia et al., 2019). Similarly to the risk-consistent argument above, a classifier-consistent approach provides theoretical guarantees that the model learned from the noisy-label data is consistent to the optimal model, where by increasing the noisy-label training set, the learned model will converge to the optimal classifier learned from clean-label samples (Xia et al., 2019). Due to this theoretical guarantee, this strategy consists of one of the most studied noisy-label learning techniques.

Let us start with the discussion present in (Song et al., 2022; Han et al., 2020b). The optimization considered by label transition methods is (see Fig. 4.41):

$$\theta_1^*, \theta_2^* = \arg\min_{\theta_1, \theta_2} \frac{1}{|\mathcal{D}|} \sum_{(\mathbf{x}, \tilde{\mathbf{y}}) \in \mathcal{D}} -\log p(\tilde{\mathbf{y}}|\mathbf{x}, \theta_1, \theta_2), \tag{4.184}$$

where

$$p(\tilde{\mathbf{y}}|\mathbf{x}, \theta_1, \theta_2) = \sum_{\mathbf{y} \in \mathcal{Y}} p(\tilde{\mathbf{y}}|\mathbf{y}, \mathbf{x}, \theta_1) \times p(\mathbf{y}|\mathbf{x}, \theta_2), \tag{4.185}$$

with θ_1, θ_2 denoting the parameters for the label transition model (first term) and the clean-label classifier (second term), respectively. The label transition model $p(\tilde{\mathbf{y}}|\mathbf{y}, \mathbf{x}, \theta_1)$ can be defined by two types of model, namely: a stochastic matrix, or a regression module usually represented by a deep neural network. Such label transition model depends on the clean label $\mathbf{y}$ and the input data $\mathbf{x}$ when handling instance-dependent noise, but, when dealing with instance-independent noise (a.k.a. asymmetric noise or class-dependent noise), the model only depends on $\mathbf{y}$, with $p(\tilde{\mathbf{y}}|\mathbf{y}, \theta_1) = p(\tilde{\mathbf{y}}|\mathbf{y}, \mathbf{x}, \theta_1)$.

After presenting these two label transition models, it is important to ask why the field did not focus only on the instance-dependent noise model since it is likely to be more effective given that it has more information to produce the label transition. The main issue with such an instance-dependent noise model is that it is in general ill-posed (Han et al., 2020b) given that we normally have an under-constrained learning problem with only a single noisy label per training sample (Menon et al., 2016; Cheng et al., 2020b). This issue is discussed by Scott (2015), who introduced a discussion for the identifiability of this instance-dependent noise model. That work (Scott,

2015) influenced the development of many solutions focused on the estimation of the instance-independent model $p(\tilde{\mathbf{y}}|\mathbf{y}, \theta_1)$ by leveraging irreducibility (Scott, 2015), anchor points (Xia et al., 2019; Liu and Tao, 2015; Yao et al., 2020b), masking (Han et al., 2018b), separability (Cheng et al., 2020b), rankability (Northcutt et al., 2021), clusterability (Zhu et al., 2021c), among other strategies (Zhang et al., 2021b; Li et al., 2021).

An early proposal of a risk-consistent estimator explored the learning of a transition matrix for binary classifiers using cross validation with noisy-label data (Natarajan et al., 2013). However, such approach was not extensible to multi-class problems because of the exponential increase in computational complexity with the number of classes. Furthermore, risk-consistent estimators tend to estimate the inverse of the transition matrix that may not be invertible, which can cause performance degradation (Xia et al., 2019; Patrini et al., 2017).

Scott (2015) explored the theory of mixture proposition estimation (MPE) to address noisy-label learning under the irreducibility assumption for binary classification problems (i.e., with labels $\{-1, +1\}$). More specifically, MPE is related to the estimation of κ in the following relation:

$$F = \kappa \times H + (1 - \kappa) \times J, \tag{4.186}$$

by observing F and H, where F, J, and H are distributions defined in a Hilbert space (Liu, 2022). The mixture proportion κ is identifiable if J is irreducible with respect to H, i.e., J cannot be written as $J = \gamma \times H + (1 - \gamma) \times F'$, with $\gamma \in [0, 1]$ and F' being another distribution. In a binary classification problem, the noisy-label learning problem can be formulated as an MPE (Yao et al., 2020c) by defining the clean-label positive and clean-label negative class conditional distributions with $p_+ = p(X|Y = +1)$ and $p_-(X|Y = -1)$, respectively. The noisy-label positive and negative class conditional distributions are defined by $\tilde{p}_+ = p(X|\tilde{Y} = +1)$ and $\tilde{p}_-(X|\tilde{Y} = -1)$, respectively. Noisy-label learning involves the estimation of λ_+ and λ_- with the following two equations (Liu and Tao, 2015):

$$\begin{aligned}
\tilde{p}_- &= \lambda_- \times p_+ + (1 - \lambda_-) \times p_-, \\
\tilde{p}_+ &= \lambda_+ \times p_- + (1 - \lambda_+) \times p_+,
\end{aligned} \tag{4.187}$$

where $\lambda_- = p(Y = +1|\tilde{Y} = -1)$ and $\lambda_+ = p(Y = -1|\tilde{Y} = +1)$ denote the mixture proportions representing the inverse label flipping rates. Given that λ_-, λ_+, p_-, and p_+ are unknown, the estimation of λ_- and λ_+ is done with the following substitution:

$$\begin{aligned}
\tilde{p}_- &= \tilde{\lambda}_- \times \tilde{p}_+ + (1 - \tilde{\lambda}_-) \times p_-, \\
\tilde{p}_+ &= \tilde{\lambda}_+ \times \tilde{p}_- + (1 - \tilde{\lambda}_+) \times p_+,
\end{aligned} \tag{4.188}$$

with $\tilde{\lambda}_- = \frac{\lambda_-}{(1-\lambda_+)}$ and $\tilde{\lambda}_+ = \frac{\lambda_+}{(1-\lambda_-)}$ being the mixture proportions. Given that we have samples from $\tilde{p}_+$ and $\tilde{p}_-$, we can estimate $\tilde{\lambda}_-$ and $\tilde{\lambda}_+$ with MPE given that, from (4.188), $\tilde{p}_+$ and $\tilde{p}_-$ correspond to F and H in (4.186), p_+ and p_- denote unobserved Js, and $\tilde{\lambda}_-$ and $\tilde{\lambda}_+$ represent the mixture proportion κ. Hence, noisy-label binary classification learning can be written as two MPE problems for the distributions $\tilde{p}_-$ and $\tilde{p}_+$. The only remaining point is then to estimate $e_- = p(\tilde{Y} = +1|Y = -1)$ and $e_+ = p(\tilde{Y} = -1|Y = +1)$ so we can recover the label transition model. This is achieved by the equivalence theorem in (Liu, 2022), which says that estimating $\{\lambda_-, \lambda_-\}$ is equivalent with identifying $\{e_-, e_-\}$.

This work inspired other developments in the field, such as leveraging the anchor point condition (Yao et al., 2020c), which can be seen as a stronger requirement of the irreducibility. In particular, Yao et al. (2020c) showed that κ in (4.186) is identifiable if there exists a subset of the Hilbert space, denoted by S, where $H(S) > 0$ and $\frac{J(S)}{H(S)} = 0$, where $H(S)$ and $J(S)$ represent the probability of the subset S from the distributions J and H. This subset S forms the anchor set that can be used to identify the label transition models. In fact, many of the early instance-independent noise approaches leverage anchor points. Anchor points are defined as samples $\mathbf{x_y}$ assumed to be a representative, or a prototype, for a particular class $\mathbf{y} \in \mathcal{Y}$, because they have $p(Y = \mathbf{y}|\mathbf{x_y}) \approx 1$. Methods that rely on anchor points (Xia et al., 2019; Liu and Tao, 2015; Yao et al., 2020b) need to extract such anchor points from $\mathcal{D}$ by classifying them as an anchor point of clean class $\mathbf{y}$ if $p(Y = \mathbf{y}|\mathbf{x_y}) = 1$. Using this anchor point assumption, the transition model can be easily obtained with

$$
\begin{aligned}
p(\tilde{Y} = \tilde{\mathbf{y}}|\mathbf{x_y}) &= \sum_{\mathbf{y'} \in \mathcal{Y}} p(\tilde{Y} = \tilde{\mathbf{y}}|Y = \mathbf{y'}, \mathbf{x_y}) p(Y = \mathbf{y'}|\mathbf{x_y}) \\
&= p(\tilde{Y} = \tilde{\mathbf{y}}|Y = \mathbf{y}, \mathbf{x_y}) p(Y = \mathbf{y}|\mathbf{x_y}) \\
&= p(\tilde{Y} = \tilde{\mathbf{y}}|Y = \mathbf{y}, \mathbf{x_y}),
\end{aligned}
\tag{4.189}
$$

assuming we have reliable estimates for $p(\tilde{Y} = \tilde{\mathbf{y}}|\mathbf{x_y})$. In practice, finding the anchor point $\mathbf{x_y}$ for which $p(Y = \mathbf{y}|\mathbf{x_y}) = 1$ will require manual or external assistance, which tends to be undesirable in the context of noisy-label learning. Therefore, it is common for methods to also propose a way to automatically select class-wise anchor points with $\mathbf{x_y^*} = \arg\max_{\mathbf{x} \in \mathcal{X}} p(\tilde{Y} = \mathbf{y}|\mathbf{x})$ (Liu and Tao, 2015) in order to estimate the transition model with (4.189). Hence, anchor points are assumed to be present in a dataset, independently if they are manually provided (Yu et al., 2018) or estimated (Liu and Tao, 2015; Patrini et al., 2017).

However, what happens when anchor points are not available? This is a question explored by Xia et al. (2019), who proposed a revised label transition model learning called Reweight T-Revision. This approach is initialized with the learning of a noisy-label learning model

$$
\theta^* = \arg\min_\theta \frac{1}{|\mathcal{D}|} \sum_{(\mathbf{x}, \tilde{\mathbf{y}}) \in \mathcal{D}} \ell(\tilde{\mathbf{y}}, f_\theta(\mathbf{x})),
\tag{4.190}
$$

which approximates the noisy-label classifier denoted by $p(\tilde{Y}|X)$. Next, the pseudo anchor points for class $\mathbf{y}$ are detected with

$$\mathbf{x_y} = \arg\max_{\mathbf{x}\in\mathcal{X}} p(\tilde{Y} = \mathbf{y}|X = \mathbf{x}) = \arg\max_{\mathbf{x}\in\mathcal{X}} f_{\theta*}^{(\mathbf{y})}(\mathbf{x}). \qquad (4.191)$$

Then, we can initialize the transition matrix using (4.189), which produces $\mathbf{T_{y,\tilde{y}}} = p(\tilde{Y} = \tilde{\mathbf{y}}|Y = \mathbf{y}, \mathbf{x_y})$ that is regarded as a prior transition model. Next, the model is fine-tuned by the minimization of the following empirical risk with respect to θ and $\Delta\mathbf{T}$:

$$\begin{aligned}
r(\theta, \Delta\mathbf{T}) &= \mathbb{E}_{(\mathbf{x},\mathbf{y})\sim p(X,Y)}[\ell(\mathbf{y}, f_\theta(\mathbf{x}))] \\
&= \mathbb{E}_{(\mathbf{x},\tilde{\mathbf{y}})\sim p(X,\tilde{Y})}\left[\frac{p(Y = \tilde{\mathbf{y}}|X = \mathbf{x})}{p(\tilde{Y} = \tilde{\mathbf{y}}|X = \mathbf{x})}\ell(\tilde{\mathbf{y}}, f_\theta(\mathbf{x}))\right] \\
&\approx \frac{1}{|\mathcal{D}|}\sum_{(\mathbf{x},\tilde{\mathbf{y}})\in\mathcal{D}}\frac{p(Y = \tilde{\mathbf{y}}|X = \mathbf{x})}{p(\tilde{Y} = \tilde{\mathbf{y}}|X = \mathbf{x})}\ell(\tilde{\mathbf{y}}, f_\theta(\mathbf{x})) \qquad (4.192) \\
&= \frac{1}{|\mathcal{D}|}\sum_{(\mathbf{x},\tilde{\mathbf{y}})\in\mathcal{D}}\frac{f_\theta^{(\tilde{\mathbf{y}})}(\mathbf{x})}{(\mathbf{T}+\Delta\mathbf{T})^\top f_\theta^{(\tilde{\mathbf{y}})}(\mathbf{x})}\ell(\tilde{\mathbf{y}}, f_\theta(\mathbf{x}))
\end{aligned}$$

where $f_\theta^{(\mathbf{y})}(\mathbf{x})$ represents the clean label predictor $p(Y = \mathbf{y}|X = \mathbf{x})$ in this second stage, and $\mathbf{T} + \Delta\mathbf{T}$ represents the stochastic label transition matrix with $\mathbf{T}$ being the prior transition model defined above in (4.191).

The learning methods above require the challenging estimation of the noisy-label class posterior to approximate the transition matrix. This issue has been addressed with dual-T estimator (Yao et al., 2020b) with the following factorization of the label transition matrix:

$$\mathbf{T_{y,\tilde{y}}} = p(\tilde{Y} = \tilde{\mathbf{y}}|Y = \mathbf{y}) = \sum_{\mathbf{y}'\in\mathcal{Y}} p(\tilde{Y} = \tilde{\mathbf{y}}|Y' = \mathbf{y}', Y = \mathbf{y})p(Y' = \mathbf{y}'|Y = \mathbf{y}), \quad (4.193)$$

where Y' is the intermediate class random variable. Note that the decomposition in (4.193) represents a divide-and-conquer approach that leverages the intermediate class to avoid the learning of the noisy class posterior for the estimation of the label transition matrix. This intermediate class enables the factorization of the original label transition matrix into the product of two easy-to-estimate transition matrices, namely: the transition matrix from clean and intermediate labels to noisy labels, and the transition matrix from clean to intermediate labels. The training involves the learning of noisy-label class posterior with (4.190), and the definition of the intermediate class posterior with $p(Y' = \mathbf{y}|X = \mathbf{x}) = f_{\theta*}^{(\mathbf{y})}(\mathbf{x})$. Then, anchor points are detected with (4.191), which are then used to estimate the transition matrix $\mathbf{T_{y,y'}} = p(Y' = \mathbf{y}|Y = \mathbf{y})$ with the model $p(Y' = \mathbf{y}|X = \mathbf{x})$ using the strategy in (4.189). The estimation $p(\tilde{Y} = \tilde{\mathbf{y}}|Y' = \mathbf{y}', Y = \mathbf{y})$ is as follows: We can then estimate intermediate class label with $\arg\max_{\mathbf{y}} p(Y' = \mathbf{y}|X = \mathbf{x})$ for training sample $\mathbf{x}$, allowing the approximation of the transition matrix $p(\tilde{Y} = \tilde{\mathbf{y}}|Y' = \mathbf{y}')$ (assumed to be equal to $p(\tilde{Y} = \tilde{\mathbf{y}}|Y' = \mathbf{y}', Y = \mathbf{y}))$ via counting, as follows:

$$p(\tilde{Y} = \tilde{\mathbf{y}}|Y' = \mathbf{y}') =$$

$$\frac{\sum_{(\mathbf{x}_i, \tilde{\mathbf{y}}_i) \in \mathcal{D}} \delta\left(\left(\arg\max_{\mathbf{y}} p(Y' = \mathbf{y}|X = \mathbf{x}_i) = \mathbf{y}'\right) \text{ AND } (\tilde{\mathbf{y}}_i = \tilde{\mathbf{y}})\right)}{\sum_{(\mathbf{x}_i, \tilde{\mathbf{y}}_i) \in \mathcal{D}} \delta\left(\left(\arg\max_{\mathbf{y}} p(Y' = \mathbf{y}|X = \mathbf{x}_i) = \mathbf{y}'\right)\right)}, \quad (4.194)$$

where $\delta(.)$ is an indicator function.

As noted in (Zhu et al., 2021c), methods based on anchor points have many disadvantages. First, when the number of classes is high and the number of training samples is small, it is hard to fit the noise distributions. Second, the accuracy of the estimations depends on the number of anchor points that are available and can be identified. Third, it is challenging to extend anchor point-based methods to more complicated label noise problems. As a result, many methods that do not depend on anchor points have been proposed, as described below.

When considering label transition matrices, it is worth noting that some label transitions are impossible to realize (e.g., the transition probability between labels car and cat should be approximately 0). However, when estimating such matrices with the approaches above, the computational resources spent for the estimation of the transition probability between such invalid pairs of labels are the same as the resources for estimating the transition probability between dog and cat, which is substantially more common. This motivates the method called Masking (Han et al., 2018b) that consists of a human-assisted learning method to mask invalid label transitions, such that it focuses on the probability estimation of valid label transitions. The incorporation of this prior label transition matrix structure is performed via a generative model that given data $\mathbf{x}$, it first generates a label $\mathbf{y} \sim p(Y|X = \mathbf{x})$, then a label transition matrix $\mathbf{T} \sim p(\mathbf{T})$ and its mask $\mathbf{T}_o \sim p(\mathbf{T}_o)$, where $p(\mathbf{T})$ is an implicit distribution modeled by neural networks, $p(\mathbf{T}_o) = p(\mathbf{T}) \frac{d\mathbf{T}}{d\mathbf{T}_o}\Big|_{\mathbf{T}_o = f(\mathbf{T})}$, with $f(.)$ being the mapping function from $\mathbf{T}$ to $\mathbf{T}_o$, and it finally generates the noisy label $\tilde{\mathbf{y}} \sim p(\tilde{Y}|Y = \mathbf{y}, T = \mathbf{T})$. Han et al. (2018b) introduced the evidence lower bound (ELBO) to estimate the log-likelihood of the noisy data, as follows:

$$\log p(\tilde{\mathbf{y}}|\mathbf{x}) \geq \mathbb{E}_{q(\mathbf{T})}\left[\log \sum_{\mathbf{y} \in \mathcal{Y}} p(\tilde{\mathbf{y}}|\mathbf{y}, \mathbf{T}) p(\mathbf{y}|\mathbf{x}) - \log\left(q(\mathbf{T}_o)/p(\mathbf{T}_o)\right)\Big|_{\mathbf{T}_o = f(\mathbf{T})}\right],$$

$$(4.195)$$

where $q(\mathbf{T})$ is the variational posterior distribution that approximates the true posterior of the label transition matrix $p(\mathbf{t})$, and $q(\mathbf{T}_o) = q(\mathbf{T}) \frac{d\mathbf{T}}{d\mathbf{T}_o}\Big|_{\mathbf{T}_o = f(\mathbf{T})}$ denotes the variational distribution of the structure $\mathbf{T}_o$. In (4.195), the first term inside the expectation represents the usual log likelihood from data $\mathbf{x}$ to noisy label $\tilde{\mathbf{y}}$, while the second term penalizes inconsistencies between the learned distribution $q(\mathbf{T}_o)$ and the manually provided prior $p(\mathbf{T}_o)$. The training algorithm explored in (4.195) leverages a generative adversarial network (GAN) (Goodfellow et al., 2020) with three modules, using a given label transition structure $\mathbf{T}_o$ (e.g., block diagonal matrix). The generator module is responsible for generating the label transition matrix $\mathbf{T}$ using $q(\mathbf{T})$. The discriminator module implements the second part inside the expectation of (4.195), while the reconstructor module is responsible for the first term inside the expectation. The main issue faced by this approach is the notoriously difficult training of the GAN model.

By assuming the rankability of training samples, the confident learning (CL) method (Northcutt et al., 2021), presented in Section 4.3.2, introduces a robust estimation for the instance-independent label transition matrix, by exploring a 3-step strategy, namely: 1) pruning noisy-label samples to avoid overfitting, 2) counting with probabilistic thresholds to estimate label noise, and 3) ranking samples for training. The main difference from the methods presented above is that instead of estimating $p(\tilde{\mathbf{y}}|\mathbf{y}, \mathbf{x})$ and $p(\mathbf{y}|\mathbf{x})$ separately, CL directly estimates $p(\tilde{\mathbf{y}}, \mathbf{y}|\mathbf{x})$ to eliminate samples where $\tilde{\mathbf{y}} \neq \mathbf{y}$. The method by Cheng et al. (2020b) assumes separability, whereby the training relies on distilled samples, selected based on the probability that their labels are identical with the annotated labels, to enable the model to converge to the Bayes optimal classifier. Hence, this model explores the pruning of inseparable training samples to avoid overfitting. Even though the approaches above do not depend on anchor points, the identification of confident samples (Northcutt et al., 2021) or inseparable samples (Cheng et al., 2020b) is as challenge as the identification of anchor points.

The assumption of feature clusterability has been explored in (Zhu et al., 2021c) to estimate the label transition matrix. Clusterability is defined as a property where the K nearest neighbors of a training sample and the sample itself have the same clean label. Let us assume clusterability to explain how to estimate $p(\tilde{Y}|Y)$ and $p(Y|X)$ in a binary classification problem, where

- $e_1 = \mathbf{T}_{1,2} = p(\tilde{Y} = 2|Y = 1)$;
- $e_2 = \mathbf{T}_{2,1} = p(\tilde{Y} = 1|Y = 2)$;
- $\mathbf{p}_1 = p(Y = 1|X)$.

The noisy labels for a training sample and its 2-nearest neighbors are denoted by $\tilde{Y}_1$ and $\tilde{Y}_2, \tilde{Y}_3$, respectively. The 2-NN clusterability assumes that $Y_1 = Y_2 = Y_3$. Following from (4.185), we have $p(\tilde{Y} = j|X = \mathbf{x}) = \sum_{i=1}^{2} p(\tilde{Y} = j|Y = i)p(Y = i|X = \mathbf{x})$. Hence, we have two first order consensus equations:

$$\begin{aligned} p(\tilde{Y}_1 = 1|X = \mathbf{x}) &= p_1(1 - e_1) + (1 - p_1)(e_2) \\ p(\tilde{Y}_1 = 2|X = \mathbf{x}) &= p_1(e_1) + (1 - p_1)(1 - e_2) \end{aligned} \qquad (4.196)$$

The second order consensus equations are:

$$p(\tilde{Y}_1 = j_1, \tilde{Y}_2 = j_2 | X = \mathbf{x}) =$$

$$= \sum_{i=1}^{2} p(\tilde{Y}_1 = j_1, \tilde{Y}_2 = j_2 | Y_1 = i, Y_2 = i) \times p(Y_1 = i | X = \mathbf{x})$$

$$= \sum_{i=1}^{2} p(\tilde{Y}_1 = j_1 | Y_1 = i) \times p(\tilde{Y}_2 = j_2 | Y_2 = i) \times p(Y_1 = i | X = \mathbf{x}),$$

$$(4.197)$$

given the 2-NN clusterability holds and the conditional independency between $\tilde{Y}_1$ and $\tilde{Y}_2$ given their clean labels. This leads to the four second-order equations for different combinations of $\tilde{Y}_1, \tilde{Y}_2$:

$$p(\tilde{Y}_1 = 1, \tilde{Y}_2 = 1 | X = \mathbf{x}) = p_1 (1 - e_1)^2 + (1 - p_1)(e_2)^2$$
$$p(\tilde{Y}_1 = 1, \tilde{Y}_2 = 2 | X = \mathbf{x}) = p_1 (1 - e_1) e_1 + (1 - p_1)(e_2)(1 - e_1)$$

$$(4.198)$$

The eight third order consensus equations are similarly defined, e.g.,

$$p(\tilde{Y}_1 = 1, \tilde{Y}_2 = 1, \tilde{Y}_3 = 1) = p_1 (1 - e_1)^3 + (1 - p_1)(e_2)^3 \qquad (4.199)$$

Such first-, second-, or third-order consensus above can be estimated with $\tilde{D}$, which are used to estimate a unique solution for the label transition matrix $\mathbf{T}$ and the clean label classifier $\mathbf{p}$. It is worth noting that the approach was extended from the binary to multi-class classification problems in (Zhu et al., 2021c).

Note that the noisy-label posterior $\tilde{\mathbf{p}} = p(\tilde{Y} | X)$ is computed from the product of the label transition matrix $\mathbf{T}_{\mathbf{y}, \tilde{\mathbf{y}}} = p(\tilde{Y} = \tilde{\mathbf{y}} | Y = \mathbf{y})$ and clean-label posterior $\mathbf{p} = p(Y | X)$, with $\tilde{\mathbf{p}} = \mathbf{T}^\top \mathbf{p}$. However, the computation of $\mathbf{p}$ from $\tilde{\mathbf{p}}$ and $\mathbf{T}$ is not always unique, so $\mathbf{p}$ and $\mathbf{T}$ may not be identifiable from $\tilde{\mathbf{p}}$, which means that multiple equivalent $\mathbf{p}$ and $\mathbf{T}$ can produce exactly the same $\tilde{\mathbf{p}}$. Such problem requires the introduction of additional assumptions, such as the assumption that anchor points exist in the training set, but the method does not need to identify them (Zhang et al., 2021b). In particular, Zhang et al. (2021b) introduce a regularization of the clean label predictions based on the observation that the "cleanest" clean class-posterior has the highest pairwise total variation, as follows:

$$\theta^*, \mathbf{T}^* = \arg \min_{\theta, \mathbf{T} \in \mathcal{T}} \mathcal{L}(\theta, \mathbf{T}) - \lambda \times \mathbb{E}_{\mathbf{x}_1 \sim p(X)} \mathbb{E}_{\mathbf{x}_2 \sim p(X)} [0.5 \| f_\theta(\mathbf{x}_1) - f_\theta(\mathbf{x}_2) \|_1]$$

$$(4.200)$$

where $\mathcal{T}$ is the space of stochastic matrices, $\lambda > 0$,

$$\mathcal{L}(\theta, \mathbf{T}) = \mathbb{E}_{\mathbf{x} \sim p(X)} \left[\mathsf{KL} \left[p(\tilde{Y} | X) \| \mathbf{T}^\top f_\theta(\mathbf{x}) \right] \right], \qquad (4.201)$$

and the second term denotes the pairwise total variation, with the expectation operators being computed with Monte Carlo approximation. Note that the optimization in (4.200) can estimate both θ and $\mathbf{T}$ using, for example, stochastic gradient descent, where $\mathbf{T}$ needs to be adjusted with column-wise softmax, so it represents a stochastic matrix. A similar strategy has been explored in (Li et al., 2021) with a simultaneous minimization of the cross entropy loss between the noisy label and model prediction, and the volume of the simplex formed by the columns of the transition matrix. Assuming that the clean-label posterior probabilities are sufficiently scattered, this strategy estimates an identifiable transition matrix and a statistically consistent classifier. More specifically, the optimization in (Li et al., 2021) is defined as:

$$\theta^*, \mathbf{T}^* = \arg \min_{\theta, \mathbf{T} \in \mathcal{T}} \text{vol}(\mathbf{T}) + \lambda \times \mathbb{E}_{(\mathbf{x}, \tilde{y}) \sim p(X, \tilde{Y})} \left[\ell(\tilde{\mathbf{y}}, \mathbf{T}^\top f_\theta(\mathbf{x})) \right] \qquad (4.202)$$

where $\mathcal{T}$ is the space of stochastic matrices, $\lambda > 0$,

$$\text{vol}(\mathbf{T}) = \log \det(\mathbf{T}), \qquad (4.203)$$

with the expectation operator being computed with Monte Carlo approximation.

A potential issue with label transition methods is that it is hard to extend them to open-set noisy-label learning problems, since images that belong to a class outside the set of training labels will not have a reliable $p(\tilde{Y}|Y)$ because the open-set class is not in $\mathcal{Y}$. Similarly, the learned label transition model will be of little use to images affected by symmetric label noise. These two issues can be addressed by introducing a label quality random variable S (Yao et al., 2018), which is a quality variable embedded in D-dimensional Gaussian space to represent the annotation quality of $\tilde{Y}$. The log likelihood of this model has the following evidence lower bound:

$$\sum_{(\mathbf{x}, \tilde{y}) \in \mathcal{D}} \log p(\tilde{y}|\mathbf{x}) \geq \sum_{(\mathbf{x}, \tilde{y}) \in \mathcal{D}} \left(\mathbb{E}_{q(\mathbf{y}|\mathbf{x}, \tilde{y})} \mathbb{E}_{q(\mathbf{s}|\mathbf{x}, \tilde{y})} \left[\log p(\tilde{y}|\mathbf{y}, \mathbf{s}) \right] \right.$$
$$- \text{KL} \left[q(\mathbf{y}|\mathbf{x}, \tilde{y}) \| p(\mathbf{y}|\mathbf{x}) \right] \qquad (4.204)$$
$$\left. - \text{KL} \left[q(\mathbf{s}|\mathbf{x}, \tilde{y}) \| p(\mathbf{s}) \right] \right),$$

where $q(\mathbf{y}|\mathbf{x}, \tilde{y})$ and $q(\mathbf{s}|\mathbf{x}, \tilde{y})$ represent variational distributions that approximate the true distributions of Y and S. Yao et al. (2018) also introduce a learning regularization for the variational distributions of Y and S based on the maximization of their mutual information, as follows:

$$\max I(Y, S|X, \tilde{Y}) \approx \frac{1}{|\mathcal{D}|} \sum_{(\mathbf{x}, \tilde{y}) \in \mathcal{D}} \left(\mathbb{E}_{q(\mathbf{y}|\mathbf{x}, \tilde{y})} \left[\log q(\mathbf{y}|\mathbf{x}, \tilde{y}) \right] \right.$$
$$\left. + \mathbb{E}_{q(\mathbf{s}|\mathbf{x}, \tilde{y})} \left[\log q(\mathbf{s}|\mathbf{x}, \tilde{y}) \right] \right), \qquad (4.205)$$

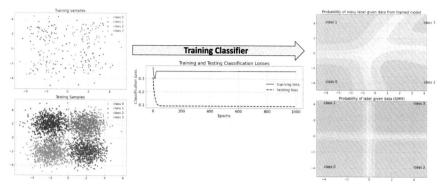

FIGURE 4.42 Label transition model.

Using the problem in Fig. 4.3, we test the label transition model from (Sukhbaatar et al., 2014) using the optimization in (4.207) with $\lambda = 0.01$.

where $I(.|.)$ denotes the mutual information operator. The optimization relies on both (4.204) and (4.205) to produce:

$$
\theta^* = \arg \min_{\theta_1, \theta_2, \theta_3, \theta_4} \sum_{(\mathbf{x}, \tilde{\mathbf{y}}) \in \mathcal{D}} \Big(- \mathbb{E}_{q_{\theta_1}(\mathbf{y}|\mathbf{x}, \tilde{\mathbf{y}})} \mathbb{E}_{q_{\theta_2}(\mathbf{s}|\mathbf{x}, \tilde{\mathbf{y}})} \big[\log p_{\theta_3}(\tilde{\mathbf{y}}|\mathbf{y}, \mathbf{s}) \big]
$$
$$
+ \mathsf{KL}\big[q_{\theta_1}(\mathbf{y}|\mathbf{x}, \tilde{\mathbf{y}}) \| p_{\theta_4}(\mathbf{y}|\mathbf{x}) \big]
$$
$$
+ \mathsf{KL}\big[q_{\theta_2}(\mathbf{s}|\mathbf{x}, \tilde{\mathbf{y}}) \| p(\mathbf{s}) \big] \qquad (4.206)
$$
$$
- \mathbb{E}_{q_{\theta_1}(\mathbf{y}|\mathbf{x}, \tilde{\mathbf{y}})} \big[\log q_{\theta_1}(\mathbf{y}|\mathbf{x}, \tilde{\mathbf{y}}) \big]
$$
$$
- \mathbb{E}_{q_{\theta_2}(\mathbf{s}|\mathbf{x}, \tilde{\mathbf{y}})} \big[\log q_{\theta_2}(\mathbf{s}|\mathbf{x}, \tilde{\mathbf{y}}) \big] \Big),
$$

which trains a model parameterized by $\theta_1, \theta_2, \theta_3, \theta_4$.

The method proposed by Sukhbaatar et al. (2014) introduces a noise layer, consisting of a label transition matrix represented by $\mathbf{T}$, on top of the prediction layer of a deep neural network (see Fig. 4.42). The optimization of such network is defined by

$$
\theta^*, \mathbf{T}^* = \arg \min_{\theta, \mathbf{T} \in \mathcal{T}} \frac{1}{|\mathcal{D}|} \sum_{(\mathbf{x}, \tilde{\mathbf{y}}) \in \mathcal{D}} \ell(\tilde{\mathbf{y}}, \mathbf{T}^\top f_\theta(\mathbf{x})) + \lambda \times \mathrm{tr}(\mathbf{T}), \qquad (4.207)
$$

where $\mathrm{tr}(.)$ denotes the trace operator, and $\mathcal{T}$ is the space of stochastic matrices. Such an optimization is sensible because under strong assumptions the minimization of the trace of $\mathbf{T}$ enables the learning of the true label transition matrix (Sukhbaatar et al., 2014). The optimization in (4.207) starts by setting $\lambda = 0$ and $\mathbf{T} = \mathbf{I}_{|\mathcal{Y}| \times |\mathcal{Y}|}$, allowing the early learning phase to fit the clean-label samples with the model $f_\theta(\mathbf{x})$. Then, λ is slowly increased such that the fitting of the noisy-label samples is done with the help of changes in $\mathbf{T}$.

One of the first instance-dependent label transition estimation approaches was proposed by Goldberger and Ben-Reuven (2017) with the introduction of a nonlinear label noise adaptation layer on top of the clean label prediction layer, similarly to (Sukhbaatar et al., 2014) explained above. Assuming that the network backbone is defined by $f_{\theta_1} : \mathcal{X} \to \mathcal{Z}$, the clean-label prediction is achieved with

$$p(Y = \mathbf{y}|X = \mathbf{x}, \theta) = \frac{\exp(\mathbf{u}_{\mathbf{y}}^{\top}\mathbf{z} + b_{\mathbf{y}})}{\sum_{\bar{\mathbf{y}} \in \mathcal{Y}} \exp(\mathbf{u}_{\bar{\mathbf{y}}}^{\top}\mathbf{z} + b_{\bar{\mathbf{y}}})}, \tag{4.208}$$

where $\mathbf{z} = f_{\theta_1}(\mathbf{x})$, $\mathbf{y} \in \mathcal{Y}$, and $\theta = \{\theta_1, \{\mathbf{u}_{\bar{\mathbf{y}}}, b_{\bar{\mathbf{y}}}\}_{\bar{\mathbf{y}} \in \mathcal{Y}}\}$. The output layer to predict the noisy label is conditioned on the clean label and the data feature, as follows:

$$p(\tilde{Y} = \tilde{\mathbf{y}}|Y = \mathbf{y}, X = \mathbf{x}, \phi) = \frac{\exp(\mathbf{v}_{\mathbf{y},\tilde{\mathbf{y}}}^{\top}\mathbf{z} + c_{\mathbf{y},\tilde{\mathbf{y}}})}{\sum_{\bar{\mathbf{y}} \in \mathcal{Y}} \exp(\mathbf{v}_{\mathbf{y},\bar{\mathbf{y}}}^{\top}\mathbf{z} + c_{\mathbf{y},\bar{\mathbf{y}}})}, \tag{4.209}$$

where $\phi = \{\mathbf{v}_{\mathbf{y},\tilde{\mathbf{y}}}, c_{\mathbf{y},\tilde{\mathbf{y}}}\}_{\mathbf{y},\tilde{\mathbf{y}} \in \mathcal{Y}}$, and $\mathbf{z} = f_{\theta_1}(\mathbf{x})$, allowing the formulation of the c-model as follows:

$$p(\tilde{Y} = \tilde{\mathbf{y}}|X = \mathbf{x}, \theta, \phi) = \sum_{\mathbf{y} \in \mathcal{Y}} p(\tilde{Y} = \tilde{\mathbf{y}}|Y = \mathbf{y}, X = \mathbf{x}, \phi) \times p(Y = \mathbf{y}|X = \mathbf{x}, \theta). \tag{4.210}$$

Note that this can be simplified for the formulation of the s-model's instance-independent label transition model with

$$p(\tilde{Y} = \tilde{\mathbf{y}}|Y = \mathbf{y}, \phi) = \frac{\exp(c_{\mathbf{y},\tilde{\mathbf{y}}})}{\sum_{\bar{\mathbf{y}} \in \mathcal{Y}} \exp(c_{\mathbf{y},\bar{\mathbf{y}}})}, \tag{4.211}$$

where $\phi = \{c_{\mathbf{y},\tilde{\mathbf{y}}}\}_{\mathbf{y},\tilde{\mathbf{y}} \in \mathcal{Y}}$, and

$$p(\tilde{Y} = \tilde{\mathbf{y}}|X = \mathbf{x}, \theta, \phi) = \sum_{\mathbf{y} \in \mathcal{Y}} p(\tilde{Y} = \tilde{\mathbf{y}}|Y = \mathbf{y}, \phi) \times p(Y = \mathbf{y}|X = \mathbf{x}, \theta). \tag{4.212}$$

Training is based on the following optimization:

$$\theta^*, \phi^* = \arg\max_{\theta, \phi} \frac{1}{|\mathcal{D}|} \sum_{(\mathbf{x}, \tilde{\mathbf{y}}) \in \mathcal{D}} \log \left(\sum_{\mathbf{y} \in \mathcal{Y}} p(\tilde{Y} = \tilde{\mathbf{y}}|Y = \mathbf{y}, X = \mathbf{x}, \phi) \times \right.$$
$$\left. p(Y = \mathbf{y}|X = \mathbf{x}, \theta) \right). \tag{4.213}$$

The algorithm consists of first training the model $p(Y = \mathbf{y}|X = \mathbf{x}, \theta)$ using $\mathcal{D}$ without the output layer to predict the noisy label, disregarding the fact that the training labels are noisy. Next, the label predictions from this model are treated as clean, allowing the initialization of the bias parameters in the output layer to predict the noisy label, as follows:

$$c_{\mathbf{y},\tilde{\mathbf{y}}} = \log \left(\frac{\sum_{(\mathbf{x}_i,\tilde{\mathbf{y}}_i)\in\mathcal{D}} \delta(\tilde{\mathbf{y}}_i = \tilde{\mathbf{y}}) \times p(Y = \mathbf{y}|X = \mathbf{x}_i, \theta)}{\sum_{(\mathbf{x}_i,\tilde{\mathbf{y}}_i)\in\mathcal{D}} p(Y = \mathbf{y}|X = \mathbf{x}_i, \theta)} \right) \tag{4.214}$$

$$\mathbf{v}_{\mathbf{y},\tilde{\mathbf{y}}} = \mathbf{0} \text{ for all } \mathbf{y}, \tilde{\mathbf{y}} \in \mathcal{Y},$$

where $\delta(.)$ is the indicator function. The training of the c-model in (4.213) is challenged by the lack of a regularization to mitigate the identifiability issue. This problem motivated the development of instance-dependent label transition methods that make strong assumptions about the problem.

One example of a label transition method that makes a strong assumption about the problem is the one by Xia et al. (2020), who assume that the label noise of a training image depends only on its image parts. Specifically, assume that the training samples are denoted by $\mathbf{x}_i \in \mathbb{R}^D$ for $i \in \{1, ..., |\mathcal{D}|\}$, the part-based representations are learned with non-negative matrix factorization (NMF) with:

$$\mathbf{W}^*, \{\mathbf{h}^*(\mathbf{x}_i)\}_{i=1}^{|\mathcal{D}|} = \arg \min_{\mathbf{W}, \{\mathbf{h}(\mathbf{x}_i)\}_{i=1}^{|\mathcal{D}|}} \sum_{i=1}^{|\mathcal{D}|} \|\mathbf{x}_i - \mathbf{Wh}(\mathbf{x}_i)\|_2^2, \tag{4.215}$$

where $\mathbf{W} \in \mathbb{R}^{D \times R}$ is the matrix of image parts (each of the R columns of $\mathbf{W}$ represents an image part), and $\mathbf{h}(\mathbf{x}_i) \in \mathbb{R}_+^R$ (s.t. $\|\mathbf{h}(\mathbf{x}_i)\|_1 = 1$) denotes the combination coefficients to reconstruct $\mathbf{x}_i$. Assuming that we can estimate the part-dependent transition matrices, denoted by $\mathbf{P}^{(j)} \in [0, 1]^{|\mathcal{Y}| \times |\mathcal{Y}|}$, for each learned image part $\mathbf{W}_j$, for $j \in \{1, ..., R\}$ as defined in (4.215), the instance-dependent label transition matrix for sample $\mathbf{x}_i$ is defined by

$$\mathbf{T}(\mathbf{x}_i) = \sum_{j=1}^{R} \mathbf{h}^{(j)}(\mathbf{x}_i) \times \mathbf{P}^{(j)}, \tag{4.216}$$

where $\mathbf{h}^{(j)}(\mathbf{x}_i)$ represents the jth component of $\mathbf{h}(\mathbf{x}_i)$, learned from (4.215). The part-dependent label transition matrices can be learned using anchor points, so assuming that $\mathbf{x}^{(\mathbf{y})}$ is an anchor point for the class $\mathbf{y}$ (i.e., $p(Y = \mathbf{y}|X = \mathbf{x}^{(\mathbf{y})}) = 1$), we have

$$p(\tilde{Y} = \tilde{\mathbf{y}}|X = \mathbf{x}^{(\mathbf{y})}) = \sum_{\mathbf{c}\in\mathcal{Y}} p(\tilde{Y} = \tilde{\mathbf{y}}|Y = \mathbf{c}, X = \mathbf{x}^{(\mathbf{y})}) p(Y = \mathbf{c}|X = \mathbf{x}^{(\mathbf{y})}) = \mathbf{T}_{\mathbf{y},\tilde{\mathbf{y}}}(\mathbf{x}).$$
$$\tag{4.217}$$

Given that we have R part-dependent transition matrices, we will need at least R anchor points per class to be able to robustly estimate $\{\mathbf{P}^{(j)}\}_{j=1}^{R}$, as follows:

$$\{\mathbf{P}^{(j)*}\}_{j=1}^{R} = \arg \min_{\{\mathbf{P}^{(j)}\}_{j=1}^{R}} \sum_{\mathbf{y}\in\mathcal{Y}} \sum_{l=1}^{K} \|\mathbf{T}_{\mathbf{y},:}(\mathbf{x}_l^{(\mathbf{y})}) - \sum_{j=1}^{R} \mathbf{h}^{(j)}(\mathbf{x}_l^{(\mathbf{y})}) \times \mathbf{P}_{\mathbf{y},:}^{(j)}\|_2^2 \tag{4.218}$$

$$\text{s.t. } \|\mathbf{P}_{\mathbf{y},:}^{(j)}\|_1 = 1, \mathbf{y} \in \mathcal{Y}, j \in \{1, ..., R\}, K \geq R,$$

where $\mathbf{T}_{\mathbf{y},:}(\mathbf{x}_l^{(\mathbf{y})})$ and $\mathbf{P}_{\mathbf{y},:}^{(j)}$ denote the row of these two matrices related to class $\mathbf{y}$. The training algorithm starts with a pre-training of the model to learn the image features, then, the optimization in (4.215) is run to estimate the matrix of image parts $\mathbf{W}^*$ and the reconstruction coefficients for the training samples $\{\mathbf{h}^*(\mathbf{x}_i)\}_{i=1}^{|\mathcal{D}|}$. Next, the part-dependent transition matrices are learned with (4.218). The last step consists of estimating the instance-dependent transition matrix with (4.216). After learning the instance-based transition matrix, the training focuses on learning the clean label classifier $f_\theta(.)$ that is used for testing.

In instance-dependent label transition methods, most columns of the transition matrix do not have much influence on the class posterior estimation. Also, as shown in Sections 4.3.3 and 4.2.3, some training samples are more reliable than others. These facts are explored in (Zhang and Sugiyama, 2021) with an instance-confidence embedding to model instance-dependent noise that relies on a variational approximation that avoids the estimation of a noise transition matrix. In particular, each training sample is associated with a confidence parameter denoted by $w \in [0, 1]$ that is computed from the function $g_\phi : \mathcal{X} \to [0, 1]$, where $w = 0$ means that the training sample is ambiguous or mislabeled. In detail, this paper (Zhang and Sugiyama, 2021) uses a variational approximation to the true noisy-label posterior distribution $p(\tilde{Y}|X)$, which is defined by $q_{\theta,\phi}(\tilde{Y}|X)$, with the variational lower bound of the expected log-likelihood, defined by

$$\theta^*, \phi^* = \arg\max_{\theta,\phi} \frac{1}{|\mathcal{D}|} \sum_{(\mathbf{x},\tilde{\mathbf{y}}) \in \mathcal{D}} \log q_{\theta,\phi}(\tilde{Y} = \tilde{\mathbf{y}} | X = \mathbf{x}). \quad (4.219)$$

In (4.219), the variational noisy-label posterior function is defined by:

$$q_{\theta,\phi}(\tilde{Y}|X) = h(f_\theta(\mathbf{x}), g_\phi(\mathbf{x})), \quad (4.220)$$

where $h : \Delta^{|\mathcal{Y}|-1} \to \Delta^{|\mathcal{Y}|-1}$ is a transformation function that returns a categorical distribution with the following properties: it is potentially non-linear and it is an argmax-preserving function. In practice, when the confidence from $g_\phi : \mathcal{X} \to [0, 1]$ is approximately one, then $h(\mathbf{p}, 1) = \mathbf{p}$, but when the confidence is approximately zero, then $h(\mathbf{p}, 0) = \mathbf{u} = \left[\frac{1}{|\mathcal{Y}|}, ..., \frac{1}{|\mathcal{Y}|}\right]$ (i.e., it is a uniform probability vector of size $|\mathcal{Y}|$). Possible examples for the function $h(.)$ are:

$$h(\mathbf{p}, w) = w \times \mathbf{p} + (1 - w) \times \mathbf{u},$$

$$h(\mathbf{p}, w) = \frac{\mathbf{p}^w}{\left((\mathbf{1}_{|\mathcal{Y}|})^\top \mathbf{p}^w\right)}, \quad (4.221)$$

where $\mathbf{1}_{|\mathcal{Y}|}$ is a column vector with $|\mathcal{Y}|$ ones. The function $g_\phi(.)$ in (4.220) is defined as an instance embedding, with a single trainable parameter for each training sample. The idea of exploring confidence for training samples has also been explored in (Berthon et al., 2021), but following a different strategy, where it is assumed that confidence scores are available for the training samples. For example, this can be computed from the multiple annotations present in multi-rater annotator problems. A confidence score in this case is defined as:

$$r = p(Y = \tilde{\mathbf{y}} | \tilde{Y} = \tilde{\mathbf{y}}, X = \mathbf{x}). \tag{4.222}$$

This allows the training set to be defined by $\mathcal{S} = \{(\mathbf{x}, \tilde{\mathbf{y}}, r)_i\}_{i=1}^{|\mathcal{S}|}$. The transition matrix is estimated first with respect to its diagonal terms:

$$\mathbf{T}_{\mathbf{y},\mathbf{y}}(\mathbf{x}) = p(\tilde{Y} = \mathbf{y} | Y = \mathbf{y}, X = \mathbf{x})$$

$$= p(Y = \mathbf{y} | \tilde{Y} = \mathbf{y}, X = \mathbf{x}) \frac{p(\tilde{Y} = \mathbf{y} | X = \mathbf{x})}{p(Y = \mathbf{y} | X = \mathbf{x})} \tag{4.223}$$

$$= r \times \beta_{\mathbf{y}}(\mathbf{x}),$$

where $\beta_{\mathbf{y}}(\mathbf{x}) = \frac{p(\tilde{Y}=\mathbf{y}|X=\mathbf{x})}{p(Y=\mathbf{y}|X=\mathbf{x})}$. The non-diagonal terms of the transition matrix are estimated with:

$$\mathbf{T}_{\mathbf{y},\tilde{\mathbf{y}}}(\mathbf{x}) = p(\tilde{Y} = \tilde{\mathbf{y}} | Y = \mathbf{y}, X = \mathbf{x})$$

$$= p(\tilde{Y} = \tilde{\mathbf{y}}, \tilde{Y} \neq \mathbf{y} | Y = \mathbf{y}, X = \mathbf{x})$$

$$= p(\tilde{Y} = \tilde{\mathbf{y}} | \tilde{Y} \neq \mathbf{y}, Y = \mathbf{y}, X = \mathbf{x}) \times p(\tilde{Y} \neq \mathbf{y} | Y = \mathbf{y}, X = \mathbf{x}) \tag{4.224}$$

$$= \alpha_{\mathbf{y},\tilde{\mathbf{y}}}(\mathbf{x}) \times (1 - \mathbf{T}_{\mathbf{y},\mathbf{y}}(\mathbf{x})),$$

where $\alpha_{\mathbf{y},\tilde{\mathbf{y}}}(\mathbf{x}) = p(\tilde{Y} = \tilde{\mathbf{y}} | \tilde{Y} \neq \mathbf{y}, Y = \mathbf{y}, X = \mathbf{x})$ denotes the probability that a sample $\mathbf{x}$ with clean label $\mathbf{y}$ has a noisy label $\tilde{\mathbf{y}}$ given that $\tilde{Y} \neq \mathbf{y}$. The training for the clean-label classifier first initializes $\beta_{\mathbf{y}}(\mathbf{x}) = 1$ for all training samples, and follows the steps: 1) train noisy-label classifier $h_\phi(\mathbf{x})$ to approximate $p(\tilde{Y}|X)$ using all samples from $\mathcal{S}$; 2) estimate the diagonal of the transition matrix with (4.223) for each $\mathbf{y} \in \mathcal{Y}$ and train the clean label classifier $f_\theta(\mathbf{x})$ to approximate $p(Y|X)$ for one epoch; 3) update $\beta_{\mathbf{y}}(\mathbf{x}) = \frac{h_\phi^{(\mathbf{y})}(\mathbf{x})}{f_\theta^{(\mathbf{y})}(\mathbf{x})}$ (where $h_\phi^{(\mathbf{y})}(\mathbf{x})$ represents the prediction probability of class $\mathbf{y}$, and similarly for $f_\theta^{(\mathbf{y})}(\mathbf{x})$). The estimation of $\alpha_{\mathbf{y},\tilde{\mathbf{y}}}(\mathbf{x})$ in (4.224) is performed with the off diagonal terms of the transition matrix using an instance-independent label transition model, which implies that $\alpha_{\mathbf{y},\tilde{\mathbf{y}}}(\mathbf{x}) = \alpha_{\mathbf{y},\tilde{\mathbf{y}}}$. Taking the expectation with respect to $p(X)$ on both sides of (4.224), we have:

$$\alpha_{\mathbf{y},\tilde{\mathbf{y}}} = \frac{\mathbb{E}_{p(X)}[\mathbf{T}_{\mathbf{y},\tilde{\mathbf{y}}}(\mathbf{x})]}{1 - \mathbb{E}_{p(X)}[\mathbf{T}_{\mathbf{y},\mathbf{y}}(\mathbf{x})]}, \tag{4.225}$$

which is computed with Monte-Carlo estimation using the anchor points present in $\mathcal{S}$.

Instead of learning the transition matrix between clean and noisy labels, Yang et al. (2021) propose the learning of the Bayes-label transition matrix between Bayes optimal labels and noisy labels. Assuming that the Bayes label is represented by Y^*, a key observation from this paper is that while the clean label posterior is defined by a soft categorical distribution, where $P(Y|X) \in \Delta^{|\mathcal{Y}|-1}$, the Bayes optimal labels are obtained by maximizing the clean label posterior with $Y^*|X = \arg\max_Y P(Y|X)$, forming a one-hot vector. Then, (Yang et al., 2021) directly estimates the transition matrix $T_{y,\tilde{y}}^*(x) = p(\tilde{Y} = \tilde{y}|Y^* = y^*, X = x)$ that relates the Bayes optimal distribution and noisy distribution. A critical point of this method is how to find Bayes optimal labels for training, which rely on noisy dataset distillation from (Cheng et al., 2020b) to collect a set of distilled examples $(x, \tilde{y}, y^*)$ from $\mathcal{D}$, where $\tilde{y}$ is the noisy label, and y^* is the inferred Bayes optimal label. These distilled samples are noisy-label samples $(x, \tilde{y}) \in \mathcal{D}$ that satisfy $\tilde{\eta}_y(x) > \frac{1+\rho_{max}}{2}$, which are assigned to the inferred Bayes optimal label, i.e., $y^* = y$, where $\tilde{\eta}_y(x)$ is the noisy class posterior of x for y and the ρ_{max} is the upper bound to the noise rate. The selection of distilled samples will form the distilled set $\mathcal{S} = \{(x, \tilde{y}, y^*)_i\}_{i=1}^{|\mathcal{S}|}$. The Bayes label transition model is then trained with the following optimization:

$$\phi^* = \arg\min_\phi \frac{1}{|\mathcal{S}|} \sum_{(x,\tilde{y},y^*)\in\mathcal{S}} \ell(\tilde{y}, T_\phi(x)^\top y^*), \quad (4.226)$$

where $T_\phi : \mathcal{X} \to \mathcal{T}$, with $\mathcal{T}$ denoting the space of $|\mathcal{Y}| \times |\mathcal{Y}|$ stochastic matrices. The last training stage comprises the optimization of the clean-label classifier $f_\theta : \mathcal{X} \to \Delta^{|\mathcal{Y}|-1}$ with

$$\theta^* = \arg\min_\theta \frac{1}{|\mathcal{S}|} \sum_{(x,\tilde{y})\in\mathcal{D}} \ell(\tilde{y}, T_\phi(x)^\top f_\theta(x)). \quad (4.227)$$

Instance-dependent or instance-independent label transition methods are one of the most studied techniques in noisy-label learning. This technique can provide some theoretical guarantees, such as classification consistency, where the learned model will converge to the optimal classifier learned from clean-label samples with an increase in the size of the noisy-label training set (Xia et al., 2019). However, the identifiability problem, particularly for instance-dependent methods, is still an open research problem being actively studied (Liu, 2022). Also, the assumptions made (e.g., separability (Cheng et al., 2020b), rankability (Northcutt et al., 2021), clusterability (Zhu et al., 2021c)) to avoid the use of anchor points still need further investigation. Nevertheless, the methods presented in this section are critical for the understanding of noisy-label learning.

4.5.2 Graph-based models

Graph neural networks (GNN) are generalizations of convolutional networks to a non-Euclidean space (Bronstein et al., 2017) that have been widely studied in machine learning (Hamilton et al., 2017). The extension of GNN to noisy-label learning is not straightforward because of the presence of noise corrupting the edges and nodes of the graph, which can cause a performance deterioration. Hence, much of the work using GNNs is focused on how to make it robust to corrupted labels.

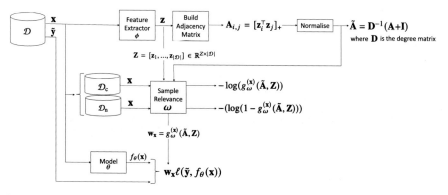

FIGURE 4.43 Graph-based models.

The graph-based model in (Iscen et al., 2020) explores an adjacency graph, denoted by $\tilde{\mathbf{A}}$, which contains a graphical representation of the training samples, where samples that are closer in the feature space $\mathcal{Z}$ have large pairwise adjacency value, and samples far from each other have low adjacency value. After estimating $\tilde{\mathbf{A}}$, we train a graph convolutional network (GCN), denoted by $g_\omega(\tilde{\mathbf{A}})$ to learn how to differentiate clean and noisy samples, as in (4.229). The last step is then to optimize the classifier $f_{\theta(\mathbf{x})}$ with a classification loss weighted by the training sample relevance, as in (4.229).

One of the first papers exploring GNNs for noisy-label learning is (Iscen et al., 2020), which proposes a few-shot learning method that is trained with small clean-label training set, denoted by $\mathcal{D}_c$, and a large noisy-label training set $\mathcal{D}_n$, where the GNN is a binary classifier that discriminates training samples as clean-label or noisy-label, as shown in Fig. 4.43. The union of the two sets forms $\mathcal{D} = \mathcal{D}_c \bigcup \mathcal{D}_n$. Assuming we have a feature extractor $z_\phi : \mathcal{X} \to \mathcal{Z}$ that produces training sample embeddings $\mathbf{z} \in \mathcal{Z} \subset \mathbb{R}^Z$, the GNN first needs to compute an adjacency matrix $\mathbf{A} \in \mathbb{R}^{|\mathcal{D}| \times |\mathcal{D}|}$, where $\mathbf{A}_{i,j} = [\mathbf{z}_i^\top \mathbf{z}_j]_+$ if $\mathbf{z}_i$ and $\mathbf{z}_j$ are reciprocal nearest neighbors (otherwise $\mathbf{A}_{i,j} = 0$), with $\mathbf{z} = z_\phi(\mathbf{x})$, and $[.]_+$ being the ReLU operator (Nair and Hinton, 2010). This matrix is then modified to have non-zero diagonals as follows: $\tilde{\mathbf{A}} = \mathbf{D}^{-1}(\mathbf{A}+\mathbf{I})$, where $\mathbf{D} = \mathrm{diag}((\mathbf{A}+\mathbf{I})\mathbf{1})$ represents the degree of matrix $\mathbf{A}+\mathbf{I}$ and $\mathbf{1}$ is a vector of ones. The class-wise graph convolutional network (GCN) is defined by

$$g_\omega(\tilde{\mathbf{A}}, \mathbf{Z}) = \sigma\left(\mathbf{\Omega}_2^\top [\mathbf{\Omega}_1^\top \mathbf{Z}\tilde{\mathbf{A}}]_+ \tilde{\mathbf{A}}\right), \tag{4.228}$$

where $\mathbf{Z} = [\mathbf{z}_1, ..., \mathbf{z}_{|\mathcal{D}|}] \in \mathbb{R}^{Z \times |\mathcal{D}|}$, $\omega = \{\mathbf{\Omega}_1 \in \mathbb{R}^{Z \times M}, \mathbf{\Omega}_2 \in \mathbb{R}^{M \times 1}\}$, $[.]_+$ is the ReLU operator (Nair and Hinton, 2010), and $\sigma(a) = (1 - \exp(-a))^{-1}$ is the sigmoid function, with $a \in \mathbb{R}$. The output of $g_\omega(\tilde{\mathbf{A}}, \mathbf{Z})$ in (4.228) is a vector of size $|\mathcal{D}|$ indicating the relevance of each sample $\mathbf{x}$ (i.e., when the output for sample $\mathbf{x}$ is approximately 1, then the sample is relevant, otherwise, it is not relevant). The learning of ω is based on a binary classification of training samples into 1 (clean label) or 0 (noisy label),

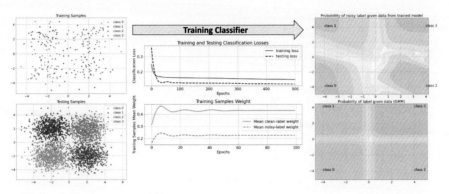

FIGURE 4.44 Graph-based methods.

Using the problem in Fig. 4.3, we test the graph-based method proposed in (Iscen et al., 2020) using the sample weighting optimization from (4.229), which lasts 100 epochs with $\lambda = 1$, and the model training in (4.230) that takes 500 epochs.

with

$$\omega^* = \arg\min_{\omega} -\frac{1}{|\mathcal{D}_c|} \sum_{(\mathbf{x},\tilde{\mathbf{y}})\in\mathcal{D}_c} \log(g_{\omega}^{(\mathbf{x})}(\tilde{\mathbf{A}}, \mathbf{Z})) - \frac{\lambda}{|\mathcal{D}_n|} \sum_{(\mathbf{x},\tilde{\mathbf{y}})\in\mathcal{D}_n} (\log(1 - g_{\omega}^{(\mathbf{x})}(\tilde{\mathbf{A}}, \mathbf{Z}))),$$

(4.229)

where $g_{\omega}^{(\mathbf{x})}(\tilde{\mathbf{A}}, \mathbf{Z})$ represents the relevance prediction for sample $\mathbf{x}$. The learning of the classifier is then based on a sample weighting technique, as follows:

$$\theta^* = \arg\min_{\theta} \frac{1}{\mathbf{1}^\top \mathbf{w}} \sum_{(\mathbf{x},\tilde{\mathbf{y}})\in\mathcal{D}} \mathbf{w}_{\mathbf{x}} \ell(\tilde{\mathbf{y}}, f_{\theta}(\mathbf{x})),$$

(4.230)

where $\mathbf{w} = g_{\omega}(\tilde{\mathbf{A}}, \mathbf{Z})$, and $\mathbf{w}_{\mathbf{x}} = g_{\omega}^{(\mathbf{x})}(\tilde{\mathbf{A}}, \mathbf{Z})$ is the relevance of sample $\mathbf{x}$. We show the experiment with the GCN model trained with (4.229) and (4.230) in Fig. 4.44.

A general method to handle graph corruption is presented in (Wang et al., 2020), where the paper assumes that the input graph, represented by the adjacency matrix $\mathbf{A} \in \{0, 1\}^{|\mathcal{D}|\times|\mathcal{D}|}$, has redundant edges. Such assumption and the formulation proposed in (Wang et al., 2020) can be potentially used in noisy-label learning. More specifically, the proposed approach consists of a GCN that has the following encoder

$$\mathbf{Z} = f(\Omega_2^\top f(\Omega_1^\top \mathbf{X}\tilde{\mathbf{A}})\tilde{\mathbf{A}}),$$

(4.231)

where $\mathbf{Z} \in \mathbb{R}^{Z\times|\mathcal{D}|}$ is the matrix containing the input data embeddings, $\mathbf{X} \in \mathbb{R}^{X\times|\mathcal{D}|}$ represents the original training sample matrix, $f(.)$ denotes a non-linear activation function, $\tilde{\mathbf{A}}$ is defined above in (4.228), $\Omega_1 \in \mathbb{R}^{X\times M}$, and $\Omega_2 \in \mathbb{R}^{M\times Z}$. The GCN decoder is defined by

$$\tilde{\mathbf{A}}' = \sigma(\mathbf{Z}^\top \mathbf{Z})$$

(4.232)

that produces the reconstructed input matrix $\tilde{\mathbf{A}}$. The training is then achieved by minimizing the reconstruction error with a binary cross entropy loss between $\mathbf{A}$ and $\tilde{\mathbf{A}}$. To increase the robustness of this optimization, Wang et al. (2020) introduce a cross-graph approach that uses a co-teaching strategy with the optimization in (4.232).

The use of graphs to address noisy-label learning with open-set noise (i.e., training samples that do not belong to any of the training classes) has been considered in (Wu et al., 2021b). The proposed noisy graph leaning (NGC) leverages a nearest neighbor graph built with training sample embeddings to remove open-set samples and to correct the instance-dependent label noise. More specifically, NGC starts by building a K nearest neighbor (KNN), where training samples are denoted by graph nodes and edges represent sample similarities, with

$$
\mathbf{A}_{i,j} = \begin{cases} [\mathbf{z}_i^\top \mathbf{z}_j]_+, & \text{if } i \neq j \text{ and } \mathbf{z}_i \in \mathcal{N}_K(\mathbf{z}_j) \\ 0, & \text{otherwise} \end{cases}, \tag{4.233}
$$

where $z_\phi : \mathcal{X} \to \mathcal{Z}$ produces training sample embeddings $\mathbf{z} \in \mathcal{Z} \subset \mathbb{R}^Z$, and $\mathcal{N}_k(\mathbf{z}_j)$ represents the set of K nearest neighbors of $\mathbf{z}_j$. Then, the labels are propagated in the graph by first defining the one-hot label matrix $\tilde{\mathbf{Y}} = [\tilde{\mathbf{y}}_1, ..., \tilde{\mathbf{y}}_{|\mathcal{D}|}] \in \{0, 1\}^{|\mathcal{Y}| \times |\mathcal{D}|}$. Then, we compute the degree of each node in the adjacency matrix $\mathbf{A}$ from (4.233) with $d_i = \sum_j \mathbf{A}_{i,j}$ for the estimation of the pseudo labels $\hat{\mathbf{Y}} = [\hat{\mathbf{y}}_1, ..., \hat{\mathbf{y}}_{|\mathcal{D}|}] \in [0, 1]^{|\mathcal{Y}| \times |\mathcal{D}|}$, with

$$
\hat{\mathbf{Y}}^* = \arg\min_{\hat{\mathbf{Y}}} \frac{\alpha}{2} \sum_{i,j=1}^{|\mathcal{D}|} \mathbf{A}_{i,j} \left\| \frac{\hat{\mathbf{y}}_i}{\sqrt{d_i}} - \frac{\hat{\mathbf{y}}_j}{\sqrt{d_j}} \right\|^2 + (1 - \alpha)\|\tilde{\mathbf{Y}} - \hat{\mathbf{Y}}\|_F^2, \tag{4.234}
$$

where $\alpha \in [0, 1]$ and $\|.\|_F$ represents the Frobenius norm. Samples are then removed from the graph using predictive confidence and geometric data structure, with

$$
\mathbf{w}_i = \begin{cases} \delta(i \in \mathcal{S}), & \text{if } \hat{Y}_{i,\tilde{\mathbf{y}}_i} > \frac{1}{|\mathcal{Y}|} \\ \delta(\max_k \hat{\mathbf{Y}}_{i,k} > \eta) \times \delta(i \in \mathcal{S}), & \text{otherwise} \end{cases}, \tag{4.235}
$$

where $\mathcal{S}$ is the largest connected component of the class with the largest prediction probability in $\hat{\mathbf{y}}_i$ from (4.234). Note that in (4.235), samples are removed when: 1) graph nodes in the largest connected component of class $\mathbf{y}$ have a different label produced by (4.234); and 2) uncertain prediction of one of the in-distribution labels, with maximum probability less than η. The method also includes a contrastive learning of the training sample embeddings, taking into account the graph connections. Then the training is based on minimizing the cross-entropy loss using the weighted and re-label training samples and the contrastive learning loss mentioned above.

The use of graphs to address noisy-label learning problems has received relatively little attention, compared with other techniques presented in this chapter. An interesting advantage is that it is an elegant technique that can perform sample selection and re-label simultaneously. Nevertheless, there are some challenges involved in the approaches presented in this section, such as: how to construct the adjacency matrix, how to train the feature extractor for building the adjacency matrix, and how to integrate the GNN training with the classifier training.

4.6 Conclusions

In this chapter, we presented the core techniques developed for addressing noisy-label learning, as presented in the hierarchy from Fig. 4.1. Even though noisy-label learning explores a wide range of ideas and strategies, they all aim to solve the problem of overfitting noisy-label samples during the optimization of classifiers and regressors.

The ideas proposed are divided into four topics: loss function, data processing, training algorithm, and model architecture. Loss function methods work by modifying the usual classification and regression losses with losses or regularization functions that show robustness to noisy labels (Zhang and Sabuncu, 2018; Liu et al., 2020), losses that weight training samples (Liu and Tao, 2015), losses that correct the model prediction or the training label (Patrini et al., 2017; Reed et al., 2014), losses that enable the adaptation of model trained with noisy labels to a domain where labels are clean (Konstantinov and Lampert, 2019). Data processing techniques aim to modify training data or labels to make the model more robust to noisy labels. For instance, adversarial training (Alayrac et al., 2019; Fatras et al., 2019; Zhu et al., 2021b), removal of noisy-label data from the training set (Jiang et al., 2017; Shen and Sanghavi, 2019; Chen et al., 2019; Han et al., 2018c), separation of clean and noisy-label data to be trained using different strategies (Li et al., 2020a), use of multiple labels per training sample (Tanno et al., 2019), prior data knowledge exploration (Seo et al., 2019; Han et al., 2018b; Luo et al., 2019), and data augmentation (Nishi et al., 2021) represent effective data processing techniques to handle noisy-label learning. Training algorithms consist of modifying the optimization of models, which are exemplified by meta-learning (Ren et al., 2018; Dehghani et al., 2017), self-supervised pre-training (Zheltonozhskii et al., 2022), training with multiple models (Jiang et al., 2017; Malach and Shalev-Shwartz, 2017; Han et al., 2018c; Yu et al., 2019a; Wei et al., 2020), semi-supervised learning (Li et al., 2020a; Ding et al., 2018), probabilistic graphical model (Lawrence and Schölkopf, 2001; Xiao et al., 2015; Vahdat, 2017; Yao et al., 2021a; Garg et al., 2023; Bae et al., 2022), and active learning (Bouguelia et al., 2018; Bernhardt et al., 2022; Goh and Mueller, 2023). Model architecture techniques modify the model's network structure to enable to inclusion of new modules, such as a label transition method (Scott, 2015; Liu and Tao, 2015) or a graph neural network (Iscen et al., 2020).

As we shall see in the next chapter, top-performing approaches usually rely on multiple techniques, such as sample selection, self-supervised pre-training, multiple models, data augmentation, and semi-supervised learning (Li et al., 2020a). In fact, it is hard to obtain state-of-the-art results in any of the noisy-label learning benchmarks without exploring multiple techniques. Current papers tend to start from a top-performing method and change just one of the modules to improve results at least in a subset of the benchmarks. Nevertheless, it is important to recognize that some techniques are currently dominating the solutions, including: separation of clean and noisy-label data to be trained using different strategies (Li et al., 2020a), data augmentation (Nishi et al., 2021), self-supervised pre-training (Zheltonozhskii et al., 2022), training with multiple models (Jiang et al., 2017; Malach and Shalev-Shwartz, 2017; Han et al., 2018c; Yu et al., 2019a; Wei et al., 2020), semi-supervised learning (Li et al., 2020a; Ding et al., 2018), probabilistic graphical model (Lawrence and Schölkopf, 2001; Xiao et al., 2015; Vahdat, 2017; Yao et al., 2021a; Garg et al., 2023; Bae et al., 2022), and label transition method (Scott, 2015; Liu and Tao, 2015). Next, we present the currently best methods for the main noisy-label learning benchmarks, and we will refer back to this chapter and explain only the main differences, with respect to what has already been presented.

Benchmarks, methods, results, and code

5.1 Introduction

In this chapter, we present the most accurate methods in the field for various benchmarks representing the many types of noisy-label problems introduced in Chapter 2. We summarize each method by explaining it with respect to the techniques introduced in Chapter 4. We also aim to provide a summary of the most successful techniques being explored by the field to mitigate the noisy-label learning problem in Section 5.10. This chapter is up-to-date with the methods published until July 2023, but new methods will be proposed almost on a monthly basis, so it is important for the reader to understand that by the time this book is published, the methods contained in this chapter are likely to no longer represent to most accurate for at least some of the benchmarks. In Chapter 6, we provide some ideas on how to find the next generation of state-of-the-art approaches.

5.2 Closed set label noise problems

Let us start with the **CIFAR-10** (Krizhevsky et al., 2014) and **CIFAR-100** (Kryzhevsky et al., 2014) datasets that have been heavily explored for the assessment of noisy-label learning methods. Using these two datasets, the **closed-set symmetric label noise problems** (Tanaka et al., 2018; Patrini et al., 2017) relied on noise rate $\eta \in \{20\%, 50\%, 80\%, 90\%\}$ and the **closed-set asymmetric label noise problems** (Tanaka et al., 2018; Patrini et al., 2017) relied on noise rate $\eta = 40\%$, as explained in Section 2.7.1.1. The results shown in Table 5.1 and Table 5.2 are obtained using the same PreActResNet-18 (He et al., 2016b) model for all approaches, which allows a reasonably fair comparison between the proposals.

Before describing the top performing methods for the two benchmarks in Table 5.1 and Table 5.2, let us first explain DivideMix (Li et al., 2020a),[1] which is a rather influential method that relied on many of the techniques presented in Chapter 4. As depicted in Fig. 5.1, DivideMix is an approach that trains two models, similarly to

---

[1] https://github.com/LiJunnan1992/DivideMix.

Table 5.1 Test accuracy (%) on the closed-set symmetric label noise benchmark on CIFAR-10 and CIFAR-100 (Tanaka et al., 2018; Patrini et al., 2017). Test accuracy (%) under closed set symmetric label noise using the best and last training results. [†]: needs a clean validation set.

Dataset		CIFAR-10				CIFAR-100			
Symmetric noise rate		20%	50%	80%	90%	20%	50%	80%	90%
Cross-Entropy	Best	86.8	79.4	62.9	42.7	62.0	46.7	19.9	10.1
(Li et al., 2020a)	Last	82.7	57.9	26.1	16.8	61.8	37.3	8.8	3.5
Co-teaching+	Best	89.5	85.7	67.4	47.9	65.6	51.8	27.9	13.7
(Yu et al., 2019b)	Last	88.2	84.1	45.5	30.1	64.1	45.3	15.5	8.8
Meta-Learning	Best	92.9	89.3	77.4	58.7	68.5	59.2	42.4	19.5
(Li et al., 2019)	Last	92.0	88.8	76.1	58.3	67.7	58.0	40.1	14.3
M-correction	Best	94.0	92.0	86.8	69.1	73.9	66.1	48.2	24.3
(Arazo et al., 2019)	Last	93.8	91.9	86.6	68.7	73.4	65.4	47.6	20.5
DivideMix	Best	96.1	94.6	93.2	76.0	77.3	74.6	60.2	31.5
(Li et al., 2020a)	Last	95.7	94.4	92.9	75.4	76.9	74.2	59.6	31.0
ELR+	Best	95.8	94.8	93.3	78.7	77.6	73.6	60.8	33.4
(Liu et al., 2020)	Last	–	–	–	–	–	–	–	–
PES	Best	95.9	95.1	93.1	–	74.3	61.6	–	–
(Bai et al., 2021)	Last	–	–	–	–	–	–	–	–
ScanMix	Best	96.0	94.5	93.5	91.0	77.0	75.7	66.0	58.5
(Sachdeva et al., 2023)	Last	95.7	93.9	92.6	90.3	76.0	75.4	65.0	58.2
C2D	Best	96.4	95.3	94.4	93.6	78.7	76.4	67.8	58.7
(Zheltonozhskii et al., 2022)	Last	96.2	95.2	94.3	93.4	78.3	76.1	67.4	58.5
SANM(C2D)	Best	96.6	96.4	95.7	95.1	81.9	79.3	71.6	61.9
(Tu et al., 2023b)	Last	–	–	–	–	–	–	–	–
DMLP(DivideMix)[†]	Best	96.3	95.8	94.5	94.3	79.9	76.8	68.6	65.8
(Tu et al., 2023a)	Last	96.2	95.6	94.3	94.0	79.4	76.1	68.5	65.4
SSR+	Best	96.7	96.1	95.6	95.2	79.7	77.2	71.9	66.6
(Feng et al., 2021)	Last	–	–	–	–	–	–	–	–

co-teaching (Han et al., 2018c), where the training starts with sample selection using the small-loss hypothesis that divides the training set into clean and noisy datasets $\mathcal{D}_c$ and $\mathcal{D}_n$, respectively. Then, each subset is augmented with common data augmentation functions. Next, MixMatch (Berthelot et al., 2019) is used as a semi-supervised learning technique, and training for each model relies on a cross-entropy (CE) loss for the clean set, a robust mean-square error (MSE) loss for the noisy set, and a regularization that imposes a balanced distribution of predictions from the model. DivideMix produced large improvements in the CIFAR-10 and CIFAR-100 label noise benchmarks, and consequently became an influential method. Similarly to other papers published at around the same time (Nguyen et al., 2019; Arazo et al., 2019), it was clear that an effective noisy-label method would require a combination of many of the techniques presented in Chapter 4.

Table 5.2 **Test accuracy (%) on the closed-set asymmetric label noise benchmark on CIFAR-10 and CIFAR-100 (Tanaka et al., 2018; Patrini et al., 2017).** Test accuracy (%) under closed set symmetric label noise using the best and last training results. [†]: needs a clean validation set.

Dataset		CIFAR-10	CIFAR-100
Asymmetric noise rate		**40%**	**40%**
Cross-Entropy	Best	77.3	44.5
(Feng et al., 2023)	Last	–	–
Meta-Learning	Best	89.2	–
(Li et al., 2019)	Last	88.6	–
M-correction	Best	87.4	47.4
(Arazo et al., 2019)	Last	86.3	–
DivideMix	Best	93.4	72.2
(Li et al., 2020a)	Last	92.1	–
ELR+	Best	93.0	–
(Liu et al., 2020)	Last	–	–
ScanMix	Best	93.7	–
(Sachdeva et al., 2023)	Last	93.4	–
C2D	Best	94.3	77.7
(Zheltonozhskii et al., 2022)	Last	93.8	75.1
SANM(DivideMix)	Best	94.8	–
(Tu et al., 2023b)	Last	–	–
DMLP(DivideMix)[†]	Best	95.0	–
(Tu et al., 2023a)	Last	–	–
OT-Filter	Best	95.1	76.5
(Feng et al., 2023)	Last	–	–
SSR+	Best	95.5	–
(Feng et al., 2021)	Last	–	–

DivideMix has been extended in multiple ways, such as with a self-supervised pre-training method (C2D) (Zheltonozhskii et al., 2022)[2] that is more effective than the warm-up stage following an ImageNet pre-training (Li et al., 2020a), with a semi-supervised learning stage that is combined with an unsupervised semantic clustering (ScanMix) (Sachdeva et al., 2023),[3] with a robust early-learning regularization loss function (ELR+) (Liu et al., 2020),[4] or with the Optimal Transport Filter (OT-filter) (Feng et al., 2023) that is a more effective sample selection approach to select

---

[2] https://github.com/ContrastToDivide/C2D.
[3] https://github.com/ragavsachdeva/ScanMix.
[4] https://github.com/shengliu66/ELR.

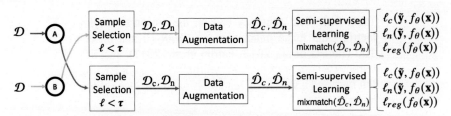

FIGURE 5.1 DivideMix (Li et al., 2020a).

Diagram of the main steps of DivideMix (Li et al., 2020a), consisting of two models Ⓐ and Ⓑ, small-loss based sample selection that divides training set $\mathcal{D}$ into clean $\mathcal{D}_c$ and noisy $\mathcal{D}_n$ sets, data augmentation (forming augmented sets $\hat{\mathcal{D}}_c$ and noisy $\hat{\mathcal{D}}_n$), semi-supervised learning with MixMatch (Berthelot et al., 2019), and regularized loss function with a robust loss for the noisy set.

samples for the subsequent semi-supervised learning by exploring the optimal transport theory (Villani, 2021).

Considering the results in Table 5.1 and Table 5.2, the top-performing methods (July/2023) to handle CIFAR-10 and CIFAR-100 symmetric and asymmetric label noise are the self-supervised adversarial noisy masking (SANM) (Tu et al., 2023b), decoupled meta label purifier (DMLP) (Tu et al., 2023a), OT-Filter (Feng et al., 2023), and sample selection and relabeling (SSR) (Feng et al., 2021). We now provide more details about some of these methods below.

SANM (Tu et al., 2023b),[5] in Fig. 5.2, explores an adversarial training process that minimizes a self-supervised image reconstruction loss and a classification loss of a masked image, where the mask size depends on the probability that the training label is noisy, computed based on the small-loss hypothesis (Li et al., 2020a). The image masking is produced based on the class-activation map (CAM) (Zhou et al., 2016), where a noisier label leads to a larger mask size. The gist of SANM is to regularize the classification loss function by adversarially masking the image given the likelihood of its label being noisy. In addition, a loss regularization in the form of a self-supervised image reconstruction (from its masked version) is explored, where images that have noisy labels will be more masked, and consequently harder to be reconstructed.

DMLP (Tu et al., 2023a)[6] is a meta-learning approach, similar to the ones presented in Section 4.4.1, which uses a noisy-label training set $\mathcal{D}_t$ and a clean-label validation set $\mathcal{D}_v$ to solve a bi-level optimization, like the one in (4.109) with an outer level training for the meta parameters and the inner level learning the model parameters, where the meta parameters are the pseudo labels for the training samples. DMLP

---

[5] https://github.com/yuanpengtu/SANM. Although github site was available, code was not available in July 2023.

[6] https://github.com/yuanpengtu/DMLP. Although github site was available, code was not available in July 2023.

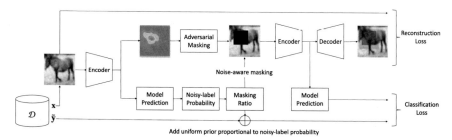

FIGURE 5.2 SANM (Tu et al., 2023b).

Diagram of the main steps of SANM (Tu et al., 2023b), consisting of an adversarial training
that minimizes a reconstruction loss and a classification loss of a masked image, where the
mask size is proportional to the probability that the training label is noisy.

argues against a coupled training of the meta parameters (represented by the pseudo
labels) and model parameters (Wu et al., 2021a) and proposes a method that pre-
trains a feature extractor, denoted by $f_{\theta_1} : \mathcal{X} \to \mathcal{Z}$, with $\mathcal{Z} \subset \mathbb{R}^Z$, using contrastive
self-supervised learning framework (Chen et al., 2020a,b). Then, the optimization
alternates the training of a simple classifier, denoted by $f_{\theta_2} : \mathcal{Z} \to \Delta^{|\mathcal{Y}|-1}$ and the
training of the pseudo labels $\{\hat{\mathbf{y}}_i\}_{i=1}^{|\mathcal{D}_t|}$ for the training samples $\{\mathbf{x}_i\}_{i=1}^{|\mathcal{D}_t|}$, as follows:

$$\{\hat{\mathbf{y}}_i\}_{i=1}^{|\mathcal{D}_t|} = \arg\min_{\{\mathbf{y}_i\}_{i=1}^{|\mathcal{D}_t|}} \frac{1}{|\mathcal{D}_v|} \sum_{j=1}^{|\mathcal{D}_v|} \ell\left(\mathbf{y}_j, f_{\theta_2^*\left(\{\mathbf{y}_i\}_{i=1}^{|\mathcal{D}_t|}\right)}\left(f_{\theta_1}(\mathbf{x}_j)\right)\right)$$

$$\text{s.t.: } \theta_2^*\left(\{\mathbf{y}_i\}_{i=1}^{|\mathcal{D}_t|}\right) = \arg\min_{\theta_2} \frac{1}{|\mathcal{D}_t|} \sum_{i=1}^{|\mathcal{D}_t|} \ell\left(\hat{\mathbf{y}}_i, f_{\theta_2}(f_{\theta_1}(\mathbf{x}_i))\right). \qquad (5.1)$$

The meta-learning training proposed in DMLP is combined with DivideMix to produce the reported results in this chapter.

   SSR (Feng et al., 2021)[7] is a relatively simple method that combines sample
re-labeling, sample selection, and a regularized training using a semi-supervised consistency loss, as shown in Fig. 5.3. Assuming a feature extractor represented by
$f_{\theta_1} : \mathcal{X} \to \mathcal{Z}$, where $\mathcal{Z} \subset \mathbb{R}^Z$, and a classifier $f_{\theta_2} : \mathcal{Z} \to \Delta^{|\mathcal{Y}|-1}$, the first stage of
sample re-labeling is achieved with:

$$\hat{\mathbf{y}} = \begin{cases} \text{OneHot}\left(f_{\theta_2}\left(f_{\theta_1}(\mathbf{x})\right)\right), & \text{if } \max\left(f_{\theta_2}\left(f_{\theta_1}(\mathbf{x})\right)\right) > \tau \\ \tilde{\mathbf{y}}, & \text{otherwise} \end{cases}, \qquad (5.2)$$

where the original training set $\mathcal{D} = \{(\mathbf{x}, \tilde{\mathbf{y}})\}$ is replaced by $\hat{\mathcal{D}} = \{(\mathbf{x}, \hat{\mathbf{y}})\}$. The second stage of sample selection relies on a K-nearest neighbor classifier, denoted

---

[7] https://github.com/MrChenFeng/SSR_BMVC2022.

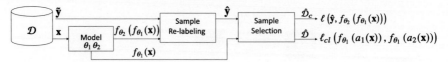

FIGURE 5.3 SSR (Feng et al., 2021).

Diagram of the three SSR steps (Feng et al., 2021), with the first step comprising a sample relabeling approach that produces a new label $\hat{\mathbf{y}}$ for sample $\mathbf{x}$ based on the model's confidence on a particular prediction. This forms the set $\hat{\mathcal{D}}$. The second step is a sample selection procedure, explained in (5.2), which forms the clean set $\hat{\mathcal{D}}_c \subset \hat{\mathcal{D}}$. The final optimization step, explained in (5.3), minimizes a classification loss for the clean samples in $\hat{\mathcal{D}}$ and a consistency loss for all samples in $\hat{\mathcal{D}}$.

by $k_N : \mathcal{Z} \to \Delta^{|\mathcal{Y}|-1}$, to select clean samples to be inserted into $\hat{\mathcal{D}}_c$ if $\hat{\mathbf{y}} =$ OneHot($k_N(f_{\theta_1}(\mathbf{x}))$). The third stage trains the classifier with $\hat{\mathcal{D}}_c$ and $\hat{\mathcal{D}}$ as follows:

$$\theta_1^*, \theta_2^* = \arg\min_{\theta_1, \theta_2} \frac{1}{|\hat{\mathcal{D}}_c|} \sum_{(\mathbf{x},\hat{\mathbf{y}}) \in \hat{\mathcal{D}}_c} \ell\left(\hat{\mathbf{y}}, f_{\theta_2}\left(f_{\theta_1}(\mathbf{x})\right)\right)$$
$$+ \frac{1}{|\hat{\mathcal{D}}|} \sum_{(\mathbf{x},\hat{\mathbf{y}}) \in \hat{\mathcal{D}}} \ell_{cl}\left(f_{\theta_1}\left(a_1(\mathbf{x})\right), f_{\theta_1}\left(a_2(\mathbf{x})\right)\right), \quad (5.3)$$

where $\ell(.)$ is the cross-entropy loss, $\ell_{cl}(.)$ is a consistency loss that penalizes low cosine similarity of the representations extracted from the augmented versions $a_1(\mathbf{x})$ and $a_2(\mathbf{x})$ of the image $\mathbf{x}$, with $a_1(.)$ and $a_2(.)$ denoting two augmentation functions.

The **instance-dependent noise (IDN) benchmarks** (Xia et al., 2020) on **CIFAR-10** and **CIFAR-100**, shown in Table 5.3, are based on noise rates $\eta \in \{20\%, 30\%, 40\%, 45\%, 50\%\}$, as explained in Section 2.7.1.1. To allow for a fair comparison, we concentrate on approaches that use the model PreActResNet-18 (He et al., 2016b), but we include two exceptions, namely CC (Zhao et al., 2022) and DISC (Li et al., 2023), to enable a more complete presentation of modern approaches. A natural technique to explore in IDN problems is the method based on the estimation of a label transition model, as depicted in Fig. 4.41. Typical examples of these approaches are the T-Revision (Xia et al., 2019),[8] and Reweight (Liu and Tao, 2015),[9] which assume the existence of anchor points (Liu and Tao, 2015), or proxy to anchor points (Xia et al., 2019) to estimate label transition matrix. Alternatively, instance-dependent label transition matrices can be learned by PTD-R-V (Xia et al., 2020),[10] as proposed in (4.216), which assumes that images can be decomposed into image parts and a separate label transition matrix can be learned for each image part. The instance-dependent transition matrix is then estimated by combining these part-based

---

[8] https://github.com/xiaoboxia/T-Revision.
[9] https://github.com/xiaoboxia/Classification-with-noisy-labels-by-importance-reweighting.
[10] https://github.com/xiaoboxia/Part-dependent-label-noise.

Table 5.3 Test accuracy (%) on the instance-dependent noise (IDN) benchmark on CIFAR-10 and CIFAR-100 (Xia et al., 2020). Most results are extracted from (Yao et al., 2021a), while results with * are from their respective papers. All results are obtained with the backbone model PreActResNet-18 (He et al., 2016b), except for CC (Zhao et al., 2022) that uses ResNet34 and DISC (Li et al., 2023) that uses PresNet-34 (He et al., 2016b).

Dataset	CIFAR-10				
IDN noise rate	20%	30%	40%	45%	50%
CE (Yao et al., 2021a)	75.81	69.15	62.45	51.72	39.42
Forward (Patrini et al., 2017)	74.64	69.75	60.21	48.81	46.27
T-Revision (Xia et al., 2019)	76.15	70.36	64.09	52.42	49.02
Reweight (Liu and Tao, 2015)	76.23	70.12	62.58	51.54	45.46
PTD-R-V (Xia et al., 2020)*	76.58	72.77	59.50	_	56.32
Decoupling (Malach and Shalev-Shwartz, 2017)	78.71	75.17	61.73	58.61	50.43
Co-teaching (Han et al., 2018c)	80.96	78.56	73.41	71.60	45.92
MentorNet (Jiang et al., 2017)	81.03	77.22	71.83	66.18	47.89
CausalNL (Yao et al., 2021a)	81.79	80.75	77.98	79.53	78.63
HOC (Zhu et al., 2021c)*	90.03	_	85.49	_	_
kMEIDTM (Cheng et al., 2022)*	92.26	90.73	85.94	_	73.77
DivideMix (Li et al., 2020a)	94.80	94.60	94.53	94.08	93.04
CC (Zhao et al., 2022)	93.68	–	94.97	–	–
DISC (Li et al., 2023)	96.48	–	95.94	–	–
InstanceGM (Garg et al., 2023)	96.68	96.52	96.36	96.15	95.90
Dataset	**CIFAR-100**				
IDN noise rate	20%	30%	40%	45%	50%
CE (Yao et al., 2021a)	30.42	24.15	21.45	15.23	14.42
Forward (Patrini et al., 2017)	36.38	33.17	26.75	21.93	19.27
T-Revision (Xia et al., 2019)	37.24	36.54	27.23	25.53	22.54
Reweight (Liu and Tao, 2015)	36.73	31.91	28.39	24.12	20.23
PTD-R-V (Xia et al., 2020)*	65.33[†]	64.56[†]	59.73[†]	_	56.80[†]
Decoupling (Malach and Shalev-Shwartz, 2017)	36.53	30.93	27.85	23.81	19.59
Co-teaching (Han et al., 2018c)	37.96	33.43	28.04	25.60	23.97
MentorNet (Jiang et al., 2017)	38.91	34.23	31.89	27.53	24.15
CausalNL (Yao et al., 2021a)	41.47	40.98	34.02	33.34	32.13
HOC (Zhu et al., 2021c)*	68.82	_	62.29	_	_
kMEIDTM (Cheng et al., 2022)*	69.16	66.76	63.46	_	59.18
DivideMix (Li et al., 2020a)	77.07	76.33	70.80	57.78	58.61
CC (Zhao et al., 2022)	79.61	–	76.58	–	–
DISC (Li et al., 2023)	80.12	–	78.44	–	–
InstanceGM (Garg et al., 2023)	79.69	79.21	78.47	77.49	77.19

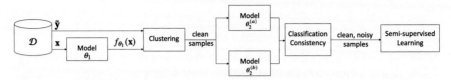

FIGURE 5.4 CC (Zhao et al., 2022).

Diagram of the two-stage sample selection proposed by the centrality and consistency (CC) approach (Zhao et al., 2022), where the first step consists of a clustering step using the features extracted by the model $f_{\theta_1}(\mathbf{x})$, with clean samples being selected based on how close they are to the class centers, and the second step detects clean samples given the classification consistency between the two classifiers $f_{\theta_2^{(a)}}(.)$ and $f_{\theta_2^{(b)}}(.)$. The clean and noisy samples from this second step are then given to the semi-supervised learning approach based on DivideMix (Li et al., 2020a).

transition matrices. Another instance-dependent label transition matrix can be estimated by HOC (Zhu et al., 2021c),[11] which relies on first-, second-, and third-order consensus from the training set to estimate a solution for the label transition matrix and the clean label classifier. The most successful transition matrix approach in Table 5.3 is the kMEIDTM, which estimates an instance-based transition matrix exploring the assumption that similar samples (which are close in the feature space) will have similar transition matrices. Such assumption is realized by embedding the transition matrix into a low-dimensional manifold. Although label transition models appear to be an appropriate technique to explore for IDN problems, results in Table 5.3 show that most of them are not competitive with other techniques described below.

Methods that explore multiple models (see Fig. 4.33), such as MentorNet (Jiang et al., 2017),[12] Co-teaching (Han et al., 2018c),[13] and Decoupling (Malach and Shalev-Shwartz, 2017),[14] have also been explored to address IDN problems. These methods were explained in detail in Section 4.4.3. They generally rely on the training of two models using some type of sample selection to mitigate the confirmation bias issue that can have a strong impact in IDN benchmarks. Results in Table 5.3 demonstrate that these multi-model approaches can be slightly better than most of label transition models in low-noise rate problems (less than or equal 30% IDN), but for larger than 30% IDN, multi-model methods are not competitive. For instance, HOC (Zhu et al., 2021c) shows more accurate classification than the multi-model approaches.

The most accurate methods proposed in the field are based on sample selection and semi-supervised learning (Zhao et al., 2022), sample selection correction and loss regularization (Li et al., 2023), and probabilistic graphical model with

---

[11] https://github.com/UCSC-REAL/HOC.
[12] https://github.com/google/mentornet.
[13] https://github.com/bhanML/Co-teaching.
[14] https://github.com/emalach/UpdateByDisagreement.

semi-supervised learning (Garg et al., 2023). The centrality and consistency (CC) method (Zhao et al., 2022),[15] shown in Fig. 5.4, is a two-stage sample selection approach, where the first stage is a class-specific feature clustering, where clean samples are assumed to be close to the class centers. More specifically, assuming a feature extractor $f_{\theta_1} : \mathcal{X} \to \mathcal{Z}$ (with $\mathcal{Z} \subset \mathbb{R}^Z$) and two classifiers $f_{\theta_2^{(a)}} : \mathcal{Z} \to \Delta^{|\mathcal{Y}|-1}$ and $f_{\theta_2^{(b)}} : \mathcal{Z} \to \Delta^{|\mathcal{Y}|-1}$, the first stage consists of a warm-up stage (i.e., training with early stopping) to train the feature extractors and the two classifiers, followed by a feature-based clustering stage. Such clustering consists of computing the class centers with

$$\mathbf{z_y} = \frac{\sum_{\hat{\mathbf{z}} \in \mathcal{Z}_\mathbf{y}} \hat{\mathbf{z}}}{\| \sum_{\hat{\mathbf{z}} \in \mathcal{Z}_\mathbf{y}} \hat{\mathbf{z}} \|_2}, \tag{5.4}$$

where $\mathcal{Z}_\mathbf{y} = \left\{ \hat{\mathbf{z}} \middle| (\mathbf{x}, \tilde{\mathbf{y}}) \in \mathcal{D}, \mathbf{z} = f_{\theta_1}(\mathbf{x}), \hat{\mathbf{z}} = \frac{\mathbf{z}}{\|\mathbf{z}\|_2}, \tilde{\mathbf{y}} = \mathbf{y} \right\}$, and $\mathbf{y} \in \mathcal{Y}$. Then, the initial sample selection is produced using a score computed from the cosine similarity between each feature and its class center, with $s = \hat{\mathbf{z}}^\top \mathbf{z_y}$, for each $\hat{\mathbf{z}} \in \mathcal{Z}_\mathbf{y}$ and $\mathbf{y} \in \mathcal{Y}$. This sample selection is achieved using the two-component Gaussian mixture model (GMM) strategy, similarly to the approach presented in (4.24), where the GMM component with the larger mean is denoted as the clean component. The clean samples are the ones with clean probabilities larger than a threshold τ_1, which form the set $\mathcal{D}_c$, with the noise set denoted by $\mathcal{D}_n$. The second stage consists of training the two classifiers with a cross-entropy classification loss and a regularization defined by

$$\mathcal{L}_{con} = -\lambda \frac{1}{|\mathcal{D}_c|} \sum_{(\mathbf{x}, \tilde{\mathbf{y}}) \in \mathcal{D}_c} d\left(\mathbf{p}^{(a)}(\mathbf{x}), \mathbf{p}^{(b)}(\mathbf{x}), \tilde{\mathbf{y}} \right) \tag{5.5}$$

that minimizes the consistency between the two classifiers defined by

$$d\left(\mathbf{p}^{(a)}(\mathbf{x}), \mathbf{p}^{(b)}(\mathbf{x}), \tilde{\mathbf{y}} \right) = w_{\tilde{\mathbf{y}}} \left\| d\left(\mathbf{p}^{(a)}(\mathbf{x}) - \mathbf{p}^{(b)}(\mathbf{x}) \right) \right\|_1, \tag{5.6}$$

with $\mathbf{p}^{(a)} = f_{\theta_2^{(a)}}(f_{\theta_1}(\mathbf{x}))$, $\mathbf{p}^{(b)} = f_{\theta_2^{(b)}}(f_{\theta_1}(\mathbf{x}))$, and $w_{\tilde{\mathbf{y}}}$ being a class weight to handle class imbalances. The last step to form the final clean and noisy sets consists of training a two-component GMM using the classification consistency score (5.6). The GMM component with the smaller mean is denoted as the clean component, and the clean samples are the ones with clean probabilities smaller than a threshold τ_2, which form the set $\hat{\mathcal{D}}_c$, with the noise set denoted by $\hat{\mathcal{D}}_n$. These two sets are then used to train a DivideMix (Li et al., 2020a) semi-supervised learning classifier.

The Dynamic Instance-specific Selection and Correction method (DISC) (Li et al., 2023),[16] displayed in Fig. 5.5, relies on strong and weak augmentations of the

---

[15] https://github.com/uitrbn/TSCSI_IDN.
[16] https://github.com/JackYFL/DISC.

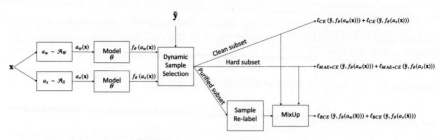

FIGURE 5.5 DISC (Li et al., 2023).

Diagram of the main steps of DISC (Li et al., 2020a), which comprises a sample selection that uses two augmented versions of the input image and an image-wise dynamic threshold to classify training samples into clean, hard, and purified subsets, where the samples in the purified subset are re-labeled. Training uses different loss functions for samples belonging to different subsets, where samples from the purified set are mixed up with samples from other sets to improve robustness to confirmation bias.

input image (Nishi et al., 2021) (see Fig. 4.26) that are used by a sample selection strategy that classifies the input image into three training subsets: clean, hard, and purified. Such sample selection uses the prediction consistency between the two views and depends on a dynamic threshold strategy for each image to select and correct noisy labels. The training proceeds with different loss functions for each of the three training subsets. More specifically, DISC trains a classifier $f_\theta : \mathcal{X} \to \Delta^{|\mathcal{Y}|-1}$ using weak and strong augmentations of the training images, denoted by $a_w(\mathbf{x})$ and $a_s(\mathbf{x})$ (with $a_w \sim \mathcal{A}_W$ and $a_s \sim \mathcal{A}_S$). The weakly augmented image-wise dynamic threshold for sample selection is defined by

$$\tau_w(t) = \lambda \times \tau_w(t-1) + (1-\lambda) \times \max_{\mathbf{y} \in \mathcal{Y}} \left(f_\theta^{(\mathbf{y})}(a_w(\mathbf{x})) \right), \quad (5.7)$$

where t is the training epoch, $f_\theta^{(\mathbf{y})}(a_w(\mathbf{x}))$ denotes the prediction for class $\mathbf{y} \in \mathcal{Y}$, and $\tau_w(0) = 0$. The threshold for the strongly augmented images is defined similarly as in (5.7), with $\tau_s(t)$ using $f_\theta^{(\mathbf{y})}(a_s(\mathbf{x}))$. The dynamic threshold for label correction is defined slightly differently, with

$$\tau'(t) = \max \left(\frac{\tau_w(t) + \tau_s(t)}{2} + \sigma, 0.99 \right), \quad (5.8)$$

where σ is a positive offset value. The clean subset of the training set $\mathcal{D}$ is defined with the training samples that the model is confident in the prediction of the training label for the weak and strong augmentations, as in

$$\mathcal{D}_c = \left\{ (\mathbf{x}, \tilde{\mathbf{y}}) | (\mathbf{x}, \tilde{\mathbf{y}}) \in \mathcal{D}, \left(f_\theta^{(\tilde{\mathbf{y}})}(a_w(\mathbf{x})) > \tau_w(t) \text{ AND } f_\theta^{(\tilde{\mathbf{y}})}(a_s(\mathbf{x})) > \tau_s(t) \right) \right\}. \quad (5.9)$$

On the other hand, the hard subset is formed with the samples that the model is confident for at least one of the augmentations, with

$$\mathcal{D}_h = \left\{ (\mathbf{x}, \tilde{\mathbf{y}}) | (\mathbf{x}, \tilde{\mathbf{y}}) \in (\mathcal{D} \setminus \mathcal{D}_c), \left(f_\theta^{(\tilde{\mathbf{y}})}(a_w(\mathbf{x})) > \tau_w(t) \text{ OR } f_\theta^{(\tilde{\mathbf{y}})}(a_s(\mathbf{x})) > \tau_s(t) \right) \right\}. $$
$$(5.10)$$

The purified, or commonly known in the literature as label-corrected, subset is formed with

$$\mathcal{D}_p = \left\{ (\mathbf{x}, \hat{\mathbf{y}}) | (\mathbf{x}, \tilde{\mathbf{y}}) \in \left(\mathcal{D} \setminus \left(\mathcal{D}_c \bigcup \mathcal{D}_h \right) \right), \left(\frac{f_\theta^{(\hat{\mathbf{y}})}(a_w(\mathbf{x})) + f_\theta^{(\hat{\mathbf{y}})}(a_s(\mathbf{x}))}{2} > \tau'(t) \right), \right.$$
$$\left. \hat{\mathbf{y}} = \arg\max_{\mathbf{y} \in \mathcal{Y}} \left(\frac{f_\theta^{(\mathbf{y})}(a_w(\mathbf{x})) + f_\theta^{(\mathbf{y})}(a_s(\mathbf{x}))}{2} \right) \right\}. $$
$$(5.11)$$

To avoid the confirmation bias issue in the training with $\mathcal{D}_p$, DISC proposes the use of a mix set, defined by

$$\mathcal{D}_m = \left\{ (\bar{\mathbf{x}}, \bar{\mathbf{y}}) | \bar{\mathbf{x}} = \gamma \times \mathbf{x} + (1 - \gamma) \times \mathbf{x}_j, \bar{\mathbf{y}} = \gamma \times \mathbf{y} + (1 - \gamma) \times \mathbf{y}_j, \right.$$
$$(5.12)$$
$$\left. (\mathbf{x}, \mathbf{y}), (\mathbf{x}_j, \mathbf{y}_j) \in \mathcal{D}_c \bigcup \mathcal{D}_h \bigcup \mathcal{D}_p \right\}$$

with j being a random index to an element in the set formed by $\mathcal{D}_c \bigcup \mathcal{D}_h \bigcup \mathcal{D}_p$ and $\gamma \sim \mathrm{Beta}(\alpha, \alpha)$. Training is conducted with a separate loss function per subset, as in

$$\theta^* = \arg\min_\theta + \frac{1}{|\mathcal{D}_c|} \sum_{(\mathbf{x}, \tilde{\mathbf{y}}) \in \mathcal{D}_c} \ell_{CE} \left(\tilde{\mathbf{y}}, f_\theta(a_w(\mathbf{x})) \right) + \ell_{CE} \left(\tilde{\mathbf{y}}, f_\theta(a_s(\mathbf{x})) \right)$$
$$+ \frac{1}{|\mathcal{D}_h|} \sum_{(\mathbf{x}, \tilde{\mathbf{y}}) \in \mathcal{D}_h} \ell_{MAE+CE} \left(\tilde{\mathbf{y}}, f_\theta(a_w(\mathbf{x})) \right) + \ell_{MAE+CE} \left(\tilde{\mathbf{y}}, f_\theta(a_s(\mathbf{x})) \right)$$
$$+ \frac{1}{|\mathcal{D}_m|} \sum_{(\bar{\mathbf{x}}, \bar{\mathbf{y}}) \in \mathcal{D}_m} \ell_{BCE} \left(\bar{\mathbf{y}}, f_\theta(a_w(\bar{\mathbf{x}})) \right) + \ell_{BCE} \left(\bar{\mathbf{y}}, f_\theta(a_s(\bar{\mathbf{x}})) \right),$$
$$(5.13)$$

where $\ell_{CE}(.)$ and $\ell_{BCE}(.)$ represent the CE and BCE losses defined in (2.13), and $\ell_{MAE+CE}(.)$, defined in (4.3), is the noise-robust loss that combines CE and MAE losses (Zhang and Sabuncu, 2018).

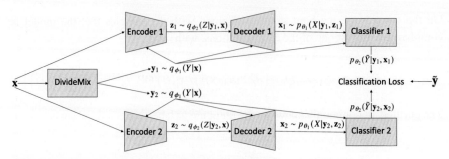

FIGURE 5.6 PGM (Yao et al., 2021a; Garg et al., 2023).

Diagram of the PGM approaches (Yao et al., 2021a; Garg et al., 2023) that are based on a classifier, denoted by $q_{\phi_1}(Y|\mathbf{x})$ and trained with co-teaching (Han et al., 2018c) (as in the PGM in (Yao et al., 2021a)), or DivideMix (Li et al., 2020a) (as in (Garg et al., 2023)). This classifier allows for the sampling of (pseudo) "clean" labels $\mathbf{y}_1, \mathbf{y}_2 \in \mathcal{Y}$, which are used by the encoder $q_{\phi_2}(Z|\mathbf{y}, \mathbf{x})$ to produce low-dimensional image representations $\mathbf{z}_1, \mathbf{z}_2 \in \mathcal{Z}$. Next, the input image is reconstructed given the low-dimensional representations and (pseudo) "clean" labels with $p_{\theta_1}(X|\mathbf{y}, \mathbf{z})$, to produce images $\mathbf{x}_1, \mathbf{x}_2 \in \mathcal{X}$. Then, a noisy-label classifier, conditioned on the (pseudo) "clean" labels and reconstructed images, denoted by $p_{\theta_2}(\tilde{Y}|\mathbf{y}, \mathbf{x})$, is trained to produce the training noisy labels.

Probabilistic graphical models have been heavily explored for IDN problems, with the CausalNL (Yao et al., 2021a)[17] and InstanceGM (Garg et al., 2023)[18] models, both depicted in Fig. 4.37(d). As explained in Section 4.4.5, both approaches are based on two encoders, two decoders, two classifiers, and a robust noisy-label classifier, such as co-teaching (Han et al., 2018c) and DivideMix (Li et al., 2020a). We summarize the functionality of PGM methods in Fig. 5.6.

The Polynomial Margin Diminishing (PMD) Noise benchmark (Zhang et al., 2021c) on **CIFAR-10 and CIFAR-100** (Krizhevsky and Hinton, 2009) is shown in Table 5.4. Recall from Chapter 2 that PMD is an instance-dependent noise, where noisy labels appear at a higher rate for the samples located near the decision boundaries, compared with samples far from the boundaries. This benchmark has not been widely used by researchers in the field, but it is a reasonably challenging problem that deserves more attention by the community. The backbone model used in this benchmark is the PreActResNet-18 (He et al., 2016b) in (Smart and Carneiro, 2023) and PreActResNet-34 (He et al., 2016b) in PLC and Cross-Entropy (Zhang et al., 2021c). An important point about this benchmark is the noise rate of 70% on both CIFAR-10 and CIFAR-100. For CIFAR-10, this 70% noise rate may effectively swap the labels of a particular class, as observed by Smart and Carneiro (2023). This occurs because

---

[17] https://github.com/a5507203/Instance-dependent-Label-noise-Learning-under-a-Structural-Causal-Model.

[18] https://github.com/arpit2412/InstanceGM.

Table 5.4 Test accuracy (%) on the instance-dependent noise Polynomial Margin Diminishing (PMD) benchmark on CIFAR-10 and CIFAR-100 (Zhang et al., 2021c). Cross-entropy and PLC results are from (Zhang et al., 2021c), and BootLN(M)(+TTA) are from (Smart and Carneiro, 2023). The backbone model used in this benchmark is the PreActResNet-18 (He et al., 2016b) in (Smart and Carneiro, 2023) and PreActResNet-34 (He et al., 2016b) in PLC and Cross-Entropy (Zhang et al., 2021c).

Dataset	CIFAR-10		
Noise type and rate	Type-I 35%	Type-II 35%	Type-III 35%
Cross-Entropy (Zhang et al., 2021c)	78.11	76.65	76.89
PLC (Zhang et al., 2021c)	82.80	81.54	81.50
BootLN(M) (Smart and Carneiro, 2023)	94.00	93.76	94.23
BootLN(M) + *TTA* (Smart and Carneiro, 2023)	94.39	94.19	94.23
Noise type and rate	Type-I 70%	Type-II 70%	Type-III 70%
Cross-Entropy (Zhang et al., 2021c)	41.98	45.57	43.42
PLC (Zhang et al., 2021c)	42.74	46.04	45.05
BootLN(M) (Smart and Carneiro, 2023)	19.18	27.28	19.94
BootLN(M) + *TTA* (Smart and Carneiro, 2023)	19.71	27.17	20.21
Dataset	CIFAR-100		
Noise type and rate	Type-I 35%	Type-II 35%	Type-III 35%
Cross-Entropy	57.68	57.83	56.07
PLC (Zhang et al., 2021c)	60.01	63.68	63.68
BootLN(M) (Smart and Carneiro, 2023)	68.25	68.14	68.22
BootLN(M) + *TTA* (Smart and Carneiro, 2023)	70.13	69.35	70.13
Noise type and rate	Type-I 70%	Type-II 70%	Type-III 70%
Cross-Entropy	39.32	39.30	40.01
PLC (Zhang et al., 2021c)	45.92	45.03	44.52
BootLN(M) (Smart and Carneiro, 2023)	58.69	58.03	57.90
BootLN(M) + *TTA* (Smart and Carneiro, 2023)	59.39	58.95	58.95

with such 70% IDN noise rate, some classes have 'flipped' to another class, as observed between classes 'cats' and 'dogs' or classes 'trucks' and 'airplanes'. On the other hand, such phenomenon is not observed in CIFAR-100 because the 70% noisy samples are more evenly distributed among many neighbors, so the class label cannot swap with a particular class.

The top methods for the PMD noise benchmark are the Progressive Label Correction (PLC) (Zhang et al., 2021c)[19] and the Bootstrapping the Relationship Between Images and their Clean and Noisy Labels (BootLN) (Smart and Carneiro, 2023).[20] PLC (Zhang et al., 2021c) is essentially a pseudo-labeling approach that starts with a warm-up training of the classifier $f_\theta : \mathcal{X} \to \Delta^{|\mathcal{Y}|-1}$. The pseudo-labeling

---

[19] https://github.com/pxiangwu/PLC.
[20] https://github.com/btsmart/bootstrapping-label-noise.

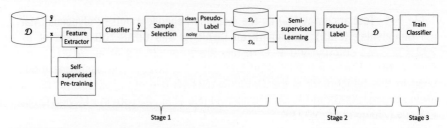

FIGURE 5.7 BootLN (Smart and Carneiro, 2023).

Diagram of BootLN (Smart and Carneiro, 2023) which takes as input the image $\mathbf{x}$ (after being processed by a feature extractor) and noisy label $\tilde{\mathbf{y}}$ to output a clean label $\bar{\mathbf{y}}$. Training is divided into 3 stages: 1) bootstrapping: self-supervised pre-training of the feature extractor + training with early stopping + sample selection and pseudo-labeling of clean samples; 2) semi-supervised learning with pseudo-clean set $\mathcal{D}_c$ assumed to be labeled and noisy set $\mathcal{D}_n$ assumed to be un-labeled, followed by a pseudo-labeling of the whole training set to form $\bar{\mathcal{D}}$; and 3) training of the classifier with $\bar{\mathcal{D}}$.

stage takes each training sample $(\mathbf{x}, \tilde{\mathbf{y}}) \in \mathcal{D}$ and checks if $\tilde{\mathbf{y}} \neq \mathrm{OneHot}(f_\theta(\mathbf{x}))$ and $\max_{\mathbf{y} \in \mathcal{Y}} \left(f_\theta^{(\mathbf{y})}(\mathbf{x}) \right) > \tau(t)$, where $\tau(t)$ is the prediction confidence threshold at training epoch t. In such case, the training set $\mathcal{D}$ updates the training sample $(\mathbf{x}, \tilde{\mathbf{y}})$ with the new label $\left(\mathbf{x}, \mathrm{OneHot}(f_\theta(\mathbf{x})) \right)$. The model is then re-trained with the updated training set, the threshold $\tau(t)$ is slightly reduced, and a new round of label correction is performed.

BootLN (Smart and Carneiro, 2023), depicted in Fig. 5.7, is a three-stage approach to train the modified (M) classification model $f_\theta : \mathcal{X} \times \mathcal{Y} \to \Delta^{|\mathcal{Y}|-1}$ that takes as input not only an image $\mathbf{x} \in \mathcal{X}$, but also the given noisy label $\tilde{\mathbf{y}} \in \mathcal{Y}$ to predict the clean label distribution (Gu et al., 2022; Inoue et al., 2017; Veit et al., 2017). Such modified model aims to learn patterns associated with the transition between noisy to clean labels. BootLN also considers the training of a normal (N) classifier defined by $f_\theta : \mathcal{X} \to \Delta^{|\mathcal{Y}|-1}$, which does not take the noisy label as input. In the first training stage, referred to as bootstrapping, the model is pre-trained with self-supervision (Chen et al., 2020a) and trained with early stopping with

$$\theta^* = \arg\min_\theta \frac{1}{|\mathcal{D}|} \sum_{(\mathbf{x}, \tilde{\mathbf{y}}) \in \mathcal{D}} \mathbb{E}_{a \sim \mathcal{A}_S} \left[\ell_{CE}(\tilde{\mathbf{y}}, f_\theta(a(\mathbf{x}), \mathbf{0}_{|\mathcal{Y}|})) \right], \quad (5.14)$$

where $\ell_{CE}(.)$ is the cross-entropy loss, $a(.)$ represents a data augmentation sampled from a set of strong data augmentations $\mathcal{A}_S$, and $\mathbf{0}_{|\mathcal{Y}|}$ is a vector of $|\mathcal{Y}|$ zeros. The initial pseudo clean labels are produced with

$$\bar{\mathbf{y}} = \mathbb{E}_{a \sim \mathcal{A}_W} \left[f_{\theta^*}(a(\mathbf{x}), \mathbf{0}_{|\mathcal{Y}|}) \right], \quad (5.15)$$

where $a(.)$ denotes an augmentation function sampled from the set of weak augmentation functions $\mathcal{A}_W$. The method then relies on sample selection and pseudo-labeling of clean samples, which forms the following clean and noisy sets:

$$\mathcal{D}_c = \{(\mathbf{x}, \tilde{\mathbf{y}}, \hat{\mathbf{y}}) | (\mathbf{x}, \tilde{\mathbf{y}}) \in \mathcal{D}, \hat{\mathbf{y}} = \mathsf{OneHot}(\bar{\mathbf{y}}), \text{ where } \max_{c \in \{1, \dots, |\mathcal{Y}|\}} \bar{\mathbf{y}}(c) > \tau\}$$

$$\mathcal{D}_n = \{(\mathbf{x}, \tilde{\mathbf{y}}) | (\mathbf{x}, \tilde{\mathbf{y}}) \in \mathcal{D}, \max_{c \in \{1, \dots, |\mathcal{Y}|\}} \bar{\mathbf{y}}(c) \leq \tau\}. \tag{5.16}$$

The second stage involves a semi-supervised learning (SSL) (Sohn et al., 2020) that uses the clean and noisy sets defined in (5.16) to pseudo-label the samples in $\mathcal{D}_n$. The SSL uses the following optimization:

$$\theta^* = \arg\min_{\theta} + \frac{1}{|\mathcal{D}_c|} \sum_{(\mathbf{x}, \tilde{\mathbf{y}}, \hat{\mathbf{y}}) \in \mathcal{D}_c} \mathbb{E}_{a \sim \mathcal{A}_W}[\ell(\hat{\mathbf{y}}, f_\theta(a(\mathbf{x}), \tilde{\mathbf{y}}))]$$

$$+ \frac{1}{|\mathcal{D}_n|} \sum_{(\mathbf{x}, \tilde{\mathbf{y}}) \in \mathcal{D}_n} \delta(\max \bar{\mathbf{y}} > \tau) \mathbb{E}_{a \sim \mathcal{A}_S}[\ell(\mathsf{OneHot}(\bar{\mathbf{y}}), f_\theta(a(\mathbf{x}), \tilde{\mathbf{y}}))], \tag{5.17}$$

where $\delta(.)$ represents an indicator function, $\bar{\mathbf{y}} = \mathbb{E}_{a \sim \mathcal{A}_W}[f_\theta(a(\mathbf{x}), \tilde{\mathbf{y}})]$, and $\mathsf{OneHot}(.)$ returns the one-hot vector from the categorical distribution $\bar{\mathbf{y}}$. This SSL stage enables the pseudo-labeling of the whole training set with:

$$\bar{\mathcal{D}} = \left\{ (\mathbf{x}, \tilde{\mathbf{y}}, \mathsf{OneHot}(\bar{\mathbf{y}})) | (\mathbf{x}, \tilde{\mathbf{y}}) \in \mathcal{D}, \bar{\mathbf{y}} = \mathbb{E}_{a \sim \mathcal{A}_W}\left[f_{\theta^*}(a(\mathbf{x}), \mathbf{0}_{|\mathcal{Y}|}) \right] \right\}. \tag{5.18}$$

The third stage simply trains the modified (M) or normal (N) model with strong and mixup (Zhang et al., 2018) augmentations using the training set $\bar{\mathcal{D}}$ from (5.18). An interesting point about the testing procedure of BoostLN is that the authors ran the method with and without test-time augmentation, where results with test-time augmentation (TTA) tend to be surprisingly better. This suggests that there is potential in the use of TTA, which is a technique relatively unexplored by the field. Also, the modified model (M) that takes image and noisy-label in the input showed better results than the normal (N) model that only takes the input image, indicating that BoostLN can uncover some relationship between the given noisy label and produced clean label. One important point is the cases with 70% noise rate in CIFAR-10, where BoostLN shows rather poor results. The reason for this poor results is related to the issue explained above, where this 70% noise rate can effectively swap the labels between two classes in CIFAR-10.

The results of **the instance-dependent noise RoG benchmarks** introduced by Lee et al. (2019) on **CIFAR-10 and CIFAR-100** (Krizhevsky and Hinton, 2009) are shown in Table 5.5. In RoG, noisy labels are provided by trained models VGG-13 (that produces a noise rate of 34% on CIFAR-10 and 37% on CIFAR-100) (Simonyan and Zisserman, 2015), DenseNet-100 (that produces a noise rate of 32% on CIFAR-10 and 34% on CIFAR-100) (Huang et al., 2017), and ResNet-34 (that produces a noise rate of 38% on CIFAR-10 and 37% on CIFAR-100) (He et al., 2016b). The backbone model used in this benchmark is the PreActResNet-18 (He et al., 2016b) in (Smart and Carneiro, 2023; Cordeiro et al., 2022) and ResNet-44 (He et al., 2016b)

Table 5.5 Instance-dependent noise RoG benchmark on CIFAR-10 and CIFAR-100 (Lee et al., 2019). D2L+RoG and CE+RoG results are from (Lee et al., 2019), PropMix result is from (Cordeiro et al., 2022), and BootLN(N)(+TTA) results are from (Smart and Carneiro, 2023). The backbone model used in this benchmark is the PreActResNet-18 (He et al., 2016b) in (Smart and Carneiro, 2023; Cordeiro et al., 2022) and ResNet-44 (He et al., 2016b) in D2L+RoG and CE+RoG (Lee et al., 2019).

Dataset	CIFAR-10		
Noise rate	**DenseNet (32%)**	**ResNet (38%)**	**VGG (34%)**
D2L + RoG (Lee et al., 2019)	68.57	60.25	59.94
CE + RoG (Lee et al., 2019)	68.33	64.15	70.04
PropMix (Cordeiro et al., 2022)	84.25	82.51	85.74
BootLN(N) (Smart and Carneiro, 2023)	93.26	92.05	93.29
BootLN(N)+ *TTA* (Smart and Carneiro, 2023)	93.87	92.66	93.86
Dataset	**CIFAR-100**		
Noise rate	**DenseNet (34%)**	**ResNet (37%)**	**VGG (37%)**
D2L + RoG (Lee et al., 2019)	31.67	39.92	45.42
CE + RoG (Lee et al., 2019)	61.14	53.09	53.64
PropMix (Cordeiro et al., 2022)	60.98	58.44	60.01
BootLN(N) (Smart and Carneiro, 2023)	62.47	64.91	64.98
BootLN(N)+ *TTA* (Smart and Carneiro, 2023)	63.40	65.74	66.10

in D2L+RoG and CE+RoG (Lee et al., 2019). In this benchmark, the top performing method is BoostLN (Smart and Carneiro, 2023) explained above, but using the normal (N) model instead of the modified (M) model. Again, the use of TTA is noticeably advantageous. The other approaches listed in Table 5.5 are the Robust Generative classifier (RoG) (Lee et al., 2019)[21] and PropMix (Cordeiro et al., 2022).[22] RoG (Lee et al., 2019), explained in Section 4.4.5, takes a discriminative model $f_\theta : \mathcal{X} \to \Delta^{|\mathcal{Y}|-1}$ pre-trained on the noisy-label dataset, and transforms it into a generative model, which is naturally more robust to training noise. PropMix (Cordeiro et al., 2022) extends DivideMix (Li et al., 2020a), by starting with a self-supervised pre-training (Chen et al., 2020a,b; He et al., 2020), followed by a warm-up training. Next, PropMix introduces a two-stage sample selection, with the first stage to select clean and noisy samples, similarly to the sample selection in DivideMix (Li et al., 2020a) that uses a Gaussian mixture model (GMM), and the second stage to separate the noisy samples into easy and hard again using a GMM classifier. After discarding the hard noisy samples, the method pseudo-labels the easy-noisy samples and trains the model with the clean and easy-noisy samples with MixUp (Zhang et al., 2018) augmentation. Such MixUp augmentation is advantageous because, differently from MixMatch (Berthelot et al., 2019) used in DivideMix (Li et al., 2020a), it is not limited by the size of the clean subset.

---

[21] https://github.com/pokaxpoka/RoGNoisyLabel.
[22] https://github.com/filipe-research/PropMix.

Table 5.6 Test accuracy (%) on the CIFAR-10N and CIFAR-100N instance-dependent noise benchmarks (Wei et al., 2021a). Results are collected from the cited papers in each row. The backbone model used in this benchmark is the PreActResNet-18 (He et al., 2016b) for all methods, except for the methods marked with †, which have been trained with a ResNet-34.

Dataset	CIFAR-10N						CIFAR-100N		
Noise type	Clean	Rnd1	Rnd2	Rnd3	Aggr	Wrst	Crs	Fin	
Noise rate	0%	17.23%	18.12%	17.64%	9.03%	40.21%	25.60%	40.20%	
CE† (Liu et al., 2022c)	92.92	85.02	86.46	85.16	87.77	77.69	76.70	55.50
ELR+† (Liu et al., 2020)	95.39	94.43	94.20	94.34	94.83	91.09	78.57	66.72
CORES† (Cheng et al., 2020a)	94.16	94.45	94.88	94.74	95.25	91.66	73.87	55.72
SOP+ (Liu et al., 2022c)	96.38	95.28	95.31	95.39	95.61	93.24	78.91	67.81
ProMix (Wang et al., 2022)	–	96.97	–	–	97.39	96.16	–	73.39

A real-world instance-dependent noise introduced in the training images of CIFAR-10 and CIFAR-100 (Krizhevsky et al., 2014) formed the **CIFAR-10N, CIFAR-100N benchmarks** (Wei et al., 2021a), with results shown in Table 5.6. These two benchmarks have gained well-deserved attention since this is a well-designed noisy-label learning benchmark. One method that works particularly well is the ELR+ (Liu et al., 2020) that consists of DivideMix (Li et al., 2020a) trained with a robust early-learning regularization loss function. Another competitive approach in this benchmark is the COnfidence REgularized Sample Sieve (CORES) method (Cheng et al., 2020a),[23] that consists of a dynamic sample selection approach that progressively filters out noisy-label training samples using the peer loss. In particular, recall from (4.6) that the peer loss is defined by

$$\ell_{peer}(\tilde{\mathbf{y}}, f_\theta(\mathbf{x})) = \ell(\tilde{\mathbf{y}}, f_\theta(\mathbf{x})) - \ell(\tilde{\mathbf{y}}_i, f_\theta(\mathbf{x}_j)), \tag{5.19}$$

where the training samples $(\mathbf{x}_i, \tilde{\mathbf{y}}_i)$ and $(\mathbf{x}_j, \tilde{\mathbf{y}}_j)$ are randomly sampled from $\mathcal{D}$ with replacement. CORES (Cheng et al., 2020a) defines two independent and uniform random variables X_i and $\tilde{Y}_j$ where $p(X_i = \mathbf{x}_i|\mathcal{D}) = p(\tilde{Y}_j = \tilde{\mathbf{y}}_j|\mathcal{D}) = \frac{1}{|\mathcal{D}|}$ for all $i, j \in \{1, ..., |\mathcal{D}|\}$. The peer loss has the following equivalent form (Cheng et al., 2020a):

$$\ell_{peer}(\tilde{\mathbf{y}}, f_\theta(\mathbf{x})) = \mathbb{E}_{(\mathbf{x}_i, \tilde{\mathbf{y}}_j) \sim p(X_i, \tilde{Y}_j|\mathcal{D})} \left[\ell(\tilde{\mathbf{y}}, f_\theta(\mathbf{x})) - \ell(\tilde{\mathbf{y}}_j, f_\theta(\mathbf{x}_i)) \right]$$

$$= \ell(\tilde{\mathbf{y}}, f_\theta(\mathbf{x})) - \sum_{i=1}^{|\mathcal{D}|} p(X_i = \mathbf{x}_i|\mathcal{D}) \mathbb{E}_{\tilde{\mathbf{y}}_j \sim p(\tilde{Y}_j|\mathcal{D})} \left[\ell(\tilde{\mathbf{y}}_j, f_\theta(\mathbf{x}_i)) \right]$$

$$= \ell(\tilde{\mathbf{y}}, f_\theta(\mathbf{x})) - \mathbb{E}_{\tilde{\mathbf{y}}_j \sim p(\tilde{Y}_j|\mathcal{D})} \left[\ell(\tilde{\mathbf{y}}_j, f_\theta(\mathbf{x})) \right], \tag{5.20}$$

where $p(\tilde{Y}_j|\mathcal{D})$ represents the distribution of Y_j given dataset $\mathcal{D}$. Instead of training directly with the loss function in (5.20), Cheng et al. (2020a) propose a sample selection approach to improve training convergence using the second term of this loss function. The selection is achieved with:

$$w(\mathbf{x}, \tilde{\mathbf{y}}) = \delta \left(\left(\ell(\tilde{\mathbf{y}}, f_\theta(\mathbf{x})) - \mathbb{E}_{\tilde{\mathbf{y}}_j \sim p(\tilde{Y}_j|\mathcal{D})} \left[\ell(\tilde{\mathbf{y}}_j, f_\theta(\mathbf{x})) \right] \right) < \tau \right), \tag{5.21}$$

where $\tau = \frac{1}{|\mathcal{Y}|} \sum_{\mathbf{y} \in \mathcal{Y}} \ell(\mathbf{y}, f_\theta(\mathbf{x})) - \mathbb{E}_{\tilde{\mathbf{y}}_j \sim p(\tilde{Y}_j|\mathcal{D})} \left[\ell(\tilde{\mathbf{y}}_j, f_\theta(\mathbf{x})) \right]$, where the optimization is performed with:

$$\theta^* = \arg\min_\theta \frac{1}{|\mathcal{D}|} \sum_{(\mathbf{x}, \tilde{\mathbf{y}}) \in \mathcal{D}} w(\mathbf{x}, \tilde{\mathbf{y}}) \times \left(\ell(\tilde{\mathbf{y}}, f_\theta(\mathbf{x})) - \mathbb{E}_{\tilde{\mathbf{y}}_j \sim p(\tilde{Y}_j|\mathcal{D})} \left[\ell(\tilde{\mathbf{y}}_j, f_\theta(\mathbf{x})) \right] \right). \tag{5.22}$$

Sparse Over-Parameterization (SOP) (Liu et al., 2022c)[24] introduces a loss correction approach exploring the idea that a relatively small percentage of samples have

---

[23] https://github.com/UCSC-REAL/cores.
[24] https://github.com/shengliu66/SOP.

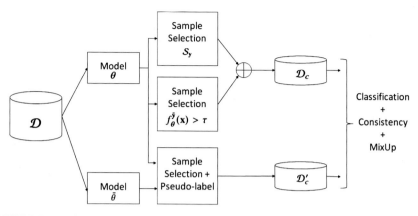

FIGURE 5.8 ProMix (Wang et al., 2022).

ProMix (Wang et al., 2022) relies on two models, three separate sample selection approaches, and one pseudo-labeling mechanism to train a model by combining a classification loss with two robust losses, one based on consistency training using a strong image augmentation and another loss based on MixUp (Zhang et al., 2018).

noisy labels. SOP aims to minimize the discrepancy between $f_\theta(\mathbf{x}) + \mathbf{s}_i$ and $\tilde{\mathbf{y}}_i$ enforcing sparsity of $\mathbf{s}_i$ with over-parameterization $\mathbf{s}_i = \mathbf{u}_i \odot \mathbf{u}_i - \mathbf{v}_i \odot \mathbf{v}_i$. The SOP's optimization is defined as

$$\theta^*, \{\mathbf{u}_i^*, \mathbf{v}_i^*\}_{i=1}^{|\mathcal{D}|} = \arg \min_{\theta, \{\mathbf{u}_i, \mathbf{v}_i\}_{i=1}^{|\mathcal{D}|}} \frac{1}{|\mathcal{D}|} \sum_{i=1}^{|\mathcal{D}} \ell(\tilde{\mathbf{y}}_i, f_\theta(\mathbf{x}_i) + \mathbf{s}_i)$$
$$\text{s.t. } \mathbf{s}_i = \mathbf{u}_i \odot \mathbf{u}_i \odot \tilde{\mathbf{y}}_i - \mathbf{v}_i \odot \mathbf{v}_i \odot (1 - \tilde{\mathbf{y}}_i) \tag{5.23}$$
$$\mathbf{u}_i \in [-1, 1]^{|\mathcal{Y}|}, \ \mathbf{v}_i \in [-1, 1]^{|\mathcal{Y}|}, \ i \in \{1, ..., |\mathcal{D}|\},$$

where $\odot$ is the element-wise vector product. The SOP+ in Table 5.6 adds a consistency regularizer that minimizes the Kullback-Leibler (KL)-divergence between the predictions from the augmented images and the predictions of the images generated with Unsupervised Data Augmentation (UDA). The SOP+ also minimizes the KL divergence between the probability distribution of class labels and the mean prediction of the training set.

ProMix* (Wang et al., 2022),[25] depicted in Fig. 5.8, is another approach that is relatively similar to DivideMix (Li et al., 2020a) since it explores sample selection and semi-supervised learning. The main contribution of ProMix is the sample selection method that comprises two parts. The first part is a class-wise small-loss selection that targets the selection of class-balanced pseudo-clean datasets, where the subset for each class is defined by $\mathcal{S}_\mathbf{y} = \{(\mathbf{x}, \tilde{\mathbf{y}}) | (\mathbf{x}, \tilde{\mathbf{y}}) \in \mathcal{D}, \mathbf{y} = \text{OneHot}(f_\theta(\mathbf{x}))\}$. Then, the

---

[25] https://github.com/Justherozen/ProMix.

cross-entropy loss values for the samples of the set $\mathcal{S}_\mathbf{y}$ are computed and ranked, where $k = \min\left(\rho \times \frac{|\mathcal{D}|}{|\mathcal{Y}|}, |\mathcal{S}_\mathbf{y}|\right)$ samples per class $\mathbf{y} \in \mathcal{Y}$ are selected. For the second part of the sample selection, samples with high classification confidence on the training label are selected with $f_\theta^{(\tilde{\mathbf{y}})}(\mathbf{x}) > \tau$. Samples that satisfy either one of the conditions in the first part or the second part are selected as clean to form $\mathcal{D}_c \subset \mathcal{D}$, and the noisy subset is defined by $\mathcal{D}_n = \mathcal{D} \setminus \mathcal{D}_c$. The samples in the noisy subset are then pseudo-labeled by a pair of models, namely the $f_\theta(.)$ above and another model $f_{\bar{\theta}}(.)$ with the same architecture but different parameters, where the selection of a clean sample depends on the following condition:

$$\left(\max_{\mathbf{y}\in\mathcal{Y}} f_\theta^{(\mathbf{y})}(\mathbf{x}) > \tau\right) \text{ AND } \left(\max_{\mathbf{y}\in\mathcal{Y}} f_{\bar{\theta}}^{(\mathbf{y})}(\mathbf{x}) > \tau\right)$$
$$\text{AND } \left(\text{OneHot}(f_\theta(\mathbf{x})) = \text{OneHot}(f_{\bar{\theta}}(\mathbf{x}))\right). \tag{5.24}$$

Then the samples that meet this condition are re-labeled as $(\mathbf{x}, \text{OneHot}(f_\theta(\mathbf{x})))$, which are added to $\mathcal{D}_c'$. The training of the two models is based on the optimization that minimizes a classification loss (CE loss), consistency loss (using a strong image augmentation), and a MixUp loss (Zhang et al., 2018), as follows:

$$\theta^*, \bar{\theta}^* = \arg\min_{\theta, \bar{\theta}} \sum_{(\mathbf{x}, \tilde{\mathbf{y}}) \in \mathcal{D}_c \bigcup \mathcal{D}_c'} \ell_{CE}(\tilde{\mathbf{y}}, f_\theta(\mathbf{x})) + \ell_{CE}(\tilde{\mathbf{y}}, f_{\bar{\theta}}(\mathbf{x}))$$
$$+ \beta \times \ell_{CE}(\tilde{\mathbf{y}}, f_\theta(a_S(\mathbf{x}))) + \beta \times \ell_{CE}(\tilde{\mathbf{y}}, f_{\bar{\theta}}(a_S(\mathbf{x})))$$
$$+ \beta \times \ell_{CE}(\tilde{\mathbf{y}}^m, f_\theta(\mathbf{x}^m)) + \beta \times \ell_{CE}(\tilde{\mathbf{y}}^m, f_{\bar{\theta}}(\mathbf{x}^m)), \tag{5.25}$$

where $a_S \sim \mathcal{A}_S$ represents a strong augmentation function, $\mathbf{x}^m = \sigma \times a_W(\mathbf{x}) + (1 - \sigma) \times a_W(\mathbf{x}_j)$, and $\mathbf{y}^m = \sigma \times \tilde{\mathbf{y}} + (1 - \sigma) \times \tilde{\mathbf{y}}_j$, are samples obtained via MixUp (Zhang et al., 2018), with $\sigma \sim \text{Beta}(\xi, \xi)$, for $\xi = 4$, and $a_W \sim \mathcal{A}_W$ represents a weak augmentation function.

Similarly to the IDN applied in CIFAR-10 and CIFAR-100 in Table 5.3, the same IDN proposed by Xia et al. (2020) is applied to the **Fashion-MNIST IDN benchmark** (Xiao et al., 2017) in Table 5.7, and to the **SVHN IDN benchmark** (Netzer et al., 2011) in Table 5.8. The backbone model for the F-MNIST benchmark is ResNet-18 (He et al., 2016b), and for the SVHN benchmark, ResNet-34 (He et al., 2016b). The main results in these two datasets have been produced by the multi-model approach MentorNet (Jiang et al., 2017), and label transition methods Reweight (Liu and Tao, 2015), T-Revision (Xia et al., 2019), PTD-R-V (Xia et al., 2020), and kMEIDTM (Cheng et al., 2022). All these approaches have already been presented above under other benchmarks. The state-of-the-art in these datasets is the Bayes-label Transition Matrix (BLTM) (Yang et al., 2022).[26]

---

[26] https://github.com/ShuoYang-1998/BLTM.

Table 5.7 Test accuracy (%) on Fashion-MNIST (Xiao et al., 2017) under various IDN noise rates (Xia et al., 2020). Results for CE, MentorNet, Reweight, T-revision, and PTD-R-V are collected from (Xia et al., 2020), and results from kMEI-DTM (Cheng et al., 2022) and BLTM-V (Yang et al., 2022) are from their papers. The backbone model used in this benchmark is the ResNet-18 (He et al., 2016b) for all methods.

Dataset	Fashion MNIST				
IDN noise rate	**10%**	**20%**	**30%**	**40%**	**50%**
CE (Xia et al., 2020)	88.54	88.38	84.22	68.86	51.42
MentorNet (Jiang et al., 2017)	90.00	87.02	86.02	80.12	58.62
Reweight (Liu and Tao, 2015)	90.33	89.70	87.04	80.29	65.27
T-Revision (Xia et al., 2019)	91.56	90.68	89.46	84.01	68.99
PTD-R-V (Xia et al., 2020)	92.01	91.08	89.66	85.69	75.96
kMEIDTM (Cheng et al., 2022)	91.96	90.83	89.61	85.81	76.43
BLTM-V (Yang et al., 2022)	96.93	95.55	92.24	83.43	76.89

Table 5.8 Test accuracy (%) of different methods on SVHN (Netzer et al., 2011) under various IDN noise rates (Xia et al., 2020). Results for CE, MentorNet, Reweight, T-revision, and PTD-R-V are collected from (Xia et al., 2020), and results from kMEI-DTM (Cheng et al., 2022) and BLTM-V (Yang et al., 2022) are from their papers. The backbone model used in this benchmark is the ResNet-34 (He et al., 2016b) for all methods.

Dataset	SVHN				
IDN noise rate	**10%**	**20%**	**30%**	**40%**	**50%**
CE (Xia et al., 2020)	90.77	90.23	86.33	65.66	48.01
MentorNet (Jiang et al., 2017)	90.28	90.37	86.49	83.75	40.27
Reweight (Liu and Tao, 2015)	92.49	91.09	90.25	84.48	45.46
T-Revision (Xia et al., 2019)	94.24	94.00	93.01	88.63	49.02
PTD-R-V (Xia et al., 2020)	94.44	94.23	93.11	90.64	58.09
BLTM-V (Yang et al., 2022)	96.37	95.12	94.69	88.13	78.71
kMEIDTM (Cheng et al., 2022)	96.38	95.66	94.68	92.20	80.22

BLTM (Yang et al., 2022), shown in Fig. 5.9, aims to model an instance-dependent label transition matrix from Bayes optimal labels to noisy labels and learn the classifier to predict the Bayes optimal labels. While the clean label posterior is a categorical distribution denoted by $p(Y|X)$ (defined as in Chapter 2) that is used for sampling clean labels, the Bayes optimal labels are defined as one-hot vectors that maximize the clean label posteriors with $(Y^*|X = \mathbf{x}) = \arg\max_{\mathbf{y} \in \mathcal{y}} p(Y = \mathbf{y}|X = \mathbf{x})$. The proposed modeling of the instance-dependent label transition matrix for sample $\mathbf{x}$ from

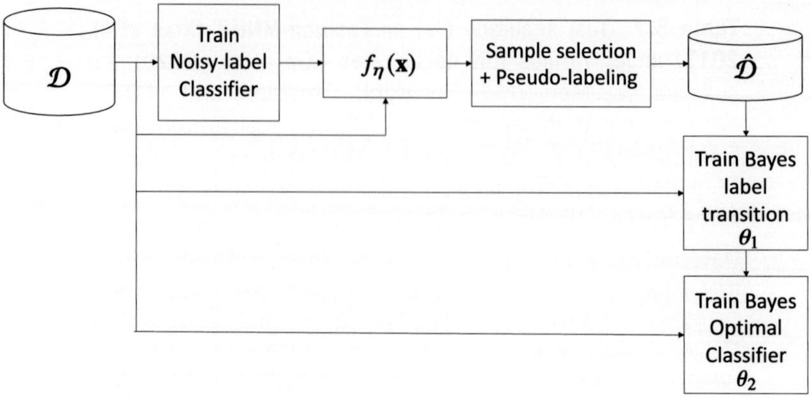

FIGURE 5.9 BLTM (Yang et al., 2022).

BLTM (Yang et al., 2022) is a 4-stage training approach to estimate the instance-dependent label transition matrix from Bayes optimal labels to noisy labels and learn the classifier to predict the Bayes optimal labels. The first stage trains the classifier $f_\eta : \mathcal{X} \to \Delta^{|\mathcal{Y}|-1}$ from the noisy-label dataset $\mathcal{D}$. The second stage distills the dataset $\mathcal{D}$ by selecting samples where $\max_{\hat{\mathbf{y}}} f_\eta^{(\hat{\mathbf{y}})} > \frac{1+\rho_{max}}{2}$, where ρ_{max} denotes a noise rate upper-bound. The third stage trains the Bayes label transition network $\mathbf{T}_{\theta_1} : \mathcal{X} \to \mathbb{R}^{|\mathcal{Y}| \times |\mathcal{Y}|}$ with (5.26), and the fourth stage trains the Bayes optimal posterior classifier $f_{\theta_2} : \mathcal{X} \to \Delta^{|\mathcal{Y}|-1}$ with (5.27).

Bayes optimal labels to noisy labels is defined by $\mathbf{T}^*(X = \mathbf{x}) = p(\tilde{Y}|Y^*, X = \mathbf{x})$, which can then be used to estimate the Bayes optimal labels with $p(Y^*|X = \mathbf{x}) = (\mathbf{T}^*(X = \mathbf{x})^\top)^{-1} p(\tilde{Y}|X = \mathbf{x})$, where $p(\tilde{Y}|X = \mathbf{x})$ can be estimated from the noisy-label training set $\mathcal{D}$. The fact that the Bayes optimal label posteriors are represented by one-hot vectors has two advantages (Yang et al., 2022): 1) it is possible to find a set of samples with theoretically guaranteed Bayes optimal labels in a noisy-label dataset; and 2) the solution space to find the Bayes-label transition matrix is smaller than the solution space for the clean-label transition matrix. BLTM first collects a set of distilled examples $(\mathbf{x}, \tilde{\mathbf{y}}, \hat{\mathbf{y}})$ to form the distilled training set $\hat{\mathcal{D}}$, where $f_\eta^{(\hat{\mathbf{y}})}(\mathbf{x}) > \frac{1+\rho_{max}}{2}$, with $f_\eta^{(\hat{\mathbf{y}})}(\mathbf{x})$ being the noisy label posterior probability distribution of $\mathbf{x}$ for the one-hot label $\hat{\mathbf{y}} \in \mathcal{Y}$ (obtained from a model trained with the noisy-label dataset $\mathcal{D}$), ρ_{max} representing the noise rate upper bound, $\tilde{\mathbf{y}}$ denoting the noisy label, and $\hat{\mathbf{y}}$ the theoretically guaranteed Bayes optimal label (Cheng et al., 2020b). Next, BLTM estimates a Bayes label transition network $\mathbf{T}_{\theta_1} : \mathcal{X} \to \mathbb{R}^{|\mathcal{Y}| \times |\mathcal{Y}|}$ using the following optimization:

$$\theta_1^* = \arg\min_{\theta_1} \frac{1}{|\hat{\mathcal{D}}|} \sum_{(\mathbf{x}, \tilde{\mathbf{y}}, \hat{\mathbf{y}}) \in \hat{\mathcal{D}}} \tilde{\mathbf{y}}^\top \log \left(\hat{\mathbf{y}}^\top \mathbf{T}_{\theta_1}(\mathbf{x}) \right). \tag{5.26}$$

Table 5.9 Test accuracy (%) for the instance-dependent noise benchmark Red Mini-ImageNet (CNWL) (Jiang et al., 2020). Results are collected from (Jiang et al., 2020; Xu et al., 2021; Cordeiro et al., 2022; Garg et al., 2023; Albert et al., 2022). Methods marked with "-SS" have been pretrained with self-supervised consistency learning (Caron et al., 2021). All methods use PreActResNet-18 (He et al., 2016b) as backbone model, except for DSOS that uses Inception-ResNetV2 (Szegedy et al., 2017).

Dataset	Red Mini-ImageNet					
Noise rate	20%	30%	40%	50%	60%	80%
CE (Xu et al., 2021)	47.36	–	42.70	–	37.30	29.76
MixUp (Zhang et al., 2018)	49.10	–	46.40	–	40.58	33.58
DivideMix (Li et al., 2020a)	50.96	–	46.72	–	43.14	34.50
MentorMix (Jiang et al., 2020)	51.02	–	47.14	–	43.80	33.46
FaMUS (Xu et al., 2021)	51.42	–	48.06	–	45.10	35.50
InstanceGM (Garg et al., 2023)	58.38	–	52.24	–	47.96	39.62
PropMix-SS (Cordeiro et al., 2022)	61.24	–	56.22	–	52.84	43.42
InstanceGM-SS (Garg et al., 2023)	60.89	–	56.37	–	53.21	44.03
DSOS (Albert et al., 2022)	–	69.84	–	66.14	–	55.26

Then, we train the classifier $f_{\theta_2} : \mathcal{X} \to \Delta^{|\mathcal{Y}|-1}$ to predict the Bayes optimal labels with

$$\theta_2^* = \arg\min_{\theta_2} \frac{1}{|\hat{\mathcal{D}}|} \sum_{(\mathbf{x},\tilde{\mathbf{y}}) \in \mathcal{D}} \tilde{\mathbf{y}}^\top \log\left(f_{\theta_2}(\mathbf{x})^\top \mathbf{T}_{\theta_1^*}(\mathbf{x})\right). \tag{5.27}$$

In Tables 5.7 and 5.8 the BLTM-V applies the transition matrix revision technique (Xia et al., 2019) to boost performance.

As detailed in Section 2.7.1.1, another **IDN benchmark** was proposed by Jiang et al. (2020) using the **Mini-ImageNet** (Vinyals et al., 2016) and **Stanford Cars** (Krause et al., 2013) datasets. Even though (Jiang et al., 2020) proposes four benchmarks, the field has concentrated on only two of them, the Red Mini-ImageNet and the Red Stanford Cars, so we present results for these two benchmarks in Tables 5.9 and 5.10, where the base models are the PreActResNet-18 (He et al., 2016b) and Inception-ResNetV2 (Szegedy et al., 2017).

Most approaches that produce competitive results in these benchmarks have been presented before, such as MixUp (Zhang et al., 2018), DivideMix (Li et al., 2020a), FaMUS (Xu et al., 2021), self-supervised pre-trained PropMix (PropMix-SS) (Cordeiro et al., 2022), and self-supervised pre-trained InstanceGM (Instance-GM-SS) (Garg et al., 2023).

The two methods that are new in Tables 5.9 and 5.10 are the MentorMix (Jiang et al., 2020) and the Dynamic Softening of Out-of-distribution Samples (DSOS) (Al-

Table 5.10 Test accuracy (%) for the instance-dependent noise benchmark Red Stanford Cars (CNWL) (Jiang et al., 2020). All results are from DSOS (Albert et al., 2022). All methods use Inception-ResNetV2 (Szegedy et al., 2017) as backbone model.

Dataset	Red Stanford Cars			
Noise rate	0%	30%	50%	80%
CE (Albert et al., 2022)	90.8	80.4	70.6	43.3
MentorNet (Jiang et al., 2017)	90.20	81.10	72.00	51.00
MixUp (Zhang et al., 2018)	91.90	85.60	79.10	55.70
MentorMix (Jiang et al., 2020)	91.80	87.80	80.40	58.60
DSOS (Albert et al., 2022)	91.38	88.36	82.04	62.36

bert et al., 2022). MentorMix (Jiang et al., 2020)[27] uses the MentorNet (Jiang et al., 2017) optimization, defined in (4.123), with a MixUp (Zhang et al., 2018) augmentation. The DSOS (Albert et al., 2022)[28] is a dynamic pseudo-labeling method that is designed to deal with both closed-set and open-set label noise, with a solution that involves a sample selection method to separate training samples into clean, closed-set label noise, and open-set label noise, as explained in (4.72). Then, DSOS tries to correct the closed-set label noise using confident predictions, and the open-set label samples are trained to produce a high-entropy prediction. More specifically, DSOS is trained with:

$$\theta^* = \arg\min_\theta \frac{1}{|\mathcal{D}|} \sum_{i=1}^{|\mathcal{D}|} \ell\left(h(\mathbf{x}_i, \tilde{\mathbf{y}}_i, u_i, v_i, \theta), f_\theta(\mathbf{x}_i)\right), \tag{5.28}$$

where $u_i \in \{0, 1\}$ corresponds to the probability given $s_{DSOS}(\mathbf{x}, \tilde{\mathbf{y}})$ in (4.72) for the left-most Beta mixture component being superior to 0.5 (i.e., $u_i = 0$ indicates a clean sample); $v_i \in [0, 1]$ represents the posterior probability of the right-most Beta mixture component (i.e., $v_i \approx 0$ indicates an open-set noisy-label sample), and

$$h(\mathbf{x}_i, \tilde{\mathbf{y}}_i, u_i, v_i, \theta) = \frac{\exp\left(\frac{v_i \times \hat{\mathbf{y}}_i}{\alpha}\right)}{\sum_{c=1}^{|\mathcal{Y}|} \exp\left(\frac{v_i \times \hat{\mathbf{y}}_i(c)}{\alpha}\right)} \tag{5.29}$$

with $\alpha \in [0, 1]$, and

$$\hat{\mathbf{y}}_i = (1 - u_i) \times \tilde{\mathbf{y}}_i + u_i \times f_\theta(\mathbf{x}_i). \tag{5.30}$$

The optimization in (5.28) involves the dynamic evaluation of $\{u_i\}_{i=1}^{|\mathcal{D}|}$ and $\{v_i\}_{i=1}^{|\mathcal{D}|}$ at every epoch, and the gist of the training is to force the model to produce a uniform

---

[27] http://www.lujiang.info/cnlw.html.
[28] https://github.com/PaulAlbert31/DSOS.

Table 5.11 Test accuracy (%) for the instance-dependent noise benchmark Animal-10N (Song et al., 2019). All results are from (Tu et al., 2023b) and (Smart and Carneiro, 2023). All methods use the VGG-19 (Simonyan and Zisserman, 2015) backbone model.

Dataset	Animal-10N
CE (Tu et al., 2023b)	79.4
DISC (Li et al., 2023)	87.1
SSR+ (Feng et al., 2021)	88.5
BootLN(M) (Smart and Carneiro, 2023)	88.5
SANM(SSR) (Tu et al., 2023b)	89.3
BootLN(M) + *TTA* (Smart and Carneiro, 2023)	89.4

Table 5.12 Test accuracy (%) for the instance-dependent noise benchmark Food-101N (Lee et al., 2018). All results are from (Li et al., 2023). All methods use the ResNet-50 (He et al., 2016a) backbone model.

Dataset	Food-101N
CE (Li et al., 2023)	81.67
CleanNet (Lee et al., 2018)	83.95
PLC (Zhang et al., 2021c)	83.40
Co-learning (Tan et al., 2021)	87.57
DISC (Li et al., 2023)	89.02

prediction for open-set samples ($v_i \approx 0$), to predict its own output for closed-set noisy labels ($v_i \approx 1$, $u_i = 1$), and to predict the training label for clean samples ($u_i = 0$). The final proposed training for DSOS includes MixUp data augmentation and an entropy-based regularization.

The **Animal-10N benchmark** (Song et al., 2019) shown in Table 5.11 is a small, but challenging dataset that has been explored by many researchers to assess the robustness of noisy-label learning methods to IDN noise. The main approaches tested in this benchmark are DISC (Li et al., 2023), SSR+ (Feng et al., 2021), BootLN(M) (Smart and Carneiro, 2023), SANM(SSR) (Tu et al., 2023b), and BootLN(M) + *TTA* (Smart and Carneiro, 2023). All these methods have been explained before and rely on the backbone model VGG-19 (Simonyan and Zisserman, 2015), where the top approaches SANM(SSR) and BootLN(M)+TTA show almost the same result. Both approaches combine many techniques, such as adversarial training, semi-supervised learning, sample selection, pseudo-labeling, and self-supervised pre-training.

The **Food-101N benchmark** (Lee et al., 2018) in Table 5.12 is becoming more popular over the last few years, given that it presents a challenging problem for noisy-

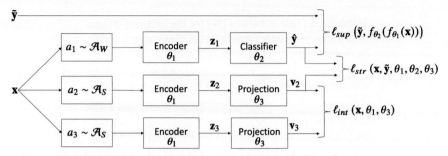

FIGURE 5.10 Co-learning (Tan et al., 2021).

Co-learning (Tan et al., 2021) is a multi-model approach that shares the encoder and has a classifier and projection heads, where training consists of minimizing the classification loss $\ell_{sup}(.)$ (with MixUp augmentation), the intrinsic similarity loss $\ell_{int}(.)$ that enforces image features to be robust to strong data augmentations in $\mathcal{A}_S$, and the structural similarity loss $\ell_{str}(.)$ that enforces similarity between pairs of images with respect to classifier and projection outputs.

label learning, as explained in Section 2.7.1.1. All methods explore the ResNet-50 backbone model (He et al., 2016a). CleanNet (Lee et al., 2018)[29] is a method that estimates the weight of each training image for training an image classifier. It achieves this goal by training a label noise estimator that needs a small clean validation set to train a reference encoder to produce clean-label class prototypes to represent each class. Then, by training a query encoder for all training images, CleanNet penalizes discrepancies between image representations, produced by this encoder, and prototypes of their classes. Using this discrepancy, CleanNet formulates a loss re-weighting method to train the image classifier, similarly to methods in Section 4.2.3. PLC (Zhang et al., 2021c) is a pseudo-labeling method that has been already discussed before. Even though competitive, PLC and CleanNet show results with lower accuracy, compared with the newer methods presented below.

Co-learning (Tan et al., 2021)[30] is a multi-model approach comprising a shared encoder, denoted by $f_{\theta_1}: X \to Z$ (with $Z \subset \mathbb{R}^Z$), with two heads, the classifier head $f_{\theta_2}: Z \to \Delta^{|\mathcal{Y}|-1}$ and the projection head $f_{\theta_3}: Z \to V$ (with $V \in \mathbb{R}^V$), where training is achieved with the following optimization function (see Fig. 5.10):

$$\theta_1^*, \theta_2^*, \theta_3^* = \arg\min_{\theta_1,\theta_2,\theta_3} \frac{1}{|\mathcal{D}|} \sum_{(\mathbf{x},\tilde{\mathbf{y}})\in\mathcal{D}} \ell_{sup}\left(\tilde{\mathbf{y}}, f_{\theta_2}(f_{\theta_1}(\mathbf{x}))\right) + \ell_{int}\left(\mathbf{x},\theta_1,\theta_3\right)$$
$$+ \ell_{str}\left(\mathbf{x},\tilde{\mathbf{y}},\theta_1,\theta_2,\theta_3\right), \tag{5.31}$$

[29] https://kuanghuei.github.io/CleanNetProject/.
[30] https://github.com/chengtan9907/Co-learning-Learning-from-noisy-labels-with-self-supervision.

where the supervised loss $\ell_{sup}(.)$ is defined with MixUp (Zhang et al., 2018) augmentation, as follows

$$
\begin{aligned}
\ell_{sup}\left(\bar{\mathbf{y}},\, f_{\theta_2}(f_{\theta_1}(\mathbf{x}))\right) =&\ \lambda \times \ell_{CE}\left(\bar{\mathbf{y}},\, f_{\theta_2}(f_{\theta_1}(a_1(\mathbf{x})))\right) \\
&+ (1-\lambda) \times \ell_{CE}\left(\bar{\mathbf{y}},\, f_{\theta_2}(f_{\theta_1}(a_2(\mathbf{x}_m)))\right)
\end{aligned}
\tag{5.32}
$$

with $a_1, a_2 \sim \mathcal{A}_W$ represent two weak augmentation functions, $m \in \{1, ..., |\mathcal{D}|\}$ representing a randomly chosen training sample, and

$$
\begin{aligned}
\bar{\mathbf{x}} &= \lambda \times \mathbf{x} + (1-\lambda) \times \mathbf{x}_m, \\
\bar{\mathbf{y}} &= \lambda \times \tilde{\mathbf{y}} + (1-\lambda) \times \tilde{\mathbf{y}}_m,
\end{aligned}
\tag{5.33}
$$

with $\lambda \sim \mathsf{Beta}(\alpha, \alpha)$. Also in (5.31), the intrinsic similarity loss $\ell_{int}(.)$ enforces training samples to have intrinsic similarity through strong data augmentations with

$$
\begin{aligned}
\ell_{int}(\mathbf{x}, \theta_1, \theta_3) =&\ \ell_{InfoNCE}\left(f_{\theta_3}(f_{\theta_1}(a_1(\mathbf{x}))),\, f_{\theta_3}(f_{\theta_1}(a_2(\mathbf{x})))\right) + \\
&\ \ell_{InfoNCE}\left(f_{\theta_3}(f_{\theta_1}(a_2(\mathbf{x}))),\, f_{\theta_3}(f_{\theta_1}(a_1(\mathbf{x})))\right),
\end{aligned}
\tag{5.34}
$$

where $a_1, a_2 \sim \mathcal{A}_S$ denote two strong augmentation functions, and

$$
\ell_{InfoNCE}(\mathbf{v}_1, \mathbf{v}_2) = -\log \frac{\exp(d(\mathbf{v}_1, \mathbf{v}_2)/\tau)}{\sum_{i,j=1; i \neq j}^{|\mathcal{D}|} \exp(d(\mathbf{v}_1^{(i)}, \mathbf{v}_2^{(j)})/\tau)}
\tag{5.35}
$$

with $d(\mathbf{v}_1, \mathbf{v}_2) = \frac{\mathbf{v}_1^{\top}\mathbf{v}_2}{\|\mathbf{v}_1\|\|\mathbf{v}_2\|}$, τ is a temperature parameter, $\mathbf{v}_1^{(i)} = f_{\theta_3}(f_{\theta_1}(a_1(\mathbf{x}_i)))$, and $\mathbf{v}_2^{(j)} = f_{\theta_3}(f_{\theta_1}(a_2(\mathbf{x}_j)))$ (here, $a_1, a_2 \sim \mathcal{A}_S$). The last term in (5.31) is the structural similarity loss $\ell_{str}(.)$ that enforces the similarity between pairs of samples with respect to the predictions from the classifier and projection heads, as follows:

$$
\ell_{str}\left(\mathbf{x}, \tilde{\mathbf{y}}, \theta_1, \theta_2, \theta_3\right) = \sum_{j=1}^{|\mathcal{D}|} \mathsf{p}(\|\mathbf{v} - \mathbf{v}_j\|_2) \log \frac{\mathsf{p}(\|\mathbf{v} - \mathbf{v}_j\|_2)}{\mathsf{p}(\|\hat{\mathbf{y}} - \hat{\mathbf{y}}_j\|_2)},
\tag{5.36}
$$

where $\mathsf{p}(d) = \exp\left(\frac{0.5 \times d^2}{(0.5)^2}\right)$, $\mathbf{v} = f_{\theta_3}(f_{\theta_1}(\mathbf{x}))$, $\mathbf{v}_j = f_{\theta_3}(f_{\theta_1}(\mathbf{x}_j))$, $\hat{\mathbf{y}} = f_{\theta_2}(f_{\theta_1}(\mathbf{x}))$, and $\hat{\mathbf{y}}_j = f_{\theta_2}(f_{\theta_1}(\mathbf{x}_j))$.

The other top-performing method in Table 5.12 is DISC (Li et al., 2023), which is a feature selection and loss regularization already presented above and depicted in Fig. 5.5.

The **Clothing1M benchmark** (Xiao et al., 2015) in Table 5.13 is one of the most explored benchmarks to compare noisy-label learning methods. All methods in this table use the ResNet-50 (He et al., 2016a) backbone model. The results from the top-performing methods e.g., C2D (Zheltonozhskii et al., 2022), AugDesc (Nishi et al., 2021), PGDF (Chen et al., 2021a), and SANM(DivideMix) (Tu et al., 2023b) are all between 74% and 75%, with DMLP(DivideMix) (Tu et al., 2023a) reaching 78% because it relies on a clean validation set.

Table 5.13 Test accuracy (%) for the instance-dependent noise benchmark Clothing1M (Xiao et al., 2015). Results are collected from the cited papers. All methods use the ResNet-50 (He et al., 2016a) backbone model. DMLP(DivideMix) (Tu et al., 2023a) uses a clean validation set.

Dataset	Clothing1M
CE (Tu et al., 2023b)	69.21
C2D (Zheltonozhskii et al., 2022)	74.30
AugDesc (Nishi et al., 2021)	75.11
SANM(DivideMix) (Tu et al., 2023b)	75.63
DMLP(DivideMix) (Tu et al., 2023a)	78.23

Table 5.14 Test accuracy (%) for the instance-dependent noise benchmark WebVision (Li et al., 2017). Results are collected from the cited papers. The backbone model for this experiment is the Inception-ResnetV2 model (Szegedy et al., 2017).

Dataset	WebVision		ILSVRC2012	
	Top-1	Top-5	Top-1	Top-5
ELR+ (Liu et al., 2020)	77.78	91.68	70.29	89.76
PropMix (Cordeiro et al., 2022)	78.84	90.56	–	–
NGC (Wu et al., 2021b)	79.16	91.84	74.44	91.04
FaMuS (Xu et al., 2021)	79.40	92.80	77.00	92.76
DISC (Li et al., 2023)	80.28	92.28	77.44	92.28
BootLN(M) (Smart and Carneiro, 2023)	80.88	92.76	75.96	92.20
SSR+ (Feng et al., 2021)	80.92	92.80	75.76	91.76
BootLN(M) + *TTA* (Smart and Carneiro, 2023)	83.16	94.28	79.64	94.20

The **WebVision benchmark** (Li et al., 2017) in Table 5.14 is another heavily explored benchmark of noisy-label learning methods. The backbone model for WebVision is the Inception-ResnetV2 model (Szegedy et al., 2017). Top-performing methods, such as ELR+ (Liu et al., 2020), PropMix (Cordeiro et al., 2022), NGC (Wu et al., 2021b), FaMuS (Xu et al., 2021), DISC (Li et al., 2023), BootLN(M) (Smart and Carneiro, 2023), SSR+ (Feng et al., 2021), and BootLN(M) + *TTA* (Smart and Carneiro, 2023), have all been already explained in this book. Similarly to what is being observed in Clothing1M from Table 5.13, the WebVision results in Table 5.14 seem to be quite close to each other, with the exception of BootLN(M) + *TTA* (Smart and Carneiro, 2023), which has been obtained with test-time augmentation (TTA). The use of TTA suggests an interesting note, which is the potential performance gain that other methods can achieve with TTA, which is a point that needs further study.

Table 5.15   Test accuracy (%) for CIFAR-10 with combined symmetric closed set noise and open set noise from CIFAR-100 (Sachdeva et al., 2021). Results are collected from (Sachdeva et al., 2021; Feng et al., 2021) using the best and last training results. The backbone model is the PreActResNet-18 (He et al., 2016b).

Dataset		CIFAR-10 with Open Set Noise from CIFAR-100					
	Noise rate	30%	30%	30%	60%	60%	60%
	Open Rate	0%	50%	100%	0%	50%	100%
ILON	Best	86.4	87.4	90.4	77.1	80.5	83.4
(Wang et al., 2018)	Last	73.8	80.0	87.4	45.6	55.2	78.0
RoG	Best	89.9	89.8	91.4	83.1	84.1	88.2
(Lee et al., 2019)	Last	84.5	85.9	89.8	59.5	66.3	82.1
DivideMix	Best	94.3	91.5	89.3	94.4	91.8	89.0
(Li et al., 2020a)	Last	94.0	90.9	88.7	94.3	91.5	88.7
EDM	Best	95.3	94.5	92.9	94.3	93.4	90.6
(Sachdeva et al., 2021)	Last	94.0	94.0	91.9	94.3	92.8	89.4
SSR+	Best	–	96.3	96.1	–	95.2	94.0
(Feng et al., 2021)	Last	–	96.2	96.0	–	95.2	93.9

5.3 Open set label noise problems

Open-set label noise is, together with IDN, a real-world type of label noise that can be present in training datasets, given that images not belonging to any of the training classes may be mistakenly present in the training set. For this reason, the field has introduced benchmarks to compare methods designed to address this type of label noise. Table 5.15 shows one of these benchmarks which combines **closed-set symmetric label noise in CIFAR-10 and open-set label noise using samples from CIFAR-100** (Sachdeva et al., 2021). Also, Table 5.16 shows the results of a benchmark that combines **symmetric closed set noise in CIFAR-10 and open-set noise from ImageNet32** (Sachdeva et al., 2021). The backbone model used in these experiments is the PreActResNet-18 (He et al., 2016b). The results in Tables 5.15 and 5.16 suggest that EvidentialMix (EDM) (Sachdeva et al., 2021) (presented in (4.5)) and SSR+ (Feng et al., 2021) (presented in Fig. 5.3) show the best results. Interestingly, even though SSR+ and DivideMix are general label noise methods, they show competitive or better results than EDM that has been implemented to specifically address the combined open-set and closed-set label noise problem. This suggests that the differences between open-set and closed-set label noise may not be as large as initially anticipated.

A similar benchmark to the ones above has been proposed by Albert et al. (2022), who combine **symmetric closed set noise in CIFAR-100 and open-set noise from ImageNet32** (Sachdeva et al., 2021). The backbone model for this experiment is the PreActResNet-18 (He et al., 2016b). The results in Table 5.17 show the top-performing method is the DSOS Albert et al. (2022), which has been explained above

Table 5.16   Test accuracy (%) for CIFAR-10 with combined symmetric closed set noise and open set noise from ImageNet32 (Sachdeva et al., 2021). Results are collected from (Sachdeva et al., 2021) using the best and last training results. The backbone model is the PreActResNet-18 (He et al., 2016b).

Dataset	CIFAR-10 with Open Set Noise from ImageNet32						
	Noise rate	30%	30%	30%	60%	60%	60%
	Open Rate	0%	50%	100%	0%	50%	100%
ILON	Best	85.8	88.0	91.8	77.3	81.2	87.7
(Wang et al., 2018)	Last	72.7	82.0	90.6	46.5	58.9	85.5
RoG	Best	89.5	90.2	91.9	82.9	84.5	87.8
(Lee et al., 2019)	Last	83.9	86.6	91.0	59.8	70.3	85.9
DivideMix	Best	94.3	93.4	92.4	94.7	93.2	92.5
(Li et al., 2020a)	Last	94.1	93.0	92.0	94.6	92.8	92.5
EDM	Best	95.2	94.7	93.2	94.1	94.0	91.2
(Sachdeva et al., 2021)	Last	94.8	94.5	92.5	94.1	93.4	90.9

Table 5.17   Test accuracy (%) for CIFAR-100 with combined symmetric closed set noise and open set noise from ImageNet32 Albert et al. (2022). All results are from Albert et al. (2022) using the best and last training results. The backbone model is the PreActResNet-18 (He et al., 2016b).

Dataset	CIFAR-100 with Open Set Noise from ImageNet32				
	Closed Rate	20%	20%	20%	40%
	Open Rate	20%	40%	60%	40%
CE	Best	63.68	58.94	46.02	41.39
(Albert et al., 2022)	Last	55.52	44.31	26.03	18.45
ELR	Best	63.90	57.16	31.20	22.85
(Liu et al., 2020)	Last	63.72	56.91	29.55	21.63
EDM	Best	65.11	55.65	28.51	24.15
(Sachdeva et al., 2021)	Last	64.49	54.49	10.47	01.62
JoSRC	Best	67.37	61.70	37.95	41.53
(Yao et al., 2021b)	Last	64.17	61.37	37.11	41.44
DSOS	Best	70.54	62.49	49.98	43.69
(Albert et al., 2022)	Last	70.54	62.05	49.14	42.88

and consists of a dynamic label correction method that is designed to deal with both closed-set and open-set label noise.

The second best method is the Joint Sample Selection and Model Regularization based on Consistency (JoSRC) (Yao et al., 2021b),[31] which is a mean-teacher approach (Tarvainen and Valpola, 2017) that leverages predictions from two aug-

---

[31] https://github.com/NUST-Machine-Intelligence-Laboratory/Jo-SRC.

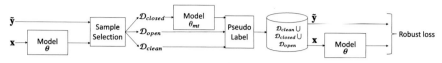

FIGURE 5.11 JoSCR (Yao et al., 2021b).

JoSCR (Yao et al., 2021b) is a multi-model approach that first selects samples to in the clean-label set $\mathcal{D}_{clean}$, closed-set $\mathcal{D}_{closed}$, and open-set $\mathcal{D}_{open}$. Then, a mean teacher (Tarvainen and Valpola, 2017) pseudo-labels samples belonging to $\mathcal{D}_{closed}$ or $\mathcal{D}_{open}$. Samples from the clean set and pseudo-labeled samples from the closed and open sets are then used to train the model with the robust loss function (5.40).

mentations of the training samples to classify them into clean or noisy, as shown in Fig. 5.11. In particular, training samples are first classified as clean if $p_{clean}(\mathbf{x}, \tilde{\mathbf{y}}) > \tau_{clean}$ using the Jensen-Shannon (JS) divergence, as follows:

$$p_{clean}(\mathbf{x}, \tilde{\mathbf{y}}) = 1 - \mathrm{JS}(f_\theta(\mathbf{x}) \| \tilde{\mathbf{y}}),$$

$$= 1 - 0.5 \times \mathrm{KL}\left(f_\theta(\mathbf{x}) \middle\| \frac{f_\theta(\mathbf{x}) + \tilde{\mathbf{y}}}{2}\right) - 0.5 \times \mathrm{KL}\left(\tilde{\mathbf{y}} \middle\| \frac{f_\theta(\mathbf{x}) + \tilde{\mathbf{y}}}{2}\right)$$

$$(5.37)$$

where JS(.) and KL(.) are the Jensen-Shannon (JS) and KL divergence operators. Hence, samples classified as clean form the dataset $\mathcal{D}_{clean}$, while the remaining samples form the $\mathcal{D}_{noisy} = \mathcal{D} \setminus \mathcal{D}_{clean}$ Then, a sample in $\mathcal{D}_{noisy}$ is classified as open-set label noise if $p_{open}(\mathbf{x}) > \tau_{open}$, where

$$p_{open}(\mathbf{x}) = \min(1, \| f_\theta(a_1(\mathbf{x})) - f_\theta(a_2(\mathbf{x}) \|_1)), \qquad (5.38)$$

where $a_1, a_2 \in \mathcal{A}$ denote two different augmentation functions sampled from $\mathcal{A}$. Samples classified as open set are inserted into $\mathcal{D}_{open} \subset \mathcal{D}_{noisy}$, while the remaining samples form $\mathcal{D}_{closed} \subset \mathcal{D}_{noisy} \setminus \mathcal{D}_{open}$. All samples are then pseudo-labeled, where samples in $\mathcal{D}_{clean}$ have their training labels modified to contain a small uniform distribution spread over all classes. Samples in $\mathcal{D}_{closed}$ are re-labeled with the mean-teacher's prediction $\tilde{\mathbf{y}} = f_{\theta_{mt}}(\mathbf{x})$, where θ_{mt} represents the mean-teacher model parameters that are updated from the model parameters during all training steps, using an exponential moving average (EMA) (Tarvainen and Valpola, 2017), as in

$$\theta_{mt} = \lambda \times \theta_{mt} + (1 - \lambda) \times \theta. \qquad (5.39)$$

Samples in $\mathcal{D}_{open}$ are re-labeled by assigning $\tilde{\mathbf{y}}$ to a uniform distribution. The training of JoSRC uses the following optimization

$$\theta^* = \arg\min_\theta \frac{1}{|\mathcal{D}|} \sum_{(\mathbf{x}, \tilde{\mathbf{y}}) \in (\mathcal{D}_{clean} \cup \mathcal{D}_{closed} \cup \mathcal{D}_{open})} \mathbb{E}_{a \sim \mathcal{A}}[\ell(\tilde{\mathbf{y}}, f_\theta(a(\mathbf{x})))] +$$

$$\rho \times \left(\mathrm{KL}[f_\theta(\mathbf{x}) \| f_\theta(a(\mathbf{x}))] + \mathrm{KL}[f_\theta(a(\mathbf{x})) \| f_\theta(\mathbf{x})] \right)$$

$$(5.40)$$

where $\rho = \delta \left((\mathbf{x}, \tilde{\mathbf{y}}) \in \left(\mathcal{D}_{clean} \bigcup \mathcal{D}_{closed} \right) \right)$ is an indicator function, and $a \sim \mathcal{A}$ is an augmentation function.

Differently from Tables 5.15 and 5.16, results in Table 5.17 suggest that DSOS and JoSRC, which have been designed to deal specifically with the combined closed-set and open-set label noise, are the best approaches tp deal with this specific problem. This apparent contradiction with the conclusion from the previous combined CIFAR-10 and open-set label noise benchmarks indicates that more study needs to be conducted until we are able to reach a more coherent analysis of the results.

5.4 Imbalanced noisy-label problems

All benchmarks presented so far assume a balanced distribution of samples per class in the training set, which facilitates the selection of noisy-label samples because samples that are hard to fit can either be located close to the classification boundary, or have a noisy label. However, when the training set contains an imbalanced distribution of samples per class, then samples belonging to minority classes (i.e., classes that have a relatively small number of training samples, compared to other classes in the training set) also tend to be hard to fit because of the dominance of majority classes in the minimization of a classification loss function. Hence, imbalanced noisy-label problems tend to be more challenging than the problems presented so far in this chapter. The combination of **symmetric label noise and imbalanced class distribution** has been proposed by three papers, referred to as FSR/RoLT/INOLML (Zhang and Pfister, 2021; Wei et al., 2021b; Hoang et al., 2022), with results shown in Tables 5.18 and 5.19. The backbone model used in this experiment is the Resnet-32 (He et al., 2016b). The baseline methods for this problem are CRUST (Mirzasoleiman et al., 2020)[32] that is a method that selects subsets of clean-label training samples to optimize the model, LDAM (Cao et al., 2019)[33] which introduces a robust loss function to minimize a margin-based generalization bound, the imbalanced-learning method BBN (Zhou et al., 2020)[34]; and HAR (Cao et al., 2020)[35] which is a data-dependent loss regularization method.

The best methods in both benchmarks (FSR (Zhang and Pfister, 2021)[36] and INOLML (Hoang et al., 2022)) are based on meta-learning approaches (see details in Section 4.4.1), which suggests that to handle imbalanced noisy-label learning problems, it is necessary to have a validation set (manually or automatically built) that contains a class balanced-distribution of clean-label samples. Another top-performing approach is the Robust Long-Tailed Learning (RoLT) (Wei et al., 2021b),

[32] https://github.com/snap-stanford/crust.
[33] https://github.com/kaidic/LDAM-DRW.
[34] https://github.com/Megvii-Nanjing/BBN.
[35] https://github.com/kaidic/HAR.
[36] https://github.com/google-research/google-research/tree/master/ieg.

Table 5.18 Test accuracy (%) in the imbalanced learning mixed with symmetric noise benchmark on CIFAR-10 (Zhang and Pfister, 2021; Wei et al., 2021b; Hoang et al., 2022). The reported results are from (Zhang and Pfister, 2021; Wei et al., 2021b; Hoang et al., 2022). The backbone model is the ResNet-32 (He et al., 2016b).

Dataset	CIFAR-10 with Symmetric Noise and Imbalanced Learning					
Noise rate	20%			40%		
Imbalanced Rate	10	50	200	10	50	200
CRUST (Mirzasoleiman et al., 2020)	65.7	41.5	34.3	59.5	32.4	28.8
LDAM (Cao et al., 2019)	82.4	–	–	71.4	–	–
LDAM-DRW (Cao et al., 2019)	83.7	–	–	74.9	–	–
BBN (Zhou et al., 2020)	80.4	–	–	70.0	–	–
HAR-DRW (Cao et al., 2020)	82.4	–	–	77.4	–	–
ROLT-DRW (Wei et al., 2021b)	85.5	–	–	82.0	–	–
FSR (Zhang and Pfister, 2021)	85.7	77.4	65.5	81.6	69.8	49.5
INOLML (Hoang et al., 2022)	90.1	80.1	66.6	89.1	78.1	61.6

Table 5.19 Test accuracy (%) in the imbalanced learning mixed with symmetric noise benchmark on CIFAR-100 (Zhang and Pfister, 2021; Wei et al., 2021b; Hoang et al., 2022). The reported results are from (Zhang and Pfister, 2021; Wei et al., 2021b; Hoang et al., 2022). The backbone model is the ResNet-32 (He et al., 2016b).

Dataset	CIFAR-100 with Symmetric Noise and Imbalanced Learning			
Noise rate	20%		40%	
Imbalanced Rate	10	100	10	100
LDAM (Cao et al., 2019)	48.1	29.7	36.7	19.7
LDAM-DRW (Cao et al., 2019)	50.4	32.3	39.4	21.2
BBN (Zhou et al., 2020)	47.9	27.8	35.2	18.2
HAR-DRW (Cao et al., 2020)	46.2	26.3	37.4	19.0
ROLT-DRW (Wei et al., 2021b)	52.4	32.7	46.3	26.6
INOLML (Hoang et al., 2022)	59.8	–	56.1	–

depicted in Fig. 5.12, which proposes new sample selection and pseudo-labeling techniques for imbalanced noisy-label learning that relies on a semi-supervised learning scheme. RoLT shows that the small-loss hypothesis does not work for imbalanced noisy-label learning problems because clean-label samples from minority classes tend to have loss values that can be larger than noisy-label samples from majority classes. Hence, RoLT proposes a new sample selection technique based on estimating class prototypes with

$$\mathbf{c_y} = \frac{1}{|\mathcal{D}^{(\mathbf{y})}|} \sum_{(\mathbf{x},\tilde{\mathbf{y}}) \in \mathcal{D}^{(\mathbf{y})}} f_{\theta_1}(\mathbf{x}), \qquad (5.41)$$

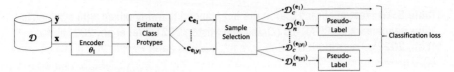

FIGURE 5.12 RoLT (Wei et al., 2021b).

RoLT (Wei et al., 2021b) consists of class-wise sample selection and pseudo-labeling method designed to handle imbalanced noisy-label learning problems. Sample selection is performed by first estimating class prototypes $\{\mathbf{c_y}\}_{\mathbf{y}\in\mathcal{Y}}$ with (5.41). Then, after selecting class-wise clean and noisy-label samples to be inserted into the sets $\mathcal{D}_c^{(\mathbf{y})}$ and $\mathcal{D}_n^{(\mathbf{y})}$, respectively, for $\mathbf{y} \in \mathcal{Y}$, RoLT pseudo-labels the samples in the noisy-label sets $\mathcal{D}_n^{(\mathbf{y})}$ for $\mathbf{y} \in \mathcal{Y}$ and trains the feature extractor $f_{\theta_1} : \mathcal{X} \to \mathcal{Z}$ and classifier $f_{\theta_2} : \mathcal{Z} \to \Delta^{|\mathcal{Y}|-1}$.

where $\mathcal{D}^{(\mathbf{y})} = \{(\mathbf{x}, \tilde{\mathbf{y}})|(\mathbf{x}, \tilde{\mathbf{y}}) \in \mathcal{D}, \tilde{\mathbf{y}} = \mathbf{y}\}$, and $f_{\theta_1} : \mathcal{X} \to \mathcal{Z}$ is a feature extractor. The sample selection is performed in a class-wise manner using the distance of each sample to its respective class prototype, computed with $d(\mathbf{x}, \mathbf{c_y}) = \| f_{\theta_1}(\mathbf{x}) - \mathbf{c_y}\|_2^2$ for $(\mathbf{x}, \tilde{\mathbf{y}}) \in \mathcal{D}^{(\mathbf{y})}$. Then, for each class, a GMM with two components is fit to $\{d(\mathbf{x}, \mathbf{c_y})\}_{(\mathbf{x},\tilde{\mathbf{y}})\in\mathcal{D}^{(\mathbf{y})}}$, where the component with the smallest mean represents the clean-label samples for class $\mathbf{y}$, where clean samples are selected with $p_{clean}(\mathbf{x}) > \tau$ to be inserted into $\mathcal{D}_c^{(\mathbf{y})}$, with the noisy set denoted by $\mathcal{D}_n^{(\mathbf{y})}$. The next step consists of pseudo-labeling the samples $(\mathbf{x}, \tilde{\mathbf{y}}) \in \mathcal{D}_n^{(\mathbf{y})}$ with:

$$\tilde{\mathbf{y}}(c) = \begin{cases} \sum_{\hat{\mathbf{y}}\in\mathcal{G}} \text{prior(clean label)} \times \mathbf{e}_c^\top \hat{\mathbf{y}}, & \text{if } \hat{\mathbf{y}} \in \mathcal{G} \\ \frac{1-\sum_{\hat{\mathbf{y}}\in\mathcal{G}} \text{prior(clean label)}}{|\mathcal{Y}|-|\mathcal{G}|}, & \text{otherwise} \end{cases}, \qquad (5.42)$$

where $\mathcal{G} = \{\mathbf{y}_{erm}, \mathbf{y}_{ncm}, \tilde{\mathbf{y}}\}$ (with $\mathbf{y}_{erm} = \arg\max_{\mathbf{y}\in\mathcal{Y}} f_{\theta_2}^{(\mathbf{y})}(f_{\theta_1}(\mathbf{x}))$, $\mathbf{y}_{ncm} = \arg\min_{\mathbf{y}\in\mathcal{Y}} \|\mathbf{c_y} - f_{\theta_1}(\mathbf{x})\|_2)$, $\mathbf{e}_c$ represents a one-hot $|\mathcal{Y}|$-dimensional vector with the value of one in the cth position, and prior(clean label) is the probability that the label $\hat{\mathbf{y}} \in \mathcal{G}$ agrees with the clean label. The parameters θ_1, θ_2 are then learned by minimizing the cross entropy loss using the original labels from the clean-label sets $\{\mathcal{D}_c^{(\mathbf{y})}\}_{\mathbf{y}\in\mathcal{Y}}$ and the pseudo-labels of the noisy-label sets $\{\mathcal{D}_n^{(\mathbf{y})}\}_{\mathbf{y}\in\mathcal{Y}}$. The extension RoLT-DRW is implemented by applying the Deferred Re-Weighting (DRW) (Cao et al., 2019) to improve the performance on minority classes.

5.5 Noisy multi-label learning

For multi-label learning, we first present results using two chest X-ray benchmarks (Liu et al., 2022a) that used **noisy multi-label training sets (Chest X-ray14 (NIH) (Wang et al., 2017b) and CheXpert (CXP) (Irvin et al., 2019))** and **clean-label testing sets (OpenI (OPI) (Demner-Fushman et al., 2016) and PadChest (PDC) (Bustos et al., 2020))**. The results from these benchmarks are presented in

Table 5.20 **Mean AUC (%) for the noisy multi-label benchmark (Liu et al., 2022a) with training on Chest X-ray14 (NIH) (Wang et al., 2017b) and testing on OpenI (OPI) (Demner-Fushman et al., 2016) and Pad-Chest (PDC) (Bustos et al., 2020)**. All results collected from (Liu et al., 2022a) with DenseNet121 (Huang et al., 2017) backbone model.

Training Set	Chest X-ray14 (NIH)	
Testing Set	OPI	PDC
ChestXNet (Rajpurkar et al., 2017)	83.69	83.29
Hermoza et al. (Hermoza et al., 2020)	86.01	83.25
Ma et al. (Ma et al., 2019)	82.80	82.41
DivideMix (Li et al., 2020a)	70.92	76.18
NVUM (Liu et al., 2022a)	88.65	85.55

Table 5.21 **Mean AUC (%) for the noisy multi-label benchmark (Liu et al., 2022a) with training on CheXpert (CXP) (Irvin et al., 2019) and testing on OpenI (OPI) (Demner-Fushman et al., 2016) and PadChest (PDC) (Bustos et al., 2020)**. All results collected from (Liu et al., 2022a) with DenseNet121 (Huang et al., 2017) backbone model.

Training Set	CheXpert (CXP)	
Testing Set	OPI	PDC
ChestXNet (Rajpurkar et al., 2017)	76.64	78.12
Hermoza et al. (Hermoza et al., 2020)	75.06	77.29
Ma et al. (Ma et al., 2019)	72.96	76.57
DivideMix (Li et al., 2020a)	69.36	65.72
NVUM (Liu et al., 2022a)	77.99	80.96

Tables 5.20 and 5.21 and all methods relied on the DenseNet121 (Huang et al., 2017) backbone model. The noisy multi-label learning problem has only recently been addressed more directly with the release of these two benchmarks, but the only approach that has been designed to address this challenge is NVUM (Liu et al., 2022a), which delivers the best result in both benchmarks. The approaches presented in (Rajpurkar et al., 2017),[37] (Hermoza et al., 2020),[38] and (Ma et al., 2019) were not designed to handle noisy-label learning, and they are present in the results because they can be considered as baseline methods in this benchmark. DivideMix (Li et al., 2020a) was extended to handle noisy multi-label learning by running a separate training for each

---

[37] https://stanfordmlgroup.github.io/projects/chexnet/.
[38] https://github.com/renato145/RpSalWeaklyDet.

label, but results indicate that it does not handle well the large class imbalances and multiple labels of both benchmarks. NVUM (Liu et al., 2022a)[39] is essentially an extension of ELR (Liu et al., 2020) to noisy multi-label learning, that trains a model $f_\theta : \mathbf{X} \to \mathcal{T}$ (where $\mathcal{T} \in \mathbb{R}^{|\mathcal{Y}|}$ is the logit space) with the following optimization:

$$\theta^* = \arg\min_\theta \frac{1}{|\mathcal{D}|} \sum_{(\mathbf{x}_i, \tilde{\mathbf{y}}_i) \in \mathcal{D}} \ell(\tilde{\mathbf{y}}, \sigma(f_\theta(\mathbf{x}_i))) + \ell_{reg}(\mathbf{t}_i, f_\theta(\mathbf{x}_i)) \tag{5.43}$$

where $\ell(.)$ is the BCE loss defined in (2.13), $\sigma(.)$ denotes the sigmoid activation function, and

$$\ell_{reg}(\mathbf{t}_i, f_\theta(\mathbf{x}_i)) = \log(1 - \sigma(\mathbf{t}_i^\top (\sigma(f_\theta(\mathbf{x}_i))))), \tag{5.44}$$

with

$$\mathbf{t}_i^{(t)} = \lambda \times \mathbf{t}_i^{(t-1)} + (1 - \lambda) \times (f_\theta(\mathbf{x}_i) - \pi) \tag{5.45}$$

representing a memory bank of logits that keeps the noisy-label early classification predictions produced by the model, which also takes into account the class prior distribution $\pi = \frac{1}{|\mathcal{D}|} \sum_{(\mathbf{x}, \tilde{\mathbf{y}}) \in \mathcal{D}} \tilde{\mathbf{y}}$ to mitigate the imbalanced learning problem that is generally present in noisy multi-label benchmarks.

Another **benchmark that uses the Chest X-ray14 (NIH)** (Wang et al., 2017b) noisy multi-label training set has been proposed in (Xue et al., 2022), which provides a **clean test set for two labels, namely Pneumothorax and Mass/Nodule**. In this benchmark, with results shown in Table 5.22, we can see results of many baseline noisy-label learning methods, such as a training with binary cross entropy (BCE), F-correction (Patrini et al., 2017), MentorNet (Jiang et al., 2017), Decoupling (Malach and Shalev-Shwartz, 2017), Co-teaching (Han et al., 2018c), and ELR (Liu et al., 2020). All of these methods have been explained before and rely on the backbone model DenseNet121 (Huang et al., 2017). The top-performing methods are NVUM (Liu et al., 2022a), described above, and the Global and Local Representation Guided Co-training (GloCal) method (Xue et al., 2022). GloCal, shown in Fig. 5.13, is a method that combines co-training with student-teacher training, exploring a self-supervised loss with global and local regularization. More specifically, GloCal co-trains two student-teacher models, denoted by $f_{\theta_{(s)}^{(A)}} : \mathcal{X} \to \Delta^{|\mathcal{Y}|-1}$, $f_{\theta_{(t)}^{(A)}} : \mathcal{X} \to \Delta^{|\mathcal{Y}|-1}$, $f_{\theta_{(s)}^{(B)}} : \mathcal{X} \to \Delta^{|\mathcal{Y}|-1}$, and $f_{\theta_{(t)}^{(B)}} : \mathcal{X} \to \Delta^{|\mathcal{Y}|-1}$, where students are trained with a set of loss functions, described below, and teachers are trained with exponential moving average (EMA), e.g., $\theta_{(t)}^{(A)} = \lambda \times \theta_{(t)}^{(A)'} + (1 - \lambda) \times \theta_{(s)}^{(A)}$ (note that $\theta_{(t)}^{(A)'}$ is the parameter of teacher A from the previous training iteration,

---

Table 5.22 Mean AUC (%) for the noisy multi-label benchmark (Xue et al., 2022) with training on Chest X-ray14 (NIH) (Wang et al., 2017b) and testing on clean-label Pneumothorax and Mass/Nodule labels from (Majkowska et al., 2020). Results are collected from (Xue et al., 2022; Liu et al., 2022a) with backbone model DenseNet121 (Huang et al., 2017).

Training Set	Chest X-ray14 (NIH)	
Testing Set	Clean-label Pneumothorax	Clean-label Mass/Nodule
BCE	87.0	84.3
F-correction (Patrini et al., 2017)	80.8	84.8
MentorNet (Jiang et al., 2017)	86.6	83.7
Decoupling (Malach and Shalev-Shwartz, 2017)	80.1	84.3
Co-teaching (Han et al., 2018c)	87.3	82.0
ELR (Liu et al., 2020)	87.1	83.2
GloCal (Xue et al., 2022)	89.1	84.6
NVUM (Liu et al., 2022a)	88.9	85.5

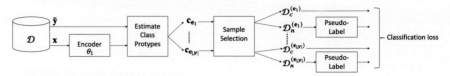

FIGURE 5.13 GloCal (Xue et al., 2022).

GloCal (Xue et al., 2022) is an approach to co-train two student-teacher models, where the selected clean and noisy samples from one model are used to train the other model. Such training involves an optimization described in (5.48) to minimize a classification loss with the clean set, a consistency loss between the teacher and student, and a local and global regularization losses. This optimization trains the student model, while the teacher model is trained with an exponential moving average using the student parameters.

and we have the same EMA update for teacher B). After computing the losses of the training samples by models A and B, the first step consists of selecting samples (using the small loss hypothesis based on fitting a two-component Gaussian mixture model (Li et al., 2020a)) to form the clean and noisy subsets for each model, denoted by $\mathcal{D}_c^{(A)}$ and $\mathcal{D}_n^{(A)}$ for model A and $\mathcal{D}_c^{(B)}$ and $\mathcal{D}_n^{(B)}$ for model B. Then, similarly to DivideMix (Li et al., 2020a), the clean and noisy subsets produced by A are used to train B, and vice-versa. Next, samples from the clean subsets are trained with cross-entropy loss, while samples from the noisy subset are trained with a global and local losses, and all samples are used to minimize a teacher-student consistency loss. Assuming that the model is represented by a feature extractor $f_{\hat{\theta}} : \mathcal{X} \to \mathcal{Z}$ and a classifier $f_{\bar{\theta}} : \mathcal{Z} \to \Delta^{|\mathcal{Y}|-1}$ (where $\theta = \{\hat{\theta}, \bar{\theta}\}$), the global loss computes the relationship between features extracted from training samples to form the $|\mathcal{D}| \times |\mathcal{D}|$ matrix

$$\mathbf{M}(i, j) = \frac{\mathbf{f}_i^\top \mathbf{f}_j}{\|\mathbf{f}_i\|_2 \|\mathbf{f}_j\|_2}, \tag{5.46}$$

which allows the minimization of the following loss

$$\ell_{glo}(\mathcal{D}) = \frac{1}{2} \left(\mathrm{KL}[\mathbf{M}_{(t)}\|[\mathbf{M}_{(s)}] + \mathrm{KL}[\mathbf{M}_{(s)}\|[\mathbf{M}_{(t)}]\right), \tag{5.47}$$

where KL[.] represents the KL divergence. This global loss aligns the inter-sample relationship of samples between the teacher and student models. The local loss minimizes the contrastive loss of augmented images, as defined in (5.35). The training also depends on the minimization of a consistency loss between the teacher and student models, defined by $\ell_{con}(\mathbf{x}) = \| f_{\theta_{(s)}^{(A)}}(\mathbf{x}) - f_{\theta_{(t)}^{(A)}}(\mathbf{x}) \|_2^2$. Hence, the student model A from GloCal is trained with

Table 5.23 Test accuracy (%) for the closed-set symmetric label noise benchmark (Xue et al., 2022) on the PatchCamelyon (PCam) dataset (Bejnordi et al., 2017; Veeling et al., 2018). All results from (Xue et al., 2022) with ResNet-34 He et al. (2016b) backbone model.

Dataset	PatchCamelyon				
Symmetric Noise Rate	0%	5%	10%	20%	40%
CE (Xue et al., 2022)	93.44	91.28	88.95	82.67	63.41
F-correction (Patrini et al., 2017)	94.22	92.60	90.54	83.24	64.10
MentorNet (Jiang et al., 2017)	93.09	92.65	91.05	85.66	69.43
Decoupling (Malach and Shalev-Shwartz, 2017)	93.03	91.73	89.74	82.85	64.13
Co-teaching (Han et al., 2018c)	93.25	92.88	91.39	86.05	76.03
ELR (Liu et al., 2020)	93.27	92.69	90.84	87.12	73.86
GloCal (Xue et al., 2022)	94.31	93.88	92.75	90.88	79.00

$$
\theta_{(s)}^{(A)*} = \arg\min_{\theta_{(s)}^{(A)}} \frac{1}{|\mathcal{D}_c^{(B)}|} \sum_{(\mathbf{x},\tilde{\mathbf{y}})\in\mathcal{D}_c^{(B)}} \ell_{CE}\left(\tilde{\mathbf{y}}, f_{\theta_{(s)}^{(A)}}(\mathbf{x})\right)
$$
$$
+ \lambda \times \left(\frac{1}{|\mathcal{D}_n^{(B)}|} \sum_{(\mathbf{x},\tilde{\mathbf{y}})\in\mathcal{D}_n^{(B)}} \ell_{InfoNCE}\left(f_{\theta_{(s)}^{(A)}}(a_1(\mathbf{x})), f_{\theta_{(s)}^{(A)}}(a_2(\mathbf{x}))\right) \right.
$$
$$
\left. + \ell_{glo}(\mathcal{D}_c^{(B)}) + \frac{1}{|\mathcal{D}|} \sum_{(\mathbf{x},\tilde{\mathbf{y}})\in\mathcal{D}} \ell_{con}(\mathbf{x}) \right)
$$

(5.48)

where $a_1, a_2 \sim \mathcal{A}$ denote augmentation functions, and $\theta_{(s)}^{(B)*}$ is similarly estimated using the clean and noisy samples from model A.

The **synthetic benchmarks using symmetric noise rates in** $\{0\%, 5\%, 10\%, 20\%, 40\%\}$ **on ISIC 2017 and PatchCamelyon**, introduced by Xue et al. (2022), are shown in Tables 5.23 and 5.24. The results in these two tables show relatively similar results as the one in Table 5.22, with GloCal Xue et al. (2022) showing the best performance, compared to other baseline methods. Xue et al. (2022) also introduced the **Inter-observer Variability benchmark based on the Gleason 2019** dataset (Nir et al., 2018), shown in Table 5.25. In this benchmark, six pathologists with high inter-observer variation annotated the images, where the clean label is obtained from the application of the Simultaneous Truth and Performance Level Estimation (STAPLE) algorithm (Warfield et al., 2004), while the noisy label is represented by the label provided by one of the pathologists. Similar to the benchmarks above, compared to the baseline methods, GloCal (Xue et al., 2022) displays the top performance. All results from these benchmarks are computed with the ResNet-34 (He et al., 2016b) backbone model.

The **DigestPath2019 and Camelyon16 benchmarks** (Da et al., 2022) are built by adding **symmetric label noise with rates in** $\{10\%, 20\%, 30\%, 40\%\}$, as shown

Table 5.24 Test accuracy (%) for the closed-set symmetric label noise benchmark (Xue et al., 2022) on the ISIC 2017 skin dataset (Codella et al., 2018). All results from (Xue et al., 2022) with ResNet-34 He et al. (2016b) backbone model.

Dataset	ISIC 2017 skin dataset				
Symmetric Noise Rate	**0%**	**5%**	**10%**	**20%**	**40%**
CE (Xue et al., 2022)	85.50	84.25	83.01	81.36	69.65
F-correction (Patrini et al., 2017)	85.63	84.32	83.82	82.88	68.60
MentorNet (Jiang et al., 2017)	85.09	83.47	83.83	82.15	70.40
Decoupling (Malach and Shalev-Shwartz, 2017)	84.98	83.39	83.13	81.64	68.63
Co-teaching (Han et al., 2018c)	85.59	83.98	83.39	83.22	74.78
ELR (Liu et al., 2020)	85.51	84.28	83.18	83.37	72.98
GloCal (Xue et al., 2022)	86.00	85.40	84.33	84.17	76.67

Table 5.25 Test accuracy (%) for the instance-dependent noise benchmark (Xue et al., 2022) on the Gleason dataset (Nir et al., 2018). All results from (Xue et al., 2022) with ResNet-34 He et al. (2016b) backbone model.

Dataset	Gleason	
Noise	**Clean training**	**Noisy training**
CE (Xue et al., 2022)	78.52	66.47
F-correction (Patrini et al., 2017)	76.75	68.92
MentorNet (Jiang et al., 2017)	79.80	68.21
Decoupling (Malach and Shalev-Shwartz, 2017)	80.66	69.63
Co-teaching (Han et al., 2018c)	79.58	71.93
ELR (Liu et al., 2020)	80.37	70.27
GloCal (Xue et al., 2022)	81.76	75.47

in Tables 5.26 and 5.27. The **real-world Chaoyang benchmark** (Zhu et al., 2021a) contains real-world closed-set instance-dependent label noise, with results shown in Table 5.28. All experiments in this table rely on the Resnet-34 (He et al., 2016b) model. Current results in these benchmarks show that the top-performing method is the Hard Sample Aware Noise Robust Learning (HSA-NRL) (Zhu et al., 2021a),[40] which is a two stage approach with the first stage comprising sample selection and pseudo-labeling, and the second stage involving a multi-model training, as depicted in Fig. 5.14. More specifically, the first stage of HSA-NRL consists of a warm-up training of the classifier $f_\theta : \mathcal{X} \to \Delta^{|\mathcal{Y}|-1}$ using the cross-entropy loss with $\mathcal{D} = \{(\mathbf{x}, \tilde{\mathbf{y}})_i\}_{i=1}^{|\mathcal{D}|}$. The prediction probability for all W epochs of the warm-up training of each training sample $\mathbf{x}_i$ is recorded as $\mathbf{p}_i \in [0, 1]^{|\mathcal{Y}| \times W}$. After sorting the training samples by their annotated-label mean prediction probability $\bar{\mathbf{p}}_i = \mathrm{mean}(\tilde{\mathbf{y}}_i^\top \mathbf{p}_i)$, the

---

[40] https://github.com/bupt-ai-cz/HSA-NRL/.

Table 5.26 Accuracy (ACC), AUC, F1 Score, Precision, and Recall (all in %) for the closed-set symmetric label noise benchmark (Zhu et al., 2021a) on the DigestPath2019 dataset (Da et al., 2022). All results from (Zhu et al., 2021a) using Resnet-34 (He et al., 2016b) backbone model.

Dataset	DigestPath2019				
	ACC	AUC	F1 Score	Precision	Recall
Symmetric Noise Rate	**10%**				
Joint (Tanaka et al., 2018)	91.49	97.62	91.25	95.41	87.45
Co-teaching (Han et al., 2018c)	91.08	98.21	90.59	97.49	84.60
INCV (Chen et al., 2019)	93.58	97.91	93.62	94.34	92.92
OUSM (Xue et al., 2019)	90.27	96.87	89.81	95.87	84.48
DivideMix (Li et al., 2020a)	92.69	97.76	92.69	93.98	91.45
HSA-NRL (Zhu et al., 2021a)	94.91	98.40	95.05	93.68	96.46
Noise rate	**Symmetric 20%**				
Joint (Tanaka et al., 2018)	88.78	95.40	89.00	88.47	89.53
Co-teaching (Han et al., 2018c)	90.33	95.86	90.12	93.49	87.00
INCV (Chen et al., 2019)	92.09	96.43	91.97	94.74	89.36
OUSM (Xue et al., 2019)	88.19	94.19	88.18	89.30	87.11
DivideMix (Li et al., 2020a)	90.53	96.09	90.46	92.51	88.51
HSA-NRL (Zhu et al., 2021a)	94.46	98.30	94.53	94.51	94.55
Noise rate	**Symmetric 30%**				
Joint (Tanaka et al., 2018)	87.17	94.72	86.41	93.34	80.44
Co-teaching (Han et al., 2018c)	86.49	93.55	86.90	85.50	88.34
INCV (Chen et al., 2019)	87.84	94.60	87.65	90.36	85.10
OUSM (Xue et al., 2019)	86.52	92.49	86.53	87.64	85.45
DivideMix (Li et al., 2020a)	88.87	95.10	88.60	92.04	85.41
HSA-NRL (Zhu et al., 2021a)	91.72	97.38	91.47	95.74	87.57
Noise rate	**Symmetric 40%**				
Joint (Tanaka et al., 2018)	84.30	91.39	84.46	84.77	84.15
Co-teaching (Han et al., 2018c)	84.92	92.98	84.94	86.02	83.89
INCV (Chen et al., 2019)	85.20	93.52	84.47	90.19	79.44
OUSM (Xue et al., 2019)	84.04	93.51	82.57	92.43	74.60
DivideMix (Li et al., 2020a)	85.96	96.87	84.49	95.97	75.46
HSA-NRL (Zhu et al., 2021a)	87.15	94.26	86.49	88.58	85.16

top $100\% - \rho\%$ of training samples are selected to form the clean subset $\mathcal{D}_c$, and the remaining samples form the unclean subset $\mathcal{D}_u$. The idea explored in this first stage is to train a noisy-label sample classifier using the training history of the prediction probability. To achieve that, we build a new dataset $\mathcal{D}_a$ formed from $\mathcal{D}_c$, where $\rho\%$ of the samples in $\mathcal{D}_c$ are flipped, with the new label replacing the old label, and the annotation $r \in \{0, 1\}$ per sample being introduced to indicate if the label was flipped ($r = 1$) or not ($r = 0$). Another warm-up training is run with $\mathcal{D}_a$, and the sample-wise prediction probability history is recorded. Next, the unclean samples from $\mathcal{D}_a$ are selected by taking the bottom $\rho\%$ of samples in terms of the mean prediction probability

Table 5.27 Accuracy (ACC), AUC, F1 Score, Precision, and Recall (all in %) for the closed-set symmetric label noise benchmark (Zhu et al., 2021a) on the Camelyon16 dataset (Bejnordi et al., 2017). All results from (Zhu et al., 2021a) using Resnet-34 (He et al., 2016b) backbone model.

Dataset	Camelyon16				
	ACC	AUC	F1 Score	Precision	Recall
Noise rate	Symmetric 10%				
Joint (Tanaka et al., 2018)	97.51	98.94	97.53	96.89	98.18
Co-teaching (Han et al., 2018c)	98.16	99.34	98.13	99.87	96.45
INCV (Chen et al., 2019)	97.87	99.23	97.84	99.57	96.17
OUSM (Xue et al., 2019)	98.08	99.37	98.06	99.55	96.61
DivideMix (Li et al., 2020a)	95.10	96.70	94.91	99.15	91.01
HSA-NRL (Zhu et al., 2021a)	98.82	99.81	98.81	99.73	97.73
Noise rate	Symmetric 20%				
Joint (Tanaka et al., 2018)	96.51	98.75	96.49	97.13	95.86
Co-teaching (Han et al., 2018c)	97.57	99.29	97.53	99.29	95.84
INCV (Chen et al., 2019)	97.65	99.33	97.62	99.42	95.87
OUSM (Xue et al., 2019)	96.57	98.90	96.52	98.33	94.78
DivideMix (Li et al., 2020a)	93.98	96.90	94.01	93.85	94.17
HSA-NRL (Zhu et al., 2021a)	98.61	99.78	98.69	99.61	97.40
Noise rate	Symmetric 30%				
Joint (Tanaka et al., 2018)	96.10	98.79	96.03	98.09	94.06
Co-teaching (Han et al., 2018c)	97.49	99.02	97.44	99.68	95.30
INCV (Chen et al., 2019)	96.28	97.64	96.24	97.41	95.10
OUSM (Xue et al., 2019)	96.43	98.73	96.32	99.63	93.22
DivideMix (Li et al., 2020a)	93.39	95.28	93.08	97.74	88.85
HSA-NRL (Zhu et al., 2021a)	98.32	99.57	98.30	99.84	96.80
Noise rate	Symmetric 40%				
Joint (Tanaka et al., 2018)	91.97	95.51	91.56	96.94	86.86
Co-teaching (Han et al., 2018c)	95.20	96.25	95.09	97.56	92.74
INCV (Chen et al., 2019)	95.40	96.26	95.28	98.06	92.65
OUSM (Xue et al., 2019)	91.98	96.35	91.32	98.64	85.11
DivideMix (Li et al., 2020a)	89.55	97.72	88.39	99.84	79.30
HSA-NRL (Zhu et al., 2021a)	98.17	99.51	98.16	99.12	97.22

$\bar{\mathbf{p}}_i \in [0, 1]$. These selected unclean samples are used to train a noisy-label sample classifier that takes as input $\mathbf{p}_i \in [0, 1]^W$ and predicts r, where $r \approx 1$ means noisy, and $r \approx 0$ represents hard. This classifier is then used to classify the samples in $\mathcal{D}_u$ into hard $\mathcal{D}_h$ or noisy $\mathcal{D}_n$. The pseudo-labeling stage consists of training the classifier $f_\theta : \mathcal{X} \to \Delta^{|\mathcal{Y}|-1}$ using cross-entropy loss with the training set $\mathcal{D}_c \bigcup \mathcal{D}_h$, and pseudo-labeling all samples in $\mathcal{D}_h \bigcup \mathcal{D}_n$ with this trained classifier. The almost-clean dataset $\mathcal{D}_o$ is built from $\mathcal{D}_c$, $\mathcal{D}_n$ after discarding samples whose labels were not changed by pseudo-labeling, and $\mathcal{D}_c$ after discarding samples whose labels were changed by pseudo-labeling. The second stage of HSA-NRL uses two models $f_{\theta_1} : \mathcal{X} \to \Delta^{|\mathcal{Y}|-1}$

Table 5.28 Accuracy (ACC), AUC, F1 Score, Precision, and Recall (all in %) for the closed-set symmetric label noise benchmark (Zhu et al., 2021a) on the Chaoyang dataset (Zhu et al., 2021a). All results from (Zhu et al., 2021a) using Resnet-34 (He et al., 2016b) backbone model.

Dataset	Chaoyang				
	ACC	AUC	F1 Score	Precision	Recall
Joint (Tanaka et al., 2018)	75.99	90.43	67.72	70.97	67.91
Co-teaching (Han et al., 2018c)	79.39	91.72	71.97	74.57	70.77
INCV (Chen et al., 2019)	80.34	92.63	74.11	76.22	73.06
OUSM (Xue et al., 2019)	80.53	93.69	73.70	74.81	73.27
DivideMix (Li et al., 2020a)	77.25	87.58	69.78	70.68	69.11
HSA-NRL (Zhu et al., 2021a)	83.40	94.51	76.54	78.33	75.45

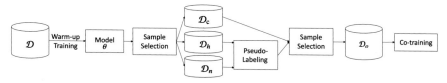

FIGURE 5.14 HSA-NRL (Zhu et al., 2021a).

HSA-NRL (Zhu et al., 2021a) is a two-stage approach that, in the first stage, explores sample selection to divide the training set $\mathcal{D}$ into clean $\mathcal{D}_c$, hard $\mathcal{D}_h$, and noisy $\mathcal{D}_n$. Then, samples in $\mathcal{D}_h$ and $\mathcal{D}_n$ are pseudo-labeled, and another round of sample selection is performed to form the almost-clean dataset $\mathcal{D}_o$. The second stage of HSA-NRL consists of a co-training approach, similar to the ones presented in Section 4.4.3.

and $f_{\theta_2} : \mathcal{X} \to \Delta^{|\mathcal{Y}|-1}$. The first model is trained to minimize a classification loss using $100\% - \rho\%$ of the samples from $\mathcal{D}_o$ that show the highest classification probabilities from the second model. The training of the second model is achieved using exponential moving average (EMA) with $\theta_2 = \lambda \times \theta_2' + (1-\lambda) \times \theta_1$ (where θ_2' is the parameter for the second model from the previous training epoch).

There are other approaches that show competitive results in Tables 5.26, 5.27, and 5.28. For instance, DivideMix (Li et al., 2020a) (explained above) presents competitive results in all benchmarks, but not quite as good as HSA-NRL. OUSM (Xue et al., 2019) is another competitive approach that relies on the small-loss hypothesis to select clean samples, followed by loss re-weighting to address imbalanced learning The INCV approach (Chen et al., 2019)[41] is also worth noting given that its results are relatively accurate with the exploration of a co-teaching approach that selects samples from the training set $\mathcal{D}$ based on an iterative cross-validation approach. These benchmarks also show a baseline result from Joint (Tanaka et al., 2018), which is a

---

[41] https://github.com/chenpf1025/noisy_label_understanding_utilizing.

Table 5.29 mAP (%) for the closed set symmetric and asymmetric segmentation noise benchmark (Yang et al., 2020) on the Pascal VOC dataset. Results are from (Yang et al., 2020), where all methods rely on Mask R-CNN (He et al., 2017) as the instance segmentation model and the ResNet-50-FPN (He et al., 2016a; Lin et al., 2017a) as the backbone model.

Dataset	Pascal VOC with Symmetric and Asymmetric Label Noise						
Noise Type	No Noise	Symmetric				Asymmetric	
Noise Rate	0%	20%	40%	60%	80%	20%	40%
LSR (Pereyra et al., 2017)	36.7	34.5	31.9	27.0	20.3	35.8	33.2
Joint (Tanaka et al., 2018)	32.7	22.7	11.5	3.8	3.8	24.6	24.3
GCE (Zhang and Sabuncu, 2018)	38.7	35.3	32.9	26.1	15.5	36.0	32.3
SCE (Wang et al., 2019c)	39.4	34.6	32.1	27.9	21.2	37.5	34.9
CE (He et al., 2017)	39.3	34.2	31.5	27.1	20.7	36.8	34.5
LNCIS (Yang et al., 2020)	39.7	38.5	38.1	33.8	25.5	37.8	35.1
Dataset	COCO with Symmetric and Asymmetric Label Noise						
Noise Type	No Noise	Symmetric				Asymmetric	
Noise Rate	0%	20%	40%	60%	80%	20%	40%
SCE (Wang et al., 2019c)	32.3	31.5	29.9	28.2	22.0	32.1	31.6
CE (He et al., 2017)	34.2	31.3	29.3	27.1	21.7	31.9	31.3
LNCIS (Yang et al., 2020)	33.7	33.1	31.3	30.8	26.6	33.3	33.0
Dataset	Cityscapes with Symmetric and Asymmetric Label Noise						
Noise Type	No Noise	Symmetric				Asymmetric	
Noise Rate	0%	20%	40%	60%	80%	20%	40%
SCE (Wang et al., 2019c)	30.2	26.1	22.3	12.6	9.3	28.0	18.6
CE (He et al., 2017)	32.5	26.0	21.0	13.3	11.6	29.8	18.9
LNCIS (Yang et al., 2020)	32.7	30.8	29.1	19.1	15.2	30.9	21.3

pseudo-labeling approach that jointly optimizes labels and model parameters, with

$$\theta^*, \{\tilde{\mathbf{y}}_i^*\}_{i=1}^{|\mathcal{D}|} = \arg\min_{\theta, \{\tilde{\mathbf{y}}_i\}_{i=1}^{|\mathcal{D}|}} \frac{1}{|\mathcal{D}|} \sum_{(\mathbf{x}_i, \tilde{\mathbf{y}}_i) \in \mathcal{D}} \ell(\tilde{\mathbf{y}}_i, f_\theta(\mathbf{x}_i)).$$

5.6 Noisy-label segmentation problems

The **symmetric and asymmetric instance segmentation noise benchmarks** presented in Table 5.29 show a consistent ranking of recently proposed approaches (Yang et al., 2020). All methods in this benchmark rely on Mask R-CNN (He et al., 2017) as the instance segmentation model and the ResNet-50-FPN (He et al., 2016a; Lin et al., 2017a) as the backbone model. The top-performing approach is the Learning with Noisy Class Labels for Instance Segmentation (LNCIS) (Yang et al., 2020)[42] that combines sample selection with an optimization that relies on a robust loss function, as shown in Fig. 5.15. LNCIS relies on Mask R-CNN (He et al., 2017) as the instance segmentation backbone, consisting of the following steps: 1) feature extrac-

---

[42] https://github.com/longrongyang/Learning-with-Noisy-Class-Labels-for-Instance-Segmentation.

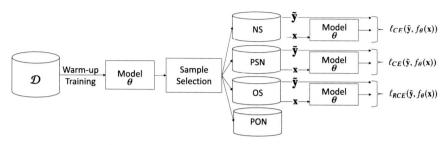

FIGURE 5.15 LNCIS (Yang et al., 2020).

LNCIS (Yang et al., 2020) combines sample selection with a robust loss function. The sample selection step takes a warmed-up model to classify samples first into positive and negative samples (NS), with the positive samples being further sub-divided into pseudo negative samples (PNS), potential noisy samples (PON), and other samples (OS). The next training stage trains the model with a robust loss function that discards samples in the PON set and uses the cross-entropy (CE) loss for NS and PSN samples and the (label noise robust) reverse cross-entropy (RCE) loss for OS samples.

tion; 2) region proposal (Girshick, 2015); 3) bounding box regression and multi-class classification; and 4) segmentation masks generation inside bounding boxes. Out of these steps, LNCIS focuses on the multi-class classification for the bounding box in step (3). Hence, the problem is related to the foreground-background and foreground-instance classifications of bounding boxes, with a training set $\mathcal{D} = \{(\mathbf{x}, \tilde{\mathbf{y}})\}$, where $\mathbf{x} \in \mathcal{X}$ is an image region, and $\tilde{\mathbf{y}} \in \mathcal{Y}$, which is the one-hot label space with one of the dimensions representing the background class; and model $f_\theta : \mathcal{X} \to \Delta^{|\mathcal{Y}|-1}$. The first stage of LNCIS comprises a sample selection process, first as positive samples (PS), i.e., samples with $\tilde{\mathbf{y}} \neq \mathbf{e}_1$, where $\mathbf{e}_1$ is the one-hot vector with the first dimension equal to 1, or negative samples (NS), i.e., samples with $\tilde{\mathbf{y}} = \mathbf{e}_1$. Positive samples are further classified into pseudo negative samples (PSN), potential noisy samples (PON), and other samples (OS), where PSN samples have $\mathbf{e}_1 = \arg\max_{\mathbf{y} \in \mathcal{Y}} f_\theta^{(\mathbf{y})}(\mathbf{x})$, PON samples have $\ell(\tilde{\mathbf{y}}, f_\theta(\mathbf{x})) > \gamma$, and OS are the training samples not classified as PSN or PON. The optimization then uses the cross-entropy loss for E_1 epochs (i.e., warm-up) with:

$$\theta^* = \arg\min_\theta \frac{1}{|\mathcal{D}|} \sum_{(\mathbf{x}, \tilde{\mathbf{y}}) \in \mathcal{D}} \ell_{CE}(\tilde{\mathbf{y}}, f_\theta(\mathbf{x})). \tag{5.49}$$

The warmed-up model is used to select training samples into NS, PSN, PON, and OS. Then, for the next E_2 epochs, LNCIS trains the model with

$$\theta^* = \arg\min_\theta \frac{1}{|\mathcal{D}|} \sum_{(\mathbf{x}, \tilde{\mathbf{y}}) \in \mathcal{D}} \delta((\mathbf{x}, \tilde{\mathbf{y}}) \text{ is NS}) \times \ell_{CE}(\tilde{\mathbf{y}}, f_\theta(\mathbf{x}))$$
$$+ \delta((\mathbf{x}, \tilde{\mathbf{y}}) \text{ is PSN}) \times \ell_{CE}(\tilde{\mathbf{y}}, f_\theta(\mathbf{x})) \tag{5.50}$$
$$+ \delta((\mathbf{x}, \tilde{\mathbf{y}}) \text{ is OS}) \times \ell_{RCE}(\tilde{\mathbf{y}}, f_\theta(\mathbf{x})),$$

where $\delta(.)$ is the indicator function, and $\ell_{RCE}(\tilde{\mathbf{y}}, f_\theta(\mathbf{x})) = -f_\theta(\mathbf{x})^\top \log(\tilde{\mathbf{y}})$ (with $\log 0$ clipped to -4) denotes the reverse cross-entropy (RCE) loss (Wang et al., 2019c) that is empirically demonstrated to be more robust to noisy labels, but converges slower than the CE loss. The optimization in (5.50) aims to achieve a good trade-off between fast convergence and noise robustness by using the CE loss with samples that are more likely to be correct and the RCE loss with samples less likely to be correct.

Table 5.29 also shows several baseline results that are competitive with the proposed LNCIS (Yang et al., 2020). A robust loss method, called LSR (Pereyra et al., 2017), which is based on adding an entropy minimization regularization, is applied to this instance segmentation noise benchmark with a surprisingly accurate result. As described above, Joint (Tanaka et al., 2018) is a pseudo-labeling approach to jointly optimize labels and model parameters, which shows competitive results, except for symmetric noise larger than 40%. Generalized cross entropy (GCE) (Zhang and Sabuncu, 2018) explores a robust loss function, which is defined as ℓ_{MAE+CE} in (4.3), which combines CE and MAE losses and produces competitive results, except for symmetric noise larger than 40%. Symmetric Cross Entropy (SCE) (Wang et al., 2019c)[43] is another robust loss function that combines the cross-entropy (CE) loss with reverse cross-entropy (RCE) loss, defined in (5.50), which displays competitive results, which are surprisingly slightly worse than the CE loss alone (He et al., 2017).

5.7 Noisy-label detection problems

Shen et al. (2020) introduce several **noisy-label detection benchmarks on Pascal VOC 2007, Pascal VOC 2012 (Everingham et al., 2010), and COCO (Lin et al., 2014)** with the goal of testing object detectors that are trained with noisy image-level labels. The results on these benchmarks are presented in Tables 5.30, 5.31, and 5.32. Table 5.30 shows detection results on PASCAL VOC 2007, with clean-label training sets (PASCAL VOC 2007) and noisy-label training sets (all others). Tables 5.31 and 5.32 show similar benchmarks with PASCAL VOC 2012 and COCO datasets. The base detection model adopted for these benchmarks is the Weakly Supervised Deep Detection Network (WSDDN) (Bilen and Vedaldi, 2016). WSSDN consists of a feature extractor that branches out into classification and detection streams that produce two normalized score matrices $\mathbf{X}_c, \mathbf{X}_d \in \mathbb{R}^{N_b \times |\mathcal{Y}|}$, where N_b is the number of region proposals. The Hadamard product of the normalized matrices from the two streams outputs the detection score matrix $\mathbf{X}_s \in \mathbb{R}^{N_b \times |\mathcal{Y}|}$ that is used to compute the image-level classification scores with $\mathbf{y}_s(k) = \sum_{r=1}^{N_b} \mathbf{X}_s(r,k)$, where $\mathbf{X}_s(r,k)$ is the score of the rth proposal and the kth category in $\mathbf{X}_s$. The training from WSDDN

---

[43] https://github.com/YisenWang/symmetric_cross_entropy_for_noisy_labels.

Table 5.30 AP (%) for the instance-dependent detection noise benchmark (Shen et al., 2020) on the Pascal VOC 2007 dataset. Results are from (Shen et al., 2020), and backbone models are as indicated in the table.

Classes	aer	bic	bir	boa	bot	bus	car	cat	cha	cow	dtb	dog	hor	mbk	per	pln	she	sfa	tra	tv	Av.
Training on PASCAL VOC 2007 trainval images with proposal/image-level annotations																					
FasterRCNN VGG16 (Ren et al., 2015)	70.0	80.6	70.1	57.3	49.9	78.2	80.4	82.0	52.2	75.3	67.2	80.3	79.8	75.0	76.3	39.1	68.3	67.3	81.1	67.6	69.9
WS-JDS VGG16 (Shen et al., 2019)	64.8	70.7	51.5	25.1	29.0	74.1	69.7	69.6	12.7	69.5	43.9	54.9	39.3	71.3	32.6	29.8	57.0	61.0	66.6	57.4	52.5
Training on Flickr-Clean and PASCAL VOC 2007 trainval images																					
Tao et al. VGG-M (Tao et al., 2018)	35.6	31.3	18.2	7.7	9.1	40.4	38.4	23.8	9.7	20.1	33.4	22.5	30.9	41.4	9.8	10.8	18.7	28.7	27.1	34.7	24.6
Tao et al. VGG16 (Tao et al., 2018)	40.6	30.1	17.8	15.9	6.4	42.9	40.5	31.5	11.4	20.3	27.4	15.7	24.1	43.8	8.9	12.2	17.7	37.3	32.1	31.0	25.4
Training on Flickr-Clean																					
fWebSOD VGG-F (Shen et al., 2020)	43.7	34.5	32.9	12.6	13.7	54.2	45.2	35.0	11.3	26.0	26.9	22.7	25.7	49.2	20.8	9.1	34.7	48.9	46.6	38.9	31.6
fWebSOD VGG-M (Shen et al., 2020)	44.3	37.8	32.5	15.0	14.1	55.2	44.5	32.4	10.9	28.0	26.8	17.9	26.2	49.6	20.2	9.7	35.4	49.4	48.9	37.2	31.8
fWebSOD VGG16 (Shen et al., 2020)	44.6	36.6	34.3	18.6	13.8	56.7	47.2	37.7	11.6	23.3	32.5	29.1	33.3	52.6	21.5	8.9	35.5	52.4	45.3	38.2	33.7
Training on Flickr-VOC																					
fWebSOD VGG-F (Shen et al., 2020)	45.4	38.1	38.9	20.1	13.8	60.8	42.9	55.2	16.1	29.2	9.4	33.3	30.9	52.9	14.5	14.9	37.8	28.8	49.2	26.8	32.9
fWebSOD VGG-M (Shen et al., 2020)	45.7	38.5	36.9	20.6	16.9	55.2	38.8	57.5	14.8	25.0	10.6	38.7	39.3	51.8	16.3	13.6	38.0	34.6	46.3	26.1	33.3
fWebSOD VGG16 (Shen et al., 2020)	45.9	39.6	39.8	21.1	14.4	60.9	39.9	61.5	15.6	32.5	14.1	44.8	45.2	51.7	18.0	13.8	38.9	32.1	47.2	23.5	35.1

Table 5.31 AP (%) for the instance-dependent detection noise benchmark (Shen et al., 2020) on the Pascal VOC 2012 dataset. Results are from (Shen et al., 2020), and backbone models are as indicated in the table.

Classes	aer	bic	bir	boa	bot	bus	car	cat	cha	cow	dtb	dog	hor	mbk	per	pln	she	sfa	tra	tv	Av.
Training on PASCAL VOC 2012 trainval images with proposal/image-level annotations																					
FasterRCNN VGG16 (Girshick, 2015)	82.3	76.4	71.0	48.4	45.2	72.1	72.3	87.3	42.2	73.7	50.0	86.8	78.7	78.4	77.4	34.5	70.1	57.1	77.1	58.9	67.0
WS-JDS VGG16 (Shen et al., 2019)	-	-	-	-	-	-	-	-	-	-	-	-	-	-	-	-	-	-	-	-	46.1
Training on Flickr-Clean and PASCAL VOC 2012 trainval images																					
Tao et al. VGG-M (Tao et al., 2018)	44.3	29.8	15.6	6.6	6.0	34.4	24.2	25.1	5.7	20.3	22.3	24.9	29.1	45.2	7.8	9.4	12.4	21.4	22.6	26.0	21.7
Training on Flickr-Clean																					
fWebSOD VGG-F (Shen et al., 2020)	41.0	15.1	29.7	10.4	13.2	47.6	42.0	36.8	10.2	16.5	13.2	28.2	20.5	39.6	15.0	8.4	28.0	38.6	9.6	38.2	25.1
fWebSOD VGG-M (Shen et al., 2020)	40.7	17.2	28.1	11.6	12.5	48.4	39.7	31.1	5.5	20.8	12.2	27.3	27.9	37.3	17.7	7.0	28.1	40.1	10.0	36.6	25.0
fWebSOD VGG16 (Shen et al., 2020)	39.6	18.1	30.7	8.4	12.0	51.2	42.5	42.6	9.4	20.4	16.1	23.5	26.9	41.6	17.1	7.9	29.1	39.0	9.6	39.9	26.3
Training on Flickr-VOC																					
fWebSOD VGG-F (Shen et al., 2020)	40.2	33.7	38.4	12.5	13.0	52.7	40.4	41.2	13.0	24.7	18.0	31.6	32.5	51.7	12.4	11.6	33.3	30.4	40.5	22.1	29.7
fWebSOD VGG-M (Shen et al., 2020)	42.6	36.7	36.9	17.5	14.8	53.6	38.3	44.4	13.7	28.8	19.2	24.6	26.8	52.2	11.3	10.5	39.1	26.6	42.9	21.4	30.1
fWebSOD VGG16 (Shen et al., 2020)	41.9	40.6	38.4	20.5	9.0	56.9	40.3	50.1	13.0	30.8	17.2	32.7	29.9	51.2	17.0	13.5	36.4	39.2	45.3	29.2	32.7

Table 5.32 AP (%) as a function of IoU and AP (%) for objects with small (S), medium (M), and large (L) areas for the instance-dependent detection noise benchmark (Shen et al., 2020) on the COCO dataset. Results are from (Shen et al., 2020), and backbone models are as indicated in the table.

Measure	AP(IoU)			AP(Area)		
	0.5:0.95	0.5	0.75	S	M	L
Training on COCO train images with proposal/image-level annotations						
FasterRCNN VGG16 (Girshick, 2015)	21.2	41.5	–	–	–	–
WS-JDS VGG16 (Shen et al., 2019)	10.5	20.3	9.2	2.2	10.9	18.3
WSDDN VGG16 (Bilen and Vedaldi, 2016)	9.5	19.2	8.2	2.1	10.4	17.2
Training on Flickr-COCO						
WSDDN VGG16 (Bilen and Vedaldi, 2016)	3.1	7.0	2.3	0.4	2.6	6.9
fWebSOD VGG16 (Shen et al., 2020)	5.4	10.6	4.6	0.6	5.1	10.7

is performed by minimizing the binary cross entropy (BCE) $\ell_{BCE}(\tilde{\mathbf{y}}, \mathbf{y}_s)$, defined in (2.13).

Shen et al. (2020) propose fWebSOD[44] that extends WSDDN to mitigate the risks associated with background label noise (i.e., missing label) by changing the model architecture with the introduction of two detection heads, namely the weak detection head and the residual detection head, with the goal of decomposing the noisy training signal, as displayed in Fig. 5.16. While the weak detection head receives the embedding from the feature extractor to branch out to the classification and detection streams, similarly to WSDDN, the residual detection receives the embedding from the feature extractor which is summed with the features from the weak detection head to branch out to the classification and detection streams. The residual detection score matrix $\mathbf{X}_u \in \mathbb{R}^{N_b \times |\mathcal{Y}|}$ produces the image-level classification scores with $\mathbf{y}_u(k) = \sum_{r=1}^{N_b} \mathbf{X}_u(r, k)$. Both the weak detection head and the residual detection head are trained to minimize the loss $(1-\lambda)^\top \ell_{BCE}(\tilde{\mathbf{y}}, \mathbf{y}_s) + \lambda^\top \ell_{BCE}(\tilde{\mathbf{y}}, \mathbf{y}_u)$, where $\lambda \in [0, 1]^{|\mathcal{Y}|}$. The idea explored by Shen et al. (2020) with this loss is that when the training label $\tilde{\mathbf{y}} \in \mathcal{Y}$ is likely to be clean, λ_y will be low, suppressing the residual detection head. On the other hand, when $\tilde{\mathbf{y}}$ is likely to be a noisy label, λ_y will be high, where the residual detection head adds noisy features to the features from the weak detection head, which are likely to produce the clean label, in order to minimize the loss with respect to the noisy label $\tilde{\mathbf{y}}$. The estimation of λ during training follows the spatially-sensitive entropy (SSE) criterion, where λ_y has high scores only for a small minority of cluttered proposals. To deal with foreground noise (i.e., when an image is labeled with a class that is not present in the image), Shen et al. (2020) propose the bagging-mixup data augmentation, consisting of using convex combinations of images containing the same foreground label. Such strategy increases the chances that the augmented image is diverse and contains at least one instance of the label.

---

[44] https://github.com/shenyunhang/NA-fWebSOD.

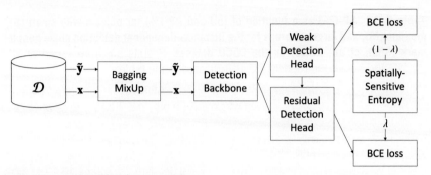

FIGURE 5.16 fWebSOD (Shen et al., 2020).

fWebSOD (Shen et al., 2020) modifies the WSDDN (Bilen and Vedaldi, 2016) object detection architecture to include two detection heads: the weak detection head and the residual detection head. A robust loss function is proposed to select (via the estimation of λ by the spatially-sensitive entropy) which head to use for the training. Essentially, if the training sample is likely to be clean, $\lambda \approx 0$ will suppress the residual detection head and train the weak detection head. However, when the sample is likely to be noisy, then $\lambda \approx 1$, which trains the residual head to "fix" the prediction of the weak detection head to fit the noisy-label from the training set. Additionally, the bagging-mixup data augmentation is used to combine training images that are annotated with the same foreground label. This increases the likelihood that the augmented image contains at least one instance of the foreground class.

Most of results in Tables 5.30, 5.31, and 5.32 show the competitive performance of the method described above (Shen et al., 2020). As baseline methods, these tables show FasterRCNN (Ren et al., 2015), WS-JDS (Shen et al., 2019), which are common visual object detection methods. The main competitor of fWebSOD is the method by (Tao et al., 2018), which consists of a multi-instance multi-label domain adaption learning framework that transfers knowledge from data collected from the web.

5.8 Noisy-label medical image segmentation problems

The noisy-label benchmark shown in Table 5.33 (Zhang et al., 2020a) forms the **IDN ISBI2015 MS lesion segmentation** (Jesson and Arbel, 2015), **IDN BraTS** (Menze et al., 2014), and the **IDN LIDC-IDRI** (Armato et al., 2011). These benchmarks contain images, each annotated by multiple labelers with different biases and competence levels, where methods are tested for the joint learning of the reliability of labelers and clean segmentation labels. The method Disentangle (Zhang et al., 2020a)[45] is a dual-model approach, with one model trained to estimate the clean

---

[45] https://github.com/moucheng2017/Learn_Noisy_Labels_Medical_Images.

Table 5.33 Dice (%), mean square error (MSE) of the labelers' confusion matrix (CM) for different methods with dense labels, and the generalized energy distance (GED) (Kohl et al., 2018) for the instance-dependent medical image segmentation noise benchmark to measure the quality of the estimated labels (Zhang et al., 2020a). All results are from (Zhang et al., 2020a).

| | IDN MSLesion | | | IDN BraTS | IDN LIDC-IDRI |
	Dice (%)	CM MSE	GED	GED	GED
CNN on mean labels (Zhang et al., 2020a)	46.55	–	–	–	–
CNN on mode labels (Zhang et al., 2020a)	47.82	–	–	–	–
Probabilistic U-net (Kohl et al., 2018)	46.15	–	1.91	3.23	1.97
Separate CNNs on annotators (Zhang et al., 2020a)	46.84	–	–	–	–
STAPLE (Warfield et al., 2004)	55.05	0.1502	–	–	–
Spatial STAPLE (Asman and Landman, 2012)	58.37	0.1483	–	–	–
Disentangle (Zhang et al., 2020a)	67.55	0.0811	1.67	3.14	1.87

segmentation labels, and the other model to characterize individual labelers using pixel-wise confusion matrices (CM) for each training image. The dataset is denoted by $\mathcal{D} = \{(\mathbf{x}, \{\tilde{\mathbf{y}}_r\}_{r=1}^{|\mathcal{S}_i|})_i\}_{i=1}^{|\mathcal{D}|}$, where the image is denoted with $\mathbf{x} \in \mathcal{X} \subset \mathbb{R}^{H \times W}$ and the segmentation label is represented with $\tilde{\mathbf{y}}_r \in \mathcal{Y} \subset \{0, 1\}^{H \times W \times |\mathcal{Y}|}$, with $|\mathcal{Y}|$ denoting the number of classes and $\mathcal{S}_i$ representing the set of annotators per training image $i \in \{1, ..., |\mathcal{D}|\}$. The training is based on the optimization defined in (4.80) (Tanno et al., 2019):

$$\theta^*, \phi^* = \arg\min_{\theta, \phi} \sum_{\left(\mathbf{x}, \{\tilde{\mathbf{y}}_j\}_{j=1}^M\right) \in \mathcal{D}} \sum_{r=1}^{|\mathcal{S}_i|} \ell\left(\tilde{\mathbf{y}}_r, \mathbf{T}_\phi(r, \mathbf{x}) \times f_\theta(\mathbf{x})\right) + \lambda \times \left(\text{tr}\left(\mathbf{T}_\phi(r, \mathbf{x})\right)\right)$$

(5.51)

where $\mathbf{T}_\phi : \mathbb{N} \times \mathcal{X} \to [0, 1]^{W \times H \times |\mathcal{Y}| \times |\mathcal{Y}|}$ represents a model that predicts the pixel-wise label transition matrix for user $r \in \{1, ..., |\mathcal{S}_i|\}$ and image $\mathbf{x}$, $f_\theta : \mathcal{X} \to [0, 1]^{W \times H \times |\mathcal{Y}|}$ denotes the model that predicts the clean label segmentation for image $\mathbf{x}$, $\text{tr}\left(\mathbf{T}_\phi(r, \mathbf{x})\right)$ denotes the trace of the pixel-wise label transition matrix predicted for each user, and $\ell(.)$ is the pixel-wise cross-entropy loss function.

Table 5.33 compares the proposed Disentangle (Zhang et al., 2020a) with: 1) clean-label segmentation produced by the mean of all of the noisy labels; 2) clean-label segmentation produced by the mode of all of the noisy labels; 3) clean-label segmentation and labelers' confusion matrices estimated by STAPLE (Warfield et al., 2004); 4) spatial STAPLE (Asman and Landman, 2012) that estimates pixel-wise confusion matrices per labeler; and 5) probabilistic UNet (Kohl et al., 2018)[46] that combines UNet (Ronneberger et al., 2015) with a conditional variational auto-encoder (Kingma and Welling, 2013) to enable the generation of an unlimited number of plausible segmentation hypotheses. Results in Table 5.33 clearly suggest that the proposed Disentangle shows the most accurate clean-label segmentations and confusion matrices.

5.9 Non-image noisy-label problems

The benchmark **IDN NEWS** (Xia et al., 2020) in Table 5.34 uses the dataset NEWS (Lang, 1995) with the same type of instance-dependent noise (IDN) presented in Tables 5.3, 5.7, and 5.8. Backbone model consists of a network with three convolutional layers and one fully connected layer. Similarly to the results in Tables 5.7 and 5.8, PTD-R-V (Xia et al., 2020) is a competitive approach for IDN NEWS, with methods T-revision (Xia et al., 2019), Re-weight (Liu and Tao, 2015), and Mentor-Net (Jiang et al., 2017) also being competitive.

The benchmark in Table 5.35 tests the robustness of text classification methods to **symmetric and asymmetric noisy-label (Zheng et al., 2021) with respect to the**

---

[46] https://github.com/SimonKohl/probabilistic_unet.

Table 5.34 **Test accuracy (%) for the instance-dependent noise benchmark on text data (Xia et al., 2020) using the NEWS dataset (Lang, 1995).** Results are from (Xia et al., 2020), and backbone model consists of a network with three convolutional layers and one fully connected layer.

Dataset	NEWS				
IDN noise rate	10%	20%	30%	40%	50%
CE (Xia et al., 2020)	69.58	66.80	63.11	58.37	54.75
MentorNet (Jiang et al., 2017)	69.03	66.92	62.87	54.35	48.35
Reweight (Liu and Tao, 2015)	70.25	68.42	65.05	59.37	57.31
T-Revision (Xia et al., 2019)	70.72	69.91	67.28	61.78	59.29
PTD-R-V (Xia et al., 2020)	71.92	71.33	69.01	63.17	62.77

Table 5.35 **Test accuracy (%) for the closed-set mean symmetric and asymmetric label noise benchmark (Zheng et al., 2021) on the text datasets AG News (Zhang et al., 2015), Amazon reviews (Xie et al., 2020), Yelp reviews (Yang et al., 2016), and Yahoo answers (Conneau et al., 2016).** Results are from (Zheng et al., 2021) and are computed using a mean over 10 noise levels using a pretrained BERT-base model.

Dataset	AG	Yelp-5	Amazon-5	Yahoo
Clean Validation Size	4 × 100	5 × 100	5 × 100	10 × 100
MWN (Shu et al., 2019)	75.91	51.27	49.49	60.18
GLC (Hendrycks et al., 2018)	83.88	60.12	60.31	68.03
MLC (Zheng et al., 2021)	85.27	62.61	61.21	73.72

datasets AG News (Zhang et al., 2015), Amazon reviews (Xie et al., 2020), Yelp reviews (Yang et al., 2016), and Yahoo answers (Conneau et al., 2016). For all these datasets, a subset of the training image is guaranteed to be clean (400 for AG News, 500 for Amazon reviews, 500 for Yelp reviews, and 1000 for Yahoo answers), while the rest of the dataset is affected by symmetric and asymmetric label noise with $\eta \in \{0\%, 10\%, 20\%, ..., 80\%, 90\%, 100\%\}$. All approaches in this experiment rely on a pre-trained BERT-base model. The top-performing approach in Table 5.35 is the Meta Label Correction (MLC) (Zheng et al., 2021), which is a meta-learning approach that defines the meta parameters as the parameters of the label correction network (LCN) $g_\alpha : \mathcal{X} \times \mathcal{Y} \rightarrow \Delta^{|\mathcal{Y}|-1}$. The optimization of MLC is as follows:

$$\alpha^* = \arg\min_{\alpha} \frac{1}{|\mathcal{D}_v|} \sum_{(\mathbf{x},\mathbf{y})\in\mathcal{D}_v} \ell(\mathbf{y}, f_{\theta^*(\alpha)}(\mathbf{x}))$$

$$\text{s.t. } \theta^*(\alpha) = \arg\min_{\theta} \frac{1}{|\mathcal{D}_t|} \sum_{(\mathbf{x},\tilde{\mathbf{y}})\in\mathcal{D}_t} \ell(g_\alpha(\mathbf{x}, \tilde{\mathbf{y}}), f_\theta(\mathbf{x})), \quad (5.52)$$

Table 5.36 Test accuracy (%) in the random noise benchmark (Garg et al., 2021) that applies symmetric label noise rates $\{10\%, 20\%, 30\%, 40\%, 50\%\}$ in the training and validation sets of the datasets TREC (Li and Roth, 2002) and AG News (Zhang et al., 2015). All results are from (Garg et al., 2021) and backbone models are the word-LSTM (Hochreiter and Schmidhuber, 1997) and word-CNN (Kim, 2014).

Symmetric noise rate	0%	10%	20%	30%	40%	50%
Dataset				TREC		
LSTM	93.8	88.0	89.4	83.4	79.6	77.6
LSTM+$\mathcal{L}_{\text{DN-H}}$	–	92.2	90.2	88.8	83.0	82.4
LSTM+$\mathcal{L}_{\text{DN-S}}$	–	92.4	90.0	87.4	83.4	82.6
CNN	92.6	88.8	89.2	84.8	82.2	77.6
CNN+$\mathcal{L}_{\text{DN-H}}$	–	91.0	90.8	89.4	81.4	81.4
CNN+$\mathcal{L}_{\text{DN-S}}$	–	92.2	91.8	88.8	77.0	77.2
Dataset				AG-News		
LSTM	92.5	91.9	91.3	90.5	89.3	88.6
LSTM+$\mathcal{L}_{\text{DN-H}}$	–	91.5	90.6	90.8	90.3	89.0
LSTM+$\mathcal{L}_{\text{DN-S}}$	–	91.8	90.8	91.0	90.3	88.6
CNN	91.5	90.9	90.6	89.3	89.2	87.4
CNN+$\mathcal{L}_{\text{DN-H}}$	–	91.3	91.0	90.3	88.3	86.6
CNN+$\mathcal{L}_{\text{DN-S}}$	–	90.9	90.4	88.7	86.6	84.5

where $f_\theta : \mathcal{X} \to \Delta^{|\mathcal{Y}|-1}$ represents the classifier, $\mathcal{D}_v = \{(\mathbf{x}, \mathbf{y})_i\}_{i=1}^{|\mathcal{D}_v|}$ is the clean validation set, $\mathcal{D}_t = \{(\mathbf{x}, \tilde{\mathbf{y}})_i\}_{i=1}^{|\mathcal{D}_t|}$ is the noisy training set (with $|\mathcal{D}_t| > |\mathcal{D}_v|$). Table 5.35 shows that MLC (Zheng et al., 2020) is more accurate than gold loss correction (GLC) (Hendrycks et al., 2018), defined in (4.36) as a loss correction approach that relies on a label transition matrix built with anchor points from the clean validation set $\mathcal{D}_v$, and MWN (Shu et al., 2019), defined in (4.113) as a meta-learning approach where the meta parameter is represented by the parameters in the sample weighting function.

Table 5.36 shows the **random noise benchmark** (Garg et al., 2021) that applies symmetric label noise rates $\{10\%, 20\%, 30\%, 40\%, 50\%\}$ in the training and validation sets of the **datasets TREC (Li and Roth, 2002) and AG News (Zhang et al., 2015)**, but it keeps their testing sets with the original clean labels. Tables 5.37 and 5.38 display the **input-conditional noise (ICN) on TREC and AG News datasets** (Garg et al., 2021), where noise is introduced as follows: 1) selectively corrupting the labels of inputs that contain the words 'How' or 'What'; and 2) flipping the label of the longest inputs in the dataset. The baseline models in this benchmark are the word-LSTM (Hochreiter and Schmidhuber, 1997) and word-CNN (Kim,

Table 5.37 Test accuracy (%) in the input-conditional noise benchmark (Garg et al., 2021) on the dataset TREC (Li and Roth, 2002). All results are from (Garg et al., 2021) and backbone models are the word-LSTM (Hochreiter and Schmidhuber, 1997) and word-CNN (Kim, 2014).

IDN noise rate	10%	20%	30%	40%	50%
IDN noise type	**Token (How/What) based**				
LSTM	89.2	84.4	77.8	76	71.8
LSTM+$\mathcal{L}_{DN\text{-}H}$	91.8	87.4	84.2	79	67.8
LSTM+$\mathcal{L}_{DN\text{-}S}$	91.8	90.6	83.8	79.2	75.6
CNN	90.4	83.8	82.4	78.8	52
CNN+$\mathcal{L}_{DN\text{-}H}$	90.0	86.6	84.4	80.6	74
CNN+$\mathcal{L}_{DN\text{-}S}$	91.2	86.8	84.2	81.8	65.2
IDN noise type	**Length based**				
LSTM	91.4	87	82.2	82.4	74.2
LSTM+$\mathcal{L}_{DN\text{-}H}$	91.6	90.2	87.4	87.4	79
LSTM+$\mathcal{L}_{DN\text{-}S}$	92	90.6	85.4	84	75
CNN	91	88	85.2	82	73.6
CNN+$\mathcal{L}_{DN\text{-}H}$	90.6	89.6	87.2	82.6	77
CNN+$\mathcal{L}_{DN\text{-}S}$	92.8	91	86.8	86	75.4

Table 5.38 Test accuracy (%) in the input-conditional noise benchmark (Garg et al., 2021) on the dataset AG News (Zhang et al., 2015). All results are from (Garg et al., 2021) and backbone models are the word-LSTM (Hochreiter and Schmidhuber, 1997) and word-CNN (Kim, 2014).

IDN noise rate	AP (7.8%)	Reuters (10.8%)	Either (18.6%)
Dataset		**AG-News**	
LSTM	82.8	85.6	75.7
LSTM+$\mathcal{L}_{DN\text{-}H}$	82.7	85.7	76.6
LSTM+$\mathcal{L}_{DN\text{-}S}$	82.8	85.5	76
CNN	83.1	85.7	76.6
CNN+$\mathcal{L}_{DN\text{-}H}$	82.4	86.2	76.1
CNN+$\mathcal{L}_{DN\text{-}S}$	82.5	86.1	76.4

2014). The method $\mathcal{L}_{DN}$ (Garg et al., 2021)[47] consists of a warm-up training to minimize the cross-entropy loss using the whole training set, then a sample selection approach produces $p(clean|\mathbf{x}, \tilde{\mathbf{y}})$ for each training sample $(\mathbf{x}, \tilde{\mathbf{y}}) \in \mathcal{D}$ using a Beta

---

[47] https://github.com/thumbe3/label-noise-nlp.

mixture model on the loss values from the warm-up stage (Arazo et al., 2019). The optimization is defined as:

$$
\theta_1^*, \theta_2^*, \theta_3^* = \arg\min_\theta \frac{1}{|\mathcal{D}|} \sum_{(\mathbf{x}, \tilde{\mathbf{y}}) \in \mathcal{D}} \ell\left(\tilde{\mathbf{y}}, f_{\theta_2}(f_{\theta_1}(\mathbf{x}))\right) + \tag{5.53}
$$
$$
\gamma \times p(clean|\mathbf{x}, \tilde{\mathbf{y}}) \times \ell\left(\tilde{\mathbf{y}}, f_{\theta_3}(f_{\theta_1}(\mathbf{x}))\right),
$$

where $f_{\theta_1} : \mathcal{X} \to \mathcal{Z}$ is a feature extractor, $f_{\theta_2} : \mathcal{Z} \to \Delta^{|\mathcal{Y}|-1}$ is a noisy-label classifier, and $f_{\theta_3} : \mathcal{Z} \to \Delta^{|\mathcal{Y}|-1}$ is a clean-label classifier. The method $\mathcal{L}_{\text{DN-S}}$ is trained with (5.53), while $\mathcal{L}_{\text{DN-H}}$ replaces $p(clean|\mathbf{x}, \tilde{\mathbf{y}})$ by the indicator function $\delta(p(clean|\mathbf{x}, \tilde{\mathbf{y}}) > 0.5)$.

Table 5.39 is a **benchmark to assess models trained with the distantly labeled Docred dataset** (Yao et al., 2019), where the training set contains 50.9% of label noise (Deng et al., 2021) and has an imbalance distribution of samples per class. All methods in this experiment use the BiLSTM backbone (Yao et al., 2019). Results on the clean-label sets Test and Dev show that the most robust method in Table 5.39 is the DisRel method (Yao et al., 2019), which minimizes a robust loss function that mitigates the negative impacts of the noisy label and class imbalance problems. DisRel minimizes a loss function defined by $\ell(\tilde{\mathbf{y}}, f_\theta(\mathbf{x})) = \sum_{n=0}^{M} \mathbf{a}_n \times f_\theta^{(\tilde{\mathbf{y}})}(\mathbf{x})^{\frac{n}{M}}$, where $M \geq 3$, $\mathbf{a} \in \mathbb{R}^{M+1}$, and $f_\theta^{(\tilde{\mathbf{y}})}(\mathbf{x})$ represents the output related to class $\tilde{\mathbf{y}}$. Competing approaches in this benchmark also rely on loss functions designed to handle imbalanced learning problems, such as the Range loss (Zhang et al., 2017b), focal loss (FL) (Lin et al., 2017b), class-balanced loss (CBL) (Cui et al., 2019) Other approaches rely on label noise robust losses, such as the bounded mean square error (BMSE) (Ghosh et al., 2017) (see Section 4.2.1), and generalized cross entropy (GCE) (Zhang and Sabuncu, 2018) (see Section 4.2.1).

Tables 5.40 and 5.41 show the **artificially noised dataset benchmarks**, obtained by modifying the human-annotated training sets with **symmetric and asymmetric label noise on datasets Docred (Yao et al., 2019) and CoNLL 2003 (Sang and De Meulder, 2003)**. For the symmetric noise, the rate is $\{20\%, 40\%, 60\%, 80\%\}$, and for the asymmetric noise, the entity pairs in the human-annotated dataset are labeled through wikidata knowledge base, then labels are flipped using noise rate $\eta \in \{20\%, 40\%, 60\%\}$. All methods use the BiLSTM backbone (Yao et al., 2019). The results in Tables 5.40 and 5.41 show a relatively similar ranking of methods, compared to the distantly labeled dataset benchmark in Table 5.39, with DisRel (Deng et al., 2021) ranked as the top-performing approach.

5.10 Conclusion

To conclude this chapter, we summarize the main techniques used by the top-performing methods for each benchmark presented in this chapter. Table 5.42 shows the techniques, presented in Chapter 4, explored by the top methods introduced in

Table 5.39 Test F1 (%), Ign F1(%), AUC (%), and Ign AUC (%) for the Dev and Test dataset for model trained in Distantly labeled Docred dataset (Yao et al., 2019), where the training set contains 50.9% of label noise and has an imbalance distribution of samples per class (Deng et al., 2021). All results are from (Deng et al., 2021) and methods are based on BiLSTM (Yao et al., 2019).

Dataset								
	Docred							
	Dev				Test			
Measures	F1	Ign F1	AUC	Ign AUC	F1	Ign F1	AUC	Ign AUC
CE (Deng et al., 2021)	48.90	43.89	46.92	42.57	48.84	44.17	46.88	42.66
GCE (Zhang and Sabuncu, 2018)	49.86	45.56	47.13	42.81	49.82	45.47	47.04	42.94
BMSE (Ghosh et al., 2017)	49.05	43.45	46.23	41.97	49.17	43.23	46.69	41.76
FL (Lin et al., 2017b)	49.53	44.43	47.21	43.05	49.82	44.38	47.03	43.02
CBL (Cui et al., 2019)	49.61	44.68	47.04	42.95	49.82	44.56	47.22	42.87
Range (Zhang et al., 2017b)	49.32	44.07	46.98	42.57	49.56	44.16	47.05	42.61
DisRel (Deng et al., 2021)	51.85	47.24	50.46	46.24	51.81	46.94	50.23	46.13

Table 5.40 Test F1 (%) and Ign F1(%) results on closed-set symmetric and asymmetric label noise (Deng et al., 2021), obtained by modifying the human-annotated training sets on Docred dataset (Yao et al., 2019). All results are from (Deng et al., 2021) and methods are based on BiLSTM (Yao et al., 2019).

Dataset		Docred						
Noise		Symmetric				Asymmetric		
Rate		20%	40%	60%	80%	20%	40%	60%
CE	F1:	49.08	47.11	43.18	35.11	48.37	42.55	30.86
(Deng et al., 2021)	Ign F1:	44.44	42.52	38.37	30.44	43.79	38.03	26.41
GCE	F1:	48.81	47.41	42.66	35.84	48.14	42.60	31.17
(Zhang and Sabuncu, 2018)	Ign F1:	44.39	42.62	38.35	30.85	43.84	38.45	26.97
BMSE	F1	49.21	47.37	43.76	35.94	48.35	43.02	31.63
(Ghosh et al., 2017)	Ign F1:	44.23	42.44	38.15	30.98	43.45	38.07	27.26
FL	F1:	49.21	47.33	43.45	35.12	48.28	42.77	30.89
(Lin et al., 2017b)	Ign F1:	44.61	42.54	38.41	30.66	43.77	38.15	26.67
CBL	F1:	49.44	47.31	43.38	35.31	48.57	42.75	31.06
(Cui et al., 2019)	Ign F1:	44.55	42.58	38.73	30.81	43.90	38.11	26.54
Range	F1:	49.15	47.13	43.32	35.25	48.66	43.98	31.54
(Zhang et al., 2017b)	Ign F1:	44.33	42.18	38.16	30.11	43.13	37.67	26.11
DisRel	F1:	50.47	49.28	46.62	39.88	49.19	46.35	36.74
(Deng et al., 2021)	Ign F1:	45.57	44.79	41.72	35.66	44.80	42.03	31.82

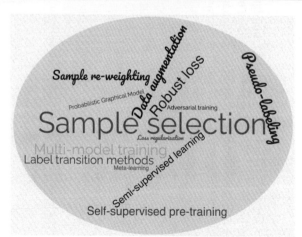

FIGURE 5.17 Word cloud of the main noisy-label learning techniques from Chapter 4.

Word cloud generated from https://www.wordclouds.com using the list of techniques from Table 5.42 weighted by how many times they are used by the top-performing methods of Chapter 5.

this chapter. In Fig. 5.17, we show the word cloud built using the list of techniques from Table 5.42 weighted by how many times they are used by the top-performing methods.

Table 5.41   Test F1 (%) and Accuracy (ACC in %) results on closed-set symmetric label noise (Deng et al., 2021), obtained by modifying the annotated training sets on CoNLL 2003 dataset (Sang and De Meulder, 2003). All results are from (Deng et al., 2021) and methods are based on BiLSTM (Yao et al., 2019).

Dataset		CoNLL 2003			
Noise		Symmetric			
Rate		20%	40%	60%	80%
CE	F1:	85.12	73.23	55.27	44.36
(Deng et al., 2021)	ACC:	82.66	70.55	52.67	41.75
GCE	F1:	84.51	73.15	56.04	46.72
(Zhang and Sabuncu, 2018)	ACC:	81.15	70.09	53.60	43.92
BMSE	F1:	80.08	71.11	54.96	44.11
(Ghosh et al., 2017)	ACC:	78.76	68.62	52.06	41.38
FL	F1:	84.76	73.51	55.36	44.27
(Lin et al., 2017b)	ACC:	81.95	70.74	52.47	40.69
CBL	F1:	83.30	72.89	55.45	44.55
(Cui et al., 2019)	ACC:	80.25	70.15	52.68	41.47
Range	F1:	82.59	73.53	54.65	44.39
(Zhang et al., 2017b)	ACC:	79.87	70.66	51.51	41.02
DisRel	F1:	85.88	74.11	56.43	47.68
(Deng et al., 2021)	ACC:	83.16	71.63	53.38	44.03

It is clear that sample selection, pseudo-labeling, robust loss, and data augmentation are the main techniques explored to handle noisy-label learning problems by the top-performing approaches. For imbalanced noisy-label learning problems, meta-learning appears to provide a good mitigation solution mostly because of the use of a balanced (pseudo-)clean validation set. It is interesting to see that even though label transition methods have theoretical guarantees of consistent performance, they do not show particularly competitive results, except in benchmarks that do not have many results available for comparison, such as the ones in Tables 5.7 and 5.8. It is clear that the current state-of-the-art approaches (in July 2023) explore a combination of many techniques. For example, SANM (Tu et al., 2023b), DMLP (Tu et al., 2023a), SSR+ (Feng et al., 2021), and InstanceGM (Garg et al., 2023) explore most of the techniques listed in Table 5.42.

A particularly concerning problem involved in the benchmarks presented in this chapter is the fact that each benchmark relies on the use of a specific backbone model, which needs to be fixed to enable a fair comparison between methods. However, new models are being proposed at a fast rate, and it is important to verify if these new models can improve the state-of-the-art results. This point is currently not well-studied in the field.

Table 5.42 Noisy-label learning techniques, from Chapter 4, explored by top-performing methods in the benchmarks of Chapter 5.

Method	Pseudo-labeling	Sample selection	Robust loss	Data augmentation	Semi-supervised learning	Multi-model training	Loss regularization	Adversarial training	Self-supervised pre-training	Meta-learning	Probabilistic Graphical Model	Label transition methods	Sample re-weighting
SSR+ (Feng et al., 2021)	✓	✓	✓	✓									
OT-Filter (Feng et al., 2023)		✓		✓	✓	✓							
SANM(C2D,DivideMix) (Tu et al., 2023b)		✓		✓	✓	✓	✓	✓	✓				
DMLP(DivideMix) (Tu et al., 2023a)		✓		✓	✓	✓					✓		
InstanceGM (Garg et al., 2023)		✓		✓	✓	✓						✓	
DISC (Li et al., 2023)	✓	✓	✓	✓									
CC (Zhao et al., 2022)		✓		✓	✓	✓							
BootLN(M) (Smart and Carneiro, 2023)	✓	✓		✓	✓				✓				
ProMix (Wang et al., 2022)	✓	✓	✓	✓	✓								
BLTM-V (Yang et al., 2022)	✓	✓	✓									✓	
kMEIDTM (Cheng et al., 2022)		✓										✓	
DSOS (Albert et al., 2022)	✓	✓	✓	✓									✓
INOLML (Hoang et al., 2022)	✓	✓									✓		✓
NVUM (Liu et al., 2022a)	✓		✓										
GloCal (Xue et al., 2022)	✓	✓	✓	✓			✓						
HSA-NRL (Zhu et al., 2021a)	✓	✓					✓						
LNCIS (Yang et al., 2020)		✓	✓										
fWebSOD (Shen et al., 2020)		✓	✓	✓									
PTD-R-V (Xia et al., 2020)												✓	
MLC (Zheng et al., 2021)										✓			
$\mathcal{L}_{DN}$ (Garg et al., 2021)	✓	✓											
DisRel (Deng et al., 2021)			✓										

Conclusions and final considerations

6

6.1 Conclusions

We conclude the book with a summary of what has been presented. The study of noisy-label learning algorithms and models is motivated by the widespread availability of poorly curated large-scale datasets that contain a substantial amount of label noise, and also of datasets that contain samples with intrinsically noisy labels. Unfortunately, the regular training of machine learning models, and deep learning models in particular, will eventually overfit the noise present in the training set labels, causing poor generalization to clean-label testing sets. Hence, the development of noisy-label learning algorithms and models aims to mitigate this overfitting issue.

Chapter 1 introduces the different types of label noise and their impacts on the learning of machine learning models. In general, label noise can be divided into closed-set (i.e., all training images belong to the set of training labels) or open-set (i.e., some training images belong to classes outside of the set of training labels). Furthermore, open-set and closed-set label noise can be subdivided into symmetric, asymmetric, and instance-dependent noise, where symmetric refers to a random flipping from the clean label to any of the other available labels, asymmetric follows a specific label transition pattern that defines the probability of pairwise flipping, and instance-dependent follows a data-specific label transition pattern. These label noise types were defined in Chapter 2, which also listed the main datasets and benchmarks used to assess noisy-label learning approaches.

Chapter 3 introduces theoretical aspects of noisy-label learning. First, we explained how the bias-variance decomposition divides the training error into bias, variance, and irreducible noise components, and how each component is affected in terms of symmetric, asymmetric, and instance-dependent noise. Second, we defined the necessary and sufficient conditions for the identifiability of the transition matrix for noisy-label learning problems. A particularly interesting identifiability condition is the need for multiple labels per training sample, which is a problem referred to as the multi-rater learning (Guan et al., 2018; Jensen et al., 2019; Jungo et al., 2018; Baumgartner et al., 2019; Sudre et al., 2019; Yu et al., 2020a). Third, we overviewed the application of Valiant's probably approximately correct (PAC) model of learning in noisy-label learning. Even though PAC learning already showed important aspects of noisy-label learning, it is still too constrained to unrealistically simple classification models and problems.

Machine Learning With Noisy Labels. https://doi.org/10.1016/B978-0-44-315441-6.00015-0

The main techniques explored in practice to mitigate the noisy-label learning problem were presented in Chapter 4. We first introduced an example of a noisy-label learning and showed how a deep learning classifier overfits to the label noise. This example was used throughout the chapter to show the functionality of each presented technique. We also proposed a new hierarchical structure to organize the available techniques in the field and briefly explained each technique. Then, in Chapter 5, we introduced the state-of-the-art methods for the main benchmarks being considered in the field. We concluded this chapter by listing the main methods and the techniques that they explore.

This book proposes solutions to all challenges listed at the end of Chapter 1. To recap, the challenges are: 1) how to define label noise models, 2) how to define the experimental setup to test the robustness of methods with respect to label noise, 3) theoretical understanding of label noise, 4) practical understanding of label noise, and 5) how to estimate rate and type of label noise in a dataset. Chapter 1 introduces the definition of label noise generation based on a label transition process (Pérez et al., 2007; Lawrence and Schölkopf, 2001), or on a label distribution (Thiel, 2008; Domingos, 2000). Even though we believe that both definitions are likely to be equivalent, this requires further study by our research community. Chapter 1 also presents many noisy-label learning benchmarks that are actively being used to assess methods. As shown in Chapter 5, no method is the best for all benchmarks, and the main challenge for the community is to understand the association between techniques and the particular problems represented by the benchmarks. For instance, if we are dealing with a symmetric closed-set label noise problem, which techniques would be more appropriate. Also, the theoretical understanding of label noise, particularly based on the application of PAC learning methods, needs to consider the complex models and learning problems that the field is studying in practice. Finally, estimating the rate and type of label noise is a relevant problem because many of the methods presented in Chapter 5 require the setting of hyper-parameters depending on the rate and type of noise (Li et al., 2020a). An alternative solution to this problem is the design of methods that are robust to all types and rates of label noise.

6.2 Final considerations and future work

We conclude the book with some considerations about future developments in the field. It is important to reiterate that this book was written in July 2023, and as with any topic in machine learning, by the time it gets published, it will already be outdated. Therefore, let us explain how the reader can find more about future publications and benchmarks. Regarding publications, the top computer vision and machine learning conferences (CVPR, ICCV, ECCV, NeurIPS, ICLR, AAAI, WACV, BMVC, ACCV) are the main source of new methods. Journals (TPAMI, TIP, PR, JMLR, TMLR) are also good sources of new methods, but the published papers tend to be more outdated than the conference papers. The PapersWithCode site[1] has the ranking of the top-performing methods on the main benchmarks, but it is not up-to-date for most of the benchmarks. The pre-print papers on arXiv[2] are also a good source of new methods, but since these papers have not been peer-reviewed (or have been rejected by some conferences and journals), the reader needs to be careful with potential problems in terms of experiments, writing, or methods. There are also many github sites that try to keep a list of relevant publications in the area. Some examples are: Awesome-Learning-with-Label-Noise,[3] Awesome-Noisy-Labels,[4] and Advances-in-Label-Noise-Learning.[5] There are also good video lectures available on YouTube, such as the lecture I gave to VinAI in 2021.[6]

Regarding the future of noisy-label learning, apart from the points already raised in the last paragraph of Section 6.1, we list below some potentially interesting topics that need to be considered by researchers. As already mentioned in the last paragraph of Section 5.10, one point that needs further investigation is the issue with the relatively old models used to evaluate noisy-label learning methods. The models that are generally used in the benchmarks are ResNet (He et al., 2016b), DenseNet (Huang et al., 2017), and Inception (Szegedy et al., 2017). These models no longer represent the state of the art in computer vision and machine learning, and need to be replaced by more modern models (Dosovitskiy et al., 2020), but the community has acted slowly to accept such new models given that this would make comparisons unfair with current approaches based on the old models.

Another interesting point about noisy-label learning is that it is related to other problems being studied by relatively different research communities. For instance, multi-rater learning (Sudre et al., 2019; Ji et al., 2021; Schaekermann et al., 2019; Becker et al., 2019; Tanno et al., 2019) (Section 4.3.4) optimizes a model using multiple labels per data point and aims to estimate the model's and annotators' uncertainty. Such set-up is quite relevant for noisy-label learning given that the identifiability of the learning from noisy labels requires a minimum number of labels per training sample (Liu, 2022; Nguyen et al., 2023). Another related research topic is that of uncertainty (Mena et al., 2021) that aims to investigate the ambiguities present in the predictions of deep learning models. In principle, uncertainty is a powerful tool to be used in sample selection and pseudo-labeling, but that is a technique that has not received enough attention. Also, multi-rater learning combined with uncertainty learning could also be used to solve noisy-label learning problems involving multiple labelers. Another interesting research topic that can be potentially useful in noisy label learning is anomaly detection (Pang et al., 2021) which aims to train a model to detect out-of-distribution samples that can be regarded as open-set noisy-label sam-

---

[1] https://paperswithcode.com.

[2] https://arxiv.org.

[3] https://github.com/subeeshvasu/Awesome-Learning-with-Label-Noise.

[4] https://github.com/songhwanjun/Awesome-Noisy-Labels.

[5] https://github.com/weijiaheng/Advances-in-Label-Noise-Learning.

[6] https://www.youtube.com/watch?v=gqrAq2138QE.

ples. In particular, there is a line of research in anomaly detection that designs training algorithms that can handle contaminated training data (Qiu et al., 2022), which is exactly the same problem as the open-set noisy-label learning problem. Finally, as noted by Liu and Tao (2015), noisy-label learning problem is fundamentally a domain adaptation problem given that the distribution of the data in the training set, with its noisy label samples, is different from the distribution of the testing set data. Hence, the whole point of noisy label learning is to take or discover the clean-label subset in the training set, and adapt the distribution of the noisy-label subset to that of the clean-label subset.

Interesting problems that deserve further investigation by researchers in the area is the impact of the combination of noisy-label problems (e.g., closed-set and open-set symmetric, asymmetric, and instance-dependent noise) on noisy-label learning models and algorithms. So far, there have been some attempts with the combination of open and closed-set label noise (Sachdeva et al., 2021) and closed-set label noise with imbalanced learning (Zhang and Pfister, 2021; Wei et al., 2021b; Hoang et al., 2022). Another important problem that has not received enough attention is the formulation of the label transition problem for multi-label problems, where the transition matrix can serve the dual purpose of modeling pairwise label noise flipping and pairwise label correlation.

Noisy-label learning has the potential to be one of the most important problems in machine learning given that the vast majority of datasets that will become available for machine learning practitioners and researchers are likely to contain relatively large amounts of noisy labels. In fact, when these datasets become available, researchers and practitioners usually assume that they contain only clean labels, but that assumption is in most cases unwarranted, which means that the dataset needs to be investigated to see how much label noise it contains. Alternatively, these datasets can be assumed to contain noisy labels, forcing researchers and practitioners to explore noisy-label learning algorithms. With the knowledge acquired from this book, we expect that the reader is better equipped to deal with the noisy-label learning problems that will be become widespread in machine learning.

Bibliography

Adamopoulou, E., Moussiades, L., 2020. Chatbots: History, technology, and applications. Machine Learning with Applications 2, 100006.

Alayrac, J.B., Uesato, J., Huang, P.S., Fawzi, A., Stanforth, R., Kohli, P., 2019. Are labels required for improving adversarial robustness? Advances in Neural Information Processing Systems 32.

Albert, P., Ortego, D., Arazo, E., O'Connor, N.E., McGuinness, K., 2022. Addressing out-of-distribution label noise in webly-labelled data. In: Proceedings of the IEEE/CVF Winter Conference on Applications of Computer Vision, pp. 392–401.

Algan, G., Ulusoy, I., 2021. Image classification with deep learning in the presence of noisy labels: A survey. Knowledge-Based Systems 215, 106771.

Ali, K.M., Pazzani, M.J., 1996. Error reduction through learning multiple descriptions. Machine Learning 24, 173–202.

Amid, E., Warmuth, M.K., Anil, R., Koren, T., 2019a. Robust bi-tempered logistic loss based on Bregman divergences. Advances in Neural Information Processing Systems 32.

Amid, E., Warmuth, M.K., Srinivasan, S., 2019b. Two-temperature logistic regression based on the Tsallis divergence. In: The 22nd International Conference on Artificial Intelligence and Statistics. PMLR, pp. 2388–2396.

Amsaleg, L., Chelly, O., Furon, T., Girard, S., Houle, M.E., Kawarabayashi, K.I., Nett, M., 2015. Estimating local intrinsic dimensionality. In: Proceedings of the 21st ACM SIGKDD International Conference on Knowledge Discovery and Data Mining, pp. 29–38.

Angluin, D., Laird, P., 1988. Learning from noisy examples. Machine Learning 2, 343–370.

Arazo, E., Ortego, D., Albert, P., O'Connor, N., McGuinness, K., 2019. Unsupervised label noise modeling and loss correction. In: International Conference on Machine Learning. PMLR, pp. 312–321.

Arazo, E., Ortego, D., Albert, P., O'Connor, N.E., McGuinness, K., 2020. Pseudo-labeling and confirmation bias in deep semi-supervised learning. In: 2020 International Joint Conference on Neural Networks (IJCNN), pp. 1–8.

Armato III, S.G., McLennan, G., Bidaut, L., McNitt-Gray, M.F., Meyer, C.R., Reeves, A.P., Zhao, B., Aberle, D.R., Henschke, C.I., Hoffman, E.A., et al., 2011. The lung image database consortium (LIDC) and image database resource initiative (IDRI): A completed reference database of lung nodules on CT scans. Medical Physics 38, 915–931.

Arpit, D., Jastrzębski, S., Ballas, N., Krueger, D., Bengio, E., Kanwal, M.S., Maharaj, T., Fischer, A., Courville, A., Bengio, Y., et al., 2017. A closer look at memorization in deep networks. In: International Conference on Machine Learning. PMLR, pp. 233–242.

Asman, A.J., Landman, B.A., 2012. Formulating spatially varying performance in the statistical fusion framework. IEEE Transactions on Medical Imaging 31, 1326–1336.

Awasthi, P., Balcan, M.F., Haghtalab, N., Urner, R., 2015. Efficient learning of linear separators under bounded noise. In: Conference on Learning Theory. PMLR, pp. 167–190.

Awasthi, P., Balcan, M.F., Haghtalab, N., Zhang, H., 2016. Learning and 1-bit compressed sensing under asymmetric noise. In: Conference on Learning Theory. PMLR, pp. 152–192.

Azadi, S., Feng, J., Jegelka, S., Darrell, T., 2015. Auxiliary image regularization for deep CNNs with noisy labels. arXiv preprint. arXiv:1511.07069.

Bae, H., Shin, S., Na, B., Jang, J., Song, K., Moon, I.C., 2022. From noisy prediction to true label: Noisy prediction calibration via generative model. In: International Conference on Machine Learning. PMLR, pp. 1277–1297.

Bahri, D., Jiang, H., Gupta, M., 2020. Deep k-nn for noisy labels. In: International Conference on Machine Learning. PMLR, pp. 540–550.

Bai, Y., Yang, E., Han, B., Yang, Y., Li, J., Mao, Y., Niu, G., Liu, T., 2021. Understanding and improving early stopping for learning with noisy labels. Advances in Neural Information Processing Systems 34, 24392–24403.

Baumgartner, C.F., Tezcan, K.C., Chaitanya, K., Hötker, A.M., Muehlematter, U.J., Schawkat, K., Becker, A.S., Donati, O., Konukoglu, E., 2019. Phiseg: Capturing uncertainty in medical image segmentation. In: International Conference on Medical Image Computing and Computer-Assisted Intervention. Springer, pp. 119–127.

Becker, A.S., Chaitanya, K., Schawkat, K., Muehlematter, U.J., Hötker, A.M., Konukoglu, E., Donati, O.F., 2019. Variability of manual segmentation of the prostate in axial t2-weighted MRI: A multi-reader study. European Journal of Radiology 121, 108716.

Bejnordi, B.E., Veta, M., Van Diest, P.J., Van Ginneken, B., Karssemeijer, N., Litjens, G., Van Der Laak, J.A., Hermsen, M., Manson, Q.F., Balkenhol, M., et al., 2017. Diagnostic assessment of deep learning algorithms for detection of lymph node metastases in women with breast cancer. JAMA 318, 2199–2210.

Bellemare, M.G., Danihelka, I., Dabney, W., Mohamed, S., Lakshminarayanan, B., Hoyer, S., Munos, R., 2017. The Cramer distance as a solution to biased Wasserstein gradients. arXiv preprint. arXiv:1705.10743.

Bengio, Y., Bastien, F., Bergeron, A., Boulanger-Lewandowski, N., Breuel, T., Chherawala, Y., Cisse, M., Côté, M., Erhan, D., Eustache, J., et al., 2011. Deep learners benefit more from out-of-distribution examples. In: Proceedings of the Fourteenth International Conference on Artificial Intelligence and Statistics, JMLR Workshop and Conference Proceedings, pp. 164–172.

Bengio, Y., Louradour, J., Collobert, R., Weston, J., 2009. Curriculum learning. In: Proceedings of the 26th Annual International Conference on Machine Learning. ACM, pp. 41–48.

Bernhardt, M., Castro, D.C., Tanno, R., Schwaighofer, A., Tezcan, K.C., Monteiro, M., Bannur, S., Lungren, M.P., Nori, A., Glocker, B., et al., 2022. Active label cleaning for improved dataset quality under resource constraints. Nature Communications 13, 1161.

Berthelot, D., Carlini, N., Goodfellow, I., Papernot, N., Oliver, A., Raffel, C.A., 2019. Mixmatch: A holistic approach to semi-supervised learning. Advances in Neural Information Processing Systems 32.

Berthon, A., Han, B., Niu, G., Liu, T., Sugiyama, M., 2021. Confidence scores make instance-dependent label-noise learning possible. In: International Conference on Machine Learning. PMLR, pp. 825–836.

Bhowmick, A., Hazarika, S.M., 2018. E-mail spam filtering: A review of techniques and trends. In: Advances in Electronics, Communication and Computing, pp. 583–590.

Bi, Y., Jeske, D.R., 2010. The efficiency of logistic regression compared to normal discriminant analysis under class-conditional classification noise. Journal of Multivariate Analysis 101, 1622–1637.

Bilen, H., Vedaldi, A., 2016. Weakly supervised deep detection networks. In: Proceedings of the IEEE Conference on Computer Vision and Pattern Recognition, pp. 2846–2854.

Bishop, C., 2006. Pattern Recognition and Machine Learning. Springer.

Blanchard, G., Lee, G., Scott, C., 2010. Semi-supervised novelty detection. Journal of Machine Learning Research 11, 2973–3009.

Blum, A., Frieze, A., Kannan, R., Vempala, S., 1998. A polynomial-time algorithm for learning noisy linear threshold functions. Algorithmica 22, 35–52.

Blum, A., Mitchell, T., 1998. Combining labeled and unlabeled data with co-training. In: Proceedings of the Eleventh Annual Conference on Computational Learning Theory, pp. 92–100.

Blumer, A., Ehrenfeucht, A., Haussler, D., Warmuth, M., 1986. Classifying learnable geometric concepts with the Vapnik-Chervonenkis dimension. In: Proceedings of the Eighteenth Annual ACM Symposium on Theory of Computing, pp. 273–282.

Bossard, L., Guillaumin, M., Gool, L.V., 2014. Food-101 – mining discriminative components with random forests. In: European Conference on Computer Vision. Springer, pp. 446–461.

Bouguelia, M.R., Nowaczyk, S., Santosh, K., Verikas, A., 2018. Agreeing to disagree: Active learning with noisy labels without crowdsourcing. International Journal of Machine Learning and Cybernetics 9, 1307–1319.

Boyd, S., Boyd, S.P., Vandenberghe, L., 2004. Convex Optimization. Cambridge University Press.

Branson, S., Van Horn, G., Perona, P., 2017. Lean crowdsourcing: Combining humans and machines in an online system. In: Proceedings of the IEEE Conference on Computer Vision and Pattern Recognition, pp. 7474–7483.

Briggs, F., Huang, Y., Raich, R., Eftaxias, K., Lei, Z., Cukierski, W., Hadley, S.F., Hadley, A., Betts, M., Fern, X.Z., et al., 2013. The 9th annual MLSP competition: New methods for acoustic classification of multiple simultaneous bird species in a noisy environment. In: 2013 IEEE International Workshop on Machine Learning for Signal Processing (MLSP). IEEE, pp. 1–8.

Bronstein, M.M., Bruna, J., LeCun, Y., Szlam, A., Vandergheynst, P., 2017. Geometric deep learning: Going beyond Euclidean data. IEEE Signal Processing Magazine 34, 18–42.

Bustos, A., Pertusa, A., Salinas, J.M., de la Iglesia-Vayá, M., 2020. PadChest: A large chest X-ray image dataset with multi-label annotated reports. Medical Image Analysis 66, 101797.

Caiafa, C.F., Sun, Z., Tanaka, T., Marti-Puig, P., Solé-Casals, J., 2021. Machine learning methods with noisy, incomplete or small datasets.

Caicedo, J.C., Goodman, A., Karhohs, K.W., Cimini, B.A., Ackerman, J., Haghighi, M., Heng, C., Becker, T., Doan, M., McQuin, C., et al., 2019. Nucleus segmentation across imaging experiments: The 2018 data science bowl. Nature Methods 16, 1247–1253.

Cao, K., Chen, Y., Lu, J., Arechiga, N., Gaidon, A., Ma, T., 2020. Heteroskedastic and imbalanced deep learning with adaptive regularization. arXiv preprint. arXiv:2006.15766.

Cao, K., Wei, C., Gaidon, A., Arechiga, N., Ma, T., 2019. Learning imbalanced datasets with label-distribution-aware margin loss. Advances in Neural Information Processing Systems 32.

Caron, M., Touvron, H., Misra, I., Jégou, H., Mairal, J., Bojanowski, P., Joulin, A., 2021. Emerging properties in self-supervised vision transformers. In: International Conference on Computer Vision, pp. 9650–9660.

Chang, H.S., Learned-Miller, E., McCallum, A., 2017. Active bias: Training more accurate neural networks by emphasizing high variance samples. Advances in Neural Information Processing Systems 30.

Charoenphakdee, N., Lee, J., Sugiyama, M., 2019. On symmetric losses for learning from corrupted labels. In: International Conference on Machine Learning. PMLR, pp. 961–970.

Chen, P., Liao, B.B., Chen, G., Zhang, S., 2019. Understanding and utilizing deep neural networks trained with noisy labels. In: International Conference on Machine Learning. PMLR, pp. 1062–1070.

Chen, T., Kornblith, S., Norouzi, M., Hinton, G., 2020a. A simple framework for contrastive learning of visual representations. In: International Conference on Machine Learning. PMLR, pp. 1597–1607.

Chen, W., Zhu, C., Chen, Y., Li, M., Huang, T., 2021a. Sample prior guided robust model learning to suppress noisy labels. arXiv preprint. arXiv:2112.01197.

Chen, X., Fan, H., Girshick, R., He, K., 2020b. Improved baselines with momentum contrastive learning. arXiv preprint. arXiv:2003.04297.

Chen, Y., Shen, X., Hu, S.X., Suykens, J.A., 2021b. Boosting co-teaching with compression regularization for label noise. In: Proceedings of the IEEE/CVF Conference on Computer Vision and Pattern Recognition, pp. 2688–2692.

Cheng, D., Liu, T., Ning, Y., Wang, N., Han, B., Niu, G., Gao, X., Sugiyama, M., 2022. Instance-dependent label-noise learning with manifold-regularized transition matrix estimation. In: Proceedings of the IEEE/CVF Conference on Computer Vision and Pattern Recognition, pp. 16630–16639.

Cheng, H., Zhu, Z., Li, X., Gong, Y., Sun, X., Liu, Y., 2020a. Learning with instance-dependent label noise: A sample sieve approach. arXiv preprint. arXiv:2010.02347.

Cheng, J., Liu, T., Ramamohanarao, K., Tao, D., 2020b. Learning with bounded instance and label-dependent label noise. In: International Conference on Machine Learning. PMLR, pp. 1789–1799.

Cheng, M.M., Mitra, N.J., Huang, X., Torr, P.H., Hu, S.M., 2014. Global contrast based salient region detection. IEEE Transactions on Pattern Analysis and Machine Intelligence 37, 569–582.

Chung, J.S., Nagrani, A., Zisserman, A., 2018. VoxCeleb2: Deep speaker recognition. arXiv preprint. arXiv:1806.05622.

Codella, N.C., Gutman, D., Celebi, M.E., Helba, B., Marchetti, M.A., Dusza, S.W., Kalloo, A., Liopyris, K., Mishra, N., Kittler, H., et al., 2018. Skin lesion analysis toward melanoma detection: A challenge at the 2017 International Symposium on Biomedical Imaging (ISBI), hosted by the International Skin Imaging Collaboration (ISIC). In: 2018 IEEE 15th International Symposium on Biomedical Imaging (ISBI 2018). IEEE, pp. 168–172.

Conneau, A., Schwenk, H., Barrault, L., Lecun, Y., 2016. Very deep convolutional networks for text classification. arXiv preprint. arXiv:1606.01781.

Cordeiro, F.R., Belagiannis, V., Reid, I., Carneiro, G., 2022. PropMix: Hard sample filtering and proportional mixup for learning with noisy labels. In: British Machine Vision Conference.

Cordeiro, F.R., Carneiro, G., 2020. A survey on deep learning with noisy labels: How to train your model when you cannot trust on the annotations? In: 2020 33rd SIBGRAPI Conference on Graphics, Patterns and Images (SIBGRAPI). IEEE, pp. 9–16.

Cordts, M., Omran, M., Ramos, S., Rehfeld, T., Enzweiler, M., Benenson, R., Franke, U., Roth, S., Schiele, B., 2016. The cityscapes dataset for semantic urban scene understanding. In: Proceedings of the IEEE Conference on Computer Vision and Pattern Recognition, pp. 3213–3223.

Cubuk, E.D., Zoph, B., Mane, D., Vasudevan, V., Le, Q.V., 2019. Autoaugment: Learning augmentation strategies from data. In: Proceedings of the IEEE/CVF Conference on Computer Vision and Pattern Recognition, pp. 113–123.

Cubuk, E.D., Zoph, B., Shlens, J., Le, Q.V., 2020. Randaugment: Practical automated data augmentation with a reduced search space. In: Proceedings of the IEEE/CVF Conference on Computer Vision and Pattern Recognition Workshops, pp. 702–703.

Cui, Y., Jia, M., Lin, T.Y., Song, Y., Belongie, S., 2019. Class-balanced loss based on effective number of samples. In: Proceedings of the IEEE/CVF Conference on Computer Vision and Pattern Recognition, pp. 9268–9277.

Da, Q., Huang, X., Li, Z., Zuo, Y., Zhang, C., Liu, J., Chen, W., Li, J., Xu, D., Hu, Z., et al., 2022. DigestPath: A benchmark dataset with challenge review for the pathological detection and segmentation of digestive-system. Medical Image Analysis 102485.

Daily, M., Medasani, S., Behringer, R., Trivedi, M., 2017. Self-driving cars. Computer 50, 18–23.

Daniely, A., 2016. Complexity theoretic limitations on learning halfspaces. In: Proceedings of the Forty-Eighth Annual ACM Symposium on Theory of Computing, pp. 105–117.

Davis, J., Goadrich, M., 2006. The relationship between precision-recall and ROC curves. In: Proceedings of the 23rd International Conference on Machine Learning, pp. 233–240.

Dawid, A.P., Skene, A.M., 1979. Maximum likelihood estimation of observer error-rates using the em algorithm. Journal of the Royal Statistical Society. Series C. Applied Statistics 28, 20–28.

Decatur, S.E., 1997. PAC learning with constant-partition classification noise and applications to decision tree induction. In: Sixth International Workshop on Artificial Intelligence and Statistics. PMLR, pp. 147–156.

Dehghani, M., Severyn, A., Rothe, S., Kamps, J. Learning to learn from weak supervision by full supervision. In: NIPS Workshop on Meta-Learning.

Delany, S.J., Segata, N., Mac Namee, B., 2012. Profiling instances in noise reduction. Knowledge-Based Systems 31, 28–40.

Demner-Fushman, D., Kohli, M.D., Rosenman, M.B., Shooshan, S.E., Rodriguez, L., Antani, S., Thoma, G.R., McDonald, C.J., 2016. Preparing a collection of radiology examinations for distribution and retrieval. Journal of the American Medical Informatics Association 23, 304–310.

Dempster, A.P., Laird, N.M., Rubin, D.B., 1977. Maximum likelihood from incomplete data via the em algorithm. Journal of the Royal Statistical Society, Series B, Methodological 39, 1–22.

Deng, J., Dong, W., Socher, R., Li, L.J., Li, K., Fei-Fei, L., 2009. ImageNet: A large-scale hierarchical image database. In: IEEE Conference on Computer Vision and Pattern Recognition. CVPR 2009. IEEE, pp. 248–255.

Deng, L., Yang, B., Kang, Z., Yang, S., Wu, S., 2021. A noisy label and negative sample robust loss function for DNN-based distant supervised relation extraction. Neural Networks 139, 358–370.

Der Kiureghian, A., Ditlevsen, O., 2009. Aleatory or epistemic? does it matter? Structural Safety 31, 105–112.

DeVries, T., Taylor, G.W., 2017. Improved regularization of convolutional neural networks with cutout. arXiv preprint. arXiv:1708.04552.

Diakonikolas, I., Gouleakis, T., Tzamos, C., 2019. Distribution-independent PAC learning of halfspaces with Massart noise. Advances in Neural Information Processing Systems 32.

Diakonikolas, I., Kane, D.M., Kontonis, V., Tzamos, C., Zarifis, N., 2020. A polynomial time algorithm for learning halfspaces with Tsybakov noise. arXiv preprint. arXiv:2010.01705.

Diakonikolas, I., Kane, D.M., Kontonis, V., Tzamos, C., Zarifis, N., 2021. Efficiently learning halfspaces with Tsybakov noise. In: Proceedings of the 53rd Annual ACM SIGACT Symposium on Theory of Computing, pp. 88–101.

Dietterich, T.G., 2000. An experimental comparison of three methods for constructing ensembles of decision trees: Bagging, boosting, and randomization. Machine Learning 40, 139–157.

Ding, Y., Wang, L., Fan, D., Gong, B., 2018. A semi-supervised two-stage approach to learning from noisy labels. In: 2018 IEEE Winter Conference on Applications of Computer Vision (WACV). IEEE, pp. 1215–1224.

Diplaris, S., Tsoumakas, G., Mitkas, P.A., Vlahavas, I., 2005. Protein classification with multiple algorithms. In: Panhellenic Conference on Informatics. Springer, pp. 448–456.

Domingos, P., 2000. A unified bias-variance decomposition. In: Proceedings of 17th International Conference on Machine Learning. Morgan Kaufmann, Stanford, pp. 231–238.

Dosovitskiy, A., Beyer, L., Kolesnikov, A., Weissenborn, D., Zhai, X., Unterthiner, T., Dehghani, M., Minderer, M., Heigold, G., Gelly, S., et al., 2020. An image is worth 16x16 words: Transformers for image recognition at scale. arXiv preprint. arXiv:2010.11929.

Druzhkov, P., Kustikova, V., 2016. A survey of deep learning methods and software tools for image classification and object detection. Pattern Recognition and Image Analysis 26, 9–15.

Elisseeff, A., Weston, J., 2001. A kernel method for multi-labelled classification. Advances in Neural Information Processing Systems 14.

Elmore, R.T., Wang, S., 2003. Identifiability and estimation in finite mixture models with multinomial coefficients. Technical Report. Technical Report 03-04. Penn State University.

Elson, J., Douceur, J.R., Howell, J., Saul, J., 2007. Asirra: A CAPTCHA that exploits interest-aligned manual image categorization. CCS 7, 366–374.

Erhan, D., Courville, A., Bengio, Y., Vincent, P., 2010. Why does unsupervised pre-training help deep learning? In: Proceedings of the Thirteenth International Conference on Artificial Intelligence and Statistics, JMLR Workshop and Conference Proceedings, pp. 201–208.

Everingham, M., Van Gool, L., Williams, C.K., Winn, J., Zisserman, A., 2010. The pascal visual object classes (VOC) challenge. International Journal of Computer Vision 88, 303–338.

Fatras, K., Damodaran, B.B., Lobry, S., Flamary, R., Tuia, D., Courty, N., 2019. Wasserstein adversarial regularization (war) on label noise. arXiv preprint. arXiv:1904.03936.

Fawzi, A., Moosavi-Dezfooli, S.M., Frossard, P., 2016. Robustness of classifiers: From adversarial to random noise. Advances in Neural Information Processing Systems 29.

Feldman, V., Gopalan, P., Khot, S., Ponnuswami, A.K., 2006. New results for learning noisy parities and halfspaces. In: 2006 47th Annual IEEE Symposium on Foundations of Computer Science (FOCS'06). IEEE, pp. 563–574.

Feldman, V., Guruswami, V., Raghavendra, P., Wu, Y., 2012. Agnostic learning of monomials by halfspaces is hard. SIAM Journal on Computing 41, 1558–1590.

Feng, C., Ren, Y., Xie, X., 2023. OT-filter: An optimal transport filter for learning with noisy labels. In: Proceedings of the IEEE/CVF Conference on Computer Vision and Pattern Recognition, pp. 16164–16174.

Feng, C., Tzimiropoulos, G., Patras, I., 2021. SSR: An efficient and robust framework for learning with unknown label noise. arXiv e-prints.

Fisher, R.A., 1936. The use of multiple measurements in taxonomic problems. Annals of Eugenics 7, 179–188.

Frénay, B., Verleysen, M., 2014. Classification in the presence of label noise: A survey. IEEE Transactions on Neural Networks and Learning Systems 25, 845–869.

Gal, Y., et al., 2016. Uncertainty in deep learning.

Gamberger, D., Lavrac, N., Dzeroski, S., 2000. Noise detection and elimination in data preprocessing: Experiments in medical domains. Applied Artificial Intelligence 14, 205–223.

Garg, A., Nguyen, C., Felix, R., Do, T.T., Carneiro, G., 2023. Instance-dependent noisy label learning via graphical modelling. In: Proceedings of the IEEE/CVF Winter Conference on Applications of Computer Vision, pp. 2288–2298.

Garg, S., Ramakrishnan, G., Thumbe, V., 2021. Towards robustness to label noise in text classification via noise modeling. In: Proceedings of the 30th ACM International Conference on Information & Knowledge Management, pp. 3024–3028.

Ghosh, A., Kumar, H., Sastry, P.S., 2017. Robust loss functions under label noise for deep neural networks. In: Proceedings of the AAAI Conference on Artificial Intelligence.

Gidaris, S., Singh, P., Komodakis, N., 2018. Unsupervised representation learning by predicting image rotations. arXiv preprint. arXiv:1803.07728.

Girshick, R., 2015. Fast R-CNN. In: Proceedings of the IEEE International Conference on Computer Vision, pp. 1440–1448.

Goh, H.W., Mueller, J., 2023. ActiveLab: Active learning with re-labeling by multiple annotators. In: ICLR Workshop on Trustworthy ML.

Goh, H.W., Tkachenko, U., Mueller, J., 2022. CrowdLab: Supervised learning to infer consensus labels and quality scores for data with multiple annotators. In: NeurIPS Human in the Loop Learning Workshop.

Goldberger, J., Ben-Reuven, E., 2017. Training deep neural-networks using a noise adaptation layer. In: International Conference on Learning Representations.

Goodfellow, I., Pouget-Abadie, J., Mirza, M., Xu, B., Warde-Farley, D., Ozair, S., Courville, A., Bengio, Y., 2020. Generative adversarial networks. Communications of the ACM 63, 139–144.

Goodfellow, I.J., Shlens, J., Szegedy, C., 2014. Explaining and harnessing adversarial examples. arXiv preprint. arXiv:1412.6572.

Gou, J., Yu, B., Maybank, S.J., Tao, D., 2021. Knowledge distillation: A survey. International Journal of Computer Vision 129, 1789–1819.

Gretton, A., Smola, A., Huang, J., Schmittfull, M., Borgwardt, K., Schölkopf, B., 2009. Covariate shift by kernel mean matching. Dataset Shift in Machine Learning 3, 5.

Gu, K., Masotto, X., Bachani, V., Lakshminarayanan, B., Nikodem, J., Yin, D., 2021. An instance-dependent simulation framework for learning with label noise. arXiv preprint. arXiv:2107.11413.

Gu, K., Masotto, X., Bachani, V., Lakshminarayanan, B., Nikodem, J., Yin, D., 2022. An instance-dependent simulation framework for learning with label noise. Machine Learning, 1–26.

Guan, M., Gulshan, V., Dai, A., Hinton, G., 2018. Who said what: Modeling individual labelers improves classification. In: Proceedings of the AAAI Conference on Artificial Intelligence.

Guruswami, V., Raghavendra, P., 2009. Hardness of learning halfspaces with noise. SIAM Journal on Computing 39, 742–765.

Hamilton, W.L., Ying, R., Leskovec, J., 2017. Representation learning on graphs: Methods and applications. arXiv preprint. arXiv:1709.05584.

Han, B., Niu, G., Yao, J., Yu, X., Xu, M., Tsang, I., Sugiyama, M., 2018a. Pumpout: A meta approach for robustly training deep neural networks with noisy labels.

Han, B., Niu, G., Yu, X., Yao, Q., Xu, M., Tsang, I., Sugiyama, M., 2020a. SIGUA: Forgetting may make learning with noisy labels more robust. In: International Conference on Machine Learning. PMLR, pp. 4006–4016.

Han, B., Yao, J., Niu, G., Zhou, M., Tsang, I., Zhang, Y., Sugiyama, M., 2018b. Masking: A new perspective of noisy supervision. Advances in Neural Information Processing Systems 31.

Han, B., Yao, Q., Liu, T., Niu, G., Tsang, I.W., Kwok, J.T., Sugiyama, M., 2020b. A survey of label-noise representation learning: Past, present and future. arXiv preprint. arXiv:2011.04406.

Han, B., Yao, Q., Yu, X., Niu, G., Xu, M., Hu, W., Tsang, I., Sugiyama, M., 2018c. Coteaching: Robust training of deep neural networks with extremely noisy labels. Advances in Neural Information Processing Systems 31.

Han, J., Luo, P., Wang, X., 2019. Deep self-learning from noisy labels. In: Proceedings of the IEEE/CVF International Conference on Computer Vision, pp. 5138–5147.

Han, Z., Gui, X.J., Cui, C., Yin, Y., 2020c. Towards accurate and robust domain adaptation under noisy environments. arXiv preprint. arXiv:2004.12529.

Hasan, M.K., Pal, C., 2019. A new smooth approximation to the zero one loss with a probabilistic interpretation. ACM Transactions on Knowledge Discovery from Data 14, 1–28.

Haussler, D., 2018. Decision theoretic generalizations of the PAC model for neural net and other learning applications. In: The Mathematics of Generalization. CRC Press, pp. 37–116.

He, K., Fan, H., Wu, Y., Xie, S., Girshick, R., 2020. Momentum contrast for unsupervised visual representation learning. In: Proceedings of the IEEE/CVF Conference on Computer Vision and Pattern Recognition, pp. 9729–9738.

He, K., Gkioxari, G., Dollár, P., Girshick, R., 2017. Mask R-CNN. In: Proceedings of the IEEE International Conference on Computer Vision, pp. 2961–2969.

He, K., Zhang, X., Ren, S., Sun, J., 2016a. Deep residual learning for image recognition. In: Proceedings of the IEEE Conference on Computer Vision and Pattern Recognition, pp. 770–778.

He, K., Zhang, X., Ren, S., Sun, J., 2016b. Identity mappings in deep residual networks. In: Computer Vision – ECCV 2016: 14th European Conference, Proceedings, Part IV 14. Amsterdam, The Netherlands, October 11–14, 2016. Springer, pp. 630–645.

Hendrycks, D., Mazeika, M., Wilson, D., Gimpel, K., 2018. Using trusted data to train deep networks on labels corrupted by severe noise. Advances in Neural Information Processing Systems 31.

Hendrycks, D., Mu, N., Cubuk, E.D., Zoph, B., Gilmer, J., Lakshminarayanan, B., 2019. Augmix: A simple data processing method to improve robustness and uncertainty. arXiv preprint. arXiv:1912.02781.

Hermoza, R., Maicas, G., Nascimento, J.C., Carneiro, G., 2020. Region proposals for saliency map refinement for weakly-supervised disease localisation and classification. In: Medical Image Computing and Computer Assisted Intervention – MICCAI 2020: 23rd International Conference, Proceedings, Part VI 23. Lima, Peru, October 4–8, 2020. Springer, pp. 539–549.

Heskes, T., 1998. Bias/variance decompositions for likelihood-based estimators. Neural Computation 10, 1425–1433.

Heskes, T., 2000. The use of being stubborn and introspective. In: Prerational Intelligence: Adaptive Behavior and Intelligent Systems Without Symbols and Logic, Volume 1, Volume 2, Prerational Intelligence: Interdisciplinary Perspectives on the Behavior of Natural and Artificial Systems, Volume 3. Springer, pp. 1184–1200.

Hoang, D.A., Nguyen, C., Belagiannis, V., Carneiro, G., et al., 2022. Maximising the utility of validation sets for imbalanced noisy-label meta-learning. arXiv preprint. arXiv:2208.08132.

Hochreiter, S., Schmidhuber, J., 1997. Long short-term memory. Neural Computation 9, 1735–1780.

Houle, M.E., 2017. Local intrinsic dimensionality I: An extreme-value-theoretic foundation for similarity applications. In: Similarity Search and Applications: 10th International Conference, Proceedings 10. SISAP 2017, Munich, Germany, October 4–6, 2017. Springer, pp. 64–79.

Hu, S., Worrall, D., Knegt, S., Veeling, B., Huisman, H., Welling, M., 2019a. Supervised uncertainty quantification for segmentation with multiple annotations. In: Medical Image Computing and Computer Assisted Intervention – MICCAI 2019: 22nd International Conference, Proceedings, Part II 22. Shenzhen, China, October 13–17, 2019. Springer, pp. 137–145.

Hu, W., Li, Z., Yu, D., 2019b. Simple and effective regularization methods for training on noisily labeled data with generalization guarantee. arXiv preprint. arXiv:1905.11368.

Hu, W., Niu, G., Sato, I., Sugiyama, M., 2018. Does distributionally robust supervised learning give robust classifiers? In: International Conference on Machine Learning. PMLR, pp. 2029–2037.

Huang, G., Liu, Z., Van Der Maaten, L., Weinberger, K.Q., 2017. Densely connected convolutional networks. In: Proceedings of the IEEE Conference on Computer Vision and Pattern Recognition, pp. 4700–4708.

Huang, L., Zhang, C., Zhang, H., 2020. Self-adaptive training: Beyond empirical risk minimization. Advances in Neural Information Processing Systems 33, 19365–19376.

Ibrahim, S., Fu, X., Kargas, N., Huang, K., 2019. Crowdsourcing via pairwise co-occurrences: Identifiability and algorithms. Advances in Neural Information Processing Systems 32.

Inoue, N., Simo-Serra, E., Yamasaki, T., Ishikawa, H., 2017. Multi-label fashion image classification with minimal human supervision. In: Proceedings of the IEEE International Conference on Computer Vision Workshops, pp. 2261–2267.

Irvin, J., Rajpurkar, P., Ko, M., Yu, Y., Ciurea-Ilcus, S., Chute, C., Marklund, H., Haghgoo, B., Ball, R., Shpanskaya, K., et al., 2019. CheXpert: A large chest radiograph dataset with uncertainty labels and expert comparison. In: Proceedings of the AAAI Conference on Artificial Intelligence, pp. 590–597.

Iscen, A., Tolias, G., Avrithis, Y., Chum, O., Schmid, C., 2020. Graph convolutional networks for learning with few clean and many noisy labels. In: Computer Vision – ECCV 2020: 16th European Conference, Proceedings, Part X 16. Glasgow, UK, August 23–28, 2020. Springer, pp. 286–302.

Jabbari, S., 2010. PAC-learning with label noise. Master's thesis. University of Alberta, Edmonton, Alberta, Canada.

Jensen, M.H., Jørgensen, D.R., Jalaboi, R., Hansen, M.E., Olsen, M.A., 2019. Improving uncertainty estimation in convolutional neural networks using inter-rater agreement. In: International Conference on Medical Image Computing and Computer-Assisted Intervention. Springer, pp. 540–548.

Jesson, A., Arbel, T., 2015. Hierarchical MRF and random forest segmentation of ms lesions and healthy tissues in brain MRI. In: Proceedings of the 2015 Longitudinal Multiple Sclerosis Lesion Segmentation Challenge, pp. 1–2.

Ji, W., Yu, S., Wu, J., Ma, K., Bian, C., Bi, Q., Li, J., Liu, H., Cheng, L., Zheng, Y., 2021. Learning calibrated medical image segmentation via multi-rater agreement modeling. In: Proceedings of the IEEE/CVF Conference on Computer Vision and Pattern Recognition, pp. 12341–12351.

Jiang, H., Wang, J., Yuan, Z., Wu, Y., Zheng, N., Li, S., 2013. Salient object detection: A discriminative regional feature integration approach. In: Proceedings of the IEEE Conference on Computer Vision and Pattern Recognition, pp. 2083–2090.

Jiang, L., Huang, D., Liu, M., Yang, W., 2020. Beyond synthetic noise: Deep learning on controlled noisy labels. In: International Conference on Machine Learning. PMLR, pp. 4804–4815.

Jiang, L., Zhou, Z., Leung, T., Li, L.J., Fei-Fei, L., 2017. MentorNet: Regularizing very deep neural networks on corrupted labels. arXiv preprint. arXiv:1712.05055.

Jindal, I., Nokleby, M., Chen, X., 2016. Learning deep networks from noisy labels with dropout regularization. In: 2016 IEEE 16th International Conference on Data Mining (ICDM). IEEE, pp. 967–972.

Johnson, J.M., Khoshgoftaar, T.M., 2019. Survey on deep learning with class imbalance. Journal of Big Data 6, 1–54.

Joo, W., Lee, W., Park, S., Moon, I.C., 2020. Dirichlet variational autoencoder. Pattern Recognition 107, 107514.

Jungo, A., Meier, R., Ermis, E., Blatti-Moreno, M., Herrmann, E., Wiest, R., Reyes, M., 2018. On the effect of inter-observer variability for a reliable estimation of uncertainty of medical image segmentation. In: Medical Image Computing and Computer Assisted Intervention – MICCAI 2018: 21st International Conference, Proceedings, Part I. Granada, Spain, September 16-20, 2018. Springer, pp. 682–690.

Kaiser, T., Ehmann, L., Reinders, C., Rosenhahn, B., 2022. Blind knowledge distillation for robust image classification. arXiv preprint. arXiv:2211.11355.

Karim, N., Rizve, M.N., Rahnavard, N., Mian, A., Shah, M., 2022. Unicon: Combating label noise through uniform selection and contrastive learning. In: Proceedings of the IEEE/CVF Conference on Computer Vision and Pattern Recognition, pp. 9676–9686.

Karimi, D., Dou, H., Warfield, S.K., Gholipour, A., 2020. Deep learning with noisy labels: Exploring techniques and remedies in medical image analysis. Medical Image Analysis 65, 101759.

Karimi, M., Jannach, D., Jugovac, M., 2018. News recommender systems—survey and roads ahead. Information Processing & Management 54, 1203–1227.

Karpathy, A., Toderici, G., Shetty, S., Leung, T., Sukthankar, R., Fei-Fei, L., 2014. Large-scale video classification with convolutional neural networks. In: Proceedings of the IEEE Conference on Computer Vision and Pattern Recognition, pp. 1725–1732.

Karpathy, A., et al., 2016. Cs231n convolutional neural networks for visual recognition. Neural Networks.

Kaster, F.O., Menze, B.H., Weber, M.A., Hamprecht, F.A., 2011. Comparative validation of graphical models for learning tumor segmentations from noisy manual annotations. In: Medical Computer Vision. Recognition Techniques and Applications in Medical Imaging: International MICCAI Workshop, Revised Selected Papers 1. MCV 2010, Beijing, China, September 20, 2010. Springer, pp. 74–85.

Katakis, I., Tsoumakas, G., Vlahavas, I., 2008. Multilabel text classification for automated tag suggestion. In: Proceedings of the ECML/PKDD. Citeseer, p. 5.

Kearns, M.J., Schapire, R.E., Sellie, L.M., 1992. Toward efficient agnostic learning. In: Proceedings of the Fifth Annual Workshop on Computational Learning Theory, pp. 341–352.

Kearns, M.J., Vazirani, U., 1994. An Introduction to Computational Learning Theory. MIT Press.

Khetan, A., Lipton, Z.C., Anandkumar, A., 2017. Learning from noisy singly-labeled data. arXiv preprint. arXiv:1712.04577.

Kim, B.S., 1984. Studies of multinomial mixture models. Ph.D. thesis. Citeseer.

Kim, T., Ko, J., Choi, J., Yun, S.Y., et al., 2021. Fine samples for learning with noisy labels. Advances in Neural Information Processing Systems 34, 24137–24149.

Kim, Y., 2014. Convolutional neural networks for sentence classification. arXiv preprint. arXiv:1408.5882.

Kim, Y., Yim, J., Yun, J., Kim, J., 2019. NLNL: Negative learning for noisy labels. In: Proceedings of the IEEE/CVF International Conference on Computer Vision, pp. 101–110.

Kingma, D.P., Ba, J., 2014. Adam: A method for stochastic optimization. arXiv preprint. arXiv:1412.6980.

Kingma, D.P., Welling, M., 2013. Auto-encoding variational Bayes. arXiv preprint. arXiv:1312.6114.

Kohl, S., Romera-Paredes, B., Meyer, C., De Fauw, J., Ledsam, J.R., Maier-Hein, K., Eslami, S., Jimenez Rezende, D., Ronneberger, O., 2018. A probabilistic U-net for segmentation of ambiguous images. Advances in Neural Information Processing Systems 31.

Köhler, J.M., Autenrieth, M., Beluch, W.H., 2019. Uncertainty based detection and relabeling of noisy image labels. In: CVPR Workshops, pp. 33–37.

Kong, K., Lee, J., Kwak, Y., Kang, M., Kim, S.G., Song, W.J., 2019. Recycling: Semi-supervised learning with noisy labels in deep neural networks. IEEE Access 7, 66998–67005.

Konstantinov, N., Lampert, C., 2019. Robust learning from untrusted sources. In: International Conference on Machine Learning. PMLR, pp. 3488–3498.

Krause, J., Deng, J., Stark, M., Fei-Fei, L., 2013. Collecting a large-scale dataset of fine-grained cars. In: Second Workshop on Fine-Grained Visual Categorization.

Krause, J., Sapp, B., Howard, A., Zhou, H., Toshev, A., Duerig, T., Philbin, J., Fei-Fei, L., 2016. The unreasonable effectiveness of noisy data for fine-grained recognition. In: European Conference on Computer Vision. Springer, pp. 301–320.

Krizhevsky, A., Hinton, G., 2009. Learning multiple layers of features from tiny images. Technical Report. Citeseer.

Krizhevsky, A., Nair, V., Hinton, G., 2014. CIFAR-10 and CIFAR-100 datasets. https://www.cs.toronto.edu/~kriz/cifar.html.

Krizhevsky, A., Sutskever, I., Hinton, G.E., 2012. ImageNet classification with deep convolutional neural networks. In: Advances in Neural Information Processing Systems, pp. 1097–1105.

Kruskal, J.B., 1976. More factors than subjects, tests and treatments: An indeterminacy theorem for canonical decomposition and individual differences scaling. Psychometrika 41, 281–293.

Kruskal, J.B., 1977. Three-way arrays: Rank and uniqueness of trilinear decompositions, with application to arithmetic complexity and statistics. Linear Algebra and Its Applications 18, 95–138.

Kuan, J., Mueller, J., 2022. Model-agnostic label quality scoring to detect real-world label errors. In: ICML DataPerf Workshop.

Kumar, H., Manwani, N., Sastry, P., 2020. Robust learning of multi-label classifiers under label noise. In: Proceedings of the 7th ACM IKDD CoDS and 25th COMAD, pp. 90–97.

Kumar, M., Packer, B., Koller, D., 2010. Self-paced learning for latent variable models. Advances in Neural Information Processing Systems 23.

Lachenbruch, P.A., 1966. Discriminant analysis when the initial samples are misclassified. Technometrics 8, 657–662.

Laine, S., Aila, T., 2016. Temporal ensembling for semi-supervised learning. arXiv preprint. arXiv:1610.02242.

Laird, P.D., 2012. Learning From Good and Bad Data, vol. 47. Springer Science & Business Media.

Lake, B.M., Salakhutdinov, R., Tenenbaum, J.B., 2015. Human-level concept learning through probabilistic program induction. Science 350, 1332–1338.

Lakshminarayanan, B., Pritzel, A., Blundell, C., 2017. Simple and scalable predictive uncertainty estimation using deep ensembles. Advances in Neural Information Processing Systems 30.

Lambert, Z., Petitjean, C., Dubray, B., Kuan, S., 2020. SegTHOR: Segmentation of thoracic organs at risk in CT images. In: 2020 Tenth International Conference on Image Processing Theory, Tools and Applications (IPTA). IEEE, pp. 1–6.

Lang, K., 1995. Newsweeder: Learning to filter netnews. In: Machine Learning Proceedings 1995. Elsevier, pp. 331–339.

Laudon, K.C., Traver, C.G., 2013. E-commerce. Pearson, Boston, MA.

Lawrence, N., Schölkopf, B., 2001. Estimating a kernel fisher discriminant in the presence of label noise. In: 18th International Conference on Machine Learning (ICML 2001). Morgan Kaufmann, p. 306.

LeCun, Y., 1998. The MNIST database of handwritten digits. http://yann.lecun.com/exdb/mnist/.

LeCun, Y., Bengio, Y., Hinton, G., 2015. Deep learning. Nature 521, 436.

Lee, K., Yun, S., Lee, K., Lee, H., Li, B., Shin, J., 2019. Robust inference via generative classifiers for handling noisy labels. In: International Conference on Machine Learning. PMLR, pp. 3763–3772.

Lee, K.H., He, X., Zhang, L., Yang, L., 2018. CleanNet: Transfer learning for scalable image classifier training with label noise. In: Proceedings of the IEEE Conference on Computer Vision and Pattern Recognition, pp. 5447–5456.

Levina, E., Bickel, P., 2004. Maximum likelihood estimation of intrinsic dimension. Advances in Neural Information Processing Systems 17.

Li, J., Socher, R., Hoi, S.C., 2020a. DivideMix: Learning with noisy labels as semi-supervised learning. arXiv preprint. arXiv:2002.07394.

Li, J., Song, Y., Zhu, J., Cheng, L., Su, Y., Ye, L., Yuan, P., Han, S., 2019. Learning from large-scale noisy web data with ubiquitous reweighting for image classification. IEEE Transactions on Pattern Analysis and Machine Intelligence 43, 1808–1814.

Li, M., Soltanolkotabi, M., Oymak, S., 2020b. Gradient descent with early stopping is provably robust to label noise for overparameterized neural networks. In: International Conference on Artificial Intelligence and Statistics. PMLR, pp. 4313–4324.

Li, W., Wang, L., Li, W., Agustsson, E., Van Gool, L., 2017. WebVision database: Visual learning and understanding from web data. arXiv preprint. arXiv:1708.02862.

Li, X., Liu, T., Han, B., Niu, G., Sugiyama, M., 2021. Provably end-to-end label-noise learning without anchor points. In: International Conference on Machine Learning. PMLR, pp. 6403–6413.

Li, X., Roth, D., 2002. Learning question classifiers. In: COLING 2002: The 19th International Conference on Computational Linguistics.

Li, Y., Han, H., Shan, S., Chen, X., 2023. Disc: Learning from noisy labels via dynamic instance-specific selection and correction. In: Proceedings of the IEEE/CVF Conference on Computer Vision and Pattern Recognition, pp. 24070–24079.

Lin, T.Y., Dollár, P., Girshick, R., He, K., Hariharan, B., Belongie, S., 2017a. Feature pyramid networks for object detection. In: Proceedings of the IEEE Conference on Computer Vision and Pattern Recognition, pp. 2117–2125.

Lin, T.Y., Goyal, P., Girshick, R., He, K., Dollár, P., 2017b. Focal loss for dense object detection. In: Proceedings of the IEEE International Conference on Computer Vision, pp. 2980–2988.

Lin, T.Y., Maire, M., Belongie, S., Hays, J., Perona, P., Ramanan, D., Dollár, P., Zitnick, C.L., 2014. Microsoft coco: Common objects in context. In: European Conference on Computer Vision. Springer, pp. 740–755.

Litjens, G., Kooi, T., Bejnordi, B.E., Setio, A.A.A., Ciompi, F., Ghafoorian, M., Van Der Laak, J.A., Van Ginneken, B., Sánchez, C.I., 2017. A survey on deep learning in medical image analysis. Medical Image Analysis 42, 60–88.

Liu, F., Chen, Y., Tian, Y., Liu, Y., Wang, C., Belagiannis, V., Carneiro, G., 2022a. NVUM: Non-volatile unbiased memory for robust medical image classification. In: International Conference on Machine Image Computing and Computer-Assisted Intervention.

Liu, S., Liu, K., Zhu, W., Shen, Y., Fernandez-Granda, C., 2022b. Adaptive early-learning correction for segmentation from noisy annotations. In: Proceedings of the IEEE/CVF Conference on Computer Vision and Pattern Recognition, pp. 2606–2616.

Liu, S., Niles-Weed, J., Razavian, N., Fernandez-Granda, C., 2020. Early-learning regularization prevents memorization of noisy labels. Advances in Neural Information Processing Systems 33, 20331–20342.

Liu, S., Zhu, Z., Qu, Q., You, C., 2022c. Robust training under label noise by over-parameterization. In: International Conference on Machine Learning. PMLR, pp. 14153–14172.

Liu, T., Tao, D., 2015. Classification with noisy labels by importance reweighting. IEEE Transactions on Pattern Analysis and Machine Intelligence 38, 447–461.

Liu, W., Wang, H., Shen, X., Tsang, I. The emerging trends of multi-label learning. IEEE Transactions on Pattern Analysis and Machine Intelligence.

Liu, Y., 2022. Identifiability of label noise transition matrix. arXiv preprint. arXiv:2202.02016.

Liu, Y., Guo, H., 2020. Peer loss functions: Learning from noisy labels without knowing noise rates. In: International Conference on Machine Learning. PMLR, pp. 6226–6236.

Liu, Y., Tian, Y., Chen, Y., Liu, F., Belagiannis, V., Carneiro, G., 2022d. Perturbed and strict mean teachers for semi-supervised semantic segmentation. In: Proceedings of the IEEE/CVF Conference on Computer Vision and Pattern Recognition, pp. 4258–4267.

Liu, Y., Wang, J., 2021. Can less be more? when increasing-to-balancing label noise rates considered beneficial. Advances in Neural Information Processing Systems 34, 17467–17479.

Long, P.M., Servedio, R.A., 2008. Random classification noise defeats all convex potential boosters. In: Proceedings of the 25th International Conference on Machine Learning, pp. 608–615.

Lukasik, M., Bhojanapalli, S., Menon, A., Kumar, S., 2020. Does label smoothing mitigate label noise? In: International Conference on Machine Learning. PMLR, pp. 6448–6458.

Luo, Y., Guo, Y., Li, W., Liu, G., Yang, G., 2020. Fluorescence microscopy image datasets for deep learning segmentation of intracellular orgenelle networks. IEEE Dataport.

Luo, Y., Liu, G., Guo, Y., Yang, G., 2022. Deep neural networks learn meta-structures from noisy labels in semantic segmentation. In: Proceedings of the AAAI Conference on Artificial Intelligence, pp. 1908–1916.

Luo, Y., Zhu, J., Pfister, T., 2019. A simple yet effective baseline for robust deep learning with noisy labels. arXiv preprint. arXiv:1909.09338.

Lyu, Y., Tsang, I.W., 2019. Curriculum loss: Robust learning and generalization against label corruption. arXiv preprint. arXiv:1905.10045.

Ma, C., Wang, H., Hoi, S.C., 2019. Multi-label thoracic disease image classification with cross-attention networks. In: Medical Image Computing and Computer Assisted Intervention – MICCAI 2019: 22nd International Conference, Proceedings, Part VI 22. Shenzhen, China, October 13–17, 2019. Springer, pp. 730–738.

Ma, X., Huang, H., Wang, Y., Romano, S., Erfani, S., Bailey, J., 2020. Normalized loss functions for deep learning with noisy labels. In: International Conference on Machine Learning. PMLR, pp. 6543–6553.

Ma, X., Wang, Y., Houle, M.E., Zhou, S., Erfani, S., Xia, S., Wijewickrema, S., Bailey, J., 2018. Dimensionality-driven learning with noisy labels. In: International Conference on Machine Learning. PMLR, pp. 3355–3364.

Maas, A., Daly, R.E., Pham, P.T., Huang, D., Ng, A.Y., Potts, C., 2011. Learning word vectors for sentiment analysis. In: Proceedings of the 49th Annual Meeting of the Association for Computational Linguistics: Human Language Technologies, pp. 142–150.

Madry, A., Makelov, A., Schmidt, L., Tsipras, D., Vladu, A., 2017. Towards deep learning models resistant to adversarial attacks. arXiv preprint. arXiv:1706.06083.

Maiti, A., Elberink, S.O., Vosselman, G., 2022. Effect of label noise in semantic segmentation of high resolution aerial images and height data. ISPRS Annals of the Photogrammetry, Remote Sensing and Spatial Information Sciences 2, 275–282.

Majkowska, A., Mittal, S., Steiner, D., Reicher, J., McKinney, S., Duggan, G., Eswaran, K., Cameron Chen, P., Liu, Y., Kalidindi, S., et al., 2020. Chest radiograph interpretation with deep learning models: Assessment with radiologist-adjudicated reference standards and population-adjusted evaluation. Radiology 294, 421–431.

Malach, E., Shalev-Shwartz, S., 2017. Decoupling "when to update" from "how to update". Advances in Neural Information Processing Systems 30.

Mammen, E., Tsybakov, A.B., 1999. Smooth discrimination analysis. The Annals of Statistics 27, 1808–1829.

Mandal, D., Bharadwaj, S., Biswas, S., 2020. A novel self-supervised re-labeling approach for training with noisy labels. In: Proceedings of the IEEE/CVF Winter Conference on Applications of Computer Vision, pp. 1381–1390.

Manwani, N., Sastry, P., 2013. Noise tolerance under risk minimization. IEEE Transactions on Cybernetics 43, 1146–1151.

Massart, P., Nédélec, É., 2006. Risk bounds for statistical learning. The Annals of Statistics 34, 2326–2366.

Mena, J., Pujol, O., Vitria, J., 2021. A survey on uncertainty estimation in deep learning classification systems from a Bayesian perspective. ACM Computing Surveys 54, 1–35.

Menon, A.K., Rawat, A.S., Reddi, S.J., Kumar, S., 2020. Can gradient clipping mitigate label noise? In: International Conference on Learning Representations.

Menon, A.K., Van Rooyen, B., Natarajan, N., 2016. Learning from binary labels with instance-dependent corruption. arXiv preprint. arXiv:1605.00751.

Menze, B.H., Jakab, A., Bauer, S., Kalpathy-Cramer, J., Farahani, K., Kirby, J., Burren, Y., Porz, N., Slotboom, J., Wiest, R., et al., 2014. The multimodal brain tumor image segmentation benchmark (BraTS). IEEE Transactions on Medical Imaging 34, 1993–2024.

Michalek, J.E., Tripathi, R.C., 1980. The effect of errors in diagnosis and measurement on the estimation of the probability of an event. Journal of the American Statistical Association 75, 713–721.

Miech, A., Zhukov, D., Alayrac, J.B., Tapaswi, M., Laptev, I., Sivic, J., 2019. Howto100m: Learning a text-video embedding by watching hundred million narrated video clips. In: Proceedings of the IEEE/CVF International Conference on Computer Vision, pp. 2630–2640.

Milletari, F., Navab, N., Ahmadi, S.A., 2016. V-net: Fully convolutional neural networks for volumetric medical image segmentation. In: 2016 Fourth International Conference on 3D Vision (3DV). IEEE, pp. 565–571.

Minaee, S., Kalchbrenner, N., Cambria, E., Nikzad, N., Chenaghlu, M., Gao, J., 2021. Deep learning-based text classification: A comprehensive review. ACM Computing Surveys 54, 1–40.

Mintz, M., Bills, S., Snow, R., Jurafsky, D., 2009. Distant supervision for relation extraction without labeled data. In: Proceedings of the Joint Conference of the 47th Annual Meeting of the ACL and the 4th International Joint Conference on Natural Language Processing of the AFNLP, pp. 1003–1011.

Mirzasoleiman, B., Cao, K., Leskovec, J., 2020. Coresets for robust training of deep neural networks against noisy labels. Advances in Neural Information Processing Systems 33, 11465–11477.

Miyato, T., Maeda, S.I., Koyama, M., Ishii, S., 2018. Virtual adversarial training: A regularization method for supervised and semi-supervised learning. IEEE Transactions on Pattern Analysis and Machine Intelligence 41, 1979–1993.

Nair, V., Hinton, G.E., 2010. Rectified linear units improve restricted Boltzmann machines. In: Proceedings of the 27th International Conference on Machine Learning (ICML-10), pp. 807–814.

Nassif, A.B., Shahin, I., Attili, I., Azzeh, M., Shaalan, K., 2019. Speech recognition using deep neural networks: A systematic review. IEEE Access 7, 19143–19165.

Natarajan, N., Dhillon, I.S., Ravikumar, P.K., Tewari, A., 2013. Learning with noisy labels. Advances in Neural Information Processing Systems 26.

Nettleton, D.F., Orriols-Puig, A., Fornells, A., 2010. A study of the effect of different types of noise on the precision of supervised learning techniques. Artificial Intelligence Review 33, 275–306.

Netzer, Y., Wang, T., Coates, A., Bissacco, A., Wu, B., Ng, A.Y., 2011. Reading digits in natural images with unsupervised feature learning.

Nguyen, C., Do, T.T., Carneiro, G., 2023. Towards the identifiability in noisy label learning: A multinomial mixture approach. arXiv preprint. arXiv:2301.01405.

Nguyen, D.T., Mummadi, C.K., Ngo, T.P.N., Nguyen, T.H.P., Beggel, L., Brox, T., 2019. Self: Learning to filter noisy labels with self-ensembling. arXiv preprint. arXiv:1910.01842.

Nigam, N., Dutta, T., Gupta, H.P., 2020. Impact of noisy labels in learning techniques: A survey. In: Advances in Data and Information Sciences. Springer, pp. 403–411.

Nir, G., Hor, S., Karimi, D., Fazli, L., Skinnider, B.F., Tavassoli, P., Turbin, D., Villamil, C.F., Wang, G., Wilson, R.S., et al., 2018. Automatic grading of prostate cancer in digitized histopathology images: Learning from multiple experts. Medical Image Analysis 50, 167–180.

Nishi, K., Ding, Y., Rich, A., Hollerer, T., 2021. Augmentation strategies for learning with noisy labels. In: Proceedings of the IEEE/CVF Conference on Computer Vision and Pattern Recognition, pp. 8022–8031.

Noroozi, M., Favaro, P., 2016. Unsupervised learning of visual representations by solving jigsaw puzzles. In: Computer Vision – ECCV 2016: 14th European Conference, Proceedings, Part VI. Amsterdam, The Netherlands, October 11–14, 2016. Springer, pp. 69–84.

Northcutt, C., Jiang, L., Chuang, I., 2021. Confident learning: Estimating uncertainty in dataset labels. Journal of Artificial Intelligence Research 70, 1373–1411.

Novotny, D., Albanie, S., Larlus, D., Vedaldi, A., 2018. Self-supervised learning of geometrically stable features through probabilistic introspection. In: Proceedings of the IEEE Conference on Computer Vision and Pattern Recognition, pp. 3637–3645.

Oakden-Rayner, L., 2020. Exploring large-scale public medical image datasets. Academic Radiology 27, 106–112.

Olver, S., Townsend, A., 2013. Fast inverse transform sampling in one and two dimensions. arXiv preprint. arXiv:1307.1223.

Ortego, D., Arazo, E., Albert, P., O'Connor, N.E., McGuinness, K., 2021. Multi-objective interpolation training for robustness to label noise. In: Proceedings of the IEEE/CVF Conference on Computer Vision and Pattern Recognition, pp. 6606–6615.

Otsu, N., 1979. A threshold selection method from gray-level histograms. IEEE Transactions on Systems, Man and Cybernetics 9, 62–66.

Paletz, S.B., Chan, J., Schunn, C.D., 2016. Uncovering uncertainty through disagreement. Applied Cognitive Psychology 30, 387–400.

Pang, G., Shen, C., Cao, L., Hengel, A.V.D., 2021. Deep learning for anomaly detection: A review. ACM Computing Surveys 54, 1–38.

Patrini, G., Rozza, A., Krishna Menon, A., Nock, R., Qu, L., 2017. Making deep neural networks robust to label noise: A loss correction approach. In: Proceedings of the IEEE Conference on Computer Vision and Pattern Recognition, pp. 1944–1952.

Pechenizkiy, M., Tsymbal, A., Puuronen, S., Pechenizkiy, O., 2006. Class noise and supervised learning in medical domains: The effect of feature extraction. In: 19th IEEE Symposium on Computer-Based Medical Systems (CBMS'06). IEEE, pp. 708–713.

Pereyra, G., Tucker, G., Chorowski, J., Kaiser, Ł., Hinton, G., 2017. Regularizing neural networks by penalizing confident output distributions. arXiv preprint. arXiv:1701.06548.

Pérez, C.J., Girón, F.J., Martín, J., Ruiz, M., Rojano, C., 2007. Misclassified multinomial data: A Bayesian approach. RACSAM 101, 71–80.

Pestian, J., Brew, C., Matykiewicz, P., Hovermale, D.J., Johnson, N., Cohen, K.B., Duch, W., 2007. A shared task involving multi-label classification of clinical free text. In: Biological, Translational, and Clinical Language Processing, pp. 97–104.

Pleiss, G., Zhang, T., Elenberg, E., Weinberger, K.Q., 2020. Identifying mislabeled data using the area under the margin ranking. Advances in Neural Information Processing Systems 33, 17044–17056.

Polyak, B.T., Juditsky, A.B., 1992. Acceleration of stochastic approximation by averaging. SIAM Journal on Control and Optimization 30, 838–855.

Potsdam, I., 2018. 2D semantic labeling dataset. Accessed: April.

Qiu, C., Li, A., Kloft, M., Rudolph, M., Mandt, S., 2022. Latent outlier exposure for anomaly detection with contaminated data. In: International Conference on Machine Learning. PMLR, pp. 18153–18167.

Rajpurkar, P., Irvin, J., Zhu, K., Yang, B., Mehta, H., Duan, T., Ding, D., Bagul, A., Langlotz, C., Shpanskaya, K., et al., 2017. ChexNet: Radiologist-level pneumonia detection on chest X-rays with deep learning. arXiv preprint. arXiv:1711.05225.

Ralaivola, L., Denis, F., Magnan, C.N., 2006. CN = CPCN. In: Proceedings of the 23rd International Conference on Machine Learning, pp. 721–728.

Raykar, V.C., Yu, S., Zhao, L.H., Jerebko, A., Florin, C., Valadez, G.H., Bogoni, L., Moy, L., 2009. Supervised learning from multiple experts: Whom to trust when everyone lies a bit. In: Proceedings of the 26th Annual International Conference on Machine Learning, pp. 889–896.

Raykar, V.C., Yu, S., Zhao, L.H., Valadez, G.H., Florin, C., Bogoni, L., Moy, L., 2010. Learning from crowds. Journal of Machine Learning Research 11.

Reddy, C.K., Cutler, R., Gehrke, J., 2019. Supervised classifiers for audio impairments with noisy labels. arXiv preprint. arXiv:1907.01742.

Reed, S., Lee, H., Anguelov, D., Szegedy, C., Erhan, D., Rabinovich, A., 2014. Training deep neural networks on noisy labels with bootstrapping. arXiv preprint. arXiv:1412.6596.

Ren, M., Zeng, W., Yang, B., Urtasun, R., 2018. Learning to reweight examples for robust deep learning. In: International Conference on Machine Learning. PMLR, pp. 4334–4343.

Ren, S., He, K., Girshick, R., Sun, J., 2015. Faster R-CNN: Towards real-time object detection with region proposal networks. Advances in Neural Information Processing Systems 28.

Rodrigues, F., Pereira, F., Ribeiro, B., 2013. Learning from multiple annotators: distinguishing good from random labelers. Pattern Recognition Letters 34, 1428–1436.

Rolnick, D., Veit, A., Belongie, S., Shavit, N., 2017. Deep learning is robust to massive label noise. arXiv preprint. arXiv:1705.10694.

Ronneberger, O., Fischer, P., Brox, T., 2015. U-net: Convolutional networks for biomedical image segmentation. In: International Conference on Medical Image Computing and Computer-Assisted Intervention. Springer, pp. 234–241.

Rosenblatt, F., 1958. The perceptron: A probabilistic model for information storage and organization in the brain. Psychological Review 65, 386.

Sachdeva, R., Cordeiro, F.R., Belagiannis, V., Reid, I., Carneiro, G., 2021. EvidentialMix: Learning with combined open-set and closed-set noisy labels. In: Proceedings of the IEEE/CVF Winter Conference on Applications of Computer Vision, pp. 3607–3615.

Sachdeva, R., Cordeiro, F.R., Belagiannis, V., Reid, I., Carneiro, G., 2023. ScanMix: Learning from severe label noise via semantic clustering and semi-supervised learning. Pattern Recognition 134, 109121.

Salimans, T., Zhang, H., Radford, A., Metaxas, D., 2018. Improving GANs using optimal transport. arXiv preprint. arXiv:1803.05573.

Sánchez, J.S., Pla, F., Ferri, F.J., 1997. Prototype selection for the nearest neighbour rule through proximity graphs. Pattern Recognition Letters 18, 507–513.

Sang, E.F., De Meulder, F., 2003. Introduction to the CoNLL-2003 shared task: Language-independent named entity recognition. arXiv preprint. arXiv:cs/0306050.

Sanyal, A., Dokania, P.K., Kanade, V., Torr, P.H., 2020. How benign is benign overfitting? arXiv preprint. arXiv:2007.04028.

Schaekermann, M., Beaton, G., Habib, M., Lim, A., Larson, K., Law, E., 2019. Understanding expert disagreement in medical data analysis through structured adjudication. Proceedings of the ACM on Human–Computer Interaction 3, 1–23.

Scott, C., 2015. A rate of convergence for mixture proportion estimation, with application to learning from noisy labels. In: Artificial Intelligence and Statistics. PMLR, pp. 838–846.

Scott, C., Blanchard, G., Handy, G., 2013. Classification with asymmetric label noise: Consistency and maximal denoising. In: Conference on Learning Theory. PMLR, pp. 489–511.

Sculley, D., Cormack, G.V., 2008. Filtering email spam in the presence of noisy user feedback. In: CEAS. Citeseer.

Sensoy, M., Kaplan, L., Kandemir, M., 2018. Evidential deep learning to quantify classification uncertainty. Advances in Neural Information Processing Systems 31.

Seo, P.H., Kim, G., Han, B., 2019. Combinatorial inference against label noise. Advances in Neural Information Processing Systems 32.

Settles, B., 2012. Active learning. In: Synthesis Lectures on Artificial Intelligence and Machine Learning, vol. 6, pp. 1–114.

Shanmugam, D., Blalock, D., Balakrishnan, G., Guttag, J., 2021. Better aggregation in test-time augmentation. In: Proceedings of the IEEE/CVF International Conference on Computer Vision, pp. 1214–1223.

Shen, Y., Ji, R., Chen, Z., Hong, X., Zheng, F., Liu, J., Xu, M., Tian, Q., 2020. Noise-aware fully webly supervised object detection. In: Proceedings of the IEEE/CVF Conference on Computer Vision and Pattern Recognition, pp. 11326–11335.

Shen, Y., Ji, R., Wang, Y., Wu, Y., Cao, L., 2019. Cyclic guidance for weakly supervised joint detection and segmentation. In: Proceedings of the IEEE/CVF Conference on Computer Vision and Pattern Recognition, pp. 697–707.

Shen, Y., Sanghavi, S., 2019. Learning with bad training data via iterative trimmed loss minimization. In: International Conference on Machine Learning. PMLR, pp. 5739–5748.

Shiraishi, J., Katsuragawa, S., Ikezoe, J., Matsumoto, T., Kobayashi, T., Komatsu, K.I., Matsui, M., Fujita, H., Kodera, Y., Doi, K., 2000. Development of a digital image database for chest radiographs with and without a lung nodule: receiver operating characteristic analysis of radiologists' detection of pulmonary nodules. American Journal of Roentgenology 174, 71–74.

Shorten, C., Khoshgoftaar, T.M., 2019. A survey on image data augmentation for deep learning. Journal of Big Data 6, 1–48.

Shrivastava, A., Gupta, A., Girshick, R., 2016. Training region-based object detectors with online hard example mining. In: Proceedings of the IEEE Conference on Computer Vision and Pattern Recognition, pp. 761–769.

Shu, J., Xie, Q., Yi, L., Zhao, Q., Zhou, S., Xu, Z., Meng, D., 2019. Meta-weight-net: Learning an explicit mapping for sample weighting. In: Advances in Neural Information Processing Systems.

Simonyan, K., Zisserman, A., 2015. Very deep convolutional networks for large-scale image recognition. In: International Conference on Learning Representation.

Sloan, R.H., 1995. Four types of noise in data for PAC learning. Information Processing Letters 54, 157–162.

Sluban, B., Gamberger, D., Lavrač, N., 2014. Ensemble-based noise detection: Noise ranking and visual performance evaluation. Data Mining and Knowledge Discovery 28, 265–303.

Smart, B., Carneiro, G., 2023. Bootstrapping the relationship between images and their clean and noisy labels. In: Proceedings of the IEEE/CVF Winter Conference on Applications of Computer Vision, pp. 5344–5354.

Smyth, P., Fayyad, U., Burl, M., Perona, P., Baldi, P., 1994. Inferring ground truth from subjective labelling of Venus images. Advances in Neural Information Processing Systems 7.

Sohn, K., Berthelot, D., Carlini, N., Zhang, Z., Zhang, H., Raffel, C.A., Cubuk, E.D., Kurakin, A., Li, C.L., 2020. Fixmatch: Simplifying semi-supervised learning with consistency and confidence. Advances in Neural Information Processing Systems 33, 596–608.

Song, H., Kim, M., Lee, J.G., 2019. Selfie: Refurbishing unclean samples for robust deep learning. In: International Conference on Machine Learning. PMLR, pp. 5907–5915.

Song, H., Kim, M., Park, D., Shin, Y., Lee, J.G., 2022. Learning from noisy labels with deep neural networks: A survey. IEEE Transactions on Neural Networks and Learning Systems.

Spolaôr, N., Cherman, E.A., Monard, M.C., Lee, H.D., 2013. A comparison of multi-label feature selection methods using the problem transformation approach. Electronic Notes in Theoretical Computer Science 292, 135–151.

Srivastava, N., Hinton, G., Krizhevsky, A., Sutskever, I., Salakhutdinov, R., 2014. Dropout: A simple way to prevent neural networks from overfitting. Journal of Machine Learning Research 15, 1929–1958.

Sudre, C.H., Anson, B.G., Ingala, S., Lane, C.D., Jimenez, D., Haider, L., Varsavsky, T., Tanno, R., Smith, L., Ourselin, S., et al., 2019. Let's agree to disagree: Learning highly debatable multirater labelling. In: International Conference on Medical Image Computing and Computer-Assisted Intervention. Springer, pp. 665–673.

Sukhbaatar, S., Bruna, J., Paluri, M., Bourdev, L., Fergus, R., 2014. Training convolutional networks with noisy labels. arXiv preprint. arXiv:1406.2080.

Sun, C., Shrivastava, A., Singh, S., Gupta, A., 2017. Revisiting unreasonable effectiveness of data in deep learning era. In: Proceedings of the IEEE International Conference on Computer Vision, pp. 843–852.

Szegedy, C., Ioffe, S., Vanhoucke, V., Alemi, A., 2017. Inception-V4, Inception-ResNet and the impact of residual connections on learning. In: Proceedings of the AAAI Conference on Artificial Intelligence.

Szegedy, C., Vanhoucke, V., Ioffe, S., Shlens, J., Wojna, Z., 2016. Rethinking the inception architecture for computer vision. In: Proceedings of the IEEE Conference on Computer Vision and Pattern Recognition, pp. 2818–2826.

Székely, G.J., Rizzo, M.L., 2013. Energy statistics: A class of statistics based on distances. Journal of Statistical Planning and Inference 143, 1249–1272.

Tan, C., Xia, J., Wu, L., Li, S.Z., 2021. Co-learning: Learning from noisy labels with self-supervision. In: Proceedings of the 29th ACM International Conference on Multimedia, pp. 1405–1413.

Tanaka, D., Ikami, D., Yamasaki, T., Aizawa, K., 2018. Joint optimization framework for learning with noisy labels. In: Proceedings of the IEEE Conference on Computer Vision and Pattern Recognition, pp. 5552–5560.

Tanno, R., Saeedi, A., Sankaranarayanan, S., Alexander, D.C., Silberman, N., 2019. Learning from noisy labels by regularized estimation of annotator confusion. In: Proceedings of the IEEE/CVF Conference on Computer Vision and Pattern Recognition, pp. 11244–11253.

Tao, Q., Yang, H., Cai, J., 2018. Zero-annotation object detection with web knowledge transfer. In: Proceedings of the European Conference on Computer Vision (ECCV), pp. 369–384.

Tarvainen, A., Valpola, H., 2017. Mean teachers are better role models: Weight-averaged consistency targets improve semi-supervised deep learning results. Advances in Neural Information Processing Systems 30.

Thiel, C., 2008. Classification on soft labels is robust against label noise. In: International Conference on Knowledge-Based and Intelligent Information and Engineering Systems. Springer, pp. 65–73.

Thomee, B., Shamma, D.A., Friedland, G., Elizalde, B., Ni, K., Poland, D., Borth, D., Li, L.J., 2016. YFCC100M: The new data in multimedia research. Communications of the ACM 59, 64–73.

Thongkam, J., Xu, G., Zhang, Y., Huang, F., 2008. Support vector machine for outlier detection in breast cancer survivability prediction. In: Advanced Web and Network Technologies, and Applications: APWeb 2008 International Workshops: BIDM, IWHDM, and DeWeb, Revised Selected Papers 10. Shenyang, China, April 26–28, 2008. Springer, pp. 99–109.

Thulasidasan, S., Bhattacharya, T., Bilmes, J., Chennupati, G., Mohd-Yusof, J., 2019. Combating label noise in deep learning using abstention. arXiv preprint. arXiv:1905.10964.

Tibshirani, R., 1996. Regression shrinkage and selection via the lasso. Journal of the Royal Statistical Society, Series B, Methodological 58, 267–288.

Traganitis, P.A., Pages-Zamora, A., Giannakis, G.B., 2018. Blind multiclass ensemble classification. IEEE Transactions on Signal Processing 66, 4737–4752.

Trohidis, K., Tsoumakas, G., Kalliris, G., Vlahavas, I.P., et al., 2008. Multi-label classification of music into emotions. In: ISMIR, pp. 325–330.

Tschandl, P., Rosendahl, C., Kittler, H., 2018. The HAM10000 dataset, a large collection of multi-source dermatoscopic images of common pigmented skin lesions. Scientific Data 5, 1–9.

Tu, Y., Zhang, B., Li, Y., Liu, L., Li, J., Wang, Y., Wang, C., Zhao, C.R., 2023a. Learning from noisy labels with decoupled meta label purifier. In: Proceedings of the IEEE/CVF Conference on Computer Vision and Pattern Recognition, pp. 19934–19943.

Tu, Y., Zhang, B., Li, Y., Liu, L., Li, J., Zhang, J., Wang, Y., Wang, C., Zhao, C.R., 2023b. Learning with noisy labels via self-supervised adversarial noisy masking. In: Proceedings of the IEEE/CVF Conference on Computer Vision and Pattern Recognition, pp. 16186–16195.

Vahdat, A., 2017. Toward robustness against label noise in training deep discriminative neural networks. Advances in Neural Information Processing Systems 30.

Vaihingen, I., 2018. 2D semantic labeling dataset. Accessed: April.

Valiant, L.G., 1984. A theory of the learnable. Communications of the ACM 27, 1134–1142.

Van Engelen, J.E., Hoos, H.H., 2020. A survey on semi-supervised learning. Machine Learning 109, 373–440.

Van Horn, G., Branson, S., Loarie, S., Belongie, S., Perona, P., 2018. Lean multiclass crowd-sourcing. In: Proceedings of the IEEE Conference on Computer Vision and Pattern Recognition, pp. 2714–2723.

Van Rooyen, B., Menon, A., Williamson, R.C., 2015. Learning with symmetric label noise: The importance of being unhinged. Advances in Neural Information Processing Systems 28.

Vapnik, V.N., Chervonenkis, A.Y., 2015. On the uniform convergence of relative frequencies of events to their probabilities. In: Measures of Complexity. Springer, pp. 11–30.

Veeling, B.S., Linmans, J., Winkens, J., Cohen, T., Welling, M., 2018. Rotation equivariant CNNs for digital pathology. In: International Conference on Medical Image Computing and Computer-Assisted Intervention. Springer, pp. 210–218.

Veit, A., Alldrin, N., Chechik, G., Krasin, I., Gupta, A., Belongie, S., 2017. Learning from noisy large-scale datasets with minimal supervision. In: Proceedings of the IEEE Conference on Computer Vision and Pattern Recognition, pp. 839–847.

Villani, C., 2021. Topics in Optimal Transportation, vol. 58. American Mathematical Soc.

Vinyals, O., Blundell, C., Lillicrap, T., Wierstra, D., et al., 2016. Matching networks for one shot learning. Advances in Neural Information Processing Systems 29.

Wang, C., Han, B., Pan, S., Jiang, J., Niu, G., Long, G., 2020. Cross-graph: Robust and unsupervised embedding for attributed graphs with corrupted structure. In: 2020 IEEE International Conference on Data Mining (ICDM). IEEE, pp. 571–580.

Wang, G., Li, W., Aertsen, M., Deprest, J., Ourselin, S., Vercauteren, T., 2019a. Aleatoric uncertainty estimation with test-time augmentation for medical image segmentation with convolutional neural networks. Neurocomputing 338, 34–45.

Wang, H., Xiao, R., Dong, Y., Feng, L., Zhao, J., 2022. ProMix: Combating label noise via maximizing clean sample utility. arXiv preprint. arXiv:2207.10276.

Wang, M., Deng, W., 2018. Deep visual domain adaptation: A survey. Neurocomputing 312, 135–153.

Wang, R., Liu, T., Tao, D., 2017a. Multiclass learning with partially corrupted labels. IEEE Transactions on Neural Networks and Learning Systems 29, 2568–2580.

Wang, X., Hua, Y., Kodirov, E., Robertson, N.M., 2019b. IMAE for noise-robust learning: Mean absolute error does not treat examples equally and gradient magnitude's variance matters. arXiv preprint. arXiv:1903.12141.

Wang, X., Peng, Y., Lu, L., Lu, Z., Bagheri, M., Summers, R.M., 2017b. ChestX-ray 8: Hospital-scale chest X-ray database and benchmarks on weakly-supervised classification and localization of common thorax diseases.

Wang, Y., Kucukelbir, A., Blei, D.M., 2017c. Robust probabilistic modeling with Bayesian data reweighting. In: International Conference on Machine Learning. PMLR, pp. 3646–3655.

Wang, Y., Liu, W., Ma, X., Bailey, J., Zha, H., Song, L., Xia, S.T., 2018. Iterative learning with open-set noisy labels. In: Proceedings of the IEEE Conference on Computer Vision and Pattern Recognition, pp. 8688–8696.

Wang, Y., Ma, X., Chen, Z., Luo, Y., Yi, J., Bailey, J., 2019c. Symmetric cross entropy for robust learning with noisy labels. In: Proceedings of the IEEE/CVF International Conference on Computer Vision, pp. 322–330.

Warfield, S.K., Zou, K.H., Wells, W.M., 2004. Simultaneous truth and performance level estimation (staple): An algorithm for the validation of image segmentation. IEEE Transactions on Medical Imaging 23, 903–921.

Wei, C., Lee, J., Liu, Q., Ma, T., 2018. On the margin theory of feedforward neural networks.

Wei, H., Feng, L., Chen, X., An, B., 2020. Combating noisy labels by agreement: A joint training method with co-regularization. In: Proceedings of the IEEE/CVF Conference on Computer Vision and Pattern Recognition, pp. 13726–13735.

Wei, J., Zhu, Z., Cheng, H., Liu, T., Niu, G., Liu, Y., 2021a. Learning with noisy labels revisited: A study using real-world human annotations. arXiv preprint. arXiv:2110.12088.

Wei, T., Shi, J.X., Tu, W.W., Li, Y.F., 2021b. Robust long-tailed learning under label noise. arXiv preprint. arXiv:2108.11569.

Wei, Y., Liang, X., Chen, Y., Shen, X., Cheng, M.M., Feng, J., Zhao, Y., Yan, S., 2016. STC: A simple to complex framework for weakly-supervised semantic segmentation. IEEE Transactions on Pattern Analysis and Machine Intelligence 39, 2314–2320.

Welinder, P., Branson, S., Perona, P., Belongie, S., 2010. The multidimensional wisdom of crowds. Advances in Neural Information Processing Systems 23.

Wheway, V., 2001. Using boosting to detect noisy data. In: Advances in Artificial Intelligence. PRICAI 2000 Workshop Reader: Four Workshops Held at PRICAI 2000, Revised Papers 6. Melbourne, Australia, August 28–September 1, 2000. Springer, pp. 123–130.

Whitehill, J., Wu, T.f., Bergsma, J., Movellan, J., Ruvolo, P., 2009. Whose vote should count more: Optimal integration of labels from labelers of unknown expertise. Advances in Neural Information Processing Systems 22.

Wilcox, R.R., 2011. Introduction to Robust Estimation and Hypothesis Testing. Academic Press.

Wilson, D.R., Martinez, T.R., 2000. Reduction techniques for instance-based learning algorithms. Machine Learning 38, 257–286.

Wu, P., Zheng, S., Goswami, M., Metaxas, D., Chen, C., 2020. A topological filter for learning with label noise. Advances in Neural Information Processing Systems 33, 21382–21393.

Wu, Y., Shu, J., Xie, Q., Zhao, Q., Meng, D., 2021a. Learning to purify noisy labels via meta soft label corrector. In: Proceedings of the AAAI Conference on Artificial Intelligence, pp. 10388–10396.

Wu, Z.F., Wei, T., Jiang, J., Mao, C., Tang, M., Li, Y.F., 2021b. NGC: A unified framework for learning with open-world noisy data. In: Proceedings of the IEEE/CVF International Conference on Computer Vision, pp. 62–71.

Xia, X., Liu, T., Han, B., Gong, M., Yu, J., Niu, G., Sugiyama, M., 2021. Sample selection with uncertainty of losses for learning with noisy labels. arXiv preprint. arXiv:2106.00445.

Xia, X., Liu, T., Han, B., Wang, N., Gong, M., Liu, H., Niu, G., Tao, D., Sugiyama, M., 2020. Part-dependent label noise: Towards instance-dependent label noise. Advances in Neural Information Processing Systems 33, 7597–7610.

Xia, X., Liu, T., Wang, N., Han, B., Gong, C., Niu, G., Sugiyama, M., 2019. Are anchor points really indispensable in label-noise learning? Advances in Neural Information Processing Systems 32.

Xiao, H., Rasul, K., Vollgraf, R., 2017. Fashion-MNIST: A novel image dataset for benchmarking machine learning algorithms. arXiv preprint. arXiv:1708.07747.

Xiao, T., Xia, T., Yang, Y., Huang, C., Wang, X., 2015. Learning from massive noisy labeled data for image classification. In: Proceedings of the IEEE Conference on Computer Vision and Pattern Recognition, pp. 2691–2699.

Xie, M.K., Huang, S.J., 2021. Partial multi-label learning with noisy label identification. IEEE Transactions on Pattern Analysis and Machine Intelligence.

Xie, Q., Dai, Z., Hovy, E., Luong, T., Le, Q., 2020. Unsupervised data augmentation for consistency training. Advances in Neural Information Processing Systems 33, 6256–6268.

Xu, Y., Cao, P., Kong, Y., Wang, Y., 2019. L_DMI: A novel information-theoretic loss function for training deep nets robust to label noise. Advances in Neural Information Processing Systems 32.

Xu, Y., Zhu, L., Jiang, L., Yang, Y., 2021. Faster meta update strategy for noise-robust deep learning. In: Conference on Computer Vision and Pattern Recognition.

Xue, C., Dou, Q., Shi, X., Chen, H., Heng, P.A., 2019. Robust learning at noisy labeled medical images: Applied to skin lesion classification. In: 2019 IEEE 16th International Symposium on Biomedical Imaging (ISBI 2019). IEEE, pp. 1280–1283.

Xue, C., Yu, L., Chen, P., Dou, Q., Heng, P.A., 2022. Robust medical image classification from noisy labeled data with global and local representation guided co-training. IEEE Transactions on Medical Imaging 41, 1371–1382.

Yan, S., Zhang, C., 2017. Revisiting perceptron: Efficient and label-optimal learning of halfspaces. Advances in Neural Information Processing Systems 30.

Yang, L., Meng, F., Li, H., Wu, Q., Cheng, Q., 2020. Learning with noisy class labels for instance segmentation. In: European Conference on Computer Vision. Springer, pp. 38–53.

Yang, S., Yang, E., Han, B., Liu, Y., Xu, M., Niu, G., Liu, T., 2021. Estimating instance-dependent label-noise transition matrix using DNNs. arXiv preprint. arXiv:2105.13001.

Yang, S., Yang, E., Han, B., Liu, Y., Xu, M., Niu, G., Liu, T., 2022. Estimating instance-dependent Bayes-label transition matrix using a deep neural network. In: International Conference on Machine Learning. PMLR, pp. 25302–25312.

Yang, Z., Yang, D., Dyer, C., He, X., Smola, A., Hovy, E., 2016. Hierarchical attention networks for document classification. In: Proceedings of the 2016 Conference of the North American Chapter of the Association for Computational Linguistics: Human Language Technologies, pp. 1480–1489.

Yao, J., Wang, J., Tsang, I.W., Zhang, Y., Sun, J., Zhang, C., Zhang, R., 2018. Deep learning from noisy image labels with quality embedding. IEEE Transactions on Image Processing 28, 1909–1922.

Yao, Q., Yang, H., Han, B., Niu, G., Kwok, J.T.Y., 2020a. Searching to exploit memorization effect in learning with noisy labels. In: International Conference on Machine Learning. PMLR, pp. 10789–10798.

Yao, Y., Liu, T., Gong, M., Han, B., Niu, G., Zhang, K., 2021a. Instance-dependent label-noise learning under a structural causal model. Advances in Neural Information Processing Systems 34, 4409–4420.

Yao, Y., Liu, T., Han, B., Gong, M., Deng, J., Niu, G., Sugiyama, M., 2020b. Dual t: Reducing estimation error for transition matrix in label-noise learning. Advances in Neural Information Processing Systems 33, 7260–7271.

Yao, Y., Liu, T., Han, B., Gong, M., Niu, G., Sugiyama, M., Tao, D., 2020c. Towards mixture proportion estimation without irreducibility. arXiv preprint. arXiv:2002.03673.

Yao, Y., Sun, Z., Zhang, C., Shen, F., Wu, Q., Zhang, J., Tang, Z., 2021b. Jo-SRC: A contrastive approach for combating noisy labels. In: Proceedings of the IEEE/CVF Conference on Computer Vision and Pattern Recognition, pp. 5192–5201.

Yao, Y., Ye, D., Li, P., Han, X., Lin, Y., Liu, Z., Liu, Z., Huang, L., Zhou, J., Sun, M., 2019. Docred: A large-scale document-level relation extraction dataset. arXiv preprint. arXiv:1906.06127.

Yu, H.F., Jain, P., Kar, P., Dhillon, I., 2014. Large-scale multi-label learning with missing labels. In: International Conference on Machine Learning. PMLR, pp. 593–601.

Yu, S., Krishnapuram, B., Steck, H., Rao, R., Rosales, R., 2007. Bayesian co-training. Advances in Neural Information Processing Systems 20.

Yu, S., Zhou, H.Y., Ma, K., Bian, C., Chu, C., Liu, H., Zheng, Y., 2020a. Difficulty-aware glaucoma classification with multi-rater consensus modeling. In: Medical Image Computing and Computer Assisted Intervention – MICCAI 2020: 23rd International Conference, Proceedings, Part I 23. Lima, Peru, October 4–8, 2020. Springer, pp. 741–750.

Yu, X., Han, B., Yao, J., Niu, G., Tsang, I., Sugiyama, M., 2019a. How does disagreement benefit co-teaching? arXiv preprint. arXiv:1901.04215v1.

Yu, X., Han, B., Yao, J., Niu, G., Tsang, I., Sugiyama, M., 2019b. How does disagreement help generalization against label corruption? In: International Conference on Machine Learning. PMLR, pp. 7164–7173.

Yu, X., Liu, T., Gong, M., Tao, D., 2018. Learning with biased complementary labels. In: Proceedings of the European Conference on Computer Vision (ECCV), pp. 68–83.

Yu, X., Liu, T., Gong, M., Zhang, K., Batmanghelich, K., Tao, D., 2020b. Label-noise robust domain adaptation. In: International Conference on Machine Learning. PMLR, pp. 10913–10924.

Zhai, X., Kolesnikov, A., Houlsby, N., Beyer, L., 2022. Scaling vision transformers. In: 2014 IEEE Conference on Computer Vision and Pattern Recognition (CVPR). IEEE.

Zhang, C., 2018. Efficient active learning of sparse halfspaces. In: Conference on Learning Theory. PMLR, pp. 1856–1880.

Zhang, C., Bengio, S., Hardt, M., Recht, B., Vinyals, O., 2017a. Understanding deep learning requires rethinking generalization. In: Proceedings of the International Conference on Learning Representation.

Zhang, C., Bengio, S., Hardt, M., Recht, B., Vinyals, O., 2021a. Understanding deep learning (still) requires rethinking generalization. Communications of the ACM 64, 107–115.

Zhang, H., Cisse, M., Dauphin, Y.N., Lopez-Paz, D., 2018. Mixup: Beyond empirical risk minimization. In: International Conference on Learning Representations.

Zhang, J., Wu, X., Sheng, V.S., 2016. Learning from crowdsourced labeled data: a survey. Artificial Intelligence Review 46, 543–576.

Zhang, L., Tanno, R., Xu, M.C., Jin, C., Jacob, J., Cicarrelli, O., Barkhof, F., Alexander, D., 2020a. Disentangling human error from ground truth in segmentation of medical images. Advances in Neural Information Processing Systems 33, 15750–15762.

Zhang, M., Gao, J., Lyu, Z., Zhao, W., Wang, Q., Ding, W., Wang, S., Li, Z., Cui, S., 2020b. Characterizing label errors: Confident learning for noisy-labeled image segmentation. In: International Conference on Medical Image Computing and Computer-Assisted Intervention. Springer, pp. 721–730.

Zhang, M.L., Zhou, Z.H., 2013. A review on multi-label learning algorithms. IEEE Transactions on Knowledge and Data Engineering 26, 1819–1837.

Zhang, X., Fang, Z., Wen, Y., Li, Z., Qiao, Y., 2017b. Range loss for deep face recognition with long-tailed training data. In: Proceedings of the IEEE International Conference on Computer Vision, pp. 5409–5418.

Zhang, X., Zhao, J., LeCun, Y., 2015. Character-level convolutional networks for text classification. Advances in Neural Information Processing Systems 28.

Zhang, Y., Liang, P., Charikar, M., 2017c. A hitting time analysis of stochastic gradient Langevin dynamics. In: Conference on Learning Theory. PMLR, pp. 1980–2022.

Zhang, Y., Niu, G., Sugiyama, M., 2021b. Learning noise transition matrix from only noisy labels via total variation regularization. In: International Conference on Machine Learning. PMLR, pp. 12501–12512.

Zhang, Y., Sugiyama, M., 2021. Approximating instance-dependent noise via instance-confidence embedding. arXiv preprint. arXiv:2103.13569.

Zhang, Y., Zheng, S., Wu, P., Goswami, M., Chen, C., 2021c. Learning with feature-dependent label noise: A progressive approach. In: International Conference on Learning Representation.

Zhang, Z., Li, Y., Wei, H., Ma, K., Xu, T., Zheng, Y., 2021d. Alleviating noisy-label effects in image classification via probability transition matrix. arXiv preprint. arXiv:2110.08866.

Zhang, Z., Pfister, T., 2021. Learning fast sample re-weighting without reward data. In: International Conference on Computer Vision.

Zhang, Z., Sabuncu, M., 2018. Generalized cross entropy loss for training deep neural networks with noisy labels. Advances in Neural Information Processing Systems 31.

Zhang, Z., Zhang, H., Arik, S.Ö., Lee, H., Pfister, T., 2020c. Distilling effective supervision from severe label noise. In: Conference on Computer Vision and Pattern Recognition, pp. 9291–9300.

Zhao, G., Li, G., Qin, Y., Liu, F., Yu, Y., 2022. Centrality and consistency: Two-stage clean samples identification for learning with instance-dependent noisy labels. In: Computer Vision – ECCV 2022: 17th European Conference, Proceedings, Part XXV. Tel Aviv, Israel, October 23–27, 2022. Springer, pp. 21–37.

Zheltonozhskii, E., Baskin, C., Mendelson, A., Bronstein, A.M., Litany, O., 2022. Contrast to divide: Self-supervised pre-training for learning with noisy labels. In: Proceedings of the IEEE/CVF Winter Conference on Applications of Computer Vision, pp. 1657–1667.

Zheng, G., Awadallah, A.H., Dumais, S., 2021. Meta label correction for noisy label learning. In: Proceedings of the AAAI Conference on Artificial Intelligence, pp. 11053–11061.

Zheng, S., Wu, P., Goswami, A., Goswami, M., Metaxas, D., Chen, C., 2020. Error-bounded correction of noisy labels. In: International Conference on Machine Learning. PMLR, pp. 11447–11457.

Zhou, B., Cui, Q., Wei, X.S., Chen, Z.M., 2020. BBN: Bilateral-branch network with cumulative learning for long-tailed visual recognition. In: Proceedings of the IEEE/CVF Conference on Computer Vision and Pattern Recognition, pp. 9719–9728.

Zhou, B., Khosla, A., Lapedriza, A., Oliva, A., Torralba, A., 2016. Learning deep features for discriminative localization. In: Proceedings of the IEEE Conference on Computer Vision and Pattern Recognition, pp. 2921–2929.

Zhou, K., Liu, Z., Qiao, Y., Xiang, T., Loy, C.C., 2022. Domain generalization: A survey. IEEE Transactions on Pattern Analysis and Machine Intelligence.

Zhou, T., Wang, S., Bilmes, J., 2021. Robust curriculum learning: From clean label detection to noisy label self-correction. In: International Conference on Learning Representations.

Zhu, C., Chen, W., Peng, T., Wang, Y., Jin, M., 2021a. Hard sample aware noise robust learning for histopathology image classification. IEEE Transactions on Medical Imaging 41, 881–894.

Zhu, J., Zhang, J., Han, B., Liu, T., Niu, G., Yang, H., Kankanhalli, M., Sugiyama, M., 2021b. Understanding the interaction of adversarial training with noisy labels. arXiv preprint. arXiv:2102.03482.

Zhu, W., Wu, O., Su, F., Deng, Y., 2022. Exploring the learning difficulty of data theory and measure. arXiv preprint. arXiv:2205.07427.

Zhu, Z., Song, Y., Liu, Y., 2021c. Clusterability as an alternative to anchor points when learning with noisy labels. In: International Conference on Machine Learning. PMLR, pp. 12912–12923.

Index

0–9

0-1 loss, 21, 22, 76, 77, 95, 98
0-1 loss function, 97
2-step sampling process, 18, 22
3-step sampling process, 18, 22

A

Abstention
    class prediction, 99
    learning, 99
Active learning, 168, 171, 172
Active passive loss, 98
Adaptive boosting algorithm (AdaBoost), 12
Adversarial
    learning, 115
    training, 95, 114–117, 190, 196, 217
Agnostic
    learning, 89
    noise, 89
Anchor points, 110, 174–179, 183, 185, 186, 198,
    246
Annotators, 84, 85, 91, 131, 132, 135, 172
Area under the margin (AUM) statistic, 122
Area under the precision and recall curve (AUPRC),
    65
Artificially noised dataset, 64
    benchmarks, 64, 248
Asymmetric, 30
    instance segmentation noise benchmarks, 236
    label noise, 13, 31, 32, 36, 38, 45, 47, 98, 100,
        110, 123, 196, 245, 248
    noise, 32, 51, 64, 77, 80, 162, 173, 248, 253
Augmented Descent (AugDesc) technique, 141
Automated data augmentation, 141
Automatic detection, 51
Auxiliary image regularizer (AIR), 101
Average precision (AP), 67

B

Backbone model, 219, 227, 231, 236, 244
Background
    class, 237
    label noise, 241
Bayes
    label, 185, 186
    optimal
        classifier, 122, 178

    distribution, 186
        label, 185, 186, 213–215
        label posteriors, 214
    rule, 166
Bayes-label Transition Matrix (BLTM), 212
Bayesian learning, 106
Benchmarks, 41, 51, 61
    artificial, 45
    classification, 45, 56
    dataset, 47
    detection, 49
    IDN, 200, 215
    IDN NEWS, 61, 244
    label noise, 194
Beta mixture model (BMM), 106, 108, 125, 127,
    129, 248
Bias-variance decomposition, 8, 73–77
Binary
    classification, 11, 65, 84, 187
        dataset, 43
        problem, 11, 73, 76, 79, 81, 83, 84, 97, 104,
            174, 178
        task, 86
    classifier, 4, 97, 187
    image classification dataset, 53
    segmentation, 55, 58
Binary cross-entropy (BCE), 228, 241
    loss, 21–23, 95, 96, 203, 228
Bounded mean square error (BMSE), 248
Bounding box, 2, 25–27, 237
    annotations, 45
    clean, 26
    coordinates, 2
    covariance, 25
    noisy, 25–27
    regression, 237
Brain tumor segmentation (BraTS), 56

C

Categorical
    distribution, 20–22, 25, 159, 160, 184, 186, 207,
        213
    distribution noisy, 21, 26
    label distribution, 10
Centrality and consistency (CC) method, 201
Chest X-ray (CXR)
    dataset, 8
    images, 1, 8

Printed in the United States
by Baker & Taylor Publisher Services